Algorithms, Software and Hardware of Parallel Computers

Edited by
J. Mikloško and V. E. Kotov

With Contributions by J. Chudík G. Dávid
V. E. Kotov J. Mikloško N. N. Mirenkov J. Ondáš
I. Plander V. A. Valkovskii

With 181 Figures

Springer-Verlag
Berlin Heidelberg GmbH 1984

Jozef Mikloško
Institute of Technical Cybernetics,
Slovak Academy of Sciences
Dúbravská 9
842 37 Bratislava
Czechoslovakia

Vadim Evgenich Kotov
Computer Centre,
Sibirian Branch of the Academy of Sciences of the USSR
Akad. Lavrentev 6
630 090 Novosibirsk — 90
USSR

ISBN 978-3-662-11108-6   ISBN 978-3-662-11106-2 (eBook)
DOI 10.1007/978-3-662-11106-2

Contents

Preface

Both algorithms and the software and hardware of automatic computers have gone through a rapid development in the past 35 years. The dominant factor in this development was the advance in computer technology. Computer parameters were systematically improved through electron tubes, transistors and integrated circuits of ever-increasing integration density, which also influenced the development of new algorithms and programming methods. Some years ago the situation in computers development was that no additional enhancement of their performance could be achieved by increasing the speed of their logical elements, due to the physical barrier of the maximum transfer speed of electric signals. Another enhancement of computer performance has been achieved by parallelism, which makes it possible by a suitable organization of n processors to obtain a performance increase of up to n times.

Research into parallel computations has been carried out for several years in many countries and many results of fundamental importance have been obtained. Many parallel computers have been designed and their algorithmic and programming systems built. Such computers include ILLIAC IV, DAP, STARAN, OMEN, STAR-100, TEXAS INSTRUMENTS ASC, CRAY-1, C mmp, CM*, CLIP-3, PEPE..

This trend is supported by the fact that:
a) many algorithms and programs are highly parallel in their structure,
b) the new LSI and VLSI technologies have allowed processors to be combined into large parallel structures,
c) greater and greater demands for speed and reliability of computers are made.

This research into parallel computations has brought with it new problems both in the creation of algorithms and programs, and in computer architecture design. These problems cannot be solved using the methods that were applied in classical serial computers. Moreover, parallel algorithms and programs are closely associated with the architecture of parallel computers so that their creation, analysis and implementation cannot be examined isolated from problems of computer architecture. In this book we examine both parallel algorithms and parallel programming, and the hardware of parallel computers. To our knowledge, there has not been published a book that covers the entire set of problems of parallel computations to this depth so far.

The book has been compiled in cooperation between members of the Institute of

Technical Cybernetics of the Slovak Academy of Sciences in Bratislava and the Computation Centre of the Siberian Branch of the Academy of Sciences of the USSR in Novosibirsk. In preparing it the editors chose the topics of the chapters so as to cover as far as possible the problems of parallel computations, and afterwards they asked some outstanding specialists in the USSR, CSSR and Hungary for their active participation in this project. This book is the result of their effort.

It consists of 12 chapters. The individual chapters are mostly surveys, though some include also the results of the authors. Chapters 1, 2, 4, 5, 6, 8 and 12 contain also short appendices, in which original solutions of some problems described in the chapter are given.

Each chapter or appendix introduces a special notation and numbering of formulae and definitions. References are always given at the end of each chapter or appendix. Although the individual chapters are related and supplement each other, the reader can study each chapter separately, too.

This are the authors of the single sections of the book: J. Chudík, J. Mikloško, I. Plander, L. Halada, O. Sýkora, M. Vajteršic, Institute of Technical Cybernetics, Slovak Academy of Sciences, Bratislava, Czechoslovakia; J. Ondáš, Institute of Control and Computational Technique, Košice, Czechoslovakia; V. E. Kotov, V. A. Valkovskii, D. Ya. Levin, A. S. Narinyani, Computer Centre, Siberian Branch of the Academy of Sciences of the USSR, Novosibirsk, USSR; N. N. Mirenkov, Mathematical Institute, Siberian Branch of the Academy of Sciences of the USSR, Novosibirsk, USSR; V. V. Ignatushchenko, Institute of Control Sciences, Moscow, USSR; and G. Dávid, I. Losonczi, A. Sárközy, Computer and Automation Institute, Hungarian Academy of Sciences, Budapest, Hungary.

The structure of the book is given by its name: algorithms, software and hardware of parallel computers. Chapters 1 to 3 are devoted to the creation and analysis of parallel algorithms and programs. The first chapter (by J. Mikloško) describes the fundamental principles of creating effective numerical algorithms; its appendix (by M. Vajteršic) describes a new fast parallel algorithm for solving biharmonic equations in the square. In the second chapter (by J. Mikloško), a survey is given of the main results of the theory of complexity of parallel algorithms. Its appendix (by L. Halada) contains results on the upper bounds of the number of steps and processors for some parallel algorithms of linear algebry. The third chapter (by V. E. Kotov and V. A. Valkovskii) is devoted to algorithms and methods for the automatic generation of parallel programs. Chapters 4 to 6 deal with the theoretical and practical problems of parallel programming. The fourth chapter (by V. E. Kotov) gives a survey of the best-known formal models of parallel computations. Chapter 5 (by V. E. Kotov) examines parallel programming languages; in its appendix (by D. Ya. Levin and A. S. Narinyani) the facilities of the high-level language SETL are described. Chaptèr 6 (by G. Dávid) and its appendix (by I. Losonczi and A. Sárközy) discusses correctness of parallel programs and their automatic synthesis. Chapters 7 to 9 deal with problems of operating systems for parallel computers. The seventh chapter (by N. N. Mirenkov) is devoted to operating systems of multiprocessor computers. In Chapter 8 (by J. Ondáš) and in Chapter 9 (by J. Ondáš) some optimal and heuristic algorithms for scheduling devices in homogeneous and inhomogeneous multiprocessor computer systems are described. The appendix of Chapter 8 (by V. V. Ignatushchenko) describes an algorithm for task scheduling with unknown execution time. The last three chapters (Chapters 10 to 12) examine hardware problems of parallel computers. Chapter 10 (by I. Plander) contains a survey of various parallel computers architectures. Chapter 11 (by J. Chudík) describes the architecture of data-flow computers, and Chapter 12 (by J. Mikloško) discusses the interrelationship of algorithm and software with the architecture of the parallel computer. Its appendix (by O. Sýkora) describes the interprocessor communication network called the generalized perfect shuffle and its possible applications.

With the demand for faster and more powerful computing resources and plans for new generations of computers, research into all aspects of parallel computation is so active that any substantial survey of results is already bound to be outdated in some respects by the time it is published. Our aim has been to provide a survey of approaches to the central problems in the area, attempting to emphasize those contributions which have had, or can be expected to have, a lasting impact upon its development. To avoid the risk of straying too far from this aim, we chose 1978 as our — admittedly somewhat arbitrary — cut-off date for research eligible for inclusion. More recent research, in VLSI, parallel algorithm design, distributed processes, programming languages for concurrent processes, and the theory of parallelism can be found in an ever-growing number of journals and conference proceedings. In so far as we have achieved our aim, the book is recommended as a source and a reference especially to students of computer science, to members of computation centres, universities and research institutes and to interested specialists and students in the fields of natural, engineering and economic sciences.

In conclusion, we would like to express our acknowledgement to the scientific editor Prof. Dr. A. Huťa, CSc. and the reviewers Assoc. Prof. Ing. Š. Neuschl, CSc., Assoc. Prof. Dr. L. Molnár, CSc. and Dr. J. Šajda, CSc., for their constructive criticism of the manuscripts; to Dr. J. Nichta and Dr. M. Kasner for translating the texts from Slovak and Russian into English; to the members of VEDA, Publishing House of the Slovak Academy of Sciences, for their understanding in solving the many problems which have arisen in the course of preparing this book, and to the management of the Institute of Technical Cybernetics of the Slovak Academy of Sciences in Bratislava as well as to the Computer Centre of the Siberian Branch of the Academy of Sciences of the USSR in Novosibirsk for having created good working conditions which have also contributed to the implementation of this ambitious project.

J. Mikloško, V. E. Kotov
Editors

Chapter 1

SYNTHESIS OF PARALLEL NUMERICAL ALGORITHMS

We live in a world which requires concurrency of actions...
K. J. Thurber [27].

In this chapter we deal with the problems of creating parallel numerical algorithms. Even though the work in this field is only at the beginning, some interesting results have already been achieved in it.

In the first section we informally classify parallelism in numerical algorithms demonstrating various types of parallelism in non-trivial parallel algorithms. The transformation of algorithms with unbounded parallelism into bounded parallelism using a decomposition algorithm, or via the decomposition of the problem is described in the second section. The third section deals with differences between serial and parallel algorithms and with their implementation on a computer. Several essential internal differences between serial and parallel computations are formulated and demonstrated on concrete examples. In the final section, the basic methods for designing parallel numerical algorithms are described, the main attention being paid to some principles for making strictly serial algorithms parallel. The methods for creating parallel algorithms are divided into five groups. Emphasis is laid mainly on methods only suited to parallel computational processes. These are vectorization of the internally serial algorithm and the asynchronous implementation of the previously strictly synchronized algorithm. The principle of the individual methods is demonstrated by examples.

We note that the chapter on the complexity of parallel algorithms and the chapter on the coherence of algorithms, software and hardware of parallel computers, are closely connected to the content of this chapter.

1.1 Parallelism in numerical algorithms

In this section we demonstrate via three examples the possibilities of rendering a numerical algorithm parallel.

Some algorithms are in their formulation highly parallel although designed for serial computation, since most of their operators can be implemented as parallel algorithms without any modifications. An algorithm containing such a natural parallelism consists of mutually independent operators, which require for their execution the results of only some few other operators. Such an algorithm was transformed into a serial process only for implementation on a serial computer.

Natural parallelism is present mainly in the algorithms of linear algebra and in the algorithms for the numerical computation of partial differential equations. It is also present in algorithms that are based on the iterative computation of the same operator over different data, e.g. identical computations dependent on many parameters, method of successive approximations, some iterative methods for solving systems of linear equations, Monte Carlo methods, numerical integration, and in complex algorithms which consist of a large number of almost independent operators, e.g. iterative computation of Dirichlet's problem by the difference method, the finite element method.

As an example of the computational process with natural parallelism we describe the parallel algorithm for matrix decomposition for the solution of Poisson's equation in a rectangle [5].

We require the function $u(x, y)$ satisfying the equation

$$\frac{\partial^2 u}{\partial x^2} + \frac{\partial^2 u}{\partial y^2} = -f(x, y) \tag{1}$$

for a given rectangle, and the condition $u(x, y) = g(x, y)$ at its boundary. We divide the given area by N lines in the direction of the x-axis with step h and by M lines in the direction of the y-axis with step k. Let $u_{ij} = u(ih, jk)$ and $f_{ij} = f(ih, jk)$. After the application of the five-point difference formula at the point u_{ij}, we obtain

$$\frac{1}{h^2} [2u_{ij} - (u_{i+1,j} + u_{i-1,j})] + \frac{1}{k^2} [2u_{ij} - u_{i,j+1} + u_{i,j-1})] = f_{ij}.$$

These equations for all points of the straight-line $x = ih$ are

$$-\mathbf{u}_{i-1} + \mathbf{A}\mathbf{u}_i - \mathbf{u}_{i+1} = \mathbf{y}_i.$$

For all internal points of the area we obtain a system of MN linear equations with NM unknows.

$$\begin{aligned}
&\mathbf{A}\mathbf{u}_1 - \mathbf{u}_2 = \mathbf{y}_1, \\
&-\mathbf{u}_{i-1} + \mathbf{A}\mathbf{u}_i - \mathbf{u}_{i+1} = \mathbf{y}_i \qquad (i = 2, 3, \ldots, N-1), \\
&-\mathbf{u}_{N-1} + \mathbf{A}\mathbf{u}_N = \mathbf{y}_N,
\end{aligned} \tag{2}$$

where $\mathbf{A}$ is a tridiagonal matrix M/M with δ on the main diagonal, ϱ^2 on the minor diagonals, where $\varrho = h/k$, $\delta = 2(1 + \varrho^2)$, $\mathbf{u}_i = (u_{i1}, u_{i2}, \ldots, u_{iM})^T$, and $\mathbf{y}_i$ is dependent on the functions $f(x, y)$ and $g(x, y)$.

Since $\mathbf{A}$ is a symmetric matrix, it follows that $\mathbf{V}^T\mathbf{A}\mathbf{V} = \mathbf{D}$, where the eigenvectors of matrix $\mathbf{A}$ are the columns $\mathbf{V}$, and $\mathbf{D}$ is a diagonal matrix with the eigenvalues of matrix $\mathbf{A}$ on the diagonal. The elements of $\mathbf{V}$, v_{ij}, and the eigenvalue λ_j, are given by

$$v_{ij} = \sqrt{\frac{2}{M+1}} \sin\left(\frac{ij\pi}{M+1}\right) \qquad (i, j = 1, 2, ..., M),$$

$$\lambda_j = \delta - 2\varrho^2 \cos\left(\frac{j\pi}{M+1}\right) \qquad (j = 1, 2, ..., M).$$

After the multiplication of each equation (2) from the left by $\mathbf{V}^T$ and after the replacement of $\mathbf{VV}^T$ by $\mathbf{I}_M$ on the right from $\mathbf{A}$, we obtain from system (2) the system

$$\begin{aligned}
&\mathbf{D}\bar{u}_1 - \bar{u}_2 = \bar{y}_1, \\
&-\bar{u}_{i-1} + \mathbf{D}\bar{u}_i - \bar{u}_{i+1} = \bar{y}_i \qquad (i = 2, 3, ..., N-1), \\
&-\bar{u}_{N-1} + \mathbf{D}\bar{u}_N = \bar{y}_N.
\end{aligned} \qquad (3)$$

where $\bar{u}_i = \mathbf{V}^T u_i$ and $\bar{y}_i = \mathbf{V}^T y_i$.

If we now gather all the equations from system (3) which contain λ_j, $j = 1, 2, ...,$ M, we obtain the system of linear equations

$$\mathbf{G}_j \bar{u}_j = \bar{y}_j \qquad (j = 1, 2, ..., M),$$

where $\mathbf{G}_j$ is a tridiagonal matrix N/N with λ_j on the principal diagonal and with -1 on the minor diagonals, where

$$\bar{u}_j = (u_{1j}, u_{2j}, ..., u_{Nj})^T \quad \text{and} \quad \bar{y}_j = (y_{1j}, y_{2j}, ..., y_{Nj})^T.$$

Thus the direct parallel algorithm for matrix decomposition for the computation of equations (2) consists of the calculation:

a) $\mathbf{V}$ and $\mathbf{D}$,
b) y_i and $\bar{y}_i = \mathbf{V}^T y_i$ $(i = 1, 2, ..., N)$,
c) $\mathbf{G}_j \bar{u}_j = \bar{y}_j$ $(j = 1, 2, ..., M)$,
d) $u_i = \mathbf{V}\bar{u}_i$ $(i = 1, 2, ..., N)$.

The values $\mathbf{V}$ and $\mathbf{D}$ are not dependent on $f(x, y)$ and $g(x, y)$ and thus for the given N and M they need only be computed once. Steps b) and d) are similar. They consist of the computation of the scalar products and can be executed in parallel. If by a suitable choice of M we compute them by means of a fast Fourier transformation, then we attain another speedup of the computation. The parallel algorithm described achieves with NM processors an almost NM-fold speedup of the computation.

A simple conversion to parallelism of a serially implemented algorithm does often not reveal the entire parallelism contained in the algorithm. Exploitation of this hidden parallelism is only possible after a modification of the original algorithm, which usually requires either the introduction of redundant operators or the addition of some new ideas to the original method which were not contained in its serial implementation, e.g. chaotic relaxation for the computation of linear equations [6], or the algorithm for the computation of eigenvalues of symmetrix matrices by Jacobi's method, eliminating simultaneously several matrix elements [21], splitting the original set of ordinary differential equations into many subsets [17].

As an example of the computational process with such artificial parallelism we should mention the parallel shooting method [4], which is the generalization of the often unstable serial shooting method for the computation of boundary-value problems.

Consider a non-linear two-point boundary-value problem on the interval $[a, b]$ $\mathbf{y}' = \mathbf{f}(x, \mathbf{y})$, $\mathbf{r}(\mathbf{y}(a), \mathbf{y}(b)) = 0$, where $\mathbf{y}$ and $\mathbf{r}$ are n-dimensional vector functions. We divide $[a, b]$ into $m-1$ subintervals $a = x_1 < x_2 < ... < x_m = b$. Let $\mathbf{p}(x)$ be some estimate of the solution of $\mathbf{y}(x)$. Let $\mathbf{Y}_j = \mathbf{p}(x_j) = (Y_{1j}, Y_{2j}, ..., Y_{nj})^T$, $j = 1, 2, ..., m$. We now solve the $m-1$ initial value problems

$$\mathbf{y}' = \mathbf{f}(x, \mathbf{y}), \ \mathbf{y}(x_j) = \mathbf{Y}_j \qquad (j = 1, 2, ..., m-1). \tag{4}$$

The solution of these problems $\mathbf{Y} = \mathbf{y}(x, \mathbf{Y}_j)$ is defined on $[x_j, x_{j+1}]$.

We define $m-1$ vector step functions in x_{j+1}, i.e.

$$\mathbf{h}_j(\mathbf{Y}_j, \mathbf{Y}_{j+1}) = \mathbf{y}(x_{j+1}, \mathbf{Y}_j) - \mathbf{Y}_{j+1} \qquad (j = 1, 2, ..., m-2),$$
$$\mathbf{h}_{m-1}(\mathbf{Y}_1, \mathbf{Y}_{m-1}) = \mathbf{r}(\mathbf{Y}_1, \mathbf{y}(x_m, \mathbf{Y}_{m-1})).$$

The method of multiple shooting is based on the application of Newton's method, where $\mathbf{Y}_j$ is iteratively modified so that $\mathbf{h}_j \to 0$, $j = 1, 2, ..., m-1$. For a given $\mathbf{Y}_j$ let $\mathbf{h}_j(\mathbf{Y}_j, \mathbf{Y}_{j+1}) \neq 0$, but $\mathbf{h}_j(\mathbf{Y}_j + \Delta \mathbf{Y}_j, \mathbf{Y}_{j+1} + \Delta \mathbf{Y}_{j+1}) = 0$. From the Taylor expansion we obtain

$$0 \approx \mathbf{h}_j(\mathbf{Y}_j, \mathbf{Y}_{j+1}) + \frac{\partial \mathbf{h}_j}{\partial \mathbf{Y}_j} \Delta \mathbf{Y}_j + \frac{\partial \mathbf{h}_j}{\partial \mathbf{Y}_{j+1}} \Delta \mathbf{Y}_{j+1} \qquad (j = 1, 2, ..., m-2),$$

$$0 \approx \mathbf{h}_{m-1}(\mathbf{Y}_1, \mathbf{Y}_{m-1}) + \frac{\partial \mathbf{r}}{\partial \mathbf{Y}_1} \Delta \mathbf{Y}_1 + \frac{\partial \mathbf{r}}{\partial \mathbf{Y}_{m-1}} \Delta \mathbf{Y}_{m-1},$$

$$\frac{\partial \mathbf{h}_j}{\partial \mathbf{Y}_j} = \frac{\partial \mathbf{y}(x_{j+1}, \mathbf{Y}_j)}{\partial \mathbf{Y}_j} = \mathbf{G}_j \quad \text{and} \quad \frac{\partial \mathbf{h}_j}{\partial \mathbf{Y}_{j+1}} = -\mathbf{I}_n,$$

where $\mathbf{G}_j$ are matrices and $\mathbf{I}_n$ is a unit matrix of order n. Since

$$\frac{\partial \mathbf{r}}{\partial \mathbf{Y}_{m-1}} = \frac{\partial \mathbf{r}}{\partial \mathbf{Y}_m} \frac{\partial \mathbf{y}(x_m, \mathbf{Y}_{m-1})}{\partial \mathbf{Y}_{m-1}},$$

if we write $\frac{\partial \mathbf{r}}{\partial \mathbf{Y}_1} = \mathbf{A}$ and $\frac{\partial \mathbf{r}}{\partial \mathbf{Y}_m} = \mathbf{B}$, we obtain a block system of linear equations of order $(m-1)n$

$$\mathbf{G}_j \Delta \mathbf{Y}_j - \Delta \mathbf{Y}_{j+1} = -\mathbf{h}_j \qquad (j = 1, 2, ..., m-2),$$

$$\mathbf{A}\Delta\mathbf{Y}_1 + \mathbf{BG}_{m-1}\Delta\mathbf{Y}_{m-1} = -\mathbf{h}_{m-1}.$$

By solving this system we obtain

$$\mathbf{E}\Delta\mathbf{Y}_1 = \mathbf{u}, \tag{5}$$

where

$$\mathbf{E} = \mathbf{A} + \mathbf{BG}_{m-1}\mathbf{G}_{m-2}\dots\mathbf{G}_1 \quad \text{and} \quad -\mathbf{u} = \mathbf{h}_{m-1} + \mathbf{BG}_{m-1}\mathbf{h}_{m-2} + \dots + \mathbf{BG}_{m-1}\dots\mathbf{G}_2\mathbf{h}_1.$$

After the calculation of $\Delta\mathbf{Y}_1$ from the system (5) we obtain recurrently

$$\Delta\mathbf{Y}_j = \mathbf{h}_{j-1} + \mathbf{G}_{j-1}\Delta\mathbf{Y}_{j-1} \qquad (j = 2, 3, \dots, m-1). \tag{6}$$

The computation of the $(k+1)$-th iteration is done by the modified Newton method $\mathbf{Y}_j^{(k+1)} = \mathbf{Y}_j^{(k)} + \lambda^{(k)}\Delta\mathbf{Y}^{(k)}$, $j = 1, 2, \dots, m-1$, $0 < \lambda^{(k)} \leqq 1$, where $\lambda^{(k)}$ is in every step chosen to assist the convergence of the iteration (4). The computation of $\mathbf{G}_j$, $\mathbf{A}$ and $\mathbf{B}$ is performed in dependence on the magnitude of $\lambda^{(k)}$ by numerical differentiation.

One iteration of the parallel shooting algorithm consists of the computation of:

a) $(m-1)$ initial value problems (4),

b) $\mathbf{G}_j$, $j = 1, 2, \dots, m-1$ and $\mathbf{A}$, $\mathbf{B}$,

c) $\mathbf{E}$ and $\mathbf{u}$,

d) $\Delta\mathbf{Y}_1$ from system (5) and $\Delta\mathbf{Y}_j$, $j = 2, 3, \dots, m-1$, from (6).

Steps a) and b) of the algorithm can be computed in parallel on $(m-1)$ and $(m+1)$ processors, respectively, while for the computation of the other steps known parallel algorithms can be applied.

Besides algorithms with natural and artificial parallelism there also exist parallel algorithms specially designed for parallel computers; their implementation on serial computers is of no value. They are algorithms for solving problems for which only complete serial algorithms have been available so far, such as recurrent relations, elimination methods for the calculation of tridiagonal systems of linear equations, one-step iterations for calculating roots of non-linear equations, one-step methods for the computation of initial values for ordinary difference equations, computation of polynomials by the Horner scheme, Gauss—Seidel iteration method. When computing these problems on a parallel computer, it was necessary to either implement the whole algorithm or design a new algorithm for their calculation. The first example of the design of such a parallelism is the algorithm for the recursive doubling of recurrent computations [12], which shows that a seemingly complete serial algorithm can contain much latent parallelism.

The direct computation of the recurrent relation $x_1 = b_1$, $x_i = a_i x_{i-1} + b_i$, $i = 2, 3, \dots, n$, requires in a strictly serial sequence $n-1$ additions and $n-1$ multiplications. But if for $m \geqq p$ we define the values

$$q_{mp} = \sum_{j=p}^{m}\left(\prod_{r=j+1}^{m} a_r\right)b_j,$$

where

$$\prod_{r=m+1}^{m} a_r = 1,$$

then $x_t = q_{t1}$ and

$$x_{2t} = \prod_{r=t+1}^{2t} a_r q_{t1} + q_{2t,t+1}. \tag{7}$$

Thus the problem has been split into two independent, structurally identical subproblems of the same complexity. This splitting may be continued, by calculating the term at q_{t1} in relation (7) recursively by the same scheme. Then the algorithm for recursive doubling consists of the following steps:

a1) $A_0(i) = a_i$, $i = 2, 3, ..., n$; $B_0(i) = b_i$, $(i = 1, 2, ..., n)$;

for $k = 1, 2, ..., \lceil \log n \rceil$ parallel computation:

b1) $B_k(i) = B_{k-1}(i) + A_k(i)B_{k-1}(i - 2^{k-1})$, $2^{k-1} < i \leqq n$,

c1) $A_k(i) = A_{k-1}(i)A_{k-1}(i - 2^{k-1})$, $2^{k-1} + 1 < i \leqq n$.

In the parallel computation of steps b1) and c1) on $B_k(i)$ and $A_k(i)$ the values of x_i, $i = 1, 2, ..., n$ and those of $\prod_{r=2}^{i} a_r$, $i = 2, 3, ..., n$ are successively obtained. It follows from the algorithm that on an n-processor computer x_i, $i = 1, 2, ..., n$, are computed with $\lceil \log n \rceil$ successive sums and $2 \lceil \log n \rceil$ successive products, i.e. with $O(\log n)$ steps.

Figure 1 shows the procedure for a three-step parallel computation of x_i, $i = 1, 2, ..., 8$. We note that it follows from the definition that $q_{t1} = b_i$.

Other application of this parallel algorithm and its additional generalizations are described by Kogge [13].

As the second example we describe a parallel algorithm for cyclic even-odd reduction [25] for the computation of a tridiagonal system of linear equations $\mathbf{A}x = \mathbf{d}$, i.e.

$$\begin{bmatrix} a_1 & c_1 & & \\ b_2 & a_2 & \cdot & \mathbf{0} \\ & \cdot & \cdot & \cdot \\ & & \cdot & \cdot & c_{n-1} \\ \mathbf{0} & & \cdot & b_n & \cdot & a_n \end{bmatrix} \begin{bmatrix} x_1 \\ x_2 \\ \\ \\ x_n \end{bmatrix} = \begin{bmatrix} d_1 \\ d_2 \\ \\ \\ d_n \end{bmatrix}, \tag{8}$$

where **A** is a regular tridiagonal matrix and $n = 2^{m+1} - 1$. Its two basic operations are elimination of odd subscript unknows from the system (8) and their computation by regressive substitution.

If for every $j = 1, 2, \ldots, 2^m - 1$ we multiply the $(2j-1)$-th equation in (8) by $-b_{2j}a_{2j-1}^{-1}$ and the $(2j+1)$-th equation by $-c_{2j}a_{2j+1}^{-1}$, then after adding them to the $2j$-th equation we obtain

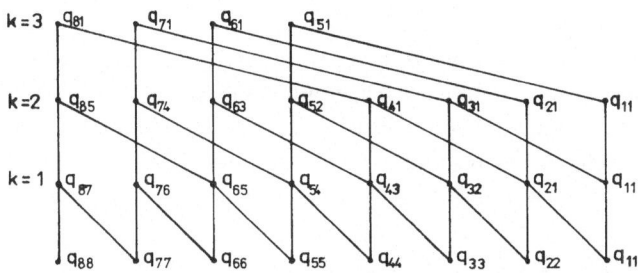

Fig. 1.

$$(-b_{2j}a_{2j-1}^{-1}b_{2j-1})x_{2j-2} + (a_{2j} - b_{2j}a_{2j-1}^{-1}c_{2j-1} - c_{2j}a_{2j+1}^{-1}b_{2j+1})x_{2j} +$$
$$+ (-c_{2j}a_{2j+1}^{-1}c_{2j+1})x_{2j+2} = d_{2j} - b_{2j}a_{2j-1}^{-1}d_{2j-1} - c_{2j}a_{2j+1}^{-1}d_{2j+1}$$
$$(j = 1, 2, \ldots, 2^m - 1). \tag{9}$$

The resulting equations comprise a tridiagonal system of equations, but only with even unknowns. It is the so-called reduction step. If we compute the even unknowns, then we obtain the odd ones from the original odd equations, which is the so-called regressive substitution step. In system (9) after rearranging the subscripts of the unknows we can again carry out a reduction step. We proceed in this way until we have one equation containing one unknown, or we can solve an arbitrary system and obtain the other unknowns by regressive substitution. Since every reduction as well as every substitution step can be executed in parallel, this algorithm can be executed on a parallel computer in a time proportional to log n.

1.2 Transformation of an algorithm with unbounded parallelism into an algorithm with bounded parallelism

It can be seen from the parallel algorithms given so far that the maximum number of processors required for their implementation is a function of n, i.e. of the size of the problem to be solved. Since the number of processors on a real computer is restricted, algorithms like this are of only theoretical importance. But in their implementation on a k-processor computer, unbounded parallelism algorithms must be transformed to k-parallel algorithms. This gives the results for unbounded parallelism great practical importance. In this section we describe two methods for this transformation: decomposition of the algorithm and decomposition of the problem.

Consider a problem P_n of size n with a given algorithm Q which solves the P_n on $p_1(n)$ processors in $t_1(n)$ time units. Our objective is to design a new algorithm R that solves the P_n on $p_2(n) < p_1(n)$ processors in $t_2(n)$ time units, where $t_2(n)$ is not much greater than $t_1(n)$.

In decomposing the algorithm each step of the original algorithm is divided into substeps, so that each of them can be executed with a smaller number of processors. If in the i-th step of the algorithm Q, q_i operations are executed, then this step changes to $\lceil q_i/p_2 \rceil$ steps of the algorithm R. Every new step consists of at least p_2 operations performed in parallel, and consequently as shown in Brent [3]

$$t_2 = \sum_{i=1}^{t_1} \lceil q_i/p_2 \rceil \le \sum_{i=1}^{t_1} (q_i + p_2 - 1)/p_2 = t_1 + \frac{1}{p_2}\left(\sum_{i=1}^{t_1} q_i - t_1\right).$$

The decomposition of the algorithm is shown by an example of the computation of a regular system of linear equations $\mathbf{A}x = \mathbf{b}$, where $\mathbf{A}$ is lower triangular matrix, i.e.

$$\begin{bmatrix} a_{11} & & & \\ a_{21} & a_{22} & & \mathbf{0} \\ \vdots & \vdots & \ddots & \\ a_{n1} & a_{n2} & \cdots & a_{nn} \end{bmatrix} \begin{bmatrix} x_1 \\ x_2 \\ \vdots \\ x_n \end{bmatrix} = \begin{bmatrix} b_1 \\ b_2 \\ \vdots \\ b_n \end{bmatrix} . \tag{10}$$

First we describe the parallel Gauss elimination, by which this system is solved on n processors in time $3n$, then we formulate its decomposition [11].

If for $i = 1, 2, \ldots, n$ we define

$$\mathbf{L}_i = \begin{bmatrix} 1 & & & & & & \\ & 1 & & & & \mathbf{0} & \\ & & \ddots & & & & \\ & & & 1/a_{ii} & & & \\ & & & \vdots & 1 & & \\ & & & \vdots & & \ddots & \\ \mathbf{0} & & & -a_{ni}/a_{ii} & & & 1 \end{bmatrix}$$

then it holds that $\mathbf{L}_n\mathbf{L}_{n-1} \ldots \mathbf{L}_1\mathbf{A} = \mathbf{I}_n$, and thus $x = \mathbf{L}_n\mathbf{L}_{n-1} \ldots \mathbf{L}_1\mathbf{b}$. Then we obtain the solution from the relation

$$y^{(1)} = \mathbf{b}, \quad y^{(i+1)} = \mathbf{L}_i y^{(i)} \quad (i = 1, 2, \ldots, n),$$

where $\mathbf{y}^{(n+1)} = \mathbf{x}$. This relation represents effectively the Gaussian elimination for system (10). It can be shown that for $i = 1, 2, \ldots, n$.

$$\mathbf{L}_i\mathbf{y}^{(i)} = \left(y_1^{(i)}, \ldots, \frac{y_i^{(i)}}{a_{ii}}, y_{i+1}^{(i)} - \frac{a_{i+1,i}}{a_{ii}} y_i^{(i)}, \ldots, y_n^{(i)} - \frac{a_{ni}}{a_{ii}} y_i^{(i)}\right)^T,$$

and thus on n processors it is possible to obtain $\mathbf{L}_i\mathbf{y}^{(i)}$ with three steps consisting of division, multiplication and subtraction. In a k-parallel implementation of this algorithm $(k < n)$ we decompose every step consisting of q_t operations $(q_t \leqq n)$ into $\lceil q_t/k \rceil$ substeps which are made up at most of k operations. By the algorithm obtained in this way $\mathbf{L}_i\mathbf{y}^{(i)}$ is computed in a time of

$$2\left\lceil \frac{n-i}{k} \right\rceil + \left\lceil \frac{n-i+1}{k} \right\rceil,$$

and consequently the sum for $i = 1, 2, \ldots, n$, i.e. the total time of computation, is

$$\frac{3}{2k} n^2 + \left(3 - \frac{7}{2k}\right)n + \frac{2}{k} - 2.$$

In decomposing a problem, we decompose it into small subproblems of size m, each of them being solved by the original algorithm G on a smaller number of processors $p_2(m)$.

We write system (10) as a block-triangular system [11]

$$\begin{bmatrix} \mathbf{A}_{11} & & & \\ \mathbf{A}_{21} & \mathbf{A}_{22} & & \mathbf{0} \\ \vdots & \vdots & \ddots & \\ \vdots & \vdots & & \ddots \\ \mathbf{A}_{m1} & \mathbf{A}_{m2} & \cdots & \mathbf{A}_{mm} \end{bmatrix} \begin{bmatrix} \mathbf{X}_1 \\ \mathbf{X}_2 \\ \vdots \\ \vdots \\ \mathbf{X}_m \end{bmatrix} = \begin{bmatrix} \mathbf{B}_1 \\ \mathbf{B}_2 \\ \vdots \\ \vdots \\ \mathbf{B}_m \end{bmatrix}, \tag{11}$$

where $m = \lceil n/p \rceil$; $\mathbf{A}_{ij}$ are square matrices of order p and $\mathbf{X}_i$, $\mathbf{B}_i$ are vectors of order p.

From system (11) we have

$$\mathbf{A}_{11}\mathbf{X}_1 = \mathbf{B}_1, \tag{12}$$

$$\mathbf{A}_{i+1,i+1}\mathbf{X}_{i+1} = \mathbf{B}_{i+1} - \sum_{j=1}^{i}\mathbf{A}_{i+1,j}\mathbf{X}_j \qquad (i = 1, 2, \ldots, m-1). \tag{13}$$

Afterwards, the computation of the solution proceeds with the following steps:
   a) computation of $\mathbf{X}_1$ with respect to (12) by algorithm Q, for $i = 1, 2, \ldots, m-1$;
   b) computation of $\mathbf{A}_{i+1,j}\mathbf{X}_j$ $(j = 1, 2, \ldots, i)$;

c) computation of the right-hand side of the relation (13);

d) computation of X_{i+1} from the relation (13) using algorithm Q.

Another method of decomposing this problem is described in [8], where the matrix **A** in system (10) is decomposed into

$$\mathbf{A} = \begin{bmatrix} \mathbf{A}_1 & 0 \\ \mathbf{A}_2 & \mathbf{A}_3 \end{bmatrix},$$

where $\mathbf{A}_1$ and $\mathbf{A}_3$ are the lower triangular matrices of order $n/2$. Then,

$$\mathbf{A}^{-1} = \begin{bmatrix} \mathbf{A}_1^{-1} & 0 \\ -\mathbf{A}_3^{-1}\mathbf{A}_2\mathbf{A}_1^{-1} & \mathbf{A}_3^{-1} \end{bmatrix}$$

and thus system (10) is solved by parallel computation of $\mathbf{A}_1^{-1}$ and $\mathbf{A}_3^{-1}$ with subsequent creation of $-\mathbf{A}_3^{-1}.\mathbf{A}_2\mathbf{A}_1^{-1}$ and $x = \mathbf{A}^{-1}b$.

1.3 Differences between serial and parallel algorithms and their implementation

There are the following internal differences between serial and parallel algorithms and their implementation:

a) Effective serial algorithms are not necessarily parallel algorithms;

b) Non-effective serial algorithms can lead to effective parallel algorithms;

c) Even algorithms that require complete serial succession of operations can contain much hidden parallelism;

d) Some parallel algorithms are obtained from serial algorithms by suitable modification;

e) Effective parallel algorithms need not be effective for serial computations;

f) The speed of convergence of serial and parallel algorithms can be different;

g) The numerical stability of serial and parallel implementation of an algorithm can be different;

h) The cost of some operations in serial and parallel implementations of the same algorithm can differ;

i) Analysis of the complexity of parallel computations can have results differing from serial computations;

j) Effectiveness and speed of implementing parallel algorithms are closely dependent on

j1) the architecture of the computer, on which these algorithms are executed;

j2) the suitability of the interconnection of its registers and processors;

j3) the suitability of the arrangement of data in the memory of the computer, which can change during computation;

k) Implementation of parallel algorithms on some types of computers requires effective methods
   - k1) for synchronization of the activity of the operators of the program being implemented;
   - k2) for solving conflicts in memory accesses;
   - k3) for distributing the work to the individual processors.

Let us demonstrate now the individual differences on concrete examples.

a) It is known that the algorithm for LR decomposition is an effective serial algorithm for solving tridiagonal systems of linear equations $\mathbf{A}x = d$, in which $\mathbf{A}$ is a positive definite or strictly diagonally dominant matrix. In this algorithm, after a recurrent use of the decomposition $\mathbf{A} = \mathbf{LR}$, where $\mathbf{L}$ is the lower and $\mathbf{R}$ the upper bidiagonal matrix, we calculate the solution successively from $\mathbf{L}y = d$ and again recurrently from $\mathbf{R}x = y$ [9]. Since each step of this computation is dependent on the preceding step, this algorithm requires both serial and parallel implementation $O(n)$ operations, and thus it is not suited for parallel computations. In the next section we shall indicate the possibility of making it parallel.

b) One of the worst algorithms for sorting on serial computers is the algorithm which determines for each element x_i of a vector how many smaller elements are there in the vector, thus determining its position in the sorted vector $p(i)$ in a sorted field. The number of the required comparisons of this algorithm is $O(n^2)$. But its parallel implementation gives the fastest known parallel algorithm for sorting, which requires on $O(\log n)$ comparisons on $O(n^2)$ processors [7].

Let $x_1, x_2, ..., x_n$ be a succession of elements of an ordered set that is to be sorted according to the relation $\leq$. If for $i, j = 1, 2, ..., n$, $j \neq i$, we define the operation

$$x_i : x_j = \begin{cases} 1, & \text{if } x_i \leq x_j, \\ 0, & \text{if } x_i > x_j, \end{cases}$$

then for the computation of $p(i)$, $i = 1, 2, ..., n$, i.e. for the implementation of all comparisons of x_i and x_j, one parallel step is needed on $n(n-1)$ processors. For the computation of $p(j) = 1 + \sum_i (x_i : x_j)$, $i, j = 1, 2, ..., n$, $j \neq i$, $\lceil \log n \rceil$ steps are required, and thus for the execution of the fastest known parallel algorithm $\lceil \log n \rceil + 1$ comparisons on $n(n-1)$ processors are needed.

c) In the case of a two-term

$$p_i = a_i p_{i-1} + b_i \qquad (i = 2, 3, ..., n), \tag{14}$$

and a three-term recurrent relation

$$q_0 = 1, \ q_1 = a_1, \ q_i = a_i q_{i-1} + b_i q_{i-2} \qquad (i = 2, 3, ..., n), \tag{15}$$

in which a_i, b_i are given, the computation of $\{p_i\}$ and $\{q_i\}$, $i = 2, 3, ..., n$, requires $O(n)$ serial computational steps. But if we write relations (14) and (15) in the form:

$$P_i = \begin{bmatrix} p_i \\ 1 \end{bmatrix} = \begin{bmatrix} a_i & b_i \\ 0 & 1 \end{bmatrix} \begin{bmatrix} p_{i-1} \\ 1 \end{bmatrix} = G_i P_{i-1}$$

and

$$Q_i = \begin{bmatrix} q_i \\ q_{i-1} \end{bmatrix} = \begin{bmatrix} a_i & b_i \\ 1 & 0 \end{bmatrix} \begin{bmatrix} q_{i-1} \\ q_{i-2} \end{bmatrix} = H_i Q_{i-1},$$

then

$$P_i = \prod_{j=2}^{i} G_j P_1 \quad \text{and} \quad Q_i = \prod_{j=2}^{i} H_j Q_1,$$

and consequently, if the required matrix products are computed in parallel, then (14) and (15) require $O(\log n)$ steps [24]. The method by which this computation is implemented is called recursive doubling and was described in this chapter in Section 1.

d) We consider the computation of the initial value problem [15]

$$y' = f(x, y), \ y(x_0) = y_0, \qquad x > x_0$$

at points $x_i = (i - 1)h$, $i = 2, 3, \ldots$, by formulae of predictor-corrector type

$$y_{i+1}^{(p)} = y_i^{(c)} + \frac{h}{2} (3f_i^{(c)} - f_{i-1}^{(c)}),$$

$$\tag{16}$$

$$y_{i+1}^{(c)} = y_i^{(c)} + \frac{h}{2} (f_{i+1}^{(p)} + f_i^{(c)}),$$

in which y_i is the approximation to $y(x_i)$, $y_i^{(p)}$ is the predicted value of y_i, $y_i^{(c)}$ is the corrected value of y_i, and $f_i^{(p)}$ and $f_i^{(c)}$ denote $f(x_i, y_i^{(p)})$ and $f(x_i, y_i^{(c)})$, respectively.

The computation using the relations (16) proceeds strictly serially in the succession $\ldots \to y_{i+1}^{(p)} \to f_{i+1}^{(p)} \to y_{i+1}^{(c)} \to f_{i+1}^{(c)} \to \ldots$ If in the first formula of (16) we write $f_i^{(c)} = f_i^{(p)}$ and instead of $y_i^{(c)}$ we substitute the second formula delayed by one step, then we obtain analogous formulae of the second order

$$y_{i+1}^{(p)} = y_{i-1}^{(c)} + 2hf_i^{(p)},$$

$$y_i^{(c)} = y_{i-1}^{(c)} + \frac{h}{2}(f_i^{(p)} + f_{i-1}^{(c)}),$$

which can proceed in parallel in two branches:

$$\ldots \to y_{i+1}^{(p)} \to f_{i+1}^{(p)} \to \ldots$$

$$\ldots \to y_i^{(c)} \to f_i^{(c)} \to \ldots$$

e) The large redundancy in the number of operations in parallel algorithms with serial implementation sometimes effectively restricts them to parallel computations only. This can be demonstrated, for instance, by an algorithms which vectorizes the serial vector of LR decomposition for the tridiagonal system of linear equations [9] and which will described in the next section of this chapter. Of the same is also the parallel algorithm for the computation of x^n which is described in the chapter on the complexity of parallel algorithms.

f) Now we consider Dirichlet's problem for the Laplace equation [23], i.e. we require the function $u(x, y)$ which in the square $0 \leqq x, y \leqq 1$ satisfies the equation

$$\frac{\partial^2 u}{\partial x^2} + \frac{\partial^2 u}{\partial y^2} = 0 \tag{17}$$

and on its boundary the boundary conditions $u(x, y) = g(x, y)$. After the discretization of the square with step $h = 1/(N + 1)$, we designate the nodes of the network as $x_i = ih$, $y_j = jh$, $i, j = 1, 2, \ldots, N + 1$. After substituting the differentiation in (17) with difference formulae we obtain for every point of the network $[x_i, y_j]$ the formula

$$u_{ij}^{(k+1)} = (u_{i-1,j}^{(k)} + u_{i,j+1}^{(k)} + u_{i+1,j}^{(k)} + u_{i,j-1}^{(k)})/4, \tag{18}$$

where $u_{ij}^{(k)}$ denotes the value of the k-th iteration for the approximate solution at the point $[x_i, y_j]$. If one processor is assigned to every point of the network, then this algorithm is highly parallel on N^2 processors, even though the speed of its convergence is small, since for the computation of the $(k + 1)$-th iteration only the values of the k-th iteration are used. It is known that in a stable iteration the application of more recent data accelerates the convergence. Thus, if we iterate successively the points of the network in rows from the left to the right and the rows from the top to the bottom, then we obtain the formula

$$u_{ij}^{(k+1)} = (u_{i-1,j}^{(k+1)} + u_{i,j+1}^{(k+1)} + u_{i+1,j}^{(k)} + u_{i,j-1}^{(k)})/4, \tag{19}$$

by which the $(k + 1)$-th iteration is computed from two adjacent values of the $(k + 1)$-th iteration and two of the k-th iteration. This algorithm converges faster than the preceding one, but its implementation is completely serial.

A simple trade-off solution is the parallel computation on N processors along the rows from the top to the bottom, i.e. by formula (18) in which $u_{i+1,j}^{(k)}$ is replaced by $u_{i+1,j}^{(k+1)}$.

A more complex, but highly parallel solution with a rate of convergence equivalent to formula (19), is the computation along the diagonals [26]. We connect the points of the net by lines parallel to the principal diagonal of the area, numbering then 1, 2, ..., $2N - 1$ from the lower left-hand corner upwards. First we calculate the values of the points of the k-th iteration on odd diagonals, then those of the $(k + 1)$-th iteration on even diagonals, then the $(k + 2)$-th iteration on odd diagonals, etc., until steady-state conditions are achieved. Since the points on the odd diagonals are only dependent on the points on the even diagonals and conversely, this computation using $N^2/2$ processors is highly effective.

g) The shooting method for the computation of boundary value problems for ordinary differential equations applied once to the whole interval is a completely serial process which is often numerically unstable. A more exact and stable algorithm for solving such problems is the so-called method of parallel shooting [4] which was described in the first section of this chapter. After splitting the entire interval into subintervals, the shooting method is applied to the subintervals in parallel, the partial solutions obtained being iterated so that the total solution is smooth and satisfies the boundary conditions. Thus, by making the method parallel, its numerical stability has been improved.

Parallelism can reduce numerical stability, for instance, in the algorithm for parallel computation of arithmetic expressions containing n variables, operations $\pm$, $\times$, $/$, and with arbitrary nesting of parentheses. Brent [3] has constructively shown that every such expression can be calculated in time $4 \log n$ on $3(n - 1)$ processors. As numerical experiments show, this parallel algorithm is not always numerically stable.

h) Serial implementation of the Gauss—Jordan elimination with partial pivotization requires for the solution of a system of n linear equations with n unknowns $O(n^3)$ arithmetic operations and $O(n^2)$ comparisons. Thus the cost of arithmetic operations exceeds substantially the cost of pivotization. The parallel implementation of this method requires $O(n)$ arithmetic steps and $O(n \log n)$ comparative steps [10] on $O(n^2)$ processors, so that the cost of pivotization may exceed the cost of arithmetic operations. Therefore, in [22] an algorithm has been designed, in which by the application of Given's transformation a system of linear equations is solved with $O(n)$ arithmetic steps without any pivotization being necessary on $O(n^2)$ processors.

We note that if only $O(n)$ processors are available, then the parallel Gauss—Jordan method with partial pivotization needs $O(n^2)$ arithmetic steps and $O(n \log n)$ comparative steps, so that the cost of some operations in the parallel computation may also be dependent on the number of processors.

i) The results in the analysis of the complexity of parallel algorithm of some matrix operations, which differ from the results for serial computations, have been described in the third section of the chapter on the complexity of parallel algorithms. We have also shown that for some matrix computations the data transfers between the memories of the processors of a given computer rather than the arithmetic operations are the limiting factor in the effectiveness of the computations.

j) The importance of the suitability of the architecture of the parallel computer to the programs and algorithms used is frequently emphasized in the chapter on the relationships between algorithms, hardware and software of parallel computers, in which examples j2) and j3) are the interconnection of processors with a "perfect shuffle" network, and the skew method of matrix storage in the matrix processor.

Problems connected with k) are described and solved in several chapters in this book.

We note that problems j) and k) also arise in serial computation, but their importance has increased with the application of parallel algorithms on parallel computers.

1.4 Methods for creating parallel algorithms

The transition from serial algorithms to parallel algorithms opens new possibilities for creating algorithms. In this section we describe some methods for designing parallel algorithms, while more attention is paid to some methods for making strictly serial algorithms parallel. The methods for making programs automatically parallel are described in a special chapter of this book and therefore are not mentioned here.

We divide the methods for creating parallel algorithms into these 5 groups:

a) Restructuring of a given algorithm as an algorithm numerically equivalent which contains a greater degree of parallelism.

b) Splitting of a given problem into subproblem that are solved in parallel; the solution of the whole problem is obtained by combining the solutions of the subproblems.

c) The "divide et impera" technique: a task of size n is split into two independent tasks of identical complexity of size $n/2$, and this splitting can be continued recursively.

d) Vectorization of the internally serial algorithm; a direct serial algorithm is converted to an iterative method which rapidly converges to the solution under certain conditions.

e) Asynchronous parallel implementation of a serial, strictly synchronized algorithm.

We note that methods a), b) and c) have also been used to render serial computations effective; but methods d) and e) are new and are only suitable for parallel computational processes.

Now we describe the individual techniques with concrete examples. In case a) the transformation can be executed by various algebraic rearrangements, or suitable formulae which are more parallel than the original formulae, can be used. Arithmetic expressions are the fundamental part of every numerical algorithm. An enhancement of their parallelism can be achieved by exploitation of the associative, commutative and distributive laws. For example, the expressions [14] $(((a + b) + c) + d)$ requires three steps for computation. By means of the associative law we obtain $(a + b) + (c + d)$ with two parallel steps. Again, the expression $a + bc + d$ requires 3 steps, but after the application of the commutative law we obtain $a + d + bc$ with two parallel steps.

The expression $a(bcd + e)$ is calculated in 4 parallel steps, nothing being improved by the associative and commutative laws. But when using the distributive law we obtain $abcd + ae$, which can be calculated in three parallel steps. Therefore algorithms have been designed which transform general arithmetic expressions into their parallel equivalents.

An algorithm which exploits in an optimal manner the associative and commutative laws has been described by Baer and Bovet [1]; an algorithm in which the distributive law is exploited has been described by Muraoka [16].

We show the application of a suitable formula for parallel computation using the following example [18].

Given a triangular matrix $\mathbf{A}$ of order n with a unit diagonal, i.e. $\mathbf{A} = \mathbf{I}_n - \mathbf{L}$ is the upper triangular matrix, the serial recurrent computation of $\mathbf{A}^{-1}$ requires $O(n^3)$ arithmetic operations. The parallel computation is based on the fact that in the matrices $\mathbf{L}^j$, $j = 2, 3, \ldots, n - 1$, along the minor diagonals, the number of zeros increases until $\mathbf{L}^s = 0$, for $s \geq n$.

Nevertheless, since

$$(\mathbf{I}_n - \mathbf{L})(\mathbf{I}_n + \mathbf{L} + \mathbf{L}^2 + \ldots) = \mathbf{I}_n,$$

then we obtain the formula for inversion

$$\mathbf{A}^{-1} = \mathbf{I}_n + \mathbf{L} + \mathbf{L}^2 + \ldots + \mathbf{L}^{n-1} = (\mathbf{I}_n + \mathbf{L}^{2^{m-1}})(\mathbf{I}_n + \mathbf{L}^{2^{m-2}}) \ldots (\mathbf{I}_n + \mathbf{L}),$$

where $m = \lceil \log n \rceil$. Thus the parallel algorithm for the computation of $\mathbf{A}^{-1}$ consists of the calculation of:

a) $\mathbf{L}^2, \mathbf{L}^4, \mathbf{L}^8 \ldots$ $(O(\log^2 n)$ steps$)$,
b) $(\mathbf{I}_n + \mathbf{L}^2), (\mathbf{I}_n + \mathbf{L}^4), \ldots$ (one step),
c) $\prod_{i=0}^{m}(\mathbf{I}_n + \mathbf{L}^{2^{i-1}})$ $(O(\log^2 n)$ steps$)$,

i.e. on $O(n^3)$ processors it is executed in $O(\log^2 n)$ steps.

We demonstrate the method b) applied to the parallelization of the numerical computation of an initial value problem for ordinary differential equations

$$y' = f(x, y), \quad y(a) = y_0, \quad a \leqq x \leqq b. \tag{20}$$

Most standard numerical methods for computing (20) are completely serial procedures. The algorithm described by Nievergelt [17] consists of a multiple parallel application of a numerical method for solving many initial value problems in the subinterval of the interval required and by interpolation of the results between the solutions obtained.

After splitting $[a, b]$ into m equal subintervals $[x_{i-1}, x_i]$, $x_0 = a$, $x_m = b$, $i = 1, 2, \ldots, m$ we obtain in some way a crude estimate of y_i for the solution of $y(x_i)$, $i = 1, 2, \ldots, m - 1$. On every straightline $y = x_i$ in the vicinity of the point $y_i^{(0)}$ we choose M_i values of y_{ij}, $i = 1, 2, \ldots, m - 1$, $j = 1, 2, \ldots, M_i$.

We obtain the initial problems

$$
\begin{aligned}
y' &= f(x, y), & y(a) &= y_0, & a &\leqq x \leqq x_1 \\
y' &= f(x, y), & y(x_i) &= y_{ij}, & x_i &\leqq x \leqq x_{i+1},
\end{aligned}
\tag{21}
$$

$$(j = 1, 2, \ldots, M_i), \quad (i = 1, 2, \ldots, m - 1),$$

which we solve in parallel on $1 + \sum_{i=1}^{m-1} M_i$ processors by some mathematical method M. In the time which is needed for one application of the method M, we obtain solutions of all these initial problems. Then, by interpolation we obtain the required solution of (20), i.e. $y_1, y_2, \ldots, y_m$ at points $x_1, x_2, \ldots, x_m$. We regard the solution (21) by M as y_1; by interpolation with M_i branches of the solution in $[x_1, x_2]$ we determine for y_1 on the straightline $x = x_2$ the value y_2, etc. Similarly we proceed until we arrive at y_m at $x_m = b$. It is interesting that for linear equations it suffices to choose $M_i = 2$, $i = 1, 2, \ldots, m - 1$; the accuracy of the method described is the same as if method M was used on the whole interval $[a, b]$. The method of splitting tasks into subtasks was also employed in designing the parallel shooting algorithm that we described in the first section of this chapter.

We demonstrate the method c), i.e. the "divide et impera" method with the technique suggested by Pease [19], by which a system of n linear equations with n unknowns $\mathbf{A}\mathbf{x} = \mathbf{b}$ is solved on n processors with $O(n^2 \log n)$ steps.

For the sake of simplicity let $n = 2^m$. The system being solved is transformed into the form

$$
\begin{bmatrix} \mathbf{I} & \mathbf{F}_1 \\ \mathbf{F}_2 & \mathbf{I} \end{bmatrix}
\begin{bmatrix} \mathbf{x}_1 \\ \mathbf{x}_2 \end{bmatrix}
=
\begin{bmatrix} \mathbf{g}_1 \\ \mathbf{g}_2 \end{bmatrix},
$$

where $\mathbf{I}$ is a unit matrix of the order 2^{m-1}. After multiplication by the matrix

$$
\begin{bmatrix} \mathbf{I} & -\mathbf{F}_1 \\ -\mathbf{F}_2 & \mathbf{I} \end{bmatrix}
$$

we split the original system into two independent subsystems

$$(I - F_1 F_2)x_1 = g_1 - F_1 g_2,$$
$$(I - F_2 F_1)x_2 = g_2 - F_2 g_1,$$

in which the same procedure can be repeated recursively. Thus, after m steps we obtain the desired solution.

The method of recursive doubling that we have described in first section of this chapter is also an example of c).

The vectorization of an internally serial algorithm, i.e. d), along with a new way of accelerating vector iterations of a certain type is demonstrated on an example of Gaussian elimination for tridiagonal systems of linear equations $Ax = c$, where for the sake of simplicity A has the form

$$A = \begin{bmatrix} 1 & & b_1 & & \mathbf{0} & \\ a_2 & \ddots & & 1 & \ddots & b_2 & \\ & \ddots & \ddots & & \ddots & & \ddots \\ \mathbf{0} & & a_{n-1} & & 1 & & b_{n-1} \\ & & & a_n & & 1 \end{bmatrix} .$$

The classical Gaussian elimination consists of the factorization $A = (I + K)D(I + R)$ and the solution of the bidiagonal equations $(I + K)f = c$ and $(I + R)x = D^{-1}f$, which can be written in recursive form as

a) $d_1 = 1,$ $d_j = 1 - a_j b_{j-1}/d_{j-1}$ $(j = 2, 3, ..., n);$

b) $f_1 = c_1,$ $k_j = a_j/d_{j-1},$ $f_j = c_j - k_j f_{j-1}$ $(j = 2, 3, ..., n);$

c) $r_j = b_j/d_j,$ $(j = 1, 2, ..., n-1);$

    $g_j = f_j/d_j$ $(j = 1, 2, ..., n);$

    $x_n = g_n,$ $x_j = g_j - r_j x_{j+1}$ $(j = n-1, n-2, ..., 1).$

As we can see, all these recurrence relations are internally serial. Their parallelization by the vectorization of this algorithm [9] is described below.

Serial recursions in the Gaussian elimination were in [9] replaced by successive vector iterations of vectors d, f and finally by x. For example, the relation for d_j can for $j > 1$ be iterated as

$$d_j^{(i)} = 1 - a_j b_{j-1} d_{j-1}^{(i-1)} \qquad (i = 1, 2, ...), \tag{22}$$

where the upper index denotes the iteration step. In this way it is possible to compute in parallel all elements of the initial vector d under a suitable initial condition. A parallel vector iteration like this requires in general many more operations than the original serial recursion, but it is implemented with advantage on parallel computers — for example pipeline processors. It will be derived from a matrix formulation.

If a matrix A has an additive or multiplicative decomposition of the form

$A = A_K + I + A_R$ or $A = (I + K)D(I + R)$, where A_K is a matrix which has its non-zero diagonal below the principal diagonal, and A_R is a matrix which has its non-zero diagonal above the principal diagonal, then

$$D = I - A_K D^{-1} A_R, \tag{23}$$

where

$$K = A_K D^{-1}, \quad R = D^{-1} A_R.$$

Let $D = \text{diag}\,(d_1, d_2, ..., d_n)$, $K = \text{subdiag}\,(k_2, k_3, ..., k_n)$ and $R = \text{superdiag}\,(r_1, r_2, ..., r_{n-1})$. Then, for the calculation of d_j, k_j and r_j the above recurrent relations and formulae are valid.

From formula (23) follows the iteration

$$D^{(i)} = I - A_K (D^{(i-1)})^{-1} A_R \qquad (i = 1, 2, ...), \tag{24}$$

where $D^{(0)}$ is assumed to be regular. From $D^{(i)}$ it is possible to compute approximately $\bar{K} = A_K (D^{(i)})^{-1}$ and $\bar{R} = (D^{(i)})^{-1} A_R$. If $D^{(i)} = \text{diag}\,(d_1^{(i)}, d_2^{(i)}, ..., d_n^{(i)})$, then iteration (24) is identical to (22). The rate of convergence of the iterations (22) can be improved since $d_j^{(i)}$ is dependent on $d_{j-1}^{(i-1)}$ only.

If we first compute in parallel all the even indexed elements of d and then the odd indexed elements, always using the most recent values available, then the results for the odd indexed elements will be the same if the vector d had been calculated twice. In this way it is possible to speed up the convergence of all vector iterations of the form $z_j^{(i)} = F(z_{j-1}^{(i-1)})$ [9].

It follows from the bidiagonal equations in the Gaussian elimination that $f = c - Kf$ and $x = D^{-1}f - Rx$. Jacobi's iteration for these equations yields $f^{(i)} = c - Kf^{(i-1)}$, and $x^{(i)} = g - Rx^{(i-1)}$, which are again parallel vector iterations $f_j^{(i)} = c_j - k_j f_{j-1}^{(i-1)}$ and $x_j^{(i)} = g_j - r_j x_{j+1}^{(i-1)}$, and can also be speeded up as described above.

On the basis of the above, it is possible to implement the speeded up parallel Gaussian elimination by replacing the horizontal recursion by vertical iteration in these steps. For simplicity let n be an even number:

a) Let $d^{(0)}$ be given and $d_1^{(i)} = 1$ for all i;
   for $i = 1, 2, ..., ID$ compute
   $d_j^{(i)} = 1 - a_j b_{j-1}/d_{j-1}^{(i-1)}$, j even
   $d_j^{(i)} = 1 - a_j b_{j-1}/d_{j-1}^{(i)}$, j odd and > 1.

b) Let $\bar{k}_j = a_j/d_{j-1}^{(ID)}$ for all $j > 1$;
   Let $f^{(0)}$ be given and $f_1^{(i)} = c_1$ for all i;
   for $i = 1, 2, ..., IF$ compute
   $f_j^{(i)} = c_j - \bar{k}_j f_{j-1}^{(i-1)}$, j even,
   $f_j^{(i)} = c_j - \bar{k}_j f_{j-1}^{(i)}$, j odd and > 1.

c) Define $\bar{g}_j = f_j^{(IF)}/d_j^{(ID)}$ for all j;

$$\bar{r}_j = b_j / d_j^{(ID)} \text{ for all } j < n.$$

Let $\mathbf{x}^{(0)}$ be given and $x_n^{(i)} = \bar{g}_n$ for all i;

for $i = 1, 2, \ldots, IX$ compute

$$x_j^{(i)} = \bar{g}_j - \bar{r}_j x_{j+1}^{(i-1)}, \, j \text{ odd},$$

$$x_j^{(i)} = \bar{g}_j - \bar{r}_j x_{j+1}^{(i)}, \, j \text{ even and } < n.$$

The approximate solution of the system $\mathbf{Ax} = \mathbf{c}$ is $\mathbf{x}^{(IX)}$. The values ID, IF and IX can be a priori established to the desired accuracy or computed. For the rate of convergence of this iterative algorithm the following theorem is valid [9]: Let

$$\lambda = \max_j |4a_j b_{j-1}|, \quad \alpha = \max_j |a_j a_{j-1}|^{1/2}, \quad \beta = \max_j |b_j b_{j-1}|^{1/2}, \quad p = 1 - \sqrt{1-\lambda}, \quad q =$$

$1 + \sqrt{1-\lambda}$. Let $\| \ \|$ denote infinite norm. If $\lambda \leq 1$, $\alpha \leq q/2$ and $\beta \leq q/2$, then for the accelerated parallel Gaussian elimination

$$\|\mathbf{D}^{(i)} - \mathbf{D}\| < (p/q)^2 \cdot \|\mathbf{D}^{(i-1)} - \mathbf{D}\| \qquad (i = 2, 3, \ldots, ID),$$
$$\|\mathbf{f}^{(i)} - \mathbf{f}\| < (2\alpha/q)^2 \cdot \|\mathbf{f}^{(i-1)} - \mathbf{f}\| + \delta_f \qquad (i = 2, 3, \ldots, IF),$$
$$\|\mathbf{x}^{(i)} - \mathbf{x}\| < (2\beta/q)^2 \cdot \|\mathbf{x}^{(i-1)} - \mathbf{x}\| + \delta_x \qquad (i = 2, 3, \ldots, IX),$$

where δ_f and δ_x are dependent on the preceding steps and can be arbitrarily small. For $i = 1$ the reduction factors are raised to the second power.

By the parallel algorithm described it is possible that under certain conditions (e.g. diagonal dominance of matrix $\mathbf{A}$) a tridiagonal system of n linear equations can be computed on $n/2$ processors in $O(1)$ steps.

The method e) of creating parallel algorithm is demonstrated using the so-called chaotic or asynchronous algorithms.

The chaotic implementation of parallel algorithms was described by Chazan and Miranker in [6] for the iterative computation of a system of linear equations $\mathbf{x} = \mathbf{Ax} + \mathbf{b}$, where $\mathbf{A}$ is a real matrix of order n. Single components of the solution are iterated on different processors in a random order, as global variables stored in a memory shared by all processors. The iterative process ends when a certain condition is satisfied which is controlled by a processor reserved for it. To ensure the convergence of this scheme, the succession of iterations is restricted in that there must exist a fixed postive integer s, so that in the execution of the i-th iteration of some component it is possible to use a component of the j-th iteration only if $j \geq i - s$, and it is necessary that in an execution of the algorithm each component of the solution is iterated for "infinitely many" times. It is proved in [6] that this process will converge, if $\varrho(|\mathbf{A}|) < 1$, where $\varrho(|\mathbf{A}|)$ is the spectral radius of matrix $|\mathbf{A}|$, i.e. of the matrix whose every element is replaced by its absolute value. The larger is s in this chaotic process, i.e. the older are the indices of iterations which can be used (which adversely effects its convergence), the less its operators will be blocked by waiting for suitable input data, the fewer housekeeping operations will be needed, and the faster the entire process will be executed. So far, no attention has been paid to looking for an optimal value of s. Work has been published on the extension of the chaotic principle to non-linear systems [20].

The repeated checking of the status of single iterations and also the form of synchronization cannot be avoided in the implementation of chaotic algorithms. Its disadvantage is also in its narrow applicability in numerical mathematics and in its restriction to iterative methods. Therefore, from the aspect of the effectiveness of the implementation and the range of application, the so-called asynchronous implementation of algorithms is preferable. We give below only some results from [2], making use of some facts and ideas from Chapter 12 of this book.

Suppose we have to solve a task that requires sequences of n subtasks $w_1, w_2, ..., w_n$ under the following conditions:

c1: subtask w_i, $i = 2, 3, ..., n$ cannot start before w_{i-1} has finished;

c2: in the computation of w_i, $i = 1, 2, ..., n$, there is no parallelism;

c3: the execution time of each subtask w_i, $i = 1, 2, ..., n$, is a random variable.

Conditions c1 and c2 mean that the subtasks constitute a strictly serial algorithm, c3 represents asynchronous operation of a multiprocessor computer.

In the algorithm to be described next, we make use of the variation in execution times of its individual subtasks to increase the parallelism of the execution. Under a parallel algorithm we understand a set of asynchronous processes communicating through global variables. We also assume that for every process that can be activated, a free processor is always available.

The algorithm in which $k \geq 1$ and asynchronous processes P_i, $i = 1, 2, ..., k$, are used for the solution of our task, consists of the following steps:

a) if no subtask has been completed by any process, then a free process starts executing subtask w_1,

b) otherwise, if the last subtask w_n has not yet been completed by any process, then a free process starts executing a subtask which is unfinished and ready for execution.

For a linear arrangement of the subtasks, step b) defines explicitly the task to be implemented.

Let $t_1, t_2, ..., t_i < t_{i+1}$ be the termination times of the subtasks by the processes. The next scheme shows a possible task schedule, in which they are executed by three processes P_1, P_2 and P_3:

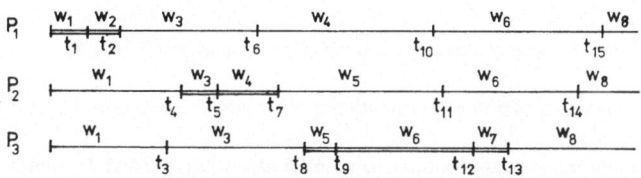

We can see that if P_3 completes w_3 at a time t_8, then P_2 will have completed w_4. Therefore, P_3 avoids w_4 and after w_3 it starts executing w_5. Similarly, P_1 avoids w_5

and w_7 and P_2 avoids w_2 and w_7. If each of the processes executes 6 subtasks, then the algorithm implements w_1, w_2, ..., w_8 and consequently we have obtained the speedup that results not from the distribution of the work among processes, but from the time variation in the execution of single subtasks. It can also be seen that at any time at least one process performs useful computations which are represented by double lines in the scheme.

The algorithm described makes algorithms parallel by the exploitation of the asynchronous behaviour of a multiprocessor computer. It yields substantial speedup if the variation of the duration of the subtasks is relatively large. It can also be used for creating parallel algorithms containing a set of dynamically generated subtasks which are represented by a directed graph. The algorithm possesses good reliability properties and according to [2] its extension to creating algorithms, in which the execution of a subtask by a process can be interrupted by some other process would be interesting, since its effectiveness would be enhanced by the interruption of processes that do not perform useful work. In [2] programs are given for the implementation of the algorithm described with k processes both with critical sections and without them, their correctness being proven. Analytical techniques for obtaining formulae for speedup with respect to the algorithm containing one process are also described.

REFERENCES

[1] BAER, J. L. and BOVET, D. P.: Compilation of arithmetic expressions for parallel computations. Proc. IFIP Congress, Edinburgh 1968. North-Holland Publ. Co., Amsterdam, 1968, pp. 340—346.

[2] BAUDET, G. M., BRENT, R. P. and KUNG, H. T.: Parallel execution of a sequence of tasks on an asynchronous multiprocessor. Tech. Report, Comp. Sci. Dep., Carnegie-Mellon Univ., Pittsburgh, Penn., 1977.

[3] BRENT, R. F.: The parallel evaluation of general arithmetic expressions. J. ACM, *21*, 1974, 2, 201—206.

[4] BULIRSCH, R.: Die Mehrzielmethode zur numerischen Lösung von nichtlinearen Randwertproblemen und Aufgaben der optimalen Steuerung. In: Flugbahnoptimierung. Carl-Cranz Gesellschaft 1971.

[5] BUZBEE, B. L.: A fast Poisson solver amenable to parallel computation. IEEE Trans. on Computers, *C-22*, 1973, 8, 793—796.

[6] CHAZAN, D. and MIRANKER, W.: Chaotic relaxation. Linear Algebra and Its Appl., *2*, 1969, 199—222.

[7] CSANKY, L.: On the parallel complexity of some computational problems. Dissertation. Univ. of California, Berkeley, 1974.

[8] HELLER, D.: A determinant theorem with applications to parallel algorithms. SIAM J. Numer. Anal., *11*, 1974, 559—568.

[9] HELLER, D., STEVENSON, D. K. and TRAUB, J. F.: Accelerated iterative methods for the solution of tridiagonal systems on parallel computers. J. ACM, *23*, 1976, 636—654.

[10] HELLER, D.: A survey of parallel algorithms in numerical linear algebra. Tech. Report, Comp. Sci. Dep., Carnegie-Mellon Univ., Pittsburgh, Penn., 1976.

[11] HYAFIL, L. and KUNG, H. T.: Parallel algorithms for solving triangular systems with small parallelism. Tech. Report, IRIA Laboria, Rocquencourt, 1975, 97.

[12] KOGGE, P. and STONE, H. S.: A parallel algorithm for the efficient solution of a general class of recurrence equation. IEEE Trans. on Computers, C-22, 1973, 8, 786—790.

[13] KOGGE, P.: Parallel solution of recurrence problems. IBM J. Res. Develop., 18, 1974, 138—148.

[14] KUCK, D. J.: Parallel processing of ordinary programs. Advances in Computers, Vol. 15. Academic Press, New York, 1977, pp. 119—179.

[15] MIRANKER, W. K. and LINIGER, W. M.: Parallel methods for the numerical integration of ordinary differential equations. Math. Comp., 21, 1967, 304—320.

[16] MURAOKA, Y.: Parallelism exposure and exploitation in programs. Tech. Report No. 71-424. Comp. Sci. Dep., Univ. of Illinois, 1971.

[17] NIEVERGELT, J.: Parallel methods for integrating ordinary differential equations. Comm. ACM, 7, 1964, 737—743.

[18] ORCUTT, S. E., JR.: Computer organization and algorithms for very high-speed computations. Dissertation. Stanford Univ., 1974.

[19] PEASE, M. C.: The C(2, m) algorithm for matrix inversion. Tech. Report, Stanford Res. Inst., Menlo Pork, California, 1974.

[20] ROBERT, F., CHARNAY, M. and MUSY, F.: Itérations choatiques sérieparalleles pour des equations non linéaires de point fixe. Apl. Math., 1975, 1, 1—38.

[21] SAMEH, A.: On Jacobi and Jacobi-like algorithm for a parallel computer. Math. Comp., 25, 1971, 115—123.

[22] SAMEH, A. H. and KUCK, D. J.: On stable parallel linear system solvers. J. ACM, 25, 1978, 81—91.

[23] STONE, H. S.: Problems of parallel computation. In: Complexity of Sequential and Parallel Numerical Algorithms. J. F. Traub (Editor). Academic Press, New York, 1973, pp. 1—16.

[24] STONE, H. S.: An efficient parallel algorithm for the solution of tridiagonal system of equations. J. ACM, 20, 1973, 27—38.

[25] STONE, H. S.: Parallel tridiagonal solvers. ACM Trans. on Math. Software, 1, 1975, 4, 289—307.

[26] VAJTERŠIC, M.: Parallel algorithms for fast computation of numerical solution of Laplace equation. Proc. 3rd Symposium on Algorithms, High Tatras, 1975. Bratislava, 1975, pp. 151—161.

[27] THURBER, K. J.: Large-Scale Computer Architecture, Parallel and Associative Processors. Hayden Book Co., Rochelle Park, N. J., 1976.

Appendix

AN IMPROVED APPLICATION OF THE SECOND BUNEMAN'S VARIANT TO PARALLEL COMPUTATION OF THE SEMIDIRECT PROCESS

1. Introduction. Numerical solution of partial differential equations even on large sequential computers is expensive in both computing time and storage. One of the most frequently occurring problems is the biharmonic one, since it arises in many applications. The finite-difference approximation of this problem leads to the need to solve large sparse linear systems of equations. In order to solve them efficiently, a sequence of vector and matrix operations must be executed. Such operations are well suited for execution on the parallel and vector processors that have appeared recently. Compared to sequential methods, parallel organization can bring a significant speedup of the computations.

The purpose of this appendix is to present an original parallel technique for solving the first biharmonic boundary value problem on a rectangular domain. This parallel algorithm is fast in terms of parallel arithmetic complexity. As for the wide class of parallel algorithms in linear algebra [8], we shall assume a parallel computer in which

  (i) any number of processors can be used at any time;

  (ii) each processor can perform any of the four arithmetic operations in one time step, and all processors execute the same instruction type or are idle (SIMD);

  (iii) there are no memory or data alignment penalties.

We shall adopt this computer model despite the fact that our algorithm can also be implemented on a limited number of processors. As far as condition (iii) is concerned, it is not difficult to add the cost of additional operations to the time required for the arithmetic ones, if the details of the computer are known. The semidirect process, which is based on the iterative procedure for the split biharmonic operator, is described in Section 2 of this appendix. Our modification of the original semidirect process is also given. In Section 3 we discuss first the second Buneman's variant of the cyclic odd-even reduction algorithm for solving the discrete Poisson equation [2]. Then we suggest how to apply this algorithm to evaluate one iteration vector of the modified semidirect process effectively.

As the result of splitting the biharmonic equation, we have two Poisson equations, which depend on one another. These equations can be dealt with by applying directly a parallel algorithm for solving blocktridiagonal systems, as discussed in the survey [6]. The parallel matrix decomposition algorithm was directly applied to solve this coupled pair of difference equations in $24 \log n$ parallel steps on n^2 processors for a grid of n^2 mesh points [7]. (For the integer n of the form $n = 2^{m+1} - 1$, we write $\log n$ instead of $m + 1$.) Based on an analysis of the semidirect process [9], we found a better application of the matrix decomposition algorithm in only $14 \log n$ steps [10]. The unstable algorithm of the cyclic odd-even reduction, the algorithm CORF in [2], was applied in $12 \log n$ steps per iteration [11]. The first Buneman's variant [2], based on the odd-even reduction, is stable and the result of its application are $20 \log n$ steps per iteration [11]. We show that our parallel application of the second Buneman's variant requires, again on n^2 processors, $19 \log n$ steps per iteration. Since the asymptotic number of iteration is $O(n^{1/2} \log n)$ for an accuracy $\varepsilon = O(n^{-2})$ [3], the above algorithms compute the solution with accuracy ε in $O(n^{1/2} (\log n)^2)$ steps. Hence, of the three parallel algorithms based on the cyclic odd-even approach, the algorithm given in this appendix is the most effective in practice in terms of parallel arithmetic complexity.

2. Semidirect process for solving the biharmonic problem. Assuming a unit square R, the first biharmonic boundary value problem in R consists in finding the function $u(x, y)$ so that

$$u_{xxxx}(x, y) + 2u_{xxyy}(x, y) + u_{yyyy}(x, y) = f(x, y) \quad (x, y) \in R \tag{1a}$$

where $u(x, y)$ and its outward normal derivative $u_n(x, y)$ satisfy the described conditions

$$u(x, y) = g(x, y); \quad u_n(x, y) = h(x, y) \quad (x, y) \in \bar{R} \tag{1b}$$

on the boundary $\bar{R}$ of R. The above system is equivalent to the system [5]

$$u_{xx}(x, y) + u_{yy}(x, y) = v(x, y) \quad (x, y) \in R \tag{2a}$$

$$u(x, y) = g(x, y) \quad (x, y) \in \bar{R} \tag{2b}$$

$$v_{xx}(x, y) + v_{yy}(x, y) = f(x, y) \quad (x, y) \in R \tag{2c}$$

$$v(x, y) = u_{xx}(x, y) + u_{yy}(x, y) - c[u_n(x, y) - h(x, y)] \quad (x, y) \in \bar{R} \tag{2d}$$

with a non-zero constant c.

In order to obtain the numerical solution of the boundary value problems (1a), (1b) a regular grid of mesh points with a mesh size of $(n + 1)^{-1}$, for some positive integer n, is superimposed on the domain. Setting $c = 2(n + 1)$, some of the discretizations in [5] are used for the normal derivative in (2d). The discretization leads to the following linear system [3]

$$\begin{bmatrix} \mathbf{A} & -(n + 1)^{-2}\mathbf{I} \\ 2(n + 1)^2\mathbf{L} & \mathbf{A} \end{bmatrix} \begin{bmatrix} \boldsymbol{u} \\ \boldsymbol{v} \end{bmatrix} = \begin{bmatrix} \boldsymbol{s} \\ \boldsymbol{t} \end{bmatrix}. \tag{3}$$

The matrix

$$\mathbf{A} = (-\mathbf{I}, \mathbf{B}, -\mathbf{I})_{n^2} \tag{4}$$

is symmetric blocktridiagonal of order n^2.

The tridiagonal matrix

$$\mathbf{B} = (-1, 4, -1)_n \tag{5}$$

and the identity matrix $\mathbf{I}$ are both of order n. The discretization formula for the normal derivative [5, p. 336] leads to a matrix $\mathbf{L}$ of the form

$$\mathbf{L} = \mathbf{E} + \mathbf{F} \tag{6}$$

with $\mathbf{E} = (\mathbf{I}, \mathbf{0}, ..., \mathbf{0}, \mathbf{I})_{n^2}$ and $\mathbf{F} = (\mathbf{C}, \mathbf{C}, ..., \mathbf{C})_{n^2}$, where $\mathbf{C} = (1, 0, ..., 0, 1)_n$. The values of the boundary functions (1b) and of the right-hand side of (1a) are involved in the constant vectors $\boldsymbol{s}$ and $\boldsymbol{t}$. The system (3) is solved by the semidirect procedure, where smoothing with a parameter ω is incorporated [3—5, 7, 9—11]. After eliminating the vectors which involve values of the function v, one iteration of this process can be expressed as [9]

$$\boldsymbol{U}^{(k+1)} = [2\omega\boldsymbol{I} - 2(1-\omega)^2\boldsymbol{A}^{-2}\boldsymbol{L}]\boldsymbol{U}^{(k)} - \omega^2\boldsymbol{U}^{(k-1)} + (1-\omega)^2\boldsymbol{q} \quad (k=1,2,\ldots), \quad (7)$$

with $\boldsymbol{U}^{(0)}=\boldsymbol{0}$, $\boldsymbol{U}^{(1)}=(1-\omega)\boldsymbol{A}^{-1}\boldsymbol{s}$ and $\boldsymbol{q}=\boldsymbol{A}^{-1}\boldsymbol{s}+(n+1)^{-2}\boldsymbol{A}^{-2}\boldsymbol{t}$. The iterative process (7) is continued until

$$\|\boldsymbol{U}^{(k+1)} - \boldsymbol{U}^{(k)}\| < \delta \tag{8}$$

for a given $\delta > 0$ where the norm is $\|.\|_\infty$. The number of iterations needed to satisfy (8), for $\delta = O(n^{-2})$ and for optimal ω [4], is $O(n^{1/2} \log n)$ [9].

The vector $\boldsymbol{u}^{(k+1)} = \boldsymbol{A}^{-2}\boldsymbol{L}\boldsymbol{U}^{(k)}$ plays the most important role in the iteration of (7). This vector can be obtained from $\boldsymbol{L}\boldsymbol{U}^{(k)}$ by twofold straightforward implementation of one of the parallel blocktridiagonal solvers, which are reviewed in [6]. However, such a strategy cannot reduce the time required for one iteration. Instead, we transform the iterative process (7), using the matrix $\boldsymbol{T} = (\boldsymbol{Q}, \boldsymbol{Q}, \ldots, \boldsymbol{Q})_{n^2}$, where [2] $\boldsymbol{Q}_{ij} = (2/(n+1))^{1/2} \sin(ij\pi/(n+1))$ for $i, j = 1, \ldots, n$. We obtain

$$\begin{aligned}
\bar{\boldsymbol{U}}^{(k+1)} = \boldsymbol{T}\boldsymbol{U}^{(k+1)} &= \boldsymbol{T}[2\omega\boldsymbol{I} - 2(1-\omega)^2\boldsymbol{A}^{-2}\boldsymbol{L}]\boldsymbol{U}^{(k)} - \omega^2\boldsymbol{T}\boldsymbol{U}^{(k-1)} + (1-\omega)^2\boldsymbol{T}\boldsymbol{q} = \\
&= 2(1-\omega)\omega\bar{\boldsymbol{U}}^{(k)} - (1-\omega)^2\bar{\boldsymbol{U}}^{(k-1)} - 2(1-\omega)^2\bar{\boldsymbol{u}}^{(k+1)} + (1-\omega)^2\bar{\boldsymbol{q}} \\
&\quad (k=1,2,\ldots),
\end{aligned} \tag{9}$$

where $\bar{\boldsymbol{U}}^{(0)}=\boldsymbol{0}$, $\bar{\boldsymbol{U}}^{(1)}=(1-\omega)\boldsymbol{T}\boldsymbol{A}^{-1}\boldsymbol{s}$.

The transformation does not change the spectral radius of the original iterative process (7). Hence, the asymptotic number of iterations is also $O(n^{1/2} \log n)$, if optimal ω and $\delta = O(n^{-2})$ are assumed for the process (9). In order to satisfy the criterion (8) with $\delta > 0$ for the iterative process (9), the new criterion is [10]

$$\|\bar{\boldsymbol{U}}^{(k+1)} - \bar{\boldsymbol{U}}^{(k)}\| < \delta n^{-1/2}.$$

The semidirect process (7) can be replaced by the process (9) without increasing the asymptotic number of iterations. Moreover, this substitution makes it possible to achieve new complexity estimates for the parallel computation of one iteration. However, the double solution of the discrete Poisson equations, required in (3), is held in the vector $\bar{\boldsymbol{u}}^{(k+1)}$. There is an efficient way to obtain this vector. Writing $\boldsymbol{L}\boldsymbol{U}^{(k)}=\boldsymbol{y}$, we first introduce the vector

$$\bar{\boldsymbol{x}} = \boldsymbol{T}\boldsymbol{A}^{-1}\boldsymbol{y}; \tag{10}$$

the solution is therefore

$$\bar{u}^{(k+1)} = \mathbf{T}\mathbf{A}^{-1}\mathbf{T}\bar{x}. \tag{11}$$

In order to obtain one iteration vector in less than 24 log n steps [7], using n^2 processors, it is necessary to develop a fast parallel algorithm for solving the systems (10), (11). One such technique is proposed in the following section.

3. Application of the second Buneman's variant. Prior to a discussion on parallel solution of the systems (10) and (11), we state briefly the second Buneman's variant of the cyclic odd-even reduction algorithm [2] for solving the system $\mathbf{A}\mathbf{z} = \mathbf{w}$, where the matrix $\mathbf{A}$ is given in (4) and the two real general vectors

$$\mathbf{z}^T = (\mathbf{z}_1^T, \mathbf{z}_2^T, ..., \mathbf{z}_n^T) \quad \text{and} \quad \mathbf{w}^T = (\mathbf{w}_1^T, \mathbf{w}_2^T, ..., \mathbf{w}_n^T)$$

have both n blocks $\mathbf{z}_i, \mathbf{w}_i, i = 1, ..., n$, each of them involving n real components.

In the first stage of the reduction phase, the right-hand side vectors $\mathbf{w}_j^{(1)}, j = 2, 4, ..., n - 1$, are computed from

$$\mathbf{w}_j^{(0)} = \mathbf{w}_j \qquad (j = 1, 2, ..., n) \tag{12a}$$

using

$$\mathbf{w}_j^{(1)} = \mathbf{w}_{j-1}^{(0)} - 2\mathbf{B}^{-1}\mathbf{w}_j^{(0)} + \mathbf{w}_{j+1}^{(0)} \qquad (j = 2, 4, ..., n - 1). \tag{12b}$$

We write $p = 2^{r-2}$ for notational simplicity. Then from the remaining stages of the reduction process, the vectors $\mathbf{w}_j^{(r)}$ are expressed for $r = 2, ..., m$ and $j = 2^r, 2 \cdot 2^r, ..., n - 2^r - 1$ as

$$\begin{aligned}
\mathbf{w}_j^{(r)} &= \mathbf{w}_{j-2p}^{(r-1)} - \mathbf{w}_{j-p}^{(r-2)} + \mathbf{w}_j^{(r-1)} - \mathbf{w}_{j+p}^{(r-2)} + \mathbf{w}_{j+2p}^{(r-1)} + \\
&\quad + (\mathbf{B}^{(r-1)})^{-1}(\mathbf{w}_{j-3p}^{(r-2)} - \mathbf{w}_{j-2p}^{(r-1)} + \mathbf{w}_{j-p}^{(r-2)} - 2\mathbf{w}_j^{(r-1)} + \\
&\quad + \mathbf{w}_{j+p}^{(r-2)} - \mathbf{w}_{j+2p}^{(r-1)} + \mathbf{w}_{j+3p}^{(r-2)}).
\end{aligned} \tag{12c}$$

Defining $\mathbf{B}^{(0)} = \mathbf{B}$, where $\mathbf{B}$ was introduced in (5), the recurrence relation for the matrices $\mathbf{B}^{(r)}$ is $\mathbf{B}^{(r)} = 2\mathbf{I} - (\mathbf{B}^{(r-1)})^2$, $r = 1, ..., m$. The solution vectors $\mathbf{z}_j$ are determined successively, in log n stages, for $r = m, m - 1, ..., 0$ and $j = 2^r, 3 \cdot 2^r, ..., n - 2^r - 1$, by

$$\mathbf{z}_j = \frac{1}{2}(\mathbf{w}_{j-2p}^{(r-1)} + \mathbf{w}_{j+2p}^{(r-1)} - \mathbf{w}_j^{(r)}) + (\mathbf{B}^{(r)})^{-1}(\mathbf{w}_j^{(r)} - \mathbf{z}_{j-4p} - \mathbf{z}_{j+4p}), \tag{13}$$

where $\mathbf{z}_0 = \mathbf{z}_{n+1} = \mathbf{w}_{j-1/2}^{(-1)} + \mathbf{w}_{j+1/2}^{(-1)}\mathbf{w}_j^{(0)} = \mathbf{0}$.

It is not advantageous to use the algorithm just described to solve the systems (10), (11). Since the matrices $\mathbf{B}^{(r)}$ fill rapidly, their inversions cause a computational difficulty in (12c) and (13). In [2] this obstacle is avoided by expressing the matrix $\mathbf{B}^{(r)}$ as a product of 2^r tridiagonal symmetric matrices for all $r = 1, ..., m$. Although all the matrix computations can be performed using the factorized form, it requires a recursive solution of $2^{(r-1)}$ tridiagonal systems for each r and j.

The eigenvalues of the matrices $\mathbf{B}^{(r)}$, $r = 1, 2, \ldots, m$, are given by

$$\mathbf{D}_j^{(r)} = 2 - (\mathbf{D}_j^{(r-1)})^2 \qquad (j = 1, \ldots, n),$$

where

$$\mathbf{D}_j^{(0)} = 2(2 - \cos{(j\pi/(n+1))}) \qquad (j = 1, \ldots, n) \ [2].$$

As given in [11], the decomposition property [2]

$$\mathbf{B}^{(r)} = \mathbf{Q}\mathbf{D}^{(r)}\mathbf{Q} \qquad (r = 0, 1, \ldots, m) \tag{14}$$

will also be used to solve efficiently the systems (10) and (11). Writing $\bar{\mathbf{y}}_j^{(r)} = \mathbf{Q}\mathbf{y}_j^{(r)}$ for each r and j, the formulae (12a)—(12c) can be modified to determine the right-hand side vectors of (10), as follows

$$\bar{\mathbf{y}}_j^{(0)} = \mathbf{Q}\mathbf{y}_j, \qquad (j = 1, \ldots, n), \tag{15a}$$

$$\bar{\mathbf{y}}_j^{(1)} = \mathbf{Q}\mathbf{y}_j^{(1)} = \mathbf{Q}(\mathbf{y}_{j-1}^{(0)} - 2\mathbf{B}^{-1}\mathbf{y}_j^{(0)} + \mathbf{y}_{j+1}^{(0)}) =$$
$$= \bar{\mathbf{y}}_{j-1}^{(0)} - 2(\mathbf{D}^{(0)})^{-1}\bar{\mathbf{y}}_j^{(0)} + \bar{\mathbf{y}}_{j+1}^{(0)} \qquad (j = 2, 4, \ldots, n-1), \tag{15b}$$

$$\bar{\mathbf{y}}_j^{(r)} = \mathbf{Q}\mathbf{y}_j^{(r)} = \bar{\mathbf{y}}_{j-2p}^{(r-1)} - \bar{\mathbf{y}}_{j-p}^{(r-1)} + \bar{\mathbf{y}}_j^{(r-1)} - \bar{\mathbf{y}}_{j+p}^{(r-1)} + \bar{\mathbf{y}}_{j+2p}^{(r-1)} +$$
$$+ (\mathbf{D}^{(r-1)})^{-1}(\bar{\mathbf{y}}_{j-3p}^{(r-2)}) - \bar{\mathbf{y}}_{j-2p}^{(r-1)} + \bar{\mathbf{y}}_{j-p}^{(r-2)} - 2\bar{\mathbf{y}}_j^{(r-1)} +$$
$$+ \bar{\mathbf{y}}_{j+p}^{(r-2)} - \bar{\mathbf{y}}_{j+2p}^{(r-1)} + \bar{\mathbf{y}}_{j+3p}^{(r-2)}) \tag{15c}$$
$$(r = 2, 3, \ldots, m), \ (j = 2^r, 2 \cdot 2^r, \ldots, n - 2^r - 1).$$

The decomposition property (14) can be used to evaluate the solution vectors $\bar{\mathbf{x}}_j = \mathbf{Q}\mathbf{x}_j$ of (10) in the following manner:

$$\bar{\mathbf{x}}_j = \mathbf{Q}\mathbf{x}_j = \frac{1}{2}\mathbf{Q}(\mathbf{y}_{j-2p}^{(r-1)} + \mathbf{y}_{j+2p}^{(r-1)} - \mathbf{y}_j^{(r)}) + \mathbf{Q}(\mathbf{B}^{(r)})^{-1}(\mathbf{y}_j^{(r)} - \mathbf{x}_{j-4p} - \mathbf{x}_{j+4p}) =$$

$$= \frac{1}{2}(\bar{\mathbf{y}}_{j-2p}^{(r-1)} + \bar{\mathbf{y}}_{j+2p}^{(r-1)} - \bar{\mathbf{y}}_j^{(r)}) + (\mathbf{D}^{(r)})^{-1}(\bar{\mathbf{y}}_j^{(r)} - \bar{\mathbf{x}}_{j-4p} - \bar{\mathbf{x}}_{j+4p}) \qquad (j = 1, \ldots, n), \tag{16}$$

with $\bar{\mathbf{x}}_0 = \bar{\mathbf{x}}_{n+1} = \bar{\mathbf{y}}_{j-1/2}^{(-1)} + \bar{\mathbf{y}}_{j+1/2}^{(-1)} - \bar{\mathbf{y}}_j^{(0)} = \mathbf{0}$.

Once $\bar{\mathbf{x}}_j$ are obtained, the reduction phase for the right-hand side vectors $\bar{\mathbf{x}}_j^{(r)}$ of (11) can be executed as in (15a)—(15c):

$$\bar{\mathbf{x}}_j^{(0)} = \bar{\mathbf{x}}_j \qquad (j = 1, \ldots, n), \tag{17a}$$

$$\bar{\mathbf{x}}_j^{(1)} = \bar{\mathbf{x}}_{j-1}^{(0)} - 2(\mathbf{D}^{(0)})^{-1}\bar{\mathbf{x}}_j^{(0)} + \bar{\mathbf{x}}_{j+1}^{(0)} \qquad (j = 2, 4, \ldots, n-1), \tag{17b}$$

$$\bar{\mathbf{x}}_j^{(r)} = \bar{\mathbf{x}}_{j-2p}^{(r-1)} - \bar{\mathbf{x}}_{j-p}^{(r-1)} + \bar{\mathbf{x}}_j^{(r-1)} - \bar{\mathbf{x}}_{j+p}^{(r-1)} + \bar{\mathbf{x}}_{j+2p}^{(r-1)} +$$
$$+ \ (\mathbf{D}^{(r-1)^{-1}}(\bar{\mathbf{x}}_{j-3p}^{(r-2)} - \bar{\mathbf{x}}_{j-2p}^{(r-1)} + \bar{\mathbf{x}}_{j-p}^{(r-2)} - 2\bar{\mathbf{x}}_j^{(r-1)} +$$
$$+ \ \bar{\mathbf{x}}_{j+p}^{(r-2)} - \bar{\mathbf{x}}_{j+2p}^{(r-1)} + \bar{\mathbf{x}}_{j+3p}^{(r-2)}) \tag{17c}$$
$$(r = 2, 3, \ldots, m)$$
$$(j = 2^r, 2 \cdot 2^r, \ldots, n - 2^r - 1).$$

After inserting the matrix $(\mathbf{B}^{(r-1)})^{-1}$ as expressed by (14) into (17), we obtain the required solutions $\bar{u}_j^{(k+1)}$

$$\bar{u}_j^{(k+1)} = \frac{1}{2}\,(\bar{x}_{j-2p}^{(r-1)} + \bar{x}_{j+2p}^{(r-1)} - \bar{x}_j^{(r)}) +$$
$$+ (\mathbf{D}^{(r)})^{-1}(\bar{x}_j^{(r)} - \bar{u}_{j-4p}^{(k+1)} - \bar{u}_{j+4p}^{(k+1)}) \qquad (j = 1, \ldots, n), \tag{18}$$

where

$$\bar{u}_0^{(k+1)} = \bar{u}_{n+1}^{(k+1)} = \bar{x}_{j-1/2}^{(-1)} + \bar{x}_{j+1/2}^{(-1)} - \bar{x}_j^{(0)} = \mathbf{0}.$$

As seen from (15b), (15c), (16), (17b), (17c), (18), instead of solving a sequence of tridiagonal linear algebraic systems, only a multiplication by the diagonal matrices is required.

Having stated formulae (15a)—(18) for evaluating the vector $\bar{u}^{(k+1)}$, we can estimate the arithmetic complexity of the parallel computation of the iteration vector $\bar{U}^{(k+1)}$ from $\bar{U}^{(k-1)}$ and $\bar{U}^{(k)}$, as required in (9). Using (6), we express the vectors $\bar{y}_j$, $j = 1, \ldots, n$, as follows

$$\bar{y} = \mathbf{T}\mathbf{L}U^{(k)} = \mathbf{E}\bar{U}^{(k)} + \mathbf{T}\mathbf{F}\mathbf{T}\bar{U}^{(k)}. \tag{19}$$

Here, the expressions $\mathbf{Q}\mathbf{C}\mathbf{Q}\bar{U}_i^{(k)}$, $i = 1, \ldots, n$ should be computed. For each $i = 1, \ldots, n$, two vector products of the n component vectors are to be evaluated. We recall that the vector product of two real vectors with n components can be calculated by n processors in $\log n + 1$ steps [1]. One step is for n multiplications while $\log n$ steps are required for $n - 1$ additions. Since in each addition step more than $(n + 1)/2$ processors are idle, two vector products of n component vectors can be obtained by n processors in $2 + \log n$ steps. Hence, the time for $2n$ vector products with n^2 processors is $\log n + 2$. Further, it is easy to see that formula (15b) can be obtained in 3 steps.

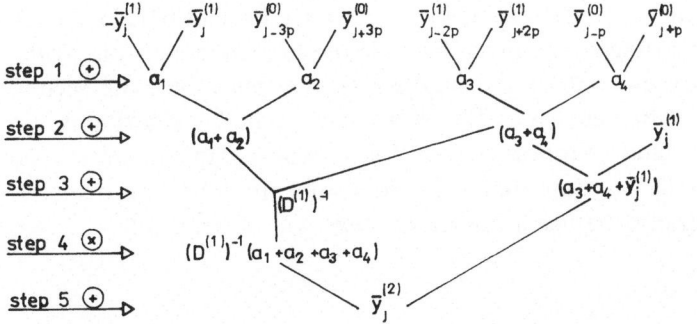

Fig. 1.

To describe the evaluation of formula (15c) for the vector $\bar{y}_j^{(2)}$, we write $a_1 = (-\bar{y}_j^{(1)}) + (-\bar{y}_j^{(1)})$, $a_2 = \bar{y}_{j-3p}^{(0)} + \bar{y}_{j+3p}^{(0)}$, $a_3 = \bar{y}_{j-2p}^{(1)} + y_{j+2p}^{(1)}$ and $a_4 = \bar{y}_{j-p}^{(0)} + \bar{y}_{j+p}^{(0)}$.

Taking into account the condition (ii) from Section 1, the SIMD computational strategy for evaluating the vector $\bar{y}_j^{(2)}$ consists of 5 steps, as shown in Fig. 1.

Since there are $4n^2/(n-5)$ processors available for each $\bar{\mathbf{y}}_j^{(2)}$, the four additions and the two additions for both steps 2 and 3 can be performed with n^2 processors simultaneously. The vectors $\bar{\mathbf{y}}_j^{(r)}$ for the succeeding reduction phases $r = 3, \ldots, m$, can be computed in a similar manner, since the number of processors available is $n^2/((n-1)/2^r - 1) > 4n$ for each vector. The vectors $\bar{\mathbf{x}}_j$ are to be computed in $\log n$ stages, starting at $r = m$. At the r-th stage, $r = m, \ldots, 0$, the number of processors available for computing each vector $\bar{\mathbf{x}}_j$ is $2^r n^2/(n+1) + 2^r$. Therefore, writing $\mathbf{b}_1 = \bar{\mathbf{y}}_{j-2p}^{(r-1)} + \bar{\mathbf{y}}_{j+2p}^{(r-1)}$ and $\mathbf{b}_2 = -\bar{\mathbf{x}}_{j-4p} + (-\bar{\mathbf{x}}_{j+4p})$, the computational strategy shown in Fig. 2 can be used for the evaluation of formula (16).

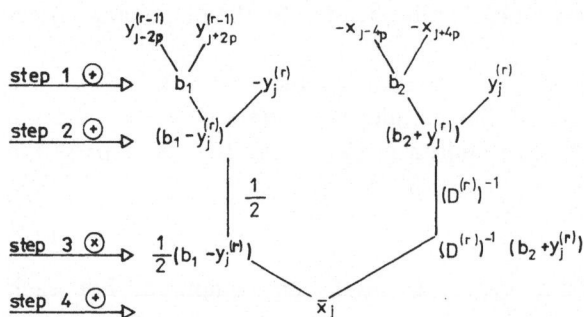

Fig. 2.

It is obvious that the number of steps is 4 for each $r = m, \ldots, 0$. Formulae (17b), (17c) and (18) can also be computed in this way. The remaining vector operations in (9) have a complexity $O(1)$, so that the total time is $18 \log n$, using n^2 processors.

Compared to the complexity in a parallel environment of the first Buneman's variant of processes (9), (11), the technique just described is faster. This reduction by $\log n$ in the number of parallel steps is due to the fact that the vector $\mathbf{TFT}\bar{\mathbf{U}}^{(k)}$ in (19) can be calculated by n^2 processors in $\log n + 2$ steps instead of $2 \log n + 2$. Despite this, it is an interesting comparison, because the sequential versions of the both Buneman variants require the same number of multiplications, the second one, however, requires more additions [2]. Both these parallel algorithms are stable, as shown in [2], and therefore suited for practical implementation on a parallel computer. Finally, we note that if n^2 processors are not at our disposal, the above technique can also be used, but more steps will be required.

REFERENCES

[1] BORODIN, A. and MUNRO, I.: The Computational Complexity of Algebraic and Numeric Problems. American Elsevier, New York, 1975.

[2] BUZBEE, B. L., GOLUB, G. H. and NEILSON, C. W.: On direct methods for solving Poisson's equations. SIAM J. Numer. Anal., 7, 1970, 627—656.

[3] EHRLICH, L. W.: Solving the biharmonic equation in a square: A direct versus a semidirect method. Comm. ACM, *16*, 1973, 711—714.

[4] EHRLICH, L. W. and GUPTA, M. M.: Some difference schemes for the biharmonic equation. SIAM J. Numer. Anal., *12*, 1975, 773—790.

[5] GUPTA, M. M.: Discretization error estimates for certain splitting procedures for solving first biharmonic boundary value problems. SIAM J. Numer. Anal., *12*, 1975, 364—377.

[6] HELLER, D.: Direct and iterative methods for block tridiagonal linear systems. Tech. Report, Dep. Comp. Sci., Carnegie-Mellon Univ., Pittsburgh, Penn., 1977.

[7] SAMEH, A. H., CHEN, S. C. and KUCK, D. J.: Parallel Poisson and biharmonic solvers. Computing, *17*, 1976, 219—230.

[8] SAMEH, A. H.: Numerical parallel algorithms — a survey. In: High-Speed Computers and Algorithms Organization. Academic Press, New York, 1977, pp. 207—228.

[9] VAJTERŠIC, M.: A fast algorithm for solving the first biharmonic boundary value problem. Computing, *23*, 1979, 171—178.

[10] VAJTERŠIC, M.: A fast parallel solving the biharmonic boundary value problem on a rectangle. Proc. 1st Eur. Conf. on Parallel and Distributed Processing, Toulouse 1979, pp. 136—141.

[11] VAJTERŠIC, M.: Fast parallel biharmonic semidirect solvers. Proc. 1979 Int. Conf. on Parallel Processing. IEEE Press, Bellaire 1979, p. 135.

Chapter 2

COMPLEXITY OF PARALLEL ALGORITHMS

In this chapter we discuss the analysis of parallel algorithms, especially their complexity. The complexity of serial algorithms is usually measured by the number of arithmetic operations. But the complexity of parallel algorithms is measured by the time, in which they can be implemented on a k-processor computer.

In the first part we demonstrate the difference between the problems of serial and parallel algorithms and their complexity for an algorithm for the calculation of x^n, and give an informal description of a model of parallel computation.

In the second part, the definition of bounded and unbounded parallelism is given. Bounded parallelism is explained using an algorithm for the computation of a polynomial value, and unbounded parallelism using the fastest known parallel algorithm for matrix inversion. It can be seen from this example that even some old, almost forgotten algorithms can be significant in the context of parallelism.

The third part deals with the problems of upper and lower bounds in connection with the complexity of parallel algorithms. Two known results for lower bounds together with some of their consequence are given. The results are also described, and it follows from these that data transfer between processors may be the limiting factor in the effectiveness of parallel computations.

In the fourth and last part, the speedup of parallel algorithms is defined and related theoretical results are explained using linear and non-linear recurrent relations as examples. In conclusion, the possibility of comparing an a priori selection of suitable parallel algorithms is explained.

2.1 Parallel computation of x^n

Investigation into the complexity of parallel algorithms brings new ideas and surprising results. We demonstrate this on the parallel algorithm for the calculation of x^n which instead of $\lceil \log n \rceil$ steps of pairwise multiplications requires $\lceil \log n \rceil + 2$ addition steps and 2 division steps [14].

Let F be a field of complex numbers and $F(x)$ be a field of rational expression in x over F. The time required for addition, multiplication and division in $F(x)$ is denoted by A, M and D.

As Kung [14] has stated, there is a serial algorithm for the computation of x^n in time $M(\log n + O(\log n/\log \log n))$. If division is not used, then the lower bound for the time of the parallel computation of x^n is $\lceil \log n \rceil M$ irrespective of the number of processors used. It follows from the above that without the operation of division no parallel algorithm can be essentially faster than a serial algorithm for the computation of this problem. But the whole situation is changed when division is used.

Kung's algorithm for computing x^n consists of the computation:
a) compute r_i, and s_i, $i = 1, 2, ..., n$, where r_i are the roots of the equation $x^n = 1$ and $s_i = r_i / n$,
b) $a_i = x - r_i$ $(i = 1, 2, ..., n)$,
c) $b_i = s_i / a_i$ $(i = 1, 2, ..., n)$,
d) $c = \sum_{i=1}^{n} b_i$,
e) $d = 1/c$,
f) $y = d + 1$.

It follows from the identity $\sum_{j=1}^{n} \dfrac{r_j}{x - r_j} = \dfrac{n}{x^n - 1}$ that $y = x^n$. The step a) does not depend on x and thus it can be executed once and for all at the beginning of the computation. The steps b) to f) can be performed on an n-processor computer in times A, $A \lceil \log n \rceil A$, D, A, and thus for the computation of x^n by this algorithm the time $T_n = \lceil \log n \rceil A + 2(A + D)$ is required. If $M > A$ and $\lceil \log n \rceil > 2(A + D)/(M - A)$, then the algorithm described is faster than the previous best parallel algorithm for the computation of x^n which needs time $S_n = \lceil \log n \rceil M$. Since $\lim_{n \to \infty} S_n / T_n = M/A$, for a large n the new algorithm is M/A-times faster. Kung derived analogous algorithms [14] for the parallel computation of $\{x^2, x^3, ..., x^n\}$,

$$\prod_{i=1}^{n} (x + a_i) \quad \text{and} \quad \sum_{i=0}^{n} a_i x^i.$$

If x in these expressions is a square matrix or a multiple precision number, then the multiplication time of such operands is far greater than the additive time and consequently, these algorithms are still more effective.

In analysing the complexity of parallel algorithms, we consider next an idealized model of parallel computation [4, 12], in which all processors are identical, and have an arbitrarily large common memory that can be simultaneously accessed by all of them. Each processor can execute one binary arithmetic operation in a common time unit — the so-called computational step. The time of the other operations will be regarded as negligible. We also assume that no memory conflicts arise during the computational process, and no delays are caused by the execution of instructions by the control unit or data transfer between the processors and memory.

All input data are stored in memory before the beginning of the computation.

Before the execution of each operation, the processor reads its operands from the memory and writes the result to the memory after the execution of one step. It is clear that k operations implemented in parallel are regarded as only one computational step.

2.2 Bounded and unbouded parallelism

A synthesis and analysis of parallel algorithms can be carried out under the assumption that a k-processor computer is available, where $k > 1$ is a fixed number — the so-called bounded parallelism — or k is not bounded, i.e. we assume we always have at our disposal a sufficient number of processors — the so-called unbounded parallelism.

Definition 1. A given algorithm implemented on a k-processor computer will be called k-parallel. The algorithm whose k-parallel implementation requires t-parallel steps is described as k-computable in a time t.

In the next definition, the numbers of processors in unbounded parallelism are divided into two cases.

Definition 2. Let a parallel algorithm solve a problem of size n on k_n processors. If for a certain polynomial K and for all n, $k_n \leq K(n)$, then the number of processors will be considered polynomially bounded and in other cases polynomially unbounded.

It is obvious that from the practical aspect parallel algorithms are of importance to bounded parallelism. Algorithms for unbounded parallelism are of interest mainly from the theoretical aspect, since they give the limits of parallel computations and allow a deeper understanding of the intrinsic structure of algorithms. The methods for transforming unbounded parallel algorithms into their k-parallel implementations are described in a separate chapter of this book. Now, let us describe some examples of parallel algorithms and indicate their complexity for bounded and unbounded parallelism. First we describe a k-parallel implementation of an algorithm for the computation of the value of the polynomial $p_n(x) = \sum_{i=0}^{n} a_i x^i$. The Horner scheme is not suitable for parallel calculations, since it requires the computation of n products and n sums in a strictly serial order. For this reason Dorn [1] has suggested a method by which $p_n(x)$ is divided into k polynomials which are calculated in parallel by the Horner scheme. For instance, for $k = 2$:

$$b_n = a_n, \quad b_{n-1} = a_{n-1}, \quad b_j = a_j + x^2 b_{j+2} \quad (j = n-2, \ldots, 0),$$

where

$$p_n(x) = b_0 + b_1 x.$$

The parallel computation of $p_n(x)$ on a $k < n/2$-processor computer can be implemented as

$$p_n(x) = \sum_{i=0}^{k-1} q_i(x)x^i,$$

where

$$q_i(x) = \sum_{j=0}^{m} a_{i+kj}x^{kj}, \qquad i = 0, 1, ..., k-1,$$
$$m = \lfloor (n-i)/k \rfloor.$$

This algorithm is k-computable in a time of $2n/k + 2 \log k$. For a k-parallel computation of arithmetic expressions with n separate variables, an arbitrary structure of brackets, and adding and multiplying operations Brent [2] has designed an algorithm, which is k-computable in a time of $4 \log n + 2(n-1)k$; an arithmetic expression which also contains division is k-computable in a time $4 \log n + 10(n-1)/k$, these two results being the best possible ones, with the exception of the constant. In unbounded parallelism such arithmetic expressions without division are computed on $n-1$ processors and if division is included on $3(n-1)$ processors in a time of $4 \log n$.

Unbounded parallelism with a polynomially limited number of processors is described for the fastest known parallel algorithm for computing the inverse of a square matrix.

All parallel versions of known algorithms for computing the inverse of a square matrix $\mathbf{A}$ of order n require $O(n)$ computational steps, so that for some time it was assumed that this was the lower bound of this problem. In 1974, Csanky [4] found that by making the classical Le Verrier method from 1840 parallel, $\mathbf{A}^{-1}$ can be calculated on $O(n^4)$ processors with $O(\log^2 n)$ steps.

If the eigenvalues of matrix $\mathbf{A}$ are λ_j, $j = 1, 2, ..., n$, its characteristic polynomial is

$$\det |\lambda \mathbf{I}_n - \mathbf{A}| = \lambda^n + c_1 \lambda^{n-1} + ... + c_n. \tag{1}$$

It follows from the Caley—Hamilton theorem that $f(\mathbf{A}) = \mathbf{0}$, i.e. that

$$\mathbf{A}^{-1} = -(\mathbf{A}^{n-1} + c_1 \mathbf{A}^{n-2} + ... + c_{n-2}\mathbf{A} + c_{n-1}\mathbf{I}_n)/c_n. \tag{2}$$

We denote the trace of matrix $\mathbf{A}$ by

$$\text{tr}(\mathbf{A}) = \sum_{i=1}^{n} a_{ii} \quad \text{and} \quad s_i = \text{tr}(\mathbf{A}^i) = \sum_{j=1}^{n} \lambda_j^i \quad (i = 1, 2, ..., n).$$

From Newton's relationship between the roots and coefficients of the polynomial (1) it follows that the coefficients $c_i = 1, 2, ..., n$, can be computed from

$$
\begin{pmatrix}
1 & & & \\
s_1 & 2 & & \\
s_2 & s_1 & 3 & \\
\vdots & & & \\
s_{n-1} & s_{n-2} & s_1 & n
\end{pmatrix}
\begin{pmatrix}
c_1 \\
c_2 \\
\vdots \\
c_n
\end{pmatrix}
=
\begin{pmatrix}
s_1 \\
s_2 \\
\vdots \\
s_n
\end{pmatrix}
. \tag{3}
$$

The parallel computation of $\mathbf{A}^{-1}$ can then be executed in the following stages (the number of steps required is given in brackets):

    a) the computation of $\mathbf{A}^i$, $i = 1, 3, \ldots, n$, in the orders
        $\mathbf{A}^2$; $\mathbf{A}^3$, $\mathbf{A}^4$; $\mathbf{A}^5$, $\mathbf{A}^6$, $\mathbf{A}^7$, $\mathbf{A}^8$, etc. $(O(\log^2 n))$,

    b) the computation of s_i, $i = 1, 2, \ldots, n$, $(O(\log n))$,

    c) the solution of system (3) $(O(\log^2 n))$,

    d) the computation of $\mathbf{A}^{-1}$ from (2) $(O(\log n))$.

Thus, the inverse $\mathbf{A}^{-1}$ can be computed in parallel on $O(n^4)$ processors in $O(\log^2 n)$ steps. This excellent theoretical result, however, is only of small practical importance, since the computation of c_i from system (3) is very sensitive to rounding errors in the traces s_i, i.e. this algorithm is numerically unstable. A stable parallel algorithm with less than $O(n)$ steps has not yet been found.

We add that with the polynomially unbounded number of $O(n!)$ processors it is possible to solve a system of n linear equations with n unknowns using Cramer's rule in a time of $O(\log n)$. But a result like this has neither practical nor theoretical importance.

2.3 Analysis of parallel algorithms

For every problem solved on a computer, there exists a parameter in that is the measure of its size, such as the order of a matrix, number of digits, degree of the polynomial, number of graph vertices, and the like. In analysing the complexity of algorithms and problems, it is necessary to define their complexity as a function of the parameter n.

Definition 3. The arithmetic complexity C_n of the parallel computation of a problem P_n of size n is the smallest number of steps required to obtain a solution with arbitrary input data. Asymptotic complexity is the behaviour of C_n as n tends to ∞.

In the analysis of parallel algorithms the basic quantities to be examined are the upper and lower bounds of the time in which it is possible to solve a given problem by some algorithm from a given class of algorithms. The fastest known parallel algorithms determine the upper bounds of the time required for the computation of a given problem. After they have been determined, there arises a question whether for the solution of this problem it is possible to find a faster algorithm or whether an algorithm with minimal execution time is known, i.e. whether the so-called lower bound of the execution time has been achieved. Thus, the lower bound determines the complexity of the problem under examination, i.e. the minimum amount of time needed for its solution by an arbitrary parallel algorithm.

The problem of the upper and lower bounds, i.e. the design of fast algorithms and the analysis of algorithm classes with the object of searching for optimal algorithms involve the specific computational complexity of algorithms.

Definition 4. We say that a problem P_n is finite with respect to the class of algorithms A, if there exists an algorithm $a \in A$ which solves P_n in a maximum time of C_n, where $C_n < \infty$ for $n < \infty$. If such an algorithm does not exist, then P_n is an infinite problem with respect to A.

The theory of optimal algorithms for finite problems, e.g. the computation of a polynomial at a given point, or matrix multiplication, is concerned with the so-called algebraic computational complexity [17], and for finite problems — computation of polynomial roots, computation of solutions of eliptical partial differential equations — it is concerned with the so-called analytic computational complexity [17]. Here, we have to deal mainly with finite problems.

The main results on the design of fast parallel algorithms are described in another chapter of this book. Now let us mention two known results on the lower bounds and some consequences, too.

A simple lower bound for the parallel computation of a problem with N input data has been derived by Heller [7], on the basis of the analysis of a set of binary trees. He has found that for the parallel computation of one result of a problem with N input data on k processors at least $m(k, N)$ steps are needed, where

$$m(k, N) = \min (s, n) + \max (0, [(N - 2^s)/k]),$$
$$s = \lceil \log k \rceil \quad \text{and} \quad n = \lceil \log N \rceil.$$

The generalization of this lower bound, derived by Munro and Paterson, is in [15].

Theorem 1. If for the computation of one value of Q at least q operations are needed, then an arbitrary algorithm employing k processors for the calculation of Q must contain at least $m(k, q + 1)$ steps.

A proof of the above statement is given by the class of optimal algorithms for the computation of $A_n = a_1 \circ a_2 \circ \ldots \circ a_N$, where $\circ$ is an arbitrary associative operation. These algorithms are known under the name of "log-sum" algorithms or "log-product" algorithms, since their original application was with $\circ$ equal to $+$ or $\times$ with $k = \lceil N/2 \rceil$ and $m(k, N) = \lceil \log N \rceil$. With regard to the number of processors required for the computation of A_N in the minimal time, Muraoka [16] has asserted that if $n = \lceil \log N \rceil$ and

$$k(N) = \begin{cases} [(N - 2^{n-2})/2], & \text{for} \quad 2^{n-1} < N \leq 3 \cdot 2^{n-2} \\ N - 2^{n-1}, & \text{for} \quad 3 \cdot 2^{n-2} \leq N \leq 2^n \end{cases}$$

then $m(k(N), N) = n$ and $m(k(N) - 1, N) = n + 1$, i.e. $k(N)$ is the minimum number of processors required for the computation of A_N with n steps. Another consequence of Theorem 1 is that the computation of the product of two vectors of order n is [1]:

a) for a k-parallel computation with $k < n$ optimal with

$$[2n - 2^{\lceil \log k \rceil}/k] + \lceil \log k \rceil \text{ steps,}$$

b) for unbounded parallelism optimal with $\lceil \log n \rceil + 1$ steps.

From b) it follows that the product of two matrices of order n can also be optimally computed for unbounded parallelism with $\lceil \log n \rceil + 1$ steps.

The second lower bound, derived by Kung [14], is comprised in the following statement:

Theorem 2. If $f(x)$ belongs to the field of rational expressions in x with $\deg f(x) = n$, then for the computation of $f(x)$ on k processors a minimum of $\lceil \log n \rceil U$ steps is required for all values of k, where U is the minimum time required for adding, multiplying and dividing operations.

A consequence of this assertion is, for instance, that the lower bound for the computation of x^n is $\lceil \log n \rceil A$. Since the upper bound $\lceil \log n \rceil A + 2(A + D)$ is determined by the algorithm described in the first section of this chapter, this algorithm for $n \to \infty$ is asymptotically optimal.

The consequence of Theorem 2 for the speedup of non-linear relations will be mentioned in the following section.

We note that analysis of the complexity of parallel algorithms can bring results different from serial computations. For instance, it is known that the serial complexity of the computation of the multiplication of two matrices and matrix inversion is the same. This does not hold in the case unbounded parallelism. For the multiplication of two square matrices of order n on $O(n^3)$ processors in the classical way, the number of steps is $\lceil \log n \rceil + 1$ and for Strassen's algorithm on $k \leq O(n^{\log 7})$ processors it is $3\lceil \log n \rceil + 1$. But for the inversion of a square matrix of order n on $k = O(n^4/\log n)$ processors the number of steps is $O(\log^2 n)$ [7].

Csanky [5] has proved that in unbounded parallelism the complexity of a parallel computation of matrix inversion, of the calculation of a determinant, and of the solution of a system of linear equations is the same, being bounded from below by $2\lceil \log n \rceil$ and bounded from above by $O(\log^2 n)$. In contrast to serial computations, the upper bound is in this case produced neither by Gaussian elimination nor by Strassen's method, but by Le Verrier's method mentioned above.

In our model of parallel computation the number of parallel steps which were arithmetic operations was the measure of complexity. As in serial calculations, this measure of computation cost is not necessarily the most realistic one. In parallel computations, the important criteria of complexity are limitations of a non-arithmetic nature resulting from the architecture of a given parallel computer.

Thus, for instance, in [6] it is shown that under certain assumptions for some matrix computations on some parallel computers, data transfer between separate memories rather than arithmetic operations are the limiting factor for computational effectiveness.

Suppose our model of parallel computation [6] has a large number of independent processors, that need not execute the same instruction in the same step. Let each processor have its own memory, and let a communication network exist between the processors, so that the data from one processor be available to only a small number of processors in a single step. The data transfer from one processor to another requires therefore several transfers through directly connected processors.

Let us further assume that at the start of the computation each element of the given matrices is represented in the computer only once and that there are no two elements from this matrix stored in the memory of the same processor.

We define the function $\varrho(k)$ as the maximum number of processors which the data, that are in only one processor at the start of computation, reach through the communication network with k or computation, reach through the communication network with k or less transfer steps.

Now we mention two theorems and their consequences from [6]:

Theorem 3. For the model of parallel computation described, the multiplication of two matrices of order N requires a minimum of s data transfer steps, where $\varrho(2s) \geqq N^2$.

Theorem 4. For the model of parallel computation described, the inversion of a matrix of order N or the solution of a system of N linear equations with N unknowns requires a minimum of s of data transfer steps, where $\varrho(s) \geqq N^2$.

If the processors are connected in a two-dimensional regular network — each with four neighbours — then $\varrho(k) = 2k^2 + 2k + 1$. From Theorems 3 and 4 the following consequence follows for this case:

For matrix multiplication $s \geqq \frac{1}{2} \sqrt{N^2/2 - 1/4} - 1/4$, or for large $N s \geqq 0.35N$, approximately. For inversion, or solution of a system of linear equations $s \geqq \sqrt{N^2/2 - 1/4} - 1/2$ or for large $N s \geqq 0.7 N$, approximately.

Thus, the solution of the above problems on the given parallel architecture requires $O(N)$ data transfer steps, even though the number of parallel steps of the arithmetic operations is significantly smaller, $O(\log N)$ or $O(\log^2 N)$, respectively.

2.4 Speedup of parallel algorithms

In this section we shall discuss the speedup of parallel algorithms that indicates how many times faster a problem or algorithm can be computed in parallel than serially.

Speedup is considered differently for finite and for infinite problems [18].

Let P_n be a finite problem and $a(P_n, k)$ be an algorithm for a k-parallel computation of P_n requiring $t(a(P_n, k))$ steps. The speedup $a(P_n, k)$ is defined as

$$s(a(P_n, k)) = \frac{T(P_n, 1)}{t(a(P_n, k))},$$

where $T(P_n, 1)$ is the minimum number of steps to solve P_n on one processor using an arbitrary algorithm. For most problems, $T(P_n, 1)$ is not known, and therefore it can only be estimated. This definition is applied to the given algorithm.

The next definition is applied to the given problem P_n, in which we introduce optimal speedup as the measure of the internal parallelism P_n.

We define optimal speedup as

$$S(P_n, k) = \frac{T(P_n, 1)}{T(P_n, k)},$$

where $T(P_n, k)$ is the minimum number of steps of the k-parallel computation of P_n.

It is obvious that for every k and $n: 1 \leqq S(P_n, k) \leqq k$. In designing parallel algorithms we aim at the optimal speedup to be linear in k, i.e. that all processors are effectively exploited. For $n \to \infty$ we want the asymptotic speedup to be of the form $ck - g(P_n, k)$, where $c \in (0, 1]$ is a constant independent of k and approximately equal to 1, and $0 \leqq g(P_n, k) = O(1)$. The function $g(P_n, k)$ is the loss from the application of parallelism in solving small problems. For large problems it is outweighed by the gain from parallelism [7].

Linear speedup is not always possible. For many important problems we have a speedup of $ck/\log k$, which is also acceptable. As we shall see, there also are problems whose speedup is only $\log k$, and also those which have for arbitrary k and n only a constant speedup. Such problems are not suitable for parallel computation.

In the computation of the speedup of an infinite problem we do not try to minimize the total time, but to maximize the measure of effectiveness [18]. This can be illustrated on the computation of the root α of the scalar function $f(x) = 0$. Suppose that for a given x_0 we have the iteration $x_{i+1} = \varphi(x_i)$, $i = 0, 1, \ldots$, in which x_i converges to α. The effectiveness of this iteration is dependent on the rate of its convergence and on the time required for one step of the iteration. The rate of convergence is specified by the order of the iteration. We say that an iteration is of order p, if $x_{i+1} - \alpha = O((x_i - \alpha)^p)$. Let $T(\varphi)$ be the execution time of the computation of x_{i+1} from x_i, then we define the measure of efficiency as

$$e(\varphi) = \frac{\log p(\varphi)}{T(\varphi)}.$$

It can be shown [18] that efficiency is inversely proportional to the total computation time of α for the precision of ε, where ε is a small number. Consequently, we want to maximize the efficiency. Let $E(1)$ be the optimal efficiency of the solution to this problem on a sequential computer. Then we define the speedup of the given algorithm $b(k)$ as $v(b(k)) = e(b(k))/E(1)$, and the optimal speedup as $V(k) = E(k)/E(1)$, where $E(k)$ is the optimal efficiency of a k-parallel computation. Now, let us formulate some theoretical results with their possible speedup, on an example of linear and non-linear recurrent relations.

For the linear recurrent relation we assume that each of its arithmetic operations takes one time unit. For the computation of x_n from the relation

$$x_0 = a_1, \quad x_i = b_i x_{i-1} + a_{i+1} \qquad (i = 1, 2, \ldots, n) \tag{4}$$

Hyafil and Kung [10] have proved that for every k and n $S(x_n, k) \leq (2k + 1)/3$, even if we assume that the overhead connected with the organization of this computation does not cause any delay. For example, for $k = 16$ or 64 the speedup of even an idealized computation can be at most only 11, or 43. The reason that in the computation of this problem generally a 70 % speedup can be expected, lies in the internal dependence of the variables of this relation. In (4) there are certain internal restrictions which, independent of the nature of the parallel computer, prevent the speedup from being k-fold.

Similarly, for all k and for all $n \geq k$ [8]:

$$S(x_n, k) \leq \frac{2k + 1}{3 + (c_1 \log k - c_2)(k + 0.5)/n}, \tag{5}$$

where c_1 and c_2 are positive constants.

For the linear recurrent relation of order p

$$x_i = \sum_{j=i-p}^{i-1} a_{ij} x_j + b_i \qquad (i = 1, 2, \ldots, n), \tag{6}$$

for every p, k and n

$$S(x_n, k) = \frac{2p}{2p + 1} k + c_3,$$

where c_3 is a constant and thus $2p/(2p + 1) < 1$; even in a k-parallel computation of x_n in relation (6) we cannot obtain an optimal speedup.

Even under these restrictions with $k \to \infty$ and the speedup of linear relations is $O(n/\log n)$, i.e. for $n \to \infty$ it is unbounded. Now, let us examine the theoretical speedup limits of some non-linear relations. In this case the situation is essentially worse. We shall see that the theory of some non-linear relations differs completely from that of linear ones, since for some non-linear relations, irrespective of the number of processors and the extent of the problem, the speedup is bounded by a constant. Thus, for these simple problems, a way to create effective parallel algorithms is not yet known.

The non-linear recurrence relation is defined as

$$x_i = \varphi(x_{i-1}, x_{i-2}, \ldots, x_{i-p}) \qquad (i = 1, 2, \ldots, n), \tag{7}$$

where φ is a non-linear rational function, i.e. $\varphi = \varphi_1/\varphi_2$, and where φ_1 and φ_2 are polynomials whose degrees are prime numbers. The degree of relation (7) is defined as

$$\deg \varphi = \max (\deg \varphi_1, \deg \varphi_2).$$

The following assertion [14] is valid:

Theorem 5. If relation (7) has a deg $\varphi > 1$, then for every k and n it holds that $S(x_n, k) \leq c$, where c is a constant.

Thus, the computation of the relation (7) cannot be essentially speeded up by parallelism.

The method of proving Theorem 5 is based on Theorem 2. We shall give a short proof of the relation $y_{i+1} = \varphi(y_i)$, where $\varphi(x)$ belongs to the field of rational expressions in x and deg $\varphi = d$. It follows from Theorem 2 that for every k $T(y_n, k) \geq \lceil n \log d \rceil U$. If the time of the serial computation of $\varphi(x)$ is $T(\varphi)$, then y_n may be calculated by a serial computer in a time of $nT(\varphi)$, and consequently for every k and n:

$$S(y_n, k) = \frac{T(\varphi)}{\lceil \log d \rceil U} = c,$$

i.e. this problem can only be speeded up by the constant.

Let us consider, for example, the known relation for the computation of $\sqrt{a}$

$$y_i = \left(y_{i-1} + \frac{a}{y_{i-1}}\right)/2 \qquad (i = 1, 2, \ldots, n), \tag{8}$$

which is of second degree.

Let us assume that we calculate with real numbers and every arithmetic operation requires a time U. Then the serial computation of y_n lasts $3nU$ and by Theorem 2 an arbitrary parallel algorithm lasts at least $\lceil \log 2^n \rceil U$, i.e. $\lceil n \rceil U$. Thus, the speedup of relation (8) is at most three-fold for every k and n. No parallel algorithm using an arbitrary number of processors can be essentially faster than the serial procedure in relation (8), which is completely different from linear relations which have a speedup $O(n/\log n)$.

The results described are so far probably the only non-trivial example of a type of problem that cannot be essentially speeded up by parallelism. Thus, the dependence between variables in non-linear relations is "stronger" than in linear relations. Hyafil and Kung [8] are of the opinion that especially the study of these dependences, or the discovery of the properties that prevent speedup make the basis for a deeper understanding of parallel computation. From Theorem 5 it follows that the only non-linear relation that can have an unbounded speedup is the relation

$$x_i = \left(\sum_{j=i-p}^{i-1} a_{ij} x_j + b_i \right) \Big/ \left(\sum_{j=i-q}^{i-1} c_{ij} x_j + d_i \right), \tag{9}$$

which is of the first degree.

For instance, for continued fractions

$$x_i = a_i + \frac{b_i}{x_{i-1}} \qquad (i = 1, 2, \ldots, n),$$

Kogge [11] has proved that

$$k/2 + c_4 \geq S(x_n, k) \geq \begin{cases} c_5 n / \log n & \text{if } k \geq n \\ 2k/5 & \text{for all } k \text{ and } n \to \infty \end{cases} \tag{10}$$

where c_4 and c_5 are constants.

It follows from the above results that algorithms containing division are more difficult to compute in parallel than algorithms without division. It is interesting that Brent [3] derived the same result for the parallel computation of arithmetic expressions. Thus, the relation

$$x_i = \frac{a_i x_{i-1} + b_i}{c_i x_{i-1} + d_i}$$

can be speeded up, since it is possible to transform it into a continued fraction. But the following assertion [9] shows that the speedup of relation (9) is bounded.

Theorem 6. If in relation (9) either $p > 1$, or $q > 1$, then for every k and n $S(x_n, k) \leq c_6$, where c_6 is a constant.

The results given for the theoretical bounds of the speedup achieved by parallelism offer basic methods for testing the efficiency of algorithms and their implementations on parallel computers. Algorithm design for theoretical computers also frequently leads, to the design of efficient algorithms for real computers. With respect to the practical choice of a suitable parallel computer, it is more advantageous to define the speedup, efficiency, and computational cost of the given algorithm as $S_k = T_1/T_k$, $E_k = S_k/k$, and $C_k = kT_k$, respectively [13], where T_k, $k \geq 1$, is the number of steps on a k-processor computer. A suitable measure for comparing algorithms is then the ratio $S_k/C_k = E_k S_k/T_1$, so that in designing algorithms we try to maximize the product of efficiency and speedup. In the next scheme we give the values of S_k/C_k for various parallel computations with arrays of size n [13]

$$a) \quad \begin{array}{l} \text{b) } O(\log^{-1} T_1) - \text{c) } O(\log^{-2} T_1) - \text{d) } O(\log^{-4} T_1) \\ O(1) \\ \text{e) } O(T_1^{-1/4}) - \text{f) } O(T_1^{-1/3}) - \text{g) } O(T_1^{-1/2}) - \text{h) } O(T_1^{-2/3}) \end{array} \quad \text{i) } O(T_1^{-1}),$$

where the single items denote:
a) array of arithmetic expressions; search for an unsorted list;
b) fast Fourier transformation; direct solution of Poisson equation;
c) multiply two matrices with $k = n^3$; arithmetic expressions; linear recurrent relations;
d) multiply n matrices with $k = n^4$; triangular systems with $k = n^3/64$;
e) multiply n matrices with $k = n^3$;
f) multiply two matrices with $k = n^2$; systems of linear equations with $k = n^2$;
g) multiply n matrices with $k = n^2$; triangular systems with $k = n$;
h) multiply two matrices with $k = n$; systems of linear equations with $k = n$;
i) search a sorted list; non-linear recurrent relations; serial computations.

The fastest parallel algorithm are on the left and the slowest on the right in the scheme. The lower line represents algorithms with less than maximum speedup. The upper line contains the best known speedup values. We can see that one problem can appear in several items; e.g. multiplication of n matrices is given for $k = n^2$, n^3, n^4, with the maximum value of S_k/C_k occurring with $k = n^3$.

REFERENCES

[1] BORODIN, A. and MUNRO, I.: The Computational Complexity of Algebraic and Numeric Problems. American Elsevier, New York, 1975.
[2] BRENT, R. P.: The parallel evaluation of arithmetic expressions in logarithmic time. Proc. Complexity of Sequential and Parallel Numerical Algorithms. J. F. Traub (Editor). Academic Press, New York, 1973, pp. 83—102.
[3] BRENT, R. P.: The parallel evaluation of general arithmetic expression. J. ACM, 21, 1974, 201--206.
[4] CSANKY, L.: Fast parallel matrix inversion algorithms. Tech. Report, Univ. of California, Berkeley, 1974.
[5] CSANKY, L.: On the parallel complexity of some computational problems. Dissertation. Univ. of California, Berkeley, 1974.
[6] GENTLEMAN, W. M.: Some complexity results for matrix computations on parallel processors. J. ACM, 25, 1978, 112—115.
[7] HELLER, D.: A survey of parallel algorithms in numerical linear algebra. Tech. Report, Comp. Sci. Dep., Carnegie-Mellon Univ., Pittsburg, Penn., 1976.
[8] HYAFIL, L. and KUNG, H. T.: Bounds on the speedup of parallel evaluation of recurrences. Tech. Report, Comp. Sci. Dep., Carnegie-Mellon Univ., Pittsburgh, Penn., 1975.
[9] HYAFIL, L. and KUNG, H. T.: Parallel evaluation of recurrences and parallel algorithms for solving band linear systems. Tech. Report, Comp. Sci. Dep., Carnegie-Mellon Univ., Pittsburgh, Penn., 1975.
[10] HYAFIL, L. and KUNG, H. T.: The complexity of parallel evaluation of linear recurrences. Tech. Report, IRIA 1975, Rocquencourt, 96.

[11] KOGGE, P. M.: Parallel solution of recurrence problems. IBM J. Res. Develop., *18*, 1974, 138—148.

[12] KUCK, D. J.: Multioperation machine computational complexity. Proc. Complexity of Sequential and Parallel Numerical Algorithms. J. E. Traub (Editor). Academic Press, New York, 1973, pp. 17—47.

[13] KUCK, D. J.: Parallel processing or ordinary programs. Advances in Computers, Vol. 15. Academic Press, New York, 1977, pp. 119—179.

[14] KUNG, H. T.: New algorithms and lower bounds for the parallel evaluation of certain rational expressions. Tech. Report, Comp. Sci. Dep., Carnegie-Mellon Univ., Pittsburgh, Penn., 1974.

[15] MUNRO, I. and PATERSON, M.: Optimal algorithms for parallel polynomial evaluation. J. Comp. Syst. Sci., 7, 1973, 189—198.

[16] MURAOKA, Y.: Parallelism exposure and exploitation. Dissertation. Dep. Comp. Sci., University of Illinois, Urbana, 1971.

[17] TRAUB, J. F.: An introduction to some current research in numerical computational complexity. Tech. Report. Comp. Sci. Dep., Carnegie-Mellon Univ., Pittsburgh, Penn., 1973.

[18] TRAUB, J. F.: Parallel algorithms and parallel computational complexity. Proc. IFIP Congress. North-Holland Publ. Co., Amsterdam, 1974, pp. 685—687.

Appendix

A PARALLEL ALGORITHM FOR SOLVING BAND SYSTEMS AND MATRIX INVERSION

1. Introduction. Recently, several studies have appeared about the solution of systems of linear equations $\mathbf{A}x = b$ on parallel computers, where $\mathbf{A}$ is a real n by n dense, triangular or tridiagonal matrix [1—6]. Essentially less effort has so far applied to this problem on parallel computers if the matrix has a different structure, e.g. a band structure with non-scalar constant coefficients, although there are studies of this for serial computers.

Thus, while there exist several parallel algorithms requiring only $O(\log n)$* time steps to solve tridiagonal systems, there are currently no such fast algorithms for band systems with bandwith $2m + 1$, where $m > 1$.

In this paper, a new parallel direct algorithm for solving such systems is discussed. This algorithm on an SIMD type parallel machine requires $(2 + \log 2m)\log n + O(m \log m)$ time steps using not more than $(3m^2 + m)n$ processors. For a tridiagonal system this are $3 \log n + O(1)$ steps using $4n$ processors, which is the lowest time we know of for solving tridiagonal systems. The algorithm can be formally interpreted as a parallel shooting method. It is based on the factorization of $\mathbf{A}$ as in [7].

---

*Throughout this paper $\log p = \lceil \log_2 p \rceil$, and the unit of time is referred to as a step.

The problem of solving the system for a band matrix has been transformed to the solving of systems with a banded lower triangular matrix. The algorithm is a generalization of the algorithm published in [1] for a tridiagonal system.

We also develop some parallel direct algorithm for inverting such a band matrix. Its application is advantageous if the computation of $\mathbf{A}^{-1}$ is part of the solution of $\mathbf{A}\mathbf{x} = \mathbf{b}$ and it is necessary to compute only selected rows or columns of $\mathbf{A}^{-1}$. If $\mathbf{A}$ is a symmetric matrix, the solution of both problems together requires $(4 + \log 4m^2) \log n + O(m \log m)$ time steps using $mn^2/4 + O(m^2 n)$ processors.

We assume throughout that any number of processors can be used at any time, but we give bounds for this.

All processors are assumed to perform the same operation during each time step, and each arithmetic operation, or the determination of the maximum magnitude of two numbers can be performed in one step.

2. A parallel band system solver. Let us consider the linear system of equations $\mathbf{A}\mathbf{x} = \mathbf{b}$, where $\mathbf{A}$ is a non-singular band matrix of order n with bandwidth $2m + 1$, i.e. $a_{ij} = 0$ for $|i - j| > m$ and $a_{i,i+m} \neq 0$ for $i = 1, 2, \ldots, n - m$. We assume a situation which frequently occurs in practice, $m \ll n$ in the worse case, $m < n/3$. Such a system can be written in the form

$$\begin{bmatrix} \mathbf{C} & \mathbf{T} \\ \mathbf{0}_m & \mathbf{S} \end{bmatrix} \begin{bmatrix} \mathbf{x}^{(1)} \\ \mathbf{x}^{(2)} \end{bmatrix} = \begin{bmatrix} \mathbf{b}^{(1)} \\ \mathbf{b}^{(2)} \end{bmatrix}, \tag{1}$$

where $\mathbf{T}$ and $\mathbf{0}_m$ are square matrices of order $n - m$ and m. In particular, $\mathbf{T}$ is a lower band triangular matrix with bandwith $2m + 1$ and $\mathbf{0}_m$ is a zero matrix. The submatrices $\mathbf{C}$ and $\mathbf{S}$ are generally rectangular and have the size $(n - m) \times m$ and $m \times (n - m)$. The vectors $\mathbf{x} = (x_1, x_2, \ldots, x_n)$ and $\mathbf{b} = (b_1, b_2, \ldots, b_n)$ are partitioned into $\mathbf{x}^{(i)}$ and $\mathbf{b}^{(i)}$, $i = 1, 2$, conformably with $\mathbf{A}$.

Since $\mathbf{T}$ is a non-singular matrix we obtain from the first equation of (1)

$$\mathbf{x}^{(2)} = \mathbf{T}^{-1}(\mathbf{b}^{(1)} - \mathbf{C}\mathbf{x}^{(1)}). \tag{2}$$

Let us assume the existence of a fast parallel method for the solution of triangular linear systems. Let $\mathbf{y}^{(i)}$, $i = 0, 1, 2, \ldots, m$ be solutions of such systems with the following right-hand side vectors

$$\mathbf{T}(\mathbf{y}^{(0)}\mathbf{y}^{(1)} \ldots \mathbf{y}^{(m)}) = (\mathbf{b}^{(1)}\mathbf{C}). \tag{3}$$

Thus, (2) can be expressed as

$$\mathbf{x}^{(2)} = \mathbf{y}^{(0)} - \sum_{k=1}^{m} x_k \mathbf{y}^{(k)}, \tag{4}$$

i.e. the last $n - m$ elements of $\mathbf{x}$ are the linear combination of the first m. When applying (4) to the second equation of (1), we obtain

$$-\mathbf{S}(\mathbf{y}^{(1)}\mathbf{y}^{(2)} \ldots \mathbf{y}^{(m)})\mathbf{x}^{(1)} = \mathbf{b}^{(2)} - \mathbf{S}_{\mathbf{y}}^{(0)}. \tag{5}$$

The following equality can be proved by the decomposition of $\mathbf{A}$

$$\det(\mathbf{A}) = \det(\mathbf{T}) \quad \det(\mathbf{S}(\mathbf{y}^{(1)}\mathbf{y}^{(2)} \ldots \mathbf{y}^{(m)}))(-1)^{mn-m}.$$

Then non-singularity of the matrix $\mathbf{S}(\mathbf{y}^{(1)} \ldots \mathbf{y}^{(m)})$ follows immediately from the assumptions. The elements of this matrix, the same as the vector of the right-hand side of (5), can be obtained by extension of the triangular system of (3) to the system

$$\begin{bmatrix} \mathbf{T} & \mathbf{O}_{n-m} \\ \mathbf{S} & \mathbf{I}_m \end{bmatrix} (\mathbf{z}^{(0)}\mathbf{z}^{(1)} \ldots \mathbf{z}^{(m)}) = \begin{bmatrix} \mathbf{b}^{(1)} & \mathbf{C} \\ \mathbf{b}^{(2)} & \mathbf{O}_m \end{bmatrix}. \tag{6}$$

Thus we obtain the following assertion.

Lemma 1. Let $\mathbf{A}$ be a non-singular band matrix of order n with bandwith $2m + 1$ and let the elements of the uppermost line above the diagonal be non-zero. Then the solution of the system $\mathbf{Ax} = \mathbf{b}$ satisfies

$$\begin{bmatrix} z_{n-m+1}^{(1)} & z_{n-m+1}^{(2)} & \cdots & z_{n-m+1}^{(m)} \\ z_{n-m+2}^{(1)} & z_{n-m+2}^{(2)} & \cdots & z_{n-m+2}^{(m)} \\ \vdots & \vdots & & \vdots \\ z_n^{(1)} z_n^{(2)} & & \cdots & z_n^{(m)} \end{bmatrix} \begin{bmatrix} x_1 \\ x_2 \\ \vdots \\ x_m \end{bmatrix} = \begin{bmatrix} z_{n-m+1}^{(0)} \\ z_{n-m+2}^{(0)} \\ \vdots \\ z_n^{(0)} \end{bmatrix}, \tag{7}$$

$$x_{m+i} = z_i^{(0)} - \sum_{k=1}^{m} x_k z_i^{(k)} \quad (i = 1, 2, \ldots, n-m), \tag{8}$$

Where $z_i^{(k)}$ is the i-th component of the vector $\mathbf{z}^{(k)}$, which is the solution of (6).

Hence, the direct parallel algorithm for solving $\mathbf{Ax} = \mathbf{b}$ of order n can be divided into 3 stages. We present it with the time required.

Stage E1. The solution of the lower band triangular system (6) of order n. There are fast parallel algorithms for solving such systems. Algorithm II [2] requires the smallest number of steps and processors. If we apply this algorithm to solve (6) in such a way that it solves simultaneously $m + 1$ band triangular systems differing from each other only at the right-hand side, then this stage requires $(2 + \log 2m) \log n - (1/2)(\log^2 2m + \log 2m) + 3$ steps using not more than $(3m^2 + m)n - 8m^3$ processors.

Stage E2. The solution of the dense system (7) of order m. Solving this system by Gaussian elimination with pivoting requires $3m(\log m - 1) + O(\log^2 m)$ steps using $(m - 1)^2$ processors.

Stage E3. The computation of (8). The computation of (8) consists of $n - m$ independent scalar products of two vectors of order $m + 1$. This can be performed in $1 + \log(m + 1)$ steps using $(m - 1)(n - m)/2$ processors.

Thus we have proved the following theorem.

Theorem 1. Let $\mathbf{A}$ be a matrix as in Lemma 1. Then the solution of $\mathbf{Ax} = \mathbf{b}$ requires $(2 + \log 2m)\log n + O(m \log m)$ steps using not more than $(3m^2 + m)n$ processors.

We can see that it needs $3 \log n + O(1)$ steps and $4n$ processors for a tridiagonal matrix. The comparison with Theorem 3.1 of [2] shows that the complexity of computation of a band system with bandwidth $2m+1$ and the lower band triangular systems with bandwidth $2m+1$ is the same, for $m \ll n$. The difference is only in the number of processors used. The band system requires 6 times more processors.

Although quite satisfactory from the point of view of algebraic complexity, like many shooting methods, also this algorithm suffers from an exponential growth in roundoff error and from the possibility of over-or underflow. These drawbacks are due to the parallel algorithm for solving lower band triangular systems (6).

On the other hand, the algorithm does not fail, if any of the leading principal submatrices is singular. It can also be used for solving a band system with a different number of non-zero super and subdiagonal lines or matrices of the semi-band form, but the elements of the uppermost line above the diagonal must be non-zero.

3. A parallel matrix inversion algorithm. Let us assume that it is necessary to obtain the solution of $\mathbf{A}\mathbf{x} = \mathbf{b}$, and also to compute some rows or columns of $\mathbf{A}^{-1}$. Such a problem can occur, for example, if we want to obtain the solution of the equation $\mathbf{B}\mathbf{v} = \mathbf{w}$ on the basis of the solution $\mathbf{A}\mathbf{x} = \mathbf{b}$, where $\mathbf{B}$ differs only slightly from $\mathbf{A}$, and so is naturally thought of as a modification of $\mathbf{A}$ [8]. Therefore, it is useful to have algorithms which make it possible, using the results obtained from solving $\mathbf{A}\mathbf{x} = \mathbf{b}$, to compute some selected rows or columns of $\mathbf{A}^{-1}$. Such a parallel algorithm is developed below. It is based on the following assertion.

Lemma 2. Let $\mathbf{A}$ be a matrix as in Lemma 1. Then for the elements α_{ij}, of matrix $\mathbf{A}^{-1}$, $i \le j$, $i = 1, ..., n$ the following relations hold

I1.
$$
\begin{bmatrix}
\alpha_{1n-m+1} & \alpha_{1n-m+2} & \cdots & \alpha_{1n} \\
\alpha_{2n-m+1} & \alpha_{2n-m+2} & \cdots & \alpha_{2n} \\
\vdots & \vdots & & \vdots \\
\alpha_{mn-m+1} & \alpha_{mn-m+2} & \cdots & \alpha_{mn}
\end{bmatrix}
=
\begin{bmatrix}
z_{n-m+1}^{(1)} & z_{n-m+1}^{(2)} & \cdots & z_{n-m+1}^{(m)} \\
z_{n-m+2}^{(1)} & z_{n-m+2}^{(2)} & \cdots & z_{n-m+2}^{(m)} \\
\vdots & \vdots & & \vdots \\
z_n^{(1)} & z_n^{(2)} & \cdots & z_n^{(m)}
\end{bmatrix}^{-1}
\tag{9}
$$

I2. $(\alpha_{j1}, \alpha_{j2}, ..., \alpha_{jn-m})\mathbf{T} = -(\alpha_{jn-m+1}, \alpha_{jn-m+2}, ..., \alpha_{jn})\mathbf{S}$ (10)
$(j = 1, 2, ..., m)$.

I3. $\alpha_{m+ij} = -\sum_{k=1}^{m} \alpha_{kj} z_i^{(k)}$ (11)
$(j = m+1, m+2, ..., n)$, $(i = 1, 2, ..., j-m)$.

Proof. Let us consider the matrix $\mathbf{A}^{-1}$ in the form

$$
\mathbf{A}^{-1} = \begin{bmatrix} \mathbf{M}_1 & \mathbf{M}_2 \\ \mathbf{M}_3 & \mathbf{M}_4 \end{bmatrix},
$$

where $\mathbf{M}_2$ and $\mathbf{M}_3$ are square matrices of order m and $n - m$, respectively. Matrices $\mathbf{M}_1$ and $\mathbf{M}_4$ are partitioned conformably with $\mathbf{M}_2$ and $\mathbf{M}_3$.

I1. From the equation $\mathbf{AA}^{-1} = \mathbf{I}_n$ we have

$$\mathbf{CM}_2 + \mathbf{TM}_4 = \mathbf{O}_{(n-m)\times m}$$
$$\mathbf{SM}_4 = \mathbf{I}_m. \tag{12}$$

By eliminating $\mathbf{M}_4$ we obtain

$$-\mathbf{S}(\mathbf{y}^{(1)}\mathbf{y}^{(2)} \ldots \mathbf{y}^{(m)})\mathbf{M}_2 = \mathbf{I}_m,$$

i.e.

$$\mathbf{M}_2 = (-\mathbf{S}(\mathbf{y}^{(1)}\mathbf{y}^{(2)} \ldots \mathbf{y}^{(m)}))^{-1} = \begin{bmatrix} z^{(1)}_{n-m+1} & z^{(2)}_{n-m+1} \cdots & z^{(m)}_{n-m+1} \\ \vdots & \vdots & \vdots \\ z^{(1)}_n & z^{(2)}_n & \cdots & z^{(m)}_n \end{bmatrix}^{-1} \tag{13}$$

I2. (10) follows from $\mathbf{A}^{-1}\mathbf{A} = \mathbf{I}_n$, since $\mathbf{M}_1\mathbf{T} = -\mathbf{M}_2\mathbf{S}$.

I3. Let α_j represent the j-th column of $\mathbf{A}^{-1}$, where $m < j \leqslant n$.

Then $\mathbf{A}\alpha_j = \mathbf{e}_j$, where $\mathbf{e}_j$ is the j-th column of $\mathbf{I}_n$. According to Lemma 1, the last $n - m$ components of α_j satisfy

$$\alpha_{m+ij} = z^{(0j)}_i - \sum_{k=1}^m \alpha_{kj} z^{(k)}_i \qquad (i = 1, 2, \ldots, n-m), \tag{14}$$

where $\mathbf{y}^{(0j)}$ is the solution of the band triangular system

$$\begin{bmatrix} \mathbf{T} & \mathbf{0}_{n-m} \\ \mathbf{S} & \mathbf{I}_m \end{bmatrix} \mathbf{y}^{(0j)} = \mathbf{e}_j.$$

It can easily be seen that $y^{(0j)}_i = 0$, for $i = 1, 2, \ldots, j-1$, and therefore (14) reduces to (11).

The algebraic complexity of stages I1—I3 is as follows:

Stage I1. The computation of any column of the matrix inverse of order m by Gaussian elimination with pivoting requires $3m(\log m - 1) + O(\log^2 m)$ steps using $(m - 1)^2$ processors. All columns can be computed in the same time using not more than $m(m - 1)^2$ processors.

Stage I2. System (10) can be readily adapted, so that Algorithm II [2] may be used for its solution. This stage requires with a computation of the right-hand side vector $(2 + \log 2m) \log (n - m) - (1/2)(\log^2 2m + \log 2m - 2 \log m) + 4$ steps and $3m^2n + mn - 8m^3$ processors.

Stage I3. The computation of (11) consists of $(n - m)(n - m + 1)/2$ independent scalar products of two vectors of length m which can be performed using $(1/4)$ $(mn^2 - (2m - 1)mn) + O(m^3)$ processors in $\log m + 1$ steps.

Thus, we can introduce the following theorem:

Theorem 2. Let $\mathbf{A}$ be a matrix as in Lemma 1. Knowing the elements $z^{(j)}_i$,

$j = 1, 2, ..., m$; $i = n - m + 1, ..., n$, the upper triangular matrix of $\mathbf{A}^{-1}$ can be computed in $(2 + \log 2m) \log (n - m) + O(m \log m)$ steps using $(1/4)$ $(mn^2 - (2m - 1)mn) + O(m^3)$ processors.

From the above theorem one can observe that, for a symmetric matrix $\mathbf{A}$ and for a value of n which is a power of 2, the solution of $\mathbf{A}x = \mathbf{b}$ and $\mathbf{A}^{-1}$ can be obtained in $(4 + \log 4m^2) \log n + O(m \log m)$ steps using $mn^2/4 + O(m^2 n)$ processors. For a tridiagonal symmetric matrix this means $6 \log n + O(1)$ steps using $n(n - 1)/4 + O(1)$ processors.

If $\mathbf{A}$ is not symmetric and all its elements in the lowermost line below the diagonal are non-zero, it is possible to compute the lower triangular matrix of $\mathbf{A}^{-1}$ in such a way that the stages E1, I1, I2, I3, to be applied to the matrix $\mathbf{A}^\mathrm{T}$ ($\mathbf{A}^\mathrm{T}$ denote the transpose of $\mathbf{A}$). The number of time steps remains the same, but the number of processors is doubled in such a case.

The algorithm for the computation of $\mathbf{A}^{-1}$ has the same drawbacks as the algorithm for solving $\mathbf{A}x = \mathbf{b}$. Therefore, it is reasonable when implementig these algorithms to use double precision arithmetics. This will stabilize the algorithms and reduce the error bounds in practice.

REFERENCES

[1] SAMEH, A. H. and KUCK, D. J.: On stable parallel linear system solvers. J. ACM, 25, 1978, 1, 81—91.
[2] SAMEH, A. H. and BRENT, R. P.: Solving triangular system on a parallel computer. SIAM J. Numer. Anal., 6, 1977, 1101—1113.
[3] CHEN, S. C., KUCK, D. J. and SAMEH, A. H.: Practical parallel band triangular system solvers. ACM Trans. on Math. Software, 3, 1978, 270—277.
[4] CHEN, S. CH. and KUCK, D. J.: Time and parallel processors bounds for linear recurrence systems. IEEE Trans. on Computers, 24, 1975, 7, 701—717.
[5] STONE, H. S.: An efficient parallel algorithm for the solution of a tridiagonal linear system of equations. J. ACM, 20, 1973, 1, 27—38.
[6] EVANS, D. J. and HATZOPOULOS, M. A.: A parallel linear system solver. Int. J. Comp. Math., 7, 1979, 227—238.
[7] BANK, R. E. and ROSE, D. J.: An $O(n^2)$ method for solving constant coefficient boundary value problems in two dimensions. SIAM J. Numer. Anal., 12, 1975, 4, 529—540.
[8] BUZBEE, B. L.: A capacitance matrix technique. In: Sparse Matrix Computations. J. R. Bunch and D. J. Rose (Editors). Academic Press, New York, 1976.

Chapter 3

AUTOMATIC CONSTRUCTION OF PARALLEL PROGRAMS

With the increasing complexity of problems to be solved and system structures, the difficulties of program construction has grown. In the first place, this holds for parallel programs which do not use the conventional step-by-step representation of computations. There are two ways to relieve the difficulties: to increase the level of computer instructions and thus to bring them closer to the programmer's thinking, or to make parallel programming more automatic which will increase its efficiency. In the last few years, parallel processing has been actively studied within the framework of both approaches. The present contribution is confined to the second approach and disregards the hardware representation and semaphore technique of parallelism. It does not claim to give an exhaustive historical overview of parallel programming techniques. The interested reader is referred to reviews [1—3] which complement each other and give a good idea of the state-of-the-art at the turn of the 70s.

Three stages will be distinguished in automating programming. In the first stage, some services for simplifying coding may be offered to the programmer: certain programming rules or methods, a set of auxiliary procedures facilitating manual coding (including parallel programs), etc. In the second stage, the procedural approach is implemented, i.e. the programmer is offered an algorithmic high-level language which is translated or interpreted automatically. Finally, the third level, that of the problem-oriented non-procedural language, requires an automatic program generation system based, as a rule, on a description of object area semantics. In response to an input non-procedural request, the system automatically constructs or locates the required program and plans the computations. At the first of the above automation stages, the programmer constructs parallel program structures manually, automation just facilitating his work. At the second stage, the programmer need not concern himself with the parallel structures and can even write the program in sequential form, if convenient. At the third stage, the programmer need not even concern himself with the algorithmic aspect of the problem and just defines the data and describes the desired results. This chapter confines itself to the second stage of automation. It is the automatic generation of parallel structures that is the main problem at this stage, because the methods of parallel program translation and interpretation with an adequate introduction of parallelism at the computer level does not, in principle, differ from its sequential-program counterpart. The major emphasis is, therefore placed in this chapter on automatic parallelization and the parallelazition of the interpretation of programs. This accounts for the fact that the term "automatic construction of parallel programs" is synonymous with "automatic parallelization" in the literature.

Program parallelization techniques can be classified with respect to the following parameters:

— the degree of automation: manual, automatic, and completely automatic, as described above;

— the elementary block size: macro-parallelization and micro-parallelization. The former manipulates larger program parts (procedures, subprograms) and is usually implemented by software. The latter transforms the structure at the instruction level and can be implemented in hardware;

— the analyzed part: local and global. The local parallelization covers only a small observable neighbourhood of each point of the program, and the resulting program has essentially the same structure. One can establish a correspondence between the parts of the initial and parallelized programs. Global parallelization alters completely the program so that it can be changed beyond recognition;

— the allowance for the specificity of particular statements: structural and special. The structural parallelization abstracts itself from the particular interpretation of statements and deals only with program schemes that indicate logical and data paths. The special parallelization allows for the specific nature of particular operations and is, mostly, the prerogative of computational techniques. The special parallelization is more profound and subtle, while the structural parallelization is more universal. For instance, although the non-existence of maximal parallelization algorithms for simply interpreted programs has been shown [4], such an algorithm exists for rather wide classes of programs;

— dynamism: static and dynamic. A static parallelization is done before program execution; there is a final product, a parallel program that can be stored and called for repeated execution. A dynamic parallelization is performed while the computation is in progress; it allows for the current computational environment and is, therefore, more flexible. However, it does not provide a complete parallel program. These modes correspond to translation and interpretation, respectively;

— parallelization depth: maximal and optimal. The maximum parallelization takes into account the whole potential parallelism of a program independently of its complexity and its implementation on a particular computer. Optimal parallelization reveals only that aspect of parallelism which optimizes some characteristics (usually, the computation time) of the program in an implementation on a particular computer;

— in addition, parallelization can be classified as explicit and implicit. The term "implicit" is applied to the preprocessing of a program with the aim to restructure it without isolating explicit parallel branches, so as to achieve the desired degree of parallelism through subsequent (usually, dynamic) parallelization.

Under any parallelization technique, the first step is the detection of independent statements or program segments. The following types of connections the prevent parallel execution are recognized in program:

a) Control connection. In contrast to the connection below, this one is of directive nature, is explicitly indicated and does not require special analysis for its recognition. It leads to the following implicit connections.

b) Data connection. Statement B is data-dependent on statement A if A generates data used by B. A data connection exists if A and B are connected through a path (e.g. shared memory location), and if there is a computational path from A to B, where A is the last statement influencing B via this path.

c) Logical connection. Statement B is logically dependent on statement A, if the execution or non-execution of B depend on the results of the execution of statement A.

d) A concurrent connection means that statement A and B cannot be permuted or executed concurrently because of the lack or incorrect use of resources. In the case of shared memory, this happens when condition

$$(\text{In}(A) \cap \text{Out}(B)) \cup (\text{In}(B) \cap \text{Out}(A)) \cup (\text{Out}(A) \cap \text{Out}(B)) = \emptyset \qquad (1)$$

is not met, where In and Out denote complete sets of input and output variables of appropriate statements. In the program there is a great variety of elements requiring fundamentally different approaches to the detection of the above connections. This paper discusses in detail three typical program structures: expressions, cycles, and branched sequential structures which include statements and branches. The paper also discusses some types of arrays. From among other important program elements, only recursion is not discussed properly, because it can be effectively parallelized only by using computational techniques discussed elsewhere in this book.

3.1 Expression transformation

All programming languages, inclusive of non-procedural ones, involve various forms of expression. In the most abstract form, an expression is defined as a term over sets of atoms $A = C \cup X$ (where X are variables, C are constants) and sets of operation symbols $F = \{f_1^{n_1}, f_2^{n_2}, \ldots\}$; the index n_i, signifying that the operation f_i is n_i-ary usually omitted. Operations can be language operations, standard and defined functions, and conditional expressions if $(p, e_1, e_2) =$, if p then e_1 else e_2, where e_i is an expression and p is a logical expression. In the last case, it is convenient to assume that all the three arguments of the conditional expression are computed in parallel. Each expression is represented by a tree and also by an expression in reversed Polish notation obtained by traversing the tree anti-clockwise. Trees and Polish notations for expressions $e_1 = f_1(f_1(x, c), f_2(a, b))$ and $e_2 = f_1(x_1, f_2(f_3(a, f_4(b)), x_2))$ are shown in Fig. 1.

The number of tree levels is referred to as the expression depth. It is, for example, equal to 3 for e_1 and 5 for e_2.

If operations involved in an expression have two or more operands, the argument expressions can be computed in parallel, provided there is an appropriate hardware

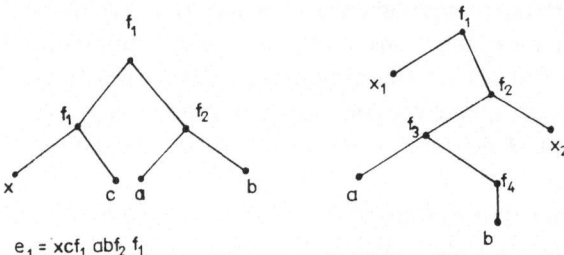

$e_1 = xcf_1 \, abf_2 \, f_1$

$e_2 = x_1 abf_4 \, f_3 x_2 f_2 f_1$ Fig. 1. Trees for the expressions e_1 and e_2.

support. For example, $f_1(x, c)$ and $f_2(a, b)$ in e_1 can be computed concurrently, but this is not possible for e_2. Let us assume that all operations are executed in unit time. In this case, the total execution time $T(e)$ of the parallel computation of the expression e is the number of levels minus one. For instance, $T(e_1) = 2$, $T(e_2) = 4$. The mean parallelism $p(e)$ of expression e is defined as the number of operations divided by the execution time: $P(e_1) = 3/2$, $P(e_2) = 1$. The maximum number N of symbols in a level is the number of processors required for parallel implementation: $N(e_1) = 2$, $N(e_2) = 1$.

The fact that particular functions f_i usually satisfy some special relations initiating equivalence relation over all the expression set E creates the prerequisite for expression parallelization. For arithmetic expressions these relations are: associativity, commutativity and distributivity; for logic expressions these are the de Morgan laws; for standard functions there are special relations such as $\sin^2(x) + \cos^2(x) = 1$. For example, if in expressions e_1, e_2 symbols f_1 and f_2 designate addition, f_3 designates subtraction, and f_4 designates unary minus, they will be rewritten as follows:

$$e_1 = (x + c) + (a + b); \quad e_2 = x_1 + ((a - (-b)) + x_2).$$

On the basis of the laws of arithmetic, e_1 can be rewritten as $e_1' = x + (c + (a + b))$, and e_2 as $e_2' = (x_1 + x_2) + (a + b)$. The trees of these expressions are shown in Fig. 2. The execution time of the first expression has increased to three, and the execution time of the second expression is reduced to one.

The problem of expression parallelization is stated as follows: construct an algorithm assigning to each expression e an expression $\bar{e}$ equivalent to e and having the minimum execution time in the class $\{e': e' \sim e\}$. In doing so, a constraint can be imposed on the number of processors $N(\bar{e})$ or a requirement can be set that the number of operations should not increase. This sometimes occurs when employing distributivity, e.g. $a(b+c) = ab + ac$. Obviously, under such a formulation there

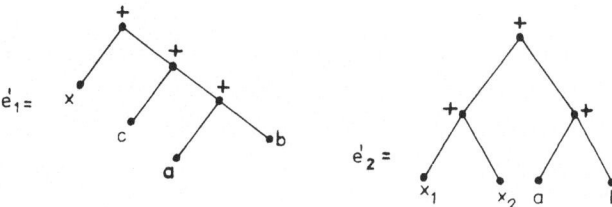

Fig. 2. Trees for the expressions e'_1 and e'_2.

always exists an algorithm, at least one using complete selection. Therefore, it is of interest to estimate its complexity and the number of passes required for its execution.

According to our classification, the expression parallelization algorithms below can be described as a local special static implicit micro-parallelization. As for maximal parallelism, some of the algorithms below do not provide maximum parallelization, but rather give an approximation to it and enhance compilation. In addition to the overview of existing methods, we present some estimates of the execution time, the number of processors and algorithm complexity. The objective classification of parallelization techniques was a difficult task for those writers who preferred the classification proposed in [5], although it was not based on deep principles. Emphasis was placed upon the axiomatic technique and that based on distributivity. As signs of arithmetic operations, we make use of $+$, $-$, $*$, $/$, $\uparrow$, μ, of which the latter two represent raising to a power and unary minus, respectively. In informal presentations, the multiplication sign $*$ is sometimes omitted. The operation priority, Pr, is introduced: $\mathrm{Pr}(\mu) = 4$, $\mathrm{Pr}(\uparrow) = 3$, $\mathrm{Pr}(*) = \mathrm{Pr}(/) = 2$, $\mathrm{Pr}(+) = \mathrm{Pr}(-) = 1$.

Some parentheses can be omitted if they are not necessary owing to the priority relation. Moreover, in the case of a succession of equal-priority associative operations, the parentheses can also be omitted, but the expression is interpreted ambiguously: $a + b + c$ can be interpreted as $(a + b) + c$ or as $a + (b + c)$. It is worthy of mention that initially this possibility of equivalent expression transformations led the programmers in a direction away from parallelization, viz. to the economization of memory allocated for partial results. For example, in expression e_1 the results $x + c$ and $a + b$ should be stored simultaneously, i.e. two memory units were required, while successive addition, e'_1, required only one memory unit. The first optimizing transformations for computers with few registers were oriented directly to the reduction of partial results. Already at this stage a drawback in unconsidered automatic permutation of parentheses set by the programmer was observed. Transformations, such as that of e_1 to e_1' or vice versa may result in an overflow or loss of accuracy for certain values of x, c, a and b. This holds especially for the distributive law. If, for example, a and b are large positive numbers, and c is a large negative number, $b + c$ in expression $a * (b + c)$ is not so large as to lead to an overflow. However, in $a * b + a * c$ the multiplication of a by b and a by c can result in an overflow. This has stimulated the development of standards regulating the application of equivalence expressions in programming languages. This trend is taken into account in the methods described below, except of those in the last subsection.

Before proceeding to particular methods, we must make one remark. It is implied in the formulation of the parallelization problem that the output of an algorithm should be an arithmetic expression in conventional linear notation. In actual systems, however, it is preferable to have an output notation close to the "processor language", e.g. a stack of operations and operands. The methods proposed here often translate expressions to just such a quintuple (operand 1, operator, operand 2, result, level) — each corresponding to one operation and defining the execution sequence.

Methods based on precedence comparison

Compilation methods are usually classified as direct or syntactic. Direct methods parse a string on the basis of some properties unambigously defining the structure of the decomposed units. This section is devoted to a technique using operation precedence relations as such a property. The technique stems from [6] and is based on associativity and commutativity relations. One can, therefore, assume that the input string is an expression in parenthesis-free notation. The method is built around separation in the expression of subexpressions involving highest-priority operations. Superated subexpressions of equal depth are "glued" into a larger subexpression, resulting in an expression having equal-depth subexpressions. Below, a more detailed description is given of a version of the algorithm. It is deliberately simplified to emphasize the main aspects of the method and applicable to expressions containing only $+$ and $*$.

Current information is stored in the following locations: x for scanned operands, y for scanned operations, l for an operation to the left of the current operand, r for an operation to the right of the current operand, *"Out"* for the output expression, and T_i for temporary results. In addition, the vector stack, $St = (St_1, St_2)$, is used, where St_1 contains operands and St_2 contains operations. Sc is the procedure for scanning the next symbol of the input string. The symbol $\rightarrow \ldots$ stands for transfer.

The input string is assumed to be bounded on both sides by blanks $\Box$, $\Pr(\Box) = 0$. Initially, r and Out contain blanks.

Step 1. $Sc \rightarrow x$, $Sc \rightarrow y$, $r \rightarrow l$, $y \rightarrow r$. The next operand and the sign of the following operations are scanned. Operation (blank) to the left of operand x is moved to location 1, that to the right of x is moved to location r.

Step 2. If $St = \emptyset \vee \Pr(l) < \Pr(r) \vee \Pr(St_2) < \Pr(l)) \wedge \Pr(r) \neq 0$, then go to Step 3, else go to Step 4.

Step 3. $x \rightarrow St_1$, $y \rightarrow St_2$, go to Step 1. Store operand and operation and proceed to the scanning of the next pair (operand, operation).

Step 4. If $\Pr(l) = \Pr(St_2)$, go to Step 5, else go to Step 6.

Step 5. $Out\ T_{ky} \rightarrow Out$. If $\Pr(y) = 0$, then end of parsing, else go to Step 1. Here, $T_k = (St_1, St_1, x)$ is the temporary result.

Thus, when two operations of equal precedence are found, the first one, together with its adjacent operands is grouped into a partial result T_k; then the second operation is written, and the whole is attached to the output string. T_k is further regarded by the algorithm as an atomic operand.

Step 6. $Out\ xy \rightarrow Out$, if $y = \sqcup$, end of parsing, else Step 1. If there are not two equal-precedence operations and priorities begin to decrease, only the operand and operation are attached to the output string.

This algorithm describes a pass resulting in the "convolution" of some subexpressions into temporary results T_k. The algorithm is repeated until the whole expression has been reduced. Below, the expression $e = a + b + c * d * l * f + g$ is shown after a series of passes.

1. The input string $\sqcup a + b + c * d * l * f + g \sqcup$.
2. The result of the 1st pass, $\sqcup T_1 + T_2 * T_3 + g \sqcup$,
   where $T_1 = (a + b)$, $T_2 = (c * d)$, $T_3 = (l * f)$.
3. The result of the 2nd pass, $\sqcup T_4 + T_5 \sqcup$,
   where $T_4 = (T_2 * T_3)$, $T_5 = (T_1 + g)$.
4. The result of the 3rd pass $\sqcup T_6 \sqcup$, $T_6 = (T_4 + T_5)$.
5. The output string $\sqcup\ (((c * d) * (l * f)) + ((a + b) + g))$.

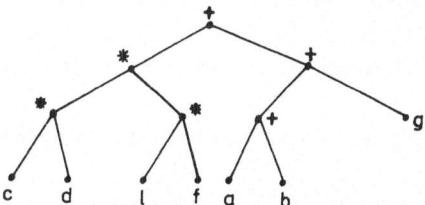

Fig. 3. Tree for the expression $(c*d)*(l*f) + + ((a+b)+g)$.

Figure 3 shows the tree of the output expression. The execution time, $T(\bar{e}) = 3$, is the same as the number of passes required. Partial results T_k generated in the i-th pass are at the i-th execution level. The expression generated can be represented as a stack of quintuples:

Level	Operation	1st operand	2nd operand	Result
1	+	a	b	T_1
1	*	c	d	T_2
1	*	l	f	T_3
2	*	T_2	T_3	T_4
2	+	T_1	g	T_5
3	+	T_4	T_5	T_6

The algorithm described has been proved [7] to lead to expressions with minimal execution time. It has, however, some disadvantages, the major one being the multiple passes: the number of passes required is equal to the execution time of the expression generated. To eliminate multiple passes, one has to keep data about the level of generated constructs when parsing. A one-pass version of the method proposed [5] is as follows.

Operand levels and precedence operations are added to the stack of operations and operands. The input expression is scanned and accumulated in the stack until a closing parenthesis or lower priority operation occur. The stack is then emptied quintuple-by-quintuple (operand 1, operation, operand 2, result, execution level). For the generation of the next quintuple,

max {operand 1 level, operand 2 level} + 1,

is taken as the value of its level. The algorithm is somewhat heuristic and does not always result in minimal-depth expressions. Experimental results show that the depth of the resulting expression is close to the minimum and approaches it asymptotically with greater input expression lengths. Although the decomposition is done in a single pass which is very important for implementation in compilers, the algorithm is not much simpler than the previous one, because the difficulties in this case are concentrated on operations with stacks. For this reason, it would be interesting to estimate the real algorithm complexity against some permanent elementary steps. Both the upper and lower bounds of the execution time of minimized expression are of interest.

Expressions of the form $a_1 + a_2 + \ldots + a_n$ readily lead to a lower bound for time of $\log_2 n$.

Similar estimates for algorithms using only associativity and commutativity are considered in [8, 9].

As demonstrated in [8], any expression e with n operands and parenthesis depth d can be transformed into $\bar{e}$, so that $T(\bar{e}) \leqslant \lceil \log n \rceil + 2d + 1$, the number of required processors being $N(\bar{e}) = \lceil n/2 - d \rceil$. As one can see from the formula, the estimate approaches the lower bound log n for small values of d. [9] gives the complexity estimate of the transformation algorithm without proof. If an expression has N symbols (identifiers, numbers, operations), the additional time for its compilation into a form with maximum parallelism is $13N + 8$. Here, reading into and out of the stack and memory are elementary steps. Note that estimates have been obtained for expressions involving no exponentiation and no unary minus.

Methods based on Polish notation

In many compilers, the expression, prior to code generation, is represented in reverse Polish notation, and this has stimulated the development of parallelization methods where the expression is the input string. Parallelization techniques perform analysis by exploiting some specific properties of the Polish notation such as parentheses-free writing the preservation of the original order of the operands. The most complete description of these methods is contained in [5]. The simplest idea of using Polish notation lies in "convoluting" subexpressions that have atomic operands (i.e. triples (⟨operand⟩, ⟨operand⟩, ⟨operation⟩)) into partial results. More precisely, the algorithm may be formulated as follows. One moves along the input string until one finds a sequence of the form: ⟨operand 1⟩ ⟨operand 2⟩ ⟨operation⟩. Any expression in Polish notation contains at least one such triple. Having found such a sequence, the following quintuple is generated: (execution level, operation, operand 1, operand 2, result) where the execution level is equal to the number of passes along the sequence. Having reached the end of the expression, we begin a new pass using previously unused symbols and partial results as operands. Quintuples of the same level can be executed in parallel. However, the method does not provide maximum parallelism, because it does not regroup operations of equal precedence. For instance, for the above expression, e, the transformation sequence is as follows:

1. Input string $ab + cd * l * f * g + +$.
2. Result of the 1st pass, $T_1 T_2 l * f * g + +$, where $T_1 = ab +$, $T_2 = cd *$.
3. Result of the 2nd pass, $T_1 T_3 f * g + +$, where $T_3 = T_2 l *$.
4. Result of the 3rd pass, $T_1 T_4 g + +$, where $T_4 = T_3 f *$.
5. Result of the 4th pass, $T_1 T_5 +$, where $T_5 = T_4 g +$.
6. Result of the 5th pass $T_6 = T_1 T_5 +$.
7. Output string in conventional notation

   $(a + b) + ((((c * d) * l) * f) + g)$.

Only T_1 and T_2 can be executed concurrently and the execution time of the resulting expression is 5, not 3 as for the previous method.

An improved technique described in [5] leads to a minimal-depth expression in three passes including the reduction to Polish notation. It is in essence as follows: both atomic and compound operands related by one operation are joined at each pass. These expressions are generated as sequences, their execution level being calculated as above. In order to scan all the operations in a single pass, the Polish notation is scanned from the left to the right. Since the method does not use the distributive property, the estimate of generated expression depth is the same as in the above method. The authors do not give a step-by-step estimate of the algorithm complexity.

Syntax-driven technique

For the reduction of expressions to a form with maximum parallelism a method was proposed [10] based on the syntax of arithmetic expressions written in normal Backus form as follows:

$\langle$expression$\rangle ::= \langle$term$\rangle\{$additive operation$\langle$term$\rangle\}$*
$\langle$term$\rangle ::= \langle$factor$\rangle\{$multiplicative operation $\langle$factor$\rangle\}$*
$\langle$factor$\rangle ::= \langle$primary$\rangle\{\uparrow\langle$primary$\rangle\}$*
$\langle$primary$\rangle ::= \langle$variable$\rangle(\langle$expression$\rangle)$
$\langle$variable$\rangle ::= A\,|\,B\,|\,...\,|\,Z.$

In this notation, the additive operation is $+$ or $-$, the multiplicative operation is * or /. During the decomposition of the input string, we try to construct from two neighbouring terms an expression, if the operation is addition, or a term, if the operation is multiplication. This method is referred to as the precedence method: the operation precedence is defined by the expression grammar. The order of parsing is such that factors are recognized before terms, terms are recognized before expressions. A reverse Polish notation is generated at the output. The expression depth minimization is provided by searching for two subexpressions of level $K-1$ when trying to generate an expression of level K. The algorithm is presented as an ALGOL procedure having the following grammar-defined structure:

procedure EXPRESSION
procedure TERM
⋮
call FACTOR
⋮
end TERM
procedure FACTOR
⋮
call PRIMARY
⋮

end   FACTOR
procedure PRIMARY
                 ⋮
end   PRIMARY
input
while   addition statements are scanned
execute   TERM
end   EXPRESSION

Thus, the procedure TERM is called in a while loop. If an operation occurs, i.e. other than addition, TERM calls FACTOR providing factors to TERM. In the course of the addition operation, it groups terms by two. The resulting units are again grouped by two, etc., i.e. it tries to construct a complete binary tree. The FACTOR procedure groups multiplication statements in a similar manner and calls PRIMARY for the generation of variables. For the expression $a + b + c * d * l * f + g$, the sequence of calls is shown in Fig. 4, and the resulting sequence will be

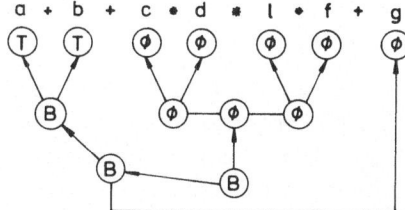

Fig. 4. Tree of calls for $a + b + c*d*l*f + g$.

$ab + g + cd * lf * * +$ or $((a + b) + g) + ((c * d) * (l * f))$ in conventional notation. The method gives a minimal-depth expression. No algorithm complexity estimates are given in the literature. A single pass is required for transformation due to recursion. However, fast compilation cannot be expected.

Axiomatic approach

The danger of an indiscriminate application of equivalent transformations to expression depth minimization has already been noted. An approach proposed for a more concrete definition of the scope of allowable transformations [7] involves the formal description of all such transformations. [7] gives a system of axioms for arithmetic expressions allowing transformations corresponding to ANSF (American National Standard for FORTRAN).

Let E be some set of expressions over atoms A and operations F. Let $e_1 = e_0(x \leftarrow e_2)$ denote the result of the substitution of expression e_2 for atom x in the expression e_0. A finite binary relation over the set E is referred to as a system of axioms Σ. Expressions e and e_1 are termed equivalent, $e \overset{\Sigma}{\sim} e_1$, if

a) $e = e_1$, or
b) $(e, e_1) \in \Sigma \vee (e_1, e) \in \Sigma$, or
c) $\exists e_2 (e \overset{\Sigma}{\sim} e_2 \wedge e_2 \overset{\Sigma}{\sim} e_1)$, or

d) $\exists e_2, e_3, e_4, e_5, x (e_2 \overset{\Sigma}{\sim} e_3 \wedge e_4 \overset{\Sigma}{\sim} e_5 \wedge e =$
$$= e_2(x \leftarrow e_4) \wedge e_1 = e_3(x \leftarrow e_5)).$$

Thus, two expressions are equivalent if they result from the substitution of equivalent expressions into equivalent ones.

Let some set of values V and I be given, i.e. a mapping is given which assigns to each atom x a value $\bar{x}$ from V, and to each operation sign f^n a function $\bar{f}^n : V^n \to V$.

Then, for each expression e its value $\bar{e}$ is assigned according to the following rules:

a) if $e = x$, $x \in A$, then $\bar{e} = \bar{x}$;
b) if $e = f(e_1, ..., e_n)$, then $\bar{e} = \bar{f}(\bar{e}_1, ..., \bar{e}_n)$.

These expressions give the formal equivalence corresponding to the semantic equivalence usually defined as equivalence of values. The problem described in the opening of this section requires a stronger formal equivalence than the equivalence of values. It should exclude, for example, the equality $a * (b + c) = a * b + a * c$. For arithmetic expressions without ↑, a system of such axioms is given below, satisfying the ANSF requirements. The system consists of three groups of axioms. The first group contains axioms of associativity and commutativity for additive operations:

1. $(x + y) + z = x + (y + z)$,
2. $(x + y) - z = x + (y - z)$,
3. $(x - y) - z = x - (y + z)$,
4. $(x - y) + z = (x + z) - y$,
5. $x + y = y + x$.

The second group contain similar axioms for multiplication and division resulting from the substitution of $*$ and $/$ for $+$ and $-$. The third group relates the unary minus to other operations:

1. $x + (\mu y) = x - y$,
2. $\mu(x - y) = y - x$,
3. $\mu(\mu x) = x$
4. $\mu(x * y) = (\mu x) * y$,
5. $\mu(x/y) = (\mu x)/y$,

6. $\mu(x/y) = x/(\mu y)$,

7. $i(\mu x) = \mu(ix)$.

In the last expression, i designates an identity operation which plays an auxiliary role and facilitates the formal reconfiguration of expressions.

This system of axioms underlies the two expression parallelization algorithms described in [7]. The expressions are limited to those which have at most one entry of some atom. The first algorithm is similar to that of Baer and Bovet [6] described above and provides the minimal expression depth. The second generates an equivalent expression containing minimal number of steps for computers like the IBM-360.

The use of the distributive property

In equivalent transformations, the above algorithms use only associative and commutative relations. They are applicable not only to numerical expressions but also to those with values from any commutative ring, e.g. matrices. This section adds the distributive relation specific to the numerical field. The appropriate algorithms are published in [9, 11—13] together with estimates of complexity and minimized expressions. Methods based on the distributive property are usually based on the deliberate removal of parentheses, the reduction of execution time often leading to a greater total number of operations. The transformation of expression $a*(b*c*d+l)$ to a parallel form with maximum parallelism results, for instance, in 5 operations instead of 4: $(a*b)*(c*d)+(a*l)$.

The most popular technique "cuts" the tree into two halves and removes some parentheses, repeating the procedure until atoms are reached. Consider an example from [11]. The expression $a(b+c(d+l(f+gh)))$ requires 7 computational steps.

The removal of parentheses results in $ab+acd+aclf+aclgh$, requiring 5 steps with the best order of computations: $(((ab)+((ac)d))+((ac)(lf)))+((ac)((lg)h)))$. At the first step of the procedure, the expression is cut between d and l and the missing factors are added to the right-hand side: $a(b+cd)+acl(f+gh)$. Now, only four time units are required for execution in the order given by $(a(b+(cd)))+(((ac)l)(f+gh)))$. The existence of minimal-depth tree algorithms of this type cannot be readily proved. Therefore, estimates of the expression execution time and transformation complexity are the basic criteria for the quality of an algorithm. Special expressions using only $+$, $-$, $*$ are considered in [11]. Any such expression with n different atoms has been shown to be computable in at most $2.465 \log n + O(1)$ steps, provided there are enough processors. If an expression has exactly 2^k atoms, it can be implemented in $3k-4$ steps. The number of processor $N(\bar{e})$ is also estimated in [11]; in particular,

$O(n^{1.71})$ suffice for implementation of the first case, while the second case requires 4^{k-2} processors. For a given number of processors p, the estimated execution time is $[n/p]+[\log p]-1$.

A corresponding estimate was derived in [12] for expressions with division: $4 \log n + 10(n-1)/p$. In [13] some estimates are generalized to include arbitrary operation delays and are improved. It is also shown, that a division-free expression is computable in a time of the order of $2.08 \log n$, while an expression containing division requires a time of $2.88 \log n + 1$, 2.08 and 2.88 being the positive roots of the equations $z^4 = 2z + 1$ and $z^2 = z + 1$, respectively. The authors believe that these coefficients are the best, because there are expressions requiring this time, apart from the additive constant.

The upper bound of complexity of the transformation algorithm for expressions of a general form, as derived in [13], is $O(n^{1.44})$. A complexity estimate of expression transformations using the distributive property was also given in [9], which asserts that the additional restructuring time for the compilation of the expression e with N symbols is $31N \log N$ for the Brent algorithm [12].

To conclude this section, we note that estimates for special types of expressions, e.g. polynomials, are significantly lower. We shall not deal with special cases and conclude by noting that any arithmetic expression with n operands can be computed in a time of the order of $\log n$ with about n processors. Although this result looks strong, expressions with n greater than ten are unfortunately rare, and the high quality of the asymptotical estimates has little application.

3.2 Parallel cycle execution

The further computations are parallelized, the larger is the effect. As shown in [14], the overwhelming majority of computations are repeated by executed program segments that are mostly given by loop statements. It is suggested in [14] that the proportion of repeated computations will grow with time, and this leads to the conclusion that parallelization of cyclic expressions is of primary importance.

Among other merits of loop parallelization there are the character and large size of the code to be parallelized, the fact that each branch is usually executed after parallelization by the same program, the data allocation to branches being the only requirement. In spite of this, it was only comparatively recently, in the early 70s, that feasibility studies of loop expression parallelization entered their major phase. Previously, branched sequential structures and parallel numerical methods attracted more attention. These two areas were the starting points in tackling loop parallelization. Both of them are treated in this section. First, the necessary definitions are given along with some simple sufficient conditions for parallelization. The second subsection describes the nested loop parallelization method, which can be effectively applied to the programming of complicated computational procedures, such as recalculation over a grid. An automatic parallelization method based on the structural study of relationships between loop iterations is described in the third subsection.

Basic concepts and simple parallelization conditions

A repeating segment can be, generally, defined as a pair $L = (O, T)$, where T is the body of the segment, a mapping (possibly with parameters) over some set M of memory locations. M may involve the parameters of the body. The loop organizer O is a predicate over M indicating the current possible application of T. $L(i)$ denotes the i-th application of T, and is referred to as the i-th iteration. All types of loops used in algorithmic languages comply with this definition. We shall mostly deal with loops of type **DO** and **WHILE.**

$$\begin{aligned} &\textbf{FOR} \quad I = i_0, i_1, h \quad \textbf{DO} \ \langle \text{body} \rangle \\ &\textbf{WHILE} \ \ P(x_1, \ldots, x_n) \cdot \textbf{DO} \ \langle \text{body} \rangle \end{aligned} \tag{2}$$

where i_0, i_1, h, x_i are variables or constants. The first loop specifies the execution of the body for the parameter value I, from the lower limit i_0 to the upper limit i_1 with step h. The second loop specifies the repetition of the body as long as the repetition condition $P(x_1, \ldots, x_n)$ is true. Loops are classified as loops with constant limits (i_0 and i_1 are symbolic or numerical constants), loops with fixed limits (i_0 and i_1 are variables determined before entering the loops and unchanged by the loop body), and loops with variable limits (their limits and number of repetitions are determined during loop execution only). There is a program fragment shown below containing loops of the first, second and third types:

$$\begin{aligned} &\textbf{FOR} \quad I = 0, 9 \quad\quad \textbf{DO} \ \ x(I) := c(I); \\ &\textbf{FOR} \quad I = 0, x(1) \quad \textbf{DO} \ \ y(I) := f(y(I)); \\ &\textbf{WHILE} \ \ |x - f(x)| \geqslant \varepsilon \quad \textbf{DO} \ \ x := f(x); \end{aligned}$$

where $c(I)$ and ε are constants, and f is a function. The step value 1 is omitted. The first loop writes 10 constants to a one-dimensional array. The second one transforms an array y from 0 to the element with index $x(1)$ defined by the first loop prior to entering the second loop. The third loop may be regarded as a computation of successive approximations by some formula, where the number of iterations is unpredictable and depends on the rate of convergence. Note that the decomposition of a loop into organizers and bodies is not absolute. The same iterative process could have been programmed as follows:

$$\begin{aligned} &m := 1; \ \textbf{FOR} \ I = 1, m \ \textbf{DO} \\ &x(I) := f(x(I-1)); \\ &\textbf{IF} \ |x(I) - x(I-1)| \geqslant \varepsilon \ \textbf{THEN} \ m := I+1; \end{aligned}$$

this is a loop with limit m which is repeated until a sufficiently good approximation is achieved. It is not clear how to classify the conditional expression: as a body, or as an organizer. On the one hand it is inside the body; on the other it performs organizing functions as is clear from the comparison with notations like **WHILE.**

For variable-limit loops, an integer look-ahead function $u(n)$ can be defined whose value for the argument n is a number $m > 0$, so that if n iterations of a loop have been executed, m more iterations must take place. Look-ahead functions allow dynamic loop parallelization [26]. However, this section is devoted to static methods only.

If there are two loops in a program, they may be either disjoint, or intersecting, or embedded. In accordance with the structured method, we exclude intersecting loops from our discussion. The sequence of embedded loops

$$(O_1, (O_2, (...(O, T)...))) \qquad (3)$$

is termed a nested loop. If in a sequence of embedded loops each loop has only one embedded loop, it can be reduced to (3). This reduction is illustrated below, FORTRAN label being used for indicating the body end.

Initial loop	Transformed loop
FOR $I = 1, 10$ **DO** 1	**FOR** $I = 1, 10$ **DO** 1
$x(I) := c(I)$	**FOR** $J = 1, 20$ **DO** 2
FOR $J = 1, 20$ **DO** 2	$x(I) := c(I)$
2 $y(J, I) := f(y(J-1, I))$	$y(J, I) := f(y(J-1, I))$
1 $x(I) := g(x(I))$	$x(I) := g(x(I))$
	2 **END**
	1 **END**

This transformation which duplicates computation cannot be recommended for practical purposes and is just an illustration of the generality of the results to follow.

Let L be a nested loop:

FOR $I_1 = a_1, b_1, h_1$ **DO**
FOR $I_2 = a_2, b_2, h_2$ **DO**
$\qquad \vdots$
FOR $I_n = a_n, b_n, h_n$ **DO**
$\qquad \langle \text{body} \rangle$

An n-dimensional integer space with coordinate axes $I_1, I_2, ..., I_n$ is called the iteration space of nested loop L. The execution of the body with indices I_1 at the K_1-th iteration, I_2 at the K_2-th iteration, ..., is represented by the point $(K_1, K_2, ..., K_n)$ of this space and is denoted by $L(K_1, K_2, ..., K_n)$. Apart from (2) further discussion is carried out within the framework of some programming language with I/O, expression assignment, conditional branching and **GÓ TO**. The problem of loop parallelization can be formulated as that of intraloop (inside loop body) parallelization or interloop parallelization (concurrent execution of different loop iterations). The loop body may be regarded a conventional program fragment, possibility-containing loops. It is, therefore, the interloop parallelization that allows for specific loop segment parallelization, and we shall focus our attention on it. For parallel segments, some statements [15] defining explicit parallelism may be used to indicate the segment type: vector, asynchronous or parallel sequential (in particular, pipeline). The most popular statement defining parallelism of repeated segments is

FOR $I = i_0, i_1, h$ **PAR DO** $\langle$body$\rangle$

which prescribes the execution of a concurrent independent body for indices I from i_0 to i_1 with step h.

Now we shall give some simple conditions for parallel execution. Let $\text{In}(L(i))$ and $\text{Out}(L(i))$ denote sets of used and generated variables at the i-th iteration of loop L. The necessary condition of parallel execution (1), as applied to loops, states that the i-th and j-th iterations can be executed concurrently if

$$(\text{In}(L(i)) \cap \text{Out}(L(j))) \cup (\text{In}(L(j)) \cap \text{Out}(L(i))) \cup$$
$$\cup (\text{Out}(L(i)) \cap \text{Out}(L(j))) = \emptyset. \tag{4}$$

A simple condition follows: if there is in a loop body a simple variable used before generation, the loop cannot be parallelized. This concerns the vector parallelism, i.e. a concurrency of data exchange after the execution of all the iterations involved. If the computation is asynchronous, the very presence of the simple variable x limits parallelization, because it leads to competition between iterations for the location x. For indexed variables, (4) gives the following condition: a loop can be parallelized and executed asynchronously, if all the input and output arrays are different and the values of the indices of each output array are different in different iterations. This difference is present, for example, in linear expressions of indices. The comparison of index sets gives a subtler test. The next condition necessary for parallelization is the lack of references from the loop body, which for the loops is a reformulation of the logic connection condition. If there is a GO TO statement in the body or a conditional branch controlled by a pointer variable which takes the value of the label of a statement lying outside the loop body, the loop cannot be parallelized, at least for vector or asynchronous execution, because it is not clear at which iteration control is to be transferred out of the loop body. Thus, even the second iteration cannot be carried out concurrently with the first one. Now, we shall give one more simple technique for loop parallelization, that of loop unwinding. If a loop has fixed limits, one can write all the iterations in succession, substituting particular index values. For bounded loops, the unwinding can be done during computation prior to entering the loop. In both cases, parallelization analysis is reduced to a linear segment analysis for which methods have been developed. For variable limit loops, the body sometimes happens to split into two parts: one determining the number of iterations and one carrying out calculations used later by other statements. An example of such a loop has already been given. If the amount of computation of the first part is appreciably smaller than that of the second, unwinding-like computations can be performed according to the method of mixed computations [31]. At each iteration, one can perform the limit-determining part, and then parallelize and compute the rest as a fixed-limit loop. The above unwinding techniques are of little use in actual computations. In practice, loop unwinding implies the computation of the indices of the variables in all the iterations in order to investigate their interrelation structure.

Method of hyperplanes and coordinates are the names given by Lamport [16, 17] to a parallelization technique for nested loops of **DO**-type. A similar technique the "wave-front method" was termed by Kuck [2]. The technique looks for a family of planes in the iteration space satisfying the following condition: all the iterations $(K_1, ..., K_n)$ lying in any of the planes can be executed in parallel. For loops with linear expressions as indices, such a family is usually a family of hyperplanes having some vector v as normal. If one succeeds in determining the vector v, renaming of variables can be defined that one of the axes of the iteration space lies along this vector. This implies that loop iterations can with respect to a new variable be executed concurrently, i.e. **FOR** ... **PAR DO** ... is substituted for **FOR** ... **DO** .... Sometimes an equivalent change in the loop body (permutation of statements, storing a value in an additional location) allows the parallelization of synchronous parallel computations to be executed without change of variables. As the result, the hyperplane family is parallel to one of the coordinate hyperplanes. The above transformations underlie the methods of hyperplanes and coordinates.

We begin with an illustration of the hyperplane method taken from [16]. Let nested **DO** loops be given:

FOR $I = 1, L$ **DO**
FOR $J = 2, M$ **DO**
FOR $K = 2, N$ **DO** (5)

$$x(J, K) := (x(J + 1, K) + x(J, K + 1) + X(J - 1, K) + \\ + x(J, K - 1)) * 0.25.$$

Let us assume that a method of recalculation over the grid is given, the iteration space of this nest is three-dimensional, and all the iterations can be represented as integer points of the parallelepiped $[1, L] \times [2, M] \times [2, N]$. Our objective is to find a hyperplane family in the iteration space so that point iterations lying in the hyperplane satisfy condition (1). The relations between the iterations (Fig. 5) show that each iteration takes information from its four neighbours, those which are nearer to the origin obtain information from a level one higher. For example, for recalculation of $J = 3$, $K = 3$, $I = 2$ the information is taken from points $a = (4, 3)$

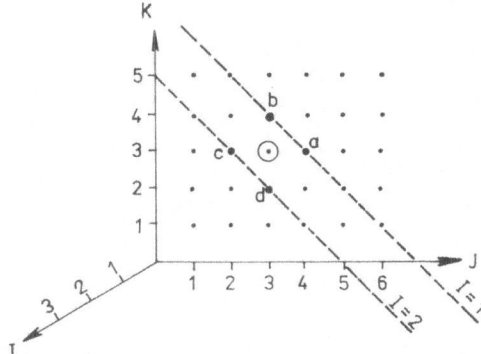

Fig. 5. Possible dependence of iterations for loop (5).

and $b = (3, 4)$ which have not yet been recalculated, i.e. they lie in the level $I = 1$, and from points $c = (2, 3)$ and $d = (3, 2)$ lying in the level $I = 2$. Hence, a hypothesis can be formulated that a plane drawn through points a, b, c, d contains mutually independent iterations, because the dependent iteration "jumps out" of the plane. Moreover, one can assume that any plane drawn through the straight-lines $K + J = c$ and $K + J = c + 2$ one level higher (where c is constant) is the required plane. One can easily see that this is so in our example. Hence, one can rewrite the nested loops (5), so that it alters the inclination of axis I until it becomes perpendicular to these planes.

This is done by the change: $\bar{I} = 2I + J + K$, transforming the loops as follows:

FOR $\bar{I} = 6, 2*L + M + N$ **DO**
FOR $\{(J, K) : 1 \leqslant J \leqslant L, 2 \leqslant K \leqslant N, 2 \leqslant \bar{I} - 2*J - K \leqslant M\}$ **DO CONC**
$\quad x(\bar{I} - 2*J - K, K) := (x(\bar{I} - 2*J - K + 1, K)$ (6)
$+ x(\bar{I} - 2*J - K, K + 1) + x(\bar{I} - 2*J - K - 1, K)$
$+ x(\bar{I} - 2*J - K, K - 1)) * 0.25.$

The statement **FOR S DO CONC** ⟨body⟩ [16, 17] defines the asynchronous execution of all the iterations whose coordinates belong to set S and is a multi-dimensional analogue of the statement **FOR ... PAR DO** .... (6) defines the following order of the iteration calculation: the loop **FOR** $\bar{I}$ ... selects all hyperplanes intersecting the domain $[1, L] \times [2, M] \times [2, N]$, and inside each reference of this loop all the iterations belonging to the plane are executed simultaneously and independently.

For the nested loop of a general **DO**-type

FOR $I_1 = l_1, r_1$ **DO**
$$\vdots \qquad\qquad\qquad\qquad\qquad (7)$$
FOR $I_n = l_n, r_n$ **DO**
$\quad$ ⟨body⟩

Ref. [16] proves a theorem representing them in a similar form:

FOR $J_1 = \lambda_1, \mu_1$ **DO**
$$\vdots \qquad\qquad\qquad\qquad\qquad (8)$$
FOR $J_K = \lambda_K, \mu_K$ **DO**
FOR S **DO CONC**
$\quad$ ⟨body⟩.

Here, all the loops should obey the following conditions:
a) contain no I/O statements;
b) contain no references outside the body;
c) contain no calls of procedures and functions that can change data;
d) the index expressions of variables should not contain variables changed by this loop; and
e) each case of a variable generated in the body should have the form $x(I_{j_1} + m_1, \dots, I_{j_r} + m_r)$, j_i being the same for any two cases of this variable.

Theorem [16]. If the nested loop (7) satisfies the conditions a) to e), it can be rewritten for $K = 1$ as (8). A corresponding transformation algorithm is given in [16]. If there are $K - 1$ $(K > 1)$ indices I_j in (7), which are not related to a variable generated by the body, the theorem holds for this value of K.

The coordinate method is illustrated by the following example:

FOR $I = 2, M$ **DO**
FOR $J = 1, N$ **DO**
$x(I, J) := y(I, J) + z(I);$
$z(I) := y(I - 1, J);$
$y(I, J) := (x(I + 1), J)\uparrow 2.$

Write iterations of this foop for $M = 4$ and $N = 2$:

$$L(2, 1) = \begin{cases} x(2, 1) := y(2, 1) + z(2); \\ z(2) := y(1, 1); \\ y(2, 1) := (x(3, 1))\uparrow 2; \end{cases}$$

$$L(2, 2) = \begin{cases} x(2, 2) := y(2, 2) + z(2); \\ z(2) := y(1, 2); \\ y(2, 2) := (x(3, 2))\uparrow 2; \end{cases}$$

$$L(3, 1) = \begin{cases} x(3, 1) := y(3, 1) + z(3); \\ z(3) := y(2, 1); \\ y(3, 1) := (x(4, 1))\uparrow 2; \end{cases}$$

$$L(3, 2) = \begin{cases} x(3, 2) := y(3, 2) + z(3); \\ z(3) := y(2, 2); \\ y(3, 2) := (x(4, 2))\uparrow 2; \end{cases}$$

$$L(4, 1) = \begin{cases} x(4, 1) := y(4, 1) + z(4); \\ z(4) := y(3, 1); \\ y(4, 1) := (x(5, 1))\uparrow 2; \end{cases}$$

$$L(4, 2) = \begin{cases} x(4, 2) := y(4, 2) + z(4); \\ z(4) := y(3, 2); \\ y(4, 2) := (x(5, 2))\uparrow 2. \end{cases}$$

By applying the hyperplane method we deduce that the iterations shown by "stripes" at an angle of 45° can be executed in parallel and asynchronously too. All in all, the iteration space has four stripe-hyperplanes, thus the loop execution time reduces from six to four. The implementation time can be reduced still more on synchronous computers of ILLIAC IV type. Let us see what prevents us from executing the loop in two trains $\{(2, 1), (3, 1), (4, 1)\}$ and $\{(2, 2), (3, 2), (4, 2)\}$, i.e. by selecting hyperplanes along the coordinate I. The first obstacle is that the operations are connected through the array y; iteration $(3, 1)$, for example, uses information from location $y(2, 1)$ generated by iteration $(2, 1)$. Since $(2, 1)$ is generated at the third step and required at the second step, the order of computations is violated. To avoid this, we can rearrange assignments $z(I) := y(I-1, J)$ and $y(I, J) := (x(I+1, J))\uparrow 2$ in the loop body, making use of their mutual independence. In addition to the dependence on array y, we have a collision at array x, too. Iteration $(3, 1)$, for instance, performs first the assignment $x(3, 1) := y(3, 1) + z(3)$, thus destroying the value required for $(2, 1)$ at the third execution level. To prevent this, the value of $x(3, 1)$ can be stored in an auxiliary array $u(I)$ and later used for squaring. After these transformations the loop becomes:

FOR $J = 1, N$ **DO**
FOR $\{I: 2 \leqslant I \leqslant M\}$ **DO SIM**
$u(I) := x(I+1, J)$;
$x(I, J) := y(I, J) + z(I)$;
$y(I, J) := (u(I))\uparrow 2$;
$z(I) := y(I-1, J)$,

where the statement **FOR** S **DO SIM** orders the synchronous execution of operations. Ref. [16] gives a general algorithm for transformations of this sort.

For pipeline computations and some types of loops with references, the methods based on the separation of independent planes in the iteration space have been further developed in [17]. Independently of Lamport and Nuriev [18] has also developed a method similar to that of hyperplanes. Nuriev's approach lies in determining the dependence between iterations by solving systems of equations made up of index expressions of arrays having the same name. The required family of planes is determined as the complement to the solution space of such systems.

Parallelepiped method

In spite of their obvious fundamental character, the methods of the above subsection have a number of disadvantages limiting their practical application. For example, the hyperplane method is applicable to nested loops only; it does not work for simple loops. It also does not work if the angle between the hyperplane is normal and one of the coordinate axes is close to zero. This method also requires deep analysis and a large amount of computation. Finally, the sections of the iterations which can be executed in parallel decrease in size, which entails overhead in the allocation of iterations between processors. The coordinate method is better in this respect, but can only be used on synchronous computers. All in all, this technique is to be regarded more an approach to better numerical methods than an automatic parallelization method.

A more practical method for parallelizing loops [19] is based on the determination of sections of independent iterations in the form of n-dimensional parallelepipeds of the same size. To attain a greater degree of parallelism, the largest possible parallelepiped faces should be determined. The algorithm is oriented to this goal. In the case of the simple loop

$$\textbf{FOR } I = l, r, h \quad \textbf{PAR DO } \langle \text{body} \rangle \tag{9}$$

the problem is posed as determination of the maximum p providing an equivalence of loop (9) to the language construct

$$
\begin{aligned}
&\textbf{FOR } J = 0, p - 1 \quad \textbf{PAR DO} \\
&\textbf{FOR } I = l + J, r, h * p \quad \textbf{DO} \\
&\qquad \langle \text{body} \rangle,
\end{aligned}
\tag{10}
$$

where the variable I is assumed to be local to each branch. The expression (10) defines the order of computations shown in Fig. 6. First, iterations are successively formed in trains of p items, then branches are "pulled out" of them. If the iterations inside each train are independent and a branch synchronization is provided after each train, then form (10) is equivalent to loop (9).

Before proceeding to a solution, we consider a special case of loop (9), conventionally written

1st branch	1st iteration	$(p+1)$-th iteration	$(np-1)$-th iteration
2 nd branch	2nd iteration	$(p+2)$-th iteration	$(np+2)$-th iteration
p-th branch	p-th iteration	$2p$-th iteration	$p(n+1)$-th iteration
1st train		2nd train	$(n+1)$-th train

Fig. 6. Realization scheme of language construct (10).

FOR $I = 0,\ r$ **DO** $\langle \text{body}(x(a * I + b),\ x(\alpha * I + \beta)) \rangle$.

The loop body structure may be complex, in particular it may involve nested loops and branching statements which do not transfer control out of the loop body. Symbols $x(a * I + b)$ and $x(\alpha * I + \beta)$ designate two entries of a, b into the body that can influence each other during parallel computation of loop iterations. According to condition (1), this can happen at least one of them is an output variable of the loop body. So far, we confine ourselves to the case where these variables form a single pair relating to loop iterations, for example,

$$\textbf{FOR } I = 1,\ 12 \quad \textbf{DO}$$
$$x(I + 15) := x(4 * I - 3). \tag{11}$$

The detection and visible representation of all relations between iterations is the first step in the determination of p. The problem of determining data connections is that of the determination of all integer pairs (I, K), so that a) $0 \le I \le r$, $0 \le K \le r$, b) $I \ne K$ and c) $aK + b = \alpha I + \beta$. If these relations are satisfied, the I-th and K-th iterations are connected through location $x(aI + b)$ and they should be executed successively. Let $\alpha \ne 0$; outherwise, the problem is trivial. Relation b) leads to

$$K = \frac{aI + b - \beta}{\alpha} = \frac{a}{\alpha}\,I + \frac{b - \beta}{\alpha} = cI + d,$$

where $c = a/\alpha$, $d = (b - \beta)/\alpha$. Thus, the dependence between iterations is given by a linear equation, and the integer points of the square $[0, r] \times [0, r]$ through which it passes, except points or the diagonal, are the required iteration pairs. If $K > I$, there is a direct relation, i.e. iteration I generates information for iteration K. If $I > K$, there is a reverse relation, i.e. iteration I cannot be executed before K, because it "jams" information required for iteration K. Figure 7 shows a graph of the loop (11).

The dependence relation of the iteration can be given by a list of dependent pairs

$$(I_1, K_1),\ \ldots,\ (I_n, K_n);\ 0 \le I_j \le r,\ 0 \le K_j \le r. \tag{12}$$

We assume that $\forall j$, $K(I_j < K_j \wedge I_j \ge I_k \leftrightarrow j \ge k)$. Otherwise, we can permute "unordered" pairs. To determine completely the dependence between the iterations, a transitive closure of the dependence relation should be used. It can be readily shown by induction that for integers c and d the sequence of iterations dependent on the I-th iteration is

$$K_n(I) = Ic^n + \frac{d(c^n - 1)}{c - 1}.$$

This is applicable to the generation of autonomous branches of iterations and also to the a priori estimation of loop parallelism [30].

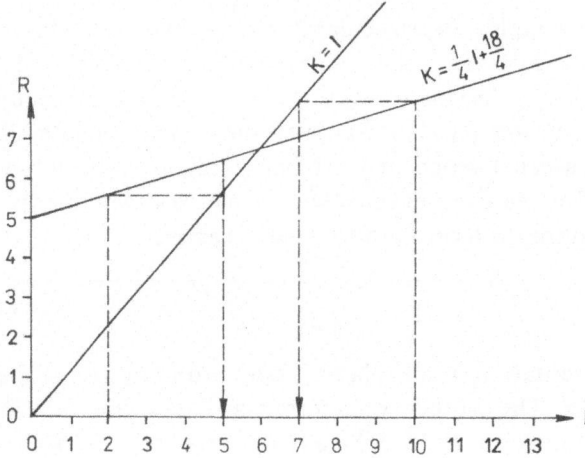

Fig. 7. Dependence for loop (11).

Consider a more general loop:
FOR $I = l, \, r, \, h$ **DO** $\langle \text{body}(x(a * I + b), \, x(\alpha * I + \beta)) \rangle$

where l and r are the initial and final limits, and h is a step. Perform the substitution $I' = (I - l)/h$. If I varies from l to r with step h, then I' varies from 0 to $[(r - l)/h]$ with a unit step.

Thus, the execution of this loop is reduced to the execution of the special loop discussed above. Generally, when the body has several input and output variables, the dependence between operations is given by straight-lines constructed for each pair of variables which have the same name and where one is the output variable.

When the iteration interrelations are known, one can construct various modes of parallel loop execution. The first mode is based upon successive construction, beginning from the first iteration, of maximal possible trains which are as a rule of different length. If the first p iterations are independent and one of them is connected to a $(p + 1)$-th iteration, then the first train will involve the 1st, 2nd, ..., p-th iterations, the second train will involve the $(p + 1)$-th, ..., $(p + q)$-th iterations, so that the $(p + q + 1)$-st iteration is connected to one of the iterations of the

a) 1. $x(16) := x(1)$ 5. $x(20) := x(17)$ 10. $x(25) := x(37)$
    2. $x(17) := x(5)$ 6. $x(21) := x(21)$ 11. $x(26) := x(41)$
    3. $x(18) := x(9)$ 7. $x(22) := x(25)$ 12. $x(27) := x(45)$
    4. $x(19) := x(13)$ 8. $x(23) := x(29)$
                            9. $x(24) := x(33)$

       1st train   2 nd train   3rd train

b) 1. $x(16) := x(1)$ 4. $x(19) := x(13)$ 7. $x(22) := x(25)$
    2. $x(17) := x(5)$ 5. $x(20) := x(17)$ 8. $x(23) := x(29)$
    3. $x(18) := x(9)$ 6. $x(21) := x(21)$ 9. $x(24) := x(33)$

       1st train   2nd train   3rd train

                           10. $x(25) := x(37)$
                           11. $x(26) := x(41)$
                           12. $x(27) := x(45)$

                                    4th train

B) 1. $x(16) := x(1)$ 5. $x(20) := x(17)$ 9. $x(24) := x(33)$
    2. $x(17) := x(5)$ 6. $x(21) := x(21)$ 10. $x(25) := x(37)$
    3. $x(18) := x(9)$ 7. $x(22) := x(25)$ 11. $x(26) := x(41)$
    4. $x(19) := x(13)$ 8. $x(23) := x(29)$ 12. $x(27) := x(45)$

       1st train   2nd train   3rd train

Fig. 8. Various types of iteration distribution.

second train. If for the sequence (12) one defines $M(N) = \min\{K_j\}$, where min extends to j so that I_j, $K_j > N$, the number of the last iteration in the t-th train is

$$l_0 = 0; \quad l_t = M(l_{t-1}) - 1.$$

The distribution described is shown in Fig. 8a for loop (11). This algorithm has the same drawback as algorithms obtained by the hyperplane method, i.e. it has trains of different lengths. As a result, one is confronted with the problem described at the very beginning of this section — the problem of determining the maximum p which allows the loop to be executed by trains of p iterations. Consider a version of this problem where the dependence is defined by the straight-line $K = cI + d$. Let (I_1, K_1), (I_2, K_2) be the first two pairs of connected iterations, then other dependent pairs are defined by

$$(I_n, K_n): I_n = I_1 + (I_2 - I_1)(n - 1); \quad K_n = K_1 + (K_2 - K_1)(n - 1).$$

We aim at $p = \min |K_n - I_n|$ which is optimal in the sense it ensures computational correctness to all possible loop distributions by trains, including cases where the first train is incomplete. We seek for a solution disregarding the last condition. Perform the transformations

$$K_n - I_n = (K_1 - I_1) + ((K_2 - K_1) - (I_2 - I_1))(n - 1) =$$
$$= (K_1 - I_1) + ((K_2 - I_2) - (K_1 - I_1))(n - 1) = u + (v - u)(n - 1),$$

where $u = K_1 - I_1$, $v = K_2 - I_2$. To determine u and v, I_1, K_1, I_2, K_2 are necessary and can be determined by conventional selection. The value of $|u + (v - u)(n - 1)|$ is a minimum if $|u - (u - v)(n - 1)|$ is a minimum or, assuming that $u \neq v$ and, $|u/(u - v) - (n - 1)|$ is a minimum. If $u/(u - v) > 0$, the minimum is reached when $n - 1$ is closest to $u/(u - v)$. In this case

$$p = \left| (u - v) \min \left\{ \frac{u}{u - v} - \left[\frac{u}{u - v} \right], \left[\frac{u}{u - v} \right] + 1 - \frac{u}{u - v} \right\} \right|,$$

and n is either $[u/(u - v)] + 1$, or $[u/(u - v)] + 2$. If $u/(u - v) < 0$ or $u = v$, the minimum is reached at $n = 1$ and is equal to $|u| = |K_1 - I_1|$. In Fig. 7, the first case corresponds to the straight-line intersecting the diagonal $K = I$. $|K_n - I_n|$ is minimal when K_n and I_n are closest to the point where the line intersects the diagonal. The second case occurs when the straight-line does not intersect the diagonal in the first quarter: the distance between K_n and I_n increases with n and is minimal for $n = 1$. These observations facilitate the computation of p. The pairs nearest to the point of intersection suffice for its determination. For loop (11), if pair (6.6) is excluded, then (2.5) and (7.10) are such pairs. Since both have a difference of 3, the loop can be executed by trains of 3 iterations (Fig. 8b). It is clear that the value of p is not a minimum for the particular distribution (10). For a special distribution, p can be improved as shown in Fig. 8b. However, the number p defined by the procedure described above satisfies a peculiar "heredity" condition: for any number less than p (10) also defines the correct computation. This is used when the dependence between iterations is defined by several straightlines. Then the number p satisfying all the lines is determined as the least number p determined for any line. For $p = 4$, the order of computation is as follows

FOR $J = 0, 3$ **PAR DO**
FOR $I = J + 1, 12, 4$ **DO**
$x(I + 15) := x(4*I - 3)$;
SYNCH $(J, I, 1)$,

where **SYNCH** is a synchronization statement for iterations defined by index I in branches defined by index J. The third position indicates the synchronization step. For example, if a loop is to be parallelized between a smaller number of processors (e.g. two processors), one can already perform grouping by two synchronizing branches after every two trains:

FOR $J = 0, 1$ **PAR DO**
FOR $I = J + 1, 12, 2$ **DO**

$x(I+15) := x(4*I-3)$;
SYNCH $(J, I, 2)$.

In its simplest form, the method can be applied to a nested loop via the coordinates: appropriate p's calculated for each coordinate are the lengths of the sides of the parallelepiped. The determination of p for a coordinate involves the computation of p for each pair of variables having the same name (one of them being an output variable), selecting the minimum one, and then selecting the maximum number from the p's for the positions.

This method was implemented for FORTRAN programs on the BESM-6 computer.

3.3 Parallelization of program schemata

This section considers parallelization algorithms for some program abstractions referred to as program schemata or flow diagrams [24]. Ref. [23] is a most fundamental contribution to the problem of parallelism within the framework of branched sequential structures. Among existing computational models, the program schemata is the most popular object of parallelization. Whereas the list of references devoted to expression and loop parallelization consists of about three dozen publications, the number of papers about parallelization of various modifications of schemata runs to over one hundred. Parallelization studies of general program models were initiated by the static approach described in [20, 21]. The idea of this approach, which is well-illustrated by acyclic scheme structures, lies in determination of logic, data and concurrency relations between statements followed by their distribution between levels. The 1st level contains statements independent of other statements; the 2nd level has statements depending only on those of the 1st level; the 3rd level consists of statements depending on the two previous levels, etc. Different authors refer to the resulting construct either as a p-algorithm, or level-parallel form, or level algorithm. Figure 9 exemplifies a loop-free structure of appropriate form.

For acyclic structures, this method gives a solution, which is, in a sense, complete. Having identified levels, one has to organize effective computations (distribute statements between processors, describe activation conditions, etc.). The situation changes radically if there are loops generated by conditional branchings: instead of the dependence between statements, one has a dependence between their execution which can be structurally very complicated. This section describes various approaches to problems caused by loops. The first method leading up to the studies of Kotov and Narinyani transforms the sequential scheme into an asynchronous program whose statements are activated by special predicates, trigger functions. Depending on whether the trigger functions are explicitly formulated or they are generated (possibly of rather large "intermediate units") and checked each time the statement activation condition is considered, the method can be classified as static or dynamic. The methods below are dynamic, i.e. they determine the statements that are to be activated at a given time by analysing the current computing situation.

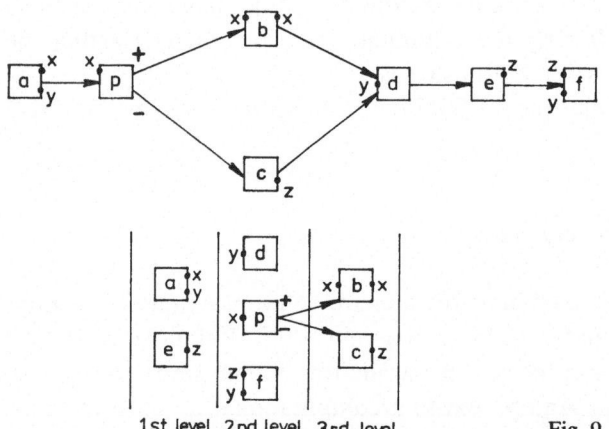

1st level 2nd level 3rd level   Fig. 9. Scheme and corresponding level form.

Transformation of schemata into asynchronous programs

When the operational environment changes unpredictably during computation, it is difficult to generate a rigid parallel program which can adequately be implemented on a computer. A program allocated to n processors of an n-processor computer system can be suspended for a long time if one of the processors is occupied by a higher priority job. To avoid such situations, programs are needed which can adjust themselves to the current operational environment and can be efficiently executed by either single or multiple processors. The present subsection introduces one model of such programs: asynchronous programs or A-programs. Program schemata are a special case of this model, i.e. there is an algorithm transforming every scheme into an equivalent A-program.

Prior to describing the method proper, we shall introduce the necessary formal definitions. Let $X = \{x, y, z, ...\}$ be some set of variables (memory locations). Let $F = \{a, b, c, ...\}$ be a set of functional symbols, and $P = \{p, q, r, ...\}$ be a set of predicate symbols. A positive integer locality is assigned to each functional and predicate symbol. The assignment statement over memory X is an expression such as $x := a(y, ..., z)$, where $a \in F$; $x \in X$ is a statement output variable, $(y, ..., z)$ is an input variable vector of length n, where n is the locality of the symbol a. The conditional statement over memory X is a predicate term such as $p(x, ..., y)$, where $p \in P$. $(x, ..., y)$ is an input variable vector of length n, and n is the locality of p. A program scheme is a directed graph with a statement assigned to each vertex.

The graph has a unique initial vertex entered by no arc and to which the statement input $(x, ..., y)$ is assigned, and a unique output vertex left by no arc and to which the statement output $(x, ..., y)$ is assigned. At any other vertex than these

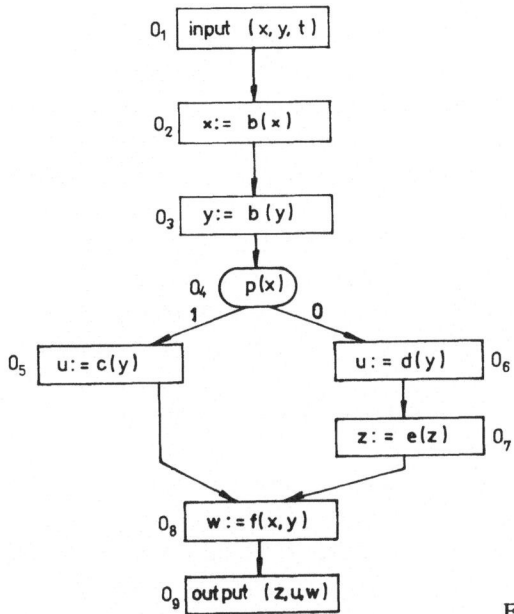

Fig. 10. Program scheme in ALGOL-like notation.

there originate one (transforming vertex) or two (conditional or recognizing vertex) arcs. In the former case, an assignment statement is assigned to the vertex; in the latter case, it is a conditional statement. The arcs coming from the conditional vertex are labelled 0-arc and 1-arc. The program scheme is transformed into a program by means of an interpretation assigning to each variable from X some element of a set of values Δ, to each functional symbol of locality n a function from Δ_n into Δ, and to each predicate symbol of locality n predicate from Δ_n into $\{1, 0\}$, where 1 and 0 are regarded as true and false.

The program execution is performed by means of successive movement along the structure graph, beginning at the input vertex in accordance with the predicates computed in conditional vertices, and the memory state changes by transformers. An example of the scheme is shown in Fig. 10. In this subsection, only free schemata, i.e. only structures where any path from the initial vertex is "confirmed" by some interpretation are considered.

The program scheme is the source object of a global parallelization algorithm to be described below. The algorithm results in an asynchronous A-scheme with maximum parallelism equivalent to the graph. Strict definitions of A-schemes, A-schemes with maximum parallelism, A-programs and equivalence relations can be found in [22]. Here we only recall that an A-scheme is a finite set of units each having:

a) an information statement which is a non-interpreted assignment statement over non-interpreted memory X;

b) an interpreted predicate over special interpreted control memory termed a trigger function and indicating the readiness of a unit for computation;

c) an interpreted control predicate over control memory. An example of A-scheme is given below.

The algorithm for transformation of schemata into maximally asynchronous A-schemata consists of three stages: analysis of the source scheme, reduction to a special form, and "framing" of statements by trigger functions and control statements. The analysis of the source scheme has to reveal information, logic and concurrency connections between statements, as well as transitive information-logic relations. One can say that there is an information connection between two vertices O and O_1, if:

a) O is an assignment statement $x := \ldots$, or initial statement "inputting" x, and O_1 involves x as an input variable, and

b) there is a path from O to O_1 which does not involve any transformer with the variable x on the left-hand side.

The recognizer O and outcoming arc (O, O_1) are referred to as logically essential for the vertex O_2, if:

a) any path over the graph from O_1 to the final statement passes through O_2, and

b) there is a path from O to the final statement that does not pass through O_2.

Thus, the recognizer O decides whether the statement O_2 is to be executed or not.

Framing of scheme statements is done at the third stage according to the previously determined information and logic connections. However, the scheme should have been reduced by this time to a form, so that no disturbance may occur in computations due to concurrency connections, i.e. only statements which are not executed in parallel can have such connections. This is provided by transitive information-logic dependence between different statement executions. However, if the concurrency connection is readily detected in the appearance of the scheme, the transitive connection is intrinsically dynamic: various entries into the computations of the same statement pair can be both dependent and independent. The existence of transitive information-logic connections between all the statement pairs requires a rather complicated analysis of the structure. In order to ensure such a dependence between all the concurrent entries, the so-called scheme reduction is performed.

A scheme is referred to as reduced if, for any pair of statement executions, the existence of a concurrency connection between them implies a transitive information-logic connection. There are two methods to perform reduction of structures:

1. introduction of fictitious connections between statements (e.g., information

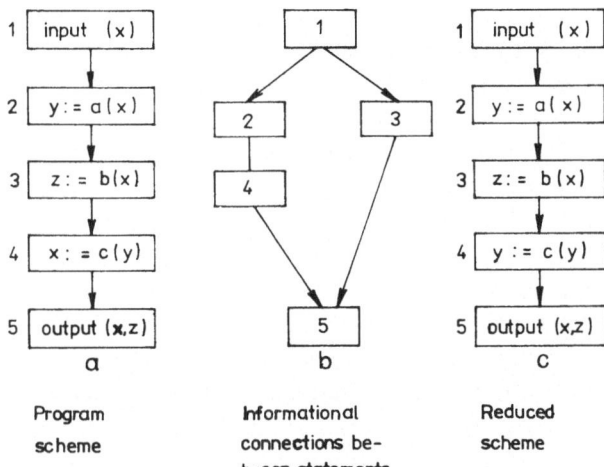

Fig. 11. Location renaming.

connection-transfers) with the aim to prevent the parallel execution of concurrent statements, and

2. renaming of statement inputs and outputs, so that concurrency over a corresponding location is eliminated. It is only the second method which provides maximal parallelism and is, therefore, used in the algorithm. Figure 11a shows a scheme without logic connections and Fig. 11b shows its graph of information connections. There is a concurrency connection between Statements 3 and 4 involving location x, but there is no transitive (in this case, information) connection. The structure of Fig. 11c has resulted from the reduction by location renaming that eliminates the concurrency connection. The scheme of Fig. 10 has also been reduced.

Generally, simple memory transformations do not achieve reduction of a structure preserving the potential parallelism of the source structure, and statement duplications or other structural changes are required. In particular, reduced structures can require arrays. Typically this happens when each current value generated by a loop body should be sent to a new location because the previous values were left unused. Thus, the degree of parallelism grows at the expense of memory size.

The reduced scheme can be directly translated into an A-scheme by framing its statements by trigger functions and control statements. According to the example given in Fig. 10, the third stage is as follows. For each vertex O_i, we denote by A_k^i a set of statements with an information connection to the k-th input O_i. For instance, $A_1^2 = \{O_1\}$, $A_1^8 = \{O_2\}$, $A_1^9 = \{O_1, O_7\}$. Arc (O_k, O_l) is referred to as complementing statement O_j with respect to statement O_i, if any path $(O_l, ..., O_i)$ does not contain O_j, but there is a path $(O_k, ..., O_i)$ containing O_j. In our example, arc (O_4, O_5) complements O_6 with respect to O_9. The desired A-scheme results from the following three steps:

1. Introduce the control memory by assigning a control variable α_i to each transformer O_i, and a pair of control variables α_i^0 and α_i^1 to each recognizer. The initial values of all the control variables are assumed to be zero.

2. Assign a control statement of type $\alpha_i := 1$ to each transformer, and a pair of statements $\alpha_i^0 := 1$ and $\alpha_i^1 := 1$ to each recognizer. Control statements follow information statements, and together they are parallel scheme statements. Within the recognizer, each control statement is put into an appropriate alternative.

3. Let statement O_i have n input variables. Assign to it a trigger function which is the conjunction of $n + 1$ predicates: $P_0^i \wedge P_1^i \wedge ... \wedge P_n^i$. Predicate P_0^i has the form $\alpha_i < \Sigma \alpha_j^k$, where α_j^k are control variables of arcs essential for O_i. The predicate P_0^i delays the initiation of statement O_i until one of the statements, logically essential to O_i, is not executed and a confirmation that O_i will be executed is obtained. Thus, in the parallel program, P_0^i represents logic connections of statement O_i. Each of the predicates $P_k^i (1 \leq k \leq n)$ corresponds to the k-th input of the statement and, in its turn, it is the conjunction of predicates $P_{k1}^i \wedge P_{k2}^i \wedge ... \wedge P_{km}^i$. Predicate P_{kj}^i corresponds to statement O_j from set A_k^i and has the form $\alpha_i < \Sigma \alpha_l' + \alpha_j$, where α_l' are control variables assigned to arcs complementing O_i with respect to O_j. Thus, predicate P_{kj}^i represents a potentially essential information connection between O_i and O_j. For an initial statement without input variables, the trigger function is $\alpha_1 = 0$.

The resulting set of units forms an A-scheme with maximum parallelism in the class of A-schemata equivalent to the source scheme. For the example given in Fig. 10, the final A-scheme is as follows ($\rightarrow$ separates the trigger function from the statement, units are separated by commas):

$$\{\alpha_1 = 0 \rightarrow (\text{input } (x, y, z); \ \alpha_1 := 1),$$
$$\alpha_2 < \alpha_1 \rightarrow (x := a(x); \ \alpha_2 := 1),$$
$$\alpha_3 < \alpha_1 \rightarrow (y := b(y); \ \alpha_3 := 1),$$
$$\alpha_4^1 + \alpha_4^0 < \alpha_2 \rightarrow (\text{if } p(x) \text{ then } \alpha_4^1 := 1 \text{ else } \alpha_4^0 := 1),$$
$$\alpha_5 < \alpha_4^1 \wedge \alpha_4 < \alpha_3 \rightarrow (u := c(y); \ \alpha_5 := 1),$$
$$\alpha_6 < \alpha_4^0 \wedge \alpha_6 < \alpha_3 \rightarrow (u := d(y); \ \alpha_6 := 1),$$
$$\alpha_7 < \alpha_4^0 \wedge \alpha_7 < \alpha_1 \rightarrow (z := l(z); \ \alpha_7 := 1),$$
$$\alpha_8 < \alpha_2 \wedge \alpha_8 < \alpha_3 \rightarrow (w := f(x, y); \ \alpha_8 := 1),$$
$$\alpha_9 < \alpha_1 \wedge \alpha_9 < \alpha_4^1 + \alpha_7 \wedge \alpha_9 < \alpha_4^0 + \alpha_5 \wedge \alpha_9 < \alpha_4^1 + \alpha_6 \wedge$$
$$\wedge \alpha_9 < \alpha_8 \rightarrow (\text{output } (z, u, w); \ \alpha_9 := 1)\}.$$

The notation of the A-scheme looks somewhat bulky, because the whole control is written in an explicit form. Implicit representations, such as those used in data-flow programs simplify greatly the outward appearance of the scheme.

If an A-scheme is generated from a scheme of general form then the framing of information statements is done in the same way, the predicates P^i_{kj}, however, become more complex. A brief description of the general-case algorithm is given in [2].

Dynamic parallelization of program schemata

The difficulties of graph representation of parallel programs equivalent to a given scheme gave rise to a models which were not related to the graph structure. Keller [25] was one of the first who studied such models. His schemata were a modification of Karp—Miller's program schemata [23], which led to a proof of some fundamental results for determinacy and equivalence. Ref. [25] is devoted to transforming a scheme into a form with maximum parallelism.

Let a finite set of statement symbols $B = \{b, c, d, ...\}$ over memory ω, an input set $D(b) \subset \omega$, an output set $R(b) \subset \omega$ and a set of alternatives $\Sigma(b) = \{b_1, ..., b_{k(b)}\}$ assigned to each statement b, be given. A finite or infinite sequence $X = X_1 X_2 ... X_n ...$ is referred to as a process X, where X_n is either the initiation symbol $\bar{b}$ of a statement b, or the termination symbol b_i of b when the i-th alternative is selected. An arbitrary finite initial segment of process X is termed the prefix of process X. The function φ assigning to each prefix X a subset of statements $\varphi(x) \leqslant B$ which are possible after the completion of X is called Keller's scheme (K-scheme). Processes that can be generated by the K-scheme φ beginning with an empty prefix are referred to as permissible by scheme φ.

Standard program schemata defined as graphs over statements and recognizers are a special case of K-schemes. The scheme of Fig. 12a, for example, can be presented as the K-scheme of Fig. 12b. Also a general K-scheme can be represented only by a graph with an infinite number of vertices.

Now, a number of definitions [25] are given which are necessary for the presentation of the method. The set of all finite and infinite processes permissible by scheme φ is called Comp φ, and the set of prefixes of these processes is Pref φ. The quadruple $i = (\Delta, \delta_0, F, G)$, where Δ is a value set, $\delta_0 : \omega \to \Delta$ is the initial state of the memory ω, $F = \{F_b, F_c, ...\}$ is a set of operations, $F_b : \Delta^{D(b)} \to \Delta^{R(b)}$, and $G = \{G_b, G_c, ...\}$ is a set of predicates: $G_b : \Delta^{D(b)} \to \Sigma(b)$, is referred to as an interpretation I. The function F_b represents the memory transformation: after each application of the operation, the memory changes its state. Depending on the memory state, function G_b selects an alternative. Thus, the statement is both a transformer and a recognizer. The interpretation I defines in a conventional manner the set of executable computations of scheme φ: Comp $(\varphi, I) \subseteq$ Comp (φ), and the prefixes of these processes Pref $(\varphi, I) \subseteq$ Pref (φ). Scheme φ is referred to as determinate, if for any I any two processes from Comp (φ, I) define the same sequence of memory states. Hence, determinate schemes give the same results for the same source data. The determinate schemes φ and φ' are termed equivalent, if for all I any pair of processes $X \in$ Comp (φ, I), $Y \in$ Comp (φ', I) defines the same memory state sequence. If

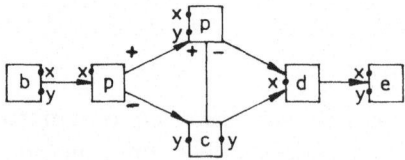

K-scheme ψ: $B = \{b, c, d, e, p, q\}$; $\Sigma b = \{b_1\}$, $\Sigma c = \{c_1\}$, $\Sigma d = \{d\}$, $\Sigma e = \{e_1\}$, $\Sigma p = \{p_1, p_2\}$, $\Sigma q = \{q_1, q_2\}$.

If one assigns: $x \to 1$, $y \to 2$, then

b) $D(b) = \Phi$, $R(b) = \{1, 2\}$; $\qquad\qquad D(e) = \{1, 2\}$, $R(e) = \Phi$;
$D(c) = \{2\}$, $R(c) = \{2\}$; $\qquad\qquad\quad D(p) = \{1\}$, $R(p) = \Phi$;
$D(d) = \{1\}$, $R(d) = \Phi$; $\qquad\qquad\quad D(q) = \{1, 2\}$, $R(q) = \Phi$.

Values of scheme ψ:

$\psi(\varepsilon) = \{b\}$, $\qquad\qquad\qquad\qquad \psi(b_1 p_1 q_1) = \{c\}$,
$\psi(b_1) = \{p\}$, $\qquad\qquad\qquad\qquad \psi(b_1 p_1 q_1 c_1) = \{d\}$,
$\psi(b_1 p_1) = \{q\}$, $\qquad\qquad\qquad\quad \psi(b_1 p_1 c_1 d_1) = \{e\}$,
$\psi(b_1 p_2) = \{c\}$, $\qquad\qquad\qquad\quad \psi(b_1 p_1 q_1 c_1 d_1 e_1) = \Phi$.

Fig. 12. Graph-scheme φ and equivalent K-scheme ψ.

$$\forall I(\text{Comp } (\varphi, I)) \subseteq \text{Comp } (\varphi', I)),$$

holds for φ and φ', then scheme φ' computes scheme φ. The computability relation is, evidently, a partial ordering. A scheme is said to have maximum parallelism if it is the maximum element with respect to this order. The problem of maximum parallelization is posed as that of constructing an algorithm defining for an arbitrary determinate scheme φ its equivalent with maximum parallelism, scheme φ'. As far as more precise definitions and problem formulation are concerned, the reader is referred to [25].

Parallelization in the Keller method is done by means of a look-ahead function $\Gamma_\varphi(X)$, which is defined for $X \in$ Pref φ and gives a set of statements, so that
   a) they must be executed by any process $Y \in$ Comp φ continuing X,
   b) prior to their execution in each process no statement is executed that competes with them for memory, and
   c) $b \notin \varphi(X)$.

Thus, $\Gamma_\varphi(X)$ gives a set of statements which can be executed immediately after X although this is not obligatory. The idea of parallelization lies in the optimal rearrangement of such statements, so that they are executed as soon as this becomes possible. Consider the parallelization transformation by scheme ψ in Fig. 12. For the arguments of this example, function Γ_ψ is as follows:

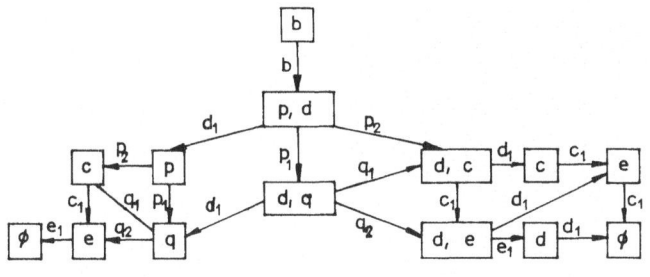

Fig. 13. Maximally parallel scheme for ψ.

$$\Gamma_\psi(\varepsilon) = \{b\}, \qquad \Gamma_\psi(b_1 p_1 q_1) = \{c, d\},$$
$$\Gamma_\psi(b_1) = \{p, d\}, \qquad \Gamma_\psi(b_1 p_1 q_1 c_1) = \{d, l\},$$
$$\Gamma_\psi(b_1 p_1) = \{q, d\}, \qquad \Gamma_\psi(b_1 p_1 q_1 c_1 d_1) = \{l\},$$
$$\Gamma_\psi(b_1 p_2) = \{c, d\}, \qquad \Gamma_\psi(b_1 p_1 q_1 c_1 d_1 e_1) = \emptyset.$$

If ψ' is defined so that it satisfies the condition $\psi'(X) = \psi(X) \cup \Gamma_\psi(X)$, an equivalent to the scheme with maximum parallelism results, graphical representation is shown in Fig. 13. Roughly speaking, it is obtained from ψ by the rearrangement of statements to input vertex b and the duplication of a part of the scheme, if required. For instance, statement d which is executed in every path and requires information x which, being generated by b, can be changed by no statement prior to d, is "pulled" into the second vertex previously occupied by statement p. However, it is necessary to connect one more copy of that part of the scheme which is entered immediately after the execution of α to the vertex (p, d). The rearrangements of other statements resulted in additional duplications some of which were linked together and others (e.g., l) were not, in order not to confuse the situation. In any case, the resulting scheme has a finite number of states. But the duplication procedure does not terminate in a finite number of steps for all schemes. For the scheme of Fig. 14a, for example, the procedure reaches beyond the class of finitely representable schemes (Fig. 14b), because the pulling of statement b into vertex c necessitates the duplication of the whole of the scheme from c, and a similar pulling for the copy. A new pulling entails a new duplication, etc., ad infinitum. The most part of [25] is dedicated to special types of tests of the coding of infinite graph structures of this type; schemes with counters, queues, etc. are examined. In particular, the scheme of Fig. 14b can be implemented with one counter indicating the number of executions of the loop b—c—b.

While [25] tries to obtain a "final" form of the resulting scheme, [26] is restricted to the dynamic analysis of parallelism and is oriented towards obtaining an algorithm "accompanying" computations and detecting all the statements that must be executed in a given computational environment. The rejection of the static approach has led in some respects to an improvement of the ideas given in [25]. In

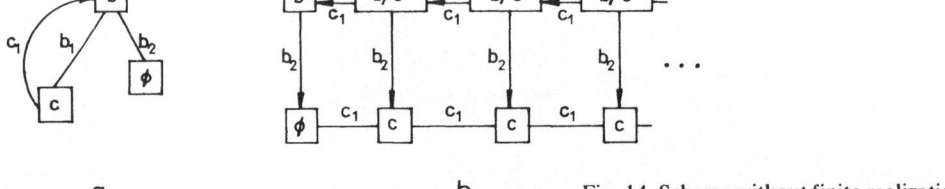

a   b   Fig. 14. Scheme without finite realization.

particular, Keller's formalism has been extended by the introduction of arrays, the use of a much weaker relation then equivalence is, and the organization of conflict-free processing. All this has made possible the formal semantic proof of an assertion giving necessary and sufficient existence conditions for the maximum parallelization algorithm in terms of look-ahead functions.

As before, let $B = \{b, c, d, \ldots\}$ be sets of statements, $Db = (n_1, \ldots, n_p)$, $Rb = (m_1, \ldots, m_q)$ be the input and output sets of statement b and $\Sigma b = \{b_1, \ldots, b_k\}$ be the set of alternatives for statement b. The computations are defined as a sequence of statement acts $X = (X_1, X_2, X_3, \ldots)$ where the act is a triple $X_i = (b_s, DX_i, RX_i)$, where $b_s \in \Sigma b$, $DX_i = (n_1[i_1], \ldots, n_p[i_p])$, $RX_i = (m_1[j_1], \ldots, m_q[j_q])$; $n[i]$ is a variable n with index i. An act represents the event of deactivating statement b, which has operated over inputs DX_i, placed the result in locations RX_i and computed the alternative b_s. From all the processes, a set of data — supported processes — is selected, where the input data for each act are computed by previous acts, or they belong to the source data for which a special finite subset of locations Ω is allocated. For processes X, set $t(X) = \{t(X_1), t(X_2), \ldots\}$ is defined, where $t(X_i)$ is a t-history of act X_i, i.e. a term over a set of statements and locations Ω defining the execution of act X_i. A process is referred to as regular, if:

$$\forall X_i \in X(RX_i = (m_1[\tilde{t}(X_i)], \ldots, m_q[\tilde{t}(X_i)])),$$

i.e. if locations with index $\tilde{t}(X_i)$ are used, where $\tilde{t}(X_i)$ is the number of term $t(X_i)$ under some single valued, enumeration method, an analogue of hash-addressing. Denote the set of finite regular processes by w^*, and the set of regular processes by w.

A vector function $\{S = \{S_b, S_c, \ldots\}$ is referred to as a program scheme over B, where for all $b \in B$, S_b: $w^* = \to 2^{\omega^{Db}}$, i.e. the component S_b is defined over regular processes and its value is some subset of the vectors from the memory locations "feeding" the inputs of statement b. The following condition should be observed: $\langle S(Xa^b) \rangle \leftrightarrow Da^b \in S_b(X)$, where a^b is some act of statement b, and the notation $\langle S(X) \rangle$ indicates that function S is defined over argument X. Thus, after the execution of a sequence of acts X, scheme S gives for each statement b a set $S_b(X)$ of vectors over memory ω, which can be processed. Thereafter, statement b can be activated independently and concurrently with other statements or itself over any of these vectors. After the completion of statement b over vector v, act $a^b = (b_s, Da^b, Ra^b)$ is added to the history, where b_s is a computed alternative. $Da^b = v$ are input data for the act, and $R_i a^b$, the i-th component of vector Ra^b, is equal to $m_i[\tilde{i}(a^b)]$, i.e. the result is hashed into locations with index $\tilde{i}(a^b)$. Denote by w^S the sets $X \in w^*$ over which the scheme S is defined by Pass S — a set of finite or infinite maximum sequences of "terminated" processes permissible by scheme S. The interpretation I of scheme S is defined similarly as in Keller's schemes. The operation is defined for each pair I and X: $I \cdot X$ denotes the memory state after the execution of a sequence of acts X under interpretation I. The content of location $n[i]$ is denoted as $I \cdot X(n[i])$. If X is infinite, the limiting memory state is taken to be $I \cdot X$. For interpretation I, sets Comp $I \subseteq w$ and Pref $I \subseteq w^*$ are also determined. They consist of all processes coordinated by I and their finite prefixes. Sets of prefixes and processes in scheme S permissible under interpretation I are defined by Boolean functions of the sets introduced:

Pref $(S, I) = $ Pref $I \cap w^S$,
Comp $(S, I) = $ Comp $I \cap$ Pass S,

Pref $S = \bigcup_{I \in \text{Int}}$ Pref (S, I),

Comp $S = \bigcup_{I \in \text{Int}}$ Comp (S, I),

where Int is the set of all interpretations. If $w^S = $ Pref S, the scheme is called free. A scheme is said to be without repetition if there are no two identical acts in each $X \in$ Pref S. The class F of free schemes includes that of schemes without repetition, RF.

Schemes S and S' are called t-equivalent $(S \overset{t}{\sim} S')$ if $\forall I\, \forall X \in$ Comp (S, I) $\forall Y \in$ Comp (S', I) $(t(X) = t(Y))$, i.e. if under any interpretation sets of t-histories of their computation are identical. Schemes are called f-equivalent, $(S \overset{f}{\sim} S')$, if $\forall I\, \forall X \in$ Comp (S, I) $\forall Y \in$ Comp $(S', I)(I \cdot X = I \cdot Y)$, i.e. if the memory states after the termination of any of their computations are identical. Scheme S is called

t-determinate if: $S \overset{t}{\sim} S$, and f-determinate if: $S \overset{f}{\sim} S$. The closeness between the relations $\overset{t}{\sim}$ and $\overset{f}{\sim}$ is shown by

Lemma.

a) $S \overset{t}{\sim} S' \to S \overset{f}{\sim} S'$;

b) if $\forall b(Rb \neq \emptyset)$, then $S \overset{f}{\sim} S' \to S \overset{t}{\sim} S'$.

The computability of scheme S by scheme S' is defined differently from [25]. The definition of computability as the inclusion of the process set of one scheme into the process set of another scheme does not cover cases of computability with permissible repeated acts. We define computability as the inclusion of prefixes into repeated acts. Let $Rf\text{pref}(S, I)$ denote a set of sequences, each obtained by the omission of repeated acts from some $Z \in \text{Pref}(S, I) \cdot S'$ computes S, if $\forall I(Rf\text{pref}(S, I) \subseteq Rf\text{pref}(S', I)$. Further, introduce set

$$\text{Comp}(S \mid X) = \{Z \in \text{comp } S: \forall i, j(t(Z_i) = t(X_j) \to \Sigma Z_i = \Sigma X_j)\},$$

containing processes of scheme S coordinated by X. Function $V(S, X) =$
$\bigcap\limits_{Z \in \text{Comp}(S \mid X)} t(Z)$ defines a set of t-histories generated by such processes. Finally, the look-ahaed function is defined as follows:

$$\Gamma(S, X) = \{t \in V(S, X): t = b(t_1, \ldots, t_n) \to \forall i(t_i \in t(X) \cup \Omega)\} \setminus t(X).$$

It gives a set of t-histories, each computed in any process coordinated by X, all pieces of their input information being computed by acts X or belonging to source data, while they themselves are not computed by acts X. Informally, $\Gamma(S, X)$ denotes the set of acts ready for execution after the computation of X and necessarily computed under any continuation of process X. $\Gamma(S, X)$ is determined over the set $Q(S)$, defined as follows:

a) the empty sequence ε belongs to $Q(S)$;
b) if $Z \in Q(S)$, then $\{Z_a \in w^*: t(a) \in \Gamma(S, Z)\} \subseteq Q(S)$.

The major result of [26] is summarized as:

Theorem. There is an algorithm assigning to each t-determinate scheme S of some class Φ a t-determinate scheme without repetition S'; t is equivalent to S and has maximum parallelism in class $\{S'': S'' \overset{t}{\sim} S\}$ only if the function $\Gamma(S, X)$ is effective over the set $\bigcup\limits_{S \in \Phi}(\{S\} \times Q(S))$, the parallelization algorithm being constructively definable by the function $\Gamma(S, X)$.

Some corollaries are presented below.

Corollary 1. There is no maximum parallelization algorithm for the class of standard schemes [24]. Hence, there is no such algorithm in the classes of K-schemes and in the class of all schemes. This result demonstrates that maximum parallelization is hampered not only by statement interpretation, as shown in [4], but also by the complexity of the logic and information structure. The corollary is proved by the reduction of the unsolvable totality problem to that of the computation of $\Gamma(S, \varepsilon)$.

Corollary 2. The problem of maximum parallelization is solvable in the class of free schemes with finite representation. The proof is built around the fact that function $\Gamma(S, X)$ can be computed as a selection of some set of processes with limited duration. A method for the computation of a look-ahead function is described in detail in the following subsection.

Corollary 3. The problem of maximum parallelization is solvable in the class of free schemes with finite representation and fixed-limit loops. The addition of these loops does not essentially change the situation from the point of view of the computability of the look-ahead function. Moreover, the corollary also holds in the class of schemes with bounded limit loops, because the loop limits are determined before the loop computability is tested.

Computation of look-ahead function and parallelization algorithms

The above theorem gives a method for the generation of a scheme with maximum parallelism via scheme S for an effective look-ahead function, but all the constructs and algorithms are described in set-theory terms and are intrinsically selective. In this sense, the theorem reveals only the feasibility of parallelization, and does not perform the task of fitting the program into an actual multiprocessor system with memory and timing constraints. These issues are discussed in [27, 28].

Dynamic analysis methods are based on the use of some information about the current state of the computation. Recording of acts executed in the course of computation is accompanied by a look-ahead winding up of the program, showing the place of the implemented part of the computations within the context of the program as a whole. The essential problems here are the optimal recording of this information and the selection of an appropriate look-ahead value to reveal all possible parallelism at each step. The present subsection is devoted to these problems. Let the standard program scheme S be given by control graph L [24] and let an equivalent maximally asynchronous scheme S' be required. The equivalence relation coincides with that of the above subsection; the notion of computability implies the inclusion of sets of computations under each interpretation I; the resulting program is regarded as a vector function $S' = \{S_b, S_c, ...\}$, where S_b gives a set of collections of arguments to be processed by statement b. The current state of the computation is referred to as configuration. The configuration ψ is a sequence of path segments of scheme S and its subschemes $\psi = \xi_1 \Delta_1 \xi_2 \Delta_2 \dots \xi_n \Delta_n$. The path segment $\xi_i = (b \dots c)$ from vertex b to vertex c represents the computation fragment executed. The subscheme $\Delta_i = \{b, \dots, c\}$ consists of vertices, which are included in at least one simple path from b to c and represent a program fragment to be executed. Both segments and subschemes can be duplicated. If $\xi_i \Delta_i \xi_{i+1} = (b \dots c)\{d \dots e\} (f \dots g)$, the arrows point from c to d and from l to f in graph L, i.e. successive elements are linked together. The first element of the configuration begins with input statement O, and the last one ends with output statement Θ. The i-th pair is written $\psi^i \Delta_i$ and is called the i-th component. Let $\psi^i = (b \dots c)\{d \dots e\}$.

The following notation is introduced.

ψ_0^i is a set of entries of subscheme $\{d \dots e\}$ on all paths from d to e;

ψ_1^i is a sequence of entries of statements of segment $(b \dots c)$;

$\psi_2^i \subseteq \psi_0^i$ is a set of entries representing currently operating statements.

$\psi_3^i = \psi_0^i \setminus \psi_2^i$ is a set of entries which are not operating and have not acted as yet, but are executed in the i-th component;

$\psi_4^i({}^j a)$ is defined for $a \in \psi_3^i$, ${}^j a$ designating the j-th input of statement a. The last entry into a segment ξ_k, $k \leqslant i$ influencing input ${}^j a$ is the value of this function:

$\psi_5^i({}^j a)$ is defined for $a \in \psi_3^i$ and is a set of entries into fragments Δ_i, which occurred there after $\psi_4^i({}^j a)$ but before a, and which may destroy the data generated by entry $\psi_4^i({}^j a)$, if computations are continued, and if

$$\psi_5^i = \bigcup_{j \in In(a)} \psi_5^i({}^j a).$$

One of the possible configurations for the example of Fig. 9 is as follows:

$$\psi = \xi_1 \Delta_1 \xi_2 \Delta_2 = a\left\{p \begin{matrix} \nearrow b \\ \searrow c \end{matrix}\right\} d\ e\{f\};$$

$$\psi_1^1 = \{a\}, \ \psi_1^2 = \{d, e\}, \ \psi_2^1 = \{p\}, \ \psi_2^2 = \emptyset,$$
$$\psi_3^1 = \emptyset, \ \psi_3^2 = \{f\}, \ \psi_4^2({}^1 f) = e, \ \psi_4^2({}^2 f) = a,$$
$$\psi_5^2({}^1 f) = \psi_5^2({}^2 f) = \psi_5^2(f) = \emptyset.$$

It describes a situation, where statements a, d, e have been executed, p operates and f can be activated.

Scheme S', which provides maximum parallelism and is equivalent to S, is defined by the following rules:

1. Initially, the process is empty, and the corresponding configuration ψ is $\{0 \dots \Theta\}$.

2. Let a process X and a configuration ψ, be there at time t and let an entry $\eta(a)$ into the configuration correspond to each act a of process X. Then, for an arbitrary statement b, φ_b consists of vectors $v = (c_1^{i_1}, \dots, c_m^{i_m})$ (where c_k^i is the output of statement c_k, $c_k \in X$) so that there is a component ψ^i for which

$$\eta(b) \in \psi_3^i \wedge \forall_k(\psi_4^i({}^k b) = (\eta\ (c))^{i_k}) \wedge \psi_5^i = \emptyset.$$

Thus, statement b can be activated over vector v if it must be executed and if vector v is stabilized, that is if it cannot be changed in any further continuation of the process.

3. The configuration at the points at which statements are activated or deactivated is changed as follows: if statement b is activated over component ψ^i, it passes from set ψ_3^i to set ψ_2^i. If it is deactivated, b passes to ψ_1^i.

In doing so, b can be linked to ξ_i or ξ_{i+1}, resulting in the contraction of fragment Δ_i, or the generation of a new segment. In the latter case, Δ_i is partitioned into two fragments and the components are re-enumerated.

Rules 1—3 define completely the scheme φ'. A more thorough analysis makes processing possible in such a way that the configuration size is independent of time and is only determined by the number of components which can be interpreted as the number of parallel branches. This demonstrates the main possibility of organizing a real-time parallelism analysis. Nevertheless, complexity estimates for the analysis of configurations defined by graphs are too high and have high overheads. Urschler has described [28] a stack-implementation of these ideas which is most convenient for stack computers. This method, however, is applicable to a somewhat narrower class of schemes.

Conclusion

This contribution describes three basic methods for the parallelization of intrinsically and structurally different program elements: expressions, loops, and graph-schemes. The practical application of these methods is very different. Algorithms for restructuring arithmetic expressions are available as programs or in a form which can be easily programmed, and can be built into existing compilers with little change.

Loop parallelization algorithms require more programming for their implementation, because the loop (more precisely, the loop body) can contain all language elements. A parallelization program, as described in [19], has about 2000 statements in a high-level language. The implementation of parallelization methods for schemes is still more difficult. Numerous publications are devoted to this issue which has been scarcely touched in the present paper. The statement "enlargement" is of prime importance in the case of parallelization methods which need much time as far as analysis is concerned. A segmentation method oriented to further parallelization is described in [29]. The common problem of estimating potential program parallelism is treated in [30]. Many other aspects of parallel programming have been omitted in this chapter. The algebraic approach actively pursued by the Kiev and Polish schools has not been discussed and the relations discovered recently between the non-procedural approach and single-assignment languages have not been mentioned either. Only little space has been devoted to some other techniques for asynchronism enhancement, e.g. variable renaming. Some understanding of this problem can be obtained in [2, 24].

On the whole, theoretical studies in the domain of automatic parallelization have reached their summit and in some areas — like arithmetic expressions approach — their conclusion, too. Currently, the major task is to collect dispersed studies and thus make of them a consistent picture of optimal methods which would show the directions to be followed in the development of suitable software and hardware. The authors would like to conclude the paper by expressing their hope that this generation of programmers will see this happen.

REFERENCES

[1] BAER, J. L.: A survey of some theoretical aspects of multiprocessing. ACM Comp. Surveys, 5, 1973, 1, 31—80.

[2] KOTOV, V. E.: Teoriya parallelnogo programmirovaniya. Prikladnye aspekty. Kibernetika, 1974, 1, 1—16; 2, 1—18.

[3] KUCK, D. J.: A survey of parallel machine organization and programming. ACM Comp. Surveys, 9, 1977, 1, 29—59.

[4] BERNSTEIN, A. J.: Analysis of programs for parallel processing. IEEE Trans. on Electric Computing, EC-15, 1966, 5, 757—763.

[5] RAMAMOORTHY, C. V., PARK, J. H. and LI, H. F.: Compilation techniques for recognition of parallel processable tasks in arithmetic expressions. IEEE Trans. on Computers, C-22, 1973, 11, 986—998.

[6] BAER, J. L. and BOVET, D. P.: Compilation of arithmetic expressions for parallel computations. Proc. IFIP Congress, Edinburgh 1968. North-Holland Publ. Co., Amsterdam, 1968, pp. 340—346.

[7] BEATTY, J. C.: An axiomatic approach to code optimization for expressions. J. ACM, 19, 1972, 4, 613—640.

[8] KUCK, D. and MURAOKA, Y.: Bounds on the parallel evaluation of arithmetic expressions using associativity and commutativity. Acta Informatica, 3, 1974, 3, 203—216.

[9] TOWLE, R. A. and BRENT, R. P.: On the time required to parse an arithmetic expression for parallel processing. Proc. 1976 Int. Conf. on Parallel Processing, New Jersey, 1976, p. 254.

[10] STONE, H. S.: One-pass compilation of arithmetic expressions for a parallel processor. Comm. ACM, 10, 1967, 4, 220—223.

[11] BRENT, R., KUCK, D. and K. MARUYAMA, K.: The parallel evaluation of arithmetic expressions without division. IEEE Trans. on Computers C-22, 1973, 5, 532—534.

[12] BRENT, R. P.: The parallel evaluation of general arithmetic expressions. J. ACM, 21, 1974, 2, 201—206.

[13] MULLER, D. E. and PREPARATA, F. P.: Restructuring of arithmetic expressions for parallel evaluation. J. ACM, 23, 1976, 3, 534—543.

[14] KOSAREV, YU. G.: Rasparallelivanie po tsiklam. In: Vychislitelnye sistemy, Vol. 24. Izd. IM SO AN SSSR, Novosibirsk, 1976, pp. 3—20.

[15] KOTOV, V. E.: Yazyki parallelnogo programmirovaniya (preprint). Izd. VC SO AN SSSR, Novosibirsk, 1979.

[16] LAMPORT, L.: The parallel execution of DO loops. Comm. ACM, 17, 1974, 2, 83—93.

[17] LAMPORT, L.: The hyperplane method for an array computer. Proc. Sagamore Computer Conf. on Parallel Processing, Aug. 1974. In: Lecture Notes in Computer Sciences, Vol. 24. Springer-Verlag, Berlin—Heidelberg—New York, 1975, pp. 113—131.

[18] NURIEV, R. M.: Neobkhodimye i dostatochnye usloviya sushchestvennoi rasparallelivaemosti programm po tsiklam. Tekh. Kib., 1976, 2, 105—111.

[19] VALKOVSKII, V. A.: Rasparallelivanie po tsiklam na nebolshoe chislo vetvei. In: Vychislitelnye sistemy, Vol. 70. Izd. IM CO AN SSSR, Novosibirsk, 1977, pp. 90—97.

[20] EVREINOV, E. V. and KOSAREV, YU. G.: Odnorodnye universalnye vychislitelnye sistemy vysokoi proizvoditelnosti. Izd. Nauka, Novosibirsk, 1966.

[21] POSPELOV, D. A.: Vvedenie v teoriyu vychislitelnykh sistem. Izd. Sovietskoe radio, Moscow, 1972.

[22] KOTOV, V. E. and NARINYANI, A. S.: On transformation of sequential programs into asynchronous parallel programs. Proc. IFIP Congress 68, Edinburgh 1968. North-Holland, Amsterdam, 1969, pp. 351—357.

[23] KARP, R. M. and MILLER, R. E.: Parallel program schemata. J. Comp. Syst. Sci., 3, 1969, 2, 147—195.

[24] KOTOV, V. E.: Vvedenie v teoriyu skhem programm. Izd. Nauka, Novosibirsk, 1978.

[25] KELLER, R. M.: Parallel program schemata and maximal parallelism. I. Fundamental results. J. ACM, 20, 1973, 3, 514—537.

[26] VALKOVSKII, V. A.: Parallelnye operatornye skhemy nad massivami peremennych i problema maksimalnogo rasparallelivaniya. Kibernetika, 1979, 5, 52—63.

[27] VALKOVSKII, V. A.: Ob odnom algoritme desekventsii. Kibernetika, 1974, 2, 77—88.

[28] URSCHLER, G.: The inherent parallelism of flow diagrams. Tech. Report 25.129, 1972.

[29] VALKOVSKII, V. A. and KASYANOV, V. N.: Krupnoblochnaya segmentatsiya i rasparallelivanie skhem programm. Programmirovanie, 1976, 1, 16—26.

[30] VALKOVSKII, V. A.: Metod otsenki vnutrennei parallelnosti algoritma. Tekh. Kib., 1977, 5, 21—39.

[31] ERSHOV, A. P.: O sushchnosti translyatsii. Programmirovanie, 1977, 5, 21—39.

Chapter 4

FORMAL MODELS OF PARALLEL COMPUTATIONS

Formal models of parallel programs and processes were developed for a variety of reasons. Some served as tools for elucidating fundamental properties and laws of parallel computations. Others were used as a rational for new programming constructs introduced into parallel programming languages, and for the verification of new methods for constructing parallel programs. Finally, models of a third category were employed for the improvement of techniques for the structural and semantic analysis of parallel programs, for the development of automatic systems of program verification, synthesis and optimization. Such a variety of objectives, naturally, leads to a wide range of models, differing mostly in the detailed modelling of constructs and phenomena. Relatively recent reviews [1—4] describe some parallel computation models. To avoid repeating these, especially their factual aspects, we confine the discussion here to several models representative of a certain class of problem, and comment on them from the point of view of current problems in parallel computation theory. The review begins with the first group of models (parallel program schemes) intended mostly for the study of the basic laws of parallel programming.

4.1 Program schemes

The theory of program schemes or schematology began with the classical paper of Yanov [5] and after a period of active development in the 60s it reached its culmination at the time of publication of papers of Luckham, Park and Paterson [6], Letichevskii [7], and Karp and Miller [8]. The schematological approach stems from the desire to study program schemes, instead of programs themselves which are more complicated. The schemes describe to some degree the enumeration of the structural properties of the programs (e.g., that they consist of statements which in turn consist of operations, variables, etc.), but abstract themselves from the particular meaning of variables, operations, and functions. Figure 1 shows an **ALGOL**-like program and its scheme that preserves the program structure but replaces integer variables (in the sense of **ALGOL**-60), operations for multiplication and subtraction, and the "equal to zero" predicate by abstract symbols for the variables x and y, functional symbols f, g and a (constant), and the abstract predicate symbol p. In contrast to the program, the scheme S is not a specification of an algorithm (a computable function), but it can generate the program (S, I) (with present initial data) if the interpretation I is given, i.e. if domains of possible values, initial values, functions, and predicates are assigned to appropriate symbols. Various interpretations lead to completely different programs having the same structure. Thus, the scheme models a class of programs having similar structural

```
begin integer x, y;                    begin
start (x);                             start (x);
y := 1;                                y := a;
l1: if x = 0 then go to l2             l1: if p(x) then go to l2;
x := x × y;                            y := g(x, y);
x := x − 1;                            x := h(x);
go to l1;                              go to l1;
l2: stop(y)end                         l2: stop(y)end
```

Fig. 1. Program and program scheme.

properties. The following properties of programs are defined and analysed: equivalence of a pair of programs (both programs either compute the same result or they diverge), emptiness (the program diverges), halting (the program is executed in finite time and halts at some result), determinancy (the program always has the same result). Similarly, these ideas are transferred to program schemes: a corresponding property or relation should hold for all the programs (or pairs of programs) resulting from all the possible interpretations of schemes (or pairs of schemes). For instance, scheme S is empty if program (S, I) is empty for any interpretation I.

Three interacting levels can be seen in programming languages: the level of computation control, the level of operations and functions, and the level of data structures, each of them containing suitable software. Since schemes reflect program structures, the corresponding levels can also be identified in them. The majority of program schemes can be defined by triples $S = (M, A, C)$, where M is a (finite) set of memory elements, A a finite set of statements, C the control.

Memory elements are abstractions of locations, queues, stacks, etc. Scheme statements model statements, such as assignment or conditional statements. Parallel programming requires a control level which is developed higher than in sequential languages. Therefore, parallel program models give much prominence to the control level. Control is the most critical part of any parallel scheme. The extent to which a given model is specified is largely defined by the organization of the control, and the degree and method of its description. In some models, the control involves special control variables, functions and statements, in other, simpler models, control is represented by elementary graph-like structures. Chronologically, these simple models (e.g., bilogical graphs [9]), were the first to appear. The models were later enriched by new details and became more and more general, allowing a deeper study of more fundamental properties of parallel computations. The Narinyani metasystems (or, more precisely, the class of metasystems described in [3] which includes the majority of existing models of parallel computations as special cases) seem to be the most general models.

4.2 Karp—Miller schemes

In the Karp—Miller scheme $S = (M, A, C)$, two finite ordered sets of memory elements (locations) are assigned to each statement $a \in A$: input set $\text{In}(a) \in M^n$ and output set $\text{Out}(a) \in M^l$, where $M^i = \underbrace{M \times \dots \times M}_{i}$, n and l are the lengths of the sets. Moreover, "control" symbols (initiation symbol $\bar{a}$ and $k(a)$ termination symbols $a_1, a_2, \dots, a_{k(a)}$) are assigned to each a. These symbols are used by control for the organization of the computations in the interpreted scheme.

In the Karp—Miller scheme, control C is an automat on (Q, q_0, Σ, τ), where Q is a control state set (possibly infinite), $q_0 \in Q$ an initial control state, $\Sigma = \Sigma_i \bigcup \Sigma_t$ a set of control symbols consisting of the set of all initiation symbols $\Sigma_i = \bigcup_{a \in A} \{\bar{a}\}$ and the set of all termination symbols $\Sigma_t = \bigcup_{a \in A} \{a_1, \dots, a_{k(a)}\}$, τ a partial function of transitions from $Q \times \Sigma$ into Q, which is completely defined over $Q \times \Sigma_t$.

An example of control for a scheme with $A = \{a, b, c\}$ and $\Sigma = \{\bar{a}, \bar{b}, \bar{c}, a_1, a_2, b_1, c_1\}$ is given in Fig. 2. Control is represented by a graph whose vertices are states, with an arc marked σ vertex q to vertex q' if and only if $\tau(q, \sigma) = q'$.

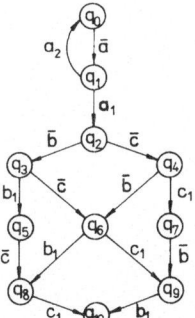

Fig. 2. Control graph of Karp—Miller scheme.

A parallel program (S, I) is the result of the interpretation of the scheme S. An interpretation I is defined, if there are

— an interpretation domain $D(m)$ for all $m \in M$;

— an initial memory state V_0 belonging to the set of memory states $\mathcal{V} = \underset{m \in M}{\times} D(m)$;

— two functions F_a: $\underset{m \in In(a)}{\times} D(m) \to \underset{m \in Out(a)}{\times} D(m)$ and G_a: $\underset{m \in In(a)}{\times} D(m) \to$ $\{a_1, ..., a_{k(a)}\}$ for each a.

Using the value of the input set, function F_a computes the values of the output set of the statement a, and function G_a generates the control symbol.

The execution of the program (S, I) consists in moving along the control graph from the vertex q_0, according to the current memory states and the values of functions F_a and G_a computed using them. The computation state is characterized by a triple $\alpha = (V, q, \mu)$, where $V \in \mathcal{V}$ is the current memory state, q is the control state, and μ is a function assigning a queue $\mu(a)$ to each $a \in A$. Queue $\mu(a)$ is the sequence $d_1, ..., d_k$, where $d_i \in \underset{m \in In(a)}{\times} D(m)$ (the sequence can be empty).

The following operations are applicable to queues:

add $(\mu(a), d) = \mu'(a) = d_1, d_2, ..., d_k,$

acc $(\mu(a)) = d_k,$

new $(\mu(a)) = \mu'(a) = d_1, ..., d_{k-1}.$

Initially, $\alpha_0 = (V_0, q_0, \mu_0)$, where $\mu_0(a)$ is an empty queue for all $a \in A$. Let $\alpha = (V, q, \mu)$ and let control be at the vertex q of the control graph. If no arc leaves q, the execution of the program (S, I) is completed and V is its result. Otherwise, further motion takes place along an arbitrary arc marked by a symbol $\bar{a}$ from Σ_i, or an arc marked by a_j from Σ_t. The latter is possible only if $\mu(a)$ is not empty and $a_j = G_a(W)$, where $W = acc(\mu(a))$.

If symbol $\bar{a}$ is chosen, state α changes to
$\alpha = (V', q', \mu')$, where
$V' = V, q' = \tau(q, \bar{a}),$

$$\mu'(b) = \begin{cases} \mu(b), \text{ if } b \neq a, \\ \text{add}\left(\mu(a), \underset{m \in In(a)}{\times} V(m)\right). \end{cases}$$

$V(m)$ is a value of location m with memory state V.

If the symbol a_j is chosen, the state α changes to $\alpha = (V', q', \mu')$, where $q' = \tau(q, a_j),$

$$V'(m) = \begin{cases} V(m) \text{ if } m \notin Out(a), \\ F_a(W)(m) \text{ if } m \in Out(a), \end{cases}$$

$$\mu'(b) = \begin{cases} \mu(b) \text{ if } b \neq a, \\ \text{new}(\mu(a)) \text{ if } b = a. \end{cases}$$

The new execution state α' in program (S, I) is said to follow from α.

The finite or infinite sequence of execution states $\alpha_0, \alpha_1, \alpha_2, ...$, such that in program (S, I) state α_i follows from α_{i-1} $(i \geq 1)$, is referred to by Karp and Miller as the computational history of the program (S, I). The computation itself is a sequence of statement initiation and termination symbols written in the order of their occurrence in the history of the program (S, I).

One can easily see that parallel programs resulting from the interpretation of Karp—Miller schemes are indeterminate in the sense that such programs can generate multiple computational histories rather than a single history. For example, for program (S, I), where S is the scheme of Fig. 2 and I is some interpretation generating the computational history $(\bar{a}a_1\bar{b}b_1\bar{c}c_1)$, the set of possible computations is as follows

$$\left\{\begin{array}{ll}(\bar{a}a_1\bar{B}B_1\bar{c}c_1), & (\bar{a}a_1\bar{c}\bar{b}B_1c_1), \\ (\bar{a}a_1\bar{B}\bar{c}b_1c_1), & (\bar{a}a_1\bar{c}bc_1b_1), \\ (\bar{a}a_1\bar{B}\bar{c}c_1b_1), & (\bar{a}a_1\bar{c}c_1\bar{b}b_1),\end{array}\right\}.$$

It would be natural to require that all the computations of a parallel program be in some sense equivalent, i.e. that there be some invariant preserved from computation to computation. For example, for two computations to be functionally equivalent both of them should be either infinite or finite, and their histories should terminate with the same result. Then, if all the computations of program (S, I) are functionally equivalent, the program is said to be (functionally) determinate.

The scheme S is determinate if the program (S, I) is determinate for any interpretation I. Taking the set of location histories as invariant, Karp and Miller considered a "stronger" relation of computational equivalence than that of functional equivalence. The location m of the history is such a sequence of values from the interpretation domain, which consists of the initial location value $V_0(m)$ and the values $V(m)$ occurring in m after the termination of statements having m in their output sets. Karp and Miller focused their attention on the study of algorithmic decidability conditions for properties of parallel program schemes, such as determinancy, equivalence and boundedness. Determinancy and equivalence are obtained using location histories, while boundedness characterizes the maximum possible "computation width", i.e. the maximum number of concurrently executed statements. Karp and Miller have formulated some sufficiency conditions for scheme determinancy (through location histories). Similar conditions were proposed by Denning [10]. In both cases, the conditions are not constructive, being formulated mostly in terms of computation properties. Denning [10], for instance, requires that the following "determinancy axioms" be observed:

1. Persistency. A scheme is persistent if for any $\sigma_1, \sigma_2 \in \Sigma$ values of $\tau(q, \sigma_1)$ and $\tau(q, \sigma_2)$ are defined, if and only if $\tau(q, \sigma_1\sigma_2)$ and $\tau(q, \sigma_2\sigma_1)$ are defined, where $\tau(q, \sigma\sigma') = \tau(\tau(q, \sigma), \sigma')$. In other words, readiness for execution of the statement is preserved in a persistent scheme until it is initialized.

2. Finite duration. If a statement is initiated, then it is terminated in finite time.

3. Separateness. For any pair of statements $a, b \in A$ so that a and b can be executed in parallel in one possible computation

$$In(a) \cap Out(b) = Out(a) \cap In(b) = Out(a) \cap Out(b) = \emptyset.$$

4. Consistency. In any prefix of any possible computation of a scheme, the number of terminations of any statement should not exceed the number of initiations.

5. Commutativity. If $\tau(q, \sigma_1\sigma_2)$ and $\tau(q, \sigma_2\sigma_1)$ are defined, they are equal.

The basic results have been obtained for counter schemes, a subclass of Karp—Miller schemes, where control is more limited than in the general case. These schemes are discussed and acquired results are summarized in the following section.

4.3 Schemes with limited controls

The Karp—Miller schemes are a rather general model of parallel computations, this generality stemming from the "abstract" representation of control as an automation. The majority of other schemes discussed elsewhere can be regarded as special cases of Karp—Miller schemes containing a special case of the control structure and a representation of the structure more in "programmer's" terms. If, in doing so, some possibilities of Karp—Miller schemes are excluded, this happens because of some methodological reasons rather than because of the less general control mechanism.

In schemes of A-programs (or A-schemes) [2, 3, 11], the control "frames" statements of A, i.e. a partially interpreted predicate referred to as a trigger function and a partially interpreted control statement are assigned to each operator. Trigger functions and control statements are defined over the same memory $M \bigcup M_c$, where M is a non-interpreted scheme memory and M_c is an interpreted control memory. As usual, an A-program is a scheme plus an interpretation. A statement of an A-program can be initiated only if its trigger function is true for the current memory value. Statement termination always occurs as in Karp—Miller schemes. An A-program terminates if none of its statements can be initiated. An additional constraint is that the trigger functions of currently executed statements are not checked. Thus, there is no autoparallelism in Karp—Miller schemes, i.e. the next initiation of a statement is possible only after its termination (queues μ contain at most one element). An example of an A-scheme is shown in Fig. 3. The symbol $\rightarrow$ separates trigger functions from statements;

$$
\begin{aligned}
p(x) \wedge \alpha = 0 &\rightarrow (x := f(x); \alpha := 1), \\
q(y) \wedge \beta = 0 &\rightarrow (y := g(y); \beta := 1), \\
\alpha = 1 \wedge \beta > 0 &\rightarrow (z := h(x, y); \alpha := 2), \\
\beta = 1 &\rightarrow (n := e(y); \beta := 2)
\end{aligned}
$$

Fig. 3. A-scheme.

statements from A have the form of assignment statements; the control statement follows directly the assignment statement, forming with it a single entity; an A-scheme is a set of such triples. The control memory involves locations α, β whose values are integers.

A-schemes and A-programs were applied to the study of fundamental properties of parallel computations, such as determinancy and equivalence of parallel
programs [12, 13], and to the studies of automatic transformations of sequential
programs into programs with maximum parallelism [12, 14] (some authors prefer
to call them „maximally asynchronous" to distinguish definitions related to the
number of generated computations (see below) from those related to the maximum
"width" of parallel computations). The problem of maximum parallelization is
discussed in detail in Chapter 3.

The theory of A-programs and A-schemes employs a definition of equivalence
differing from that used in the studies of Karp—Miller schemes; namely, computation data-flow graphs or some derivatives are used as computation invariants. The
data-flow graph vertices are the statement entries in the computation. The vertices
are connected by arcs corresponding to the transmission of results from one
operator to another through shared memory locations. There is no information
about the locations as such. Thus, the data-flow graph indicates data exchanges
between the entries of statements in the computation. Figure 4 demonstrates

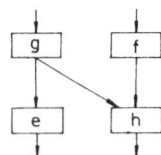

Fig. 4. Data graph.

a data-flow graph of equivalent computations generated by the A-scheme in
Figure 3 under some interpretation, where $p(x)$ and $q(y)$ are true. In this scheme,
α and β are control variables whose initial values are 0.

Equivalence relations with respect to location histories and data-flow graphs are
incompatible; examples of computations can be given that are equivalent in one
sense but not in the other. The data-flow graph equivalence has the advantage that
it allows equivalent transformations of schemes and programs involving location
renaming. Transformations of this sort are especially useful in parallelization;
maximal parallelization cannot be achieved without them [2, 15, 16]. The latter
concept consists of two equivalent determinate parallel programs; that which has
a richer set of computations, including all the computations of another program, is
regarded as more parallel (asynchronous). This relation is transferred to schemes in
a standard manner. A scheme (program) which is not less parallel than other
schemes (programs) in the class of all the schemes (programs) equivalent to it is
described as having maximum parallelism. The literature gives various definitions
of computational equivalence. Definitions of maximum parallelism are meaningful
only with respect to the chosen definitions of equivalence. Therefore, the definition
of maximum parallelism in [14, 17] differs from that of Keller [18]. Generally, the

property of being a scheme with maximum parallelism is not recognizable. For sequential statement schemes like those considered in [6], there is an algorithm for maximum parallelization in an A-scheme under some constraints which facilitate analysis of the source scheme [2, 14, 15].

4.4 Subclasses of Karp—Miller schemes

Most results obtained in [8] concern the counter scheme which is a concrete implementation of the general Karp—Miller scheme. Similarly as in A-schemes, an interpreted control memory is introduced consisting of a finite number of control variables, called counters. The current state of this memory is represented by a vector of length h consisting of non-negative integers. The state $q = (e, \mathbf{x}) \in Q$ is a pair consisting of an element e of some special set E and vector $\mathbf{x}$. To each symbol σ of Σ a vector $\mathbf{v}(\sigma)$ is assigned, its components being non-negative if $\sigma \in \Sigma_t$. The vector $\mathbf{v}(\sigma)$ indicates the change of the state of the control memory caused by the action σ. Finally, $\theta: E \times \Sigma \to E$ is a partial function completely defined over Σ_t. The value of $\tau(q, \sigma)$ is defined if $q = (e, \mathbf{x})$, $\mathbf{x}$ is a vector, $\theta(e, \sigma)$ is defined, and $\mathbf{x} + \mathbf{v}(\sigma) \geq 0$. If the value is defined, then

$$\tau((e, \mathbf{x}), \sigma) = (\theta(e, \sigma), \mathbf{x} + \mathbf{v}(\sigma)).$$

For counter schemes, insolvability of the equivalence problem has been established [8], including the class of determinate schemes [19]. Similarly, the problems of determinacy (even in the subclass of finite counter schemes) of boundedness and some others, also turn out to be insolvable [20]. It is interesting that consideration of schemes without repetition leads to a different situation. A scheme is said to be without repetition if, for any computation and any pair of entries of the same symbol $\bar{a} \in \Sigma_t$, there exists a symbol $b_j \in \Sigma_t$ which lies between these two entries of $\bar{a}$, and $Out(b) \cap In(a) = \emptyset$. For counter schemes without repetition there is an algorithm for bounded parallelization, and if, moreover, the schemes are commutative and $\forall a \in A$, $Out(a) \neq \emptyset$, the determinacy problem is solvable. There is also an algorithm for the recognition of single-entry counter schemes [8].

Parallel operator schemes [8] represent another restriction of the general model, forming a subclass of counter schemes. In this case, the set E consists of a single element, i.e. the vector of counter values represents directly some control state. Moreover, for each operator a a counter is fixed which will be incremented by 1 at the initiation and decremented by 1 at the termination. This counter is inaccessible to other operators; it is as it counts the number of data elements in the queue $\mu(a)$. A fixed predicate of the form $\mathbf{x} + \mathbf{v}(\sigma) \geq 0$ is an initiation condition; the vector $\mathbf{x} + \mathbf{v}(\sigma)$ becomes a new state. The fixed form of the initiation conditions (trigger functions) is the major difference between parallel operator schemes and A-programs. A parallel operator scheme equivalent to the scheme of Fig. 2 is shown in Fig. 5. Counters are shown by circles and operators by squares, with initial counter values indicated inside the circles.

Parallel operator schemes have been modified by Slutz [21] so as to make

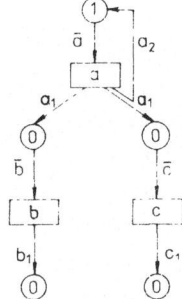

Fig. 5. Parallel statement scheme.

operator termination conditional as initiation. As a result, a greater variety of computations has been achieved with less memory. Indeed, parallelization requires more locations for the elimination of memory conflicts. In interpreted Slutz schemes, parallel executions of operators with intersecting input and output sets are allowed, but their termination should be made to occur in a required order by means of appropriate conditions.

A version of Karp—Miller schemes, where autoparallelism is excluded and operator execution is regarded as instant action was applied by Keller [18] and Logrippo [22] to the study of maximal parallelism schemes.

The above parallel program schemes and some others outside the scope of this review have some common properties:

1. They have three explicit program levels: memory, statements, and control.

2. In these models, the memory is shared by several statements that can write to and read from it. A location stores one data item that is copied on reading from, and replaced in writing to it (in Karp—Miller schemes, the queue plays an auxiliary role and is "hidden" inside the statement).

3. All the models feature the so-called asynchronous control where all operators are regarded independent and potentially parallel, and the computation is directed by checks of individual initiation conditions which permit (rather than prescribe) the execution of appropriate statements.

4. Control receives information about the state of the computations and derives from it a new "control situation". As a rule, information about the state of the computations is associated with such events like statement initiation or termination (alphabet Σ in Karp—Miller schemes).

4.5 Data-flow schemes

In contrast to the above Karp—Miller schemes where the control information is associated with statements (or more precisely, with initiations and terminations), in data-flow schemes and programs it is associated with data flow. Data-flow control is based upon the implicit principle that a statement can be initiated when its input data is ready. In this connection, a memory consisting of queues is used instead of one consisting of locations. Each queue is assigned to a certain pair of statements (distributed memory). One statement writes the data into the queue, another reads it out. The current state of the queue (data sequence) can be empty. Data written to the queue is added to the tail, and data is read from its head. Queues allow pipelining when the data flows successively through a set of concurrently executed statements. Generally, the queue "capacity" is infinite. Therefore, the scheme memory is potentially infinite, and the expressive capabilities of data-flow schemes, in particular the maximum attainable parallelism, become superior to those of finite memory schemes with locations. The situation, however, becomes more balanced if locations are supplemented by arrays. The initiation conditions of any statement are usually standard and depend on input queues: a statement can initiate computations, if any of its input queues contain at least a definite amount of data. Sometimes additional conditions (absence of data in output queues, etc.) are introduced. One can easily see that data-flow control and distributed memory eliminate shared location conflicts, thus making data-flow control completely decentralized, i.e. the control of statement readiness and decision-making about initiation are performed locally.

The Karp—Miller data-flow schemes [23] were one of the first models of this type. All statements of these schemes belong to the same type of unconditional transformers (i.e. the interpretations associate only function F_a with statement a, while function G_a is missing).

Each queue is characterized by the

— initial amount of data in it;
— number of data items eliminated when reading from it;
— number of data items added when writing to it;
— initiation threshold indicating the minimal amount of data in the queue required for the initiation of the statement for which this is an input queue.

The condition for the initiation of a statement requires that for any input queue the number of data items in it is at least equal to the initiation threshold. The initiation leads to reading from each input queue as many data items as indicated. The statement termination is unconditional and is accompanied by writing to its output queue as many data items as indicated.

A graph form of the Karp—Miller data-flow scheme is shown in Fig. 6. The vertices of the graph correspond to statements and the arcs correspond to queues, each arc being accompanied by a quadruple of numbers characterizing it as a queue. The Karp—Miller data-flow schemes have no facilities for the establish-

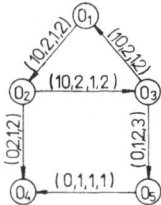

Fig. 6. Karp—Miller data-flow scheme.

ment of connection conditions for data and control (no decision functions G_a). Therefore, the class of data-flow programs resulting from the interpretation of these schemes is not universal, in the sense that arbitrary computable functions cannot be represented in it. This also eliminates the advantages offered by queues of unlimited capacity. In this connection, Karp and Miller [23], and later also Reiter [24] focused their attention on operational aspects of the model, i.e. on the derivation of quantitative and some qualitative characteristics of data-flow program operation. Karp and Miller have established necessary and sufficient conditions for queue boundedness (the number of data items in the queue cannot exceed some given number). Reiter has given an algorithm for the determination of maximum queue length, and indicated the existence of optimal scheduling strategies for statement execution resulting in minimum total computation time.

Adams' schemes [25, 26] are an important generalization of the above graph data-flow schemes, primarily because decision vertices are introduced which map (after interpretation) data from input queues onto control states assigned to output arcs (see the description of the Rodriguez schemes for details of these states). As a result, Adams' model has universal computational capabilities. Secondly, the model is enhanced by procedure description and access facilities. There are special call vertices in the "master" scheme and a set of recursively defined scheme procedures. It is also possible to simulate complex data structures. As a result, Adam's model was at one time the closest to a practical data-flow language model.

Although it has a location-oriented memory and explicit control facilities, the Rodriguez schemes should be classified as data-flow schemes, because their control is associated with data flows. Control variables either correspond to locations of uninterpreted memory M or they are "independent". A control variable reflects the "state" of a corresponding location and takes four control values: -1 (passive), 0 (empty), 1 (accessible), and 2 (blocked). Statements are divided into several types: transformers, transfer statements which copy data without changing it, **INPUT/OUTPUT** statements, **DISTRIBUTOR, MERGE, CYCLE BEGIN,** and

END of cycle, and the special "control" statements **AND** and **OR**. Transformers have sets of input and output locations as in shared memory schemes. **AND** and **OR** statements handle only control variables, cycle statements handle both locations and control variables. Each type of statement has a fixed initiation condition indicating those sets of values of control variables (related to the statement) which allow the initiation of this type of statement. The statement termination leads to a determinate change of the control variable states, i.e. the statement is treated as if it had a fixed "control function" related to its type. The control function of a two-input (1, 2), two-output (3, 4) **DISTRIBUTOR** is given by the following table:

Values of control variables

before initiation				after termination				
1	2	3	4	1	2	3	4	
1	1	0	0	0	0	−1	1	depending on the
				0	0	1	−1	distributor predicate
1	−1	0	0					
−1	1	0	0	0	0	−1	−1	
−1	−1	0	0					

As seen, **DISTRIBUTOR** can be "normally" initiated if both input variables are 1, and both output variables are 0. The scheme computes the distributor predicate for the current values of the input locations and, depending on its value, selects one of the sets of control variable values indicated on the right-hand side. If at least one input variable is passive, both output variables become passive, too.

Rodriguez has formulated the conditions for scheme determinancy and described a set of equivalent scheme transformations [26].

The schemes of Dennis [27] are a development of those of Rodriguez. They are a mathematical model of the method of parallel computation organization developed by Dennis in a series of contributions initiated by [28]. The major objective of these publications is to suggest a conceptual language which could underlie computations in future highly parallel computers. Universality, modularity and the ability to express maximal parallelism are the basic features which Dennis would like to build into his language. The version of the data-flow scheme proposed in [27] is based on a graphical scheme representation. The scheme is represented by a bipartite graph whose vertices are either actors or links, the latter being either data links or control links. Actors and links are connected by arcs type of which (data arc, or control arc with values "true" or "false") depends on the type of the corresponding link. The arcs represent memory elements which are queues that have a capacity of at most one data item. The input and output vertices are isolated. Similarly as in the Rodriguez schemes, statements can be of several types. Figure 7 shows statements of several types with their initiation rules, and rules for changing the content of the arcs after the statement. Data links are shown by circles and control links are shown by bold points. As can be seen from Fig. 7, the presence of data on each input arc and the absence of data on the output arcs are the prerequisites for the initiation of the transformer and recognizer. The same holds

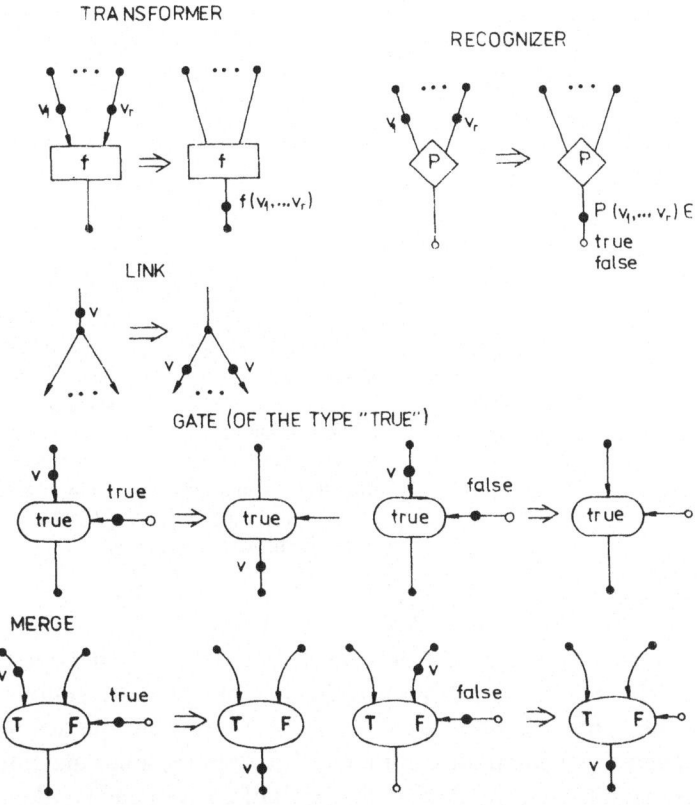

Fig. 7. Statements of Davis data-flow scheme and their operation rules
(logic statements **AND, OR, NOT** are not shown).

for logic operators and control gates. For **MERGE,** it is sufficient for data to be present on one of the arcs indicated by the control input.

Some basic issues were considered for Dennis' schemes: the determination of constraints leading to a solvable equivalence problem, equivalent transformation of schemes, etc. The translation of sequential schemes into data-flow schemes was discussed as well. Essentially new results, exceeding the scope of technical theorems applicable to this class of schemes, however, were not obtained. The operator structures of Bers [29] are, in essentials, close to the Dennis models. No special theory has been developed for them. They served merely as a conceptual scheme for a method of data-flow organization of parallel programs proposed by the present author. In doing so, attention was concentrated on constructing complex structures out of a relatively small set of basic elements, by methodical

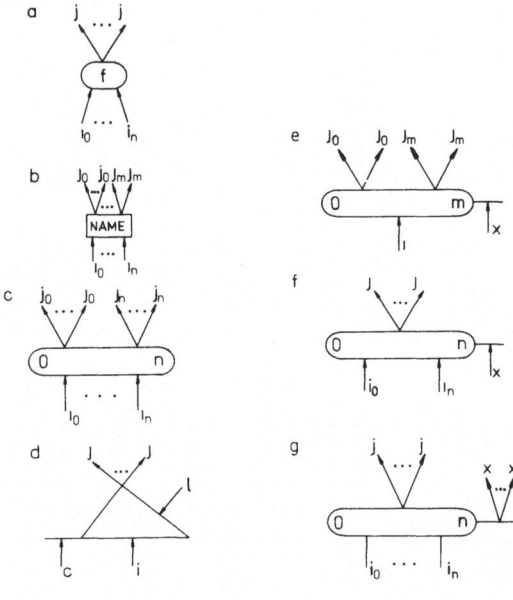

Fig. 8. Statements of Davis data-flow scheme.

a — transformer, $j = f(i_0, ..., i_n)$; b — procedure call; c — synchronizer, $j_0 = i_0, ..., j_n = i_n$; d — cycle gate; e — distributor, $j_x = i$; f — selector, initiation conditions — non-empty queues at inputs x and i_x, $j = i_x$; g —arbiter, initiation conditions — non-empty queue at one input $j = i_k$, $x = k$, where k is any input with non-empty queue.

application of an extension mechanism that allowed the substitution of some new elements for structures constructed in a certain way. Some data-flow networks developed by Davis [30, 31] are similar to those of Dennis, but they are simpler because they do not distinguish data and control links. Arcs represent queues of potentially unlimited capacity. A statement is initiated if its input queues are not empty. When a statement is initiated, the data at the head of each queue is taken and the result is put onto the output queues. The results are computed according to the function of the statement. The seven types of statements used in data-flow networks are shown in Fig. 8.

Functions and precise initiation conditions are indicated beside the statement diagrams. A statement can have several output queues which receive copies of the same data, because data read out of the queues is destroyed. The only statement using its "internal state" for the computation of results is **GATE** which is a special case of **DISTRIBUTOR** with two competing inputs i and l, and a logic input c. Depending on the input c and the statement state, one of the inputs i or l is open. In the initial state, **GATE** is open and passes on its output (inside the cycle) a data item from queue i, if logic input c is **true.** Next, **GATE** closes for i and opens for data from l. This mode of operation lasts until queue l has data and queue c has **true** items. When a **false** value reaches the input c, input i opens again to allow a data item to pass. The statements **GATE** and **DISTRIBUTOR** are both used for the organization of iterations in data-flow computations, as shown in Fig. 9a. **ARBITER** and **SELECTOR** allow parallel paths to be merged into a single pipeline, and the pipeline to be split into parallel paths. This allows the sharing of resources in data-flow computations.

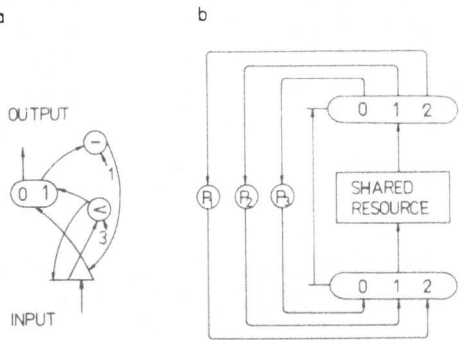

Fig. 9. Fragments of data-flow schemes.
a) Example of single iteration, logic values are coded by 0 (**false**) and 1 (**true**); b — three processes using shared resource.

Similarly as in other schemes for data-flow programs, data-flow nets are oriented to the substantiation and completion mechanisms for data-flow control in asynchronous distributed computations. Data-flow nets have become a starting-point for the development of a more detailed computational model, leading to the architecture of an asynchronous recursive computer DDM 1 (Data Driven Machine 1) [31]. The appearance of data-flow computation theory is due to the desire to define a "more natural" method of program organization namely that of the direct transformation into parallel computations of the von Neumann concept of statement programming with shared memory. Data-flow computations are likely to be more natural in "formula-like" and "network-like" problems. But by and large, the principle of argument readiness is too simple to be a universally applicable method of computation control, especially where a shared resource is essential, as in sorting, etc.

Kahn [32] has used a simple data-flow model to illustrate his method for the description of parallel language semantics. A similar but more involved model was studied for the same reason by Mazurkiewicz [33]. Generally, data-flow models are popular in studies of parallel program verification because of their naturalness.

4.6 Abstract parallel structures

There are various forms of parallelism in programs, systems and computations. For example, there may be parallelism in programs at the level of independent statements (see the above models), or macroparallelism of complex interacting processes. At the same time, these varied forms of parallelism have some properties in common that can be studied via some abstract representations of parallel systems and processes. The abstract representations are free of unneces-

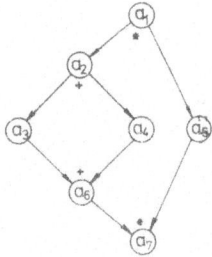

Fig. 10. Bilogical graph.

sary details of the programs and oriented to a "superficial" analysis of the control structures of parallel processes. Most abstract models are based on special graphs with special labelling.

For instance, bilogical graphs [34] are directed, their vertices corresponding to statements of a parallel program, and their arcs corresponding to control or data connections between the statements. Input and output controls are associated with each vertex, each of them being either conjunctive or disjunctive. Under disjunctive input control, statement execution can be initiated only if one and only one of the arcs entering this vertex-statement is "activated". Under conjunctive input control, statement execution is initiated only when all the arcs entering the vertex are active.

The execution of a disjunctive output control vertex terminates with the activation of one and only one outgoing arc. In the case of conjunctive output control, all the vertices leaving the vertex are activated.

A single initial vertex without input arcs and a single terminal vertex without output arcs are isolated. Weights can be associated with vertices and arcs, these are the times of statement execution and data transfer. In addition, the probability of a transfer along it can be assigned to each arc.

In an example of the bilogical graph (Fig. 10), asterisks indicate conjunctive controls and crosses indicate disjunctive controls. Bilogical graphs were predominantly used in studies of operational issues of parallel programming: estimation of expected program execution time [35], maximum number of processors required for minimum execution time of a parallel program [36].

In practice, bilogical graphs and similar models were replaced by the Petri nets which are the most popular current formalism describing the structure and interaction of parallel systems and processes. Petri nets [37] were introduced by

Holt and Commoner [38] who made the first steps towards the study and interpretation of Petri nets in the theory of parallel systems. For the same purposes Karp and Miller had independently employed systems of added vectors [8] which were later demonstrated to be mathematically equivalent to Petri nets. Subsequently, Petri net theory was developed in several directions, including mathematical theory of networks, structural theory of networks, applications of parallel programming, and application to a wide range of discrete dynamic systems. A good review of Petri net theory development and status up to 1977 was given by Peterson [39], who compiled a major bibliography on nets.

A Petri net is an ordered set $N = (P, T, F, H, M_0)$, where P is a finite non-empty set of symbols called places, T is a finite non-empty set of symbols called transitions,

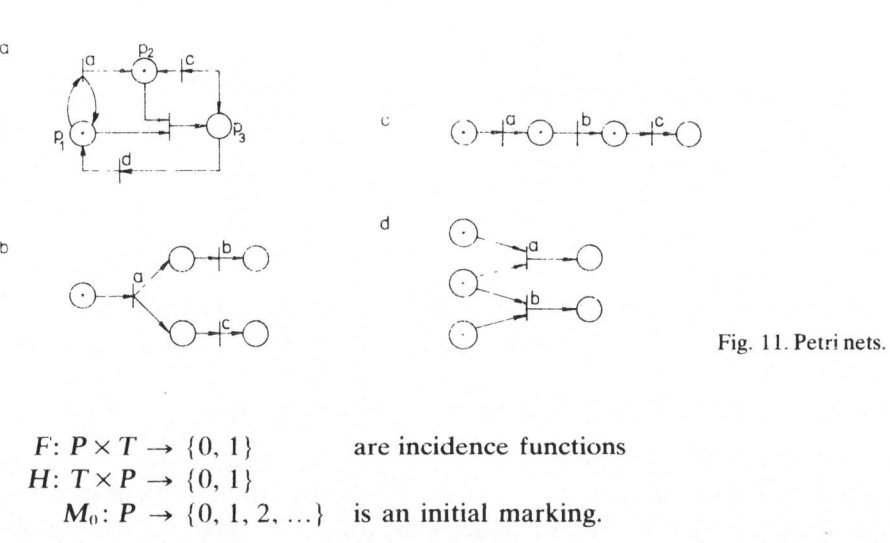

Fig. 11. Petri nets.

$$F: P \times T \to \{0, 1\}$$ are incidence functions
$$H: T \times P \to \{0, 1\}$$
$$M_0: P \to \{0, 1, 2, \ldots\}$$ is an initial marking.

The Petri net is represented by a marked directed graph with the set of vertices $P \cup T$. Places are shown by circles, transitions by boxes or bars. An arc goes from a place p to a transition t if and only if $F(p, t) = 1$; an arc goes from transition t to place p if and only if $H(t, p) = 1$. Places are marked by non-negative integers (place-marking) which are graphically represented by a number or the corresponding number of tokens inside the circles representing places.

Figure 11a shows the following Petri net

$$P = \{p_1, p_2, p_3\}, \qquad T = \{a, b, c, d\},$$

$$M_0 = \frac{\begin{array}{ccc} p_1 & p_2 & p_3 \end{array}}{\begin{array}{ccc} 1 & 1 & 0 \end{array}}$$

F:	a	b	c	d
p_1	1	1	0	0
p_2	0	1	0	0
p_3	0	0	1	1

H:	p_1	p_2	p_3
a	1	1	0
b	0	0	1
c	0	1	0
d	1	0	0

The Petri net operates by changing the markings. Each marking is a function $M: P \rightarrow \{0, 1, 2, ...\}$. The net begins to function at the initial marking M_0. Markings are changed as a result of the firing of one of the transitions.

Transition t fires for marking M if

$$\forall p \in P, M(p) - F(p, t) \geqslant 0.$$

This condition implies that each input place of the transition t, i.e. each place p contains at least one token, such that $F(p, t) = 1$.

As a result of the firing of transition t at marking M, the latter is replaced by the marking M' according to the following rule:

$$\forall p \in P, M'(p) = M(p) - F(p, t) + H(t, p).$$

In other words, the transition t takes one token from each of its input places and adds one token to each of its output places, i.e. to each place p such that $H(t, p) = 1$.

Marking M' is said to follow marking M, and marking M is said to precede marking M'. This is written $M \overset{t}{\vdash} M'$.

Transitions fire successively but indeterminately: if several transitions can fire, any one of them fires. The net stops if under some (dead-end) marking none of the transitions can fire.

Thus, the Petri net models a structure and its operational dynamics. Our definition relates to "simple" Petri nets. In the general case, the net is a multi-graph, and the firing condition requires that the number of tokens in each input place p of a transition t is at least equal to the number of arcs connecting p and t, transition t adding after firing to each of its output places P as many tokens as there are arcs going to P from t. This generalization, however, is inessential because any such net can be reduced to a simple net preserving the fundamental properties of the generalized net [40].

If the set of net places is ordered in some way, say $P = (p_1, p_2, ..., p_n)$, the marking M can be conveniently represented as a vector of length n:

$M = (M(p_1), M(p_2), ..., M(p_n))$. The following relations can be introduced naturally: equal markings $M = M'$, marking M' covering marking $M(M' \geqslant M)$, strictly covering $(M' > M)$, etc. For example, $M' \geqslant M$ if $\forall p \in P$, $M'(p) \geqslant M(p)$.

In a net, the marking M' is reachable from the marking M as a result of successive firings $\tau = t_1 t_2 \ldots t_e$, if there is a sequence of markings $M \overset{t_1}{\vdash} M_1 \overset{t_2}{\vdash} \ldots \overset{t_e}{\vdash} M_e$ (notation $M \overset{\tau}{\vdash} M'$), where τ is a word from the set T^* of all words in the alphabet T. The marking M is reachable in net N, if there exists τ such that $M_0 \overset{\tau}{\vdash} M$. Let $R(N)$ be the set of all reachable markings in N. The set of words $L(N) = \{\tau \in T^* \mid M, M_0 \overset{\tau}{\vdash} M\}$ is referred to as a (free) language of the Petri net N.

The transition t is reachable from the marking M in the net N, if there is a marking M' in $R(N)$ and a word τ such that $M \overset{\tau}{} M'$ and transition t can fire under M'. The transition is reachable in the net N if it is reachable from M_0.

The transition t is live if it is reachable from any marking in $R(N)$. A Petri net is live if all its transitions are live.

The place p is bounded if there is a number k such that $M(p) \leqslant k$ for any marking M in $R(N)$. The net N is bounded if all its places are bounded.

The Petri nets N_1 and N_2 are equivalent if $L(N_1) = L(N_2)$.

Below, there are listed some presently known properties of Petri nets:

1. There is an algorithm for boundedness verification of any Petri net [8, 40].

2. There is an algorithm which establishes that a net transition is reachable [40].

3. Problems of inclusion $(R(N_1) \leqslant R(N_2))$ and equality $(R(N_1) = R(N_2))$ of sets of reachable markings are not solvable [40].

Most interesting appears the problem of marking reachability: for a given net N and some marking M one wishes to ascertain whether M belongs to $R(N)$. This problem was demonstrated [40] to be equal to those of liveness and equivalence. The equivalence lies in the fact that (un)solvability of any of these problems implies automatically the (un)solvability of the others. Reference [41] asserts that reachability is solvable. In spite of the mistakes detected by proving, the problem is still regarded as solvable and a proof is still sought for.

Why are the Petri nets and their mathematical equivalent, vector addition systems regarded as a convenient vehicle for modelling "abstract parallelism". Firstly, because it is easy to represent by nets such things as asynchronous operation (time is not implied in the net definition), indeterminancy of parallel independent events (Fig. 11b), pipeline parallelism (Fig. 11c), resource conflicts (Fig. 11d), etc. Secondly, as a mathematical model do Petri nets lie between finite automata and Turing machines; they are much richer than automata in their expressive power and very close to Turing machines. At the same time, many net properties are solvable as is the case with finite automata.

Petri nets are applied to the analysis and design of computing devices and circuits (see [42], for example). Two approaches to the application of Petri net theory to programming begin to appear. In the first approach, standard situations occurring in parallel programs because of process interaction, resource allocation, program deadlocks, etc., are described in net terms. A situation is known, for instance, when each of two concurrent sequential processes has "critical sections". Their interaction should be organized so as to prevent their simultaneous activity in critical sections. Dijkstra [43] has solved this problem by introducing semaphores (special integer control variables) and two operations P and V over them:

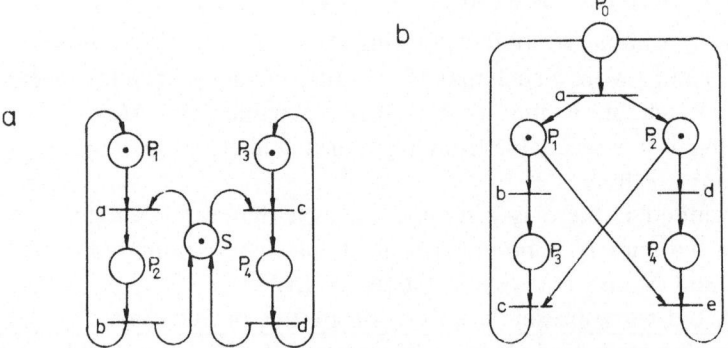

Fig. 12. Modelling of mutual exclusion and deadlock by Petri nets.

$$V(s) = s + 1,$$

$$P(s) = \begin{cases} \text{wait, if } s \leq 0, \\ s - 1, \text{ otherwise.} \end{cases}$$

A corresponding Petri net is shown in Fig. 12a. The subnet involving transitions a, b and places p_1, p_2 models one cyclic process; another process is modelled by the subnet involving transitions c, d, and places p_3, p_4. The interval between a and b is the critical section of the first process, and the interval between c and d is the critical section of the second process. Place s corresponds to the semaphore; the transitions a and c model P-operations the transitions b and d model V-operations. The net in Fig. 12b shows the so-called deadlock, where two processes conflict for two resources shown by tokens in places p_1 and p_2. Reference [44] gives some sufficient deadlock conditions formulated in terms of Petri nets. Patil [45] and other authors studied the use of Petri nets to model typical situations occurring in parallel programs.

A second application of Petri nets to programming is the formalization of control structure semantics in parallel languages. In contrast to the first approach, nets are used here for the construction and justification of expansible program mechanisms for parallel computation control, rather than for modelling individual situations.

These mechanisms should be conceptually simple, complete, capable of development, and mathematically rigorous, so that they would support development of parallel languages that are convenient, effective and adaptable to the increasing structural variety of problems and systems. For example, in parallel languages an explicit separation of description mechanisms for control structures and for statements (procedures) and data structures was proposed in [46, 48]. Description mechanisms for control structures are expansible and they centre around some Petri net algebras. In [46, 47] the control structure is programmed by means of

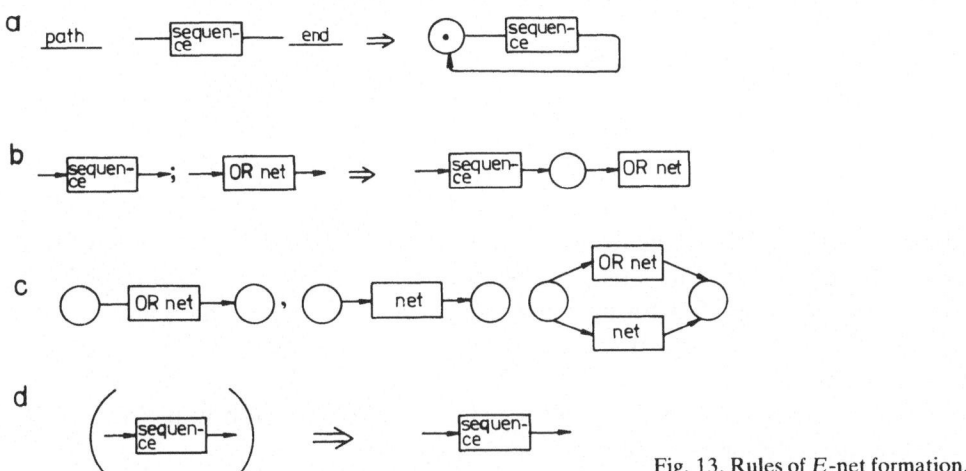

Fig. 13. Rules of E-net formation.

path expressions, semantics of which is described by Petri nets constructed of elementary nets using composition rules shown in Fig. 13. This figure shows construction rules for a special case of path expressions (E-expressions), semantics of which is described by E-nets. The syntax of E-expressions is described by the following metalinguistic formulae:

$\langle$E-expression$\rangle$ :: = **path** $\langle$sequence$\rangle$ **end**
$\langle$sequence$\rangle$ :: = sequence; $\langle$**OR**-net$\rangle$ | $\langle$**OR**-net$\rangle$
$\langle$**OR**-net$\rangle$ :: = $\langle$**OR**-net$\rangle$,$\langle$net$\rangle$ | $\langle$net$\rangle$
$\langle$net$\rangle$ :: = $\langle$transition$\rangle$ | $\langle$sequence$\rangle$

Operations over nets designated by the symbols ";", "," and special parentheses correspond to these formulae. Figure 14 shows an E-net constructed using path expressions:

path a ; $((b ; c), (d ; e))$ **end**.

E-nets are live Petri nets. Various generalizations of E-expressions and E-nets describing various existing program control constructs and standard control situations are considered in [47].

Similarly, an algebra of regular and structured nets was developed [48, 49] allowing the formal description and construction of control structures at all levels of highly parallel languages. Regular Petri nets are constructed of elementary nets by means of operations illustrated in Fig. 15 and examples. Figure 15a shows an

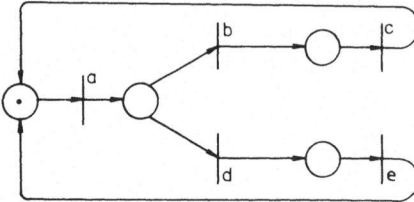

Fig. 14. E-net defined by path E-expression.

elementary net. By means of superposition (Fig. 15b) one net is laid over another, identical transitions being matched. If there are no such transitions, nets form independent parallel fragments. Marking (Fig. 15c) changes the markings of head places. Iteration (Fig. 15d) merges each "head place" with each "tail place". The join operation (Fig. 15e) forms a net from a pair of nets by merging their tail places. The exclusion operation (Fig. 15f) merges separately the head and tail places of two nets.

Let ε be a class of elementary nets each designated by a transition symbol. The net formula is defined as follows:

a) a symbol from ε is a formula;
b) if A is a formula, then $n(A)$ and $*A$ are formulae;
c) if A and B are formulae, then (A, B), $(A ; B)$ and $(A \square B)$ are formulae;
d) additional constraint: formulae of the form $(A ; B)$ and $(A \square B)$ do not simultaneously involve the same symbol in A and B.

Net formulae define the class of regular nets. Formula

$$1*(a ; ((b ; c)\square(d ; e))),$$

for example, defines the regular net shown in Fig. 14. Regular nets are a strict subclass of Petri nets. The net in Fig. 12a is not regular, but an arbitrary net can be transformed into an equivalent regular net [49]. Formulae of regular nets are directly involved in a parallel language with control types, where they define the program structure on the assumption that symbols of elementary nets are names of statements and modules [48].

An adequate description of hierarchical systems and programs is made possible by special techniques which allow one to consider externally monolithic transitions and places as subnets. For example, in [48, 49] there have been structured regular nets introduced where transitions are classified as terminal and non-terminal. The former are indivisible simple transitions, the latter are structured nets. The

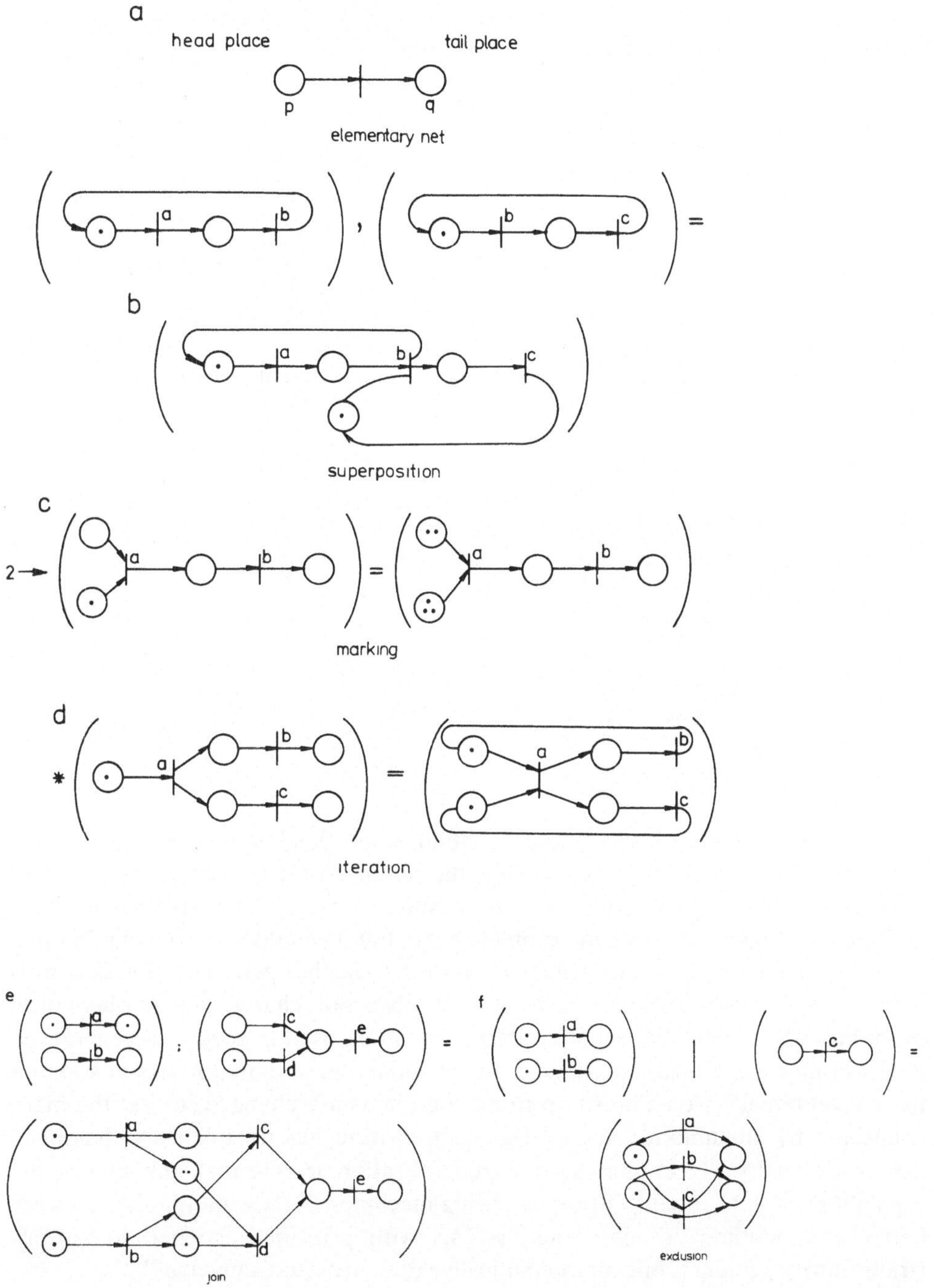

Fig. 15. Operations over structures.

"internal" net of a non-terminal transition begins to operate as soon as the transition is initiated. The non-terminal transition is completed as soon as the internal net stops its operation. Thus, the firing of a non-terminal transition is more a lengthy process than an instantaneous event. Figure 16 shows a structured net defined by the following formula:

$$(*1(t;(v,w)),(2e;d)),$$
$$t = 1(a\,\square\,b),$$
$$v = 2(c;d),$$
$$w = (2e;1f),$$

where a, b, c, d, e, f are terminal transitions and t, v, w are non-terminal transitions, the first row defining the main formula, and the other rows defining non-terminals.

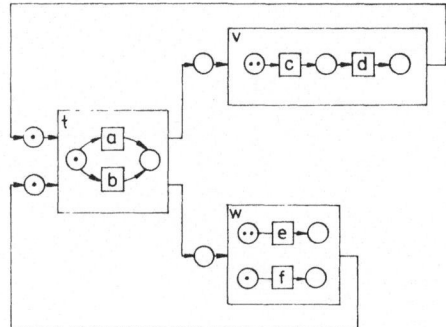

Fig. 16. Structured net.

Attempts to improve modelling capabilities of Petri nets have been made elsewhere. In generalized nets [40, 50], the number of arcs connecting a pair of vertices is arbitrary. The condition of transition firing and the rule for marking change are the same as those mentioned above, but it should be borne in mind that $F(p, t)$ and $H(t, p)$ can take values exceeding 1. Such a generalization is convenient in a number of applications, but it does not change the mathematical properties of the nets, i.e. a simple Petri net can be used instead of a generalized one. Another generalization [40] is in the introduction of inhibitor arcs in addition to "conventional" arcs. Transition firing conditions are changed so that the place connected by an inhibitor arc to a given transition has no tokens. It has been demonstrated by Hack, that such a generalization is essential and makes the capabilities of nets equal to those of Turing machines. Nets with inhibitor arcs are better at modelling asynchronous systems with priorities assigned to various (transition) fragments, but, mathematically, they are "too universal".

On the whole, Petri nets are a convenient tool not only for modelling control structures in parallel programs (which was our main topic treated above), but also for the description of data flows. However, there are no models other than program schemes that can adequately model the interaction of control and data structures. Therefore, the theory of nets can give answer to particular questions or serve as a component of the general theory of parallel programs.

4.7 Semantic issues of parallel programs

Semantic studies of programs and programming languages should, firstly, indicate methods for synthesis and correctness checking of programs and, secondly, separate and justify rigorously the basic primitives of advanced programming languages, providing effective and reliable development of complex programs. Obviously, these issues are topical for parallel programming, because the difficulties of indeterminate interaction of concurrent asynchronous processes are imposed upon those of the "traditional" logic of sequential programming.

Designers of operating systems and, generally speaking, of all sequentially-parallel programs (which are generalizations of sequential programs to which facilities are added for explicit definition of parallel processes and for synchronization) were the first to meet this problem. Asynchronous interaction of processes resulted in errors such as deadlocks or undesired writing to shared memory areas. At the first stage, one could single out typical structural situations where errors could occur, and find correct (sometimes incorrect) solutions by means of semaphores and other new linguistic constructs. This can be exemplified by the studies of mutual exclusion in [43, 52, 53]. Formalisms for the search for mathematical substantiation of correct solutions were developed by Gilbert, Chandler [54], Habermann [55], and others. To this end, Gilbert and Chandler have made use of the apparatus of finite automata. Habermann has formally described operations P and V and formulated a theorem which leads to a correctness proof of solutions of synchronization problems. To describe synchronization states, Habermann associates with each semaphore s a constant $c(s)$ and the three following variables initial values of which are assumed to be equal to zero:

$nw(s)$ — the number of executions of $P(s)$,
$ns(s)$ — the number of executions of $V(s)$,
$np(s)$ — the number of executions of the operator directly following $P(s)$.

The execution of $P(s)$ results in the following change of the synchronization state:

$nw(s): = nw(s) + 1$; **if** $nw(s) \leqslant cs(s) + n(s)$, **then**
$np(s): = np(s) + 1$.

The execution of $V(s)$ results in the following change of state:

if $nw(s) > c(s) + ns(s)$, **then** $np(s) := np(s) + 1$;
$ns(s) := ns(s) + 1$.

Habermann has established that the relation

$$np(s) = \min (nw(s), c(s) + ns(s))$$

does not change as a result of the execution of $P(s)$ and $V(s)$. Using this relation, one can demonstrate the correctness of that solution of the mutual exclusion problem which was discussed in the above section, and was presented in Fig. 12a in terms of Petri nets. Indeed, each critical section begins with the operation $P(s)$ and ends with $V(s)$. The solution is correct if at each instant at most one process is within the critical section, and no process can be delayed if all of them are outside the critical section. Let $c(s) = 1$. It follows from the Habermann relation that $np(s) \leqslant 1 + ns(s)$. Consequently, $np(s) - ns(s) = 1$, i.e. the number of processes which can be within their critical sections does not exceed 1. In the case of delayed processes, $nw(s) > 1 + ns(s)$ and, using the Habermann relation, $np(s) = ns(s)$. On the other hand, it is easy to see that $np(s) = ns(s)$ if there is no process within the critical section.

There have been proposals for many other formal systems for the identification of deadlocks and other standard situations occurring in asynchronous systems and processes. Reviews [56, 57] and some studies using Petri nets [44, 46, 47, 58, 59] can be selected from the bulky literature devoted to this problem.

Together with the development of structural methods for correctness checking, the transfer of formal methods of semantics description developed by the semantic theory of sequential programming to parallel programs was started in the 70s. This was done mostly by reducing parallel program semantics descriptions to those of sequential indeterminate programs. For example, Ashcroft and Manna [60] proposed a method for the reduction of parallel programs to equivalent indeterminate programs for which semantics formalization methods had already been developed [61]. Then, instead of proving the correctness of a given parallel program, one proves the correctness of the derived sequential program. The performance of this method was improved by some authors [62, 63], but further significant progress in this direction is unlikely.

The Hoare axiomatic method for semantic description [64], which he tried to extend to parallel programs [65], was developed by Owicki and Gries [66]. It will be recalled that in the Hoare method the expression $\{P\}S\{Q\}$ means that if proposition P about the current values of the variables is true prior to the execution of statement S, the proposition Q is true after the execution of S. In addition, A/B designates the inference rule: if A is true, B is true as well. Using these, Hoare has described a deductive system for the inference of statements about sequential programs. This system has, for example, the following axioms corresponding to statements of various types:

a) assignment: $\{P_E^x\}x:=E\{P\}$, where E is an expression (term), P_E^x is a proposition resulting from the substitution of E for any entry x in P;

b) conditional statement:

$$\frac{\{P\wedge B\}S_1\{Q\},\ \{P\wedge\neg B\}S_2\{Q\}}{\{P\}\ \text{if } B \text{ then } S_1 \text{ else } S_2\{Q\}},$$

where B is a conditional expression, S_1 and S_2 are statements;

c) loop:

$$\frac{\{P\wedge B\}S\{p\}}{\{P\}\ \text{while } B \text{ do } S\ P\wedge\neg B\}};$$

d) sequence of statements (compound statement):

$$\frac{\{P_1\}S_1\{P_2\}\ldots\{P_n\}S_n\{P_{n+1}\}}{\{P_1\}\ \text{begin } S_1;\ \ldots;\ S \text{ end } \{P_{n+1}\}}.$$

The sequential program R, constructed from the above statements is correct, if proposition $\{P\}R\{Q\}$ can be deduced from the Hoare axioms, where P and Q are propositions about the initial and final memory state.

Owicki and Gries consider parallel compound statements of the form

cobegin $S_1 \,\|\, S_2 \,\|\, \ldots \,\|\, S_n$ **coend**,

execution of which involves the asynchronous concurrent execution of its component statements. A parallel compound statement is terminated when all its component statements are terminated. Compound statements can form a hierarchy having at the lowest level assignment statements which are regarded as indivisible actions.

Concurrent statements are synchronized by an **await** statement

await B, **then** S,

where B is a conditional expression, and S does not involve another await statement or a parallel statement **cobegin**. When control tries to initiate statement S, condition B is checked and, if false, the execution of S is delayed until B becomes true, after which S is executed as an indivisible action. If there are several **await** statements, control waits until B becomes true and permits any one of them to execute its statement S, the rest continuing to wait. The computation of B is regarded as a part of the await statement.

The axioms which formally describe the semantics of these new statements are as follows:

e) **await** statement

$$\frac{\{P \wedge B\} S\{Q\}}{\{P\} \text{ await } B \text{ then } S\{Q\}},$$

f) parallel compound statement

$$\frac{\{P_1\} S_1\{Q_1\}, \ldots, \{P_n\} S_n\{Q_n\} \text{ are separated}}{\{P_1 \wedge \ldots \wedge P_n\} \text{ cobegin } S_1 \| \ldots \| S_n \text{ coend } \{Q_1 \wedge \ldots \wedge Q_n\}}.$$

The second axiom states that the result of the execution of any statement from $S_1, \ldots, S_n$ in the compound statement is the same as if it was executed in isolation, provided that the statements are separated. The latter means that either these statements have no variables in common through which they could influence each other's results, or that the common variables of statements S_i and S_j do not prevent propositions $\{P_i\} S_i\{Q_i\}$ and $\{P_j\} S_j\{Q_j\}$ from being invariant with respect to statement "interference" over these common variables. For example, proposition $Q_i: \{x \geq 0\}$ after S_i is true if S_j is an assignment statement $x := x + 1$.

In the course of the correction checking of parallel programs, Owicki and Gries add (or eliminate) special statements for assignment to separated auxiliary variables. These variables are used to store information about the program history or to mark currently executed fragments. The next axiom permits addition or elimination of assignments to auxiliary variables:

g) $$\frac{\{P\} S'\{Q\}}{\{P\} S\{Q\}},$$

where P and Q do not involve free auxiliary variables. Using the deductive Hoare system complemented by the above three axioms, Owicki and Gries have carried out illustrative proofs of some existing solutions of standard parallel programming problems.

Kahn [32] describes the mathematical semantics of a simple data-flow language using equations in the space of the queues of data circulating between statements. In the Kahn data-flow program, statements change some or all of their output queues depending on the input queues. Figure 17 shows an example of a data-flow

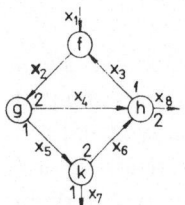

Fig. 17. Data-flow program and its related system of equations.

$x_2 = f(x_1, x_3)$; $x_5 = g_1(x_2)$; $x_4 = g_2(x_2)$; $x_7 = k_1(x_5)$;

$x_6 = k_2(x_5)$; $x_8 = h_2(x_4, x_6)$; $x_3 = h_1(x_4, x_6)$.

program on a graph whose arcs are queues of data. Functions of queue processing performed by statements satisfy the requirement that the set of all possible queues forms a lattice (with partial order $\sqsubseteq: X \sqsubseteq X'$, where X is a prefix of the sequence X'). A system of equations is constructed by a data-flow program as shown in Fig. 17. Because the queue space is a lattice (in the Scott sense), this system has a unique solution. Thus, the system describes the program structure without explicit recourse to such concepts as sets of possible computations, program execution states, etc. [54]. In the latter case, the length of the derivation of propositions about the program grows exponentially with the number of parallel processes, while in the equation method this growth is linear. It should, however, be noted that, in doing so, difficulties "accumulate" at the stage of the solution of the system of equations. Data-flow programs are the most general objects in the theory of the mathematical semantics of parallel programs. This is due to the fact that, organizationally, data-flow programs are closer to non-procedural (non-algorithmic) high-level languages. As they have no facilities for the control of shared resources and other "computer-oriented" objects, the formalization of their semantics is easier. The need for adequate methods for a strict description of the mathematical semantics of these objects is not, however, eliminated because, otherwise, one could not construct a "general" theory of parallel computations covering all the stages of parallel programming ranging from non-procedural, very high-level programs to the control of processes in a complicated hierarchical multicomponent system. In other words, "algebraic" methods for parallel computation description are required allowing, within the framework of a unique formalism, a convenient representation of a) indeterminancy, the "behavioural sub-definiteness" of parallel programs and processes involved, and b) rules for the construction of such systems from simpler units and subsystems. Among the publications stating or demonstrating the desire to pursue this approach, one should mention [33, 47, 49, 67, 68], but these are far from reaching their objectives.

Conclusion

This chapter concentrates on models oriented to structural studies of parallel computation. This seems natural, because studies of computational parallelism started with structural models. They have proved to be useful in establishing a number of fundamental facts which gave a better insight into the nature of parallel computations and the difficulties involved into their implementation. These models and the theory based on them are important especially today when practicable concepts and mechanisms for the organization of computation; which are to be embodied in future-generation highly-parallel computers and programming languages, are being explored. There is a number of approaches which have already been developed and substantiated by means of such models. Further progress in this area requires studies of more complex and variegated structures (e.g. a developed hierarchy of interacting processes) and the use of deep semantic aspects of programming.

To deal with mathematical difficulties which are bounded to occur, a conceptually simple mathematical basis is required for parallel computation theory, expecting a more active study of the problems of the semantics of computational parallelism. On the other hand, due to the stimulating influence of the growing use of parallel computation and the need to develop the architectural concepts of new generations of computers the results of the formal theory of parallel computations will be applied more often. Experimental systems and languages should soon appear, based on the above models.

REFERENCES

[1] BAER, J. L.: A survey of some theoretical aspects of multiprocessing. ACM Comp. Surveys, 5, 1973, 1, 31—80.

[2] KOTOV, V. E.: Teoriya parallelnogo programmirovaniya. Prekladnye aspekty. Kibernetika, 1974, 1, 1—16; 2, 1—18.

[3] NARINYANI, A. S.: Teoriya parallelnogo programmirovaniya. Formalnye modeli. Kibernetika, 1974, 3, 1—16; 5, 1—14.

[4] KUCK, D. J.: A survey of parallel machine organization and programming. ACM Comp. Surveys, 9, 1977, 1, 29—59.

[5] YANOV, YU. I.: O logicheskikh skhemakh algoritmov. In:Problemy kibernetiki. Vol. 1. Fizmatgiz, Moscow, 1958, pp. 78—127.

[6] LUCKHAM, D. C., PARK, D. M. R. and PETERSON, M. S.: On computer programs. J. Comp. Syst. Sci., 4, 1970, 3, 220—249.

[7] LETICHEVSKII, A. A.: Funktsionalnaya ekvivalentnost diskretnykh preobrazovatelei. Kibernetika, 1969, 2, 5—15; 1970, 2, 14—28.

[8] KARP, R. M. and MILLER, R. E.: Parallel program schemata. J. Comp. Syst. Sci., 3, 1969, 2, 147—195.

[9] ESTRIN, G., BUSSELL, B., TURN, R. and BIBB, J.: Parallel processing in a restructurable computer system. IEEE Trans. on Electronic Computers, EC-12, 1963, 6, 747—755.

[10] DENNING, P. J.: On the determinancy of schemata. In: Record of the Project MAC Conf. on Concurrent Systems and Parallel Computations. Woods Holl, Mass., New York, 1970, pp. 143—147.

[11] KOTOV, V. E. and NARINYANI, A. S.: Asinkhronnye vychislitelnye protsessy nad pamyatyu. Kibernetika, 1966, 3, 64—71.

[12] KOTOV, V. E. and NARINYANI, A. S.: On transformation of sequential programs into asynchronous parallel programs. Proc. IFIP Congress 68, Edinburgh 1968. North-Holland Publ. Co., Amsterdam, 1969, pp. 351—357.

[13] NARINYANI, A. S.: Asinkhronnye vychislitelnye protsessy nad pamyatyu. Dissertation. Novosibirsk, 1970.

[14] KOTOV, V. E.: Preobrazovanie operatornykh skhem v asinkhronnye programmy. Dissertation. Novosibirsk, 1970.

[15] VALKOVSKII, V. A. and KOTOV, V. E.: Automatic construction of parallel programs. In this book.

[16] LOGRIPPO, L.: On maximally parallel program schemes. Tech. Report 77-06. Dep. Comp. Sci., University of Ottawa, 1977.

[17] VALKOVSKII, V. A.: Ob odnom algoritme desekventsii. Kibernetika, 1974, 2, 77—88.

[18] KELLER, R. M.: Parallel program schemata and maximal parallelism. I. Fundamental results. J. ACM, 20, 1973, 3, 514—537.

[19] ITKIN, V. E. and ZWINOGRODZKI, Z.: On program schemata equivalence. J. Comp. Syst. Sci., 6, 1972, 1, 88—101.

[20] MILLER, R. E.: Some undecidability results for parallel program schemata. SIAM J. Computing, 1, 1972, 1, 119—129.

[21] SLUTZ, D. R.: Flow graph schemata. In: Record of the Project MAC Conf. on Concurrent Systems and Parallel Computations. Woods Holl, Mass., New York, 1970, pp. 129—141.

[22] LOGRIPPO, L.: Renamings and economy of memory in program schemata. J. ACM, 25, 1978, 1, 10—22.

[23] KARP, R. M. and MILLER, R. E.: Properties of a model for parallel computations: Determinancy, terminations, queueing. SIAM J. Appl. Math., 14, 1966, 1390—1411.

[24] REITER, R.: Scheduling parallel computations. J. ACM, 15, 1968, 4, 590—599.

[25] ADAMS, D. A.: A computation model with data flow sequencing. Tech. Report CS-117, Dep. Comp. Sci., Stanford Univ., 1968.

[26] RODRIGUEZ, J. E.: A graph model for parallel computations. Ph. D. Thesis. Massachusetts Institute of Technology, Cambridge, Mass., 1967.

[27] DENNIS, B., FOSSIN, B. and LINDERMAN, J. P.: Skhemy potoka dannykh. In: Teoriya programmirovaniya. VC SO AN SSSR, Novosibirsk, 1972, part 2, pp. 7—43.

[28] DENNIS, J. B.: Programming generality, parallelism and computer architecture. Proc. IFIP Congress 68, Edinburgh 1968. North-Holland Publ. Co., Amsterdam, 1969, pp. 484—492.

[29] BERS, A. A.: Operatornye struktury. In: Teoriya programmirovaniya. VC SO AN SSSR, Novosibirsk, 1972, part 2, pp. 44—82.

[30] DAVIS, A. L.: DNN's — a maximally concurrent procedural parallel process representation. Tech. Report, Dep. Comp. Sci., Univ. of Utah, Salt Lake City, 1977.

[31] DAVIS, A. L.: The architecture of DDM1: A recursively structures data-driven machine. Tech. Report. Dep. Comp. Sci., Univ. of Utah, Salt Lake City, 1977.

[32] KAHN, G.: The semantics of a simple language for parallel programming. In: Proc. IFIP Congress 1974. North-Holland Publ. Co., Amsterdam, 1974, pp. 472—475.

[33] MAZURKIEWICZ, A.: Invariants of concurrent programs. In: Proc. IFIP-INFOPOL Conf. on Inform. Processing. North-Holland Publ. Co., Amsterdam, 1977, pp. 353—372.

[34] ESTRIN, G. and TURN, R.: Automatic assignment of computations in a variable structure computer system. IEEE Trans. on Electronic Computers, EC-12, 1963, 6, 755—773.

[35] MARTIN, D. and ESTRIN, G.: Path length computations on graph models of computations. IEEE Trans. on Computers, C-18, 1969, 6, 530—536.

[36] BAER, J. L. E. and ESTRIN, G.: Bounds for maximum parallelism in a bilogic graph model of computations. IEEE Trans. on Electronic Computers, C-18, 1969, 11, 1012—1014.

[37] PETRI, C. A.: Kommunikation mit Automaten. Ph. D. Thesis. University of Bonn, 1962.

[38] HOLT, A. W. and COMMONER, F.: Events and conditions. In: Record of the Project MAC Conf. on Concurrent Systems and Parallel Computation. Woods Holl, Mass., New York, 1970, pp. 3—52.

[39] PETERSON, J. L.: Petri nets. ACM Comp. Surveys, 9, 1977, 3, 223—252.

[40] HACK, M.: Decision problems for Petri nets and vector addition systems. Tech. Memo 59, Project MAC. MIT, Cambridge, 1975.

[41] SACERDOTE, G. S. and TENNEY, R. L.: The decidability of the reachability problem for vector addition systems. COINS Tech. Report 77-3. Univ. of Massachusetts, 1977.

[42] PATIL, S. S.: Circuit implementation of Petri nets. Project MAC. MIT, Cambridge, 1972.

[43] DIJKSTRA, E. W.: Solution of a problem in concurrent programming control. Comm. ACM, 8, 1965, 9, 569.

[44] TOURLAKIS, G.: Petri nets. In: Topics in Operating Systems Revisited. Tech. Report. Dep. Comp. Sci., Univ. of Toronto, 1971.

[45] PATIL, S. S.: Limitations and capabilities of Dijkstra's semaphore primitives for coordination among processes. Project MAC. MIT, Cambridge, 1971.

[46] CAMPBELL, R. H. and HABERMANN, A. H.: The specification of process synchronization by path expressions. In: Lecture Notes in Computer Science, Vol. 16. Springer-Verlag, Berlin, 1974.

[47] LAUER, P. M. and CAMPBELL, R. H.: Formal semantics for a class of high-level primitives coordinating concurrent processes. Acta Informatica, 1975, 5, 297—332.

[48] KOTOV, V. E.: Concurrent programming with control types. In: Constructing Quality Software. North-Holland Publ. Co., Amsterdam, 1978, pp. 207—208.

[49] KOTOV, V. E.: An algebra for parallelism based on Petri nets. In: Lecture Notes in Computer Science, Vol. 64. Springer-Verlag, Berlin, 1978, pp. 39—55.

[50] HACK, M.: Petri net languages. Tech. Report 59, MIT Laboratory Comp. Sci., Boston, 1976.

[51] KELLER, R. M.: Generalized Petri nets as models for system verification. Tech. Report 202, Dep. Electr. Eng., Princeton Univ., 1975.

[52] COURTOIS, P. J., HEYMANS, F. and PARNAS, D. L.: Concurrent control with readers and writers. Comm. ACM, 14, 1971, 10, 667—668.

[53] WODEN, P. L.: Still another tool for synchronizing cooperating processes. AD 750538, Carnegie-Mellon Univ., Pittsburgh, 1972.

[54] GILBERT, P. and CHANDLER, W. J.: Interference between communicating parallel processes. Comm. ACM, 15, 1972, 6, 427—437.

[55] HABERMANN, A. N.: Synchronization of communicating processes. Comm. ACM, 15, 1972, 3, 171—175.

[56] COFFMAN, F. G., ELPHICK, M. J. and SHOSHANI, A.: System deadlocks. ACM Comp. Surveys, 3, 1971, 2, 67—78.

[57] HOLT, R. C.: Some deadlock properties of computer systems. ACM Comp. Surveys, 4, 1972, 3, 179—196.

[58] DENNIS, J. B.: Concurrency in software systems. In: Advanced Source in Software Engineering. Springer-Verlag, Berlin, 1973, pp. 111—127.

[59] LAUTENBACH, K. and SCHMID, H. A.: Use of Petri nets for proving correctness of concurrent process systems. In: Proc. IFIP Congress 74. North-Holland Publ. Co., Amsterdam, 1974, pp. 181—191.

[60] ASHCROFT, E. and MANNA, Z.: Formalization of properties of parallel programs. Machine Intelligence, 6, 1971, 17—41.

[61] MANNA, Z.: The corectness of non-deterministic programs. In: Artificial Intelligence, 1, 1970, 1—26.

[62] CADIOU, J. M. and LEVY, J. J.: Mechanizable proofs about parallel processes. Proc. 14th Annual IEEE Symp. on Switching and Automata Theory, 1973, pp. 34—48.

[63] ROSEN, B. K.: Corectness of parallel programs: The Church-Rosser approach. Theor. Comp. Sci., 2, 1976, 183—207.

[64] HOARE, C. A. R.: An axiomatic basis for computing programming. Comm. ACM, 12, 1969, 576—580.

[65] HOARE, C. A. R.: Towards a theory of parallel programming. In: Operating Systems Techniques. Academic Press, New York, 1972, pp. 220—230.

[66] OWICKI, S. and GRIES, D.: An axiomatic proof technique for parallel programs. I. Acta Informatica, 6, 1976, 319—340.

[67] WINKOWSKI, J.: An algebraic characterization of the behavior of non-sequential systems. Inf. Processing Lett., 6, 1977, 4, 105—109.

[68] MILNER, R.: Synthesis of communicating behavior. In: Lecture Notes in Computer Science, Vol. 64. Springer-Verlag, Berlin, 1978, pp. 71—83.

Chapter 5

ON PARALLEL LANGUAGES

The improvement of mechanisms for program representation of parallelism was, and still is, the central problem of parallel programming. In practice, this consists of two different problems:
— the development of methods for describing parallelism in programs modelling complex discrete systems and processes;
— the development of methods for the organization of computations on parallel multiprocessing computers.
More specifically, the problem lies in the development of parallel programming languages containing facilities for the description of task parallelism and/or the definition of computational parallelism. Both problems have many traits in common from the point of view of the basic principles underlying the mechanism of parallel structure organization. Basically, the differences between them can be reduced to the differences between high- and low-level languages.

5.1 Parallelism in programs and computations

The discussion of problems associated with parallelism in programming requires a more precise definition of this concept, the separation of its abstract and concrete forms at various stages of programming, and at various levels of the program hierarchy.

Difficulties arise from the very beginning: how to define the concepts of parallel computation (processes, statements, operations, etc.). The definitions introducing real or conditional time and leading to ideas such as "concurrent processes" or "processes that can be concurrent", lead to difficulties and ambiguities unless one considers trivial examples (e.g. a pair of processes which do not interact at all). The fact that formal theoretical definitions of parallelism based on time relations are complicated reflects these difficulties. There is another, wider possibility for defining parallelism: fragments or processes are referred to as parallel, if they are (or can be) implemented by different separate physical or virtual units. One can fully avoid the necessity of defining the parallelism relation and, instead, define the dependence relation of fragments or processes. This approach complements the above ones, and it can be characterized as "parallelism presumption": all the program fragments and actions are regarded as initially independent, i.e. parallel;

144

dependence relations are imposed on them as necessary constraints, these relations being generally dynamic.

We cannot dwell here in more detail on the definition of parallel processes, but it should be pointed out that a more precise definition of the fundamental concepts related to program parallelism is most important, because the lack of a unique basis

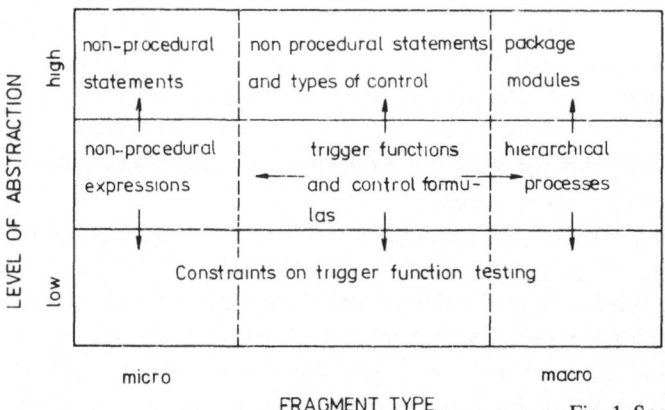

FRAGMENT TYPE

Fig. 1. Space of program control structures.

for the treatment of parallelism results (both in theory and practice) in confusion when analysing the capabilities, advantages, and disadvantages of various methods for parallelization and synchronization of parallel processes.

Thus, difficulties in classification and standardization of methods for the representation of parallel structures and processes arise already at the level of abstract parallelism. The diversity of the forms of parallelism grows significantly when one consider its practical implementation, given by the complexity of contemporary software and computer architecture. This is due to the basic complexity and variety of programs and systems, and to the excessive number of criteria for the classification of parallel structures. We confine ourselves to a simple intuitive diagram (Fig. 1) by means of which we try to identify some standard situations from among the variety of parallel structures. The diagram is a two-dimensional "space of program structures". There are two factors that influence the character of the structures, the level of abstraction (programming language) and the relative complexity of the fragments from which the structure is constructed. The level of abstraction increases upwards, and the relative complexi-ty increases from left to right. From empirical considerations, three stages were chosen for each factor, i.e. (1) low, intermediate and high levels of abstractions, and (2) micro, basic, and macro levels of fragment complexity. The high-level structures are oriented to the adequate description of problem structures, and the lower level structures are oriented to the most effective description of computations for a given system. Expression in ALGOL-like languages can exemplify microstructures; statements are basic fragments, subprograms, modules, etc. are macrofragments.

This classification makes it possible to discriminate up to nine areas in the structure space. Each of these areas is characterized by an intrinsic form of computational parallelism. For this reason special program facilities for the representation of each of these forms of parallelism are necessary. Recently, the development of parallel and structured programming has stimulated active research and the development of control structures in programming languages. However, if one traces the introduction of parallelism into programming languages up to the present time, one can see that the development of parallel control structures proceeds from the periphery of Fig. 1 to its centre. Indeed, the development from above is characteristic of non-algorithmic (non-procedural) programming methods in very high level languages, rejecting the concept of sequential parallelism in favour of problem models that are, essentially, parallel structures. From below, parallelism is developed in computer architectures beginning with concurrent operation of peripheral units and the central processor through parallel processors to microprogramming. From the right, multiprogramming is developed to take advantage of the underlying parallelism of interacting sequential processes; from the left vector, matrix pipeline and other methods are developed for the parallel processing of regular data structures.

5.2 Parallelism of interacting processes

Program facilities for the description of parallelism on the right-hand side of Fig. 1 have first appeared within the framework of the sequential-parallel approach. Facilities for explicit separation of parallel segments (branches) were added to the sequential basis of FORTRAN- and ALGOL-like languages. The segment beginning (i.e. the point of branching) and the segment end (i.e. the point of branch convergence) are indicated. During the execution of parallel-sequential programs control moves successively along the program "block diagram", splitting at the beginning of a parallel segment into as many independent copies as there are branches in the segment. At the end of the segment the control merges. In their turn, parallel segment branches can include parallel segments. In this simple form, the parallel branch concept was embodied in such constructs as **FORK—JOIN, SPLIT—ASSEMBLE, START—HALT, DO TOGETHER—HOLD, PARBEGIN—PAREND, COBEGIN—COEND,** etc. [1—7], where the segment is opened by the first primitive and closed by the second one. The hierarchy of parallel segments is "well structured", any segment can only be terminated after the termination of all its branches. To relax the last requirement, special constructs are introduced allowing the branch to terminate before it is completed [4, 5].

The above facilities are insufficient both for the description of the natural parallelism of interacting processes in tasks and for the definition of parallel computations in real environments with limited resources. Indeed, the nature of the structure of parallel segments requires with respect to control a corresponding structure, i.e. parallel branches should in general not access the same memory areas and shared resources. To overcome these limitations, parallel branch synchronization facilities are introduced which implement branch interactions by allowing access to shared resources. In doing so, branches themselves assume the nature of a more closely integrated construct (like a block in ALGOL 60) and are usually referred to as processes. A process has shared resources and "private" resources (e.g. local memory) that are inaccessible to other processes. Since a process is a sequentially parallel program fragment, a "critical section" can be isolated, in which shared resources are used. Dijkstra [7, 8], Dennis and Van Horn [5], Anderson [3] and Wirth [6] were the first to start a systematic study of the synchronization of processes executing their critical sections. The requirements below were found to be necessary for the correct organization of the interaction of processes that mutually exlude each other in critical sections:

(1) one process at most can be in its critical section;

(2) a process delay outside its critical section does not influence other processes;

(3) each process desiring to enter its critical section will, sooner or later, be given permission to do so.

Dijkstra [7] proposed a semaphore process synchronization mechanism that has won general recognition. For example, it is employed in the general-purpose programming language ALGOL 68 [9] and is implemented in hardware in existing computers. Semaphores are special variables assuming non-negative integer values only, over which only two operations P and V are defined. For the semaphore s, the operation V is equivalent to $s := s + 1$, and the operation P is equivalent to l: **if** $s > 0$, **then** $s := s - 1$ **else go to** l.

Operations P and V are regarded as indivisible, i.e. at any instant only one such operation can be executed. Semaphores are extensively used for process control in operating systems. Many typical synchronization problems stemming from complex process interactions were solved in terms of semaphores [6—8, 10—12]. This can be exemplified by the well-known problem of readers and writers [11], where several processes called "writers" place records in the buffer that are read by processes called "readers". Access to the buffer is permitted simultaneously to any number of readers and to a single writer only. Moreover, writers have priority over readers. Figure 2 shows a correct interactive organization of these processes by means of semaphores as proposed in [11], where an ALGOL-like notation complemented by semaphores is used.

The semaphore mechanism permits arbitrary process interactions. (The "limitation" of semaphores [13] is caused by special requirements, namely by the

```
                    integer readcount, writecount;
                    semaphore mutex1, mutex2, mutex3, w, r;
                    readcount = writecount = 0;
                    mutex1 = mutex2 = mutex3 = w = r = 1;

reader:                                 writer:
begin P(mutex3);                        begin P(mutex2);
P(r);                                   writecount := writecount + 1;
P(mutex1);                              if writecount = 1 then P(r);
readcount := readcount + 1;             V(mutex2);
if readcount = 1 then P(w);             P(w);
V(mutex1);                              write;
V(r);                                   V(w);
V(mutex3);                              P(mutex2);
read;                                   writecount := writecount - 1;
P(mutex1);                              if writecount = 0 then V(r);
readcount := readcount - 1;             V(mutex2)
if readcount = 0 then V(w);             end
V(mutex1)
end
```

Fig. 2. Solution to the "readers-writers" problem using semaphores.

prohibition of the use of semaphores together with conditional statements.) A "nonreliability" of semaphores, however, is generally recognized to be a disadvantage: an uncontrolled application of semaphores confuses the control structure of a parallel program, and there is a high probability of errors in descriptions of complicated interactions (see Fig. 2). Great attention has been paid in the last few years to programming technique. In particular, Dijkstra himself has developed a concept of structured programming. Semaphores do not provide for structured parallel programs simultaneously. In this connection, attempts to increase the level of synchronizing primitives and to obtain structured parallel programs were made almost immediately after the advent of semaphores. In the majority of cases, it is a question of "tying" synchronization facilities to other program objects (the semaphore, in this sense, is independent). This allows the application of implicit, latent synchronization mechanisms that are (or can be) implemented through semaphores. In the Hoare mechanism of conditional critical sections [14], shared resources through which interaction should be organized, are the object of tying. Hansen [12] has built the mechanism into PASCAL and illustrated it through the "writers-readers" problem.

In this approach, shared resources are represented by variables which are explicitly described as shared variables, i.e. in terms of PASCAL

var v: **shared** T.

The process can use shared variables only inside the structured statement called the conditional critical section:

region v **when** B **do** S,

where B is a conditional expression, and S is a statement.

The process enters the critical section (this can be done by one process only) and computes B. If its value is **true,** the process proceeds with the execution of statement S. Otherwise the process leaves the critical section and is delayed until another process terminates the operation in its critical section. Then, the delayed process can reenter the critical section and compute B. The loop will be repeated until B becomes **true** and S can be executed. If B is always **true,** the critical section is as follows: **region** v **do** S. Note that the use of shared variables outside the critical section can be observed at the syntactic level. Statement:

region v **do** S **await** B

is introduced as a "symmetrical" construct. It delays the process after the execution of S until B becomes **true.**

Figure 3 demonstrates Hansen's solution [12] of the "readers-writers" problem

```
var v, w: shared record rr, aw: integer end;
reader:  begin
             region v when aw = 0 do rr : = rr + 1
             reading;
             region v do rr : = rr − 1
         end;

writer:  begin
             region v do aw : = aw + 1 await rr = 0;
             region w do writing;
             region v do aw : = aw − 1
         end
```

Fig. 3. Solution to the "readers-writers" problem using conditional critical sections.

in terms of extended PASCAL. The variable rr is the number of "operating" readers and aw is the number of active writers.

A process is referred to as "active" from the instant it requests a shared resource until it releases it; the process is referred to as "operating" from the instant it obtains a resource until it releases it.

Hansen's solution of the "readers-writers" problem is much more compact and transparent than that using semaphores, but it is not completely correct because, as noted in [16], it does not exclude the case where some writer will be blocked by readers which have occupied the buffer and do not allow the writer to write into it. This imperfection has demonstrated that the mechanism of critical sections has limitations. This is due to the fact that, although the level of synchronization primitives was raised and they were tied to shared resources, accesses to resources were distributed all over the program. Process interaction control was therefore, distributed and decentralized, leading to "oversights" in those parts of the control algorithm which, essentially, required the intervention of a supervisor. A similar case was observed by Dijkstra [10] in his problem of the five dining philosophers, one of whom may be starved to death by both his neighbours preventing him from obtaining the two forks required to eat spaghetti. As a result, the following was proposed by Dijkstra: instead of organizing the decentralized interaction of n processes with their critical sections, the sections should be combined into the $(n + 1)$-th process which is called "secretary" and which assumes responsibility for process interactions. Such a structure of processes might be generalized to several hierarchical levels.

The concept of process-secretary was developed and implemented in a number of program synchronization mechanisms including Hoare and Hansen's monitor [17—19], Keller's sentinel [20], Campbell and Habermann's path expressions [21, 22]. Further, it is noted below when discussing asynchronous computations that the concept of a centralized process controlling the interaction of parallel processes had been developed before Dijkstra in asynchronous processes over shared memory.

The next step in increasing the level of synchronization primitives, tying them to data and centralizing the control of parallel processes is represented by a monitor [17—19], which is a set of control variables, related to some shared resources, and procedures which request and release resources. The monitor extracts from processes all of their critical sections related to given resources and transforms them into monitor procedures which are called by stating the procedure and monitor names. They are accessible to all processes in the sense that any process can try to call any procedure, but only one process can enter the procedure, the rest of them having to wait until this call is terminated. Monitor procedures can have variables local to the monitor body. This constraint prevent errors occurring with semaphores.

To allow the delay of a process calling a given procedure until an occupied resource is released and to provide information about the release of a process control, a new type of variable, "condition" is introduced. This variable is only used inside monitor procedures, with operations **wait** and **signal** which follow the identifier of the variable and are separated from it by a fullstop: "**cond. wait**", "**cond. signal**". For each event that can lead to a process delay, a variable is declared belonging to the condition type. It has no stored values, and it is only a queue of processes waiting to fulfill a given condition.

Figure 4 presents an example of a simple monitor allocating a single resource to an arbitrary number of processes calling monitor procedures in order to obtain or to free the resources. The monitor text is written in PASCAL syntax; in particular, the identifier of a variable being described and the monitor name precede the type designator and are separated from it by a colon. The variable "busy" indicates whether the resource is occupied or free. An attempt to call a busy resource causes a process delay by means of a "non-busy" variable.

A special type of sequential process is represented by the sentinel [20] which communicates with other processes through their tagged statements. These are conventional statements accompanied by a tag indicating the sentinel's queue and, possibly, some parameters, too. The sentinel coordinates processes by determining

```
resource: monitor
begin busy: Boolean;
   non-busy: condition;
   procedure acquire;
      begin if busy then non-busy.wait;
         busy : = true
      end;
   procedure release;
      begin busy : = false;
         non-busy.signal
      end;
   busy : = false
end
```

Fig. 4. Example of simple monitor.

when the execution of tagged statements is allowed. The sentinel syntax is based on that of a conventional procedure. All procedures are regarded as reentrant, the parallel versions of the sentinel operating with their own local variables. The statement

detach ⟨statement⟩

creates a process which leads to a subsequent execution of the statement. This process is concurrent with the execution of the process containing the "**detach**" statement. As a special case, a process sentinel can be generated together with the names of the sentinel queues:

detach ⟨sentinel call⟩ **queues** (⟨list of queues⟩).

The queue related to a sentinel contains statements to be executed. A statement enters the queue, if it is tagged and if the tag refers to this queue:

queues (⟨queue⟩ ⟨list of parameters⟩) ⟨statement⟩.

The sentinel controlling the statement decides whether it is executable by means of the executing statement

execute ⟨queue⟩.

The statement whose execution is permitted is eliminated from the queue. The sentinel body is a sequential program which, just like the statements described above and ordinary ALGOL-like statements, uses statements and expressions:

wait until   ⟨conditional expression⟩
empty   (⟨queue⟩)
non-empty (⟨queue⟩)

meaning of which is clarified by key words. The addition of **count**(n) after a process generation statement causes the following changes in the value of the integer variable n: the value of n is incremented by 1 when a process is initiated and decreased by 1 when it is terminated.

Figure 5 shows a sentinel solution to the "readers-writers" problem, as proposed by Keller [20]. The sentinel is generated by the statement:

detach call readers-writers **queues** (read: write).

Reading and writing into the shared buffer are tagged as follows:

queue (R) for readers,
queue (W) for writers.

```
procedure readers-writers queues (R, W);
begin integer readers;
   readers : = 0;
   loop
      wait until non-empty (R) V non-empty (W);
      if non-empty (W) then
         begin wait until readers = 0; execute W end
      else
         detach execute R count (readers);
   pool
end readers-writers;
```

Fig. 5. Sentinel coordinating processes in the "readers-writers" problem.

As can be seen from the sentinel design, its aim is to eliminate the numerous drawback of the synchronization mechanisms described above. For instance, it has explicit queues, which are missing in the definitions of semaphores and conditional critical sections. Like the monitor, also the sentinel centralizes control, but, in contrast to the monitor, it does not define the synchronization discipline or conceal the implementation mechanism, and it allows the programmer to describe them explicitly in the sentinel body. Such an approach gives the programmer more freedom and, at the same time, frees him from such habitual constructs as procedures. It is easy to compose a standard sentinel library. The mechanism of dynamically generating sentinels does not present a problem. The sentinel's drawback, in our view, is the lack of a clear conceptual basis that would enable one to disengage oneself from programming details and study the process control structure through the sentinel syntax. The path expressions of Campbell and Habermann are very useful in this context.

Path expressions [21, 22] are expressions in a special language describing the structure of the parallel program control. They consist of the names of actions and of special control operations. Actions are procedures generating processes. Path expressions are completely isolated from procedure descriptions. This ap-

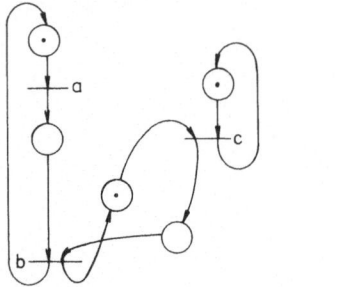

begin
process a ; b **end**
process c **end**
path c ; b **end**
$a: y: = f(x)$,
$b: x: = x - y/z$
$c: z: = f'(x)$
end

Fig. 6. Program with path expressions.

proach embodies the concept of an explicit separation of the control and processing parts of programs, which was suggested by V. M. Glushkov [23] and used to advantage in theoretical studies. Control operations generate sequences of actions (operation ";"), indeterminate selections (operation ","), cyclic repetitions of actions (brackets "**path** ... **end**"); there are facilities for the organization of accesses from various processes to the same procedures. An example of a program solving an equation by means of the Newton technique is shown in Fig. 6. As the computations of $f(x)$ and $f'(x)$ can be separated, there are two interacting concurrent processes. The first part of the program contains all controls written in the form of path expressions; the second part describes actions denoted by label. The structure and dynamics of the control are depicted graphically by a Petri net. The bars denote the net transitions, and the circles denote places containing tokens. A transition corresponds to an action; it fires if each of its input places (i.e. the places from which the arcs lead to it) contain at least one token. When a transition fires, it takes a token from each of its input places and adds a token to each of its output places, i.e. the places to which arcs go from the transition.

The concept of separation of the control part of parallel programs from their processing parts is supported by numerous publications, such as [24—27]. On the whole, the history of methods and facilities for the organization of interactions of sequentially parallel processes can be summed up as follows:

— synchronization primitives explicitly distributed between processes with simple fixed discipline (semaphores with operations P and V, events in PL/1);

— implicitly tied to shared resources distributed primitives, implicitly tied to shared resources, with additional arbitrary constraints (conditional critical sections);

— a hierarchy of subordinate and control processes;

— special partially centralized control processes tied to shared resources and controlling interactions of the processes (monitors);

— the same processes not associated with particular resources (sentinels);

— the isolation of control into an independent program level performing all the control functions, including the coordination of process interactions. This is programmed in a special language of path expressions.

The control mechanisms discussed in this section are designed for the implementation of structures and processes on the right-hand side of the space shown in Fig. 1. Many of them have been implemented in languages in common use. As there are no similar special, universally adopted mechanisms (see Sec. 4) in the middle part of this space (the assignment statement level), and as the need for such mechanisms increases, attempts are being made to extend the sequentially parallel organization of computations to the left, at least over the middle part of the structure space.

The Hoare proposal for communicating sequential processes [28] and the method of parallel branches used in uniform computer systems [29] serve as examples.

In trying to find simple solutions to the problem of structured communication between processes, Hoare introduces statements for I/O data which take over the organization of synchronized exchanges. In various processors, I/O statements from the following pairs:

$\langle$ input command $\rangle := \langle$ source $\rangle ? \langle$ variable $\rangle$

$\langle$ output command $\rangle := \langle$ destination $\rangle ! \langle$ expression $\rangle$

Source and destination are name-label of commands (statements). A pair of corresponding input and output commands form something like two halves of a split assignment statement: the value of the expression computed in the input part is assigned to the variable in the output command. If necessary, the input command is delayed until a corresponding destination is ready. Thus, the input and output commands are the main facility for a communication between the concurrent sequential processes; they also are the main facility for process synchronization. An additional synchronization is provided by what Dijkstra calls "guards" [30], i.e. statement initiation conditions which are semantically close to conditional critical sections [14, 15] or trigger functions [31].

Other objectives are pursued by the method of parallel branches used for the organization of computations in homogeneous parallel systems described in Chapter 7. This approach in essence, unites facilities for the organization of the asynchronous interaction of sequentially parallel branches — processes with some control statements characteristic of the programming of synchronous parallelism of operations over data structures. This unification is due to the desire to implement various forms of parallelism inherent in various parts of the space in Fig. 1 within the framework of a uniform system concept and, correspondingly, within the framework of a unique language for these systems. This issue is discussed below in more detail in Sections 4 and 5.

5.3 Languages for matrix and vector computers

In the previous section we discussed the development of program facilities for the control of parallel computations from the right-hand side of Fig. 1. These facilities were implemented in multiprogramming systems, and in programming languages for computer systems with a few powerful processors. As for the left-hand side of the parallel structure space, the advent of "microparallelism" has stimulated the development of computers with parallel (vector, matrix, associative) processors.

Examples of this type of computer are the STAR-100 [30], ASC Texas Instrument [33] and CRAY-1 [34] computers featuring the pipeline processing of data, the matrix computer ILLIAC-IV [35], the associative systems PEPE [36] and STARAN [37], etc. All these computers are oriented to parallel processing of data structures, such as vectors and matrices. At present, this level makes use mostly of synchronous, sequentially parallel computations. Since in traditional algorithmic programming languages complex data structures are processed by means of loops, the loop statements have been extended in the majority of existing parallel languages for computers with parallel processors. Moreover, special facilities became necessary for the control of memory data alignment, providing data delivery to the parallel processor at a maximum rate, and for the transformation of data structures. Gosden [38] has introduced program primitives for the description of a **PARALLEL FOR** statement which is a parallel modification of the ALGOL statement **for**. During the execution of the statement

PARALLEL FOR $I = K$, L, M **DO** S

a sequential loop is generated listing the values of the parameter I from K to L with step M, each new value generating branch S_J by copying S and substituting J for parameter I.

The majority of practical languages for parallel-processor computers are FORTRAN-based, because matrix and vector computers are oriented to applications where FORTRAN is habitual and where a stock of algorithms has already been built up. Moreover, a FORTRAN-based system is better adaptable to particular computer configurations than other algorithmic high-level languages.

For example, the language IVTRAN [39] — an extension of FORTRAN — has been designed for the ILLIAC IV computer. It is worthy of mention that the ILLIAC IV consists of 64 identical processing elements controlled by a single controller. During a clock period of synchronous computations, all the elements (except masked ones) perform the same instruction.

Statement **DO** k **FOR ALL** $(i_1, ..., i_n)/S$ in IVTRAN defines a "parallel loop", where k indicates the label of the last statement in the "loop" body, and i is an integer index variable referred to as the control index. The control multiple-index $(i_1, ..., i_n)$ and the logic array S of the same dimension n define the so-called index set. The body of the statement **DO FOR ALL** is executed for indices from this array, each of the indices indicating in assignment statements those elements of the n-dimensional array for which computations and assignments can be done in parallel. Let, for example, $A(I, J, K)$ be an array of dimensions $3 \times 7 \times 10$. The following fragment recomputes each element of A so that it becomes equal to the square root of its absolute value:

DO 1 **FOR ALL** $(I, J, K)/[1...3].C.[1...7].C.[1...10]$
IF$(A(I, J, K).LT.0.0)$ $A(I, J, K) = -A(I, J, K)$
1 $A(I, J, K) = SQRT(A(I, J, K)),$

where .C. is the Cartesian product.

IVTRAN also has facilities for mapping array structures into memory, and statements replacing the EQUIVALENCE statement for arrays of different structure.

A vector version of the language LRLTRAN [40] for the STAR-100 computer contains facilities for the description of various vectors including compressed vectors, bit vectors for the control of result allocation in memory, dynamic vectors, etc. The language features a rich set of operations and functions over vectors including format transformations and vector generation, unary functions with vector arguments and scalar results, and binary component-by-component operations.

The languages ASC FORTRAN [41] for the pipeline computer ASC Texas Instrument and CFD [42] for ILLIAC IV are also modifications of FORTRAN, while STARAN [43], designed for the associative STARAN system, is closer to PL/1.

As noted before, all these modifications allow for the features of the hardware systems for which they are designed. The programmer should be well aware of the specific features of the systems and the tasks they execute, in order to attain that high computation speed for which these "giants" were designed. In doing so, the effectiveness of programming has diminished because of the return, in a sense, to "manual programming". Attempts to improve the level of programming languages for vector and matrix computers can be found in TRANQUIL [44], an algorithmic high-level language for ILLIAC IV based on ALGOL 60. Sets have been introduced into it along with conventional variables and arrays. Since array allocation on memory units is of prime importance for speed enhancement in matrix and vector computers, a function mapping a given structure onto the memory can be assigned to each description. A two-dimensional array, $A[0:3, 0:3]$, is located in 4 memory units, as shown in Fig. 7a, if its description refers to the mapping function STRAIGHT. Since the data retrieval within a memory unit is sequential, the

a) Direct allocation of 4×4 matrix				b) Skewed allocation of 4×4 matrix			
0	1	2	3	0	1	2	3
a_{00}	a_{01}	a_{02}	a_{03}	a_{00}	a_{01}	a_{02}	a_{03}
a_{10}	a_{11}	a_{12}	a_{13}	a_{13}	a_{10}	a_{11}	a_{12}
a_{20}	a_{21}	a_{22}	a_{23}	a_{22}	a_{23}	a_{20}	a_{21}
a_{30}	a_{31}	a_{32}	a_{33}	a_{31}	a_{32}	a_{33}	a_{30}

Fig. 7. Versions of matrix allocation in parallel access memory.

retrieval of columns is n times slower than that of rows. If the description refers to the mapping function SKEWED, the data will be allocated as shown in Fig. 7b, and the access times for rows and columns will be "balanced". (Parallel access to memory is, for instance, discussed in [45] and also in Chapter 12.) Along with the standard mapping functions, such as STRAIGHT and SKEWED, "user-designed" functions can be generated in TRANQUIL.

In TRANQUIL Algol expressions are generalized so that arrays can be used as operands. Here, the meaning of the operation depends on the type of the operands, e.g. A/B means $A \times B^{-1}$, if A and B are matrices, B has an inverse matrix, and the dimensions are compatible.

Obvious quantors **ANY** and **ALL** are used for the generalization of relations; operations over sets, such as **UNION**, are included.

The language has sequential and parallel versions of control statements. For example, a parallel **SIM**-function (SIMULTANEOUS) in its general form is as follows:

SIM BEGIN⟨assignment⟩:...:⟨assignment⟩**END**

Within the **SIM**-function, all the statements are executed synchronously and simultaneously.

The sequential loop statement

FOR (I, J) **SEQ** $([1, 2, ..., 10], [5, 10, ..., 50])$ **DO**
$A[I] \leftarrow B[I+1] + C[J]$

is computed similarly to

$A[1] \leftarrow B[2] + C[5]$

$$A[2] \leftarrow B[3] + C[10]$$
$$\vdots$$
$$A[10] \leftarrow B[11] + C[50].$$

The parallel loop statement

FOR (I, J) **SIM** $([1, 2, 3], [4, 5])$ **DO**
$A[I, J] \leftarrow B[J, I]$

is computed as

SIM BEGIN
$A[1, 4] \leftarrow B[4, 1]$
$A[2, 5] \leftarrow B[5, 2]$
$A[3, 4] \leftarrow B[4, 3]$
    END

Sequential and parallel statements may form hierarchical construct.

The language APL developed in the early 60s by Iverson [46] makes the computer an "intellectual calculator" with a rich set of operations and functions over vectors, matrices and arrays. Control facilities at the statement level in APL are very few, but there are wide possibilities for generating "powerful" expressions allowing various on-line solutions of engineering and computational problems. With the advent of vector and matrix computers, APL was regarded a candidate for an "ideal" high-level language for them, or a basic language for the design of the architecture of an APL-computer [47—49]. The advantages gained by APL implemented in a parallel processor computer (in particular, an associative one) were revealed in [50]. For STARAN, a dialect of APL has been designed [51].

The problem of organizing synchronous parallel computations from data algebra convenient for the representation of parallel computations to the implementation of synchronous parallel statements is comprehensively discussed in [52]. The central concept of this theory is that of a periodically defined function over data structures, which generalizes the periodically defined transformations of [53].

Periodically defined functions are defined over a set of finite data structures closed with respect to basic operations over elementary structures and operations changing data structures (shifts, superpositions, cuts). Periodically defined functions are solutions to a set of the following equations (with respect to the unknown functions $f_1, \ldots, f_n$):

$$y_i = F_i(y_1, \ldots, y_n, x_1, \ldots, x_m) \qquad (i = 1, \ldots, n),$$

where $x_1, \ldots, x_m$ are data structure variables, $y_i = f_i(x_i, \ldots, x_m)$ are unknown functions, $f_i(Z_1, \ldots, Z_{n+m})$ are given functions over the data structure set. One can introduce a partial order relation $\leq$ over the data structure set, writings $s \leq t$, if s is undefined or coincides with t. This relation is extended in the usual manner to functions over the data structure set. As a result, using the well-known theorems about fixed points in partially ordered sets one can demonstrate that above system has a solution under some constraints on the right-hand sides of the equations. The regularity of the functions $F_i(Z_1, \ldots, Z_{n+m})$ is such a constraint, i.e. any of these functions can be represented as an expression, where each sum consists of summands whose ranges of values are disjoint under any set of argument values. By extending programming languages to include facilities for the definition of periodically defined functions, the implementation of simultaneous synchronous computations over data structures is made possible. An example of an assignment statement generalization allowing the description of periodically defined transformations is given in [53]. In particular, the statement

$$a[i, j] := a[i, j] - (a[i, k]/a[k, k]) \times a[k, j],$$

where $k \leq i \leq n$, $k \leq j \leq n$, describes an operation over the matrix $a[1:n, 1:n]$ for some k, $1 \leq k \leq n$. All the elements of the matrix with coordinates indicated in the statement are recomputed concurrently.

The theory of periodically defined functions appears to be a convenient basis for the development and implementation of sets of enlarged parallel operations over regular data structures on various parallel processors. Further development of this theory in the direction of asynchronous operations would allow it to be merged with the theory of asynchronous parallelism (see Sec. 5), which is further developed for the middle part of the structure space in Fig. 1.

5.4 The problem of basic parallelism

Thus, the right and left sides of the parallel structure space (Fig. 1) are developing so as to complement mutually each other. They are developing, in general, independently and towards each other, but the centre of the space (containing such basic "average power" fragments as assignment statements in ALGOL-like languages) is still empty in the sense that there are no practical and accepted methods for the definition of parallelism. Indeed, the process mechanism turns out to be rather unwieldy in this area, and synchronous parallelism does not provide the required computational flexibility. The question arises as to whether it is reasonable to develop facilities for the description of parallelism in this area. The answer is, yes, because such facilities are necessary in order to ensure the "continuity" of the parallel control structure space. The need for languages with total parallelism, i.e. with a convenient and effective definition of parallelism at any level, is dictated (1) by the development of parallelism in computer systems, where it simultaneously spreads from the periphery (peripheral devices) and kernel (parallel processors) towards the centre, and (2) by the extension of the range of problems requiring total parallelism for their effective solution.

Another question is how to develop facilities for the organization of parallelism at the statement level in the middle part of the structure space under considerations. As stated above, the techniques for communicating parallel processes (branches) and synchronous parallelism are not convenient at this level. Their combination can only be regarded as a stopgap, because the total complexity of program control becomes greater and at the same time the shortcomings of both techniques are present. It remains to find new organizational techniques for parallel structures in this area. If a new technique is to be orthogonal to the two previous ones, the complexity of the program control structure will be prohibitive. Consequently, the new technique should be more general, so that the parallel process mechanism and synchronous microparallelism are special cases.

The unique technique of total parallelism should be conceptually simple, reliable, not too difficult to implement, and suitable for a wide class of "parallel" problems. Moreover, its theoretical basis should be a complete and closed formalism allowing a strict formulation of statements about parallel programs and automatic program manipulation. The conceptual unity of parallel structures at all levels does not imply the use of the same set of program primitives for the description or definition of parallelism, because it is difficult to achieve a set that would meet the requirements of both high- and low-level languages and would at the same time be equally effective on the left and right sides of the structure space. Our aim is a unified principle for the design and development of control mechanisms in parallel programs, but the actual control primitives and their number can vary in various areas of the structure space in Fig. 1. Specifically, we find it reasonable to consider a family of "compatible" languages of various levels, whose control structures are designed through a unique principle rather than a single general-purpose languages.

5.5 Asynchronous programming

We believe that the so-called asynchronous programming technique is an acceptable unique basis for developing an adequate program mechanism over the whole space of control structures (Fig. 1). As noted above, in the sequentially parallel organization of programs, additional facilities for the definition of parallel fragments and synchronization are introduced into the sequential basis. On the contrary, in asynchronous computations all program fragments are initially regarded parallel, independent and unordered. Any constraint on their interactions (generating particular execution sequencing) is formulated as explicit or implicit individual conditions associated with fragments (readiness conditions). These conditions are related to each fragment, are dynamically checked, and enable or disable (rather than prescribe) the execution of a given fragment (statement), thus forming computations. These readiness conditions perform the overall organization of control. If a program is hierarchically structured, then each "component" fragment is internally organized in the same way. It follows from what has been said before that asynchronous programming is "complementary" to sequentially parallel programming. The relative merits of these approaches, of course, depend essentially on the internal structure of the problems programmed and the type of computing system. An analysis of the total effect of asynchronous program organization over the total space of control structures (Fig. 1) and, especially, over the middle part, convinces us that it is effective. Asynchronous programs are most flexible in the sense of describing or defining "maximum parallelism"; they model sequentially parallel programs fairly easily. All this stems from the fact that fragment parallelism and independence are put in the forefront, and that the technique is conceptually simple and corresponds to the intrinsic parallelism of the problems and the asynchronous organization of complex computer systems. Finally, we note that the asynchronous organization of parallel programs has originated from theoretical studies of promising ways of development of parallel computations and systems.

Computations in asynchronous programs are initiated by control which examines the computation status data (stored in memory or distributed somehow throughout the program) and tests the appropriate conditions of fragment readiness.

Various modifications of asynchronous programming involve the organization of the data exchange between program fragments and the nature of control.

In centralized asynchronous computations, control is a unique (possibly for some statements or for a single hierarchical level) "control process" which task is to monitor readiness conditions and to select for initiation fragments whose execution is enabled. The data (including control data) is exchanged through a common memory shared by a given group of statements.

In distributed asynchronous computations (data-flow computations and programs), the exchange of information and control data is performed through isolated or controlled direct communication paths which are dynamic memory structures, usually queues. Control is decentralized, each statement determining independently its degree of readiness to initiate computations. Most commonly, data-flow computations use implicit readiness conditions of which most frequent is the presence of data (operands, arguments) on "input paths".

In theory, extreme forms of each of these asynchronous techniques are universal in the sense that they provide flexibility, diversity of generated or described parallel structures, etc. for parallel computation. In a real environment, however, they have, as a rule, positive and negative aspects which mutually complement each other. In data-flow programming, for example, implicit readiness conditions facilitate the natural description of conflict-free parallel structures in high-level languages, and the organization of interaction through distributed program paths suits the implementation of computations in distributed computer systems. On the other hand, the data-flow organization of programs does not allow for conflict situations occurring with shared resources. This give rise to difficulties in mapping an "ideal" data-flow computation scheme onto a "real" system configuration with limited resources (including a limited number of processors). Finally, the programming of "non-data-flow" computations (e.g. the handling of complicated data structures, sorting, etc.) leads to particular difficulties. Wider possibilities for solving conflict situations are characteristic of centralized asynchronous structures where readiness conditions can be more varied, and where program structures are easier mapped onto the computer system structure, etc. On the whole, the centralized organization is more powerful than the distributed one, but it becomes cumbersome if there is no essential need for the centralized control of parallel computations. Therefore, that version of asynchronous program organization can be regarded as reasonable which has explicit facilities for the indication of fragment readiness (trigger functions) combined with implicit facilities (operands at statement inputs, etc.), the control is partially centralized, exchanges are performed through shared memory and channels, etc.

The majority of theoretical models for parallel programs were found to be asynchronous. The reverse is also true: the majority of asynchronous programming languages exist only as theoretical models or, at best, are under development. Therefore, one can familiarize oneself with them through reviews [55—58] and also from Chapter 4 of this book. The most essential contribution to the development of data-flow computation theory and to design for data-flow languages and computers has been made by a group of researchers from MIT headed by J. Dennis. Their main objective was to develop a basic language [59] that would support highly parallel computations. The data-flow language [60] has a set of statements of various types whose inputs and outputs are connected by "data exchange channels" which can be "linked" and "split". Each channel stores data of a certain type (at most a single data item). Among data-flow program statements there are "transformers" computing outputs from inputs, "recognizers" generating the logic values **true** or **false** in response to the input data, statements which pass data from one input channel to the output channel depending on the control logic input, and "gates" passing or eliminating data in the channels which contain them. The execution of a data-flow program generates a flow of data which controls statement initiation and causes computations. Generally, the data-flow program is a hierarchy of data-flow procedures which are linked to the environment through input and output channels only and which have no "global channels". Procedures are reentrant and facilities are provided for monitoring the movement of data through the procedure body.

The data-flow language of Davis [61] is similar to that of Dennis, but it is more compact because it makes hardly any distinction between data and control (logic) channels and because queues can store an arbitrary amount of data. The Davis language is also a basic language for the development of data-flow recursive computer architecture. The "feedback" from the engineering approach to the computer hardware design is felt in the structures of both languages; they incline towards a graphic representation which, despite the designer's expectations, is not simpler or more obvious for a programmer without experience in this area. The problem of structure in data-flow program has still not been well formulated.

A centralized asynchronous technique for the organization of parallel processes over shared memory was suggested in [62]. The asynchronous parallel program (A-program) is a hierarchical system of modules:

⟨A-program⟩ :: = ⟨module⟩
⟨module⟩ :: = ⟨simple module⟩ | ⟨compound module⟩
⟨compound module⟩ :: = **input** (⟨input list⟩)
   do ⟨framed module list⟩ **od**
   output (⟨output list⟩)
⟨framed module⟩ :: = ⟨trigger function⟩ ⇒ ⟨module⟩
⟨trigger function⟩ :: = ⟨logic expression⟩
⟨input⟩ :: = ⟨local variable⟩ : = ⟨external variable⟩
⟨output⟩ :: = ⟨external variable⟩ : = ⟨local variable⟩

A simple module is an "atomic" structural unit, e.g. an ALGOL-like assignment statement or procedure call.

If the trigger function of a framed module is the logic constant **true**, it can be omitted. Let M be a compound module generated by a list of framed modules M_1, M_2, ..., M_n. The local module memory consists of variables involved in

— trigger functions of submodules M_1, ..., M_n,
— right-hand sides of the inputs of submodules M_1, ..., M_n (or right-hand sides of assignment statements),
— left-hand sides of the outputs of submodules M_1, ..., M_n (or left-hand sides of assignments).

The local memory of module M is also a shared external memory of submodules M_1, ..., M_n. Thus, the memory is hierarchically structured according to the structures of the modules. A more complicated data exchange between modules is not discussed here.

Similarly as simple variables (locations), also memory can contain more complex data, e.g. stacks, queues, etc. Simple variables are assumed to be always accessible, while queues and stacks can be "empty". This provides the additional possibility of using an implicit data-flow control as well as explicit data-flow control based on trigger functions.

Figure 8 demonstrates simplified semantic of control by trigger functions. Each module goes through a succession of "passive", "tested" and "active" states. If passive, the module does not participate in computations. When it is tested, the value of its trigger function is determined. When the module is active, computations are being executed "inside the module body". Conditions defining the transition of the module from one state to another and the effect of transitions on the memory are also shown in Fig. 8.

Possible transitions	Transition condition	Effect on memory
1. Passive-tested	The framing module is active, the program or system event has occurred	Input variables are copied from the memory from trigger functions
2. Tested-passive	There are "empty" variables among input ones and variables from trigger functions, or trigger function is **false,** or there is no system resource	
3. Tested-active	There is no "empty" variable among input ones and variables from trigger functions, or trigger function is **true,** and there are all system resource	Input variables are sent into local module memory
4. Active-passive	a) transition is unconditionally possible if the module is simple	
	b) or (in the case of a compound module) if all its submodules are passive and their trigger functions are **true**	Computed local variables are sent to output external ones

Fig. 8. The execution of an A-programe module.

The trigger function is not associated with the execution of an appropriate module, it rather allows its initiation. This property together with the indeterminancy of A-program execution, makes parallel programming with trigger functions a convenient vehicle for the organization of a flexible interaction between the parallel program and the computer system. Trigger functions, as natural conditions for the initiation of actions described by the module, allow a natural definition of high-level parallelism. Thus programming with trigger functions is a convenient method for parallel programming of both low and high levels.

A simple illustrative example of an A-program consisting of a single compound module is shown in Fig. 9a. The module has three framed statements, and as a result of the computations, the output variables become equal to the maximum input variable. This program allows the parallel execution of two statements out of three. The program in Fig. 9b is functionally equivalent to the program in Fig. 9a, but it is "less parallel". Constraints added to the trigger functions have changed the set of computations and made the A-program sequentially executable. One can change the behaviour of an A-program in another manner, namely, by modifying its execution rules. Tests of trigger functions can be synchronized so as to make a new test possible only when all the active modules become passive.

If, on the contrary, only one module can be active at any time, the A-program becomes a sequential program with guarded statements [30].

a) **input** $(x := ..., y := .. , z := ...)$
    do
        $x < y \rightarrow x := x + 1,$
        $y < z \rightarrow y := y + 1,$
        $z < x \rightarrow z := z + 1$
                od
    output $(... := x, ... := y, ... := z)$

b) **input** $(x := ..., y := ..., z := ...)$
    do
        $x \leq z \wedge x < y \rightarrow x := x + 1,$
        $y \leq x \wedge y < z \rightarrow y := y + 1,$
        $z \leq y \wedge z < x \rightarrow z := z + 1$
                od
    output $(... := x, ... := y, ... := z)$

Fig. 9. A-programs.

Thus, changes in the behaviour of A-programs can be made in two ways: (a) by adding explicit constraints to trigger functions, or (b) by adding implicit constraints to the execution rule. A useful "monotonicity" is observed in both cases: new information added to the A-program reduces the indeterminacy of the execution. Thus, the result can be obtained in a step-by-step manner: first, a set of independent modules is generated, then constraints are added successively until the desired interaction between the modules is achieved.

5.6 The universal family of parallel languages

A (partially) centralized asynchronous control with trigger functions seems to be a good common basis of program mechanisms describing the parallel structures of Fig. 1. This concept is illustrated in Fig. 10, which shows a family of three "compatible" parallel languages: a high-level language, a low-level language and a basic language. The high-level language is designed to provide an adequate description of problem parallelism, and, in general, it has no constructs requiring information about the features and structure of the computer system on which it is to be implemented. The low-level language improves the computation effectiveness by using this information. The intermediate (basic) language has all the facilities necessary for the support and coordination of low and high levels. Each language has a special set of control facilities for macro-, basic- and microcontrol.

As can be seen from Fig. 10, the control of the basic language consists of trigger functions and control formulae (see below). The control mechanisms for other areas are extensions or modifications of the trigger function mechanism. The

syntactic structure of the basic language consists of three interacting sublanguages:
— control sublanguage (C-language),
— memory sublanguage (M-language), and
— expression sublanguage (E-language).

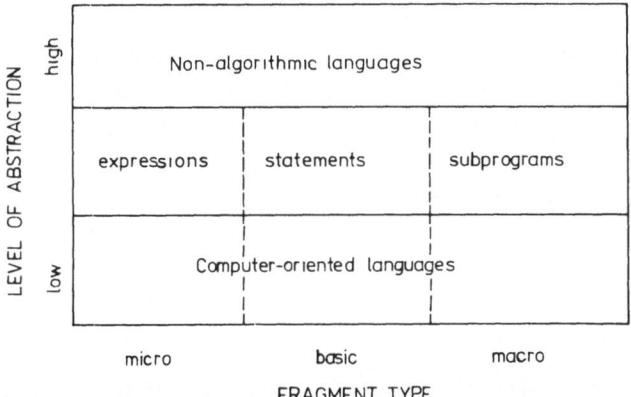

Fig. 10. Family of compatible parallel languages.

All the three sublanguages are orthogonal, but have similar syntactic structures. In each sublanguage L, the fundamental construct is the L-object which is an elementary L-object or L-formula. An L-formula is constructed or L-objects (operands), L-operations, and L-functions. Sublanguages differ in elementary objects and operations. For example, modules are elementary objects in the C-language, scalars are elementary objects in the E-language. Complex operations and functions are constructed by means of metasyntactic rules common to all the sublanguages.

As a result, a program in the basic language is a C-object (i.e. C-formula) constructed of modules and C-operations (or control operations) generating complex control structures out of the simple ones. The control operations in the language of A-programs are exemplified by brackets **do ... od**, the symbol $\Rightarrow$ connecting trigger functions to modules, and a comma separating modules.

To be able to construct high-level control mechanisms, the C-language is provided with a larger set of control operations. The control formulas generated from these operations define unconditional data-independent constraints on the order of the operand-module execution. The only facility for conditional control represent trigger functions. Control functions can be defined and described by the programmer. Control operations and the mechanism of the control function (control types) definition are described in [27]. The control structure algebra [63] is a formal basis for the control sublanguage. The semantics of control, control functions and control formulae (C-formulas) is defined by means of asynchronous structured nets which are generalizations of Petri nets. Thus, C-formulas are, in essence, formulae of nets described in [27, 63]. They resemble path expressions [21, 22] define however, more general structures.

In net formuli, the program module is represented by a net transition classified as terminal or non-terminal. The former are conventional indivisible transitions of Petri nets, the latter are structured nets. The terminal transition corresponds to a simple module, the non-terminal transition corresponds to a compound module. The "internal" net of the non-terminal transition starts operation as soon as the transition is initiated. When the internal net completes its operation, the non-terminal transition is terminated, and the initial marking of the net is restored. Figure 11 shows the structured net defined by formula

$(*1(t; (v, w)), (2e; d)),$
$t = 1(a \Box b),$
$v = 2(c; d),$
$w = (2e; 1f),$

where a, b, c, d, e, f are terminal transitions which are simple net modules, and t, v, w are non-terminal transitions.

Symbols $*$, $\Box$, $;$, $\supset$, stand here for control operations. Their semantics is described in [27, 54, 63] and is illustrated, to some extent, by the above example. The join operation "$;$" joins two nets by merging the set of the so-called tail places

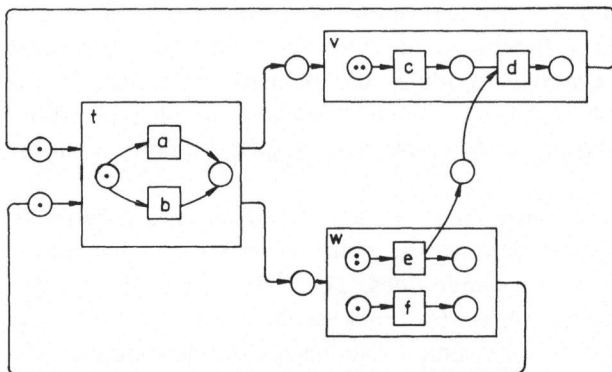

Fig. 11. Structured net.

of one net with the set of head places of the other (see fragment $(c; d)$ in Fig. 11). Two places are merged so that each place of one net is merged with each place of the other, their end markings being added. The exclusion operation "$\Box$" joins two nets by merging their head and tail place sets (see $(a \Box b)$ in Fig. 11). The iteration operation "$*$" merges head and tail place sets of the same net. The marking operation adds tokens to each head place of a net (see $2(c; d)$ in Fig. 11). Note especially operation "$,$" which superposes one net on another, resulting in the join of two structures by merging modules and transitions with identical names (e.g., transitions e and d). The operation of superposition of conditional and unconditional control structures allows the step-by-step addition of new control information (i.e. new constraints).

The program in Fig. 12 has been obtained from the A-program in Fig. 9a. Names

input $x := ..., y := ..., z := ...)$
do

$\quad 1 * (a \mid b \mid c),$
$\quad a : x < y \rightarrow x := x + 1,$
$\quad b : y < z \rightarrow y := y + 1,$
$\quad c : z < x \rightarrow z := z + 1$
$\qquad\qquad$ **od**
output $(... := x, ... := y, ... := z)$ $\qquad$ Fig. 12. Program with control formulae.

were assigned to submodules, and the control formula $1 * (a \square b \square c)$, which defines mutual exclusion for cyclically executable submodules a, b, c, is "superimposed" on the original A-program, thus adding to it new control constraints. Functionally, this program is equivalent to the A-program in Fig. 9a. However, the additional control formula reduces the set of possible computations and turns the parallel program into a sequential program with an indeterminate order of statement execution.

Control functions (or control types) are defined by the programmer by means of control formulas through conventional descriptions, e.g. mutex $(A, B, C) = 1 * (A \square B \square C)$. Control types describe typical control structures used by the programmer. This mechanism is used to design both convenient high-level control primitives and autonomous control information for the computer system. Programming with control types is discussed in more detail in [27] and implemented in [67], also in a modular language. The function of the E-language is the implementation of microparallelism in the basic language. Usually, the structure of ALGOL-like algebraic expressions is represented by trees indicating data flows. Trees are a special case of A-programs and data-flow programs. Indeed, they are programs with distributed memory and implicit trigger functions which allow the module to initiate computations only if all its data are accessible. Data-flow trees can be represented here by data-flow formulae derived from the structure of algebraic formulae, i.e. trees can be regarded as a special case of nets. For instance, a data-flow tree for the expression $(x_1 + x_2) + (x_3 + x_4)$ can be represented by the structural formula $((x_1, x_2); +, (x_3, x_4); +); +$ where ";" and "," are control operations. Note that the latter formula resembles the reverse Polish notation (if one eliminates parentheses and symbols for control operations) which can be used instead of this more detailed notation. This formula defines the net-tree in Fig. 13a, defining the parallel asynchronous computation of the expression. Another formula

$$(((((x_1, x_2); +), x_3); +), x_4); +$$
or $x_1x_2 + x_3 + x_4 +$

is defined by the tree in Fig. 13b.

a 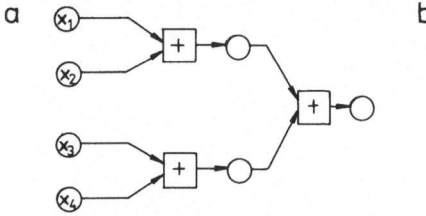 b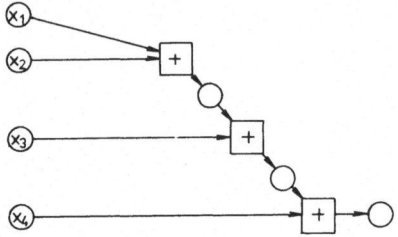

Fig. 13. Structure of expressions.

The application of this principle to operations over data structures allows the organization of parallel asynchronous, periodically definite transformations. The operations and functions of APL, in particular, can be generalized so as to make them concurrently executable.

Macrocontrol facilities are not described here; they are derived from the basic facilities, that make use of the procedure mechanism and are similar to sentinels [20].

On the whole, the basic language is hierarchically and modularly structured. The module is framed by a trigger function and, possibly, by another data item necessary for communication with other modules. The module body contains descriptions in three sublanguages:

do
    ⟨control structure description in the C-language⟩
    ⟨data structure description in the M-language⟩
    ⟨submodule list⟩
od

The right-hand sides of simple submodules (assignment statements) are programmed in the E-language. There also is a "meta-language" level that precedes the whole of the program, and in which structures common to all the sublanguages are described, e.g. the matrix of L-objects (i.e. data), modules, etc.

The main task of the low-level control is the organization of the most effective computation of a system of given computations on a system with a given configuration. As noted above, the modification of the execution rules changes the operational behaviour of the A-program. Therefore, the control sublanguage of the low-level language is constructed of trigger functions and of additional facilities for changing control modes, i.e. for imposing constraints on trigger function tests and on manipulations with modules ready for execution. Microparallelism of the low-level language (the left-hand bottom area of the space in Figs. 1 and 10) is programmed using data-flow formulae and control modes. In particular, the definition of the synchronous testing of readiness conditions generates a synchronous parallel execution of expressions and periodically defined operations and functions.

The high-level language is a non-procedural language where explicit control facilities of the basic language are replaced by implicit control facilities, or are partially omitted. Parallelism at the statement level is programmed as in non-procedural (or non-algorithmic) languages, i.e. equations relating variables are used instead of assignment statements, and computations are formed much the same as in non-procedural parametric languages [64, 65] or Lucid [66]. The microparallelism of high-level languages (the left-hand upper area of the space in Figs. 1 and 10) is expressed by

(1) non-procedural expressions that do not indicate how they should be computed,

(2) some constraints on the computation of expressions that are imposed, for instance, if there is a danger of losing accuracy because of operand permutations. These are formulated using a version of the control structure algebra.

The microparallelism implementation mechanism includes operations over complex data structures (sets, vectors, arrays) thus allowing the definition of batch operations, similar to those of APL, in parallel and non-procedural to an arbitrary degree.

Conclusion

The present contribution is a discussion of parallel programming languages of the next generation. To this end, we have briefly reviewed the history of including parallelism description and definition facilities in programming languages. This was an evolutionary process following advances in both computers and their applications. Major progress has been made in the area of control organization of concurrent sequential processes because this type of programming is characteristic of multiprogramming systems. Studies of these problems have revealed that programming of parallel computations is much more complicated than that of sequential ones. Any attempts to achieve simplification through the higher abstraction level of control primitives results in lower effectiveness (and does not prevent from errors). Therefore, we propose the concept of a family of compatible languages which have facilities adequate to the areas identified in the "control structure space" in Fig. 1. The compatibility lies in the fact that all the control mechanisms of these languages are centred around the same method for concurrent computation control, that of trigger functions. This is possible because other methods of concurrent computation control: sequentially parallel organization of computations, a mechanism for synchronous vector and matrix computations, data-flow control, non-procedural organization of high-level languages, etc. can be regarded as special cases of it. We do not discuss non-procedural languages (the upper part of the space in Fig. 1) and microprogramming languages (the lower part of the same space), because this would expand the scope of the chapter and prevent us from concentrating on the basic level of parallel computation control structures.

On the whole, the introduction of parallelism in computations is a part of a more general process of improving programming languages and computer architectures. The development of languages will be the main factor defining future computer architectures, because it is in languages that new principles of computation organization are implemented. A proper introduction of parallelism into programming languages will not complicate programming, but rather will stimulate the development of such program features as modularity, high reliability and programming efficiency, and high efficiency of program execution.

REFERENCES

[1] CONWAY, M.: A multiprocessor system design. Proc. AFIPS Fall Joint Computer Conference, 1963, pp. 139—146.

[2] OPLER, A.: Procedure-oriented languages to facilitate parallel processing. Comm. ACM, 8, 1965, 5, 306—307.

[3] ANDERSON, J. P.: Program structures for parallel processing. Comm. ACM, 8, 1965, 12, 786—788.

[4] LEHMAN, M.: A survey and preliminary results concerning parallel processing and parallel processors. Proc. IEEE, 54, 1966, 1889—1901.

[5] DENNIS, J. B. and VAN HORN, E. C.: Programming semantics for multiprogrammed computations. Comm. ACM, 9, 1966, 3, 143—155.

[6] WIRTH, N.: A note on programm structures for parallel processing. Comm. ACM, 9, 1966, 5, 320—321.

[7] DIJKSTRA, E. W.: Cooperating sequential processors. In: Programming Languages. F. Genuys (Editor). Academic Press, New York, 1968, pp. 43—112.

[8] DIJKSTRA, E. W.: Solution of a problem in concurrent programming control. Comm. ACM, 8, 1965, 9.

[9] VAN WIJNGAARDEN et al.: Report on the Algorithmic Language Algol 68. Springer-Verlag, Berlin, 1969.

[10] DIJKSTRA, E. W.: Hierarchical ordering of sequential processes. Acta Informatica, 1, 1971, 2, 115—138.

[11] COURTOIS, P. J., HEYMANS, F. and PARNAS, D. L.: Concurrent control with readers and writers. Comm. ACM, 14, 1971, 10, 667—668.

[12] HANSEN, P. B.: A comparison of two synchronizing concepts. Acta Informatica, 1, 1972, 3, 190—199.

[13] PATIL, S. S.: Limitations and capabilities of Dijkstra's semaphore primitives for coordination among processes. Project MAC, MIT, Cambridge, Mass., 1971.

[14] HOARE, C. A. R.: Towards a theory of parallel programming. In: Operating Systems Techniques. Academic Press, New York, 1972, pp. 220—230.

[15] HANSEN, P. B.: Structured multiprogramming. Comm. ACM, 15, 1972, 1, 574—578.

[16] COURTOIS, P. J., HEYMANS, F. and PARNAS, D. L.: Comments on "A Comparison of Two Synchronizing Concepts". Acta Informatica, 1, 1972, 375—376.

[17] HOARE, C. A. R.: Monitors: An operating system structuring concept. Comm. ACM, 17, 1974, 10, 549—557.

[18] HANSEN, P. B.: Operating System Principles. Prentice-Hall, Englewood Cliffs, N. J., 1973.

[19] HANSEN, P. B.: The programming language concurrent pascal. IEEE Trans. on Software Engineering, *1*, 1975, 2, pp. 199—207.

[20] KELLER, R. M.: Sentinels: A language construct for multiprocess coordination. Unpublished Memo, Dep. Comp. Sci., Univ. of Utah, Salt Lake City, 1978.

[21] CAMPBELL, R. H. and HABERMANN, A. N.: The specification of process synchronization by path expressions. In: Lecture Notes in Computer Science, Vol. 16. Springer-Verlag, Berlin, 1974.

[22] LAUER, P. E. and CAMPBELL, R. H.: Formal semantic for a class of high-level primitives coordinating concurrent processes. Acta Informatica, 1975, 5, 297—332.

[23] GLUSHKOV, V. M. and LETICHEVSKII, A. A.: Teoriya diskretnykh preobrazovatelei. In: Izbrannye voprosy algebry i logiki. IM SO AN SSSR, Novosibirsk, 1973.

[24] ROBERT, P. and VERJUS, P.: Towards autonomous descriptions of synchronization modules. Proc. IFIP Congress, North-Holland Publ. Co., Amsterdam, 1977.

[25] BEKKERS, Y., BRIOT, J. and VERJUS, J. P.: Construction of a synchronization scheme by independent definition of parallelism. In: Constructing Quality Software. North-Holland Publ. Co., Amsterdam, 1978, pp. 193—205.

[26] LEDANOIS, P. et al.: Multilevel description and simulation of parallel cooperating processes. Arbeitsber. IMND, *9*, 1977, 247—275.

[27] KOTOV, V. E.: Concurrent programming with control types. In: Constructing Quality Software. North-Holland Publ. Co., Amsterdam, 1978, pp. 207—208.

[28] HOARE, C. A. R.: Communicating sequential processes. Dep. Comp. Sci., The Queen's Univ., Belfast, 1976.

[29] MIRENKOV, N. N.: Sistemnoe parallelnoe programmirovanie. I. Preprint OVS-05. Inst. Mat. SO AN SSSR, Novosibirsk, 1978.

[30] DIJKSTRA, E. W.: Guarded commands, nondeterminancy, and formal derivation of programs. Comm. ACM, *18*, 1975, 8, 453—457.

[31] KOTOV, V. E. and NARINYANI, A. S.: On transformation of sequential programs into asynchronous parallel programs. Proc. IFIP Congress, Edinburgh 1968. North-Holland Publ. Co., Amsterdam, 1969, pp. 351—357.

[32] HENTZ, R. G. and TATE, D. P.: Control data Star-100 processor design. In: Proc. IEEE Comp. Conf., 1972, pp. 1—4.

[33] WATSON, W. J.: The Texas Instruments advanced scientific computer. In: Proc. IEEE Comp. Conf., 1972, pp. 191—193.

[34] SITES, R. L.: An analysis of the Cray-1 computer. In: Proc. 5th Annual Symp. on Computer Architecture. IEEE Inc., New York, 1978, pp. 101—106.

[35] BARNES, G. H. et al.: The ILLIAC IV computer. IEEE Trans. on Computers, *C-17*, 1968, 8, 746—757.

[36] EVENSEN, A. J. et al.: Introduction to the architecture of a 288-Element PEPE. In: Sagamore Comp. Conf. on Parallel Processing, Sagamore 1973, pp. 162—169.

[37] BATCHER, K. E.: STARAN parallel processor system hardware. In: Proc. IEEE Comp. Conf., 1974, pp. 385—387.

[38] GOSDEN, J. A.: Explicit parallel processing description and control in programs for multi- and uni-processor computers. Proc. FJCC AFIPS, *29*, 1966, 651—660.

[39] The IVTRAN Manuel. Massachusetts Computer Associates, Inc., 1973.

[40] ZWAKENBERG, R. G.: Vector extensions to LRLTRAN. SIGPLAN Notices, *10*, 1975, 3, 77—86.

[41] WEDEL, D.: FORTRAN for the Texas Instrument ASC system. SIGPLAN Notices, *10*, 1975, 3, 119—132.

[42] STEVENS, K. G.: CFD — A Fortran-like language for the ILLIAC IC. SIGPLAN Notices, *10*, 1975, 3, 72—76.

[43] LANGE, R. G.: High-level language for associative and parallel computation with Staran. In: Proc. Int. Conf. on Parallel Processing. IEEE Inc., New York, 1976, pp. 170—176.

[44] ABEL, N. E. et al.: TRANQUIL: A language for an array processing computer. In: Proc. AFIPS Spring Joint Computer Conf., Montvale, N. Y., Vol. 34. AFIPS Press, Montvale 1969, pp. 57—73.

[45] KUCK, D.: ILLIAC IV software and application programming. IEEE Trans. on Computers, C-17, 1968, 8, 758—770.

[46] IVERSON, K. E.: A Programming Language. Wiley, New York, 1962.

[47] EVANS, D. J.: Large scale scientific problem formulation using APL. SIGPLAN Notices, 10, 1975, 3, 153—163.

[48] THURBER, K. J. and MYRNA, J. W.: System design of a cellular APL computer. IEEE Trans. on Computers, 19, 1970, 4, 199—212.

[49] HASSITT, A., LAGESCHULTE, J. W. and LYON, L. E.: Implementation of a high-level language machine. Comm. ACM, 16, 1973, 4, 291—303.

[50] HARRISON, M. J. and HARRISON, W. H.: The implementation of APL on an associative processor. In: Lecture Notes in Computer Sciences. Vol. 24. Springer-Verlag, Berlin, 1975, pp. 75—96.

[51] MARZOLD, J. G.: AAPL: An array processing language. In: Lecture Notes in Computer Science, Vol. 24. Springer-Verlag, Berlin, 1975, pp. 230—237.

[52] GLUSHKOV, V. V., KAPITONOVA, Yu. V. and LETICHEVSKII, A. A.: Teoriya struktur dannykh i sinkhronnye parallelnye vychisleniya. Kibernetika, 1976, 6, 2—15.

[53] GLUSHKOV, V. M.: Teoriya avtomatov i voprosy projektirovaniya struktur tsifrovykh mashin. Kibernetika, 1965, 1, 1—12.

[54] KOTOV, V. E.: Formalnye modeli parallelnykh vychislenii. Preprint VV SO AN SSSR, Novosibirsk, 1978.

[55] BAER, J. L.: A survey of some theoretical aspects of multiprocessing. ACM Comp. Survey, 5, 1973, 1, 31—80.

[56] MILLER, R. E.: A comparison of some theoretical models of parallel computation. IEEE Trans. on Computers, C-22, 1973, 8, 710—717.

[57] KOTOV, V. E.: Theory of parallel programming. I. Survey of practical aspects. In: Advances in Information Science, Vol. 6. Plenum Press, New York, 1976, pp. 1—57.

[58] NARINYANI, A. S.: Theory of parallel programming. II. Survey of formal models. In: Advances in Information Systems Science, Vol. 6. Plenum Press, New York, 1976, pp. 58—114.

[59] DENNIS, J. B.: Programming generality, parallelism and computer architecture. Proc. IFIP Congress, Edinburgh 1968. North-Holland Publ. Co., Amsterdam, 1969, pp. 484—492.

[60] DENNIS, J. B.: First version of a data-flow procedure language. Computation Structures Group Memo 93-1, Project MAC. MIT, Cambridge, 1974.

[61] DAVIS, A. L.: DDN's — A maximally concurrent procedural parallel process representation. Comp. Sci. Dep., Univ. of Utah, Salt Lake City, 1977.

[62] KOTOV, V. E. and NARINYANI, A. S.: Asinkhronnye vychislitelnye protsessy nad pamyatyu. Kibernetika, 1966, 3, 64—71.

[63] KOTOV, V. E.: An algebra for parallelism based on Petri nets. In: Lecture Notes in Computer Science, Vol. 64. Springer-Verlag, Berlin, 1978, pp. 39—55.

[64] LYUBIMSKII, E. E.: Ob algoritmizatsii programmirovaniya i metode programmiruyushchikh programm. Dissertation. Moscow, 1958.

[65] ZADYKHAILO, I. B.: Organizatsiya tsiklicheskogo protsessa schota po parametricheskoi zapisi spetsialnogo vida. Zh. vychisl. mat. i mat. fiz., 1963, 2, 337—357.

[66] ASHCROFT, E. A. and WADGE, W. W.: Lucid, a nonprocedural language with iteration. Comm. ACM, 20, 1977, 7, 519—526.

[67] DAVID, G.: On the basic concepts of a module language. MTA SZTAKI, Közleményei, Budapest, 1978.

Appendix

HIGH LEVEL OF PROGRAMMING LANGUAGE
AND INDETERMINANCY: SETL

1. One cannot disregard the rapidly growing interest in parallel and indeterminate (asynchronous, concurrent) computations. Anxious to be up to date, the designers of new languages and new versions of existing languages believe they are obliged to offer appropriate facilities to the user. In doing so, the very fact that a new language has some parallel computation facilities is regarded as sufficient. They do not consider it necessary to justify their choice in terms of completeness and universality. As a result, the elements concerned are usually alien to the language rather than intrinsic. We believe that it is natural to try to formulate the problem more precisely.

First of all, which parallelism is implied: "external", i.e. intrinsic to the problem and the technique for its solution, and requiring from the language facilities for the description of a parallel or asynchronous problem, situation or system; or "internal", allowing program execution on a multiprocessor computer independently of the problem? Any language element can be regarded as both "internal" and "external", and its use can be convenient for one but not for the other context. Obviously, a high-level language should primarily involve facilities oriented to "external" parallelism, "internal" parallelism being implemented during the translation from the input programming language to the language of the multiprocessor computer. It is, therefore, desirable that the language facilitates the parallelization as much as possible, and is "convenient" for it. Currently, however, specific capabilities of various solutions are dictated by the following two considerations:

a) Parallel programming theory does unfortunately still not thoroughly deal with "external" parallelism. Therefore, selection of a particular "external" linguistic facility may be justified, for the time being, only by a subjective estimate of its relative convenience for describing, i.e. programming some class of problems.

b) Facilities for implementing "internal" parallelism are better: although we still cannot compare them in terms of simplicity or convenience, we can sometimes demonstrate their adequacy (or inadequacy) in terms of the maximum asynchronism of a particular program [2].

2. The language SETL [3, 4] makes it possible to generate programs in a far less algorithmic style than in the majority of programming languages. This is due to the fact that its basic constructs are set-oriented and to some extend "externally" parallel.

To begin with, let us observe that, according to the semantics of the language, operations over sets do not fix the order of elementary operations. For instance, the operation $A + B$, where A and B are sets, and " $+$ " is the set — theoretic sum, is in essence the writing of $\#B$ attachments

A **WITH** b,

where b is an element of B.

The elements of B are selected in an arbitrary manner; therefore, attachments are made independently.

Even the membership test

$x \in A$

is naturally treated as a parallel or asynchronous test of the identity of element x and $\#A$ elements of A. For some portions of the set, this test can be performed independently.

Moreover, this also applies to quantifier construction, the loop of the form

$(\forall x \in A)B(x)$,   i.e. for all x of A

execute $B(x)$, and the logic expressions

$\forall x \in A \,|\, P(x)$,
$\exists x \in A \,|\, P(x)$.

Although some of the latter constructs demonstrate "external" parallelism, they also preserve some properties of "internal" parallelism. In this sense, SETL constructs such as "set element such that..." and "subset whose elements have the property..." seem to be constructs of a very high level that obviously demonstrate "external" parallelism. We refer to constructs, such as

$(x \in A \,|\, P(x))$,
$\{x \in A \,|\, P(x)\}$,
$\{B(x), x \in A \,|\, P(x)\}$,

where $P(x)$ is an arbitrary predicate, and $B(x)$ is an arbitrary expression.

Taking into account the unlimited complexity of expressions $P(x)$ and $B(x)$, the latter construct can be regarded as a task specifier describing what should be done by a given program without indicating how it is to be done.

The application of SETL as a formal language for handling relational data basis is a convincing demonstration of the "what-rather-than-how" principle, indeterminate properties, and the "very high level" of the language. In this case, information is retrieved from the data basis by means of a request formulated without "operational" SETL facilities at all. In particular, this is achieved by using the "data basis description" which is actually a description of data structures.

Note that "indeterminacy" should be regarded as relative: in this case, the level of SETL is compared to the level of program detail in most common programming languages.

3. The totality of "external" parallelism facilities of SETL is incomplete: there is no general construct that would make it possible to form an arbitrary statement set and request execution of the statements of this set without indicating their order, i.e. where any order of execution including parallel is permissible. A number of languages have constructs of this type; the "collateral clause" of ALGOL 68 is an example of it. In contrast to SETL, these languages do not have extensive facilities for handling unordered sets. For this reason, corresponding constructs in these languages look rather artificial, as was noted above. In SETL they are quite natural and the external facilities they provide for can be used effectively. Since the introduction of parallel facilities into SETL is still purely experimental, it is reasonable to do this in stages using the experience gained from the previous stages. Using the distinction between external and internal parallelism produced above, one might start by introducing into SETL rather simple facilities providing maximum asynchronism (i.e. "internally" oriented). When evaluated later from the "external" point of view, one can complement them so as to obtain, finally, a universal set of "externally" oriented facilities that are an intrinsic part of SETL and that do also extend its philosophy.

4. Let S be a set, each element of which is an ordered pair (block) $\langle x, y \rangle$, where y is a statement and x is a binary $(0, 1)$ "trigger" function. This set is referred to as an A-program [1]. Its implementation can be represented as a recurrent process:

a) the set S' of all pairs whose trigger functions are currently 1 is selected from S;

b) the subset S'' is selected from S' in an arbitrary manner, its statements being executed in an arbitrary order (or concurrently). Then control returns to a). The process is terminated if S' is empty, or if a special stop signal is generated during the execution of S''.

Thus, for each initial memory value a set of implementations corresponds, generally, to an A-program. If all the implementations are equivalent, i.e. if any execution of the A-program leads to the same result, the program is determinate then. If the implementation set of a determinate program contains all the equivalent processes, the given A-program is as asynchronous as possible (in other words, it is as flexible as possible, it provides a maximum variety of different ways leading to the result, and offers maximum convenience to the implementing system).

It was shown in [2] that for each A-program there is a most asynchronous A-program equivalent to it. Thus, if some facilities in a language are sufficient for the implementation of an A-program, they are sufficient for the generation of most asynchronous programs. In this case, the parallelization can be performed using equivalent program transformations in the language.

5. There are classes of problems for which, from the "external" viewpoint, A-programs provide a sufficiently natural description. They include, for example, a simulation of systems consisting of many rather simple elements operating asynchronously and, to a great extent, concurrently. The function and activation conditions of each element are known. If such a system is large enough, its behaviour in all possible situations cannot, in general, be described. The only approach is to describe the given system so that the description itself is a program generating computations equivalent to the system behaviour under appropriate conditions.

The introduction of facilities for generating A-programs into SETL does not lead to any difficulties. Moreover, this turns out to be quite natural because the A-program is simply an unordered set of pairs, and its execution fits easily into the corresponding SETL constructs.

To this end, it is sufficient to introduce into SETL a special statement called the A-statement. Any set S can be an A-statement if its elements are pairs (blocks) $\langle x, y \rangle$, where x is an arbitrary Boolean function, and y is an arbitrary SETL-program (in particular an A-statement). To differentiate syntactically the A-statement from a conventional set, we enclose it by statement brackets **ADO** S **END**:. The execution of an A-statement is described in Section 4. Consider a SETL-program using A-statements, for example 1 of [1].

Let the vector $A = (a_1, a_2, ..., a_n)$ be given. The vector components must be recalculated n times, so that the k-th and $(k + 1)$-th steps are related as follows:

$$\langle a_1^{(k)}, a_2^{(k)}, ..., a_n^{(k)} \rangle \rightarrow \langle a_1^{(k+1)}, a_2^{(k+1)}, ..., a_n^{(k+1)} \rangle,$$

where

$$a_i^{(k+1)} = a_i^{(k)}/p_k, \quad p_k = a_{k-1}^{(k)}.$$

The trigger functions of the A-statements require auxiliary variables V, Z and a vector w of dimension n. The roles of the vectors A and P are clear from the problem formulation.

SETL-program:
$v = 1$; $Z = 0$; $(v1 \leqslant i \leqslant n)w(i) = 1$;
DEFINE $A1(i)$; $a(i) = a(i)/P(w(i))$; $w(i) = w(i) + 1$;
   IF $w(i)$ **EQ** i **THEN** $Z = 0$; **END**;
DEFINE P1; $P(i) = P(i) - 1$; $v = v + 1$; $Z = 1$; **END**;
$SA = \{\langle w(i) \textbf{ LT } v, A1(i) \rangle \,|\, 1 \leqslant i \leqslant n\}$;

(*SA is an A-statement consisting of n blocks recalculating asynchronously every i-th element of its vector A*.)

$SP = \{\langle Z \textbf{ EQ } O, P1 \rangle\}$,

(*SP is a block calculating the current value of Pk*.)

ADO $SA \cup SP$ **END**.

6. As already mentioned above, A-statements are sufficient and "externally" convenient and natural in numerous problems where asynchronism is an intrinsic feature. At the same time, if procedures such as the "collateral clause" of ALGOL 68 are implemented in SETL by means of A-statements, the corresponding constructs are rather bulky.

In this case, one can extend the "external" facilities by permitting the enclosure by statement brackets **ADO** ... **END** of any set of SETL-programs (in the simplest case statements) as well as A-statements, and by treating this new construct (conventionally called an S-statement) as an indication that the SETL-programs of this set can be executed in an arbitrary order.

The possibilities of the S-statement are illustrated by a formulation using a SETL-program equivalent to an A-statement **ADO A END**:

M: **IF** $(\exists x \in A)$ **HD** x **THEN**
$\quad S1 = \ni \{SS \in \mathbf{POW}\ A \mid x \in SS\}$:
$\quad S = \{\mathbf{IF\ HD}x\ \mathbf{THEN\ TL}\ x \mid Vx \in S1\}$:
$\quad$ **ADO** S **END**; **GO TO** M;;

Thus, one can use a SETL-program with an S-statement instead of an A-statement, or a SETL-program with an A-statement instead of an S-statement (the corresponding example is omitted). The introduction of both possibilities into SETL is redundant, but makes it more flexible from the point of views of "external" parallelism. Any of these alternative extensions of SETL can be exploited as a first stage in providing SETL with facilities for asynchronous parallel processes.

REFERENCES

[1] Kotov, V. E. and Narinyani, A. S.: Asinkhronnye vychislitelnye protsessy nad pamyatyu. Kibernetika, 1966, 3, 64—71.
[2] Narinyani, A. S.: Teoriya parallelnogo programmirovaniya: formalnye modeli (obzor). Kibernetika, 1974, 3, 1—15.
[3] Schwartz, J. T.: An Iterim Report on SETL Project. Tech. Report, Univ. of New York, 1972.
[4] Levin, D. Ya.: SETL-yazyk programmirovaniya vesma vysokogo urovnya. Programmirovanie, 1976, 5.

Chapter 6

PROVING CORRECTNESS AND AUTOMATIC SYNTHESIS OF PARALLEL PROGRAMS

In this paper we try to give a more or less complete review of our project on the programming technology of parallel architectures. In order to prove correctness and to generate (synthesize) parallel programs we have to describe

a) the semantic of programming languages,
b) parallelism based on semantics,
c) the analysis and synthesis of parallel programs derived by semantic deductions.

These requirements are fulfilled by a special mathematical logic, so-called Structure Logic (SL), developed for these purposes. SL gives the correct semantics of programming languages and its proof-theory supplies a mechanical theorem-proving technique. Based on this logic both sequential and parallel programs can be generated automatically.

6.1 Introduction and Motivation

Many attempts have been made in recent years to solve the problems of
— the software crisis,
— the programming of parallel computers.
In our approach we have followed the development starting from program specification through programming technology, architecture description to program analysis and synthesis [1, 2]. The method was applied first to microcomputer architecture and the automatic synthesis of microprograms (in the sense of "microprocessor-programming" and "programming microprograms") [3, 4]. Later, we extended it to structured design technology [5] and to the description of the architecture of (abstract) computer systems. The method was inspired by both mathematical logical and algebraic semantics. Here we treat the method from the logical aspect (including syntax and semantics); we will publish the algebraic model elsewhere.

Logic is meant here in its classical sense given
— the language of logic,
— the evaluation of formulae on different domains,
— the models on different domains,
our purpose can be reformulated in the following form: "Find a logic in which the models are the processors of abstract or real computer systems."

Here, the expression "abstract or real" means that to every (possibly parallel) programming language we associate its processor, which will execute the programs. The abstract or real computing system consists of a set of processors in this sense. Hence, we need a logic in which the models are the processors themselves. Starting from the structural properties of such processors, we can state:

— processors have typed data structures in which the composition of different data structures is also a data structure,
— processors have instructions, more generally, functions performed on data structures, and the result is written into an appropriate data structure,
— the composition of processors is again a processor, hence one can speak of processor structures.

These requirements are satisfied by Structure Logic (SL), which is based on many-sorted logic and extended to express structures: basically, this logic is specially designed to express statements on

— structuring the objects, called structures,
— the types of structures,
— the functions defined on structures.

In this approach, the semantic definition of a programming language is "simply" the description of a processor Structure Logic (SL). Here, the processor is a set of structures, types of structures and instructions as functions.

Using the above-mentioned processor, a program can be expressed as a statement in Structure Logic: a program expresses its abstract data structure, and the functions associated with them. The programs is only a transformation of abstract data structures. Consequently, one can describe the program by statements in Structure Logic. Thus, the specification of a program is a set of statements (more precisely: well-formed formulae) in Structure Logic. In SL the resolution principle is valid in a suitable form. Hence, the mechanical theorem-proving technique can be applied (implemented on a computer by A. Sarközy). In our case this means that starting from the specification of the program, it can be verified mechanically, and if the algorithm is not given, the system will generate the proof of the specification, and the proof itself (being constructive) is the specified program. This is frequently referred to as program synthesis.

Throughout this paper we shall use an assembly-like language and a micro-processor in various examples, however, the results presented can be applied to any other (abstract) levels.

Four cases will be analysed in this paper:

Case 0: the classical sequential architecture: one instruction stream and one data stream.

Case 1: n homogeneous processors, n data streams, where the processors execute the same instruction.

Case 2: *n* homogeneous processors, *n* data streams, where the processors execute different instruction streams (i.e. programs).

Case 3: *n* heterogeneous processors and a shared data stream.

Although mathematically it would be satisfactory that there exist some descriptions for these four cases in SL, we shall concentrate on the question of "how": how can they be described in SL? Case 0 is included in this classification not only for the purpose of completeness but also to illustrate SL by Case 0.

SL is also a programming language with novel principles in which the programmer can concentrate on the notions and concepts, on the relations to different objects and on the transformations required. The solution, i.e. the program which will execute the transformations required, is generated automatically by the system.

In the following sections we shall proceed as follows: first we shall introduce SL, then the description of parallel architectures, and finally we shall prove the correctness and deal with the synthesis of parallel programs.

Following the Summary, the Appendix contains an example and a more detailed description of SL for the reader interested in details.

6.2 Structure Logic (SL)

SL is specially designed for the description of architectures. In the introduction we stated that such a processor must have
— data structures,
— their associated types,
— functions.
In mathematical logic we have predicates, objects, variables and functions. In SL we use types and type structures instead of predicates, and data structures instead of objects and variables. Functions are defined on data structures.

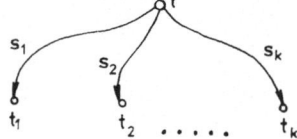

t_1 t_2 . . . . . t_k Fig. 1.

Structuring is based on the notion of selectors: if $t_1, t_2, ..., t_k$ are defined symbols, $s_1, s_2, ..., s_k$ are different symbols called selectors, then a new structure t is defined as

$$t \langle s_1 : t_1, s_2 : t_2, ..., s_k : t_k \rangle$$

and we associate the structure in Fig. 1.

Here we can use t_1, t_2, ..., t_k for types (and t also for a composed type) or for the terms of the language, i.e. objects, representing data structures. The structuring mechanism is used for both data and type structures:

If string, integer are types, then

record ⟨1: string, 2: integer, 3: integer⟩

defines a new, composed type as in Fig. 2, and if "NAME"

"SALARY", "TAX" are data, then PAYMENT ⟨1:NAME, 2:SALARY, 3:TAX⟩

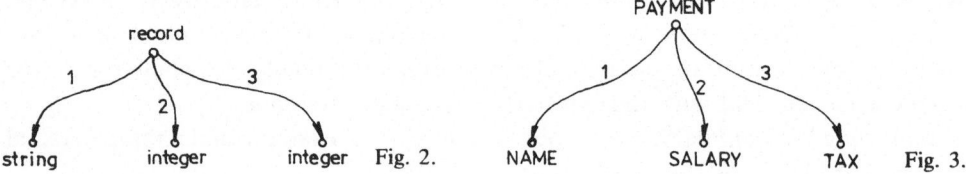

Fig. 2.   Fig. 3.

is also a data structure (Fig. 3). If NAME is a string and both SALARY and TAX are integers, then

string (NAME)
integer (SALARY)
integer (TAX)
record (PAYMENT)

are fomulae in SL and the first three are true. For structured types and data, a formula such as record (PAYMENT) can be true or false, but if in the more elementary structures, the so-called substructures are true, then record (PAYMENT) should be true (as in this case).

We denote by $t[s_i]$ a substructure of t selected by selector s_i, then

record [i] (PAYMENT[i])   (i = 1, 2, 3).

But we have

record[1] = string, PAYMENT[1] = NAME,
record[2] = integer, PAYMENT[2] = SALARY,
record[3] = integer, PAYMENT[3] = TAX,

hence, we have instead of record [i] (PAYMENT [i]):

string (NAME)
integer (PAYMENT)
integer (TAX)

which can be true or false. If true, we can say that PAYMENT is of type record.

Here we give the syntax of SL in BNF notation in a slightly modified form:
— concatenation is written using dot ".": for example, letter.letter.
set is written as {...}: i.e. a list of symbols, bracketed by { },

— symbols, occurring in a special context where they are selectors, are automatically declared as selector and in this case we write "selector", representing an arbitrary symbol;

— we assume that a set of basic-types is given. They are the predicate symbols. The user can declare the appropriate set of basic-types reflecting the elementary concepts of the lowest-level which the structures are built from. In the examples we shall use only bit (n), instructions; these are sufficient to describe hardware processors. The one essential basic-type is the selector or simply sel, and it is always assumed that the set of basic-types includes this type.

Syntax of SL

letters : : = A | ... | Z,a | b | ... | z ;

digits : : = 0 | ... | 9

externals : : = constant | reference | formulae | basic-types |
                selector | structure |
                < | > | [|] | (|) | : | , | ; | logical-connectives ;

logical-connectives : : = unary-logical-connectives |
                          binary-logical-connectives ;

unary-logical-connectives : : = $\neg$ (not)

binary-logical-connectives : : = $\rightarrow$, $\vee$, $\wedge$ (implies, or, and)

alphanumeric : : = digit | letter | letter.alphanumeric |
                digit.alphanumeric

symbol : : = letter | letter.alphanumeric

list : : = symbol | symbol.,.list

selector : : = selector | sel | "selector"

selector-domain : : = [lower-bound : upper-bound]

lower-bound : : = "selector"

upper-bound : : = "selector"

constant-declaration : : = constant list-of-symbols ;

selector-expression : : = ["selector"] | ["selector"].selector-expression

basic-type : : = {basic-type} | selector

type-declarator : : = structure

type-name : : = symbol

type-declaration : : = type-declarator.
                    .type-name{⟨"selector" : struc-type-ref⟩} ;

struc-type-ref : : = type-reference | struc-reference

type-ref : : = basic-type | type-name | type-name.
          .selector-expression | type-expression

type-expression : : = type-name⟨{"selector" : type-reference}⟩ ;

structure-reference : : = structure-name |
                  struc-name.selector expression |
                  struc-expression

structure-declarator : : = type-reference | reference (type-name)
struc-declaration : : = struc-declarator.list-of-structure-names ;
structure-name : : = symbol
structure-expression : : = structure-name.
                            .⟨ { "selector" : structure-reference} ⟩ ;
predicate-declaration : : = predicate.structure-expression ;
function-declaration : : = type-reference.function.function symbol.
                            .specification ; identities-declaration ; body ;
function-symbol : : = function-name.(list-of-formal-parameters)
function-name : : = symbol
formal-parameters : : = symbol
specification : : = declaration
identities-declaration : : = identities list-of-identities ;
identity : : = term. = term ;
term : : = symbol | function name (list-of-terms)
body : : = begin.local declaration ; list-of-structure assignments.end
local-declaration : : = declaration
structure-assignment : : = left-part. :.right-part ;
left-part : : = structure-reference | function-name
right-part : : = structure-reference | term
statement : : = structure expression.binary-logical-connective.
                .structure-expression | unary-logical-connective.
                .structure-expression
declaration-part : : = {declarations}
declaration : : = type-declaration | structure-declaration |
                    constant-declaration
description : : = formulae{statements},
program-specification : : = statement ;

What does the given description cover? First we explain the data structures and then the types:

By structures we mean objects and hierarchical interconnections between them. Instructions are mappings of structures: for example, i

$$i: s_1 \rightarrow s_2.$$

To describe the hierarchy of structures we use selectors. The selectors of a single structure must be different. Instead of their declaration the selectors are allocated by ⟨ ⟩ signs in the following form:

structure-name⟨ {selector$_i$: substructure$_i$} ⟩

For instance:
REGISTERS⟨1:ACCUMULATOR, 2:REG, 3:INST⟩
ACCUMULATOR ⟨1:CARRY, 2:VALUE⟩

The meaning of this is shown in Fig. 4.

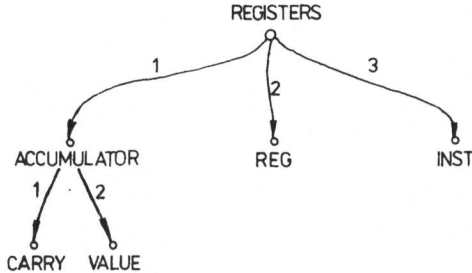

Fig. 4.

We refer also to the substructures, e.g.
REGISTERS [1] = ACCUMULATOR
REGISTERS [1] [2] = VALUE

A structure is called homogeneous if it has substructures of the same type. In this case we can shorten our notation:

structure-name⟨[*lb*: *nb*]: structures⟩,

where [*lb*: *nb*] stands for the lower-bound and the upper-bound of selectors.

Operations in structures

In accordance with the notation we now present the operations on structures. If we write $S⟨se1:S*⟩$, then structure S has a substructure $S*$; that is, if S had a substructure connected to it by the selector $se1$ before, then it is changed by $S*$, if not, a new selector $se1$ is generated and $S*$ is attached to it. Referring to the example in the Fig. 4, REGISTERS⟨1:NULL⟩ results in the Fig. 5, and REGISTERS⟨3:MOVE⟩ in Fig. 6. This operation corresponds to the μ in VDL.

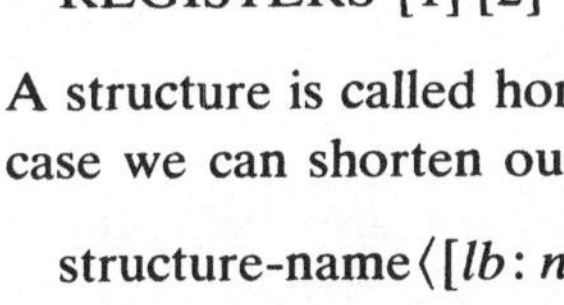

Fig. 5.

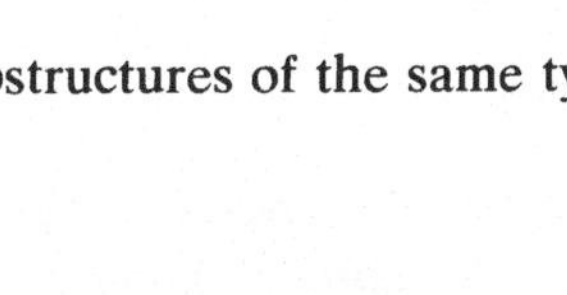

Fig. 6.

As can be seen, only those selectors are written which are changed. So REGISTERS ⟨ ⟩ would mean no change at all.

Types

As already mentioned, each structure has a type. The following rule applies: only structures of the same type can be replaced by each other. This eliminates instructions without meaning, e.g. moving data from MEMORY to the CARRY bit not knowing which part of the data is to be stored and which part is to be dropped.

Examples: If we have three basic-types, such as: bit(n) selector, instruction, then the type of every structure must be declared:

bit(1) CARRY;
bit(4) REG,VALUE;
selector j;
instruction MOVE,EXCH;

New structured types can be derived from these basic types:

type-name$\langle\{$selectors sub-types$\}\rangle$.

Examples

REGIST-TYPE: $\langle 1: \text{bit}(5), 2: \text{REG-TYPE}, 3: \text{instruction}\rangle$;
REG-TYPE$\langle[1:8]: \text{bit}(4)\rangle$;

In this way "new standard types" are introduced which can also be used in declarations. As shown, homogeneous types are treated in a similar way as homogeneous structures. In a declaration we allow the use of structures whose type has already been defined. This can be of importance if we want to emphasize that two different structures have the same substructure.

We have shown how to declare compound structures using the compound types already defined. There is no restriction on the sequence of declarations, but it is important that there should be no structure left without a type declaration at the end.

Functions

In SL (as generally in Mathematical Logic) we use a set of functions such as

function-name (parameters),

where "parameters" state the types of symbols, and functions have types. It should be noted that it is not necessary to associate meanings with function symbols, because functions represent strings which are symbolically manipulated by special syntax (and substitution rules). Hence,

+ (integer, integer),

where integer is a basic-type which has no connection with the "plus" function which adds 2 and 3, and has the result 5. In mathematical logic it is not necessary to know the value (only the type) of a function, except for equality, e.q. EQU(5, + (2,3)). That part of SL which deals with functions and constants is described in the Appendix, together with a complete description of a microcomputer.

Description of instructions

Given structures, types and functions, we can describe instructions by giving the state of the structures before and after the execution of the instruction. We have declared the syntactic form of the instructions, here we must describe their effects. For example, if we write in the declaration

instruction add(sel),

then

$$\text{REGISTERS}\langle 1:X\rangle \rightarrow \text{REGISTERS}\langle 1: +(X,\text{REG}[j]),3:\text{add}(j)\rangle$$

or the equivalent form:

$$\text{REGISTERS}\rightarrow \text{REGISTERS}\langle 1: +(\text{REGISTERS}[1], \text{REG}[j]),3:(\text{add}(j)\rangle;$$

This statement can be interpreted as follows: the instruction add(j) can be executed in an arbitrary state of the machine described by $\text{REGISTERS}\langle 1:X\rangle$, and after the execution of add(j) the state will be changed as in Fig. 7.

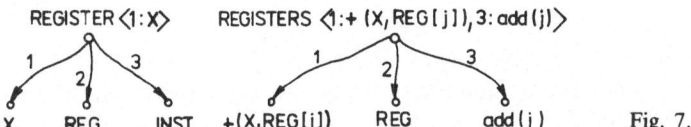

Fig. 7.

Syntactically, the set of statements describing all the instructions should be declared by

formulae{statements}.

We must stress the difference between the instruction declaration and the instruction description. In the instruction declaration we declare some of the function symbol instructions and in the parameter-list we write the appropriate types of parameters:

instruction move (selector).

The description of the instructions is the description of the changes produced in the structure by the execution of the instruction in question.

For simplicity we introduce a declaration

predicate structure-expression;

e.g., predicate $MC\langle 1:A, 2:R, 3:M, 4:SRC, 5:P, 6:s\rangle$;

for those structure-names which are used in the instruction description part. Here we can associate substructures with a structure-name in order to simplify the notation used in the description part.

6.3 Description of parallel architectures

Given the logical language SL, we have to show that a set of formulae describes (abstract or real) architectures. It is intuitively true that one can describe a given architecture by an appropriate "program" written in SL: the declaration of structures and functions and a set of logical formulae composed of types with (both unary and binary) logical connectives.

But the converse question is open: given a set of formulae in SL, does a processor implementing it exist? Or, more generally: how can one interpret a set of formulae? Hence, we have to consider interpretations in SL, before describing parallel processors.

Interpretations

Mathematically we have to choose a domain $\mathcal{D}_1$, a set $F(\mathcal{D})$ of functions defined on the domain $\mathcal{D}$, and an evaluation function v, such that
 a) for every symbol x, y, etc., $v(x)$, $v(y) \in \mathcal{D}$,
 b) for every function symbol f in SL, $v(f) \in F(\mathcal{D})$,
 c) for every type symbol t (predicate symbol) $v(t)$ is also a predicate on $\mathcal{D}$, and $v(t)$ on $\mathcal{D}$ has a value, either T or F, such that $v(t_1)$ and $v(t_2)$ have the value T, if $v(t_1 \wedge t_2)$ has the value T, if $v(t_1) = T$, then $v(\neg t_1) = F$, if $v(t_1) = F$, then $v(t_1 \rightarrow t_2) = T$, etc. One can associate true and false with the values T and F. The quadruple $\{\mathcal{D}, F(\mathcal{D}), v, \{T, F\}\}$ is called an interpretation.

Given a set S of formulae, an arbitrary domain $\mathcal{D}$ and the evaluation function v, $\mathcal{D}$ is called a model of S, if for every formula $s \in S$, $v(s) = T$, i.e. the statements in S are true.

In our case the interpretations can be constructed as in classical first-order logic with the exception of structural properties and selectors. For selectors we extend $\mathcal{D}$ by the $\dot{I}$ (set of integers) and extend v, such that if both s_1 and s_2 are selectors and $s_1 \neq s_2$, then $v(s_1) \neq v(s_2)$ and $\in \dot{I}$. In SL the following axiom is valid: for every structure t and O (t is a type, O is a data structure)

$$t(O) \leftrightarrow \bigwedge_{s \in S_t} t[s](O[s])$$

(where ↔ states the logical equivalence and S_t denotes the set of selectors of t, and $t(O)$ represents the application of t to O). This axiom expresses that a formula $t(O)$ is true if and only if its subtypes, namely $t[s]$ are true on the substructure $O[s]$ for every $s \in S_t$. Consequently,

$$v(t)(v(O)) \leftrightarrow \bigwedge_{s' \in v(S_t)} v(t[s])(v(O[s]))$$

($v(S_t)$ is the image set of S_t, i.e. the set $S_{v(t)}$). This is a fundamental formula: it can be interpreted to mean that a statement on a structure O is true if and only if it is true on lower-level substructures:

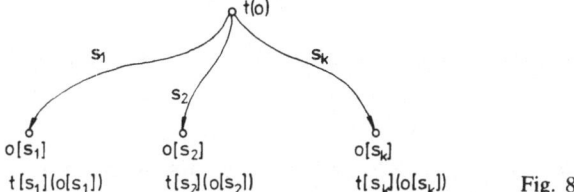

Fig. 8.

hence a lifting mechanism is provided.

It should be noted that during an evaluation, function v is a function defined on symbols, words and sentences of SL, i.e. v map strings. Hence, if for a symbol α, $v(\alpha)$ is fixed in a statement β, $\beta \in S$, then this is true for every other $\beta' \in S$. In our case if, symbols t_1, t_2, t_3, t', t'' such that $t' = \langle s_1 : t_1, s_2 : t_2 \rangle$, $t'' = \langle s_3 : t_1, s_4 : t_3 \rangle$, given in Fig. 9, then during the evaluation

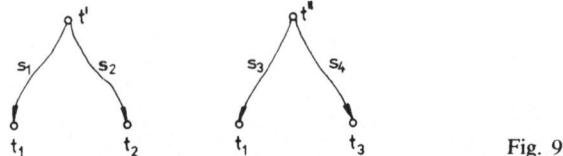

Fig. 9.

the substructure $v(t'[s_1])$ is the same as $v(t''[s_3])$, namely $v(t_1)$:

$$v(t'[s_1]) = v(t''[s_3]) = v(t_1).$$

Here we wish to remind the reader that it is possible in the syntax of SL in a structure-declaration to use a structure already defined by reference, for example:

```
structure a⟨[1 : n] : b⟩ ;
reference (a)A ;
structure machine⟨1 : bit(8), 2 : A⟩ ;
reference (machine)M1, M2.
```

How can one interpret M1 and M2? The structures described by machine are shown in Fig. 10a, and will be interpreted in such a way that A is always the same, hence, M1 and M2 are as in Fig. 10b, c.

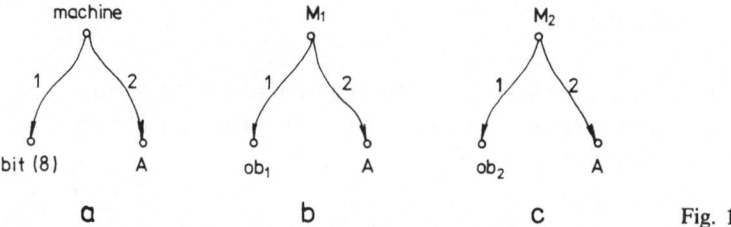

a   b   c   Fig. 10.

Here, ob_1 and ob_2 represent objects characterized by bit(8). It should also be noted, that bit(8) can be interpreted as, for example, a filing system, or a computer. The interpretation is independent of the fact that everyone reading the string "bit(8)" will associate with it the same meaning: objects, consisting of 8 bits. Returning to M1 and M2, one can see that the substructure A is the same object in both M1 and M2. This means that in a formula, such a

$$t_1(M1) \wedge t_2(M2) \rightarrow t_3(M3)$$

M1[2] and M2[1] are the same. Hence, the substructure A of M1 and M2 represents the same object, that is, A is a shared object. This feature makes it possible to describe parallel architectures. The machine described by the previous declaration and extended by

structure double $\langle 1:M1, 2:M2 \rangle$;
reference (double) M;

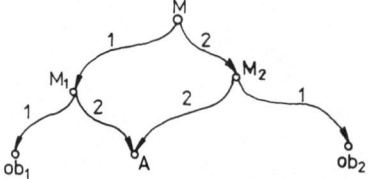

Fig. 11.

is interpreted as in Fig. 11.

Following these explanations, we turn to the description of parallel architectures. First we give an example for Case 0, used in the following way.

Case 0. This processor architecture consists of one instruction stream and one data stream. The instruction stream manipules data in registers by the use of an execution-register. Although a detailed example is given in the Appendix, here we use a simpler architecture to illustrate the power of SL.

We assume that reg, data, inst, exec are basic-types, and ZERO is a predicate with one variable symbol. Then,

structure mach $\langle 1:\text{reg},2:\text{data},3:\text{inst},4:\text{exec}\rangle$

is the type of the machine in Case 0. Also, if

reference (reg)R;
reference (data)DAT;
reference (exec)F;
reference (inst)IN,

then the objects generated by these will be similar to those in above Fig. 12; only the structure of M is not given. We add

reference (mach)M;
predicate $M\langle 1:R,2:DAT,3:IN,4:F\rangle$.

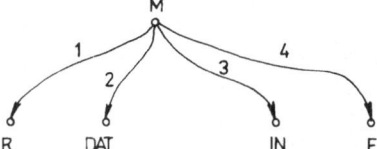

Fig. 12.

(As already mentioned, predicate declares structure-name M with the specified substructures, but this is only a notational simplification.) Given the structures, we define the following simple instruction set (sel stands for selector)

I: instruction move(sel, sel),
  store(sel, sel)
  jump(sel, sel)
  plus(sel, sel, sel),
  not(sel)
 selector s, s_1, s_2;

then

$\mathscr{F}$: $M\langle 3:IN\langle s:\text{move}(i,j)\rangle,4:s\rangle \rightarrow M\langle 1:R\langle i:DAT[j]\rangle,4:s+1\rangle$
  $M\langle 3:IN\langle s:\text{store}(i,j)\rangle,4:s\rangle \rightarrow M\langle 2:DAT\langle i:R[j]\rangle,4:s+1\rangle$
  $M\langle 3:IN\langle s:\text{plus}(i,j,k)\rangle,4:s\rangle \rightarrow M\langle 1:R\langle i:+R[j],R[k])\rangle,4:s+1\rangle$
  $M\langle 3:IN\langle s:\text{not}(i)\rangle,4:s\rangle \rightarrow M\langle 1:R\langle i:-(R[i])\rangle,4:s+1\rangle$
  $M\langle 3:IN\langle s:\text{jump}(i,s_1)\rangle,4:s\rangle \wedge \text{ZERO}(M[1][i]) \rightarrow M\langle 4:s_1\rangle$
  $M\langle 3:IN\langle s:\text{jump}(i,s_1)\rangle,4:s\rangle \wedge \neg\text{ZERO}(M[1][i]) \rightarrow M\langle 4:s+1\rangle$

Each of the first four formulae — the first one, for example — states that if the current instruction — pointed to by the object F in M[4] — is move(i,j), then the result is DAT[j], i.e. the j-th component of DAT is moved to register R[i], and both the remaining part of R and the whole of DAT remain unchanged; furthermore, the instruction to be executed next is selected by $s + 1$. The last two formulae of $\mathscr{F}$ describe "jump if zero to s_1 else continue with $s + 1$". Hence, Case 0 can be illustrated by the following program in SL. ($\mathscr{D}$ stands for declaration, $\dot{I}$ for instruction symbols, and $\mathscr{F}$ for the set of formulae)

$\mathscr{D}$: structure mach$\langle 1:\text{reg},2:\text{data},3:\text{inst},4:\text{exec}\rangle$;
  reference (reg)R; reference (data)DAT;
  reference (inst)IN; reference (exec)F;
  reference (mach)M;
  predicate M$\langle 1:\text{R},2:\text{DAT},3:\text{IN},4:\text{F}\rangle$;

$\dot{I}$: instruction move(sel, sel), store(sel, sel), jump(sel, sel),
       plus(sel, sel, sel), not(sel);
  selector S, s_1;

$\mathscr{F}$: formulae
  M$\langle 3:\text{IN}\langle s:\text{move}(i,j)\rangle,4:s\rangle \rightarrow$M$\langle 1:\text{R}\langle i:\text{DAT}[j]\rangle,4:s+1\rangle$
  M$\langle 3:\text{IN}\langle s:\text{store}(i,j)\rangle,4:s\rangle \rightarrow$M$\langle 2:\text{DAT}\langle i:\text{R}[j]\rangle,4:s+1\rangle$
  M$\langle 3:\text{IN}\langle s:\text{plus}(i,j,k)\rangle,4:s\rangle \rightarrow$M$\langle 1:\text{R}\langle i:+(\text{R}[j],\text{R}[k])\rangle,4:s+1\rangle$
  M$\langle 3:\text{IN}\langle s:\text{not}(i)\rangle,4:s\rangle \rightarrow$M$\langle 1:\text{R}\langle i:-(\text{R}[i])\rangle,4:s+1\rangle$
  M$\langle 3:\text{IN}\langle s:\text{jump}(i,s_1)\rangle,4:s\rangle \wedge \text{ZERO}(\text{M}[1][i])\rightarrow$M$\langle 4:s_1\rangle$
  M$\langle 3:\text{IN}\langle s:\text{jump}(i,s_1)\rangle,4:s\rangle \wedge \neg\text{ZERO}(\text{M}[1][i])\rightarrow$M$\langle 4:s+1\rangle$.

Case 1. n homogeneous processors with one instruction stream and n data streams can be described in such a way that the instruction streams are shared. We describe computers involved in Case 1 by two different programs.

The first is based on the fact that reg and data in $\mathscr{D}$ are the basic-types, i.e. they are not defined on a lower level. If we define them as follows:

  structure reg$\langle[1:m]:\text{reg1}\rangle,\text{reg1}\langle[1:n]:\text{reg2}\rangle$;
  structure data$\langle[1:k]:\text{data}\rangle,\text{data}\langle[1:n]:\text{data2}\rangle$,

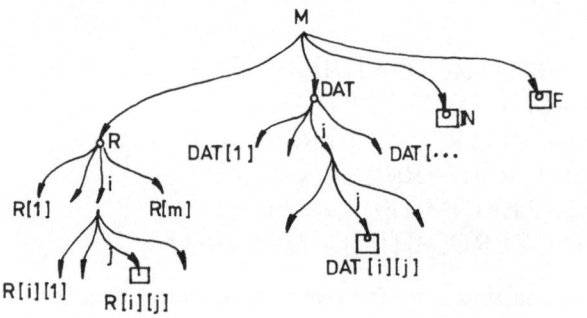

Fig. 13.

then reg2 and data2 are interpreted as words storing information, reg1 and data1 as a vector of length n between processors, and reg and data represent data streams with length m and k, respectively.

Adding these to $\mathscr{D}$, we become Fig. 13.

One component of this machine is of $R[i][j]$, $DAT[i][j]$, IN and F indicated by $\square$. The remaining parts of the program should be $\mathscr{D}$, $\dot{I}$ and $\mathscr{F}$. For example, in $\mathscr{F}$ a typical expression is

$R\langle i : DAT[j]\rangle$.

This states that the i-th component of R, $R[i]$, is changed by the j-th component of DAT, $DAT[j]$ and the other substructures of R remaining unchanged. But both $R[i]$ $DAT[j]$ have the same "scheme"

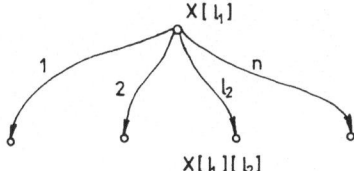

Fig. 14.

where X is either R or DAT and these finer substructures will be copied, so that $R[l_1][l_2]$ will be $DAT[l_1][l_2]$. In fact, on the l-th machine this is the effect of the instruction move(i, j).

The second description of the processor in Case 1 leads us closer to our final solution based on the interpretations discussed at the beginning of this chapter. What we have to do is to generate the objects IN and F before the composed type mach is specified. The basic-types are not redefined and the original ones are used:

$\mathscr{D}1$: reference (inst)IN, reference (exec)F;
structure mach$\langle 1 : \text{reg}, 2 : \text{data}, 3 : \text{IN}, 4 : \text{F}\rangle$;
reference (reg)R; reference (data)DAT;
reference (mach)M;
predicate M$\langle 1 : R, 2 : DAT, 3 : IN, 4 : F\rangle$,
structure machine$\langle [1 : n] : M\rangle$;
reference (machine)MM.

The structure of the processors in Case 1 is shown in Fig. 15.
The instruction stream IN and the program counter F are shared and MM consists of n processors, each of which has its own registers and data streams. M was declared to be a predicate, hence in copies of it one can refer to substructures R and

DAT directly and not as **MM**[1][1], ..., etc. The structure-declaration of the machine $\langle \square : n] : \mathbf{M} \rangle$ states that n copies of $\mathbf{M}$ are structured as a machine. Before dealing with the description of parts $\dot{I}$ and $\mathscr{F}$, some comments should be made:

— In this description n is interpreted as follows: n is fixed, but arbitrary. Fixed, because we will use it as a constant (i.e. it will not be changed or substituted), arbitrary, because every statement is valid (or not) independently of the value of n.

— In the instruction description a typical formula used is:

$$\mathbf{MM}\langle k : \mathbf{M}\langle 3 : \mathbf{IN}\langle s : \text{move}(i,j)\rangle, 4 : s\rangle\rangle \rightarrow \mathbf{MM}\langle k : \mathbf{M}\langle 1 : \mathbf{R}\langle i : \text{DAT}[j]\rangle, 4 : s+1\rangle.$$

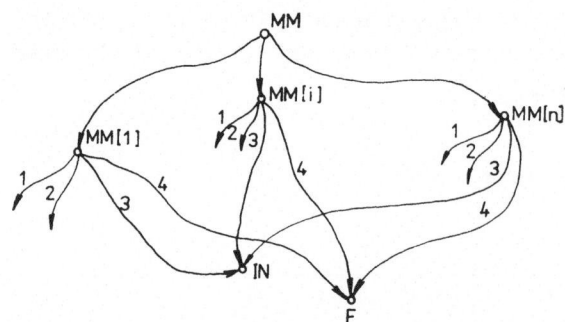

Fig. 15.

To explain this formula, one has to read it as follows: for every k, **MM**[k] is changed as described in the internal description bracketed by $\langle\ \rangle$.

Why? In Mathematical Logic these statements are totally independent. If we have two predicates P and Q, variable symbols X, Y and Z and two formulae, such as

$$\mathscr{F}_1 : P(X,Y) \wedge Q(X,X) \rightarrow \neg Q(X,Y),$$
$$\mathscr{F}_2 : P(X,Z) \wedge Q(Z,X) \rightarrow P(X,X),$$

then there is no connection between the symbols X in $\mathscr{F}_1$ and $\mathscr{F}_2$. They are totally different although the same symbols are used. However, within the same formula, for example in $\mathscr{F}_1$, the symbol X represents the same object in all its occurrences. In SL selectors can be constant (1, 2, or n — as has been mentioned) or variables (i, j, k — in our examples). Hence, in a formula

$$\mathbf{MM}\langle k : X \rangle \rightarrow \mathbf{MM}\langle k : Y \rangle,$$

if no other references are made to k in X and Y, then the formula is valid for every k, because k is arbitrary (between 1 and n). Of course, we could say the same of the selector variables i, j and s in this description of move(i, j), because the formula makes a statement based on i, j and s, i.e. for every i, j and s. Thus, they are arbitrary symbols. Consequently, the above formula can be written in SL as

$$MM\langle 1:M\langle 3:IN\langle 1:move(1,1)\rangle,4:1\rangle\rangle\rightarrow MM\langle 1:M\langle 1:R\langle 1:DAT[1]\rangle,4:2\rangle\rangle$$
$$\vdots$$
$$MM\langle n:M\langle 3:IN\langle l:move(m,k)\rangle,4:l\rangle\rangle\rightarrow$$
$$\rightarrow MM\langle n:M\langle 1:R\langle m:DAT[k]\rangle,4:l+1\rangle$$

which is a set of $n\times l\times m\times k$ formulae. They are logically "and"-ed. SL allows us to write them as one formula. From these explanations one can see that in Case 1 the set of the formal declarations of instructions is the same as in Case 2, but part $\mathscr{F}$, in which the description of the instruction is given, is modified as suggested:

$\mathscr{F}1$: formulae
$$\{MM\langle k:Y\rangle\rightarrow MM\langle k:Z\rangle\mid Y\rightarrow z\in\mathscr{F}\}.$$

Hence, the set written in $\mathscr{F}1$ is the same as in $\mathscr{F}$, but it is extended to the higher-level structure of MM containing machines M.

Case 2. n homogeneous processors, n streams and n instruction streams are given. This case is meaningless if we do not assume that they perform synchronized processes. For without synchronization they operate simultaneously and independently. A special case can be described here where only one data memory is given, and the n data streams are selected by the processors (with the exec-type component F). This subcase can be described as

reference (data) DAT;
structure mach$\langle 1:reg,2:DAT,3:inst,4:exec\rangle$,

and continued as in Case 0, but ended with

structure machine$\langle[1:n]:mach\rangle$,
reference (machine)MM,

when n processors are given. In both forms DAT is shared and the objects, i.e. the processors described by mach, have separate instruction streams, with their own instruction selectors stored in the exec-typed subobjects of the processors (4-th component). A more interesting subcase is the problem of synchronized processors. In the simplest case discussed here every processor has a special flag, 0 or 1, which represents the free or busy state of the processor.

The set of instruction-symbols $\hat{I}$ is to be extended by the instructions

start(sel), stop(sel),

which activate or halt the processor pointed to by the parameter selector; "start" is a deferred instruction: if the processor is busy then the start instruction is repeated; "stop" executes no operation if the processor to be stopped is free, else it makes it free. We concentrate on this problem only because more complicated control structures (with wait, messages, etc.) can be described in a similar way. Hence, the declaration part of the description using the basic-type flag is:

2: structure mach$\langle 1:\text{reg},2:\text{data},3:\text{inst},4:\text{exec},5:\text{flag}\rangle$

    reference (reg)R; reference (data)DAT;

    reference (inst)IN; reference (exec)F;

    reference (flag)FL;

    reference (mach)M;

    predicate M$\langle 1:\text{R},2:\text{DAT},3:\text{IN},4:\text{F},5:\text{FL}\rangle$;

    structure parallel$\langle [1:n]:\text{M}\rangle$;

    reference (parallel)MM;

    constant 0,1;

  $i2: i \cup \{\text{start(sel)}, \text{stop(sel)}\}$.

The formulae should contain the synchronization primitives. Hence,

$$F_1 \; MM\langle k: M\langle 3:x,4:s,5:0\rangle\rangle \to MM\langle k: M\langle 3:x,4:s,5:0\rangle\rangle$$

states that every processor $MM[k]$, for which $MM[k]$ is free, i.e. $MM[k][5]=0$, executes no operation, independent of the contents x and s of the instruction stream and the program-counter, because in F_1 both parts describe the same structure. Similarly,

$$F_2 \; MM\langle k: M\langle 5:0\rangle, i: M\langle 3: IN\langle s: \text{start}(k)\rangle, 4:s, 5:1\rangle\rangle$$
$$\to MM\langle k: M\langle 5:1\rangle, i: M\langle 4:s+1, 5:1\rangle\rangle$$
$$F_3 \; MM\langle k: M\langle 5:1\rangle, i: M\langle 3: IN\langle s: \text{start}(k)\rangle, 4:s, 5:1\rangle\rangle$$
$$\to MM\langle k: M\langle 5:1\rangle, i: M\langle 4:s, 5:s\rangle\rangle$$
$$F_4 \; MM\langle k: M\langle 5:1\rangle, i: M\langle 3: IN\langle s: \text{stop}(k)\rangle, 4:s, 5:1\rangle\rangle$$
$$\to MM\langle k: M\langle 5:0\rangle, i: M\langle 4:s+1, 5:1\rangle$$
$$F_5 \; MM\langle k: M\langle 5:0\rangle, i: M\langle 3: IN\langle s: \text{stop}(k)\rangle, 4:s, 5:1\rangle\rangle$$
$$\to MM\langle k: M\langle 5:0\rangle, i: M\langle 4:s+1, 5:1\rangle\rangle$$

F_2, F_3 describe start and F_4, F_5 describe stop. The processor i gives a signal to processor k to start. This can be issued only if processor i itself is in a busy state.

The original instruction set declared in i and described in $\mathscr{F}$ will be almost the same, but in every formula such as

$$X \to Y$$

in $\mathscr{F}$ we have to assume that the 5-th component is 1 (i.e. the processor is working).

We denote by T_1 and T_0 the transformations

$$T_1: X \to X\langle 5:1\rangle$$
$$T_0: X \to X\langle 5:0\rangle$$

Then $\mathscr{F}^*$ is a set:

$$\mathscr{F}^*: \{MM\langle k: T_1 X\rangle \to MM\langle k: T_1 Y\rangle \mid X \to Y \in \mathscr{F}\}$$

F_1 can be rewritten as

$$MM\langle k:T_0X\rangle \rightarrow MM\langle k:T_0X\rangle$$

for every X. Hence, it is superflous to describe the instructions when the processor is free. The new formulae, describing Case 2 are:

$$\mathscr{F}_2: \{F_1, F_2, F_3, F_4, F_5\}\cup\mathscr{F}^*.$$

Now, let us deal with the last case.

Case 3. n heterogeneous processors with shared data and with synchronization. In this typical case the synchronization can be described in a similar way as in Case 2; hence, the only case to be dealt with is when explicit synchronization is performed. The shared data is declared by

> reference (data)DAT;
> structure mach $1\langle 1:\text{reg},3:\text{inst}, ..., s_d^1:\text{DAT}, ...\rangle$;
> structure mach $2\langle ..., 2:\text{DAT},3:, ...\rangle$;
> structure mach $n\langle 1:\text{flag},s_d^n:\text{DAT}\rangle$,

where the structures mach 1, mach 2, ..., mach n contain arbitrary substructures reflecting the heterogeneity of the machines, but s_d^i selects component DAT. The remaining part of the declarations are the same as in Case 0, but n different processors are declared. Similarly to the set I in Case 0, I^1, I^2, ..., I^n represent the set of instruction symbols implemented on the processors mach 1, mach 2, ..., mach n.

The common frame is declared

> structure submachine$\langle 1:\text{mach } 1,2:\text{mach } 2, ..., n;\text{mach } n\rangle$;
> structure machine$\langle 1:\text{DAT},2:\text{submachine}\rangle$;
> reference (machine)MM.

Note that "mach i" (for arbitrary i) can have the component DAT selected by s_d^i.

In the formulae defining the instructions, the sets of formulae $\mathscr{F}^*$ for machines, such as "mach i", must be described as if they were independent, except for local structures, because there is a higher-level structure MM containing shared data DAT. For every structure-expression in $\mathscr{F}$ (or in the appropriate $\mathscr{F}^1$, $\mathscr{F}^2$, ..., $\mathscr{F}^n$ for local structure-description) we denote by H_k the following structure-transformation:

$$H_k: x \rightarrow MM\langle 1:X[s_d^i]\langle 2,MM[2][k],i:X\ s_d^i:\Omega\rangle\rangle$$

where Ω is an empty substructure and for the arbitrary substructure Z, $MM[k]Z$ represents $MM[k][\text{sel}_z]$ for that selector sel_z which selects $Z: MM[k][\text{sel}_z] = Z$: i.e., $X[s_d^i]$ represents the DAT component of X, which is copied into the shared data in such a way that every substructure-symbol in $X[s_d^i]$ is qualified by $MM[k]$. This is represented by $X[s_d^i]$ MM[2][k]. The qualification of the symbol Z is simple; it has the form

MM[2][k]Z

$X\langle s_d^i : \Omega \rangle$ means that the original DAT component is removed. For example, in $\mathscr{F}^k$ the store instruction (if $k = 2$) we write:

X: $M_k \langle 3 : \text{IN}\langle s: \text{store}(i, j)\rangle, 4: s \rangle$
Y: $M_k \langle 2 : \text{DAT}\langle i: \text{R}[j]\rangle, 4: s + 1 \rangle$,

where M_k is the predicate declared for mach k. (We took these formulae from $\mathscr{F}$ in Case 0.) Hence, we have the form

$X \to Y$

describing the instruction store (i, j).

After H_k, if $k = 2$ then $s_2^2 = 2$, on the left-hand side $X[s_d^k]$ is arbitrary, so that

$H_k X$: $\text{MM}\langle 2: \langle k: M_k \langle 3: \text{IN}\langle s: \text{store}(i,j)\rangle 4: s \rangle\rangle\rangle$,

but the right-hand side:

$H_k Y$: $\text{MM}\langle 1: \text{DAT}\langle i: \text{MM}[2][k]\text{R}[j]\rangle, \langle 2: \langle k: M_k \langle 4: s + 1, 2: \Omega \rangle\rangle\rangle$

hence,

$H_k X \to H_k Y$

has the form

$\text{MM}\langle k: M_k \langle 3: \text{IN}\langle s: \text{store}(i,j)\rangle, 4: s \rangle\rangle$
$\qquad \to \text{MM}\langle 1: \text{DAT}\langle i: \text{MM}[2][k]\text{R}[j]\rangle, k: M_k \langle 4: s + 1 \rangle\rangle$.

The transformations H_k are imbedded into a higher-level structure. $\mathscr{F}_3$, the set of formulae in Case 3 is

$\mathscr{F}_3$: $\{H_k \mathscr{F}^k, \qquad k = 1, 2, ..., n\}$

where $\mathscr{F}^k$ is a set of formulae describing mach k and

$H_k \mathscr{F}^k$: $\{H_k X \to H_k Y \,|\, X, Y; X \to Y \in \mathscr{F}^k\}$.

6.4 Specification and synthesis of parallel programs

Above we have dealt with a method for describing parallel abstract processors. Although we have treated four cases only, the others can be described by suitable applications of the techniques presented here. It is shown in this chapter how one can describe parallel programs and how the system SL generates such programs.

We know that every program $\mathscr{P}$ is only a transformation of the input data structure $\mathring{\mathscr{J}}$ into another data structure $\mathcal{O}$

$$\mathscr{P}: \mathring{\mathscr{J}} \to \mathcal{O}.$$

The data structure and the program itself are imbedded in the processor which will execute it. The processor is given by its description and the special data structures of $\mathscr{P}$ are given in $\mathscr{P}$. Hence, $\mathscr{P}$ is only a function composed of instructions.

Consequently, both $\mathring{\mathscr{J}}$ and $\mathcal{O}$ are data structures compatible with the processor, so $\mathscr{P}$ transforms the processor from a state specified by $\mathring{\mathscr{J}}$. This means that both $\mathring{\mathscr{J}}$ and $\mathcal{O}$ are structure expressions; $\mathring{\mathscr{J}}$ and $\mathcal{O}$ are called input-specification and output-specification and a formula

$$\mathring{\mathscr{J}} \to \mathcal{O}$$

is the specification of program $\mathscr{P}$. It is a well-formed formula in SL, where $\to$ represents "implies". (Readers interested in Mathematical Logic can see that this proves the correctness and adequacy of SL — hence, SL has correct semantics and is a unique model, apart from isomorphism.)

Using a description $\mathscr{A}: \mathscr{D} \cup \mathring{I} \cup \mathscr{J}$, verification means that

$$\mathscr{A} \mapsto \mathring{\mathscr{J}} \to \mathcal{O}$$

i.e. $\mathring{\mathscr{J}} \to \mathcal{O}$ can be derived from $\mathscr{A}$ logically, and the program can be proved.

What are the specification and proof? These are illustrated for Case 1. The declarations are given there, but not the formulae. In the following examples only the instructions move, plus and store are needed.

F1 : $\mathrm{MM}\langle k: \mathrm{M}\langle 3: \mathrm{IN}\langle s: \mathrm{move}(i,j)\rangle\rangle, 4: s\rangle$
        $\to \mathrm{MM}\langle k: \mathrm{M}\langle 1: \mathrm{R}\langle j: \mathrm{DAT}[i]\rangle\rangle, 4: s+1\rangle$
F2 : $\mathrm{MM}\langle k: \mathrm{M}\langle 3: \mathrm{IN}\langle s: \mathrm{store}(i,j)\rangle\rangle, 4: s\rangle$
        $\to \mathrm{MM}\langle k: \mathrm{M}\langle 2: \mathrm{DAT}\langle i: \mathrm{R}[j]\rangle\rangle, 4: s1\rangle$
F3 : $\mathrm{MM}\langle k: \mathrm{M}\langle 3: \mathrm{IN}\langle s: \mathrm{plus}(i,j,k)\rangle\rangle, 4: s\rangle$
        $\to \mathrm{MM}\langle k: \mathrm{M}\langle 1: \mathrm{R}\langle k: +(\mathrm{R}[j], \mathrm{R}[j])\rangle\rangle, 4: s+1\rangle$

Let x and y be vectors of length n. Add them componently to component and store them in z: $z(k) = x(k) + y(k)$.

DAT described by

$$\mathrm{DAT}\langle 1: x, 2: y, 3: z\rangle$$

and x, y, z are of type structure $\langle[1:n]: \text{integer}\rangle$, where integer is a basic-type. Then $\mathring{\mathscr{J}}$ contains this structure and the program $\mathscr{P}$.

$$\mathscr{P}: \mathrm{move}([1][k], 1)0\ \mathrm{move}([2][k], 2)0\ \mathrm{plus}(1,2,3)0\ \mathrm{store}([3][k], 3)$$

for every k, where 0 represents sequential execution. Hence,

$\mathring{p} \to \mathcal{O}$:

$\mathring{p}$: $MM\langle k: M\langle 2: DAT\langle 1: x, 2: y, 3: z\rangle,$
$\qquad\qquad 3: IN\langle 1: move([1][k],1),$
$\qquad\qquad\qquad 2: move([2][k], 2),$
$\qquad\qquad\qquad 3: plus(1,2,3),$
$\qquad\qquad\qquad 4: store([3][k], 3)\rangle$
$\qquad\qquad 4: 1\rangle\rangle \to$

$\mathcal{O}$: $\to MM\langle k.$
$\qquad M\langle 2: DAT\langle 3: z\langle k: +(x[k],y[k])\rangle\rangle$

We now explain this specification: DAT contains the vectors where, for example, $x[k]$ represents $DAT[1][k]$, and the program is stored in IN. The program counter points initially to 1, i.e. to the first instruction.

Before this program is verified, two remarks must be made:

a) in an expression like $IN\langle s: store(i,j)\rangle$ we state only that the s-th component contains store (i,j). This means that the others are arbitrary, so we do not write $s + 1: x_1, s + 2: x_2, \ldots$ The same is true for more complicated structures;

b) in a formula F the symbols are local. This means that if two arbitrary symbols x and y are given and x occurs in the formula, then every occurrence of x can be replaced by y, the result being written $F_{y/x}$. It can be proved that

$F \to F_{y/x}$

is valid, i.e. $F_{y/x}$ is a logical consequence of F. If X and Y are typed symbols (for example, structures in SL) then, if they have the same type, they can be substituted. With regard to symbols, one has to use their syntactic meaning. Examples of symbols are: X, 2, M, move $(x[k],2),n$.

The first step in proving program p is to use F1 with the substitutions

$\{DAT\langle 1: x, 2: y, 3: z\rangle \mid M[2], 1/s, 1/j, [1][k]/i\}$

The system rewrites F1 as

$MM\langle k: M\langle 2: DAT\langle 1: x, 2: y, 3: z\rangle,$
$\qquad\qquad 3: IN \ \langle 1: move([1][k],1), 2: move([2][k],2),$
$\qquad\qquad\qquad 3: plus(1,2,3), 4: store([3][k],3)$
$\qquad\qquad\qquad 4: 1\rangle \to$

$\to MM\langle k: M\langle 1: R\langle 1: DAT [1][k]\rangle,$
$I\dagger \qquad\qquad 2: DAT\langle 1: x, 2: y, 3: z\rangle,$
$\qquad\qquad 3: IN\langle 2: move([2][k],2), 3: plus(1,2,3),$
$\qquad\qquad\qquad\qquad 4: store([3][k],3),$
$\qquad\qquad\qquad\qquad 4: 2\rangle$

Hence, F1 can be written as $\overset{\circ}{\mathcal{J}}$, i.e. F1 derives the structure described in I_1^*. This means that we have proved mechanically (using substitutions) that the first step of the programs results in

$$I_1^* : \overset{\circ}{\mathcal{J}} \xrightarrow{\text{F1}} I_1^*.$$

A further application of F1 with substitutions

$$\{2/s, 2/j, [2][k]/i\}$$

has the result: $I_1^* \to I_2^*$, where

$$
\begin{aligned}
I_2^* = \text{MM}\langle\, k : \text{M}\langle\, 1 : & \text{R}\langle 1 : \text{DAT}[1][k], \\
& 2 : \text{DAT}[2][k], \\
2 : & \text{DAT}\langle 1 : x, 2 : y, 3 : z \rangle, \\
3 : & \text{DAT}\langle 3 : \text{plus}(1,2,3), \\
& \qquad 4 : \text{store}([3][k],3)\rangle \\
4 : & 3\rangle
\end{aligned}
$$

and the application of F3 with substitutions

$$\{3/s,\ 1/s,\ 2/j,\ 3/k\}$$
$$I_2^* \to I_3^*,$$

where

$$
\begin{aligned}
I_3^* = \text{MM}\langle\, k : \text{M}\langle\, 1 : & \text{R}\langle 1 : \text{DAT}[1][k], \\
& 2 : \text{DAT}[2][k], \\
& 3 : +(\text{DAT}[1][k], \text{DAT}[2][k])\rangle \\
2 : & \text{DAT}\langle 1 : x, 2 : y, 3 : z \rangle, \\
3 : & \text{IN}\langle 4 : \text{store}([3][k],3)\rangle \\
4 : & 4\rangle
\end{aligned}
$$

and F2 with substitutions

$$\{4/s, [3][k]/i,\ 3/j\}$$
$$I_3^* \to \mathcal{O}^*$$

$$
\begin{aligned}
\mathcal{O}^* = \text{MM}\langle\, k : \text{M}\langle\, 1 : & \text{R}\langle 1 : \text{DAT}[1][k], \\
& 2 : \text{DAT}[2][k], \\
& 3 : \text{DAT}[1][k], \text{DAT}[2][k]\rangle \\
2 : & \text{DAT}\langle 1 : x, 2 : y, \\
& \qquad 3 : \langle k : +(\text{DAT}[1][k], \text{DAT}[2][k])\rangle \rangle\rangle\rangle
\end{aligned}
$$

and $\mathcal{O}^* \to \mathcal{O}$ is an immediate consequence.

Only formulae F1, F2 and F3 were used, hence the program $\mathcal{P}$ had been proved correct to the specification, because k is arbitrary.

Of course, this proof is performed by the system SL implemented on a computer. The specification is equivalent to

$$MM\langle k: M\langle 3: \mathscr{P}, 4:1\rangle\rangle \rightarrow$$
$$\rightarrow MM\langle k: M\langle 2: DAT\langle 3: z\langle k: +(x[k], y[k])\rangle\rangle\rangle\rangle$$

where $\mathscr{P}$ stands for the program proved. We wrote the specification in a more detailed form only to ease the explanation. The set of formulae F was used as an axiom-system. If $\mathring{\mathscr{I}} \rightarrow \mathcal{O}$ is a specification of a program

$$\mathscr{P}: i_1 \circ i_2 \circ \ldots \circ i_n$$

of instructions $i_1, i_2, \ldots, i_n$, then the proof of correctness of $\mathscr{P}$ is a chain of logical consequences

$$\mathring{\mathscr{I}} \xrightarrow{\mathscr{I}_{i1}} I_1^* \xrightarrow{\mathscr{I}_{i2}} I_2^* \rightarrow \ldots \xrightarrow{\mathscr{I}_{in}} I_n^* \xrightarrow{\mathscr{I}} \mathcal{O},$$

where $\mathscr{I}_{ij}$ represents the formula describing the instruction i_j, and the deduction $I_{i_{j-1}}^* \xrightarrow{\mathscr{I}_{ij}} I_{i_j}^*$ represents an application of this formula.

The synthesis of parallel programs is just the opposite: Let a description $\mathscr{A}$ and a specification $\mathscr{I} \rightarrow \mathcal{O}$ be given; the symbol $\mathscr{P}$ represents the unknown parallel program. Find a proof of the specification using $\mathscr{A}$. The proof is program $\mathscr{P}$ itself.

In Mathematical Logic proof theory is a special branch. Here we illustrate in SL how a constructive proof can be reached in a mechanical way. We start with the definition of substitutions.

Substitution is a finite set of the form

$$\sigma: \{t_1/v_1, \ldots, t_n/v_n; \text{inst}/s; z_1/s_1, \ldots, z_k/s_k\},$$

where every v_i is a variable, s an instruction variable, s_i a selector variable, t_i a function of the same type as v_i, inst is an instruction variable or function, z_i is a selector or selector-function, and the variables are different after the symbol (stroke). If F is a formula, then $F\alpha$ is a formula obtained in such a way that a/b means that each occurrence of b is replaced by a, and σ is executed from left to right.

Clauses are formulae which contain only $\vee$ and $\neg$ ("or" and "not"). C is a resolvent of clauses C_1' and C_2', if $C_1' = C_1 \vee B_1$, $C_2' = C_2 \vee B_2$, and there are substitutions σ_1 and σ_2 for which $\neg B_1\sigma_1 = B_2\sigma_2$ implies that

$$C = P_1\sigma_1 \vee P_2\sigma_2.$$

We say that B_1 and B_2 have been resolved.

Note that we have used formulae which are clauses, because every formula was written in the form $X \rightarrow Y$, which is equivalent to $\neg X \vee Y$.

Mechanical theorem-proving methods are based on resolution. The resolution is complete in SL, i.e. it will find the proof if it exists.

The above example of the verification of programs can be repeated in reverse. The only difference is that instead of the chain described by instructions the system will try to find the proof from the expression $\mathcal{O}$. Which are the formulae from which $\mathcal{O}$ can be derived?

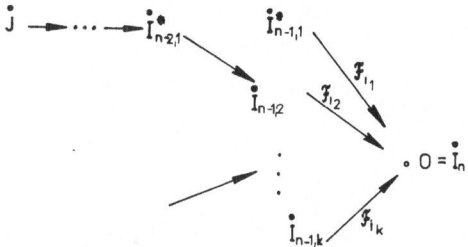

The possible $I_{n-1} = \{I^*_{n-1,1}, I^*_{n-1,2}, ..., I^*_{n-1,k}\}$ (where k is the number of formulae in $\mathcal{F}$ of $\mathcal{A}$) is formed by the resolvents of $\mathcal{O}$ and $X (\in J)$. Not every instruction can be executed in such a way that after the execution the result is $\mathcal{O}$. Remove these from I_{n-1} and repeat this construction for every element of I_{n-1}. Continue this process until $\mathcal{J}$ is contained in a set generated subsequently.

It would go beyond the limits of this paper to synthesize the above. For details see [4].

Conclusion

SL is a mathematical logic, but it is also a "programming" language as presented here. SL has correct semantics, hence every description will have the same semantic contents. Both abstract and real parallel processors can be described, and parallel programs can be specified, verified and generated. We want to obtain experience in SL with a realistic parallel architecture. Our goal is to supply the programmer with tools for systematic program development and for system development from design to implementation (inclusive of documentation). The common base presented here in the context of parallel problems is SL.

REFERENCES

[1] DÁVID, G.: Structured automatized design of microprograms. In: Large-Scale Integration. H. W. Lawson et al. (Editors). North-Holland Publ. Co., Amsterdam, 1978.
[2] DÁVID, G., KERESZTÉLY, S. and SÁRKÖZY, A.: Microprogram synthesis by theorem proving. Proc. 2nd Hungarian Computer Scientific Conference, 1977, part, 1, pp. 291—310.

[3] DÁVID, G., KERESZTÉLY, S., LOSONCZI, I. and SÁRKÖZY, A.: Logic-based description of microcomputers. Tech. Report, MTA SZTAKI Közlemények, Budapest, 1978.

[4] DÁVID, G., KERESZTÉLY, S., LOSONCZI, I. and SÁRKÖZY, A.: Microprogram synthesis. Tech. Report, MTA SZTAKI Közlemények, Budapest, 1978.

[5] DÁVID, G.: A many-stored logic based programming language. In: Logic in Programming. North-Holland Publ. Co., Amsterdam.

Appendix

FUNCTIONS IN SL, THE LANGUAGE OF ARCHITECTURES

A further description of SL is given in this Appendix. The functions and constants are described and an illustrative example is given.

Constants, function: Any identifier which has been declared formerly can be contained in the constant list. Constants are not evaluated, here. So if we use symbol 7 for a constant, it does not necessarily mean that its value is seven. On the contrary, we can give values to the constants and in this way the value of 7 can be, for example, three. The list of constants appears as follows:

constant VALUE,5,REG,
        ACC/$\langle 1:12 \rangle$/, 7/3/.

This means that the substructure connected to structure ACC by selector 1 has the value 12 and symbol 7 has the value 3.

Functions are also not evaluated, unless all their parameters are constants having a value. To declare a function, its type, name and parameter list must be given. A function transforms structures in its parameter list into a structure having the type of the function. The list of identities and the body of the function do also belong to the declaration of a function (see the syntax).

It should be noted that in a logic-based description language the various symbols used are not evaluated — they do not represent values unless this is stated explicitly. The description of a machine is handled symbolically, and the list of identities should be treated as symbolic equations. This means that in the following example $P\langle i:x \rangle$ is equivalent to (RAL: Rotate A Left four bits):

$P\langle i: \mathrm{RAL}(\mathrm{RAL}(\mathrm{RAL}, (\mathrm{RAL}(x)))) \rangle$,
or $P\langle j: \mathrm{RAL}(1) \rangle$ is equivalent to $P\langle j:2 \rangle$.

Let us consider an example of a function declaration. This function defines the instruction Rotate Left by One.

bit (5) function RAL(x); bit(5)x:

identities RAL(0) = 0,
          RAL(1) = 2,
          RAL(RAL(RAL(RAL(RAL(x))))) = x ;
begin structure$\alpha\langle 1:\text{bit}(1),2:\text{bit}(5)\rangle,\delta\langle 1:\text{bit}(5),2:\text{bit}(1)\rangle$,
     reference(α)SA, reference(δ)SO ; equivalence(SA,SD) ;
     SD[1]: x ; SD[2]: = SA[1] ;RAL: = SA[2] ;
end.

The bit(5) function RAL(x); bit(5)x ;" declares RAL to be a five-bit operation in both input x and output RAL(x). The part of "identities" states that five successive RAL's are equivalent to a no-operation NOP and it also provides information about the operation on objects 0 and 1.

The body starts with the declaration of local structures SA and SD. They are equivalenced, and hence refer to the *same* object but with different internal structures

SA[1]   SA[2]

$\underbrace{\hspace{2.5cm}}$

o o o o o o   SA : 1 + 5 bits
o o o o o o

$\underbrace{\hspace{2.5cm}}$

SD[1]   SD[2] : 5 + 1 bits

SD[1]: = X states that the higher 5 bits contain the variable to be rotated. SD[2]: = SA[1] means that the lowest bit will be filled with the highest one. RAL: = SA[2] gives us the result required.

It is possible to declare references to different elements as equivalent. This equivalence can be considered as function where the body and the list-of-identities are empty. We declare

equivalence (list-of-structures).

Example. Let us consider the description of the old-fashioned microcomputer INTEL MCS-4 a paradigm. Naturally, we have to consider only those parts of the machine, which are modified or referred to by the instructions. The MCS-4 has a 4-bit accumulator and a carry flag. It contains an SRC register of one byte (8 bits)

	o	oooo	oooooooo			
	CY	ACC	SRC	0	0	1
	CARRY	Accumulator		1	2	3
				2	4	5
				3	6	7
				4	8	9
				5	10	11
				6	12	13
				7	14	15

The 16 4-bit-long index registers belong to the central processor. They can also be used as eight 1-byte words.

As far as memory is concerned, we are interested at the moment only in RAMs and not ROMs. RAM consists of 256 4-bit-long words from which we can choose according to the contents of the SRC register.

There are 16 input-output parts with 4-bit words. These can be addressed by the four lower bits of SRC register.

The description begins with the declarative part. Here we describe the structure of the machine, i.e. the structure of the hardware.

structure $\alpha \langle [0:15]:\text{bit}(4)\rangle, \beta\langle[0:7]\text{bit}(8)\rangle$,
    $\gamma\langle[0:255]:\text{bit}(4)\rangle, \delta\langle1:\text{bit}(1):2:\text{bit}(4)\rangle$;
    $\varepsilon\langle[1:2]\text{bit}(4)\rangle$;
$\pi\langle1:\text{ref}(\delta), 2:\text{ref}(\alpha), 3:\text{ref}(\gamma), 4:\text{bit}(8), 5:\text{ref}(\alpha), 6:\text{instruction}\rangle$
bit(1) CY/0/,C/1/; bit(5) AC;
bit(4) K,ACO/O/,KO/7/,9/9/ ;
bit(8) SRC,cost ;
ref(α)R,P: ref(β)RR; ref(γ)M; ref(δ)A ;
ref(π)MC: ref(ε)SR ;
equivalence (R, RR),(SRC,SR): (A,AC) ;
   predicate MC$\langle1:A,2:R,3:M,4:SRC, 5:P, 6: SR\rangle$:
   instruction S,NOP(inst), FIM(sel,bit(8)inst),
           SRC(sel,inst), LDM(bit(4),inst),

LDR(sel,inst), XCH(sel,inst),
INC(sel,inst), ADD(sel,inst),
SUB(sel,inst), WRM(inst),
RDM(inst), SBM(inst),ADM(inst),
WRR(inst), RDR(inst), CLB(inst),
CLC(inst), IAC(inst), CMC(inst),
CMA(inst), RAL(inst), RAR(inst),
TCC(inst), DAC(inst),
TCS(inst), STC(inst).

bit(5) function ral(X); bit(5)X;
    identities ral(0) = 0, ral(1) = 2,
        ral(ral(ral(ral(ral(X))))) = X;
    begin
        structure$\alpha \langle 1:bit(1),2:bit(5)\rangle, \delta \langle 1:bit(5),2:bit(1)\rangle$:
        ref(α)SA,ref(δ)SD : equivalence(SA,SD);
        SD[1]: = X: SD[2]: = SA[1],
        ral: = SA[2];
    end;

bit(5) function rar(X); bit(5)X;
    identities rar(0) = 0, rar(2) = 1,
        rar(rar((rar(rar(rar(X)))′))″ = X;
    begin
        structure$\alpha \langle 1:bit(1),2:bit(5)\rangle$;$\delta \langle 1:bit(5),2:bit(1)\rangle$′
        ref(α)SA,ref(δ)SD; equivalence (SA,SD);
        rar: = SD[1];
    end;

bit(4) function inc (X);bit(4)X;
    begin
        structure$\alpha \langle 1:bit(1),2:bit(4)\rangle$
        bit(5)S′,ref(α)SA ; equivalence (S,SA);
        S: = X + 1;
        inc: = SA[2];
    end.

Having defined the hardware, we now consider the instructions. The trick of the description is that the formulae include the instructions, although the instructions do not exist in the machine. This makes it possible for us to generate programs. The instruction set is formulae $MC \rightarrow MC\langle 6 : NOP(s)\rangle$

$MC \rightarrow mC\langle 2 : RR\langle i : const\rangle, 6 : FIM(i, const, s)\rangle$

$MC \rightarrow MC\langle 4 : RR[i], 6 : SRC(i, s)\rangle$

$MC \rightarrow MC\langle 1 : \langle 2 : K\rangle, 6 : LDM(K, s)\rangle$

$MC \rightarrow MC\langle 1 : \langle 2 : R[i], 6 : LDR(i, s)\rangle$

$MC \rightarrow MC\langle 1 : \langle 2 : R[i]\rangle, 2 : \langle i : A[2]\rangle, 6 : XCH(i, s)\rangle$

$MC \rightarrow MC\langle 2 : R\langle i : inc(R[i]), 6 : INC(i, s)\rangle$

$MC \rightarrow MC\langle 1 : R[i] + A[2] + A[1], 6 : ADD(i, s)\rangle$

$MC \rightarrow MC\langle 1 : A[2] - R[i] - A[1], 6 : SUB(i, s)\rangle$

$MC \rightarrow MC\langle 3 : \langle SRC : A[2]\rangle, 6 : WRM(s)\rangle$

$MC \rightarrow MC\langle 1 : \langle 2 : M[SRC], 6 : RDM(s)\rangle$

$MC \rightarrow MC\langle 1 : A[2] + M[SRC] + A[1], 6 : ADM(s)\rangle$

$MC \rightarrow MC\langle 1 : A[2] - M[SRC] - A[1], 6 : SBM(2)\rangle$

$MC \rightarrow MC\langle 5 : \langle SR[2] : A[2]\rangle, 6 : WRR(s)\rangle$

$MC \rightarrow MC\langle 1 : \langle 2 : P[SR[2]], 6 : RDR(s)\rangle$

$MC \rightarrow MC\langle 1 : \langle 1 : CY, 2 : ACO\rangle, 6 : CLB(s)\rangle$

$MC \rightarrow MC\langle 1 : \langle 1 : CY\rangle, 6 : CLC(s)\rangle$

$MC \rightarrow MC\langle 1 : \langle 1 : A[1] + 1\rangle, 6 : CMC(s)\rangle$

$MC \rightarrow MC\langle 1 : \langle 1 : C\rangle, 6 : STC(s)\rangle$

$MC \rightarrow MC\langle 1 : \langle 2 : KO - A[2]\rangle, 6 : CMA(s)\rangle$

$MC \rightarrow MC\langle 1 : rar(AC), 6 : RAR(s)\rangle$

$MC \rightarrow MC\langle 1 : ral(AC), 6 : RAL(s)\rangle$

$MC \rightarrow MC\langle 1 : A[2] - 1, 6 : DAC(s)\rangle$

$MC \rightarrow MC\langle 1 : 9 + A[1], 6 : TCS(s)\rangle$

$MC \rightarrow MC\langle 1 : ACO + A[1], 6 : TCC(s)\rangle$

Chapter 7

OPERATING SYSTEMS FOR MODULAR PARTIALLY RECONFIGURABLE MULTIPROCESSOR SYSTEMS

7.1 Introduction

Design and operation aspects of operating systems (OS) for multiprocessor systems modules are connected via communication networks which can be reconfigured by program, are discussed in this chapter. The structure of an OS is analysed, along with some of the features which are due to its expansibility and to the need to organize interactions between multiple processes. Decision-making levels and OS organizational hierarchy, features of scheduling and planning algorithms are discussed as well. Attention is focused on subsystem operational modes, parallel program concepts and the interactions of program branches.

It has been commonly recognized that computer technology has entered the era of multicomputer (multiprocessor) systems designed to meet increasing demands of users on computer performance, such as speed, reliability, cost effectiveness, etc. In the development of computer systems attention is primarily being paid to the provision of a high total throughput of a flow of different, small, and weakly interacting tasks, as well as to the attainment of minimal computer time for a single complex task.

Among the various concepts for new computer facilities, a prominent place is held by modular multiprocessor systems (MMS) with programmable (reconfigurable) structures that are potentially applicable to classes and flows of tasks processed, thus providing a unique method for the implementation of the above approaches [1, 2]. The progress achieved in IC technology makes these systems even more topical. Partial and complete reconfigurability levels are usually present in MMS structures. The former is characterized by program control of interconnections between modules, while the latter also provides control of the structures of the modules themselves. It are MMS with partially reconfigurable structures that are primarily referred to in this paper, although the possibility of changing the program "stuffing" can also be regarded as a method for making a more global change to the system structure.

It should be noted that, apart from general theoretical and methodological studies, research is mostly oriented to computer hardware which differs from reconfigurable MMS. At the same time, the structure of any OS and the functions of its units depend on hardware features, as well as on the computer facilities provided, and the possibilities of their extension.

The primarily considered computer facilities are as follows:

a) the possibility of executing complex tasks requiring a high or very high speed and a very large main memory;

b) concurrent execution of complex tasks and flows of weakly related smaller tasks;

c) reliable fault-tolerant computations which should be continued until termination or even some individual modules fail, these facilities being provided within the framework of techniques for resource utilization and programming methods characteristic of third-generation computers.

Among the new features of MMS hardware, the three most important are: 1. MMS multiprocessor capability: the number of processors in the system is not fixed, the shared main memory is organized hierarchically, and a fast-access local memory is directly connected to each processor; 2. program reconfigurability of module interconnections allowing the generation of subsystems of various configurations and the control of module activity in system interactions; and 3. system uniformity implying that both modules and their interconnections are, in a sense, identical.

Our aim is to develop an OS providing new facilities and techniques for maintenance in relation to MMS hardware.

Emphasis laid on new hardware features does not mean that we are going to alter the software. In fact, we are concerned with some general (hypothetical) characteristics of the computer system which provide a framework for decisions about the relationships between software and hardware.

The creation of an OS for MMS in which many concurrent processes can occur requires, at any early stage of the software analysis, consideration of technical aspects of OS implementation, and specific approaches to all issues involved in its operation, from program generation through job definition and provision of the required computations to the presentation of the results to the user. In this chapter, a number of such factors are included at the level of definition and interpretation of the OS, considered as a collection of interacting asynchronous units, each characterized by the use of memory and processor time. This approach ensures the possibility of a formal OS study and the addition of new features to the structural elements of the model, which increase the degree of comprehension [3]. This implies that there is a set of principles limiting, at a given stage, the range of the problem and allowing OS implementation in practice. These principles involve standardization of both unit interfaces and unit structures themselves.

Some concepts related to OS and its structural peculiarities are introduced and some of its features are discussed informally. Each OS unit can be regarded as a supervisor which executes certain tasks and controls its resources. Consideration is given to subsystem operational models, the concept of a parallel algorithm, and the problem of interacts between parallel program branches.

7.2 Basic notions

The collection of modules (mini- or microcomputers), termed elementary machines (EM), connected through a program controlled communication system is referred to as the hardware of a modular multiprocessor system. The minimal EM is a "processor with memory", i.e. a module exemplified by existing microcomputers. The processor of the module has access to any MMS memory location, but the access "mechanisms" can differ for different locations. The processor has direct access to its own memory, but the memory of another module is accessed through the processor of the latter. Thus, the MMS main memory is shared and hierarchically structured as well.

The number of EM's in MMS is assumed to vary within a wide range and may extend to several hundreds or even more. The EM's are connected to form a single system by means of a distributed network switch which is a collection of elementary switches regularly connected to their nearest neighbours. A two-dimensional lattice having elementary four-directional switches at the nodes is an example of such a switch. An elementary switch is assigned to each EM; thus the number of switches is equal to that of EM's. Any EM can change by program the state of any elementary switch, thus establishing connections with any MMS hardware module and, in particular, breaking down the system into autonomous, but connected subsystems of various configurations.

An important feature is the homogeneity of system modules. The trend to homogeneity is related to the design of large (complex) systems. The homogeneity is defined for the properties of all modules. In our case it is defined by the identical interface to the other modules, availability of the processor and memory, unique instruction format, asynchronous operation, etc. At the same time, the homogeneity does not prevent the existence of different properties in modules, for example, different memory size, different instruction sets, different connections to external devices, etc.

A set of program units which provide the interface between users, or user's programs and MMS resources is referred to as an operating system. Its operation is initiated by certain changes (events) in MMS "reported" to the OS by interrupt. Events result in changes in the MMS image, a set of parameters characterizing the MMS status (multiprogramming state). Characteristics of computer systems, incoming tasks, current subsystem operation modes, OS unit states, data allocation, etc., are given by parameters which can be used as semaphores defining resources for various processes. These parameters are used by OS for decision-making and for influencing MMS. Reconfiguration of the computer system, the initiation of processors with access to memory within certain limits, timer setting and resetting, etc., are regarded as the influence of OS on MMS. Hardware faults, external interrupts, accesses to OS, etc., are regarded as system changes (events).

OS units "embedded" in the uniform hardware form a collection of functionally non-uniform firmware MMS modules. The operating system can be regarded as a quintuple of finite sets:

$$\langle S, \Phi, U, \Gamma, G \rangle,$$

which are, informally, as follows: S is a set of program units regarded as a pair of parallel subunits, where the first unit recognizes the multiprogramming state via the values of set G, and the second unit implements scheduling and control algorithms from set Φ; Φ is a set of algorithms used by OS units for taking decisions about the control of memories, processors, tasks and data, and for the initiation or interruption of processes in the computer system; U is a set of initiation vectors; to each unit in S a vector is assigned components of which are specially ordered queues. The occurrence of a record in at least one queue (if not masked) results in the initiation of the appropriate unit. A record can occur as the result of an "external" interrupt, or of the transfer of control from another OS unit; Γ is a directed graph defining the ordering relation $\rightarrow$ or $=$ between units in S; an arc goes from node i to node j (i.e. unit $S_i \rightarrow S_j$), if there are parameters in G common to both units, such that S_i has access to them for reading and writing, while S_j is only permitted to read; it is possible that $S_i \rightarrow S_j$ and $S_j \rightarrow S_i$ exist simultaneously; $S_i = S_j$ if the units do not use common parameters or have similar access to them (in contrast to writing; any operation which does not change the parameter value or state is understood as reading); and G is a set of parameters defining a multi-programming state (MPS). These can be simple variables, stacks (queues), semaphores, subprograms, etc. A domain of values is assigned to each parameter. The parameter value (state) can be changed by writing or reading (initiation or termination). The OS operation begins with certain initial values of parameters G and vectors U. Now, within the framework of the OS concept we formulate the basic OS design principles for modular multiprocessor systems.

7.3 Design philosophy and some OS properties

Within the framework of existing techniques [4—6], we formulate some principles providing the standardization of MMS OS units and their interfaces and, also, the ground work for the OS analysis via the above OS definition.

1. Constraints on unit sizes are due to the fact that each unit is executed by the resources of a single computer; in doing so, the amount of memory, resources controllable by the unit, cardinality of the subset of MPS parameters which can be analysed and used, and the maximum unit operation time are limited. This is related to OS process isolation and reliable resource control.

It follows that the number of OS units should grow with the number of EM's in MMS and the cardinality of the set G. This property is of fundamental importance because the MMS structure allows a continuous expansion of the computer system throughput within a wide range.

2. The differentiation of unit accesses to MPS parameters consists of a) a decomposition of the parameter set G into subsets $\{G; j \in J\}$, such that each unit S_i has only access to an appropriate subset (J is the set of values of the index j corresponding to the units of S), and b) dependence establishment of connections for information flow between units on the basis of intersections of subsets of parameter related to these units.

Essentially, the specification of the multiprogramming state parameters defines the types of memory organization used by OS. The assignment of a subset of these parameters to each unit localizes its scope of application. This principle, however, does not exclude dynamic access of units to common parameters within the limiting boundaries or dynamic resource allocation to appropriate parameters. The decomposition of the set G into subsets and the assignment of the subsets to units S_j is related to graph Γ. Therefore, using the information relations as defined by the graph, one can naturally introduce the notion of the OS structure and compare various OS structures. Reference [3] describes an OS structure as decentralized, uniformly centralized, or hierarchically depending on that whether Γ is a zero, complete or a cyclic graph. With an increasing number of units, their access time to common parameters can exceed some critical interval. Hence, some structures allow more universal OS than the other ones.

3. Collective schemes for unit interaction stem from the need for collective access to common parameters and collective processes, based on the need to control large numbers of concurrent processes.

An individual access of a unit to common parameters (e.g., the subset G_j) excludes the access of other units to the same data. A collective access provides simultaneous access of several or even all the units for which the parameters G_j' are common. A synchronous collective access, i.e. an access to G_j' such that any parameter from G_j' can be accessed collectively, is of prime importance to MMS OS. Individual initiation allows the initiation or interruption of only one unit, while collective initiation changes the operation of a group of units.

Supported by MMS hardware, collective schemes should organize access to common parameters so as to make the efficiency practically independent of the number of concurrently accessing units. In a similar way, the execution time of the order "right turn!" is independent of the number of men on a parade ground. However, collective schemes do not exclude individual access to common parameters. Statements defining collective interaction are important check points for the verification of system processes.

4. Standardized structure units are constructed as pairs of successive subunits.

The first subunit recognizes the situation, in particular it checks the correctness of unit initiation, and the second subunit executes certain scheduling and control algorithms. Each subunit, in its turn, makes use critical segments, i.e. segments having access to common parameters from G, of standardized canonical forms that can be validated at the syntactic level. The construction of standardized segments is centered around macro-statements **QUEUE UP** (*QU*), **CHECK QUEUE** (*CQ*), **RELEASE RESOURCE** (*RR*), **SERVE OTHER UNITS** (*SOU*) involving all the process synchronization actions required for common resource actions [3]. The following form exemplifies a standardized segment

$$QU\,;\,SOU\,;\,CQ\,;\,CR_j(i),\,RR,$$

where $CR_j(i)$ is the critical segment body which either does not use parameters required by statements QU, SOU, CQ and RR, or is constructed again according to the canonical form.

These forms make it possible to formulate sufficient conditions for a deadlock-free OS operation which can be checked either in advance or during the OS operation, by means of a special additional checking facility. It should be noted that these conditions must be preserved under variation of the number of computers in MMS and the units in OS within, theoretically, arbitrary boundaries, i.e. when checking a deadlock situation one should keep in mind that there are MMS and OS sizes such that the use of methods oriented to a single dispatcher unit becomes impossible. Thus, the concept of the standardized unit involves both high-level language facilities and canonical forms for writing critical program segments related to deadlock situations.

5. The division of unit interactions into information and control is as follows:

— information connections define access to common parameters giving access to shared resources; in doing so, all the situations that might result in deadlocks are included in the level of these connections;

— control connections define unit sequencing in strings generated by events in the computer system; problems of cycling and uniqueness of OS operation are analysed at the level of these connections.

This principle allows one to consider separately various aspects of system operational correctness.

6. Non-determinancy is used in the analysis of control connections for the following factors:

　　a) the parameters of the multiprogram state can have different structure and semantics, and they can sometimes be non-determinate, i.e. they require decision-making in an uncertain environment;

　　b) to restore an OS operation, one needs various paths from the unit which initiates interrupt processing to the units which input the control actions to the computer system;

c) a large number of units and parameters can lead to a multiplicity of processes which, although uniquely generated, cannot practically be checked at all.

It is suggested that control connections should be organized so that they would provide the introduction of non-determinancy through model simplification, i.e. by disregarding some parameters. Although these parameters will influence decision-making in the physical OS, their influence, will be within "the limits of sufficient conditions". This is a technique recommended to simplify the analysis of determinate control connections.

7. A combined checking of OS operational correctness is required because of the cardinal fact that even an absolutely debugged program can operate incorrectly owing to hardware faults, i.e. operation of complex OS is impossible without dynamic checking. Since this is unavoidable one should, when dealing with correctness checking, plan from the very beginning two stages: static (at the level of translation) and dynamic (during the OS operation). Specifically, the correctness of the canonical forms of segments and units is conveniently checked at the translation level, while the possibility of cycling is better checked during the operation of each first subunit.

8. The merging of data and organizational hierarchies of OS units reflects the fact that OS units which are separated by a data hierarchy related to graph Γ coincide with those separated by decision-making levels, i.e. through allocation of planning and control algorithms, from the set Φ to the units. Planning and control at the level of OS structure selection simplifies significantly the problem of matching intrinsically different operational modes in one computer system. Each unit can be regarded as a supervisor executing certain tasks and controlling its resources, various units having various criteria for effectiveness. This treatment of OS structure is not opposed to the levels of language hierarchy usually implied in "upward" or "downward" programming.

9. The use of the "parallel program" concept lies in the introduction of a special object which is an organized assembly of successive programs (branches) concurrent execution of which alternates with interactions between them so as to attain the goal of the algorithm of the problem. The parallel program is a single object with its own name and characteristics. When it is loaded into a system, it requires subsystems sizes and configuration of which can accommodate parallel informating processing.

The concept of a parallel program is intended for adding more structuring to multiprocessor system processes; it contributes to the localization of conflicts caused by failures and errors, the simplification of branch interaction debugging, the organization of super-reliable computations, the reduction of the execution time of a large task, etc.

The above principles can be used by programmers as a methodological basis for the design of parallel-operating systems oriented towards the control of modular multiprocessor systems with expandable resources. Taking into account the great potentialities of these systems and the necessity for efficient use of their resources, in the following section we shall discuss in more detail the decision-making levels and the organizational hierarchy of OS units.

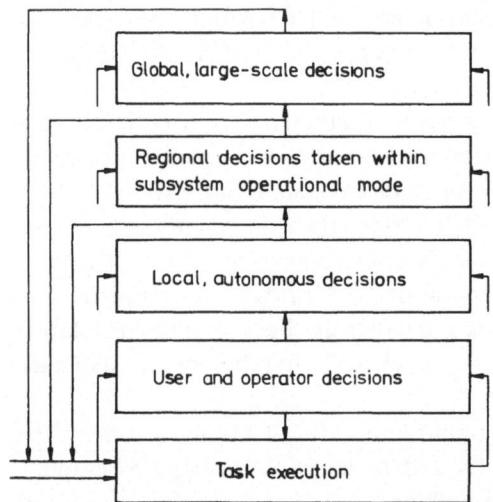

Fig. 1.

7.4 Decision-making levels and organizational hierarchy

For decision-making in complicated multiprogramming states, OS are divided into hierarchical levels, each reducing the state indeterminancy by defining and fixing some parameters for the higher level. Since each multiprogramming state is largely related (directly or indirectly) to MMS resources, their assignment to subsystems can be naturally used for classificational decomposition of the decision set into subsets corresponding to various levels. Such an approach is dictated by: 1. the EM resource autonomy necessary for conceptual and program compatibility with the OS of existing computers, and 2. the execution by MMS of complicated tasks requiring united subsystem resources.

Figure 1 shows the MMS OS with four decision levels. At the first level, decisions are made by the user. The user selects algorithms for this problems, data formats, and the techniques for writing, analysing and debugging the algorithms, etc. The operator decides about loading removable tapes or discs, putting paper in the printers, responds to OS requests, etc.

At the second level, local decisions are made concerning the analysis of the input flow of tasks and its implementation by means of EM facilities. Input tasks are classified with respect to their operational modes. Modes which are executable by the resources of a single EM are selected.

At the third level, decisions concern operational modes requiring the resources of one or more subsystems and an access to external devices. If tasks appear which cannot be executed within the framework of the existing subsystems and operating modes, demands for a higher level are generated for a new decomposition of the system into subsystems.

At the fourth level, global system decisions are taken changing the MMS functional state. These decisions are defined by operational mode priorities, task queues peculiar to these modes, hardware failures, operator's directives, etc. The above decision-making levels underlie OS organizational structure. At each decision-making level it is important to define the composition of units and to specify their method of interaction.

The organizational OS hierarchy is shown in Fig. 2 as a collection of units $\{S_{i,j}, i = 1, 2, 3; j = 1, 2, ..., j(i)\}$ distributed between three levels. This number was chosen to render planning and control algorithms more specific and as a value which usually includes the basic features of decision-making in complex systems. Units S_{1j} and S_{2j} are used for decision-making at the first and second levels in Fig. 1, and S_{3j} is used at the third and fourth levels in the same figure.

Control connections between units are confined to adjacent decision-making levels, i.e. any unit of level K can initiate units of levels $K - 1$ and $K + 1$, but cannot initiate units of its own level.

The units S_{1j} are regarded as identical and they resemble in content the OS of elementary machines. Such an OS can be constructed by adding facilities for information and control interactions with other units to the OS of some basic computer. The direct information interrelations, necessary for complicated tasks,

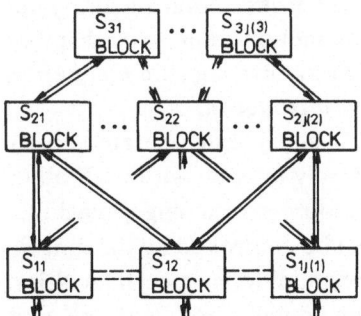

Fig. 2.

constitute the most important feature of the interactions. Here, a subsystem executing a complicated task with multiple parallel branches acts as a single computing kernel. The computation should be as efficient as possible.

Therefore interactions in the kernel should be efficient and, generally, independent of higher hierarchical levels. The units S_{2j} can be collected into subsets elements of which are identical only inside the subset. The number of subsets $J(2)$ is equal to the number of subsystem operational modes. The units of one subset control the subsystems operating in a single mode. Each unit is a supervisor controlling the resources of one or more subsystems and using an elementary machine as a unit resource. The units from different subsets are assumed to interact only through the units of adjacent levels, and the units from the same subset can interact within their decision-making level.

Units S_{3j} represent the highest level in the hierarchy. They recognize the subsystems of required structures [7], assign them to operational modes, change the decomposition of MMS into subsystems, control I/O for external devices, etc. These units are identical and interact with each other within their decision-making level. Each unit is a supervisor controlling some or all the system resources, and uses, as a unit resource, a subsystem as well as a single EM.

Note that the introduction of information connections between units of the same level must improve the efficiency of multiple interacting concurrent processes and the reliability of OS operation.

Planning algorithms implemented in the units S_{ij} should be coordinated with the aim to attain the global common objective. Each unit has to maximize the efficiency of the resources it controls. Generally, some units can use the resource throughput as a criterion for efficiency, while others use the load factor or response time to a request.

7.5 Subsystem operational modes

In order to combine the execution of complicated tasks requiring the joint resources of many EM's with flows of small tasks having non-uniform and sparse interrelations, a basic set of operational modes which involve specific techniques for resource control to be used by incoming tasks is introduced.

Autonomous mode. In this mode, the EM's of a subsystem operate mostly independently and serve flows of small tasks which rarely interact with each other and are executed with sufficient efficiency by the resources of a single machine. Each EM can have individual external devices and can be controlled by the unit S_{1j} which has the capabilities of a third-generation OS with additional special facilities. The user of such an EM can: 1. execute, translate, debug, edit and segment programs on the same computer, 2. access system information, 3. define system tasks, etc.

Parallel mode combines all the subsystem EM's for the implementation of complicated tasks represented by parallel (p-) programs (see Secs. 7.7—7.9). The two following computational modes can be identified: 1. monoprocessing — where a complicated task occupies all the resources and the tasks are executed sequentially, and 2. multiprocessing — where each subsystem EM executes a branch belonging to a different p-program.

Monoprocessing is intended for large and involved tasks. The representation of the p-program as an ensemble of branches obtained at the level of the programming system allows one to make major decisions about concurrent computations at the level of preliminary, static parallelization. While the autonomous mode is, primarily, oriented to collective access and can be used to improve the level of service in MMS, the parallel processing mode is, mostly, oriented to a high throughput when complicated tasks are executed, and to the allocation of all the resources to pure computation.

Operating system mode. An EM or subsystem is considered to operate in this mode if it executes some units S_{ij}. Since the EM hardware is directly connected to the EM OS, each system machine has to operate in the OS mode and execute units S_{1j}. However, not every machine deals with units S_{2j} and S_{3j}; this reflects certain properties of centralization in MMS resource control. It seems reasonable to allocate subsystems for permanent (during a time interval) operation in the OS mode with the aim to execute units S_{2j} and S_{3j}. Then the OS units S_{1j} are spatially dispersed over all the machines, and the units S_{2j} and S_{3j} are localized in some subsystems.

Preventive and recovery mode. A subsystem is considered to operate in preventive mode if it is executing test programs or is under repair. The measures of this mode are regarded as preventing rather than excluding the possibility of an EM fault or failure. Therefore, any mode should be able to interact quickly with the preventive and recovery mode. Reliable computations impose on OS additional requirements due to the subsystem structure rearrangement which must take place when an EM failure occurs, the rearrangement of p-programs for the execution of computations on a lower-rank subsystem, the duplication of computations in subsystems, and the need for unit restarting.

A priority is assigned to each operational mode thus characterizing its right to MMS resources. The operating system mode has the highest priority, then follows that of the preventive measures. The priorities of these modes are absolute; those of autonomous operation and parallel processing are defined either at the time of system generation, or by operator's directives and can be either absolute or relative.

7.6 General remarks about planning and control algorithms

The composition and effectiveness of these algorithms depend largely on both the absolute EM cost and the ratios of EM processor and memory costs, the cost of external devices, etc. The relative contribution of the processor and memory (especially that of the processor) to the total cost of the computer hardware has significantly dropped now, and this trend is still striking. The costs of electronic components decrease 10 times each 5—6 years. Small computers are expected to appear which would have one or more LSI circuits and would be equal in their capabilities to existing minicomputers. Their cost is estimated to be $ 1 to $ 100. When designing a modular multiprocessor environment consisting of such computers, one does not necessarily need to load processors and memories completely. This is why planning and control algorithms become much simpler. In essence, there is no need to control processors, since every EM processor can be regarded as a constituent of the memory unit. In memory allocation, every EM can be conveniently treated as a unit resource completely assigned to a single process. Then multiprogramming mode is centred around the distribution of EM's and subsystems between tasks, each subsystem operating in monoprogram mode. This allows one to isolate better the processes, to diminish the failure propagation rate, and to arrange more precisely check points by relating them to statements which define process interactions.

Since in this approach each unit S_{1j} has only facilities for interactions with other OS units, their implementation in hardware is advisable.

Multidimensionality of the MMS structure provides additional possibilities to solve the memory partition problem. A subset of memory units can be, in particular, regarded as an entity if appropriate EM's form a connected subsystem. Some existing memory and data control algorithms can be used if the system is decomposed into two subsystems: the control subsystem, which is specialized in the execution of the units S_{2j} and S_{3j} and has direct connections to all the external devices, and the computing kernel which is oriented to "pure" computations.

The characterization of the OS would be incomplete without discussing the use of multiprocessor subsystem resources for the execution of a single complicated task. Therefore, the rest of this chapter is devoted to the concept of a parallel program.

7.7 Concept of parallel algorithm

The term parallel refers to programming which results in special objects, parallel programs which are organized ensembles of sequential programs (branches) which can be executed concurrently, interact with one another and should be performed in accordance with the given algorithm. All the actions in the system are regarded as the execution over a shared memory of a finite set of statements implementing specific mappings over the memory [8]:

$$S = \{S_k, \ k \in K\},$$

where K is a set of values of index k, and each statement (referred to as a c-statement in order to stress its composite structure) is a triple

$$S_k = ([SI(k)]; BODY(k); [SI(k)],$$

where $SI(k)$ is a system interaction statement; square brackets indicate that any (including the empty) subset of successively executable statements from the set $SI = \{SI(j), j \in J\}$ is allowed as contents; $BODY(k)$ is a subprogram which transforms the contents of memory location and does not involve statements from SI.

The set of system interaction statements includes those of interaction, data exchange, and successor selection which initiates and interrupts the execution of c-statements. The activation (execution) of a c-statement depends on the conjunction of two conditions: its presence in the successor list and the validity of the predicates in the system-interaction statements.

An explicit separation of data-exchange and successor selection statements in the structure of c-statements is oriented towards a more effective use of computer system resources, in particular of its hierarchical main memory, and to the simplification of computation planning in the system. Specific descriptions of system interaction statements related to the concept of the p-algorithm are given below. The execution of tasks on single-processor computers requires sequential algorithms written as a sequence of statements:

$$S_1, S_2, ..., S_k$$

each having the form $S_i = (BODY(i); [\Phi, UB, CB])$ where UB means the unconditional transfer to one of the c-statements $S_j \in \{S_l, l = \overline{1,k}\} S_j \neq S_l$, CB is a conditional transfer statement, and Φ is a stop statement. It is assumed in this sequential algorithm that only one c-statement is executed at each time, its name (number) being in the algorithm statement counter, i.e. the successor list cannot involve more than one element.

Definition. Quadruple $\langle S, S', H, CB \rangle$ is referred to as a p-algorithm over shared memory, where S is a finite set of c-statements; $S' \subseteq S$ is a subset of statements initiating the execution simultaneously or within a finite time interval (t_1, t_2) of each statement belonging to the corresponding counter from H; H is a set of counters with one-to-one correspondence to the elements of S'; CB is a set of system interaction statements including successor selection statements capable of: 1. generating new counters or eliminating the existing ones, and 2. assigning successors over any subset of existing counters;* the halt statement which

---

*If several assignments come to the same counter, the statement which selects the current c-statement gives priority to the first statement to arrive and cancels the other statements.

eliminates its own counter. The execution of the p-algorithm is completed when the last counter has been eliminated. The totality of c-statements executed on a counter is termed a "p-algorithm branch". Here, we consider p-algorithms in which each branch is a sequential algorithm, and where the order of c-statements and the results are unambiguously defined by common source data and are independent of the computation rates in other branches. In such a p-algorithm, no order is imposed on the execution of the c-statements, but there is an order for the c-statements of each individual branch. The waiting time of an event, required for a statement from SI is included in the execution time of this statement. The concept of the p-algorithm is specified below using the description of system interaction statements.

7.8 Individual system interaction statements

These statements assign an individual access by branches to shared data and an individual process initiation. Let X be a vector whose components are semaphore variables intended for process synchronization of parallel algorithm branches. Then the statement

CHANGE $X(B)$

can be accessed by each branch. The vector B has the same dimension as X; the components of B can be positive or negative and are added to the corresponding components of X; the operation of changing X is indivisible. The vector X is also used (though implicitly) in other individual interaction statements. Note that the combination of synchronous action and access to shared arrays in a single statement is practically convenient because reading and writing are related to the most frequently used critical intervals. This fact is reflected in the following statements.

The statement **READ** $D(D1, b, B)$ inputs the data array D in the place of $D1$, B is the same as the vector described under **CHANGE** $X(B)$. Reading is executed and X is changed if the condition specified by the vector b is fulfilled (the dimension of b is the same as that of X). The components of the vector b indicate the components of X to be used and the logic functions to be performed over these semaphores. In the MINIMAX system [9, 13], the vectors $b = (1, 0, 1, ..., 1)$ and $b = (-1, 0, -1, ..., -1)$ define conjunction and disjunction, respectively, over the components of the vector X corresponding to the 1's in b. Execution of the statement is delayed until the given condition is false.

The statement **WRITE** $D(D1, b, B)$ outputs the data array D instead of $D1$; b and B are as above. The introduction of **READ** and **WRITE** statements is due to the fact that the arrays D and $D1$ are located, from the point of view of the p-algorithm branch, at different levels of the main memory, i.e. in different system computers. In other words, only those data are selected which the branch accesses without system interaction statements, and which are accessed through these statements only. Both statements are indivisible in the sense that they block the access of other branches to vector X (during predicate verification and changing of semaphore values) and to arrays D and $D1$ (during data transfers).

The statement **DO** $S_j(i, b, B)$ initiates the execution of the c-statement S_j in the branch i, i.e. the process executed by the blocks of branch i will go from the passive state to the active state, or from the active state related to the execution of some c-statement S_k to the active state related to the execution of the c-statement S_j. The statement **DO** defines a new counter if S_j is the first statement executed in branch i.

7.9 Collective system interaction statements

As a rule, these statements define the collective (concurrent) access of branches to common data or they generate several processes simultaneously. They have been constructed on the basis of interaction schemes identified by the analysis of a large number of problems [10]. Collective interaction schemes do not use explicit semaphore variables because, relying on definite standard events, they use special program variables δ_i values of which define the active or passive condition of the branch towards the collective interaction executed: if $\delta_i = 1$, then branch i participates in such interactions; if $\delta_i = 0$, it considers the corresponding statements empty; if $\delta_i = 2$, the execution of the collective interaction statement reduces to the delay of the transfer of control to the next statement, the duration of the delay being defined by the interaction execution time in branches with $\delta_i = 1$. The collective interaction is activated if each branch passes from $\delta_i \neq 0$ to its copy of the statement defining this interaction.

The statement **GENERAL BRANCH** $(b, F, List)$ defines the generalized conditional transfer in all branches with $\delta_i = 1$; b is a logical function which is computed over the set $F = \{F_i, i \in I\}$, where F_i is a variable defined in branch i; $List$ is a list of pairs of blocks, control being transferred to the first element of a pair in each branch with $\delta_i = 1$ if $b(F) = \textbf{true}$, otherwise control is transferred to the second element of the pair.

The statement **EXCHANGE** $(l, B, List)$ defines the collective access of all branches with $\delta_i = 1$ to the array B; l is the number of a branch that can read B without statements from SI; $List$ is a list of arrays into which B is rewritten; $Li \in List$ is an array accessed by branch i without statements from SI. The exchange, called "broadcast exchange", broadcasts simultaneously data from one branch to all other branches with $\delta_i = 1$. It is reasonable to have several collective exchange operations for the sake of programming convenience and effectiveness and in order to "hide" from the programmer the system structure, i.e. to prevent him from using the operation **SYSTEM SETTING.**

The statement **CYCLE BROADCAST EXCHANGE** (*List* 1, *List* 2) defines a broadcast exchange in a cycle with respect to l values of which are the numbers of branches with $\delta_i = 1$; *List* 1 is a list of broadcast arrays, element i of the list corresponding to the name of the array from branch i; *List* 2 is a list of arrays into which the arrays of *List* 1 are rewritten.

The statement **SHIFT EXCHANGE** (*T*, *List* 1, *List* 2) defines an array shift between branches; *T* defines a shift to the right (the branch number i increases), to the left (i decreases), a cyclic shift, etc. This statement features a parallel sequential shift in two or three stages independent of the number of branches rather than a sequential shift: at the first stage, odd branches transfer data to even branches ($1 \rightarrow 2, 3 \rightarrow 4, ..., n-1 \rightarrow n$); at the second stage, even branches transfer data to odd branches ($2 \rightarrow 3, 4 \rightarrow 5, ..., n-2 \rightarrow n-1$); the cyclic shift and the odd number of branches require a third stage ($n \rightarrow 1$).

The statement **COLLECTION EXCHANGE** (*l*, *B*, *List*) means collecting the data transfer (exchange) from all branches with $\delta_i = 1$ into branch number l; B is the array in which all the data contained in the arrays from the *List* are collected.

The statement **GENERAL GO TO** (*List*) defines a general unconditional change of all branches with $\delta_i = 1$ to c-statements indicated in *List* (element $L_i \in List$ is a label to which branch i should transfer control). The main difference between this statement and other collective interactions is that there is no need for statement copy in other branches. The **GENERAL GO TO** statement is assumed to be able to define new p-algorithm counters and the corresponding branches.

An arbitrary use of system interaction statements does not necessarily lead to the required p-algorithms. Sufficient conditions of definiteness and absence of dead-lock of p-programs are formulated in [11]. These conditions are recommended as pragmatic rules for parallel programming.

Conclusion

The ideas presented in this contribution could underlie studies of the general properties of the environment of large programs and serve as methodological guidelines for programmers developing parallel operating systems for the control of modular multiprocessor systems with increasing resources. The proposed principles define the rules of the OS structural organization, and make its operation more regular and stable. The use of information and language hierarchy makes it possible introduce a set of basic subsystem operational modes and hence enable the execution of different tasks on the same computer system. It should be emphasized that the organizational hierarchy is one of the most important aspects of any large program which can be regarded as a complex system involving decision-making.

The proposed methodology of operating system development directly indicates those parameters of a multiprogram state, the units or subunits, which are most promising for hardware implementation. Indeed, the specification of the MPS parameters defines, essentially, the types of memory organization in the computer system, while lower-level units in the OS hierarchy, guarantee for subunits recognizing MPS, and statements implementing collective interaction between processes, are supporting high processing speed in the system. The introduction of the parallel program as a special object in the computer system results in a reasonable distribution of tasks which control computations in the multiprocessor system, among the hierarchical levels. The concept of the parallel algorithm provides a framework for the application of the techniques of concurrent data processing, simplifies the debugging of parallel programs, and enables the user to orient himself according to the determinate computation scheme, although many different histories can be assigned to each program in the system.

To conclude, let us note that the above ideas and results were obtained and partially implemented in the MINIMAX project [9, 13].

REFERENCES

[1] EVREINOV, E. V. and KOSAREV, YU. G.: Universalnye odnorodnye vychislitelnye sistemy vysokoi proizvoditelnosti. Izd. Nauka, Novosibirsk, 1966.

[2] MARCHUK, G. I. and KOTOV, V. E.: Modulnye asinkhronnye rozvivayushchiesya sistemy. Preprint VC SO AN SSSR, Novosibirsk, 1978.

[3] MIRENKOV, N. N.: Odnorodnye vychislitelnye sistemy. Strukturnaya organizatsiya operatsionnykh sistem, Vols. 1, 2. Preprints OVS-01, OVS-02, IM SO AN SSSR, Novosibirsk, 1977.

[4] DIJKSTRA, E. W.: The structure of the "THE" multiprogramming system. Comm. ACM, 11, 1968, 5, 341—347.

[5] HANSEN, P. B.: Structured multiprogramming. Comm. ACM, 15, 1972, 7, 574—578.

[6] GLUSHKOV, V. M. and VELBITSKII, I. V.: Tekhnologiya programirovaniya i problemy ee avtomatizatsii. USIM, 1976, 6, 75—92.

[7] MIRENKOV, N. N. and FOSHERMAN, S. B.: Algoritmy raspoznavaniya podsistem zadannykh struktur v OVS. In: Vychislitelnye sistemy, Vol. 63. Novosibirsk, 1975, pp. 44—53.

[8] NARINYANI, A. S.: Teoriya parallelnogo programmirovaniya. Formalnye modeli. Kibernetika, 1974, 1, 1; 2, 1.

[9] MIRENKOV, N. N.: MINIMAKS — vychislitelnaya sistema kollektivnogo polzovaniya. In: Vychislitelnye sistemy, Vol. 60. Novosibirsk, 1974, pp. 115—128.

[10] KOSAREV, YU. G.: O skhemakh obmena mezhdu vetvyami parallelnykh algoritmov. In: Vychislitelnye sistemy, Vol. 51. Novosibirsk, 1972, pp. 70—76.

[11] MIRENKOV, N. N.: Sistemnoe parallelnoe programmirovanie. Preprints OVS-05, OVS-06, Institut matematiki SO AN SSSR, Novosibirsk, 1978.

[12] VINOKUROV, V. G., DMITRIEV, YU. K., EVREINOV, E. V., KOSTELYANSKII, V. M., LEKHNOVA, G. M., MIRENKOV, N. N., REZANOV, N. N. and KHOROSHEVSKII, V. G.: Odnorodnaya vychislitelnaya sistema iz mini-mashin. In: Vychislitelnye sistemy, Vol. 51. Novosibirsk, 1972, pp. 127—146.

[13] KHERBEL, V. G., KOLOSOVA, YU. I., KORNEEV, V. D., KRYLOVA, E. G. and MIRENKOV, N. N.: Programmnoe obespechenie sistemy MINIMAKS. Preprint OVS-09, Institut matematiki SO AN SSSR, Novosibirsk, 1979.

Chapter 8

ALGORITHMS FOR SCHEDULING HOMOGENEOUS MULTIPROCESSOR COMPUTERS

8.1 Introduction

Advances in hardware technology and computer architecture have led to designs and implementations of computer systems containing several processors, referred to as multiprocessor systems (MS). Since these computers are capable of executing several tasks simultaneously in parallel, one of the most important problems connected with the implementation of a given computational process is the problem of effective exploitation of the resources of such a multiprocessor computer together with the problem of scheduling individual sections of the computational process on the individual processor or other resources of a multiprocessor system or, which is equivalent, assigning individual resources to individual sections of the computational process.

There are several approaches to the solution of the problem of scheduling the execution of computational processes on MS, related to various criteria for the efficiency of the exploitation of resources. We always assume that the scheduling mechanism is part of the operating system of a given MS and that the scheduling problem does not involve such functions of the operating system as, for example, interaction between processes, ensuring access to resources, synchronization, information protection. We suppose that the function of the scheduling mechanism is only the determination of the beginning of the execution of every part of the computational process, the determination of the duration of this execution, and the determination of the resources used in this execution, and that the other functions of the operating system are designed in such a way that they can ensure the execution of a given computational process in accordance with the design of the scheduling mechanism. We have to design the principles of scheduling according to the type of the MS and its architecture. There are several ways to use a given multiprocessor system and, consequently, to solve the scheduling problem — scheduling in separated systems, coordinated scheduling, master-slave scheduling, and equivalent scheduling [16].

All these methods of scheduling have the common property that they contain specific algorithms for assigning MS devices to single tasks or parts of the computational process. In the following sections of this chapter we deal with some designs of these algorithms and review some known scheduling algorithms.

8.2 Models and basic concepts

In general, a multiprocessor computer, MS, is considered to consist of various resources, i.e. devices executing, or in some other way participating in the execution of operations. These resources can be divided into main (processors) and (secondary I/O channels, memory, disks, tapes, ...). Formally, we regard a multiprocessor system as a pair:

MS = (P, R), where $P = \{P_1, ..., P_m\}$ is a set of processors,

R = (TR, M) is a pair determining the types of secondary resources,

$TR = \{TR_1, TR_2, ..., TR_p\}$ and the numbers of resource units of the given types,

M = $\{m_1, ..., m_p\}$. It is assumed here that in the MS there are m_i identical resource units of type TR_i, $i = 1, ..., p$.

The processors $P_1, ..., P_m$ can be identical or have different speeds, or it can be functionally different.

We want to execute some computational process on the given MS. We use the basic model of a computational process and its atomic units as given in [2] and [5]:

Task: an atomic calculating unit with non-specified internal operations and relationships, but with specified external functional relationship to other tasks, requirements for resources, time required for its execution, input and output variables, ...

Calculating process: is then defined as a set of tasks, T, on which a partial ordering representing the necessary precedences for the execution of the single tasks in the process is given.

Task system, TS, is a pair TS = $(T, <)$, where $T = \{T_1, ..., T_m\}$ is a set of tasks and $<$ is the partial ordering on T. The relation is represented as follows: if $T_i < T_j$, then task T_i must be executed before starting the execution of task T_j.

We require that the partial ordering is acyclic, does not contain redundant transitive connections, and that (without less of generality) it contains a single input task without predecessors and a single output task without successors. If we implement the task system TS on the multiprocessor system MS = (P, R), the following values relate to the task $T_1, ..., T_n$:

t_{ij} the time needed for the execution of task T_i on processors P_j, $i = 1, ..., n$, $j = 1, ..., m$. In case of identical processors we write only t_i, $i = 1, ..., n$.

r_{ij} the amount of the resource unit of type TR_j required during the execution of task T_i, $i = 1, ..., n$, $j = 1, ..., p$. Here we suppose that $r_{ij} \leq m_j$ for all $i = 1, ..., n$, $j = 1, ..., p$.

The values of t_{ij}, r_{ij}, $i = 1, ..., n$, $j = 1, ..., m$, $k = 1, ..., p$, must be known in advance.

The task system TS = $(T, <)$ is often represented by a finite (weighted) oriented graph $G = (V, H)$, the set of vertices V being identical with the set T, and if $T_i < T_j$, then $(T_i, T_j) \in H$ for $i \neq j$, $i, j = 1, ..., n$. The weights of the vertices T_i (for identical processors only) are denoted by t_i. Here, H is a set of edges.

We assume that a multiprocessor system MS is available for the execution of the task system TS, where $t_{i,j}$, $r_{i,j}$ are determined for $i = 1, ..., n$, $j = 1, ..., m$, $k = 1, ..., p$. The rule by which we assign processors and other resources from the MS to tasks from the system TS, is called the schedule of TS on MS and we denote it by $S(\text{TS, MS})$ (or simply S). The process of designing the schedules $S(\text{TS, MS})$ is called the scheduling of TS on MS. By the duration of a schedule we mean the time which elapses from the beginning of the execution of TS on MS by a given schedule until the complete execution of the system TS. This duration will be denoted by: $t(S(\text{TS, MS}))$, $t(\text{TS, MS})$, or simply t.

Most frequently, we represent schedules as a Gant's diagram.

Example 1. MS consists of $m = 2$ identical processors P_1, P_2, the task system TS is $\text{TS} = (T, <)$, $t_1 = 5$, $t_2 = 4$, $t_3 = 1$, $t_4 = 3$, $t_5 = 2$, $t_6 = 1$ and is represented by the graph G (Fig. 1).

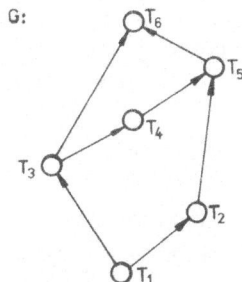

Fig. 1.

One of the possible schedules of TS on MS is given in Fig. 2. If the schedule TS is to be implementable on MS, it must satisfy the conditions:

a) the duration $t = t(\text{TS, MS})$ is finite;

b) at an arbitrary time $\tau \in (0, t)$ at most one task is assigned to each processor;

c) it obeys the precedence restrictions given by the partial ordering $<$ on TS.

We divide these scheduling algorithms into two fundamental classes according to the mode of operation of the MS.

1. Non-preemptive scheduling algorithms, in which if a task is assigned to a processor this remains on it until it is completely executed (non-preemptive scheduling).

2. Preemptive scheduling algorithms, in which the execution of a task assigned to a certain processor can be interrupted and replaced by the execution of some other task, and the execution of the original task can be also completed on some other processor (preemptive scheduling).

A special and very important subclass of the class of non-preemptive scheduling algoritm are algorithms which use priority scheduling. This scheduling method (list scheduling) is characterized by the fact that an ordered list L of tasks from TS is constructed in advance. The scheduling itself consists of scanning the task list L whenever some processor becomes idle until a task is found which is ready for execution, i.e. it has no unexecuted predecessors and the momentary capacities of

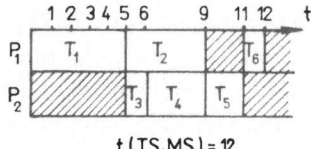

$t(TS, MS) = 12$ Fig. 2.

the secondary resources are sufficient. This task is then assigned to the idle processor and removed from the list L. In this case the scheduling algorithms consist of the design of the task list L. Algorithms for scheduling TS on MS can be designed to satisfy various requirements, such as:
   a) minimization of the execution time of TS on MS;
   b) minimization of the mean execution time of TS on MS;
   c) minimization of the number of processors and the secondary resources required for the execution of a task system in a given time. This problem occurs in designing specialized MS;
   d) achieving of the latest times allowed for the execution of the tasks of the system TS, the times being given in advance.
In this chapter we deal mainly with scheduling algorithms for the minimization of the execution time of TS on MS and thus the minimization of the duration of the schedules $S(TS, MS)$.

The minimum time in which it is possible to execute TS on MS is written $t_{opt}(TS, MS)$ or simply t_{opt}. We call the schedule $S(TS, MS)$ having duration t_{opt} the optimal time schedule or simply the optimal schedule.

The algorithm that designs the optimal schedule for TS and MS is called the optimal algorithm for scheduling TS on MS. Without loss of generality we consider only task systems $TS = (T, <)$, in which, if $< \neq \emptyset$, it is a tree, i.e. there is a single initial task, input, and a single final task, output. The initial and final tasks can be added to TS, not being taken into consideration in scheduling.

8.3 A survey of optimal and heuristic algorithms
for scheduling homogeneous
multiprocessor computers

Let us consider the general problem of optimal time scheduling of the system task $TS = (T, <)$ on a multiprocessor system MS. This problem is solvable for all TS and MS, since the sets of tasks, processors and resources are finite. In the case of preemptive scheduling, we can obtain the solution by examining simply all possibilities of assigning TS on MS. But this method requires a number of steps which increase exponentially with the number of tasks. We need, however, effective scheduling algorithms which can be used in practice, where the number of steps is a polynomial function of the number of tasks being scheduled. Great efforts have been made to obtain such effective optimal algorithms, but the results achieved have only been partial solutions in some special cases of either the task system or the multiprocessor system.

Ullman showed in 1973 [18] that the general scheduling problem is NP-complete, i.e. it belongs to that class of problems for which no algorithm with polynomial complexity has been found (such an algorithm would solve all problems of the given class in polynomial time), and it has been generally accepted that such an algorithm does not exist [1]. All this and the need for fast algorithms have resulted in the construction of heuristic algorithms and the examination of their properties.

In the following section we give a survey of the optimal algorithms in which the MS does not contain secondary resources, i.e. $MS = \{P_1, ..., P_m\}$.

8.3.1 Non-preemptive scheduling

In this section we assume that the MS consists of m identical processors $P_1, ..., P_m$.

Suppose we have a task system $TS = (T, <)$, in which partial ordering defines a tree and t_i, $i = 1, ..., n$, are identical. In this case there exists an optimal algorithm based on an assignment strategy according to the levels of tasks, i.e. their distances from the final task [10]:

Algorithm A_{LS}: $TS = (T, <)$ is a tree.

1. We construct a list L of tasks from the TS, ordered in a descending order according to the distances of the tasks from the end vertex (task), i.e. according to their level numbers.

2. We schedule the tasks TS on MS according to their order in list L.

Theorem 1. If TS is a tree and $t_1, ..., t_n$ are identical, then the algorithm A_{LS} yields the optimal schedules $S(TS, MS)$. The proof of this theorem can be found in [2, 10].

The algorithm A_{LS} can be implemented by using a suitable data structure with almost linear complexity with respect to the task number n in TS. With a small change, this algorithm can be used to obtain optimal schedules for such structures of $TS = (T, <)$ as forest, antitree or antiforest.

In case of antitree or antiforest we reverse the orientation of all edges in G and apply A_{LS} to the tree or the forest. The schedule obtained yields the optimal schedule by reading from right to left.

If $TS = (T, <)$, $t_1 = t_2 = \ldots = t_n$, with respect to any $<$, there is no known algorithm with polynomial complexity for scheduling the TS on a system MS with more than two processors, nor has it been shown that this problem is NP-complete [19].

If $m = 2$, the optimal scheduling algorithm is known [3], based on the creation of a special list of tasks and on the application of priority scheduling using the list created. We still need to define the lexicographical ordering of natural number sequences:

Let N and M be two finite, not increasing sequences of natural numbers:
$N = (n_1, n_2, \ldots, n_n)$, $M = (m_1, m_2, \ldots, m_m)$,

$n_i \geqq n_{i+1}$, $1 \leqq i \leqq n - 1$,

$m_i \geqq m_{i+1}$, $1 \leqq i \leqq m - 1$.

We say that N is lexicographically smaller than M and write $N < M$, if:
a) there exists i, $1 \leqq i \leqq n$, such that $n_j = m_j$ for $j = 1, \ldots, i - 1$
   and $n_i < m_i$

or
b) $n_i = m_i$ for all $i = 1, \ldots, n$ and $n < m$.

In the task system $TS = (T, <)$ let $S(T_i) = $ the set of all direct successors of the task T_i.

Algorithm A_{LM2}: $TS = (T, <)$, $T = \{T_1, \ldots, T_n\}$;

$$t_1 = t_2 = \ldots t_n$$
$$MS = \{P_1, P_2\}.$$

1. We construct the task list L from the TS as follows:

a) We assign to one of the final tasks, say T_i, the number $\alpha(T_i) = 1$.
b) Suppose the numbers $1, 2, \ldots, j - 1$ have already been assigned to the tasks from TS, and let these tasks constitute a set P.

   Let $T' \in \{T_i: T_i \in P \& \ (T_i, T_j) \in < \Rightarrow T_j \in P\}$.

   Let $N(T_i)$ be a decreasing sequence of numbers $\alpha(T_j)$, $T_j \in S(T_i)$ for every $T_i \in T'$. There must exist a task $T_{i_0} \in T'$ such that for $N(T_{i_0})$, $N(T_{i_0}) \leqq N(T_i)$ for every task $T_i \in T'$. For this task T_{i_0} we define $\alpha(T_{i_0}) = j$ and repeat step 1b until no tasks from TS have been assigned the number α, i.e. until T' is not identical with T.
c) We create the task list L by ordering the tasks from TS with decreasing values of α (i.e. from T).

2. We schedule the TS on MS according to the list L.

Theorem 2. For $m = 2$ and $TS = (T, <)$, where $t_1 = \ldots = t_n$ the schedules obtained by algorithm A_{LM2} are optimal.

The proof of this theorem is given in [2, 3], and [4] and is based on the determination of task sets from T, which must be preceded by complete sets in the execution.

Example 2. Schedule G on MS, for $m = 2$. List $L = (T_{12}, T_{11}, T_9, T_8, T_{10}, T_5, T_7, T_6, T_4, T_3, T_2, T_1)$. The schedule according to list L and graph G are given in Figs. 3 and 4.

The complexity of the algorithm A_{LM2} is $O(n^2)$, which is the number of steps required to construct the list L.

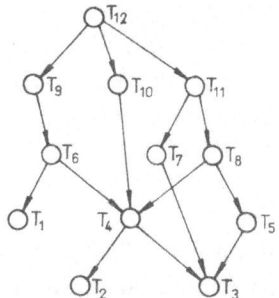

Fig. 3.

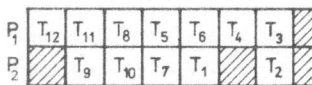

Fig. 4.

8.3.2 Preemptive scheduling

In this section again we consider a multiprocessor system consisting of m identical processors $MS = \{P_1, ..., P_m\}$. If $TS = (T, <)$ and $< = \emptyset$, i.e. a system of independent tasks, there exists an optimal scheduling algorithm of TS on MS.

Algorithm A_{PNT}: $TS = (T, <)$, $< = \emptyset$, $T_1, ..., T_n$ — independent tasks

1. Calculate $t_{opt} = \max \{t_1, ..., t_n, \sum\limits_{i=1}^{n} t_i/m\}$ and put $j = 1$, $k_1 = 1$.

2. Let $k \geqq 1$ be the smallest integer such that $\sum\limits_{i=k_1}^{k+1} t_i < t_{opt}$. Then assign the tasks

$T_{k1}, ..., T_k$ to the processor P_j, the task T_{k+1} during the interval $\left\langle \sum\limits_{i=k_1}^{k} t_i, t_{opt} \right\rangle$ to P_j.

3. Put $t_{k+1} = t_{k+1} - \left(t_{opt} - \sum\limits_{i=k_1}^{k} t_i \right)$, $k_1 = k+1$, $j = j+1$ and repeat from step 2 until j is not larger than m, or the task T_n has already been completely assigned. The tasks $T_{k_1}, ..., T_k$ are successively assigned to processors, e.g. the task T_{k_1} is assigned to the processor P_j during the interval $\langle 0, t_{k_1} \rangle$, the task T_{k_1+1} on the interval $\langle t_{k_1}, t_{k_1} + t_{k_1+1} \rangle$, etc.

The algorithm A_{PNT} is of complexity $O(n)$ and it is clear that the number of preemptions cannot exceed the number of processors m. The proof of optimality of the algorithm A_{PNT} is evident and follows from the relation for t_{opt}.

Now let $TS = (T, <)$ constitute a tree. In this case this is the known Muntz—Coffman algorithm [14] which produces optimal schedules. This algorithm consists of two parts. In the first part, the optimal "general" schedule is constructed, in which all sets of tasks (or their parts) can share processors during the defined time interval. In the second part, the optimal preemptive schedule is constructed from this general schedule by the algorithm A_{PNT}.

Algorithm A_{MC}: Muntz—Coffman

1. Assign one processor to each of the m free tasks most remote from the final task of the TS. If there exist such k tasks for the last k_1 processors, assign all k tasks to all k_1 processors. Then each task from these k tasks will be executed at a speed k_1/k. At any time at which one of the two situations described below occurs, we assign the processors, according to the above rule, to a task that is still unexecuted. These two situations are:
   a) some task has been executed from the TS;
   b) we reach the point where, if we continued be execution according to the current assignment, we would carry out some tasks faster than others more remote from the final task of the TS (the root of the tree).

2. In every time interval in which a single assignment was considered, we construct (since the tasks assigned are independent) the respective preemptive

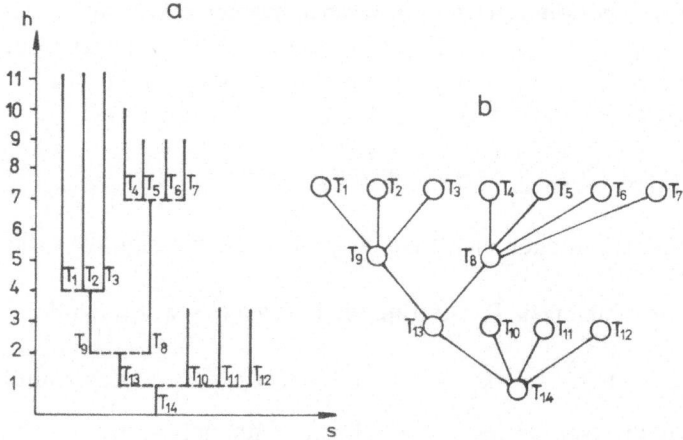

Fig. 5.

schedules using the A_{PNT} algorithm. Their concatenation gives the desired schedule.

Algorithm A_{MC} is illustrated by an example.

Example 3. The TS is shown with line segment representation in Fig. 5a, and as a tree in Fig. 5b.

$$T = T_1, \ldots, T_{14},$$

$$t_i = 7, 7, 7, 3, 2, 2, 2, 5, 2, 2\frac{1}{2}, 2\frac{1}{2}, 2\frac{1}{2}, 1, 1,$$

$$i = 1, 2, \ldots, 14, \text{MS} = \{P_1, P_2, P_3\}.$$

The general schedule is given in Fig. 6a and the desired preemptive schedule is given in Fig. 6b.

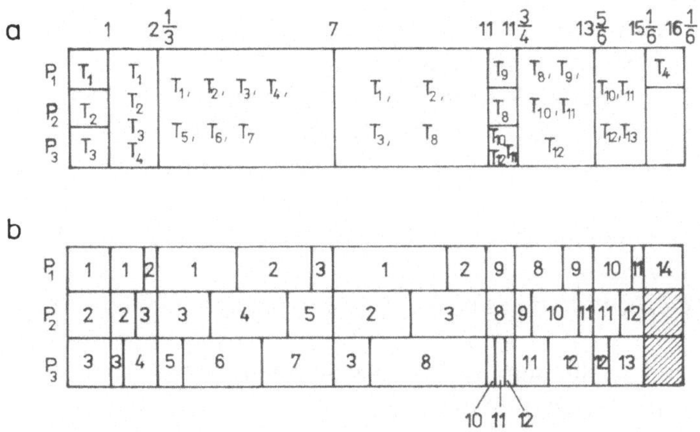

Fig. 6.

Theorem 3. Algorithm A_{MC} is optimal for the case that TS is a tree, or MS consists of two processors.

The proof of this theorem, based on the theorem that an arbitrarily close approximation to an optimal preemptive schedule for general task systems can be found if an optimal preemptive schedule for task systems with equal execution time can be found, is given in [14] and [15].

If TS is a tree, the algorithm A_{MC} has complexity $O(n \log_2 n)$, for any TS and for $m = 2$ has complexity $O(n^2)$. This algorithm can also be used if TS is a forest, antitree or antiforest, analogous to preemptive scheduling in the algorithm A_{LS}. If TS is a forest, we add to it a dummy final task T_0 with $t_0 = 0$, which is a successor of all final tasks from TS and apply A_{MC}. If TS is an antitree, we apply A_{MC} to the tree that arises from TS by reversing the orientation of all edges and apply the schedule obtained in reverse.

8.3.3 Heuristic scheduling algorithms and their properties

Since there are few cases in which effective scheduling algorithms are known, and it has been shown that most of the above scheduling problems are NP-complete in general, one of the directions in which the theory of scheduling has developed and is tending, is the design of heuristic algorithms and the investigation of their properties.

The basic feature of these algorithms is their low complexity and the recognition of relationships between the duration of the schedules that can be obtained by them and the durations of optimal schedules. These relationships make it possible for the designer of scheduling mechanisms to select that strategy (heuristic or exact) which is easy to compute and which, in a particular case, has results closest to those from the strategy which is optimal but requires heavy computation. The selected strategy should deviate markedly from the optimal strategy only exceptionally. Almost all known heuristic strategies for scheduling are based on the class of priority scheduling algorithms, i.e. they consist of the construction of a list of tasks that is to be performed on a given MS. The basic feature of this scheduling is that when a processor is free, the first ready task from the list is always assigned to it.

The well-known Graham "anomalies" of this scheduling by lists show that:

a) there exists a case when no list gives an optimal schedule for the given task system;

b) an increase in the number of processors can increase the duration of the schedule;

c) the reduction of the execution times of the tasks can increase the duration of the schedule;

d) the decrease (increase) of the number of edges of the given task system can increase (decrease) the duration of the schedule.

These and other anomalies are described in [5]. Below you may find some known results about the qualitative are given relationships between some heuristic methods — general priority scheduling, method of critical path, etc. — and the optimal strategies.

The following theorem proved in [3] or [Sehti R. in 4] states about the relationship between preemptive, priority and non-preemptive strategies:

Theorem 4 [3]. Let t_{opt}, t_L, t' be the durations of optimal non-preemptive schedules, according to the task list, and with preemption of the task system TS on m identical processors. Then:

1. $t' \leqq t_{opt} \leqq t_L$,

2. $t_L/t' \leqq 2 - \dfrac{1}{m}$,

3. $t_L/t_{opt} \leqq 2 - \dfrac{1}{m}$,

4. the bounds in 2 and 3 are the best possible ones,

5. there exists a TS, such that $t_{opt}/t' = 2m/(m+1)$.

The results of this theorem show that preemptive scheduling is best for minimizing the duration of the schedules.

Now, let us consider the strategy of the so-called critical path. In it the task list is ordered according to the durations of the critical paths from a given task to the final task of the system, i.e. in ascending order according to the so-called latest needed task-execution time, if the duration of the critical path of the whole TS is to be kept.

A comparison of optimal non-preemptive scheduling with scheduling according to the task list obtained by the critical path method (CP-scheduling) is given by Graham in [5] for the case that $< = \emptyset$, and in [4] for the case that $<$ constitutes a tree. If $t_1 = t_2 = \ldots = t_n$, then CP-scheduling yields optimal schedules.

Theorem 5 (Graham). Let t_{CP} be the duration of a schedule obtained by CP-scheduling.

If $< = \emptyset$, then $\dfrac{t_{CP}}{t_{opt}} \leqq \dfrac{4}{3} - \dfrac{1}{3m}$.

It has been proven by Graham, that if $<$ constitutes a tree, then the worst asymptotic bound of the quotients t_{CP} and t_{opt} has been $2 - 2/(m+1)$.

The critical path strategy was also examined in [8, 12] for the case of inhomogeneous MS's, in which all processors except one had the same speed. It has been shown for independent tasks that if:

$m = 3$, then $t/t_{opt} \leqq 3/2 - 1/2m$, this being the best bound,
$m = 4$, then $t/t_{opt} = 4/3$,
$m = 5$, then $t/t_{opt} = 3/2 - 1/2m$.

A hypothesis is given in [8] that 4/3 is valid for all $m \geqq 3$, and that for different speeds of all processors $t/t_{opt} \leqq 2m/(m+1)$, this being the best bound for $m = 2$.

A special aspect of scheduling, not less important than that discussed in the preceding section, is scheduling for secondary resources with limited capacities. Here we consider a general multiprocessor system $MS = (P, R)$, where $P = \{P_1, \ldots, P_m\}$ is a set of processors and $R = (TR, M)$, $TR = \{TR_1, \ldots, TR_p\}$, $M = \{m_1, \ldots, m_p\}$ is a set of resource types with respective capacities in the set M, and p is the number of resources.

In this case the schedule $S(TS, MS)$ has to fulfil a condition that at time $t \in \langle 0, t(TS, MS) \rangle$ the desired recources must not be larger than their capacity.

Garey and Graham have shown the following relations of non-preemptive scheduling and priority scheduling for limited resources:

Theorem 6 [7]. If $p = 1$, L, TS, m are arbitrary and L is a task list from TS, then $t_L/t_{opt} \leqq m$, this being the best possible bound.

Theorem 7 [6]. If $m \geqq n$, TS is any system of independent tasks, and p is arbitrary, then $t_L/t_{opt} \leqq p + 1$, this being the best possible bound.

Theorem 8. [6]. If $m \geqq 2$, p is arbitrary, and TS is any system of

$$\frac{t_L}{t_{opt}} \leqq \min \left\{ \frac{m+1}{2}, p + 2 - \frac{2p+1}{m} \right\}.$$

These results show that in this case the application of priority scheduling with a random task list does not yield the desired results. Nevertheless the analysis of one case, when $p = 1$, $< = \emptyset$, all tasks have the same duration and $m \geqq n$, shows that even in the case of secondary resources there exist heuristics which can reduce the durations of the schedules. One such algorithm is the well-known bin-packing algorithm, used, for example, in the problem of cutting rods.

Bin-packing algorithms: $p = 1$, $TS = (T, <)$, $t_1 = \ldots = t_n$, $< = \emptyset$, the processors $P_1, \ldots, P_m$ are identical. Let the requirements of tasks for a secondary resource of type TR_1 of capacity m_1 be $r_i, \ldots, r_n$. Evidently, the TS has to be executed on a given MS in a time less than or equal to n. Let us denote the time intervals $B_i = \langle i - 1, i \rangle$ by $B_1, \ldots, B_n$. If we suppose that some tasks say $T_1, \ldots, T_k$, are executed during the time interval B_i then evidently $\sum_{i=1}^{k} r_i \leqq m_1$, and we write this sum $l(B_i)$. Denote by $L_1, \ldots, L_n$ the lists of tasks executed during intervals $B_1, \ldots, B_n$.

Let L be some list of tasks from TS and let $L = (T_1, \ldots, T_n)$. We rearrange the tasks from TS according to the list with the corresponding requirements for the recource. Then there exist two fundamental bin-packing algorithms for scheduling based on the given task list L from TS.

Algorithm FF: (first-fit) $m \geqq n$
1. Put $L_i \leftarrow 0$, $l(B_i) \leftarrow \emptyset$, $1 \leqq i \leqq n$, $j \leftarrow 1$;
2. Put $k \leftarrow \min \{i \geqq 1 : l(B_i) + r_j \leqq m_1\}$;
3. If $j \leqq n$, go to 2, else stop.

The number k of non-empty lists $L_1, \ldots, L_k$ gives the duration of the schedule, and their concatenation — the list by which we can schedule a given TS on a given MS using the priority.

By changing the condition in step 2 of the algorithm FF to the condition $k \leftarrow \min \{i \geqq 1 : l(B_i) = \max \{l(B_k) : 1 \leqq k \leqq n \& l(B_k) + r_j \leqq m_1\}\}$, i.e. the first interval from $B_1, \ldots, B_n$, for which the resulting capacity unused is a minimum, we obtain another type of bin-packing algorithms — the so-called BF-algorithm (best-fit).

If we arrange the task list L in a non-increasing order, according to the requirements for the resource r_i, $i = 1, \ldots, n$, and apply FF or BF algorithms, we obtain FFD or BFD algorithms. By t_{FF}, t_{BF} we denote the durations of the schedules obtained by means of the algorithms FF and BF for a given task list.

Theorem 9 [18]. For an arbitrary list L of tasks from the TS:

$$t_{FF} \leqq 17/10 \, t_{opt} + 2 \quad \text{and} \quad t_{BF} \leqq 170/100 \, t_{opt} + 2.$$

The result of this theorem is better than that of Theorem 7, but since all t_i are equal, this is a less general result.

By means of the algorithm FFD, Coffman, Garey, and Johnson [21] have reduced the bound given by Graham, $t_{CP}/t_{opt} \leqq 4/3 - 1/3m$, for executing independent tasks to $t/t_{opt} \leqq 20/17 + c$, where c is a constant. This is scheduling without any resources added.

For preemptive scheduling the Lüdtke—Schindler result [13] for the ratio t_{LA}/t_{opt}, where t_{opt} is the duration of the optimal preemptive schedule and t_{LA} is the duration of the schedule obtained using the algorithm A_{PNT} given in 8.3.2, is known.

But here the A_{PNT} is applied to sets of independent tasks or subtasks, determined by splitting the system $TS = (T, <)$ according to the earliest possible starts of tasks. Their result $t_{LA}/t_{opt} < 1 + (m - 1)/m$ indicates the possibilities and advantages of preemptive scheduling.

8.4 Algorithms for scheduling resources of special multiprocessor computers

In this section we discuss a special case of the multiprocessor computer, in which the processors are identical, all of them have a common operating memory M and a common external memory E.

The operating memory M is divided into b independent blocks $B_1, ..., B_b$ with the same number of pages s of the same size. Let there be m processors $P_1, ..., P_m$. The other possible resources are either attached to the processors or have unlimited capacity or speed, and therefore we can ignore them. Let the total memory capacity be C, then $C = b.s.$

Let $TS = (T, <)$, $T = \{T_1, ..., T_n\}$ is a set of tasks with a partial ordering $<$, which does not have loops and redundant (transitive) branches. Let $t_1, ..., t_n$ be the execution times of the tasks $T_1, ..., T_n$, and let $m_1, ..., m_n$ be the requirements of the tasks $T_1, ..., T_n$ for operating memory. The numbers m_i, $i = 1, ..., n$, determine the number of pages, since we assume that two processors cannot possess a memory page simultaneously. The location mechanism is of no interest here.

In this case, the scheduling problem can be defined as the construction of the schedule $S(MS, TS)$, such that

1. $t(S)$, i.e. the schedule duration, is minimum;
2. at time $\tau \in \langle 0, t(S) \rangle$ the sum of all memory requirements m_i, for which the tasks are being executed, is less than or equal to C.

It is evident that this is one of the cases of scheduling with secondary resources. Since this is also an NP-complete problem where no effective scheduling algorithm is known, and it seems that no such algorithm exists, we discuss again various heuristic scheduling methods. If we use priority scheduling, using a task list.

Theorems 6 and 8 give the following results:

a) If TS, L and m are arbitrary, then $t_L/t_{opt} \leqq m$, this being the best possible bound.

b) If $m = 2$, TS is a system of independent tasks, i.e. $< = \emptyset$, and L is arbitrary, then

$$t_L/t_{opt} \leq 3(m-1)/m. \text{ If } m \geq n, \text{ then } t_L/t_{opt} \leq 2.$$

It can be seen, mainly in case a) how important the construction of a suitable task list for scheduling is.

8.4.1 Independent, equally long tasks

We assume that all t_i, $i = 1, ..., n$ are equal and that $< = \emptyset$. It is clear that the schedule duration t is $t \leq n$. We denote a set of tasks which will be executed on MS during the time interval $\langle i - 1, i \rangle$ by B_i, $i = 1, ..., n$. Let b_i be the task number in B_i and o_i be the free storage capacity, i.e.

$$o_i = C - \sum_{T_k \in TS \cap B_i} m_k.$$

It is clear that o_i must be ≥ 0, if the schedule is to be implementable.

Algorithm BP:
1. Order and renumber the tasks from TS, so that
   $m_1 \geq m_2 \geq ... m_n$.
   Put $B_i = 0$, $b_i = 0$, $o_i = C$ for $i = 1, ..., n$, $j = 1$.
2. Let $k = \min \{i \geq 1 : b_i + 1 \leq m \& o_i \geq m_j\}$.
3. Put $B_k = B_k \cup \{T_j\}$ and $j = j + 1$.
4. If $j \leq m$, go to 2, else $L = (B_1, B_2, ..., B_n)$.
5. Stop.

The number k of unempty sets B_i, $i \leq k$, determines the duration of the schedule S that is obtained by priority scheduling according to the list L. This list is obtained by taking tasks from the sets $B_1, B_2, ..., B_k$ in succession.

It is evident that if $m \geq n$, this is the so-called proper bin-packing problem.

By applying various bin-packing criteria, we can change algorithm BP into another algorithm, as in Section 3. The algorithm BPI is based on the algorithm BP.

Algorithm BPI: The tasks $T_1, ..., T_n$ are ordered as in BP.

1. Let k^* be the length of the schedule S obtained by means of algorithm BP. Let $d = \max \left\{ \left\lceil \dfrac{n}{m} \right\rceil, \sum_{i=1}^{n} m_i / C \right\}$. Evidently, $d \leq t_{opt}$. Let the task list from which we can obtain the schedule S, be L (defined in step 4 of BP), and let $k = k^*$.

2. $k = k - 1$, $B_i = \emptyset$, $b_i = \emptyset$, $o_i = C$ for $i = 1, 2, ..., k$, $j = 1$.

3. Let $\quad i = \min \{\alpha: o_\alpha = \max \{o_\beta: b_\beta = \min \{b_\gamma: 1 \leq \gamma \leq k \& b_\gamma + 1 \leq m \& o_\gamma - m_j = 0\}\}\}$. If such an i does not exist, then go to 7.

4. Put $B_\iota = B_\iota \cup \{T_\iota\}$, $j = j + 1$.

5. If $j \leqq n$, then go to 3.

6. $L = (B_1, B_2, ..., B_k)$, $k^* = k$. If $k \leqq d$, then go to 2.

7. L is the desired task list. Stop.

Using priority scheduling it is possible to create from L a schedule of duration k^*. The algorithm is of small complexity, but we have to use the elements of B_ι, $i = 1, ..., k$, logically ordered with decreasing o_ι and increasing b_ι.

Now, let us give an example of a system of independent tasks $TS = (T_1, ..., T_n)$, $t_\iota = 1$, $i = 1, ..., n$, for which the ratio of the duration of the optimal and of the worst schedules is $3/2 - 1/m$.

Let m be even. Let the tasks in TS be $T_1, ..., T_m$, $m_1 = ... = m_n = 1/2$, and T_{m+1}, ..., $T_{m+m(m-1)}$, $m_{m+1} = ... = m_{m+m(m-1)} = 1/2(m-1)$.

Let L and L' be the lists:

$L = (T_1, ..., T_m, T_{m+1}, ..., T_{m.m})$,

$L' = (T_{m+1}, ..., T_{m+m-1}, T_1, T_{m+m}, ..., T_{m+2(m-1)},$
  $T_2, ..., T_{m.m}, T_m)$.

Then for L and L' the durations of the schedules are $t_L = (3m - 2)/2$ and $t_{L'} = m$. Hence, $t_L/t_{L'} = 3/2 - 1m$. This seems to be one of the worst ratios. We can see that $t_{L'} = t_{opt}$. In this case, the algorithm BP yields the list L and the algorithm BPI the list L'. Thus, the modification BPI of the algorithm BP can significantly decrease the duration of the schedules. The algorithm BPI tries to schedule the requirement of the memory uniformly over time. This reduces the number of B_ι in which no processors are employed.

On the basis of our experience with the algorithm BPI we see that the strategy of referring tasks with the greatest memory requirements is not always suitable. What becomes more striking, if we have differing task durations.

8.4.2 Independent Tasks

We assume that the task system $TS = (T, <)$ is such that $< = \emptyset$, t_i are different and $m_\iota \leqq C$ for $i = 1, ..., n$.

In this case, the problem of optimal scheduling is again NP-complete. Consequently, it is of no value to seek for the optimal algorithm. Therefore we try to construct a suitable algorithm for constructing a list, by which we can schedule the given TS on a given MS.

Not considering the storage capacity, we know that in this case CP-scheduling yields relatively good results: $t_{CP}/t_{opt} \leqq 4/3 - 1/3m$. But the limitation of the storage capacity changes this bound to $3(m-1)/m$.

There exist many known strategies for producing priority task lists. Nevertheless, better bounds for the maximum execution time than that given above are not known for any of them. Among the simplest belong: STF (Smallest Time First), LTF (Largest Time First), SMF (Smallest Memory First), LMF (Largest Memory First), and then combinations such as LMTF.

None of these strategies considers the "uniform" distribution of memory requirements at the time of execution of the task system TS. Therefore, if the number of tasks is sufficiently large and the requirements m_i are uniformly distributed on the interval $\langle 0, C \rangle$, it might occur that all processors are idle because of shortage of memory (LMF at the beginning of scheduling), and at other times, all processors work with an extremely low memory utilization (SMF at the beginning of scheduling).

Therefore we try to design a very heuristic method of constructing schedules which will "uniformly" distribute the requirements for memory over the whole duration of the schedule. We must pay increasing attention to achieve such a distribution of the memory requirement, so that we can exploit the possibilities of MS as much as possible. We know that without memory limitations, a deviation from the optimum of less than 100% may be achieved using any priority scheduling (CP-scheduling only 1.25), this, however, can greatly worsen due to a limitation of the memory available.

Algorithm BPM: $TS = \{T_1, ..., T_n\}$, $< = \emptyset$,
$$m_i \leqq C, \ i = 1, ..., n.$$

Without loss of generality we can regard $t_1, ..., t_n$ as integers.

1. Using the LMTF strategy we construct a list L, by which the TS is executed in t_L time units, and the schedule S.

2. Put $t^*_{opt} = \max \left\{ \max\limits_{1 \leq i \leq n} t_i, \left\lceil \dfrac{t_L}{3\,\dfrac{m-1}{m}} \right\rceil, \left\lceil \dfrac{\sum\limits_{i=1}^{n} t_i}{m} \right\rceil, \left\lceil \dfrac{\sum\limits_{i=1}^{n} m_i t_i}{C} \right\rceil \right\}$.

Put $t = t_L$.

3. $t = t - 1$. Using the algorithm AMM, given below, we construct the schedule $S'(TS, MS)$ with duration t.

   a) If such S' exists, then $S \leftarrow S'$, $t_L = t$ and GO TO 3.

   b) If such S' does not exist, then if $t > t^*_{opt}$, GO TO 3.

4. The schedule S of duration t_L is the required schedule of the TS on MS. STOP.

If the duration of the desired schedule is given, the main component of BPM is the algorithm AMM for scheduling TS on MS.

Algorithm AMM: TS as in BPM, $MS = \{P_1, ..., P_m\}$, the storage capacity is C.

Let us suppose that the tasks in the TS are ordered so that for T_i, T_j: $i < j$, if $m_i > m_j \vee m_i = m_j \, \& \, t_i \geqq t_j$. Let t be the duration of the schedule required. Let $B_1, ..., B_{2n+1}$ be the sets of tasks beginning at times $\tau_1, ..., \tau_{2n+1}$. With each of these

B_i is associated the numbers o_i, the available storage capacity at time τ_i, b_i the number of free processors at time τ_i, the index k_i of the successor in the chain CHB. The chain CHB is generated during scheduling from the sets B_i, $i = 1, \ldots, 2n + 1$, and its elements determine either the time at which the execution of a task is terminated, or the time at which the execution of some task begins, or both. The chain CHB is logically ordered by increasing times τ_i.

1. Put $\tau_1 = \emptyset$, $\tau_2 = t$

$o_1 = C$, $b_i = m$, $B_i = \emptyset$ for $i = 1, \ldots, 2n + 1$

$k_1 = 2$, $k_2 = \emptyset$, i.e. from B_1 and B_2 we have created the chain $B_1 B_2$.

Let k be the index of the first B_i that has not yet been incorporated in the chain (here $k = 3$). Let INIT be the index of the first B_i in the chain CHB such that up to the time τ_{INIT} it is not possible to incorporate tasks in the schedule, because there is no free processor, or there is not enough memory, for all remaining unicorporated tasks. Let α be the index of this B_i such that, beginning at time τ_α, we want to incorporate in the schedule some task from the TS.

Initially $\alpha = 1$.

2. If TS is empty, GO TO 6.

3. In the TS we are looking from the left for the first task T_i which can be implemented beginning at time τ_α. The possibility of the implementation of T_i from the time τ_α occurs if the following conditions are satisfied:

a) $\tau_\alpha + t_i \leqq t \,\&\, b_\alpha \geqq 1 \,\&\, c_\alpha \geqq m_i$.

b) Let B be the first element in the chain CHB for which $\tau_\beta \geqq \tau_\alpha + t_i$. Then, for all B_γ between B_α and B_β in the chain CHB $b_\gamma \geqq 1$ & $c_\gamma \geqq m_i$.

4. If we find such a task from T_i, then:

let β' be the index of the predecessor B_β in CHB.

a) We implement the task T_i in the elements B_γ in CHB, beginning with the element B_α and ending with $B_{\beta'}$:

$b_\gamma = b_\gamma - 1$, $o_\gamma = o_\gamma - m_i$,

$B_\alpha + B_\alpha \cup \{T_i\}$ — the beginning of the execution of task T_i is at τ_α;

b) if $\tau_\alpha + t_i = t$, then $\alpha = \text{INIT}$ and GO TO 4.e;

c) if $\tau_\alpha + t_i = \tau_\beta$, the $\alpha = \beta$ and GO TO 4.e;

d) if $\tau_\alpha + t_i < \tau_\beta$, then:

$k_{\beta'} = k$ and $k_k = \beta$, i.e. insertion of the element B_k into CHB after the element $B_{\beta'}$,

$o_k = o_{\beta'} + m_i$, $b_k = b_{\beta'} + 1$, $\tau_k = \tau_\alpha + t_i$,

$\alpha = k$ (the beginning of the next scheduling),

$k = k + 1$;

e) erase the task T_i from TS and GO TO 2.

5. If we do not find such a task T_i from step 3, then:

a) if $\alpha = \text{INIT}$, then $\text{INIT} = k_\alpha$, $\alpha = \text{INIT}$ and GO TO 5.c;

b) if $\alpha \neq \text{INIT}$ then $\alpha = k_\alpha$;

c) if $\alpha = 2$, then GO TO 7;

d) else GO TO 2.

6. Output: schedule of duration t, in which the sets B_γ from B_1 to B_2 in the chain CHB together with the times determine which task is to be executed and when. STOP.

7. Output: AMM does not construct a schedule of TS on MS of duration t. STOP.

Example 4 shows scheduling using algorithm AMM. The description of the algorithm AMM is complex. This complexity results from the use of data structures which have been applied only recently, and which in many cases have significantly reduced the complexity of computations. This algorithm can also have additional modifications, but these are only suitable for solving very highly specialized problems, mainly in the area of

Example 4. $C = 10$, $m = 3$, $n = 10$ (Fig. 7a)

$$T_i = 1, 2, 3, 4, 5, 6, 7, 8, 9, 10,$$
$$t_i = 6, 5, 4, 2, 5, 5, 5, 3, 6, 4,$$
$$m_i = 5, 5, 4, 4, 3, 3, 2, 2, 1, 1.$$

We can see that $t_{\text{LMTF}} = 18$.

The LMTF schedule is given in Fig. 7b.

Thus, $t_{\text{opt}} = \max \{7, 9, 16, 14\} = 16$

since $\max_{i \leq 10} t_i = 7$

$$\left\lceil \frac{t_L}{3\,\dfrac{m-1}{m}} \right\rceil = 9, \quad \left\lceil \frac{\sum t_i}{m} \right\rceil = 16, \quad \left\lceil \frac{\sum t_i m_i}{C} \right\rceil = 14.$$

For $t = 18, 17$ it is possible to construct schedules AMM. The AMM-schedule for $t = 16$ is given in Fig. 7c and we can see that it is optimal.

8.4.3 Arbitrary task system

Till now, only systems of independent tasks have been dealt with in this chapter. Now we assume that $\text{TS} = (T, <)$ is general, $<$ is not empty, there is exactly one node in $<$, T_1, without ancestors (input) and exactly one node, T_n, without successors (ouptut), and $<$ has no loops. Under the assumption of finite memory this problem becomes rather complex, even for heuristic methods. We know that in this case by the application of priority scheduling using the list of task priorities we obtain the worst upper bound $t/t_{\text{opt}} \leq m$.

In such cases the critical path method, is used most frequently. As seen in Chapter 3, this method gives in some special cases the optimal schedules. But in general, when the graph $G \sim (TS, <)$ is extensive, there are only few processors and memory is limited. Hence, this method does not appear so successful. In the following section we shall suggest some modifications of CP-scheduling for the case

a

T_i	1	2	3	4	5	6	7	8	9	10
t_i	6	5	4	2	5	5	6	3	6	4
m_i	5	5	4	4	3	3	2	2	1	1

b

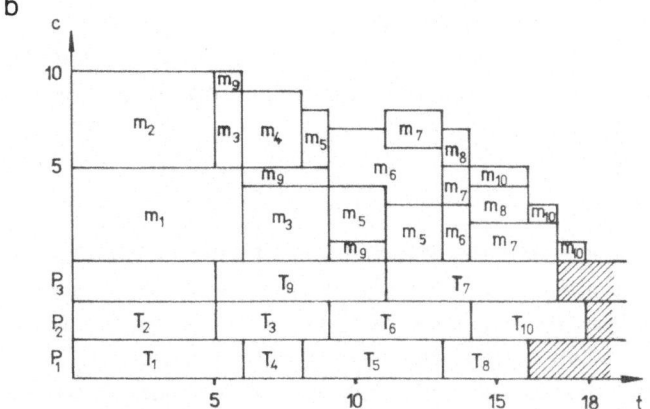

c

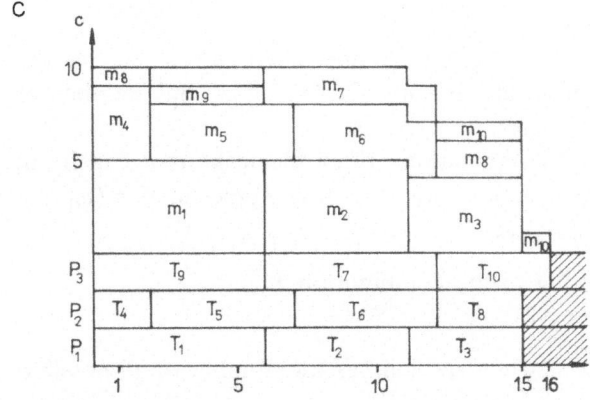

Fig. 7.

of a limited memory, which may help to exploit the possibilities of MS in specified cases. One of these methods is the algorithm OPG (scheduling in the case of limited memory for a general graph).

Algorithm OPG: $TS = (T, <)$, storage capacity C.

The assignment of tasks to processors proceeds according to the following strategy: Always when a processor becomes free or is already free, a task T_i is assigned to it, which

    a) is ready, i.e. all its predecessors have already been executed,

    b) has the minimum difference between the latest required and the earliest possible termination times,

    c) has a maximum requirement for memory which is smaller than the current free memory,

    d) has the maximum execution time.

This strategy should ensure that the course of task execution keeps to the set time t for executing G. It is obvious that this strategy can be changed, depending on the particular scheduling. But the change should not affect item a), since, if we are to keep the time t this item is of key importance.

Here, a suitable choice of strategy depends on the properties of the system TS, the number of edges, the range of the times t_i, the requirements on the memory m_i, and on their relationship.

8.4.4 Preemptive scheduling

Preemptive scheduling is a special case of scheduling. In the case of limited memory, as in the case of inhomogeneous MS, it seems that the so-called priority functioning of MS, which allows the execution of tasks to be interrupted and to continue after a certain time on a different processor (if possible), is more advantageous, since it exploits the resources and processors of MS more effectively than for homogeneous MS or MS without the limitation of the capacities of the resources.

Let $TS = \{T_1, ..., T_n\}$, $< = \emptyset$, $t_1, ..., t_n$ be unequal, and $m_1, ..., m_n$ be the memory requirements of tasks of total capacity C; let m be the number of processors.

Let us assume that we know all combinations K of the tasks that can be in memory simultaneously. These combinations are given by n-tuples of $K_i = (a_{i1}, a_{i2}, ..., a_{in})$, where a_{ij} are defined as follows:

$a_{ij} = \emptyset$, if the task T_j does not belong to the combination K_i,

$a_{ij} = 1$, if the task T_j does belong to K_i.

Clearly $\sum_{j=1}^{n} a_{ij} \leqq C$ for all $i = 1, ..., N$, where N denotes the number of all possible combinations. Now we can describe the problem of optimal preemptive scheduling by a simple linear programming model. We note that this is not a question of discrete linear programming.

    Minimize $f(x_1, ..., x_N) = \sum_{i=1}^{N} x_i$

under the conditions

$$\sum_{i=1}^{N} x_i a_{ij} r_i = t_j \text{ for } j = 1, \ldots, n$$

and $x_i \geq \emptyset$, x_i — real, for $i = 1, \ldots, N$.

Here, r_i gives the speed of task processing in the execution of the combination $K_i = (a_{i1}, \ldots, a_{in})$ and is given by

$$r_i = \min \left\{ 1, \frac{m}{\sum_{j=1}^{n} a_{ij}} \right\}.$$

We can see that $r_i = 1$, if less than m tasks are processed in the combination K_i. If more than m tasks are processed in K_i, the total speed of the computational system MS, m, must be distributed among these tasks uniformly.

There is always this solution of the problem, i.e. we always obtain the optimal solution. The solution is the x_i, $i = 1, \ldots, N$, such that $x_i > \emptyset$. Let these be $x_1, \ldots, x_k$, then the combinations are $K_1, \ldots, K_k$. Let us interpret this solution in such a way that the combination of tasks K_i is executed in the schedule for duration x_i as follows:

    a) Let K_i be such that $r_i = 1$, i.e. it contains tasks $T_1, \ldots, T_p$, where $p \leq m$. The corresponding part of the schedule of duration x_i is shown in Fig. 8a.

a

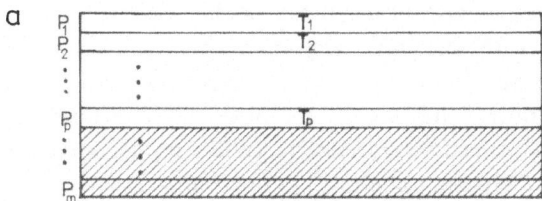

b

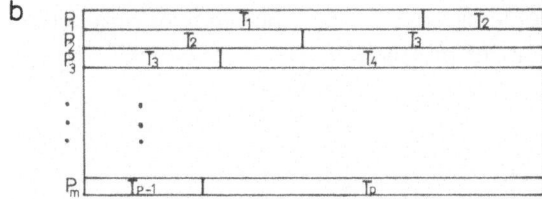

Fig. 8.

    b) Let K_i be such that $r_i < 1$, i.e. K_i contains tasks $T_1, \ldots, T_p$, where $p > m$. Then the corresponding part of the schedule of duration x_i is shown in Fig. 8b.

Consequently, this is a preemptive schedule for the tasks $T_i, \ldots, T_p$, of duration $x_i r_i$, at time x_i.

The desired schedule $S(TS, MS)$ is obtained by writing the combinations K_i, with durations x_i, in series.

This algorithm for constant m is of polynomial complexity with respect to the number of tasks, n in the TS. There are at most $O(n^m)$ possible combinations, and the solution of the linear programming model, e.g. the simplex method, is also of polynomial complexity. But it must be stated that even though the resulting complexity is polynomial, it is so high that this algorithm can only be applied to problems of the so-called static scheduling, in which a new schedule is constructed only rarely.

If $TS = (T, <)$ is an arbitrary graph, one of the simplest and most useful methods of preemptive scheduling is the so-called scheduling by levels in the graph $TS(G)$. Here, similarly as in Schindler's algorithm, we break the graph into levels in each of which there starts at least one task; in each of these levels we use some heuristic algorithm for scheduling the set of independent, equally long tasks with bounded total memory. The resultant schedule is produced by combining the schedules for the single levels. The formal description of the algorithm is analogous to that given above, and therefore it is not given here.

Conclusion

We have given a brief survey of the subject of scheduling in multiprocessor systems. Research in this sphere started relatively recently and there are still many unsolved problems. In connection with the NP-completeness of the general problem of scheduling, research currently follows several directions. This includes the design of new heuristic algorithms, the investigation of their properties including the upper bounds of the total duration. Recently, the theory of so-called probability algorithms, which generate random schedules dependent on the type of the TS and MS has been developed. The solution of all these questions is extremely important, not only from the aspect of utilizing multiprocessor systems, but also from the point of view of practical problems, such as the scheduling of production and resources, operational management of production, etc.

REFERENCES

[1] AHO, A. V., HOPCROFT, J. E. and ULLMAN, J. D.: The Design and Analysis of Computer Algorithms. Adison Wesley, Reading, Mass., 1974.
[2] COFFMAN, E. G. and DENNING, P. J.: Operating Systems Theory. Prentice-Hall, Englewood Clifs, N. J., 1973.
[3] COFFMAN, E. G. and GRAHAM, R. L.: Optimal scheduling for two processor systems. Acta Informata, *1*, 1972, 3, 200—213.

[4] COFFMAN, E. G. (Editor): Computer and Job/Shop Scheduling Theory. John Wiley & Sons, Inc., New York, 1976.

[5] GRAHAM, R. L.: Bounds on multiprocessing timing anomalies. SIAM J. Appl. Math., *17*, 1969, 2, 416—429.

[6] GAREY, M. R. and GRAHAM, R. L.: Bounds for multiprocessing scheduling with resource constraints. SIAM J. on Computing, *4*, 1975, 187—200.

[7] GAREY, M. R. and GRAHAM, R. L.: Bounds on scheduling with limited resources. Operating Systems Review, *7*, 1973, 4, 104—111.

[8] GONZALES, T., IBARRA., O. H. and SAHNI, S.: Bounds for LPT schedules on uniform processors. SIAM J. on Computing, *6*, 1977, 1, 155—166.

[9] GAREY, M. R., JOHNSON, D. S. and SETHI, R.: The complexity of flowshop and jobshop scheduling. Tech. Report 168, Dep. Comp. Sci., Pennsylvania State Univ., 1975.

[10] HU, T. C.: Parallel sequencing and assembly line problems. Operating Research, *9*, 1961, 6, 841—840.

[11] JOHNSON, S. M.: Optimal two- and three-stage production schedules. Naval Research and Logistic Quart., *1*, 1954, 1.

[12] LIU, J. W. L. and LIU, C. L.: Bounds on scheduling algorithms for heterogeneous computing systems. Tech. Report, Dep. Comp. Sci., Univ. of Illinois, 1974.

[13] LÜDTKE, H. and SCHINDLER, S.: Some properties of heuristic graph scheduling algorithms and the conjecture on Hu's algorithm. Tech. Report 75-05, Fachbereich 20 — Kybernetik, Technische Universität Berlin, 1975.

[14] MUNTZ, R. R. and COFFMAN, E. G.: Preemptive scheduling for realtime tasks on multiprocessor systems. J. ACM, *17*, 1970, 2, 324—338.

[15] HUNTZ, R. R. and COFFMAN, E. G.: Optimal scheduling on two-processor systems. IEEE Trans. on Computers, *C-18*, 1969, 11, 1014—1020.

[16] MADNICK, S. E. and DONOVAN, J. Y.: Operating Systems. McGraw-Hill Book Co., New York, 1974.

[17] SCHINDLER, S.: Quantitative aspects of optimal schedules for multiprocessor systems. Tech. Report 73-10, Fachbereich 20 — Kybernetik, Technische Universität Berlin, 1973.

[18] ULLMAN, J. D.: Polynomial complete scheduling problems. Tech. Report 9, Dep. Comp. Sci., Univ. of California, Berkeley, 1973.

[19] ULLMAN, J. D.: Polynomial completeness of the equal execution time scheduling problem. Tech. Report 115, Dep. Elect. Eng., Princeton University, 1972.

[20] ULLMAN, J. D.: The performance of a memory allocation algorithms. Tech. Report 100, Dep. Elect. Eng., Princeton University, 1971.

[21] COFFMAN, E. G., GAREY, M. R. and JOHNSON, D. S.: An application of bin-packing to multiprocessor scheduling. SIAM J. on Computing, *7*, 1978, 1, 1—17.

Appendix

UNIFORM COMPUTER SYSTEM: SCHEDULING OF JOBS WITH UNKNOWN EXECUTION TIME

1. Problem formulation. Suppose that a program can be represented as a combination of jobs (subtasks, branches, processes), for which partial ordering,

depending on data and program logic is given. Jobs should be assigned to single processors of the uniform computer system (UCS) so that these would minimize the total program execution time, T^*, taking into account the partial ordering of the jobs. Specifically, such a problem occurs in job scheduling in UCS with a common main memory; for example, the assignment of branches which are ready for execution between single control units in the programmable structure of UCS [1].

There are exact methods for optimal job assignment in UCS [2], but these are based on the assumption that the execution time of each job is given either exactly or stochastically. In practice, the execution time of a complicated program or its part (job) is, in most cases, unpredictable owing to logical branching, loops of indefinite length which occur during job execution, internal and external interrupts, conflicts in common memory, etc. In particular, the execution time of some jobs can turn out to be zero if during program execution there is no transfer of control to these jobs. We consider the problem of selecting and justifying a criterion for the assignment of program jobs to free UCS processors (with the aim of minimizing T^*) with no information available about the execution time of each job different from its upper bound (from the UCS timer, for instance).

A single UCS processor is assumed to execute one job at a time. All program jobs which are ready for execution form a job queue, Φ. If a job is assigned to a processor, it is removed from Φ. The execution of job a can be interrupted internally or externally, in which case another job from Φ can be assigned to the free processor, and the job a is added to the queue after interrupt processing. Our problem is under the above conditions formulated as follows:

A program is given in the form of a graph $G = (A, T, \Gamma)$, where vertex $a_i \in A$ corresponds to the i-th job ($i = 1, 2, ..., m$), $t_i \in T$ is the unknown execution time of

the i-th job (a random variable within an interval $\overline{0, t_{max}}$), and the set of edges Γ reflects relations between jobs depending on data and program logic. The graph G has an arbitrary number of input edges and only one output edge. The set of vertices which have only input edges forms the job front Φ_0.

The system has n processors. At the time t_{cur} when a processor is set free, there is a front of jobs $\Phi_{cur} = \{a_i, ..., a_j\}$ with unknown execution times; if the job a_i or a_j is assigned to the free processor the unknown variable, T_i or T_j, is assigned to the execution time of the remainder of the program. The free processor should be assigned to a job $a_j \in \Phi_{cur}$, so that $p(T_j \leqslant T_i) \geqslant p(T_j > T_i)$, i.e. the probability of the event $(T_j \leqslant T_i)$ is not less than that of the event $(T_j > T_i)$, where T_i, T_j are random variables. We assume that the smaller the total idle time of the system processors, i.e. the "better" the system loading at each time, the smaller the execution time of a program (T^*) or of its remainder (T_i or T_j).

2. Scheduling criterion and its estimation. The job scheduling criterion should

(i) reflect the possible (probabilistic) behaviour of the system which executes the programs, i.e. it should be a criterion for the probabilistic estimation of the possible system states, and (ii) allow for each possible ordering of jobs following a given one. In doing so, the criterion should be as straightforward as possible to ensure that only simple calculations are necessary for each program job. Program job rank (the rank of the vertex of graph G) is suggested as such a criterion.

The rank τ_i of vertex a_i is defined as the length of the maximum path over graph G beginning at this vertex and expressed as the number of vertices.

Let Q_i be a set of successor jobs of job a_i: $a_\varphi \in Q_i$ if $(a_i \, a_\varphi) \in \Gamma$. Then τ_i is defined recursively by

$$\tau_i = 1 + \max_{a_\varphi \in Q_i} \tau_\varphi. \tag{1}$$

It follows from (1) that job vertex rank is constant and independent, for instance, of logical program branches which succeed this job. This implies that the rank of each job can be computed statically, i.e. prior to actual program execution. The set of job/vertices having the same rank forms a level. Initially, assume that there are no logical branches and loops in the program.

For acyclic programs, one can obtain unique decompositions of the vertices of graph G into levels by means of the above definitions of rank and level. For the graph shown in Fig. 1a, the decomposition into levels is shown in Fig. 1b.

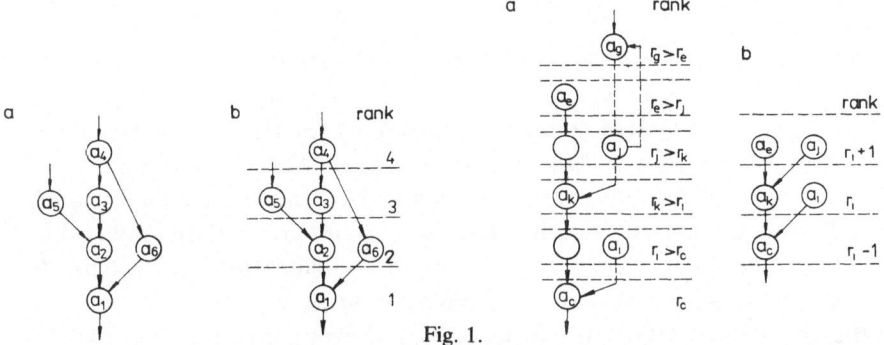

Fig. 1.

Fig. 2.

Let a system of n processors execute some program jobs including a_e, and let there be a current front of two jobs $\Phi_{cur} = \{a_i, a_j\}$ having different ranks (belonging to different levels) (Fig. 2a).

Since further system behaviour depends at any time only on the current state and is independent of the succession of events that have resulted in this state, the process under consideration is Markovian.

To reduce the number of system states under consideration, let us consider first the case where the ranks of alternative jobs and successor jobs differ at most by 1 for $n = 2$; the graph in Fig. 2a takes the form shown in Fig. 2b. Suppose a processor is currently executing job a_e. Job a_k can only be executed after the completion of both predecessor jobs a_e and a_j. Job a_c can also be executed after the completion of both jobs a_k and a_i (the AND rule).

If a job with a higher rank is assigned from Φ_{cur} to a free resource, i.e. a_j, the system changes at current time t_{cur} to the state $(a_e\ a_j)$, which will be considered the initial state for further discussion (Fig. 3a). If $t_e > t_j$, after the completion of a_j only job a_i can be assigned to the free resource, and the system changes to the state $(a_e\ a_i)$; if $t_e < t_j$, after the completion of job a_e the system changes to the state

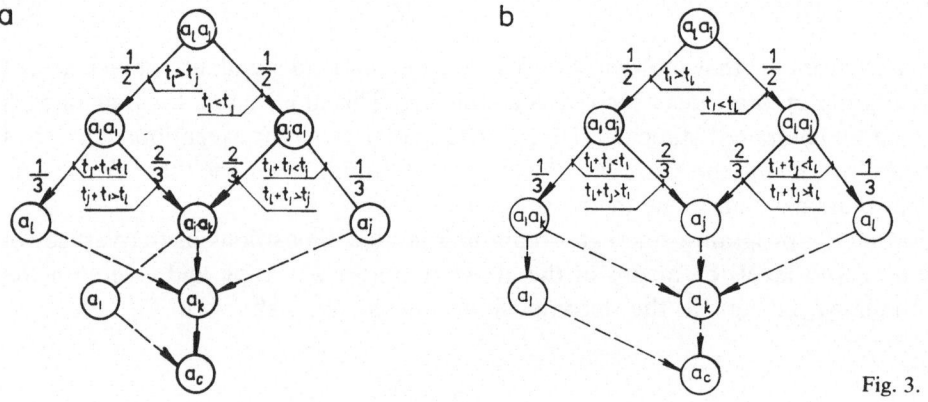

Fig. 3.

$(a_j\ a_i)$. Similarly, if $t_j < t_e + t_i$, state $(a_j\ a_i)$ is followed by state $(a_i\ a_k)$, otherwise, the system changes to state (a_j), i.e. only one of two processors is operating.

Graphs of all possible system states and transitions for the case of assignment jobs with higher (a_j) and lower (a_i) rank are shown in Figs. 3a and 3b.

We assume that jobs in both processors cannot be completed simultaneously. This is true if random variables taking values over a sufficiently large interval are used. We also neglect the execution time of job a_e before time t_{cur}.* This also applies to system behaviour at activation time, i.e. at $t_{cur} = t_0$.

Under the above assumptions the probabilities of events $p(t_e > t_j)$ and $p(t_e < t_j)$ are the same and equal to $1/2$. Similarly, $p(t_e > t_i) = p(t_e < t_i) = 1/2$.

Assign these values to the edges corresponding to transitions from the state $(a_e\ a_j)$ to the states $(a_e\ a_i)$ and $(a_j\ a_i)$ in Fig. 3a, and from the state $(a_e\ a_i)$ to the states $(a_i\ a_j)$ and $(a_e\ a_j)$ in Fig. 3b.

---

*Here we make use of a fact well known in probability theory and queueing theory: the probability that a random service interval is less than some given value is equal to the probability of the same event but beginning from some arbitrary (fixed or random) service time.

Determine the probabilities of transitions from state $(a_e\ a_i)$ to states (a_e) and $(a_i\ a_k)$, and from state $(a_j\ a_i)$ to states $(a_i\ a_k)$ (Fig. 3a), and also from state $(a_j\ a_i)$ to state $(a_i\ a_k)$, and from state $(a_e\ a_j)$ to states (a_e) and (a_j) (Fig. 3b). Since t_e, t_i, t_j are independent random variables, to determine the probabilities of the above transitions, the probability $p(a + b > c)$, i.e. the probability that the sum of the two independent random variables a and b is greater than random variable c, must be determined, where a, b and c are random variables which take values over the same interval and have the same, although unknown, distribution.

One can rigorously demonstrate that, for any probability distribution $p(a + b > c) \geq 2/3$. In particular, for a uniform (rectangular) probability distribution, $p(a + b > c) = 5/6$, while for an exponential distribution $p(a + b > c) = 3/4$.

Since, in general, the lower bound of the probability is $2/3$, this value will be used in further computations. Returning now to the system under consideration, attach probabilities $2/3$ to the edges corresponding to transitions from the states $(a_e\ a_i)$ and $(a_j\ a_i)$ to the state $(a_i\ a_k)$ (Fig. 3a), and from the states $(a_j\ a_j)$ and $(a_e\ a_j)$ to the state (a_j) (Fig. 3b). The other system transitions (edges) have probability $1/3$.

Note that the system under consideration is completely loaded in the states $(a_e\ a_j)$, $(a_e\ a_i)$, $(a_j\ a_i)$, $(a_i\ a_k)$, i.e. both processors are operating. In the other states shown in Figs. 3a and 3b, there operates one processor only.

Independently of the job assigned first to the free resource (a_j or a_i), the system changes from the initial state $(a_e\ a_j)$ or $(a_e\ a_i)$ into one of the states in which it is loaded completely. Later, however, the system can change either into the state $(a_i\ a_k)$ where it is completely loaded, or into one of the states (a_i), (a_e) where only one processor is loaded, the probabilities of system transitions into such states depending on which of the jobs with different ranks (a_j or a_i) was first assigned to the free resource. We are interested in the asymptotic behaviour of the system only before and in the states $(a_i\ a_k)$, (a_j), (a_e), since in the succeeding states (a_i), (a_k), (a_c) only a single processor will work in any case. Consider a pseudo-ergodic chain transition graph of which is shown in Fig. 4. It is generalized in the sense that it

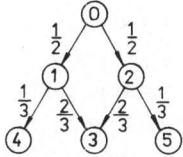

Fig. 4.

corresponds to the graphs in Figs. 3a and 3b — apart from the states (a_i), (a_k) and (a_c); vertices 0 through 5 can be regarded as the states $(a_e\ a_j)$, $(a_e\ a_i)$, $(a_j\ a_i)$, $(a_i\ a_k)$. (a_e), (a_j) of the graph in Fig. 3a, or the state $(a_e\ a_i)$, $(a_j\ a_i)$, $(a_e\ a_j)$, (a_j), $(a_i\ a_k)$. (a_e) of the graph in Fig. 3b. Evidently, as shown in Fig. 4, the system under consideration will change to state 3 with probability 2/3 and to states 4 or 5 with probability 1/6.

Referring again to the transition graphs in Figs. 3a and 3b, this means that, if the free resource first gets a job with higher rank a_j (Fig. 3a), the system will change with probability $p = 2/3$ to the state $(a_i \, a_k)$ corresponding to vertex 3 of the graph in Fig. 4, where the system is completely loaded; if a job with lower rank, a_i, is assigned (Fig. 3b), the system will change to the state $(a_i \, a_k)$ corresponding to vertex 4 of the graph in Fig. 4 with probability $p = 1/6$ only. State $(a_i \, a_k)$ is, generally, the "key" state for our consideration in the sense that a system transition into this state implies that the jobs a_e, a_j and either job a_i or a_k have been executed, so that the system has always been completely loaded. A transition into state (a_e) or (a_j) implies that only two jobs, a_j and a_i, or a_e and a_i have been executed during complete loading of the system; the jobs a_k and a_c and also, partially, job a_e (or a_j) have been executed by a single processor successively.

Thus, depending on the rank of the vertex assigned to the free resource, the probabilities of system operation under complete loading (after two intermediate states) differ by a factor of four. Referring to the problem formulation given in Section 1, this means that $p(T_j < T_i) > p(T_j > T_i)$. Let us consider again the program graph in Fig. 2a. It is assumed that alternative job ranks can differ by more than 1. First of all, consider the case where rank τ_e of job a_e executed at time t_{cur} is greater than rank τ_j, $\tau_j > \tau_i$. For the case given in Fig. 3a this means that the probability of the system changing from state $(a_e^* \, a_j^*)$ to state $(a_e^* \, a_i^*)$ increases, here a_e^*, a_j^*, and a_i^* are job sequences which have already been ordered from a_e, a_j and a_i to a_k, a_c. One can prove that under the above conditions the probability that the sum of n independent random variables is greater than that of $n-1$ random variables is greater than $1/2$; the "key" state $(a_i^* \, a_k^*)$ can be reached from the state $(a_e^* \, a_j^*)$.

Since $\tau_e > \tau_j > \tau_i$, the probability of the system changing from the initial state $(a_e \, a_i)$ to $(a_e^* \, a_j^*)$ in the case given in Fig. 3b in which job a_i with smaller rank is assigned to the free resources, is still greater; the "key" state $(a_i^* \, a_k^*)$ cannot be reached in the case of state $(a_e^* \, a_j^*)$.

It is of interest to analyse the system behaviour for a large rank difference between alternative jobs a_j and a_i, i.e. for $\tau_e \geqslant \tau_j \gg \tau_i$. As to the case given in Fig. 3b, this means that the probability of the system changing to state $(a_e^* \, a_j^*)$, from which the "key" state $(a_i^* \, a_k^*)$ cannot be reached, approaches 1. As far as the case given in Fig. 3a is concerned the probability of the system changing to the "key" state $(a_i^* \, a_k^*)$ approaches 1.

Thus, in all the cases considered above it is more reasonable to assign to the free resource a job a_j with a higher rank rather than job a_i with a lower rank, because this ensures that $p(T_j < T_i) > p(T_j > T_i)$.

3. Algorithm and experiment. The source data for job scheduling (e.g. the graph

of Fig. 5) can be tabulated similarly as in Table 1 in which the i-th row corresponds to the i-th vertex of the graph (job a_i) and indicates the predecessors and successors job a_i and its rank τ_i computed using (1). A job is regarded ready for execution and is included in Φ_{cur} if all its predecessors have already been completed. A free processor obtains the job with the higher rank from Φ_{cur}. If there are several such jobs, selection is arbitrary.

a

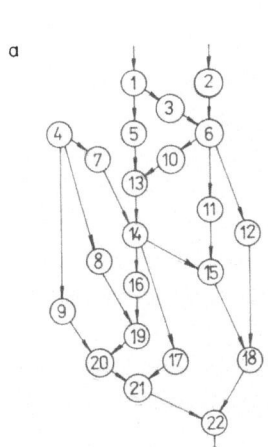

b

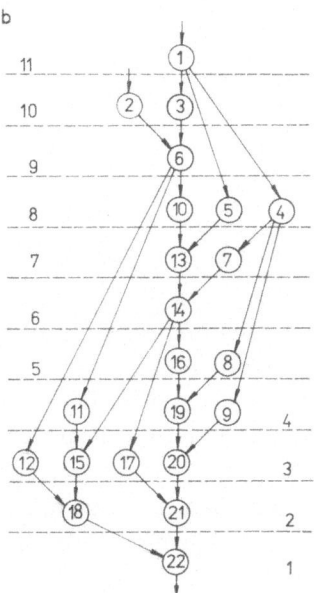

Fig. 5.

Table 1

i	Predecessor	Successor	τ_i	t_i	i	Predecessor	Successor	τ_{in}	
1	—	3, 4, 5	11	3	12	6	18	3	2
2	—	6	10	6	13	5, 10	14	7	2
3	1	6	10	8	14	7, 13	15, 16, 17	6	5
4	1	7, 8, 9	8	7	15	11, 14	18	3	7
5	1	13	8	10	16	14	19	5	6
6	2, 3	10, 11, 12	9	1	17	14	21	3	5
7	7	14	7	1	18	12, 15	22	2	3
8	4	19	5	2	19	8, 16	20	4	10
9	4	20	4	4	20	9, 19	21	3	4
10	6	13	8	3	21	17, 20	22	2	2
11	6	15	4	6	22	18, 21	—	1	4

Figure 6a illustrates a scheduling example (for $n = 2$) of the program given in Fig. 5. For comparison, Fig. 6b shows job scheduling where a job with the smallest index is assigned to the free resource from Φ_{cur}. The execution time of each job was taken to be a random number of loops between 1 to 10. In this example, the program execution time obtained using the above criterion was 55 cycles and was 14.5% less than that obtained without using criterion, 63 cycles.

a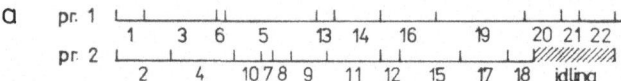

b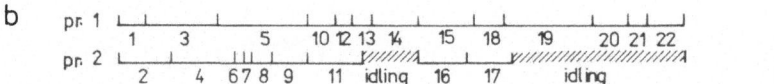

Fig. 6.

K. T. Tocheva (Institute of Control Sciences) has demonstrated on more than 300 computer experiments (for $n = 2$) over graphs having 20 to 70 vertices that the application of the above scheduling rule results in a program execution time 8% to 19% less than that based on various formal approaches: random selection of jobs from Φ_{cur}, FIFO, etc.

4. Programs with logical branches and cycles. Note that Section 2 was only devoted to programs having an arbitrary number of internal conditional branches and loops in program segments which are referred to as jobs; it is, in particular, conditional branches and loops that make the execution time of each job t_i a random variable in an interval. Note that this program interpretation holds completely for structured programs. Now, we shall consider some aspects of scheduling which arise from conditional branches between jobs.

Above the assumption has been used that each job is ready for execution only after the completion of all its predecessors. The presence of conditional branches from one job to another implies (i) that a job can be attached to a job queue after the completion of one or more, but not necessarily all predecessors, and (ii) that there are alternative successors to the given job. But the rank τ_i of the job a_i is, according to (1), constant and independent of alternative job selection during program execution.

Indeed, if for example branching occurs, as a result of the execution of job 4 (see Fig. 5), either to jobs 7, 8 or 9, only one of them, i.e. the job whose rank is comparable with those of other jobs from Φ_{cur}, will be attached to the queue; the execution time of other alternative jobs is regarded as zero and they are not attached to Φ_{cur} in this version of program execution. Here, the job set of a level may happen to Φ_{cur} be empty. The fact that the rank criterion is applied only to those jobs which are attached to Φ_{cur}, when conditions for both data and program logic readiness are met, is essential in our method. Therefore, the justification for using the rank criterion for programs with logical branches agrees with the argument given in Section 2, because the program is assumed always to have jobs that are attached to the job front using the AND, AND-OR rules. In all the above cases, the job rank is determined uniquely by (1). The situation becomes more involved if the programs clude transfer of control from one job to another inside a loop, because rank can only be determined after interrupting the loop, thus introducing ambiguity by making rank depend on the interruption point of the loop. The job rank determination rule is evidently more complicated for such programs. The aim of current work is to eastablish a simpler rule. One possible way to solve this problem is the application of an algorithm well known in graph theory for the determination of the minimal vertex permutation potential in oriented graphs; this algorithm reduces to the purposeful interruption of graph loops.

If one succeeds in interrupting "luckily" the loops between program jobs and in assigning ranks to the jobs, the transfer of control from the last job in the loop to the start of the loop, in particular, to the beginning of a program, means in our terms that job a_g is in queue Φ_{cur} (see dashed line in Fig. 2a) whose rank τ_g can be greater than that of the job being executed, τ_e. For example, Fig. 2a has $\Phi_{cur} = \{a_g, a_i\}$ at $\tau_g > \tau_i$. If a resource that became free after the execution of job a_j is given to job a_g, then, owing to the increase of $t_j^* = t_g + \ldots + t_j$, the probability that the system will change from state $(a_e^* \, a_j^*)$ (Fig. 3a) to state $(a_i^* \, a_j^*)$ increases, too, with the subsequent possibility of changing to the "key" state $(a_i^* \, a_j^*)$. If the resource is assigned to job a_i with rank $\tau_i < \tau_e < \tau_g$ (Fig. 3b), the probability increases that the system will change from state $(a_e^* \, a_j^*)$ to state $(a_e^* \, a_j^*)$, from which the "key" state cannot be reached at all. Consequently the above, scheduling rule is suitable for programs containing loops if the job that begins a loop has higher rank than the last job in the loop.

Conclusion

For all the cases considered holds the following scheduling rule: if jobs a_i and a_j from Φ_{cur} have different ranks and $\tau_j > \tau_i$, the free resource is assigned to the job a_j with higher rank. Then $p(T_j < T_i) > p(T_j > T_i)$.

REFERENCES

[1] PRANGISHVILI, I. V. and IGNATUSHCHENKO, V. V. et al.: A uniform array-based rearrangeable control system. IFAC 6th Trienal World Congress, Boston, 1975, part IVA, p. 13.3.
[2] GONZALES, M. Y.: Deterministic processor scheduling. ACM Comp. Surveys, 9, 1977, 3, 173—204.

Chapter 9

ALGORITHMS FOR SCHEDULING INHOMOGENEOUS MULTIPROCESSOR COMPUTERS

9.1 Introduction

In this chapter we discuss the problems of scheduling inhomogeneous multiprocessor systems. This case is more realistic than that of homogeneous multiprocessor systems, in which all processors are identical, but there are significantly fewer results about inhomogeneous multiprocessor systems. The multiprocessor system (MS) is represented here by the set $\{P_1, ..., P_m\}$. The processors in it can differ from each other only in speed, or, more generally, they can also differ in function.

The task system (TS) that we want to execute on the given MS is represented by the pair $\text{TS} = (T, <)$, where $T = \{T_1, ..., T_n\}$ is a set of tasks with durations $t_1, ..., t_n$ and $<$ is a partial ordering on T. The relation $T_i < T_j$ (read T_i precedes T_j) means that the execution of task T_i must be completed before the execution of task T_j begins. The elements of the matrix (s_{ij}), $1 \leq i \leq m$, $1 \leq j \leq n$, are the execution speed of the task T_j on a processor P_i when the task system is processed on the given set of processors $\{P_1, ..., P_m\}$. We assume that for all i, j $s_{ij} \geq 0$, the equality, $s_{ij} = 0$, indicates that the task T_j cannot be executed on P_j. The execution of the task T_i with a duration t_i on the processor P_i means the reduction of t_i at speed s_{ij}. The task is regarded processed when its duration is equal to zero. A special case occurs when each of the processors $P_1, ..., P_m$ performs all tasks at the same speed, i.e. if $s_{i1} = s_{i2} = ... = s_{im}$ for all $i = 1, ..., n$. Such multiprocessor system is called uniform and the execution speeds of tasks $T_1, ..., T_n$ on the processors $P_1, ..., P_m$ are written simply $s_1, ..., s_m$. The algorithm by which we assign the tasks $T_1, ..., T_n$ to the single processors $P_1, ..., P_m$ during the execution of the task system TS on the multiprocessor system MS is called the schedule of TS on MS and written $S(\text{TS}, \text{MS})$, or simply S. It is clear, as in the case of identical processors, that the execution of TS on MS according to the schedule S must be completed in a finite time, that each task from TS has to be executed, that at a given time at most one task can be assigned to the processor, and that a given task can be assigned at the given time to, at most, one processor. Similarly as in the case of identical processors, the schedules are divided into two fundamental classes, namely:

Non-preemptive schedules, in which, if a task is assigned to the processor, it must remain there until its execution is completed, and preemptive schedules, in which the execution of a task on a processor can be interrupted and replaced by the execution of some other task, and the execution of this task is continued on some other processor at the same time or later. A special and very important class of non-preemptive schedules represent the so-called list schedules, in which the tasks are executed according to some list of priorities in such a way that when a processor becomes free, that task is assigned to it whose all predecessors have already been executed and which has the highest priority. The list of priorities is, as a rule, given by the list of tasks from TS. Usually, this list is ordered according to descending priority.

Let S be the schedule of a given TS on a given MS. Let $f_i(S)$ (or simply f_i) be the time of completion of the execution of a task T_i according to the schedule S. Then define: $t(S) = \max \{f_i(S): i = 1, ..., n\}$ is the execution time of the given TS according to the given schedule S. This time is also called the duration of the schedule S. $wmt(S) = \sum_{i=1}^{n} w_i f_i(S)$ is the weighted mean execution time of TS by S, w_i, $1 \leq i \leq n$, being weights such as costs or priorities correlated with the execution time of the tasks T_i from TS. If $w_i = 1$, $i = 1, ..., n$, then this is the mean execution time of TS by S and we write it $mt(S)$.

The principal problem of scheduling is the selection of the schedule $S(TS, MS)$ from among all possible schedules of TS on MS which has the minimum duration $t(S)$ or the minimum value of $wmt(S)$. Since both TS and MS are always finite, it is obvious that the problem of finding a schedule with a minimum $t(S)$ or $wmt(S)$ is solvable. In the case of non-preemptive schedules one can use, for example, an enumerative algorithm, which computes all possible assignments of TS to MS and selects the schedule that minimizes $t(S)$ or $wmt(S)$. But this algorithm requires a number of operations which increase exponentially with n in TS, and are therefore not suitable for larger values of n. The problem is to find effective algorithms for optimal scheduling with polynomial complexity in the number of tasks n.

Despite great efforts, such an algorithm for optimal scheduling in the general case has not been found so far, nor has it been shown that this optimization couldn't be solved in less than an exponential number of operations. It has only been proven [16] that this problem belongs to the class of NP-complete problems, which includes the travelling salesman problem, the knapsack problem, the integer linear programming problem, graph coloring, satisfaction of a Boolean expression. The problems of this class are characterized as follows: if there existed an algorithm with polynomial complexity, then this would solve all members of the class of NP-complete problems. But it is generally accepted that such an algorithm does not exist. More details on NP and NP-complete problems can be found in [1, 12, 16]. Ullman in [3] gives a comprehensive survey of the results achieved in the theory of the complexity of the scheduling problem.

Because of the above reasons and the great practical importance of the scheduling problem, the general problem of scheduling was divided into various subproblems in which optimal algorithms were sought for. Again it was shown that some of these subproblems were NP-complete. For others, optimal algorithms with polynomial complexity have been found. For the subproblems for which such algorithms have not been found, various heuristic strategies and algorithms have been suggested, and their properties and upper bounds of execution time examined. In some cases, approximate algorithms with polynomial complexity have been found which produce schedules arbitrarily close to the optimal ones. In the following sections we shall survey some known results about scheduling in the inhomogeneous case.

9.2 Scheduling with minimum schedule duration

9.2.1 Non-preemptive scheduling

No algorithm producing optimal schedules has been found for the general task system $TS = (T, >)$ and an arbitrary MS. But it is clear that the scheduling problem, in our case, of non-identical processors is at least as difficult as that of identical processors, which is known to be NP-complete [16]. Moreover, it is known that the scheduling problem is NP-complete for systems containing only independent tasks, i.e. $< = \emptyset$. For this case, $< = \emptyset$, Horowitz and Sahni [10] have found an optimal algorithm for a two-processor system from which they have later developed an approximate algorithm producing schedules arbitrarily close to the optimal schedule. They have also indicated possibilities for extending these algorithms to any number of processors m. In the next section we introduce a general algorithm for optimal scheduling on an inhomogeneous MS. This algorithm of dynamic programming type consists of the successive construction of the sets $S_0, \ldots, S_n$ containing $(m + 1)$-tuples $(\tau_1, \ldots, \tau_m, \mathbf{R})$, in which τ_i is the time needed to complete activity on the processor P_i, $1 \leq i \leq m$, and $\mathbf{R}$ is a vector $(r_1, \ldots, r_n)$, in which r_j is the index of the processor to which a task T_j is assigned. These $(m + 1)$-tuples are constructed successively for all possible ways of assigning tasks to processors. To reduce the number of possible $(m + 1)$-tuples, τ_i, $1 \leq i \leq m$, cannot exceed the upper limit, t_{min}, which is some reasonable upper bound of the duration of the optimal schedule.

Since we are considering here non-preemptive scheduling only, the duration of the execution of the tasks is given by $t_{ij} = t_j / s_{ij}$, $1 \leq i \leq m$, $1 \leq j \leq n$, and without loss generality we can regard these durations as positive integers.

Algorithm ET (Exact Algorithm for Time Optimal Scheduling):

Input: the number of processors m, the number of tasks n, t_{ij}, $1 \leq i \leq m$, $1 \leq j \leq n$.

Output: optimal schedule of a given TS on a given MS.

1. $t_{\min} = \min \left\{ t, \sum_{j=1}^{n} t_{ij}, 1 \leq i \leq m \right\}$, where t is the duration of the schedule that is obtained by assigning each task to the processor on which the given task has the minimum execution time.

2. $S_0 = (0, 0, \ldots, 0, R)$.

3. for $j = 0, \ldots, n - 1$ do $S_{j+1} = \bigcup_{i=1}^{m} (S_j \oplus (i,j))$; operations $\bigcup$ and $\oplus$ are defined below.

4. In S_n choose end the $(m + 1)$-tuple that has the minimum value of $\max \{\tau_1, \ldots, \tau_m\}$ from all $(m + 1)$-tuples from S_n.

5. Stop.

The operation $\oplus$ is defined as follows:

$$S_{j-1} \oplus (i,j) = \{(\tau_1, \ldots, \tau_{i-1}, \tau_i + t_{ij}, \tau_{i+1}, \ldots, \tau_m, (r_1, \ldots, r_{j-1}, i, \ldots)) : (\tau_1, \ldots, \tau_m, R) \in S_{j-1} \ \& \ \tau_i + t_{ij} \leq t_{\min}\}.$$

The operation $\bigcup$ is defined as a union of sets in which, if for any two $(m + 1)$-tuples $(\tau_1, \ldots, \tau_m, E)$ and $(\tau'_1, \ldots, \tau'_m, R)$ $\tau_i \leq \tau'_i$, $1 \leq i \leq m$, then the $(m + 1)$-tuple $(\tau'_1, \ldots, \tau'_m, R)$ is omitted from the union. It is clear that this omission, like the limiting of the size of τ_i by the upper bound $t_{\min}$ in the definition of the operation $\oplus$, is correct, since the $(m + 1)$-tuples omitted from S_{j+1} cannot lead to a schedule which is shorter than those remaining in S_{j+1}. We evaluate the complexity of the algorithm ET. It is obvious that in every set S_i, $1 \leq i \leq n$, there are at most m^i elements. But there cannot be more than $t_{\min}^m$ of these elements, and since the sets S_i are created in n iterations, it follows that the algorithm ET is of complexity $O(\min (t_{\min}^m, m^n))$. Thus, in the worst case this algorithm is of exponential complexity with respect to the number of tasks n. But in many practical applications this algorithm is of substantially lower complexity.

Horowitz and Sahni [10] have discovered an algorithm with polynomial complexity which approximates an optimal schedule to any desired accuracy. We give this algorithm for the case of an arbitrary number of processors n.

Definition. An algorithm A is termed an E-approximate algorithm for a minimalization problem P if for any fixed arbitrary $\varepsilon > 0$, $(t - t_{opt})/t_{opt} \leq \varepsilon$. Here, t is the solution obtained by algorithm A for the problem P and t_{opt} is the optimal solution of the problem P.

Let t_{opt} be the duration of the optimal schedule and let $t_{\min}$ be the duration of the schedule defined in step 1 of algorithm ET. Obviously, $t_{\min}/m \leq t_{opt} \leq t_{\min}$. We denote by r the largest positive integer such that $t_{\min}/m \geq 10^r$. Let ε be a given deviation. Let k be the smallest integer such that $\varepsilon \geq 10^{-k}$. We divide the interval $\langle 1, 10^{r+1} \rangle$ into $n \cdot 10^{k+1}$ identical subintervals of duration $10^{r-k}/n$. An approximation algorithm is essentially an algorithm ET, where in step 2 the operation $\bigcup$ is modified as follows: if $(\tau_1, ..., \tau_m, \boldsymbol{R})$ and $(\tau_1', ..., \tau_m', \boldsymbol{R})$ are two $(m+1)$-tuples and for every i, $1 \leqq i \leqq m$, τ_i and τ_i' are in the same subinterval, then the $(m+1)$-tuple which is lexicographically larger is omitted.

Hence it follows that every set S_j, $1 \leqq j \leqq n$, constructed by the algorithm ET with the operation $\biguplus$, modified as above, has at most $(n \cdot 10^{k+1})^m$ elements. Since the sets S_j are again constructed in n iterations, the complexity of this approximative algorithm is $O(n(n \cdot 10^{k+1})^m$, and so is exponential with respect to the number of processors. It is clear that the total error is at most $n[10^{r-k}/n] \leqq 10^{r-k}$, since in passing from S_j to S_{j+1} the error is at most $10^{r-k}/n$, i.e. the length of the interval. Hence, $(t - t_{\text{opt}})/t_{\text{opt}} \leqq 10^{r-k} \leqq \varepsilon$.

The above algorithms can be simplified for uniform multiprocessor systems which reduces their complexity. For example, in the case of the approximate algorithm, an algorithm of complexity $O(10^{2k} \cdot n)$, for $m = 2$, and of complexity $O((10^k n^2)^{m-1})$ for any m is given in [10].

It is clear that both the algorithm ET and the approximate algorithm require too much memory and time. In many cases, where very fast scheduling is required, various heuristic methods are used for this reason most frequently — scheduling by priority lists. But it is necessary to know the properties of these heuristic methods, i.e. it is necessary to know the limit of the difference between this heuristic scheduling and optimal scheduling.

In the case of non-uniform MS, the strategy of assigning a task to the processor on which this task has the smallest processing time is used most frequently. We denote the duration of the schedule obtained by this strategy by t and the duration of the optimal schedule by t'. Then $t/t' \leqq m$ and this is the best possible bound. It is obvious that $t/t' \leqq m$. To prove that this is the best possible bound, consider the following task system. Let $TS = (T, <)$, $< = \emptyset$, $t_{1j} = 1$, $j = 1, ..., n$ and $t_{ij} = 1 + \varepsilon$ for $i = 2, ..., m$, $j = 1, ..., n$. It is clear that $t = n$, $t' \leqq \dfrac{n}{m}(1 + \varepsilon)$. Consequently, $t/t' \leqq m/(1 + \varepsilon)$, which for $\varepsilon \to 0$ gives the above bound. This strategy does not belong to the strategies of priority scheduling, in which the bound t/t' can be even worse.

Next we consider only uniform multiprocessor systems, in which the processor's speeds are written $s_1, ..., s_m$, and we assume that the processors are ordered in such a way that $s_1 \geqq ... \geqq s_m$.

For the general task system $TS = (T, <)$, J.W.S. Liu and C. L. Liu gave in [13] very interesting results on the duration t' of the optimal schedule and the duration t_L of the schedule obtained by priority scheduling using an arbitrary priority list L. It is worthy of mention that in priority scheduling, if a processor is free, then a free task must be assigned to it, i.e. the task for which all predecessors have already been executed, and which has the highest priority.

Theorem 1 [13]: Let $TS = (T, <)$ be an arbitrary task system, let MS be a uniform multiprocessor system with speeds $s_1 \geqq \dots \geqq s_m$. Let L be an arbitrary priority list of tasks from TS. Then,

$$t_L/t' \leqq \frac{s_m}{s_1} + 1 - \frac{s_m}{\sum\limits_{i=1}^{m} s_i} < \frac{s_m}{s_1} + 1,$$

where t' is the duration of the optimal schedule of TS on MS. From this it can be seen that the efficiency of such a uniform system can be very low and that it is very dependent of the ratios of the highest and the lowest speeds of the processors. In [15] an algorithm was suggested for uniform MS and universal TS $= (T, <)$, based on the principle of CP-scheduling. This algorithm assigns the free task, which is closest to the critical path in TS to the fastest free processor. After every assignment of a task T_j to a processor P_i, the duration t_j of the task T_j in TS changes to t_j/s_i and a new critical path for the tasks that have not started yet or are still being executed, is calculated. This algorithm, although the bound from Theorem 1 applies to it, has very good results in practice. For the system of independent tasks, i.e. $< = \emptyset$, and the multiprocessor system in which $s_1 = \dots = s_{m-1}$ and $s_m \geqq 1$, the following bounds have been proved for CP-scheduling:

$$t_{CP}/t' \leqq \frac{2(m-1+s)}{s_m+2} \quad \text{for} \quad s_m \geqq 2 \quad \text{and}$$

$$t_{CP}/t' \leqq \frac{m-1+s}{2} \quad \text{for} \quad s_m \leqq 2.$$

All bounds given above depend on the speeds of the processors in MS. It is clear that this is due to the unsuitability of priority scheduling for uniform MS. Sometimes it is by far more advantageous to process the whole task system on the fastest processor or processors of the system. This technique is provided by the algorithm MFT [8, 15].

MFT algorithm (Minimum Finish Time Strategy):

Input: $t_1 \geqq \dots \geqq t_n$, $s_1 \geqq s_2 \geqq \dots \geqq s_m$; TS is a system of independent tasks.

Output: Schedule S_{MFT} with duration t_{MFT} of the task system TS on MS.

1. Assign T_1 to processor P_1 and compute $\tau_1 = t_1/s_1$, $\tau_2 = \dots = \tau_m = 0$.

2. If the j-th task T_j has been assigned to some processor, $1 \leqq j \leqq n$, then let

$$i = \min \{\alpha: 1 \leqq \alpha \leqq m \ \& \ \tau_\alpha + t_{j+1}/s = \min \{\tau_\beta + t_{j+1}/s: 1 \leqq \beta \leqq m\}\}.$$

Assign T_{j+1} to the processor P_i and compute $\tau_i = \tau_i + t_{j+1}/s_i$.

3. If $j + 1 \leqq n$, do $j = j + 1$ and go to 2.

4. Stop. The duration of the schedule is obviously $t_{MFT} = \max \{\tau_1, \dots, \tau_m\}$.

The scheduling strategy of this algorithm can be simply stated as the assignment of a task to that processor on which the execution of the task is finished earliest. It is clear that the algorithm MFT is not a priority scheduling algorithm. It is to be expected that the ratio t_{MFT}/t', where t' is the duration of the optimal schedule will be larger than for identical processors, for which Graham [6] has shown that $t_{MFT}/t' = 1/3 - 1/3m$.

Gonzales, Ibarra and Sahni have proved in [8] the following bound given by the theorem:

Theorem 2 [8]: For a TS system of independent tasks and a uniform MS with m processors

$$t_{MFT}/t' \leqq 1 + \frac{m-1}{m+1}.$$

The proof can be found in [8].

This bound does not seem to be the best. The worst case which has been constructed is $t_{MFT}/t' < 1.5$ for $m \to \infty$. For uniform MS with one fast processor, i.e. $s_i = 1$, $i = 1, \ldots, m-1$, $s_m > 1$, the bound in [8] has been improved to:

a) $t_{MFT}/t' \leqq (1 + \sqrt{17})/4$ for $m = 2$, and this is the best possible bound.

b) $t_{MFT}/t' \leqq \dfrac{3}{2} - \dfrac{1}{2m}$ for $m > 2$, and for $m = 3$ it is the best possible bound.

The above results show that the efficiency of inhomogeneous MS is greatly dependent of the scheduling algorithm used. These results give the designer a chance to evaluate the suitability of the non-preemptive scheduling methods given above. In the following section we shall give some results for preemptive scheduling.

9.2.2 Preemptive scheduling

In this section we only discuss uniform multiprocessor systems and preemptive scheduling. For this reason a schedule is here always understood to be preemptive.

In this case, for identical processors, the optimal scheduling algorithms of a system of independent tasks of the task system in which the partial ordering $<$ is a tree, are known. For uniform processors and a system of independent tasks the optimal algorithm is known ([15], Sethi in [3]). This is based on the Muntz—Coffman optimal strategy for preemptive scheduling on identical processors, where the task system generates a tree [14].

First we describe the scheduling of equally long tasks by the algorithm IET.
IET Algorithm (Independent Equal Task Scheduling):
Input: $\tau = t_1 = t_2 = , \ldots = t_n$, $s_1 \geqq s_2 \geqq \ldots \geqq s_m$, m, n.
Output: Optimal schedule TS on MS with preemption
1. If $m > n$, then put $m = n$.
2. Put $t = n \cdot \tau / \sum_{i=1}^{m} s_i$, where t is the duration of the optimal schedule.

3. If $\tau/s_m > t$, go to 8.

4. Assign the task T_1 to the processor P_1 for the time interval $\langle 0, \tau/s_1 \rangle$.

5. Do step 6 for $T_2, T_3, \ldots, T_n$.

6. We assume that tasks $T_1, \ldots, T_{j-1}$ have been assigned to the processor $P_1, \ldots, P_{i-1}$ for intervals $\langle 0, t \rangle$ and to the processor P_i for the interval $\langle 0, c \rangle$ for some $c < t$. We consider the task T_j. If $c + \tau/s_1 \leqq t$, assign the task T_j to the processor P_i for the interval $\langle c, c + \tau/s_i \rangle$. Otherwise, assign T_j to P_i for the interval $\langle c, t \rangle$ and to P_{i+1} for the interval $\langle 0, (\tau - s_i(t-c))/s_{i+1} \rangle$.

7. Go to 9.

8. Split the interval $\langle 0, t \rangle$ into n identical intervals $I_1, \ldots, I_n$. For $i = 1, 2, \ldots, m$, for $j = 1, \ldots, n$ assign the task T_j to the processor P_i in the interval I_α, $\alpha = (i + j - 2) \bmod(n) + 1$.

9. Stop.

An IET algorithm is illustrated by the following example: Let $t_1 = \ldots = t_5 = t_6$, $s_i = 2, 1, 1$ for scheduling in the first case, i.e. via steps 4 to 6 in IET, and $s_i = 3, 2, 1$ for scheduling in the second case, i.e. via step 8 in IET. The schedules are given in Fig. 1a, b.

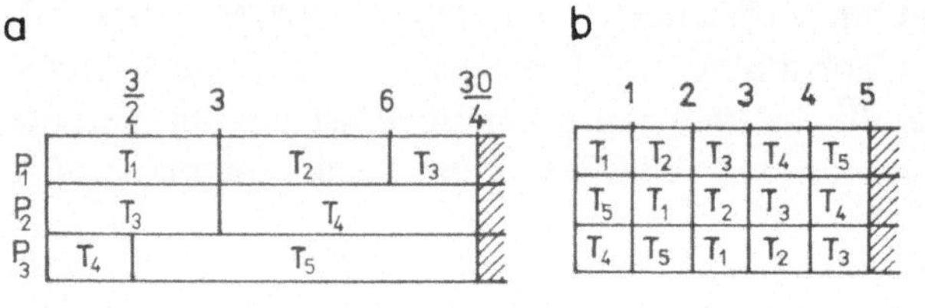

Fig. 1.

It is clear that also the first case can be scheduled by the algorithm for the second case, but in this way we reduce the number of preemptions from nm to maximum $m - 1$. Algorithm IET is part of the next algorithm IT for scheduling any system of independent tasks. Algorithm IT consists (like the Muntz—Coffman algorithm) of two parts. In its first part, the so-called general schedule (with processor sharing) is defined, from which in the second part the optimal preemptive schedule $S(TS, MS)$ is constructed using algorithm IET.

Algorithm IT (Independent Not Equal Task Scheduling):

Input: $t_1 \geqq t_2 \geqq \ldots \geqq t_n$, $s_1 \geqq s_2 \geqq \ldots \geqq s_m$, $n \geqq m$

Output: optimal preemptive schedule $S(TS, MS)$.

1. a) assign the fastest processors successively to the longest tasks;

b) if for some α tasks $T_{j+1}, \ldots, T_{j+\alpha}$, $j + \alpha < m$, $j \geqq 0$, $t_{j+1} = \ldots = t_{j+\alpha}$ is valid, assign in the general schedule all α processors $P_{j=1}, \ldots, P_{j+\alpha}$ to all α tasks $T_{j=1}, \ldots, T_{j+\alpha}$, each of them being executed during this assignment at a speed $\sum_{i=j+1}^{i+\alpha} s_i/\alpha$;

c) if for some α tasks $T_{j+1}, \ldots, T_{j+a}$ for the last β processors $P_{m-\beta+1}, \ldots, P_m$, $t_{j+1} = \ldots = t_{j+a}$ is valid, assign all β processors $P_{m-\beta+1}, \ldots, P_m$ to all tasks $T_{j+1}, \ldots,$ T_{j+a}, the duration of each being reduced at a speed $\sum\limits_{i=m-\beta+1}^{m} s_i/\alpha$.

2. At every moment after which, if continuing execution according to the current assignment, the shorter tasks or their subtasks would be executed at a greater speed than the longer tasks or their subtasks, preassign processors to tasks or their subtasks according to step 1. The number of tasks remains unchanged, but the durations change.

3. When the durations of all tasks have been reduced to zero, i.e. TS has been executed, construct the schedule $S(\text{TS}, \text{MS})$ as follows:

a) if in the general schedule the processor P_j was assigned during time interval $\langle \tau_1, \tau_2 \rangle$ to task T_j only, assign in $S(\text{TS}, \text{MS})$ during the interval $\langle \tau_1, \tau_2 \rangle$ task T_j to processor P_j;

b) if in the general schedule all α processors $P_{j+1}, \ldots, P_{j+a}$ have been assigned to all tasks $T_{j+1}, \ldots, T_{j+a}$ during the time interval $\langle \tau_1, \tau_2 \rangle$, assign tasks $T_{j+1}, \ldots, T_{j+a}$ to processors $P_{j+1}, \ldots, P_{j+a}$ using algorithm IET for the interval $\langle \tau_1, \tau_2 \rangle$;

c) if in the general schedule all β processors $P_{m-\beta+1}, \ldots, P_m$ have been assigned to tasks $T_{j+1}, \ldots, T_{j+a}$ during the interval $\langle \tau_1, \tau_2 \rangle$, assign during this interval the tasks to processors using algorithm IET;

4. Stop.

In step 2 of the algorithm IT a method should be given for determining the time at which the pre-assignment in the general schedule and thus also in $S(\text{TS}, \text{MS})$ must be made. Let the assignment F be enforced from some time for a task system with durations $t_1, \ldots, t_n$, which can already be smaller than the original ones, in the general schedule. This assigns certain subsets of a set of processors to the subsets of a set of tasks. Let F consist of parts $F_1, \ldots, F_k$. Let every F assign a set of processors of cardinality β_i starting with the processors P_{j_i} to a set of tasks of durations f_i. Let this set be of cardinality α_i, and let f be the duration of the first task in TS to which no processor has been assigned. If such task does not exist, we write $f = 0$. Then the time $\Delta\tau$, in which the given assignment F will be considered, is given by the relation

$$\Delta\tau = \min\left\{\min\left\{x : x = \frac{\alpha_i\alpha_{i+1}(f_i - f_{i+1})}{Q_i\alpha_{i+1} - Q_{i+1}\alpha_i} \ \& \ x > 0, \ 1 \le i \le k-1\right\}, \frac{\alpha_k(f_k - f)}{Q_k}\right\},$$

where $Q_i = \sum\limits_{j=j_k}^{j_i+\beta_i-1} s_j$ for $i = 1, \ldots, k$. The time $\Delta\tau$ indicates the time at which the duration of some tasks executed on processors with different speeds become equal.

The proof of the optimality of algorithm IT is trivial. It is sufficient to realize that duration of the optimal schedule t_{opt} for a given task system and a given MS is

$$t_{opt} = \max \left\{ \dfrac{\sum\limits_{i=1}^{n} t_i}{\sum\limits_{i=1}^{m} s_i}, \; \dfrac{t_1}{s_1}, \; \dfrac{t_1 + t_2}{s_1 + s_2}, \; \dots, \; \dfrac{\sum\limits_{i=1}^{m-1} t_i}{\sum\limits_{i=1}^{m-1} s_i} \right\}$$

and that the algorithm IT produces schedules of this very duration.

The following example illustrates the construction of schedules using IT. Let $t_i = 6, 5, 4, 4, 2$ for $i = 1, \dots, 5$, $< = \emptyset$, $s_i = 3, 2, 1$, $1 \le i \le 3$.

The schedule $S(TS, MS)$ is shown in Fig. 2. It is not difficult to prove that algorithm IT is optimal even for an arbitrary task system $TS = (T, <)$, but of course, only for a two-processor system, i.e. $m = 2$. It is proved in [15] that when $m \ge 3$, the IT is not optimal even for a TS-determining tree. The algorithm IT can also be used as a good heuristic method for any TS and MS.

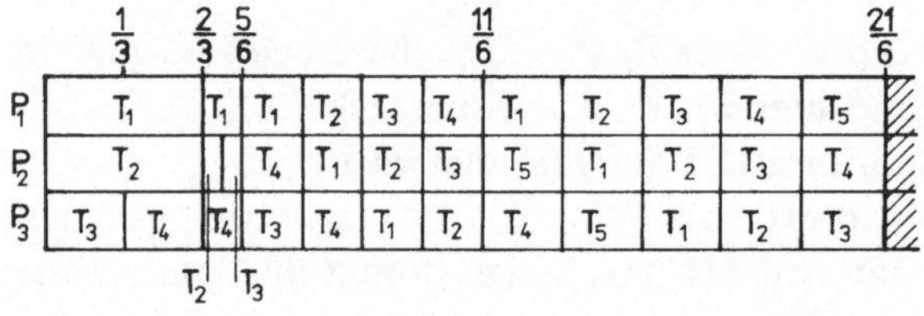

Fig. 2.

9.3 Some special problems

9.3.1 Flow-shop problem

Our scheduling model includes also the so-called flow-shop problem. Let $TS = (T, <)$ consist of n chains $C_1, \dots, C_n$, each C_i containing m tasks $T_1^i < T_2^i < \dots < T_m^i$, $i = 1, \dots, n$. Let MS consist of m processors $P_1, \dots, P_m$. For every i, $i = 1, \dots, n$, the task T_j^i can and must be executed on one processor P_j only, $j = 1, \dots, m$. The execution time of the task T_j^i on P_j is t_{ij}. The ordering in chains C_i, $i = 1, \dots, n$, indicates that the task T_j^i can be executed on the processor P_j only after the task T_j^i has already been executed on the processor P_{j-1}, $j = 2, \dots, m$. The problem is to obtain a schedule $S(TS, MS)$ with minimum duration. It is known that for $m \ge 3$ this is an NP-complete problem [9]. For $m = 2$ Johnson [11] has obtained an algorithm producing optimal schedules.

Algorithm FS (Flow-Shop Scheduling):

Input: t_{i1}, t_{i2}, $i = 1, 2, \dots, n$

Output: optimal schedule of TS on MS

1. Construct a list of chains L from TS, ordered by the following condition: chain C_i ranks before chain C_j in list L, if $\min(t_{i1}, t_{2j}) \le \min(t_{i2}, t_{j1})$.

2. Create by priority scheduling according to list L the required schedule

$S(\text{TS}, \text{MS})$. In this schedule the execution of task T_1^i must be completed on processor P_1 before the execution of task T_2^i starts on processor P_2.

Theorem [11]: Algorithm FS is optimal for the flow-shop problem with $m = 2$.

Proof is given in [11] and [3]. Algorithm FS is of complexity $O(n \log_2 n)$.

9.3.2 Scheduling with minimal WMT

A problem which is of practical importance in a wide range of applications is the scheduling with minimum weighted mean time of the execution of a task system on an inhomogeneous MS. This time is defined as $wmt(S) = \sum_{i=1}^{n} w_i f_i$, where f_i are the completion times of the execution of tasks T_i under schedule S and w_i are the weights which are known in advance, $i = 1, ..., n$. In this section we consider only the case of independent tasks, for which it has been shown that for various weights the scheduling is NP-complete [2]. If the weights $w_1, ..., w_n$ of the task $T_1, ..., T_n$ are identical, the mean execution time TS on MS is to be minimized. The problem becomes [2] the minimum cost-problem of network flow solution of which is already known ([5] and [7]). Let the execution time of tasks $T_1, ..., T_n$ on processors $P_1, ..., P_m$ be given by a matrix (t_{ij}), $i = 1, ..., m$, $j = 1, ..., n$. Let S be any schedule TS on MS and let f_j, $j = 1, ..., n$ be the completion time of the execution of task T_j according to the schedule S.

Denote the mean execution time of TS on MS by $mt(s) = \sum_{i=1}^{n} f_i$. We assume that according to S, task T_j is to be executed on processor P_i, and after T_j, exactly k tasks are executed on P_i, $0 \leq k \leq n$. It is clear that this task, T_j, contributes with its t_{ij} to the completion time f_j of the task T_j and also to the completion time of the task following T_j on P_i (there are exactly k of these). Our problem is to express the value of $mt(S)$ as the sum of an expression dependent of f_{ij} and an expression independent of f_{ij}.

Then $mt(S) = (k + 1)t_{ij} + (\text{other expressions not containing } t_{ij})$. It is clear that if T_j is the last task executed on P_i, the coefficient of t_{ij} is equal to 1; if T_j is the second last task, the coefficient is equal to 2, etc. This leads to:

$$\text{Let } \mathbf{C} = \begin{pmatrix} 1(t_{ij}) \\ 2(t_{ij}) \\ \vdots \\ n(t_{ij}) \end{pmatrix} \text{ be a matrix of size } (mn \times n).$$

The matrix $\mathbf{C}$ has elements c_{ij}, $1 \leq i \leq mn$, $1 \leq j \leq n$. From this matrix, which is a cost matrix now, we can formulate the problem of the minimum cost of the network flow N, the element c_{ij} being the unit flow cost from position x_i to position y_j. The network N is given as follows: $x_0, ..., x_{mn}, y_0, ..., y_n$ are vertices

$$\left.\begin{cases} (x_i, y_i),\ 1 \leq i \leq mn,\ 1 \leq j \leq n \\ (x_0, x_i),\ 1 \leq i \leq mn \\ (y_j, y_0),\ 1 \leq j \leq n \\ (y_0, x_0)\ \text{return edge} \end{cases}\right\} \quad \text{are edges.}$$

See Fig. 3.

The flow capacities of all edges except (y_0, x_0) are of unit type, the capacity of (y_0, x_0) is n. We denote the unit flow cost of the edge (x_i, y_i) by $c(x_i, y_i)$. We put

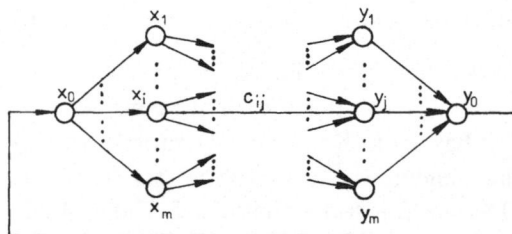

Fig. 3.

$c(x_i, y_i) = c_{ij}$ for $1 \leq i \leq mn$ and $1 \leq j \leq n$, the unit flow costs of all other edges are zero. Each possible flow in the network N is in our case determined by the function h from the set of edges of the network N to the set of natural numbers, such that $h(y_0, x_0) \leq n$ and for all other edges $h(z, z') = 1$. The value $h(z, z')$ denotes the amount of flow from the vertex c to the vertex z'. For every vertex we assume that the flow to the vertex is equal to the sum of the flows coming from it.

The optimal flow in the network for N is the function h, for which the value

$$c(h) = \sum_{i=1}^{mn} \sum_{j=1}^{n} c(x_i, y_j) \cdot h(x_i, y_j) \text{ is minimal.}$$

Theorem [2]: Let P be a scheduling problem with minimum mean execution time of the task system TS given by the matrix (t_{ij}) on MS with m processors. Let h be the optimum network flow for N, and let the schedule S of the system TS on MS be constructed as follows: if $h(x_i, y_i) = 1$, $1 \leq i \leq mn$, $1 \leq j \leq n$, then assign the task T_j to the processor $P_{i'}$, and after T_j on P_i, additional k tasks are executed, where i' and k are given by the equations:

$$i = k \cdot m + i',$$
$$0 \leq k < n,$$
$$1 \leq i \leq m.$$

Then the schedule S is the optimal solution of the problem P. The optimal flow can be obtained by known methods for obtaining the minimum cost of the network flow [5, 7], Bruno in [3]. The algorithm for the total solution of the minimization of $mt(S)$ is of complexity $O(mn^2 + n^3)$, [3, 4]. If we consider uniform MS only, this algorithm can be simplified [5] and its complexity is $O(n \log_2 n + n \log_2 m + m)$ [3].

REFERENCES

[1] AHO, A. V., HOPCROFT, J. E. and ULLMAN, J. D.: The Design and Analysis of Computer Algorithms. Adison Wesley, Reading, Mass., 1974.

[2] BRUNO, J., COFFMAN, E. G., JR. and SETHI, R.: Scheduling independent tasks to reduce mean finishing time. Comm. ACM, 17, 1974, 7, 382—387.

[3] CODDMAN, E. G., JR. (Editor): Computer and Job/Shop Scheduling Theory. John Wiley & Sons, New York, 1976.

[4] EDMONDS, J. and KARP, R.: Theoretical improvements in algorithmic efficiency for network flow problems. J. ACM, 19, 1972, 2, 248—264.

[5] FORD, R. L. and FULKERSON, D. R.: Flows in Networks. Princeton Univ. Press, Princeton, N. J., 1962.

[6] GRAHAM, R. L.: Bounds on multiprocessing timing anomalies. SIAM J. Appl. Math., 17, 1969, 2, 416—429.

[7] GASS, S. I.: Linear Programming. Methods and Applications. McGraw-Hill, New York—Toronto—London, 1958.

[8] GONZALES, T., IBARRA, O. H. and SAHNI, S.: Bounds for LPT schedules uniform processors. SIAM J. on Computers, 6, 1977, 1, 155—166.

[9] GAREY, M. R., JOHNSON, D. S. and SATHI, R.: The complexity of flowshop and job shop scheduling. Tech. report, Comp. Sci. Dep., The Pennsylvania State Univ., 1975.

[10] HOROWITZ, E. and SAHNI, S.: Exact and approximate algorithms for scheduling nonidentical processors. J. ACM, 23, 1976, 2, 317—327.

[11] JOHNSON, S. M.: Optimal two- and three-stage production schedules. Naval Res. and Logistic Quart., 1, 1954, 1.

[12] KARP, R. M.: Reducibility among combinatorial problems. In: Complexity of Computer Computations. R. E. Miller and J. W. Thatcher (Editors). Plenum Press, New York, 1972, pp. 85—104.

[13] LIU, J. W. S. and LIU, C. L.: Bounds on scheduling algorithms for heterogeneous computing systems. Information Processing, Vol. 74. North-Holland Publ. Co., Amsterdam, 1974.

[14] MUNTZ, R. R. and COFFMAN, E. G., JR.: Preemptive scheduling for real time tasks on multiprocessor systems. J. ACM, 17, 1970, 2, 324—338.

[15] ONDÁŠ, J.: Algoritmy rozdeľovania úloh na nehomogénne multiprocesorové systémy. Dissertation. Faculty of Natural Sciences, Komenský University, Bratislava, 1977. (In Slovak.)

[16] ULLMAN, J. D.: Polynomial complete scheduling problems. Tech. report No. 9, Comp. Sci. Dep., Univ. of California, Berkeley, 1973.

Chapter 10

PARALLEL PROCESSORS AND MULTICOMPUTER SYSTEMS

10.1 Introduction

The rapid development of microelectronics permits the manufacture of large-scale integrated LSI and VLSI circuits, which has a direct impact on the further development of computer systems. The cost of processors and computer systems is substantially reduced. Moreover, processors made of LSI have a higher reliability.

At present, advanced LSI technologies are available, by means of which 16-bit processors can be made with 2- or, 4-bit slices, e.g. Intel 3000, AMD 2900, Texas Instruments SBP 0400, Motorola 10 800, etc. or as one chip 16-bit microprocessors, e.g. INTEL 8086, Texas Instruments SBO 9900, on the basis of I^2L technologies.

The availability of LSI processors has brought about changes in the design and architecture of computer systems. Further increases by physical and engineering means in the rate of operation of computer systems above a certain limit, i.e. by increasing the speed of electronic circuits, is no longer practicable.

The attainable operation speed is bounded by maximum speed of propagation of electric impulses in solid-state circuits. The programs throughput of conventional single processor computer systems is also limited by the speed of the operating system which controls a multiprogram activity of the computer system in a centralized manner. The proportion of time consumed by the operating system when the number of programs processed is above a certain limit is so large that its use is inefficient.

The problems of contemporary science and technology, such as the solution of complex linear and non-linear systems of algebraic, ordinary and partial differential equations with rapidly changing parameters, initial and boundary conditions (equations for weather forecasting in meteorology, seismic data processing in geophysics, geology, etc.), spectral analysis by the Fast Fourier Transformation, computation of convolution integrals, inversion of large matrices, application of Monte Carlo methods, require large-scale computations. Problems of this type require computers whose speed is 2 to 3 orders of magnitude higher than that of conventional single-processor computers.

In addition to speed, computer systems for real-time process control have to satisfy requirements for high reliability and operational availability and easy maintainability. This cannot be achieved by third-generation conventional computers, whose mean time between failures (MTBF) is between 1000 and 10,000 h.

Since the speed and reliability of conventional computers is limited, the satisfaction of these requirements can only be achieved by a system solution based on the exploitation of the principles of parallelism in computer architecture. From this it follows that the architectures of next-generation computer systems have to achieve two main objectives as follows:

a) in the case of computers for large-scale data processing and for scientific and engineering computations maximum operational speed and program throughput;

b) in the case of computers for real time process control: high reliability and operational availability, i.e. an almost fault-free operation and easy maintainability, while also satisfying the requirement for high speed.

10.2 Classification of architectures and definition of processors

According to Flynn [1], computer systems can be classified according to the types of control, and arithmetical and logical processors into four main categories:

a) Processors with single instruction and single data stream — SISD — (Single Instruction Single Data Stream) or sequential processors.

b) Processors with multiple instruction and single data stream — MISD — (Multiple Instruction Single Data Stream) or pipeline processors.

c) Processors with single instruction and multiple data stream — SIMD — (Single Instruction Multiple Data Stream) which include array, associative, associative array and orthogonal processors.

d) Processors with multiple instruction and multiple data stream — MIMD — (Multiple Instruction Multiple Data Stream) or multiprocessor-multicomputer systems.

10.2.1 Sequential SISD processors

The activity of the SISD processor (Fig. 1a) is identical with the conventional single-address monoprocessor (P1) with single instruction stream, which corresponds to J. von Neumann's fundamental structure [2]. The instruction stream for an N-instruction program can formally be expressed by a sequence of pairs of operational codes and addresses:

$$\text{stream} = \{\langle \Phi, A \rangle\}_{i=1}^{N}, \tag{1}$$

where A is the memory address, $\Phi = R \,|\, J \,|\, B \,|\, C$ is the operation code of the following classes of instructions: R — type for inter-register and register to store operations; H — type for unconditional jumps out of the normal instruction sequence; B — type for conditional jumps; C — type for computational operations on data fetched from memory and the current contents of the registers. The register from the set $R = \{r_0, r_1, ..., r_{k-1}\}$ is implicitly determined by the instruction Φ.

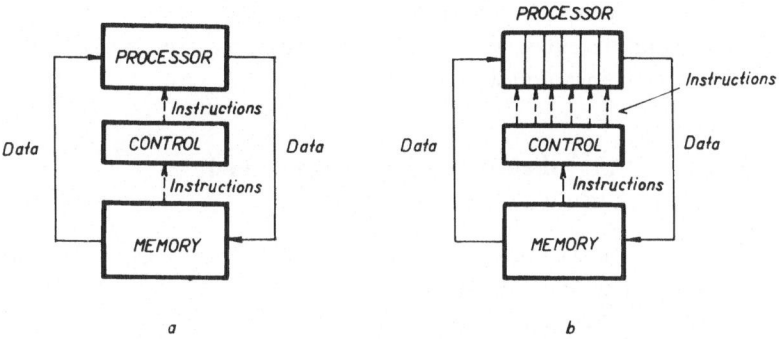

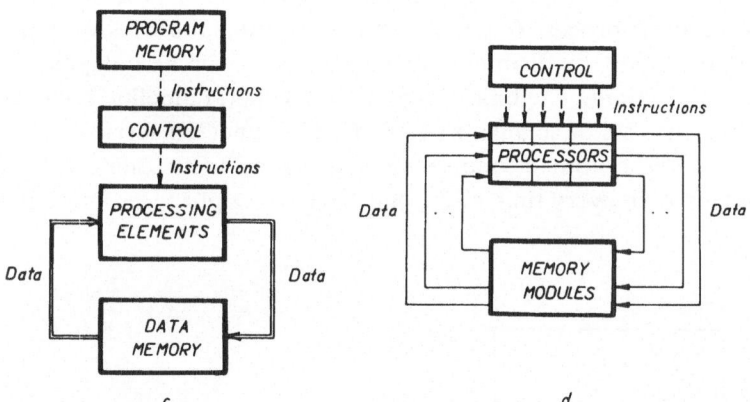

Fig. 1. Computer architectures: a — SISD; conventional series computer, b — MISD: pipeline processor, c — SIMD: Array and vector processor, d — MIMD: multiprocessor.

A single-address processor operates as follows:

$\langle R, A \rangle = (A) \leftarrow r_i,$ **incr** α

$\langle J, A \rangle = \alpha \leftarrow A$

$\langle B, A \rangle =$ **if** $\text{cond}_\Phi [r_i],$ **then** $\alpha \leftarrow a,$ **else incr** α **end**

$\langle C, A \rangle = r_i \leftarrow r_j \Phi(A),$ **incr** $\alpha,$

where **incr**: $= x \leftarrow x + 1$, α is the address of the current instruction and (A) means "the content of the word stored at the address A".

For the two-address processor P2, every instruction word contains the addresses of two operands. An N-instruction stream for P2 can be represented as

$$\text{stream} = \{\langle \Phi, A1, A2 \rangle\}_{i=1}^{N},$$

where Φ is the operation code ($\Phi = J \mid B \mid C$), and A_1 and A_2 are memory addresses. After fetching and decoding the instruction, the processor performs the following operations for each instruction:

$$\langle J, -, A_2 \rangle = \alpha \leftarrow A_2$$
$$\langle B, A1, A2 \rangle = \textbf{if } \text{cond}_\Phi \, [(A1)] \textbf{ then } \alpha \leftarrow A2 \textbf{ else incr } \alpha \textbf{ end},$$
$$\langle C, A1, A2 \rangle = (A1) \leftarrow (A1) \Phi(A2); \textbf{ incr } \alpha.$$

A two-address instruction set without registers has advantages, especially in processing a large number of instruction flows.

10.2.2 The pipeline MISD processor

A pipeline processor is an MISD processor (Fig. 1b) which works according to the principle of pipelining. The pipelining principle implies the segmentation or partition of a computational process (e.g. an instruction) into subprocesses which can be executed independently by distinct units or modules. Such an independent unit is called a pipeline segment. The block diagram of a general pipeline is shown in Fig. 2. The pipeline consists of segments A, B, C, D connected serially. After constant time intervals, the output of one segment is shifted to the next. A new operand enters segment A in every time cycle, and segment D produces an output every time cycle.

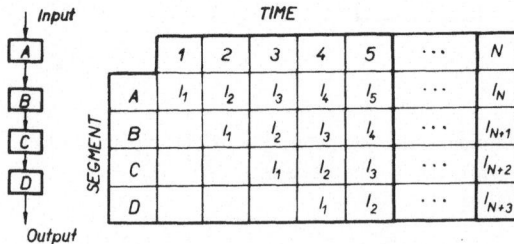

Fig. 2. Block diagram of general pipelining.

In general, parallel computers are designed to process arrays of regularly arranged data (vectors) as efficiently as possible. In addition to conventional scalar instructions, these computers have an additional set of vector instructions. For this reason they are sometimes called vector computers.

A two-address instruction extended to a multistream environment (MISD) can be written [3]:

$$\text{stream} = \{\{ \Phi, A1, A2 \longleftarrow \! \}_{i=1}^{N_j}\}_{j=1}^{M}. \tag{3}$$

The index j indicates the instruction stream which the instruction belongs to, and the index i indicates the position within the N_j-th instruction sequence for the j-th program. The transition to a two-address format of the instruction word allows an unambiguous mixing of instruction streams, which significantly simplifies the design of the processor. To take advantage of these possibilities processing units performing single elementary operations to be pipelined are needed, i.e. various processing elements must be able to complete one computation (operation) in one cycle time τ of the computer. Figure 3 shows simplified floating point addition using pipelining.

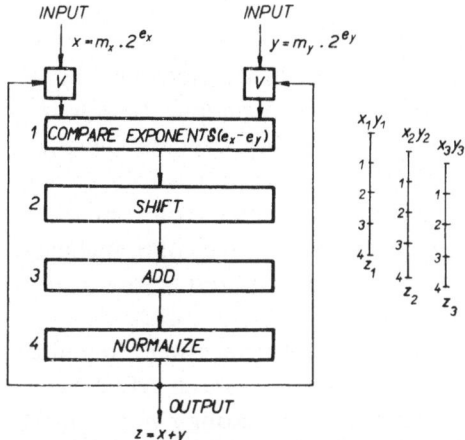

Fig. 3. Simplified diagram of pipeline floating point addition.

In this way, new arguments can be received and the results transmitted simultaneously in every cycle. To achieve the maximum processing speed, the arguments must stream steadily from the memory into the pipeline and the results from the pipeline to the memory. Such a stream speed requires a memory data stream width of at least three floating point numbers per cycle (for x_i, y_i, and z_i). This speed can, as a rule, only be achieved if data are stored in a regular way, i.e. as vectors. For this reason, pipelining is in principle a concept for vector processing and can be found in most computers designed for these purposes. The following systems can be given as examples: CDC STAR 100, Texas Instruments ASC, CRAY 1.

Pipelining levels

The principle of pipelining, which we have defined as overlapping of operations executed simultaneously, can be exploited in computer architecture at various levels: Pipelining at the gate level is used, for example, in the design of instruction processing units (IPU). An instruction passes through one segment during each cycle so that after the input of instructions into the pipeline, instructions are emitted in every cycle. In Fig. 4 the diagram of a pipelined instruction processing unit is shown.

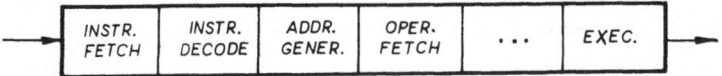

Fig. 4. Pipelined unit for instruction processing.

The above makes it evident that a pipeline can be used if a process can be divided locally into subfunctions $(s_1, \tau_1), (s_2, \tau_2), ..., (s_n, \tau_n)$, where s_i is the i-th subfunction and τ_i ($i = 1, 2, ..., n$) is the time needed for its execution. A pipeline is especially suitable for instruction processing. Computers using an instruction pipeline are more common than those using pipelined arithmetic. For example, the Floating Point Systems AP 120-B Array Transform Processor [4] contains pipelined decoding of instructions and pipelined arithmetic for vector processing.

In instruction pipelining, a continuous instruction stream into the pipeline can be interrupted, e.g. by conditional jumps. To recognize the occurrence of branching in a program, computer hardware for instruction scanning is required before instruction decoding.

Another level of pipeline application is that of the subsystem. Pipelined arithmetic units are typical examples of this. The pipelined operations ADD, MUL, DIV and SORT are found in many contemporary, even though not typically pipelined, computer structures. As an example we give decimal division using an iteration of the form

$$\frac{N_{i+1}}{D_{i+1}} = \frac{(2 - D_i)N_i}{(2 - D_i)D_i},$$

where N_0 is the dividend and D_0 the divisor. If D_0 is made smaller than 1, it can be proved that $D_0 < D_1 < 1$. During repeated iterations, D_i approaches 1 and N_i approaches the quotient N_0/D_0. In Fig. 5 a pipeline unit is shown at a subsystem level for the operation DIV, in which the above iterative method is utilized. In general, the pipeline is effective in applications where data is entered into the system in a highly structured form which can be processed iteratively.

The characteristic feature of a pipeline computer system is its reconfigurability. A typical example of such a system is the Texas Instruments ASC. Each arithmetic unit (AU) contains 8 pipeline segments (Fig. 6) for the execution of individual subfunctions of arithmetic operations. Figure 7 shows how the single segments of a dynamic pipeline are used for the execution of floating point addition and fixed point multiplication. Out of eight AU segments at time t_1, for example, four segments form the pipeline for fixed point multiplication, while at time t_2 six segments form a pipeline for floating point addition. Pipeline configurations, however, can have two or more dimensions. The pipeline segment need not be at

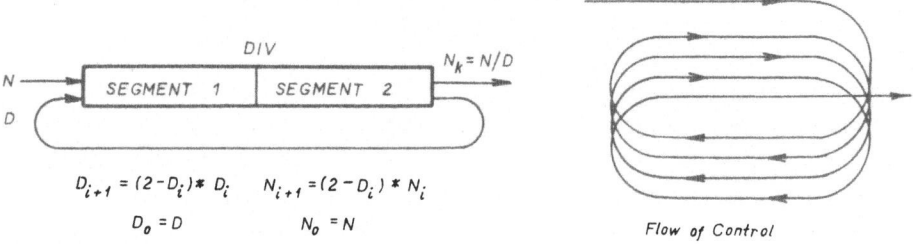

$$D_{i+1} = (2-D_i) * D_i \qquad N_{i+1} = (2-D_i) * N_i$$
$$D_0 = D \qquad N_0 = N$$

Flow of Control

Fig. 5. Division by pipelining at the subsystem level.

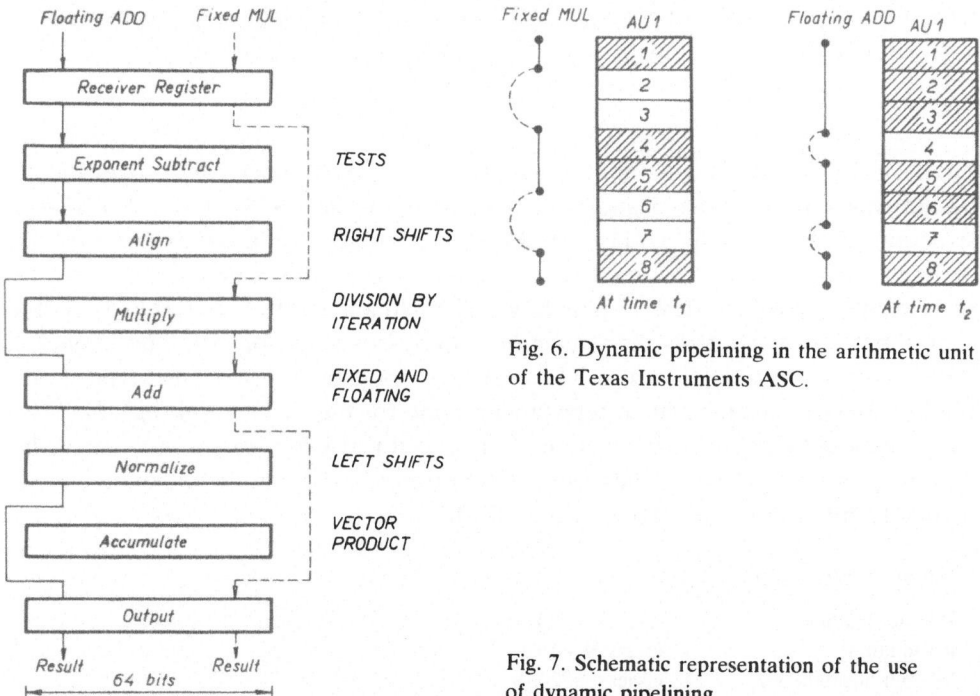

Fig. 6. Dynamic pipelining in the arithmetic unit of the Texas Instruments ASC.

Fig. 7. Schematic representation of the use of dynamic pipelining.

the hardware level; the pipeline can form a software structure of arbitrary complexity. This type of pipeline constitutes the highest system level (Fig. 8). It also includes specialized computer networks and various types of high-reliability systems (see Sections 4 and 5). The evolution of various pipeline systems containing combinations of the various types of configuration constitutes an important advance in the architecture of computer systems [5]. A generalized pipeline design involves both subsets and conventional parallel processing, as well as pipelining.

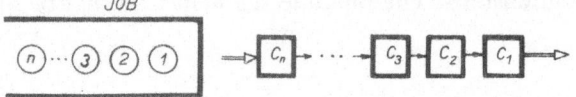

C_i – Processor, resp. Software Complex
Fig. 8. Pipelining at the system level.

The improvement of reliability is another advantage of a generalized pipeline. The reconfigurability and replicability of segments (subsegments, systems) in a generalized pipeline give a good base for the provision of graceful degradation of the system, failure diagnosis, and recovery after failure. Using pipelining techniques, it is possible to create processors with an arbitrary width of data flow (in particular 16, 32 and 64 bits) by a replication of the basic 2-, 4-, 8-bit slices of LSI microprocessors. The principle of pipelined processors and memories is, similarly as in the Texas Instruments ASC computer, utilized in the computers CDC STAR 100 (1973/74) and CRAY-1 (1976). In the following section we shall give an overview of the main examples of pipeline processor architecture.

CDC STAR 100

The CDC STAR 100 computer was the first pipelined vector processor. Its design was started in 1965 and it became available in 1973/74 [6]. The logical structure of the computer is shown in Fig. 9 [7]. The central processor unit (CPU) contains two pipelined floating point arithmetic units. Access units for data access and storing provide efficient data flow. The stream control unit (SCU) of the central processors controls the stream of data, instructions, operand modification, buffer storage and addressing. Three-address register-register instructions are used, two addresses for source registers and one for the destination register. With continuous activity in both pipelines it is possible to generate a 64- or 32-bit floating point result every synchronization period (40 ns), i.e. the maximum speed is one 32-bit result every 10 ns (i.e. 100 Mflops).

Scalar arithmetic speed:

Register loading	1280 ns
FP addition	11 cycles = 440 ns
FP multiplication	13 cycles = 520 ns
FP division	31 cycles = 1240 ns

Vector arithmetic speed:

pipeline start-up	76 cycles = 3040 ns
maximum speed	100 Mflops

The vector operation start-up is relatively slow. Therefore the vector pipeline in the CDC STAR 100 computer is effective only if the vectors have a minimum length of 100 elements. The improved CDC STAR 100 A system (1977) is faster; it has a cycle time of 13 ns. Instead of a ferrite memory, it uses bipolar memory;

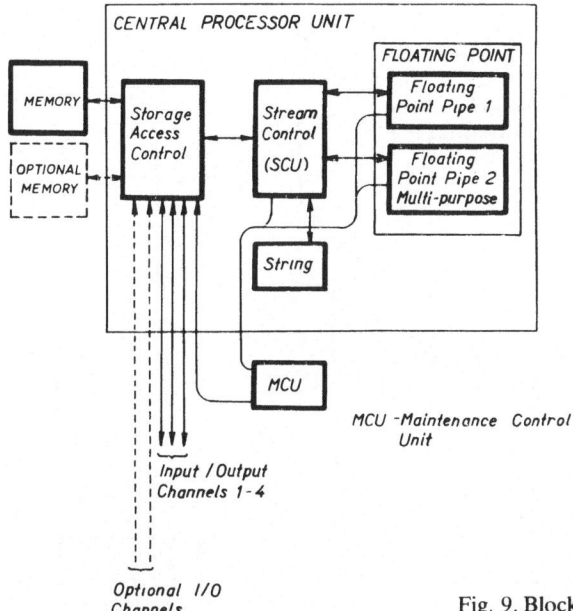

Fig. 9. Block diagram of the CDC STAR 100 computer.

moreover, it contains a new LSI-based scalar processor. The vector processor is the same as in the original STAR 100. Since 1979, a new CDC STAR 100 C vector processor has been available, which has significantly reduced pipeline start-up time, because, owing to LSI, the physical dimensions of the system are much smaller.

Texas Instruments ASC (Advanced Scientific Computer)

The Texas Instruments ASC computer became available in 1973. Its logical structure is shown in Fig. 10 [8]. It contains a 4 to 16 M-byte MOS memory with an access time of 160 ns. The cycle time is 80 ns. The central processor (CP) consists of one or two instruction processing units (IPU) for non-arithmetic segments of the instruction stream, and one to four pipelined arithmetic units (AU) for the execution of individual arithmetical and logical operations. One to four memory buffer units (MBU) provide for a smooth flow of arguments and results to and from the pipelined units. Since the CP of the Texas Instruments ASC system can contain

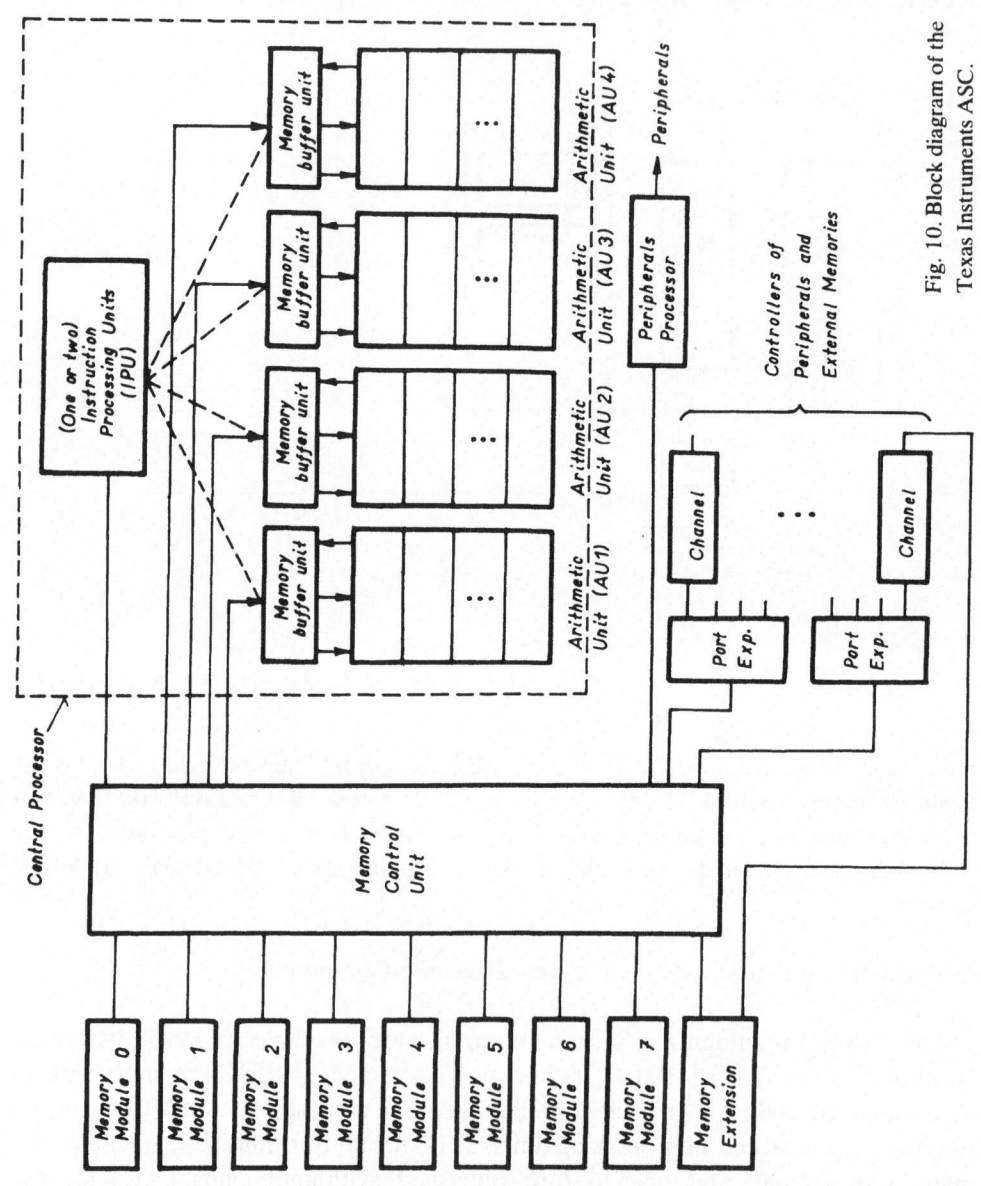

Fig. 10. Block diagram of the Texas Instruments ASC.

up to 4 pipelined AU's, a vector operation result can be obtained every 80/4 = 20 ns, which is equivalent to a speed of 50 Mflops. The speeds of arithmetic operations are:

Scalar arithmetic

Register loading	800 ns
FP addition	400 ns
FP multiplication	320 ns
FP division	1280 ns

Vector arithmetic

vector pipeline start-up	1920 ns
minimum time per segment (1 pipeline)	80 ns
minimum time per segment (4 pipelines)	20 ns
maximum speed	50 Mflops

Scalar arithmetic operations are executed similarly as in the CDC STAR 100 computer. The vector pipeline start-up is also relatively long, but shorter than in the STAR 100 computer. The maximum processing speed is one-eighth with one pipeline and one-half with four pipelines of the STAR 100.

The CRAY-1 computer

The first model of this computer was delivered in 1976. It represents the most up-to-date pipeline computer. The logical structure of the CRAY-1 computer is shown in Fig. 11 [6, 9]. The centre of the computer is a bipolar main memory with a cycle time of approximately 50 ns. The computer has 64 scalar buffer registers for 64-bit floating point words and 64 buffer registers for 24-bit addresses which are located between the main memory and the registers. It contains 8 address registers, 8 scalar registers and 8 vector registers. The access time of the registers is 6 ns. The CRAY-1 is the only computer with vector registers in which vectors of 64 elements can be stored. Longer vectors are divided by program into vectors of 64 elements. The vector arithmetic is performed between the vector registers without accessing the main memory. The computer contains 12 independent functional pipelines which execute arithmetic operations in parallel.

The speed characteristics are as follows: in combined parallel and sequential operations performing independent addition and multiplication, the mean operation time is about 7.5 ns, which is less than the cycle time (12.5 ns). The maximum operation speed of approximately 133 Mflops is achieved for matrices whose size is a multiple of the basic vector module (i.e. 64). The CRAY-1 is the fastest existing computer for matrix operations.

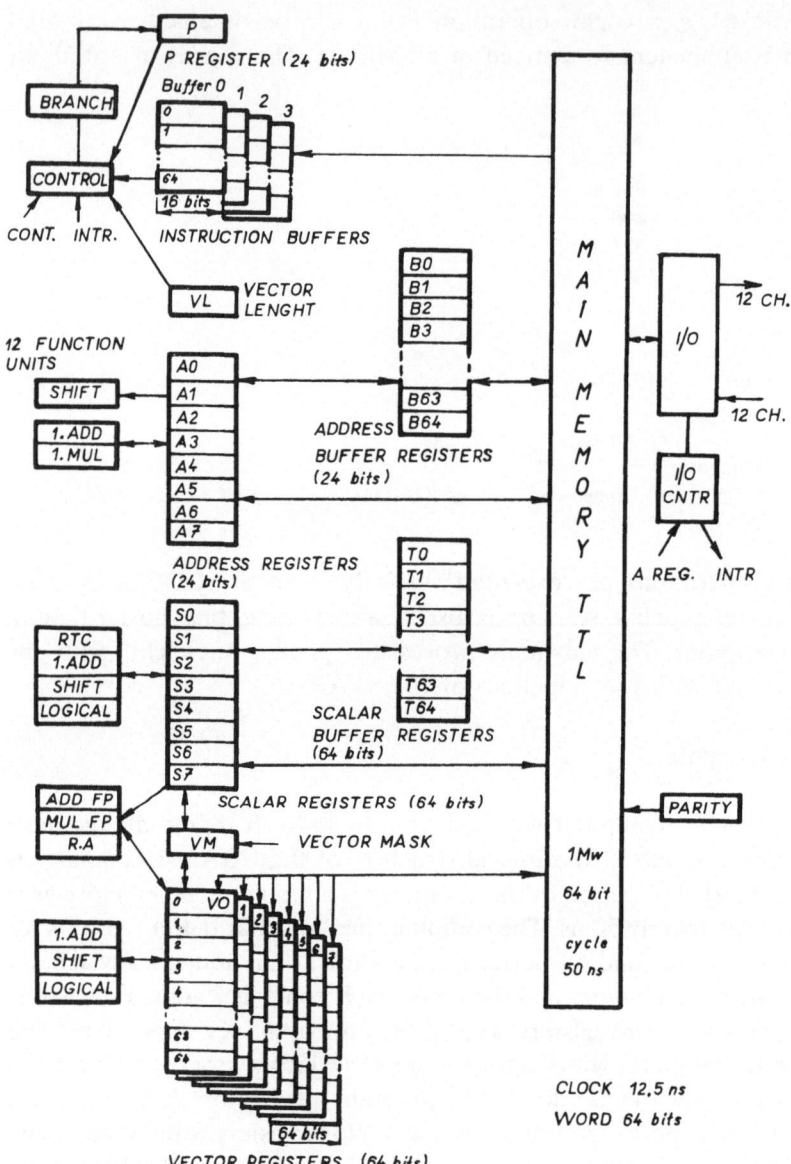

Fig. 11. Block diagram of the CRAY-1 computer.

The speed of arithmetic operations is:

Scalar arithmetic

Register loading	125 ns
FP addition	75 ns
FP multiplication	87 ns
FP division	262 ns

Vector arithmetic

Vector operation start-up	100 ns
minimum time per element	12.5 ns
maximum speed — theoretical	160 Mflops
minimum speed — measured	133 Mflops

10.2.3 Array and vector processors with SIMD architecture

In SIMD architecture (Section 10.2.2), the parallelism of the system is achieved by multiple processing units, each of which is capable to execute an autonomous specialized operation in a separate instruction stream. The architecture of array or vector processors is characterized by the fact that the same operation is performed at a given moment over a large data set in all the processing elements. An array processor can be defined as a set of interconnected processor elements (PE), often serial, each of which has a local memory and a control unit. Each PE can communicate with its four or six neighbours, as shown symbolically in Fig. 12 (for four neighbours). In SIMD architecture, the system contains only one control unit

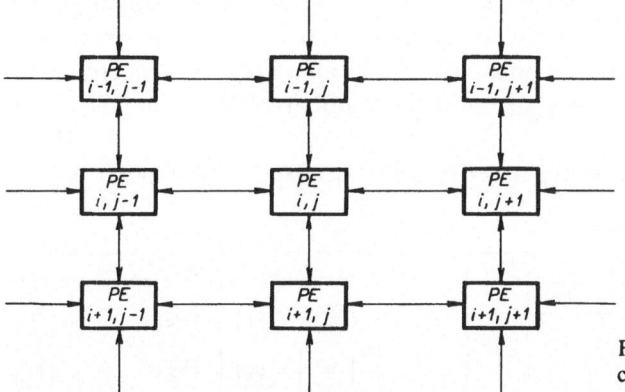

Fig. 12. Symbolic representation of communications in an array processor.

which decodes the instruction stream and sends control signals to the PE array. Moreover, the control unit of an array processor controls the input-output operations of the PE's, the data transmission between PE's, shifts, etc., and can ensure the processing of a substantial number of tasks of serial character from the instruction stream, including the masking of PE operations and memory protection.

Since individual PE's do not constitute complete central processor units (CPU) and are not capable of independent activity, the system in this case is parallel, though it is not a multiprocessor. The only variation in the activity of the array processors is the choice between performing or not performing a certain operation, by using masks. The control unit generates and distributes these activation (masking) signals. The array processor is thus suitable for bit manipulation. The array processor is also suitable for linear algebra. If, for instance, an array processor contains N processor elements (where $N = 2^n$), the array $N \times N$ is stored by columns in such way that each element of the matrix column (Fig. 13) is stored in the memory of the corresponding PE and one memory fetch transfers one column of the matrix into the vector of arithmetic units (PE). For example, the addition of two columns of an $N \times N$ matrix requires N shifts:

$$
\begin{array}{ccccccc}
a_{11} & a_{12} & a_{13}, & \ldots, & a_{1k}, & \ldots, & a_{1N} \\
& | & | & & | & & \\
a_{21} & a_{22} & a_{23}, & \ldots, & a_{2k}, & \ldots, & a_{2N} \\
& | & | & & | & & \\
a_{31} & a_{32} & a_{33}, & \ldots, & a_{3k}, & \ldots, & a_{3N} \\
\cdots & \cdots & | \cdots & \cdots & | \cdots & \cdots & \cdots \\
a_{N1} & a_{N2} & a_{N3}, & \ldots, & a_{Nk}, & \ldots, & a_{NN} \\
& | & | & & & &
\end{array}
\tag{5}
$$

$$
\vec{A}_2 + \vec{A}_3 \quad \rightarrow \quad \vec{A}_k
$$

The primary aim of an array processor is the simplification of programming through the availability of scalar and vector operations. It is possible to execute in one instruction operations over a whole vector of data. With the exception of physical constraints on the memory size and the number of PE's, there are no logical constraints.

A well-known example of array processors is the ILLIAC IV computer whose

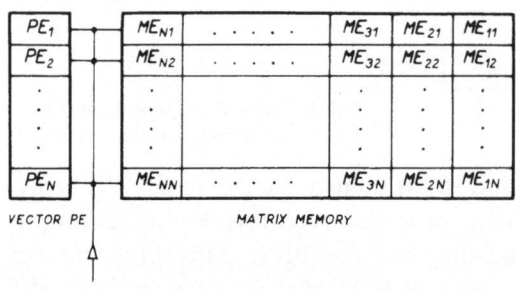

Fig. 13. Arrangement of the vector of elementary processors PE and the memory matrix ME.

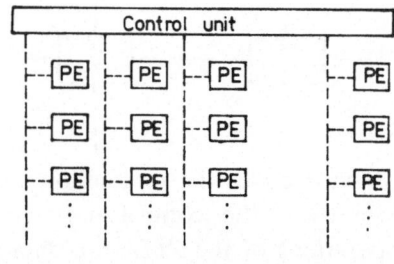

Fig. 14. Basic structure of matrix processor and its control.

predecessors are ILLIAC III and SOLOMON I and II (Fig. 14). The original design of the ILLIAC IV computer contained 256 processor elements PE [10]. Figure 15 shows one quadrant (all that has been implemented) of the array processor ILLIAC IV, which consists of 8×8 processors (PE) and has been in

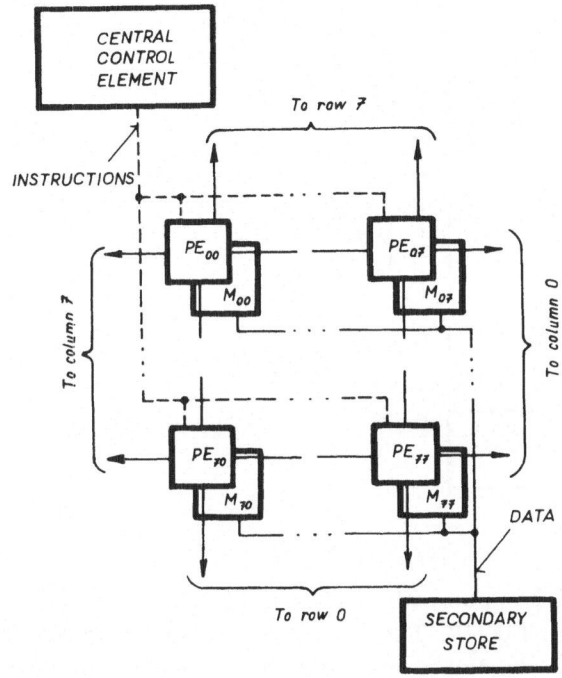

$PE_{i,j}$ – Processor element i,j
$M_{i,j}$ – Memory i,j

Fig. 15. A matrix quadrant of the ILLIAC IV computer.

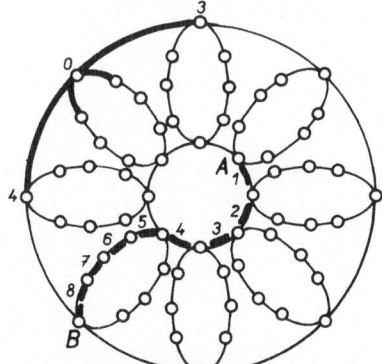

Fig. 16. Communication of processor elements within one quadrant of the ILLIAC IV computer.

operation since 1973/74. Each processor contains approximately 10^4 fast gates and has the performance of a modern single processor computer. All PE's of the quadrant are controlled by a common control unit, as a result of which all of them can execute the same operation simultaneously. The communication between processor elements (PE) within the quadrant is shown in Fig. 16. Each PE communicates with its four neighbours, for instance, 0 with 1 and 2 along the circle, and with 3 and 4 along the toroid. The longest path between the most remote PE's is 8 (4 along the toroid and 4 along the circle). The structure of quadrant

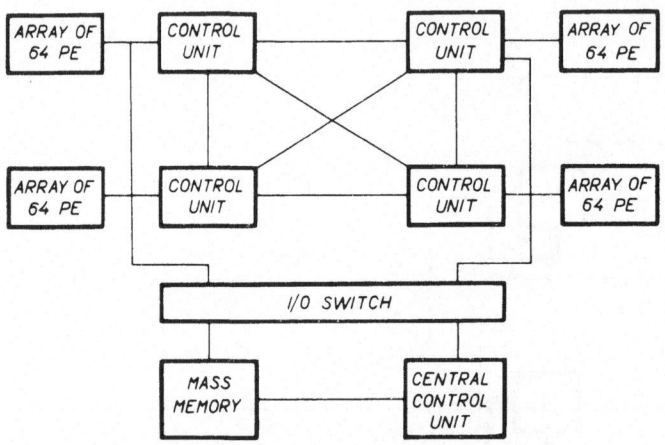

Fig. 17. Structure of the complete (four-quadrant) system of ILLIAC IV.

interconnection of the ILLIAC IV computer where each quadrant contains 64 PE's with separate control is shown in Fig. 17. The central control unit controls the activity of the control units of the quadrants, processor elements (PE), memories and peripheral devices. This maximum configuration has not been and is not to be implemented.

The technical specification of a quadrant of ILLIAC IV is as follows:

clock cycle	80 ns
number of processor elements PE	64
memory per PE	2 K (64-bit) words
number of registers per PE	4 (64-bit)
	1 (16-bit)
	1 (18-bit)

main memory; disk memory with access time 20 ms

PE floating-point arithmetic:

FP addition	560 ns
FP multiplication	720 ns
FP division	4400 ns

Because the main memory consists of a slow disk with an access time of 20 ms, a substantial amount of time is consumed by data transfer to and from the disk when tasks are processed which exceed the memory capacity of the PE's, $64 \times 2\,K = 128\,K$.

The software of the ILLIAC IV system is combersome, since there are as much as 6 additional independent program units needed to obtain one result from the program.

In evaluating the efficiency of array processors, their operational speed is supposed to increase linearly with the number of processor elements PE. But this is not completely true because of both physical properties and the nature as the applications. Array processors can only be effective if the array is completely filled with operands.

The most common applications of array processors are in the field of numerical computations in which the data consists of matrices, e.g. the solution of partial differential equations. In the application of relaxation methods, a new value for the node i, j of the space net is calculated using the present values of the adjacent nodes by the relation:

$$u_{i,j} = \frac{1}{4}\left(u_{i,j} + u_{i+1,j} + u_{i,j-1} + u_{i,j+1}\right). \tag{6}$$

The inner parallelism is explicit in these cases, and the matrix form makes the applicability of the array processor evident. To obtain solution, kN^2 steps must be executed for the execution of k iterations of an $N \times N$ network. If the matrix of processor elements in an array processor is large enough, N^2 steps are performed simultaneously, which reduces the time for obtaining the solution from kN^2 to k steps. In addition to the basic type of array processor represented by the ILLIAC IV computer, the following types are important:
— associative array processor,
— orthogonal array processor,
— pipeline array processor.
The associative array processor which we discuss in more detail in the next section is very important.

10.2.4 Associative array processor

The main reason for the difficulty in enhancing the speed of conventional computers is the functional separation of computation and memory capacities. The consequence of this separation is that there must exist certain mechanisms for data transfer between the memory and the processing units. These mechanisms are buses which are a potential bottleneck in the computer system. One method for avoiding this separation of data storage and processing is to include the calculation capacity in the memory and so create a so-called "active memory", as opposed to the conventional passive memory. The best known form of an active memory is the associative memory or content addressable memory (CAM), which is addressed by its content and not by its absolute location.

An associative array processor is a matrix-type parallel processor using associative memory, each cell of which contains a processor element (PE).

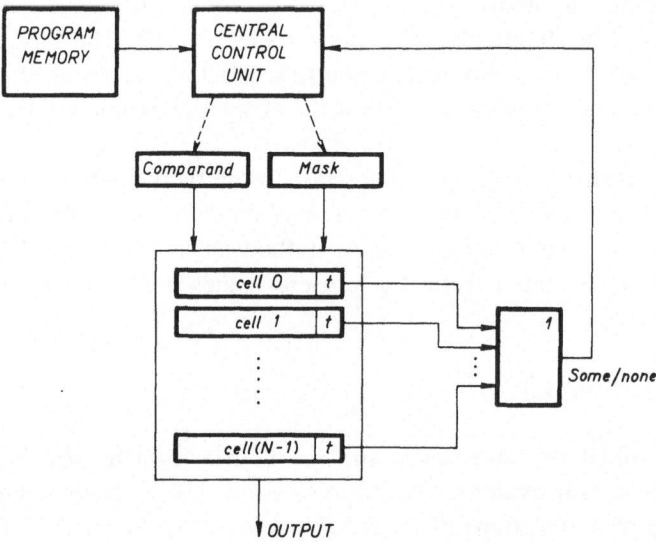

Fig. 18. Block diagram of the associative computer.

Array processors with associative memory cells are suitable for storing, selecting and processing data of large information systems. Each cell of the memory contains one memory word of a constant length W. All cells receive simultaneously the required word C and the mask M, which are transmitted by transfer channel. A memory cell is regarded selected if the condition $(C = W) \wedge M$ is satisfied for all bits. The block diagram of an associative computer with content addressable memory is shown in Fig. 18.

A content addressable memory is an ideal way to implement global operations which find the largest or the smallest word stored in memory. By a modification of these operations it is possible to divide all memory words into three groups: larger than, equal to and smaller than the content stored in reference register.

The single memory words and processor elements PE can either be arranged so that the processor elements are in every word (associative linear array processor), or they are outside the memory matrix with which they only communicate. The following four categories of associative processors are known:

— fully parallel,
— bit-serial,

— word-serial,

— block-oriented.

Because of costs, fully parallel associative processors are not equipped with large memory capacities. Word-serial parallel associative processors are technically less complex, but slower. From the aspect of the amount of circuitry and speed most effective are processors with bit-serial PE's where arithmetic operations are performed sequentially bit-by-bit over all words of the memory. Since the costs of integrated circuits are dropping rapidly at present, it will be possible to design associative processors in which each memory cell would contain a 4- to 8-bit arithmetic unit. In such a system, arithmetic operations will be executed in a serial-parallel mode. For example, a 4-bit PE is more than 20 times faster than a 1-bit PE.

An associative array processor, as compared to an array processor, can be characterized as follows: it allows memory addressing down to the bit level, the word length is arbitrary, and the number of PE's can be large owing to the low cost of integrated circuits. Arithmetic units of single memory cells work serially bit-by-bit, but they perform simultaneously the same operation assigned by the central control unit to all cells. For example, a very fast conventional computer with a memory cycle time of 0.5 µs, processing all bits in parallel, can sort and add two 32-bit items of a list in approximately 3 µs. An associative array processor working serially bit-by-bit needs approximately 25 µs for these operations. But if these operations are executed over a list of 4000 items, an associative processor still needs only 25 µs, while a conventional computer requires $3 \times 4000 = 12,000$ µs.

Typical example of an associative array processor is the STARAN computer of the firm Goodyear Aerospace Corp. [12]. Since this is a computer with several important applications, we describe it in more detail in the next section.

The associative array processor STARAN

STARAN is one of the parallel array processors that is in serial production. It has been produced since 1971 in the versions STARAN IV, STARAN S, and recently STARAN E. The STARAN computer has an SIMD-type architecture, consisting of a large number of simple processors working simultaneously under unified control. The basic architecture of the system consists of a conventionally addressed control memory for storing programs, a buffer memory for data, a control unit for generating instruction sequences and decoding instructions from the control memory and n associative modules ($n \leqq 32$).

The block diagram of an associative array module is shown in Fig. 19 [13, 14]. It consists of a multidimensional access MDA memory, a vector of processor elements PE, a permutation network and selector switching imputs to the permutation network and the multidimensional access MDA memory.

The MDA memory in the original model contains 256 words of 256 bits. It allows a multidimensional access by words, bit slices, and byte slices. The vector of associative processor elements consists of 256 one-bit PE's. The PE's communicate with each other and with the MDA memory through the permutation network PN

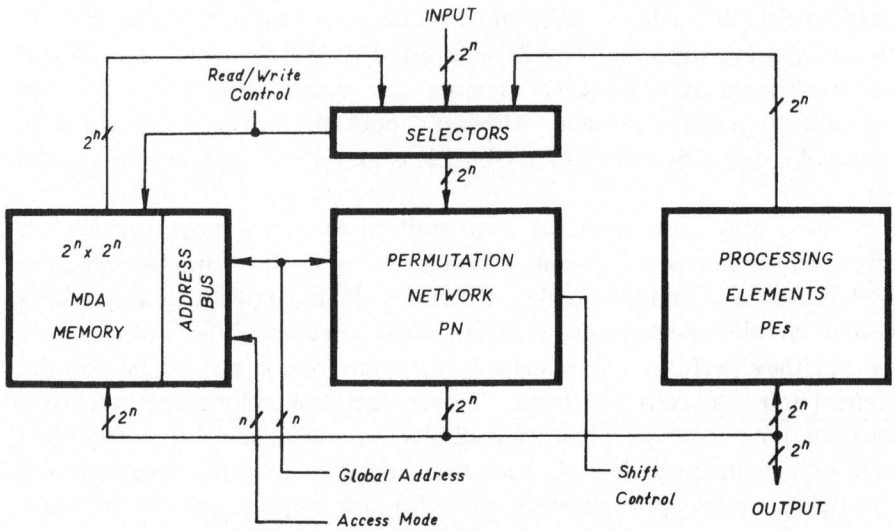

Fig. 19. Associative array module of the STARAN processor ($n = 8$).

which can shift and shuffle data. A word of 256 bits can be permuted as a whole, or it can be divided into groups of 2, 4, 8, 16, 32, 64 or 128 bits and permutations can be performed within the groups.

A multidimensional access memory allows:

a) an access by bit slices for associative operations, i.e. a parallel access to 1 bit of all words (Fig. 20a),

b) an access by word slices for input-output operations where a parallel access to all bits of one word is required (Fig. 20b),

c) an access by bytes of length 2^k, $k = 1, 2, ..., n - 1$ (Fig. 20c).

An MDA memory module is made of standard semiconductor RAM memories of bipolar or unipolar type. The inner organization of an MDA memory consisting of RAM chips can be shown as an example of a module with a capacity of 2^n words containing 2^n bits. The memory module consists of 2^n RAM chips with 2^n bits in each chip. To make possible a multidimensional access by bit-, word-, or byte-slices in one memory cycle, data in the memory must be stored in a particular way according to the following storage rule [15].

For any two n-dimensional vectors, **B** and **W**, bit **B** of word **W** is stored in the bit location of the memory chip $C = B \oplus W$.

The reversed storage rule is: For any two n-dimensional vectors, **B** and **C**, the bit location **B** of the memory chip **C** contains bit **B** of word $W = B \oplus C$.

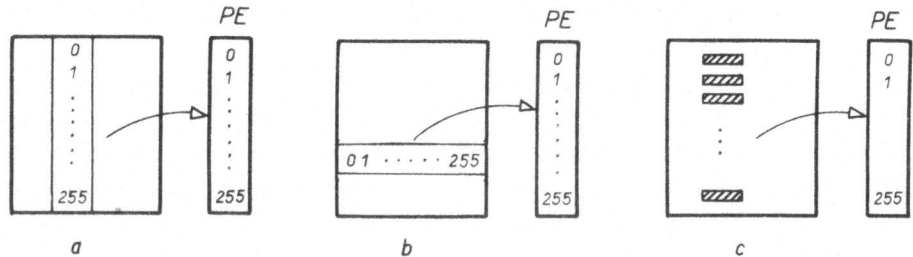

Fig. 20. Accessing MDA memory: a — bit slice access, b — word slice access, c — byte slice access.

Figure 21 illustrates the application of the storage rule to a memory module of dimensions 8×8. Elements of the given matrix a_{ij} are stored in such a way that the i-th bit-slice is stored in bit location i of all eight memory chips ($0 \leq i \leq 7$). This allows access to them in one memory cycle.

0	a_{00}	a_{11}	a_{22}	a_{33}	a_{44}	a_{55}	a_{66}	a_{77}
1	a_{01}	a_{10}	a_{23}	a_{32}	a_{45}	a_{54}	a_{67}	a_{76}
2	a_{02}	a_{13}	a_{20}	a_{31}	a_{46}	a_{57}	a_{64}	a_{75}
3	a_{03}	a_{12}	a_{21}	a_{30}	a_{47}	a_{56}	a_{65}	a_{74}
4	a_{04}	a_{15}	a_{26}	a_{37}	a_{40}	a_{51}	a_{62}	a_{73}
5	a_{05}	a_{14}	a_{27}	a_{36}	a_{41}	a_{50}	a_{63}	a_{72}
6	a_{06}	a_{17}	a_{24}	a_{35}	a_{42}	a_{53}	a_{60}	a_{71}
7	a_{07}	a_{16}	a_{25}	a_{34}	a_{43}	a_{52}	a_{61}	a_{70}

MEMORY CHIP (C)

BIT LOCATION (B) ⟶

a_{ij} = BIT i OF WORD$_j$ Fig. 21. Storage rule for an 8×8 memory module.

The access to the data in an MDA memory is implemented by assigning an access stencil which is determined by the stencil position (the global address **G**), and the stencil shape (the access mode **M**). The access stencil covers 2^n bits of a bit-, word-, or byte-slice which is accessed in one memory cycle. On the basis of both the access mode **M** and the global address **G**, the memory bus generates a local address for every memory chip, such that the local address fed to the address pins of the memory chip C is $G \oplus (MC)$.

Before the backward reading of the scrambled pattern of stored data in the processor elements or input-output channels, it is necessary to unscramble it. According to the unscrambling rule for any two n-dimensional binary vectors, G and P, when storing data in memory with the global address G and with an arbitrary mode M, the data bit from the processor element or input P is brought to the data input pin of the memory chip $C = G \oplus P$. Conversely a data bit on the data input pin of the memory chip C is sent to the processor element, or output $P = G \oplus C$. Because of the similarity of the rules for scrambling and unscrambling, since writing to and reading from memory never occur simultaneously, one common permutation network is sufficient for the two operations. Figure 18 shows the connection diagram of the permutation network between MDA memory elements and processor elements PE. Many applications require PE's to perform arithmetic and logical operations with pairs of operands which are not from the same word. This is achieved by moving data through the permutation network. The permutation network can permute a 2^n-vector read from the MDA memory in various ways, by shifts, mirroring, etc. The structure of permutation networks is to be discussed in more detail in Section 10.6.

In conclusion, it is possible to formulate the access rule by which, for any three n-dimensional binary vectors, M, G and P, when reading or writing data, the processor element P, or the input-output line will access the bit

$$(\overline{M}G) \oplus (MP) \tag{7}$$

of the memory word

$$(MG) + (\overline{M}P). \tag{8}$$

For a bit-slice access, the access mode vector is $M = (00 \dots 00)$ and the global address G specifies the bit-slice

$$B = (\overline{M}G) \oplus (MP) = (\bar{0} \cdot G) + (0 \cdot P) = G \tag{9}$$

of the word

$$W = (MG) \oplus (\overline{M}P) = (0 \cdot G) \oplus (\bar{0} \cdot P) = P = (p_1 p_2 \dots p_{n-1} p_n). \tag{10}$$

The processing element P accesses bit B of word G as shown in Fig. 20a.

For word access, the access mode is $M = (11 \dots 11)$ and the global address G specifies the word address. Thus

$$B = (\overline{M}G) \oplus (MP) = (\bar{1} \cdot G) \oplus (1 \cdot P) = P = (p_1 p_2 \dots p_{n-1} p_n) \tag{11}$$

and

$$W = (MG) \oplus (\overline{M}P) = (1 \cdot G) \oplus (\bar{1} \cdot P) = G, \tag{12}$$

i.e. the processor element P accesses the bit of that word which is given by the global address G (Fig. 20b).

Access by bytes, e.g. with length of 8 bits, is achieved by using the access mode $M = (00 \ldots 0011)$ and the global address $G = (b_1 b_2 \ldots b_{n-3} w_{n-2} w_{n-1} w_n)$. In this case, the vector of the processor element $P = (p_1 p_2 \ldots p_{n-1} p_n)$ accesses the bits

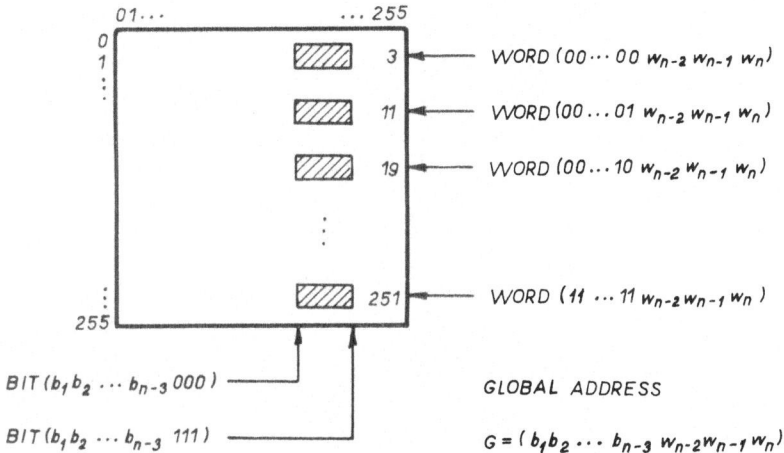

Fig. 22. Stencil for 8-bit horizontal bytes.

$$B = (\overline{M}G) \ \oplus (MP) = (11 \ldots 11000) \cdot (b_1 b_2 \ldots b_{n-3} w_{n-2} w_{n-1} w_n) \oplus$$
$$\oplus (00 \ldots 00111) \cdot (p_1 p_2 \ldots p_{n-1} p_n) =$$
$$= (b_1 b_2 \ldots b_{n-3} p_{n-2} p_{n-1} p_n) \tag{13}$$

of the words:

$$W = (MG) \oplus (\overline{M}P) = (00 \ldots 00111) \cdot (b_1 b_2 \ldots b_{n-3} w_{n-2} w_{n-1} w_n) \oplus$$
$$\oplus (11 \ldots 11000) \cdot (p_1 p_2 \ldots p_{n-1} p_n) =$$
$$= (p_1 p_2 \ldots p_{n-3} w_{n-2} w_{n-1} w_n). \tag{14}$$

In Fig. 22, a stencil is shown for 8-bit bytes, for which the right-hand side of the global address $(w_{n-2} w_{n-1} w_n)$ is (111). If the access mode M has m ones on the left-hand side, then 2^n covered bits are separate and 2^{n-m} covered words create a continuous group. Figure 23 shows the access stencil for $M = 1100 \ldots 00$ and $G = (b_1 b_2 w_3 \ldots w_{n-1} w_n)$, where from (13) and (14):

$$B = (p_1 p_2 w_3 \ldots w_{n-1} w_n), \tag{15}$$
$$W = (b_1 b_2 p_3 \ldots p_{n-1} p_n). \tag{16}$$

For a memory read cycle faster than 200 ns and a write cycle of 400 ns, the frequency width of one module is large than 1.28 gigabits/s (1.28×10^9 bit/s) for reading and 0.64 gigabits/s (0.64×10^9 bits/s) for writing.

The associative array module contains three 256-bit registers, M, X and Y, and a vector of 256 serial 1-bit processor elements PE. The register M is a masking register. The register X and Y have an independent logic capable of executing any arbitrary function from the 16 Boolean functions of two variables:

$$x_i \leftarrow \Phi(x_i, f_i), \qquad (i = 0, 1, \ldots, 255), \tag{17}$$

$$y_i \leftarrow \Phi(y_i, f_i), \qquad (i = 0, 1, \ldots, 255), \tag{18}$$

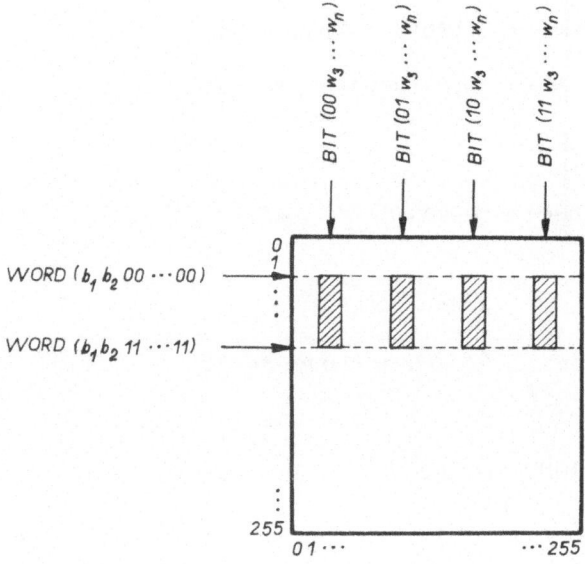

Fig. 23. Stencil for access to bits of a continuous group of words.

where x_i, y_i is the value of the i-the bit of the registers, X and Y, and f_i is the value of the i-th output of the permutation network. By using the operation EXOR, two bit slices of the fields **A** and **B** can be added in four iterative steps. In the case of n-bit fields, the basic adding cycle is performed n times. During each cycle the bit slice (A_i) of field **A** is read from the MDA memory, then (B_i) of the field **B** and the result of the summation is written in the bit slice (S_i) of the field **S**. The operation begins with the least significant bits. The graphic representation of the iterative steps for reading the fields **A** and **B** storing the result in the field **S** of the MDA memory is shown in Fig. 24. At a reading speed of 5 Mbit/s (read cycle time of 0.2 µs) per cell and with the maximum capacity of the MDA memory of $32 \times 256 = 8$ K words, the STARAN computer can execute 8 K parallel additions, for instance of 32 bit words in 6.4 µs, i.e. 1280 million additions per second. The CDC 6600 computer needs 0.2 µs for the same operation, since it executes 5 million additions per second.

In comparison with the CRAY-1 computer, which needs 12.5 ns per addition, i.e. has a speed of 810 million additions per second, the STARAN computer is 16 times faster.

In Fig. 25 the structure of the data paths of the STARAN computer is shown.

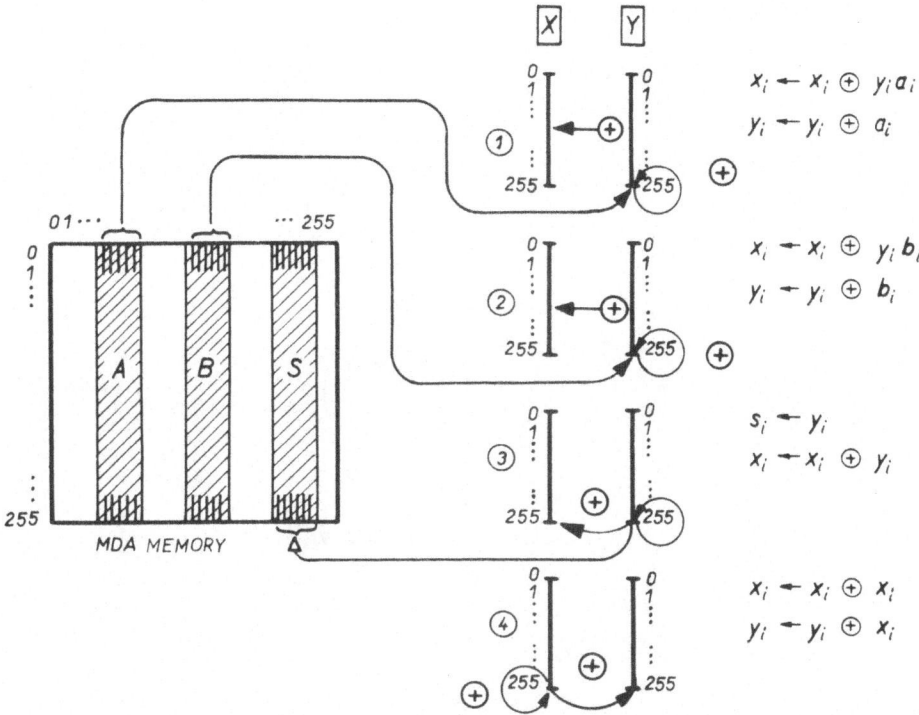

Fig. 24. Graphical representation of iterative steps of the addition of the fields $S \leftarrow A + B$.

The main difference between the single paths is the speed at which data is transferred. The fastest input-output path is a parallel PIO (80 Mbits/s array). The direct access to the MDA memory has an intermediate speed and finally the BIO channel (Buffered Input-Output) 100 to 200 Kbytes/s. The BIO channel allows connection of the STARAN computer, as a specialized precomputer, to a host computer controlling the processing of application programs.

From this it follows that the input-output operations are the bottleneck of the associative array processor. In this respect, the application of an associative processor is advantageous in applications that require few input-output operations. In Table 1, the distribution of the total processing time of some algorithms is given for an associative processor with a cycle time of 100 ns and an I/O operation speed of about 1.5 µs/byte, together with a comparison with the IBM 360/30 computer

[16]. It can be seen from Table 1 that an associative array processor is advantageous for processing algorithms from the area of artificial intelligence, image processing, tree search and other algorithms with internal parallelism.

Another serious problem in the practical use of the associative array processor is that of its programming. So far, only assembler languages are available which are "tailored" for single configurations of the computer.

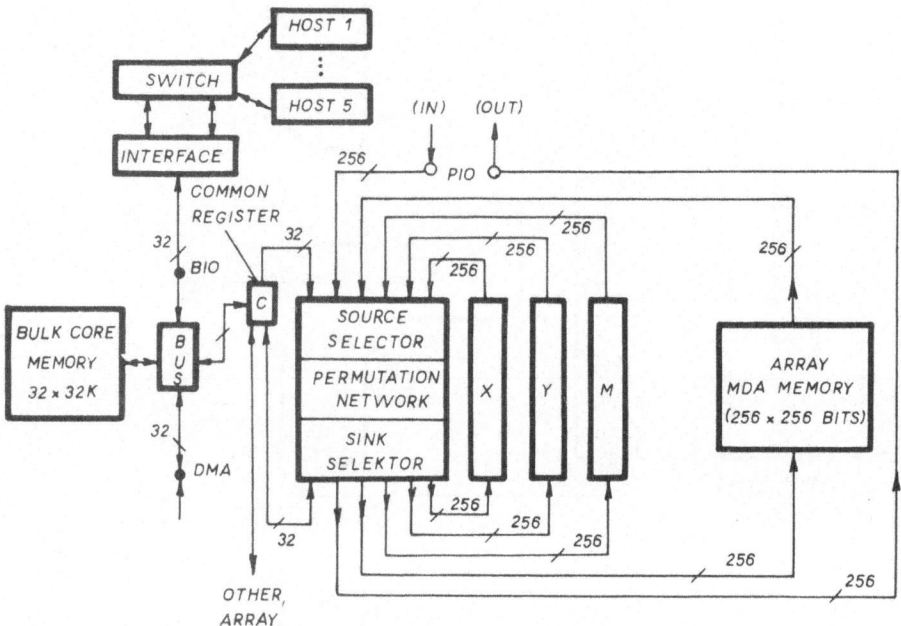

Fig. 25. Data paths of the STARAN computer.

Table 1

Algorithm	Distribution of the total processing time				
	Processing (%)	Data reorganization (%)	I/O (%)	Total processing time (ms)	Speed-up as against IBM 360/30
Image processing	97	—	3	122	610×
Sorting	70	—	30	20	110×
Matrix multiplication	31	7	62	1	78×
Fourier transformation	17	44	39	31	75×
Hadamard transformation	4	46	50	12	79×
One-dimensional filter	40	—	60	10	280×
Two-dimensional filter	50	—	50	20	510×

An example of such an assembler language is APPLE (Associative Processor Programming Language) of the STARAN computer. It contains a full set of instructions for conditional branching, register instructions, and sets of instructions for associative writing into and reading from the associative memory, associative searching in memory, associative data transfer, and associative arithmetic instructions.

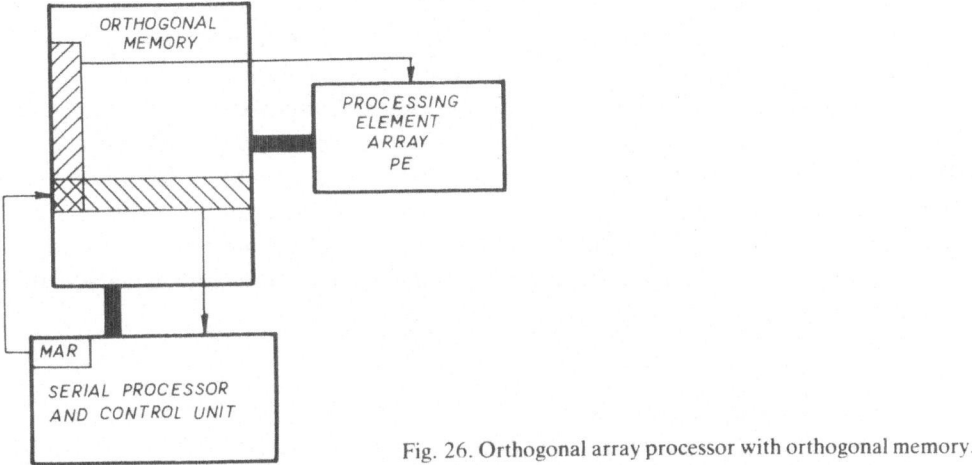

Fig. 26. Orthogonal array processor with orthogonal memory.

Associative arithmetic instructions allow addition, substraction, multiplication, and division of arrays by the content of a common register or component by component, etc. In spite of the fact that no higher programming language is available, the power of the single associative instructions of the assembler language is so high that the effectiveness of the associative array processor is unquestioned for suitable applications.

10.2.5 Orthogonal array processor

The orthogonal array processor is a special case of the associative array processor. As well as an array of elementary processors PE, it contains a serial processor that has access to the same orthogonal memory (Fig. 26). An orthogonal memory is defined as a dual access memory, i.e. with selection by word and bit slice. Some associative array processors contain an orthogonal multidimensional access memory, e.g. STARAN (Section 10.2.4), which allows more effective I/O operations to be carried out. But this does not create an orthogonal processor. Structurally, an orthogonal processor differs from a standard SIMD array processor by having a common memory for programs and data.

The use of a common memory has several advantages:

a) It simplifies the compilation of programs, since the control unit has access to capabilities of the associative processor.

b) Operations in the serial processor over programs and parallel operations over data in a set of PE processors can be executed simultaneously. Since the orthogonal processor allows more efficient computation, it is specially advantageous for scientific and engineering computations. The dual access to memory provides immediate availability of the results of condition testing and thus increases the efficiency of the control unit, mainly in processing programs with a large number of branching operations.

The orthogonal array processor can also be used in combination with some other large array processor as an efficient input-output processor. If an identical number of elementary processors are used in both the array processors, the problems of communication are significantly simplified. The data transfer from the external environment to the input-output processor can be implemented in a conventional way and data can be transferred from the input-output processor to the associative memory array in blocks.

10.2.6 Pipeline array processor

By expanding the pipeline principle (Section 10.2.2) to the array processor a pipeline array processor is produced. It consists of a processor array which, due to pipelining, has simpler hardware with fast processing. Pipeline processors require faster circuits and a more complex control. Since in a pipeline array processor the control unit controls the whole vector or the array of pipelined processors, the share of control per processor is smaller. In using bit slices with a width of n bits and a word length of N bits, the pipeline processor itself represents only an N/n-th part of the hardware of the whole processor. Pipeline array processors are not yet in quantity production.

10.2.7 MIMD multiprocessors

A multiprocessor is defined as a computer containing two or more processor units working on a common memory under integrated control. The basic multiprocessor configuration is shown in Fig. 1d. A multiprocessor can be defined in more detail as follows: A multiprocessor consists of two or more processors. If these processors have approximately equal capabilities, we speak of a symmetrical multiprocessor, otherwise an asymmetric multiprocessor system. The main memory must be accessible to and usable by all processors. According to the basic definition, a multiprocessor requires the whole memory to be common and only small local memories to exist in each processor. If the processors have large local memories, the multiprocessor is considered to be a multicomputer complex which can be centralized or distributed. Input and output must be accessible to all processors. All processors share access to I/O channels, control units and devices.

For the entire multiprocessor system there must exist one integrated operating system which controls the entire hardware and software of the computer system. The operating system must ensure interaction between processors and their programs at the job, task, data set and data element levels.

The creation of a parallel high-performance processor in the MIMD category has been considered in the past. However, the implementation of multi-microprocessor architecture was only possible with the onset of LSI technologies. The best known existing versions of LSI processors allow high-speed processing of a data stream with a width of 16 or 32 bits. For example, existing microprocessors, such as Texas Instruments 9940, Elektronika NC-80, and the like, contain 5×10^4 to 10^5 transistors per chip, and it is assumed that this density will be almost double every year. The central processor unit (CPU) contributes a relatively small part of the cost of the whole system.

Additional features and their control units, memory modules and the required software cost as much as, if not more than, the basic CPU. Therefore, the traditional processor-oriented view, in which the main objective was to keep the CPU fully employed all the time is no longer valid [17]. The instruction cycle times of typical LSI processors are 5 to 10 times longer than the cycle time of the main memory. For this reason, the main memory must be shared in time and space between several processors to improve the efficiency of the use of the memory. In this connection two problems arise concerning the alignment of system resources:

   a) Memory conflicts and the resulting reduction of system performance.

   b) Partitioning the memory (into modules) and the resulting possibility that the whole memory cannot be used.

   c) Problem of information exchange between processors.

Attaching different importance to these problems has led to the creation of various multiprocessor architectures.

Topology of multiprocessor computer architectures

The topological problem of the organization of multiple interconnected monolithic microprocessors in an effective multiprocessor structure has been solved in several ways. In the literature [18—20] there are five widely discussed classical multiprocessor organizations:

   a) multiprocessor time-shared bus,

   b) crossbar switch,

   c) n-dimensional cube,

d) matrices connecting the nearest neighbours,
e) cluster bus.

Multiprocessor time-shared common bus

The time-shared common bus represents a classical solution of the organization of a multiprocessor system that was employed in the IBM 360/67 and IBM 370 /168 computers. A set of processors Pc, a set of memory modules Mp and a set of inputs-outputs I/O have a single common bus (Fig. 27), e.g. the data bus in the

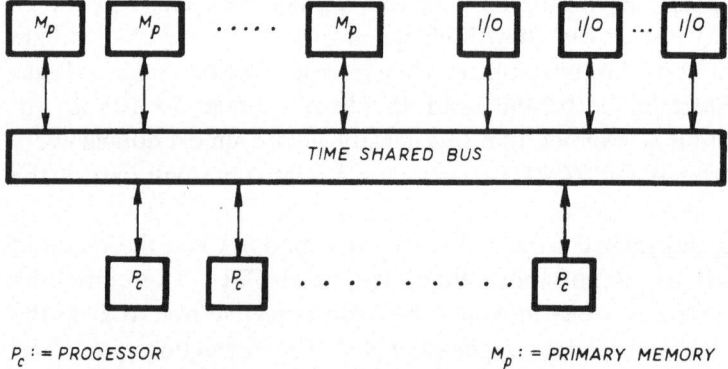

P_c := PROCESSOR M_p := PRIMARY MEMORY

Fig. 27. Multiprocessor time-shared bus.

PDP-11, the UNIBUS. It is also possible to interconnect in this way pairs of processors and memories (nodes). The bus is the bottleneck in this organization. With more than four processors the performance of the system is significantly reduced. A recently developed system utilizing a series of multiple and separate buses is the PLURIBUS multiprocessor. Since other structures have clear advantages for a greater number of processors, we do not further discuss the organization in connection with multiprocessors.

Crossbar switch

The crossbar switch is an attempt to overcome reduced throughput of the system organization of the time-shared bus. The best known example of the application of the crossbar switch is the C mmp system [21]. The crossbar switch in C mmp interconnects N Pc-processors with M Mp-memory modules, but it can also be used to interconnect nodes (Fig. 28). In view of the fact that the crossbar switch mediates all communications in a multiprocessor, it becomes a critical part of the system. Moreover, it is relatively expensive, and reduces the efficiency, system expandibility and reliability. When the number of processors is approximately equal to the number of memory modules, the cost is proportional to N^2. But the greatest weakness of this approach is the fact that this problem cannot be solved even by using LSI, because the crossbar switch remains limited by the number of

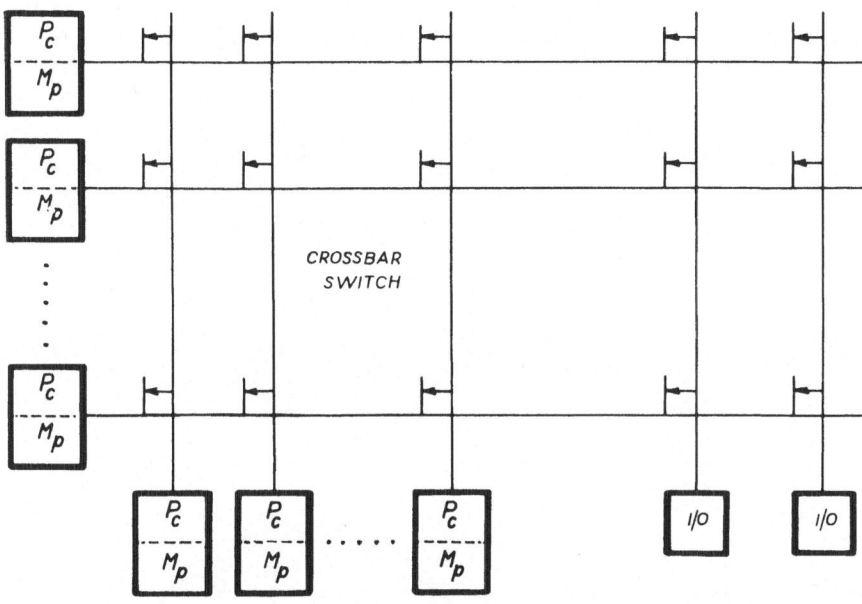

Fig. 28. Crossbar switch.

pins on the chip. It is not thought that crossbar switches which are advantageous in price can be implemented for more than several tens of processors.

n-Dimensional cube

This method uses the analogy of an *n*-dimensional cube or toroid for interconnecting 2^N processor-memory pairs (for $N > 3$ this organization is termed "hypercube"). From among all the existing systems, the ILLIAC IV system comes nearest to this method. The main characteristics of this method are:

a) The communication between processors is via redundant paths, so that no internal overloads can occur.

b) Due to multiple interconnections between the nodes, failures in one branch cannot cause the system to crash.

c) For an *n*-dimensional cube with a maximum of 2^n nodes, the maximum communication distance between two nodes is n.

For example, a three-dimensional cube requires only 3 inputs per node for 2^3 processors (Fig. 29a). The number of inputs increases with an increase in the number of nodes, e.g. 256 nodes require 8 inputs per processor. The transition from the hypercube to the toroid arrangement is shown in Fig. 29. By merging the switches T_i and B_i in each processor column i (Fig. 29b) one physical node is produced. Figure 19c shows how the toroid results in this case. In Fig. 29d the structure is shown of a toroid communication system of the ILLIAC IV computer.

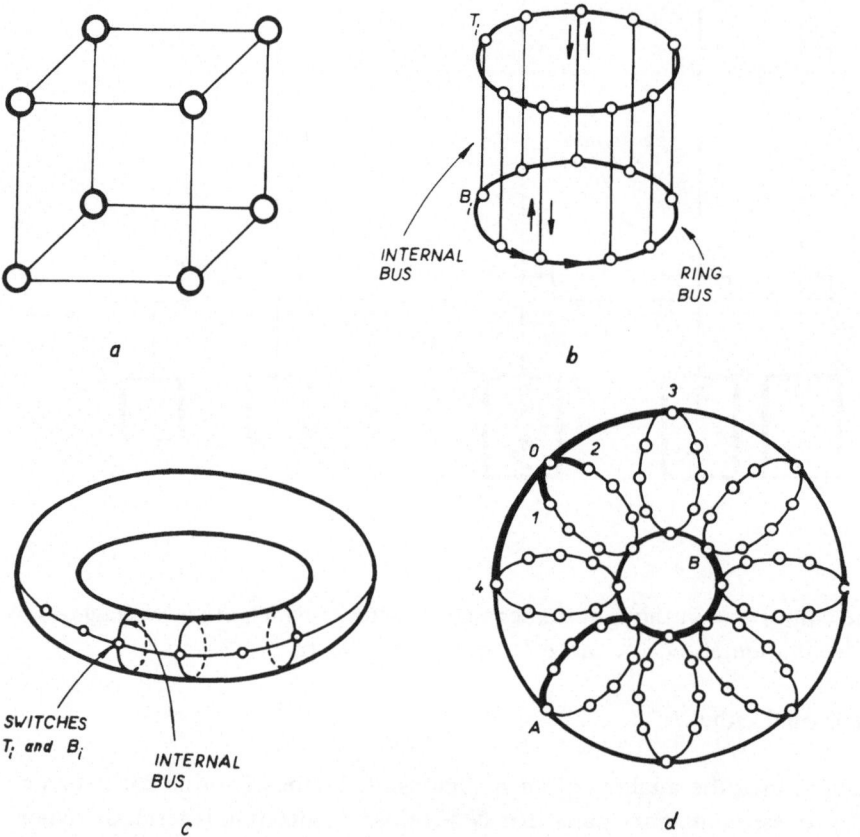

Fig. 29. a — Three-dimensional cube, b — interconnection of nedes by ring buses, c — resultant toroid architecture, d — toroid architecture of ILLIAC IV.

Matrices connecting the nearest neighbours

The organization of an n-dimensional cube can be expanded by enlarging the number of nodes per dimension. For example, some organization can be represented by a two-dimensional matrix, where the number of inputs per processor is reduced to four. This organization has the properties a) and b), but the maximum distance for N nodes is $(2N-2)$.

Cluster bus

In this organization, one or more processors are connected by a local bus to memory and I/O devices. Each of these clusters is connected to the other clusters

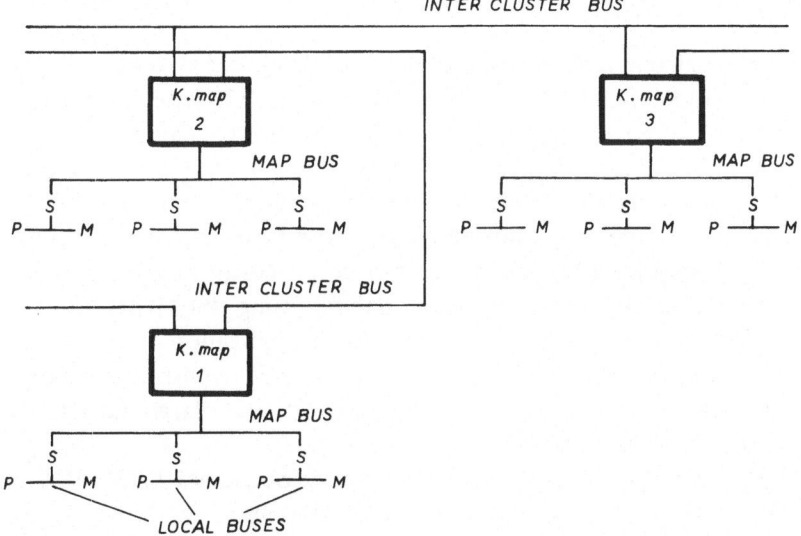

Fig. 30. Simple three-cluster structure.

via one or more global buses. The advantage of this organization is that most memory accesses are local and consequently do not load the system with redundant overheads or with a general mapping mechanism. The best known example of the cluster organization bus is the Cm* system [23].

The Cm* structure consists of pairs: processor (P) — memory (M), called computer modules Cm. The mapping processors K map perform all the functions required both for access to external memory and external access to local memory. Figure 30 shows the hierarchy of buses in the Cm* structure using the PMS language [24]. The local buses which interconnect the processors P with the memories M represent the lowest level of the bus hierarchy. The second level contains mapping buses which provide the interface between the group of computer modules Cm and the mapping processor K map through switches S. The third level in the hierarchy consists of intergroup or global buses. From the aspect of distributed multicomputer complexes, another topology which is worth considering is based on the tree structure described in Section 10.4.

10.3 Centralized processor systems

In addition to the classification of processor architecture given in Section 10.2, processors can also be divided according to their distribution in space, i.e. into centralized and distributed processor systems. Centralized processor systems can consist of MISD, SMID and MIMD processors which work on a pipeline, matrix or multiprocessor principle. Distributed multicomputer systems are mostly based on MIMD architecture. They are a set of independent mini- or microcomputers, with local and global control provided either by a processor of this set or one of a higher category.

Although there exist strong tendencies in the area of computer system architecture (see Section 10.4) to emphasize the advantage of using distributed multicomputer systems, i.e. a network of a large number of mini- or microcomputers rather than centralized processor systems, it is clear that for large-scale scientific and technical calculations and special purpose data processing in real time, centralized processor systems with extremely high throughput will also be needed in the future. Examples of problems requiring the use of centralized processor systems are, for example: large matrix calculations, spectral analysis using the Fast Fourier Transformation, solution of partial differential equations, application of the Monte Carlo method, air traffic control based on processing signals from radiolocators, seismic signal processing in geophysics, processing and updating large data bases for long-term weather forecasts, etc.

All MISD, SIMD and MIMD architectures presented in Sections 10.2.2—10.2.7 are included in the category of centralized processor systems.

Physically different, though structurally similar, are systems of centralized computer networks. A centralized computer network can be defined as a set of autonomous computers, usually mini- or microcomputers, physically distributed over a large area, each of which has its own local, though limited, main memory with access to a common secondary mass memory.

10.4 Distributed computer systems

Another form of parallelism arises when several computers are interconnected in so-called computer networks, such as ARPA, MERIT, TYMNET, CYBERNET, and others [25, 26].

For message switching and storing, as well as for connecting the computer network to large computers, minicomputers are used as elements of the network. This structure allows the execution of many functions of a centralized multiprocessor computer system (such as C mmp), but it is not restricted to one location. On the other hand, the use of distributed computer systems for the solution of some real time problems is not possible owing to time delay and limited band width of the transfer between the computers of the network. A functional diagram of the structure of a distributed computer network is shown in Fig. 31.

The importance of the interconnection of computers in networks is increasing, especially since the computer system resources are distributed and consequently

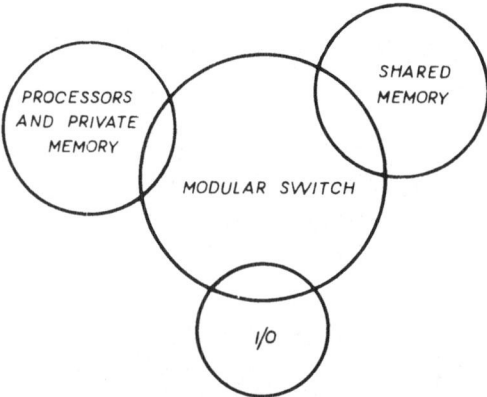

Fig. 31. Structure of distributed computer network.

also more efficiently used. This is especially important in minicomputers where the cost of a host computer is low and the costs of secondary memories for files and data bases, input-output devices and other peripherals are relatively high. Also the solution of some tasks on minicomputers is relatively expensive, because these require the use of mass (disk) memory and additional resources, such as file processing, printing, plotting, program translation from higher programming languages, floating point and double precision operations.

The parallelism implemented in distributed computer networks offers the following possibilities:

a) Parallel processing. The task being solved is partitioned into several independent subtasks using apparent or inherent parallelism.

b) Pipeline processing. The task is distributed into a certain number of subtasks which are processed in parallel on a large number of computers using cooperative subroutines. The cooperative subroutines are assigned processors which exchange intermediate results for further processing. A typical example is pattern recognition in real time, signal processing, EKG, EEG processing, and also compilation of programs and similar tasks.

c) Network processing. A set of computers works on different tasks utilizing the so-called natural parallelism [27] of the problem to be solved. The individual computers of the network are assigned special functions. The jobs are moved between specialized computers, e.g. computers for certain types of calculations, input-output processors. Specialized computers can be added to the

computer network for interpreting higher programming languages, e.g. LISP, for spectral analysis using the Fast Fourier Transformation (FFT), etc.
d) The conventional multiprogramming mode. Multiple independent programs are assigned to independent processor or sets of processors that work in a normal multiprogramming mode.

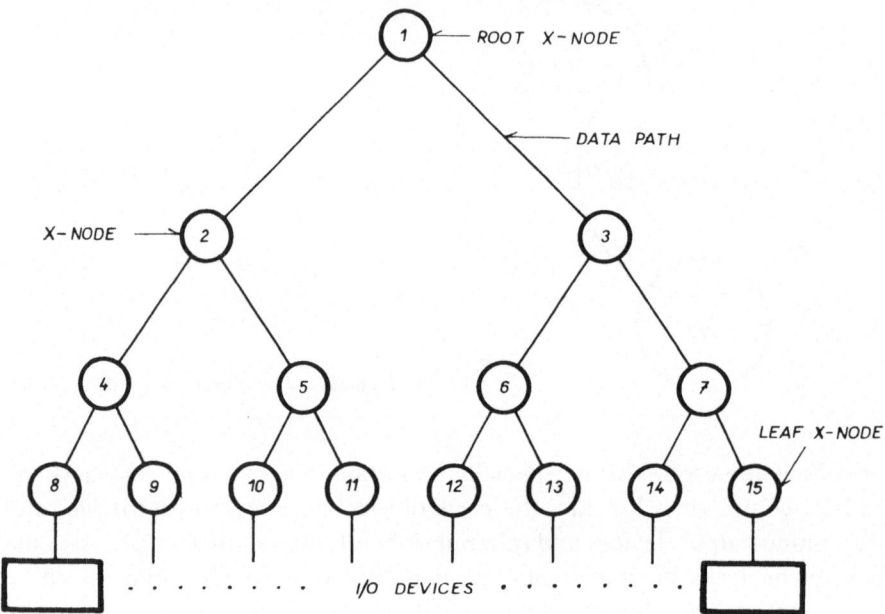

Fig. 32. Simple linear X-tree.

From the topological aspect, computer networks make use of the hierarchical control of the computer system which consists of a set of CPUs, data channels and front-end processors. In the entire computer system explicit logical control is used, where the logical control paths are isomorphic to physical information paths. An X-tree structure [20] satisfies best the principle of hierarchic control. The basic organization of the X-tree is the full binary tree with microprocessors constituting the X-nodes of the network (Fig. 32). A simple algorithm for binary tree branching has the following form:

Route (targetaddress)
if (targetaddress = nodeaddress) **then** {send to processor}
else [**while** (targetaddress→ nodeaddress) **do**
    (oldaddress: = targetaddress;
    targetaddress: = targetaddress/2);
if: (targetaddress < nodeaddress) **then** {send to parent}

else if odd (oldaddress) **then** {send to right child}
    else {send to left child}].

The X-tree structure allows the use of identical universal microprocessors for executing the functions of the CPU, control memory unit, control cache unit, control channel and disk units. Therefore, the X-tree structure is a homogeneous system making use of identical processors for all those functions in which I/O is on the lowest hierarchic level. If some node processor is overloaded, this function can be automatically transferred to the next higher node. In this way, the X-tree structure solves some of the problems of the assignment of processes to single processors and is very attractive for multiplex networks.

In conclusion we note that reconfigurable computer networks can be implemented using generalized pipelining (see Section 10.2.2). The processors of the network are partitioned into two sets according to the functions they perform. One set of processors generates sequences of instructions or data, and the other set of processors executes, or processes them. The ratio of the number of execution processors to the number of processors which generate the sequences is variable and thus the system is highly adaptive with respect to the changing external load.

The future of pipeline networks implemented by microprocessors seems to be very bright, this owing mainly to heavy cuts in hardware prices. In a microprocessor network, each microprocessor has its specialized function derived from the general principle of pipelining, which is implemented using microprocessors. In such networks, the principle of graceful degradation is implemented in a very simple manner which makes it possible to build systems with high reliability and operational availability, such as those dealt with in Section 10.5.

10.5 Fault-tolerant centralized multiprocessor and distributed multicomputer systems

The probability of fault-free behaviour of a system in a given time interval is determined by the product of the probabilities that the single components will not fail during the given interval. The larger the system, the higher the probability of failure. In addition to reducing the complexity of computer systems, there are two fundamental methods for increasing reliability: testing the system and the use of redundancy. The testing method requires that the system can be decomposed into simpler subsystems, or modules, which can be tested independently. Redundancy does not eliminate system failures, but provides fault-tolerance. The purpose of hardware redundancy is to prevent system failures caused by some random breakdown, by shutting off the faulty unit and switching over to a spare unit, or by outvoting the faulty input by other inputs that are assumed to be correct. Other forms of redundancy are: program redundancy, where special programs for the detection of failures and the recovery of activity after a failure are used; time redundancy based on repetition of computations or transfers, and finally data redundancy: check sums, back-up copies, echotests, etc.

In principle, all fault-tolerant systems can be divided into three main categories:

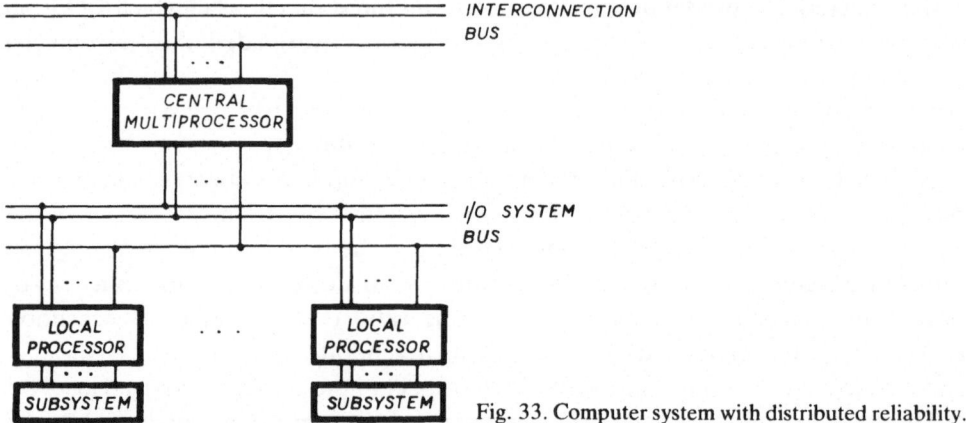

Fig. 33. Computer system with distributed reliability.

HIFT (hardware implemented fault-tolerant) systems, SIFT (software implemented fault-tolerant) systems and hybrid fault-tolerant systems which are the combination of the two preceding systems.

The architecture of hardware implemented fault-tolerant computer systems is based on intracomputer or intercomputer redundancy. The intracomputer redundancy, selective or massive, leads in both cases to non-standard designs for the basic modules of the computer: redundant logic circuits, detecting and correcting codes, etc. In accordance with technological development, the change from standard computers to intercomputer redundancy which allows the design of fault-tolerant complexes of mini- and microcomputers is natural. This approach is especially suitable for real time computer control systems, mainly in a hierarchical arrangement [28]. The design of such fault-tolerant computer systems must satisfy the following requirements: The hardware and software must be modular and so segmented that it is possible to check the successful execution of transfers between modules. The system must be resistant against hardware and software failures, and automatic diagnostics of the whole system must be possible [29]. The degradability and reconfigurability of the system must be able to deal with failures of the single parts of the system. The system must be capable of a dynamic recovery of the degraded subsystem following a failure.

The distributed reliability computer system (Fig. 33) consists, as far as reliability is concerned, of a central multiprocessor and a set of local processors communicating between each other through a fault-tolerant bus [30]. The local processors provide the local control functions and simple data processing at high operation speeds. The central computer performs global control functions including complex calculations at low operation speeds. The central computer is designed as

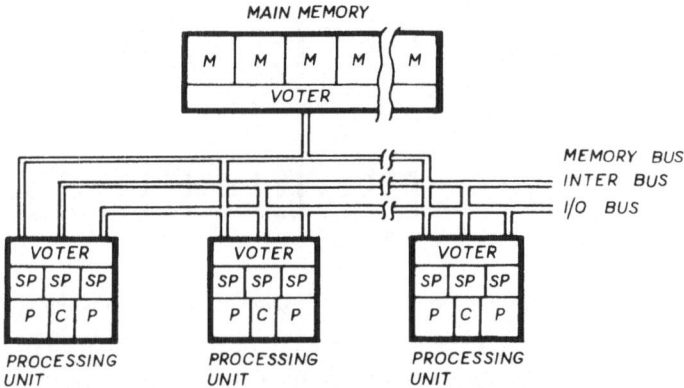

Fig. 34. Structure of a central microprocessor with high reliability. P — processor, M — memory modul, SP — scratchpad, C — comparator.

a fault-tolerant multiprocessor consisting of 6 to 9 processors (Fig. 34). Each processor is duplicated for failure detection and has a triple scratchpad store, so that the processor can locate failures and protect the data which is critical for the automatic recovery of the activity of the system and for the continuity of the data. The structure of the central computer allows graceful degradation of the system without any loss of data being processed. The main storage is modular, so that writing to several modules simultaneously and voting when reading are possible. If a failure of one of the processors or scratchpad memories occurs, the scratchpad memories transfer their entire contents to a reserved area in the main store which is accessible to the nearest disengaged processor, which continues processing from the beginning of the interrupted instruction phase. If the fault is a transient one, after having successfully completed the self-checking program, the processor is reinstated into the system.

The so-called ultrareliable computer systems are used for controlling extraordinarily important processes where the breakdown of the computer system is out of the question even for a fraction of a second. This category includes, e.g. the JPL-STAR system (Self-Testing-And-Repairing) [31], which is capable of automatic recovery following the failure of any of its parts. An error-detecting code is used for instructions and data. The decentralization of the system activity allows the localization of program failures. Replacement of a failed unit and reconfiguration of the system is performed by reconnection of inputs of the units involved. Besides the fault-tolerant systems mentioned above there also is a series of other solutions which optimize system reliability in a particular way. Such SIFT and HIFT systems include PRIME, SERF, MERCA, "A Three-Failure-Tolerant Computer System", as well as the multi-miniprocessor systems C mmp and ARPA mentioned above.

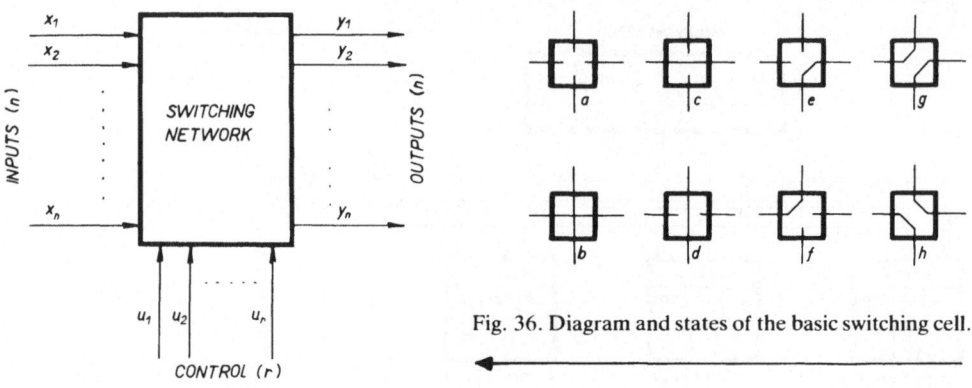

Fig. 36. Diagram and states of the basic switching cell.

Fig. 35. Block diagram of a switching network.

10.6 Switching and permutation networks

Processing of arrays, vectors or matrices, requires computer systems with a complex data access facility. This is implemented by using permutation networks. For computer systems with SIMD or MIMD architectures and for HIFT high--reliability systems, the critical problem is the design of switching and permutation networks with high reliability which are also economically viable due to the use of LSI technologies. In principle, a switching network has the form as shown in Fig. 35. The control signals u_r control the structure of connecting logic such that the n input and n output lines are connected together in some fashion. The maximum number of settings is $n!$ and the upper bound of the number of control signals is $\log_2(n!)$.

A network is called switching network if it executes the function of a switch between inputs and outputs, or it is a permutation network — if it implements permutations between inputs and outputs. The use of LSI technology for the implementation of permutation networks requires that the networks have to be universal, minimal and such that standard sets of homogeneous switching elements be available for their synthesis. The settings of such a basic switching cell, as described by Kautz [32], is shown in Fig. 36. From cells of this type it is possible to produce various types of structures of switching and permutation networks: triangular, rectangular, square, Bosé—Nelson permutation matrices, and others.

The triangular Bosé—Nelson permutation matrix [32] is shown in Fig. 37. The number of cells required is $1/2(n^2 - n)$. This number is smaller than in the square matrix that requires n^2 cells.

Nowadays, the Clos switching network [33] of the form $Q(p, q, r)$ is already classical. It contains three stages: $p \times q$, $r \times r$, and $q \times p$ with p, q, r modules,

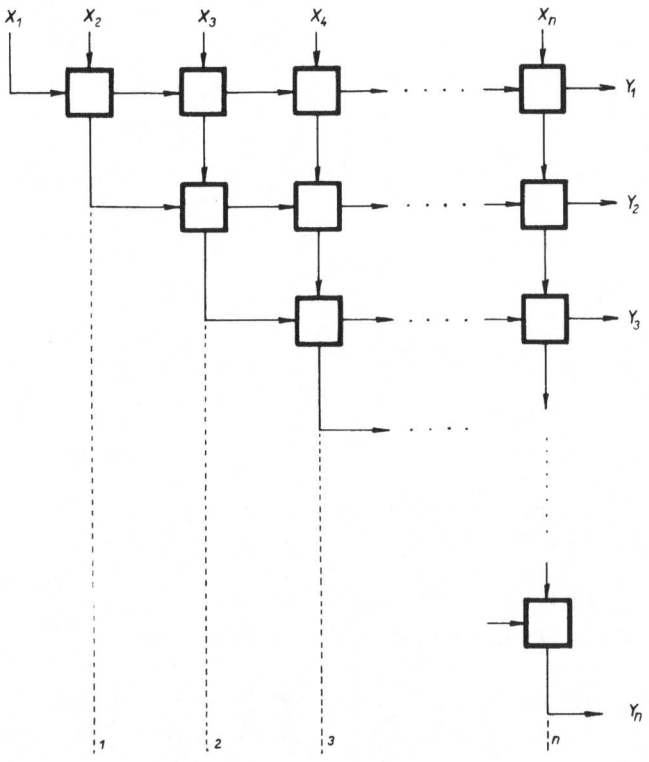

Fig. 37. Triangular Bosé—Nelson permutation array.

respectively, containing crossbar switches (Fig. 38). The network can be designed to be conflict-free. The Beneš network is derived from the Clos type network. For $Q(2, 2, 2^{n-1})$, the middle stage is replaced by $Q(2, 2, 2^{n-2})$ and this is repeated till all switches in the middle stage have size 2×2 [34—36]. This network has the same capacity as the crossbar switch, but it contains only $O(N \log N)$ gates for the $N \times N$ network. The transition time through the network is $O(\log N)$. The best known algorithm for the implementation of this arrangement (Opferman and Tsao-Wu [37]) requires $O(N \log N)$ units of time. This is too long for practical applications. Figure 39 shows the Beneš binary network $R^{(3)}$. It contains $(2n - 1)$ stages, each stage having 2^{n-1} switching modules. The switching module 2×2 can have only two states: "straight" and "exchange". This network can implement all permutations of the input vector onto the output vector without conflict.

Another possibility is the Batcher sorting network [38]. This requires $O(N \log N^2)$ gates and $O(\log N)^2$ units of time. This network is cheaper than the

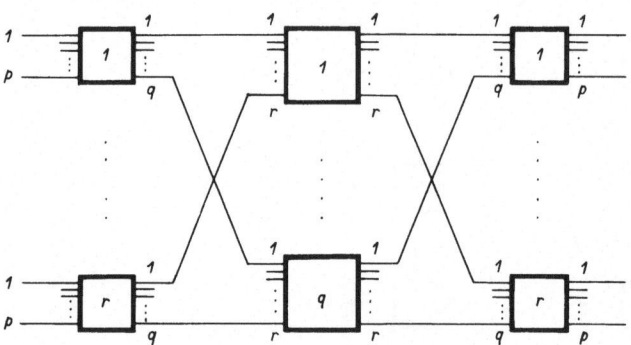

Fig. 38. Three-stage switching network by Clos.

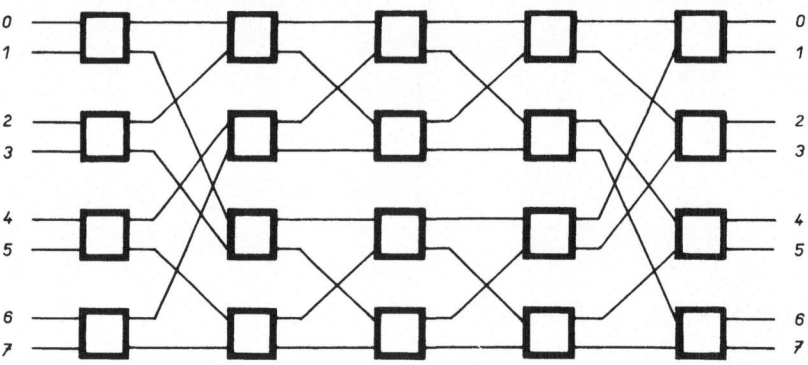

Fig. 39. Binary Beneš network $R^{(3)}$.

crossbar switch and faster than the Beneš network. Other networks suggested by Waksman [39], Thurber [40], Kautz [41], and Rohrbacher [42] can be adapted to our requirements. Currently important in parallel processing is the permutation called the perfect shuffle, which was designed by Stone [43]. Another set of switching networks, known as omega networks, was designed by Lawrie [44, 45]. A survey of a variety of interconnection networks for reconfigurable parallel processing systems described in the literature is presented in [46].

10.6.1 Omega networks

The omega network is understood interconnection network between the vector of elementary processors and the vector of memory modules. The omega network

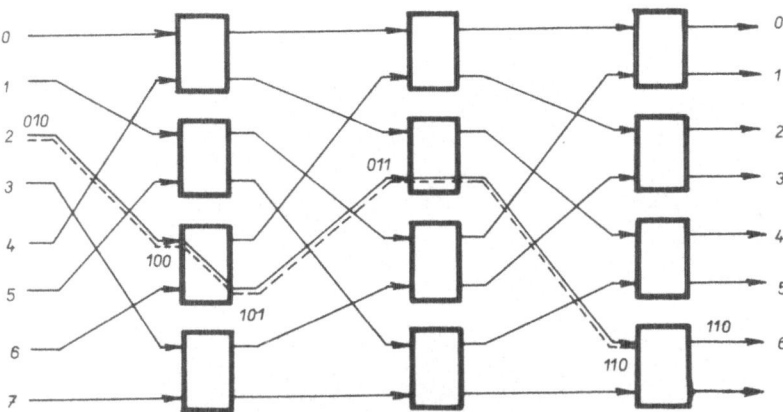

Fig. 40. 8 × 8 omega network with interconnection (010, 110).

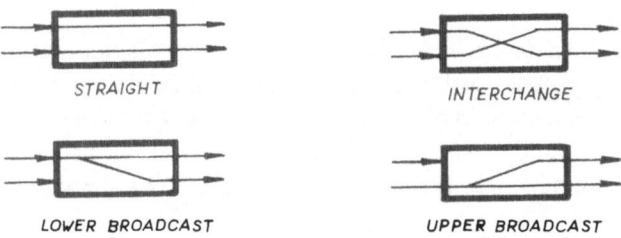

Fig. 41. Possible states of the switching cell 2 × 2.

is based on the concept of the mathematical expression of integers with omega base [47]. At the beginning we consider only networks $N \times N$, where N is a power of 2. The omega network $N \times N$ consists of $l = \log_2 N$ identical stages. Each stage consists of a perfect shuffle interconnection which is followed by $N/2$ switching elements. An example of 8×8 omega network is shown in Fig. 40.

Each switching element is in one of the four states shown in Fig. 41. The perfect shuffle [43, 48] interconnection shuffles a group of elements as in card shuffling where the element can be a word or a bit slice. The group of elements is divided into two subgroups, and the elements of these subgroups are rearranged so that the first elements of the first subgroup are output, followed by the elements of the second subgroup, etc. A perfect shuffle interconnection can take its input at the position whose binary representation is $s_1 s_2 \ldots s_l$ and swap it to the position $s_2 s_3 \ldots s_l s_1$. Then the switch can swap the output to $s_2 s_3 \ldots s_l 0$ or $s_2 s_3 \ldots s_l 1$, i.e. shuffling corresponds to a circular shift of the binary representation.

Two questions are raised in this respect. The first question is whether there exists

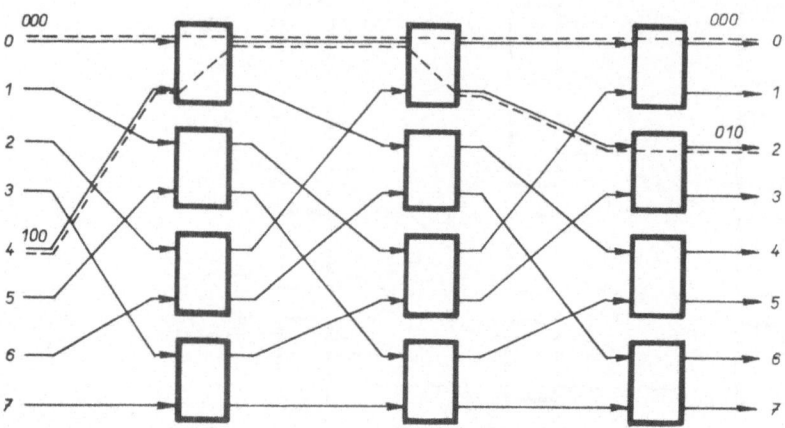

Fig. 42. Interconnection for (000, 000), (100, 010).

an algorithm which determines the necessary conditions for switching elements and which can be implemented in the same order of magnitude of time as the data require for passing through the network. The second question is, what types of input-output representations are possible. The first question concerns the existence of a fast control algorithm for the network, the second question is to be discussed only briefly here.

10.6.2 Omega network control

We show that there exists an effective algorithm for setting an omega network. First, we consider the interconnection of the input number S to the output number D. Examining Fig. 42, it is evident that there is one and only one path between the given input-output pair. Let $D = d_1 d_2 \ldots d_l$ be the determination tag, i.e. the binary representation of the output number to which the input number S can be connected, and let $S = s_1 s_2 \ldots s_l$ be the source tag, i.e. the binary representation of the input number. Beginning with the input S, the first switch to which S is connected is set so as to interconnect the input S to the upper output — if $d_1 = 0$, or to the lower output — if $d_1 = 1$. In Fig. 41, this is shown for $S = 010$, $D = 110$. Proceeding to the switch of the next stage, we again interconnect the input to the upper output — if $d_2 = 0$, or to the lower output — if $d_2 = 1$. In this way we continue interconnecting by d_i at every stage i until we obtain the output required. It can easily be seen that at any given stage i the input that has been switched to the position $s_i s_{i+1} \ldots s_l d_1 d_2 \ldots d_{i-1}$ goes through the perfect shuffle, terminates in the position $s_{i+1} s_{i+2} \ldots s_l d_1 d_2 \ldots d_{i-1} s_i$, and is then switched into the position $s_{i+1} s_{i+2} \ldots s_l d_1 d_2 \ldots d_{i-1} d_i$. Thus, after $l = \log_2 N$ operations the original input must be connected to output $d_1 d_2 \ldots d_l$. A similar algorithm can start at the output $d_1 d_2 \ldots d_l$ and work backwards through the network switching an element of stage i according to s_i. The procedure is complete in the sense that it can set any arbitrary representation that is possible in the network. We do not prove this formally (see [44, 45, 52]).

Since there exists one and only one path between any input and output, the set of paths for a given representation must be unique and this must be determined by an algorithm. But we note that the algorithm can specify sets of paths which cannot be implemented by the network. For example, Fig. 42 shows paths created for the mapping of $000 \rightarrow 000$, $100 \rightarrow 010$. These paths make use of a common connection at the output of the first stage. This condition, which is known as conflict, is not admissible, according to the definition, since it means that two different signals use one commom wire.

There are several ways of implementing omega networks, some of which are mentioned here briefly. In Fig. 43, there are 2×2 switching elements. An omega network can be constructed of elements larger than 2×2. For example, an omega network of size 8×8 can be constructed from 4×4, and 2×2 elements. Thus an omega network can be segmented according to the requirements of the architecture of the computer and according to the properties of the chips of a given LSI technology.

The use of permutation omega networks appears to be specially interesting in array and associative computers with a modular structure of processors and memories. The choice of $M = 2N$ for the number of memory modules appears to be optimal, where $N = 2^n$ is the number of processors. The wide class of permutations for processing matrices, submatrices and their slices allows such a system to operate without any conflicts. Also empty locations in memory modules can be used for another matrix or for the other half of the same matrix.

In conclusion, we may say that in SIMD and MIMD parallel computers, interconnection and permutation networks are a new component of their architecture. They are necessary for providing communication between processors and memory modules and for communication between processors and I/O devices.

Conclusion

A survey has been given of the architecture of parallel computer systems which, owing to the fast development of LSI and VLSI technologies, are now of practical importance. For complex scientific and technical calculations, it will be necessary to continue to develop large centralized supercomputers with speeds of 10^7 to 10^9 ops/s. The basis of these systems form parallel processors (pipeline, array or associative), or some combination of these.

The current fast development of microelectronics, LSI and VLSI technologies, is bringing with itself a reduction of the costs of logic circuits which are close to the costs of memory elements. It is therefore necessary to reconsider the concepts of von Neumann computer architecture, since the minimum number of logic elements does not necessarily lead to the minimum cost of the computer system, especially if software costs are also taken into account. The programming languages used at present are purely sequential which limits the possibilities of execution speed-up using parallelism.

The principle of sequential control of the computational process has remained, although highly parallel computer systems have been developed.

The von Neumann computer architecture cannot satisfy requirements of a modern computational technology. It appears that a complete replacement of all von Neumann's principles by a new system of principles which would provide a complete harmony between the computer structure and the program organization is actually the method proposed by Glushkov [49]. He has suggested new principles and the type of computer which he has called a recursive computer.

To solve the problems of artificial intelligence, pattern recognition, image processing, and scene analysis, specialized signal processors must be available which can process a large amount of data in real time. The most important operation here is the Fast Fourier Transformation (FFT). Of equal importance are also: The Inverse FFT (IFFT), convolution, correlation, "windowing", transmission function, etc. For these purposes, specialized problem-oriented parallel processors have been designed using pipelining [50].

Also specialized parallel processors have been designed for processing two-dimensional sets of data, such as binary images. The interactive image processors operating in real time, CLIP-3 and CLIP-4 (Cellular Logic Image Processor) [51] are examples of these. In addition to parallel processors of a centralized type, computer systems will be further developed for distributed processing, allowing the execution of computational and logical functions in geographically scattered physical localities with complete freedom of movement of data and programs. Distributed systems created from mini- and microprocessors, interconnected by data transfer channels, are advantageous in wide areas of data processing. Real time process control and data processing without any loss of data require the use of fault-tolerant computer systems.

From the point of view of the architecture of parallel processors and multicomputer systems, it is necessary to continue to work on hitherto not quite satisfactorily solved problems. In hardware these are: problems of connecting processors to memories, mutual interconnection of processors, implementation by hardware of synchronization primitives, addressing problems in virtual memory systems, cache memories, the need of local memory, processing of interrupts, queues, etc.

In software the following problems should be mentioned: communication between simultaneous activities, synchronization of parallel processes, deadlock prevention, scheduling of system resources, etc. These require software constructions such as: multiprocessor operating systems, reliability constructions, Petri networks, methods for preventing deadlock, processes and methods of synchronization, monitors (resource modules), critical areas and the like.

REFERENCES

[1] FLYNN, M. J.: Some computer organizations and their effectiveness. IEEE Trans. on Computers, *C-21*, 1972, 9, 948—960.

[2] NEUMAN, J., von: Collected Works. McMillan, New York, 1963.

[3] MILLER, E. F.: A multiple-stream registerless shared-resource processor. IEEE Trans. on Electronic Computers, *EC-23*, 1974, 3, 277—285.

[4] The Array Processor AP-120B. Floating Point Systems, Inc., Portland, OR 97223, USA.

[5] RAMAMOORTHY, C. V. and KIM, K. H.: Pipelining. The generalized concept and sequencing strategies. National Computer Conference 1974, pp. 289—297.

[6] HOCKNEY, R. W.: Super-computer architecture. In: Future Systems. Infotech. State of the Art Report International, 1977, Vol. 2, pp. 277—305.

[7] PURCELL, C. J.: The control data STAR-100-performance measurements. National Computer Conference, 1977, pp. 385—387.

[8] WATSON, W. J. and CARR, H. M.: Operational experience with the TI advanced scientific computer. National Computer Conference, 1974, pp. 389—397.

[9] SITES, R. L.: An analysis of the CRAY-1 computer. The 5th Annual Symposium on Computer Architecture. IEEE Press, 1968, pp. 101—106.

[10] SLOTNICK, D. L., BORCK, W. C. and MCREYNOLDS, R. C.: The SOLOMON computer. AFIPS Proc., FJCC, 22, 1962, 97—107.

[11] BARNES, J. H., BROWN, E. M., KATO, M., KUCK, D. J., SLOTNICK, D. L. and STOKES, R. A.: The ILLIAC IV COMPUTER. IEEE Trans. on Computers, *C-17*, 1968, 8, 746—757.

[12] RUDOLPH, J. A., FULMER, L. C. and MEILANDER, W. C.: The coming of age of the associative processor. Electronics, 1971, 2, 91—95.

[13] BATCHER, K. E.: STARAN parallel processor system hardware. National Computer Conference, 1974, pp. 405—410.

[14] BATCHER, K. E.: The flip network in STARAN. Proc. Int. Conf. on Parallel Processing, 1976, pp. 65—71.

[15] BATCHER, K. E.: The multidimensional access memory in STARAN. IEEE Trans. on Computer, *C-26*, 1977, 2, 174—177.

[16] WESLEY, M. A., CHANG, S. K. and HOMMENS, J. H.: A design for an auxiliary associative parallel processor. Fall Joint Computer Conf., 1972, pp. 461—472.

[17] OHMORI, K., KOIKE, N., NEZU, K. and SUZUKI, S.: MICS — a multi-microprocessor system. In: Information Processing 74. North-Holland Publ. Co., Amsterdam, 1974, pp. 98—102.

[18] ENSLOW, P. H.: Multiprocessors and Parallel Processing. J. Wiley, New York, 1974, pp. 255—273.

[19] LORIN, H.: Parallelism in Hardware and Software, Real and Apparent Concurrency. Englewood Clifs, Prentice Hall, 1971.

[20] DESPAIN, A. M. and PETTERSON, D. A.: X-tree: A tree structured multiprocessor computer architecture. The Annual Symp. on Computer Architecture, 1978, pp. 144—151.

[21] WULF, W. A. and BELL, C. G.: C mmp — a multi-miniprocessor. Fall Joint Computer Conf., 1972, pp. 765—777.

[22] GOSTELOW, A. and GOSTELOW, K. P.: A computer capable of exchanging processing elements for time. Tech. Report 77, Dep. Comp. Sci., University of California, Irvine, 1976.

[23] SWAN, R. J., FULLER, S. H. and SIEWIOREK, D. P.: The structure and architecture of Cm*A modular, multi-microprocessor. Computer Sci. Res. Rev., Carnegie-Mellon University, Pittsburgh 1976, pp. 25—46.

[24] BELL, C. G. and NEWELL, A.: The PMS and ISP descriptive systems for computer structures. Spring Joint Computer Conf. 1970, pp. 351—374.

[25] HEART, F. E. et al.: A new minicomputer/multiprocessor for the ARPA network. National Computer Conf. 1973, pp. 529—537.

[26] SHARMA, R. L., SHAN, J. C., EL-BARDAI, M. T. and SHARMA, K. K.: C-System: Multiprocessor network architecture. In: Information Processing 74. North-Holland Publ. Co., Amsterdam, 1974, pp. 19—23.

[27] KOCZOLA, L. J.: The distributed processor organization. In: Advances in Computers, Vol. 9. F. L. Alt and M. Rubinoff (Editors). Academic Press, New York, 1968, pp. 285—353.

[28] PLANDER, I.: The reliability of a hierarchic multicomputer system for real time direct industrial process control. Proc. IFIP Congress 71, Ljubljana 1971. North-Holland Publ. Co., Amsterdam 1972, pp. 1168—1173.

[29] BOGOMOLOV, A. A. and TVERDOKHLEBOV, V. A.: Diagnostika slozhnykh sistem. Izd. Naukova dumka, Kiev, 1974.

[30] HOPKINS, A. L., JR.: A fault-tolerant information processing concept for space vehicles. IEEE Trans. on Computers, C-20, 1971, 11, 1394—1403.

[31] AVIZIENIS, A. et al.: The STAR (Self-Testing-And-Repairing) computer: An investigation of the theory and practice of fault-tolerant computer design. IEEE Trans. on Computers, C-20, 1971, 11, 1312—1321.

[32] KAUTZ, W. H. et al.: Cellular interconnection arrays. IEEE Trans. on Computers, C-17, 1968, 5, 443—451.

[33] CLOS, C.: A study of non-blocking switching networks. Bell System Tech. J., 32, 1953, 3, 406—424.

[34] LANG, T. and STONE, H. S.: A shuffle-exchange network with simplified control. IEEE Trans. on Computers, C-25, 1976, 5, 496—503.

[35] LENFANT, J.: Parallel permutations of data: A Benes network control algorithm for frequently used permutations. IEEE Trans. on Computers, C-27, 1978, 7, 637—647.

[36] BENES, V. E.: Mathematical Theory of Convecting Networks and Telephone Traffic. Academic Press, New York, 1965.

[37] OPFERMAN, D. C. and TSAO-WU, N. T.: On a class of rearrangeable switching networks. Bell System Tech. J., 50, 1971, 5—6, 1579—1618.

[38] BATCHER, K. E.: Sorting networks and their applications. Proc. 1968 Spring Joint Computer Conf., AFIPS Press, 1968, pp. 307—314.

[39] WAKSMAN, A.: A permutation network. J. ACM, 15, 1968, 1, 159—163.

[40] THURBER, K. J.: Programmable indexing networks. Proc. 1970 Spring Joint Computer Conf., AFIPS Conf. Proc., Vol. 36. AFIPS Press 1970, pp. 51—58.

[41] KAUTZ, W. H., LEVIT, K. N. and WAKSMAN, A.: Cellular interconnection arrays. IEEE Trans. on Computers, C-17, 1968, 5. 443—451.

[42] ROHRBACHER, D. and POTTER, J. L.: Image processing with the STARAN parallel computer. Computer, *10*, 1977, 8, 54—59.

[43] STONE, H. S.: Parallel processing with perfect shuffle. IEEE Trans. on Computers, *C-20*, 1971, 2, 153—161.

[44] LAWRIE, D. H.: Memory processor connection networks. Tech. Report 557, Dep. Comp. Sci., University of Illinois, Urbana, 1973.

[45] LAWRIE, D. H.: Access and alignment of data in an array processor. IEEE Trans. on Computers, *C-24*, 1975, 12, 1145—1155.

[46] SPIEGEL, H. J., MCMILLEN, R. J. and MUELLER, P. T., JR.: A survey of interconnection methods for reconfigurable parallel processing systems. Proc. 1979 National Computer Conf., pp. 529—542.

[47] VINOGRADOV, I. M.: Osnovy teorii chisel. Izd. Nauka, Moscow, 1972.

[48] PEASE, M. C.: An adaption of the fast Fourier transform for parallel processing. J. ACM, *15*, 1968, 4, 252—264.

[49] GLUSHKOV, V. M., IGNATIEV, M. B. and MYASNIKOV, V. A.: Recursive machines and computing technology. In: Information Processing 74. North-Holland Publ. Co., Amsterdam, 1974, pp. 65—70.

[50] AISO, H., TOKORO, M., UCHIDA, S. et al.: A very high-speed microprogrammable pipeline signal processor. In: Information Processing 74. North-Holland Publ. Co., Amsterdam, 1974, pp. 60—64.

[51] DUFF, M. J. B., WATSON, D. M. and DEUTSCH, E. S.: A parallel computer for array processing. In: Information Processing 74. North-Holland Publ. Co., Amsterdam, 1974, pp. 94—97.

[52] PLANDER, I.: Parallel and problem-oriented processors for artificial intelligence and robotics. Počítače a umelá inteligencia, *1*, 1982, 1, 7—33.

Chapter 11

DATA FLOW COMPUTER ARCHITECTURE

11.1 Introduction

One of the main objectives in the development of computer systems architecture has been to achieve the highest possible speed and throughput. This objective was and still is obtained in two ways — by exploiting technological possibilities in the design of the computer components, and by a suitable structure and organization of the computer. The advance of computer components is very fast due to technological progress in the production of integrated circuits, where the speed and density of the components increase constantly, while the costs decrease. Increase in speed and density is not unlimited, for it has ultimate physical limits. The other method of increasing speed — improving the organization of computers — leads to the design of parallel architectures of computers. The present state of technology makes it possible to use a large number of moderately priced LSI circuits to produce distributed parallel computer systems. However, the fact that this possibility exists does not mean that designers of computer systems can make full use of it. Despite the large number of designs of various parallel architectures based on microprocessors or other LSI circuits, it can be said that technology is advancing so fast that advances in computer architecture lag behind the development of circuitry. It is the task of computer architects not only to be able to make use of existing LSI circuits, but also to influence actively their design, so that efficient computers can be based on them.

The attempt to produce parallel computer architecture with high speed and throughput is motivated by the requirement to solve large problems, mostly of parallel character, such as pattern recognition, signal and image processing, problems of artificial intelligence, nuclear physics, weather forecasting, air traffic control, control of production processes, many of which should be solved in real time. In the design of parallel systems, it is important to concentrate on simultaneous execution of as many functions as possible. Treleaven [38] has identified 6 levels of parallelism that are provided by program languages: parallelism can occur at the level of:

1. program — independent programs (multiprogramming),
2. procedure — procedures within a program,
3. statement — statements within a procedure or program,

4. arithmetic — address calculation and operand calculation can frequently be overlapped,

5. operator — separate operations within a statement,

6. pipeline — overlapping of the execution of a series of individual operation phases.

Additional types of parallelism can be derived from the structure of the data — the execution of calculations in bit slices over vectors or matrices, or from the character of the algorithm — dynamic parallelism [25], or from the technology of a computer, e.g. parallel addition or multiplication. It is to be expected that the more levels of parallelism a systems exploits, the more efficient it will be. It appears that the hypothesis of Gurd and Treleaven [25] is true: "Intuitively, any computer architecture or language that provides a mechanism for operator level parallelism should support the higher levels. Thus it is necessary to start the exploitation of parallelism at the lowest levels". Existing parallel computers make use of various levels of parallelism, but seldom of more than one, or two. In SISD systems, it is "look-ahead" techniques, in SIMD systems, it is processing by bit slices of vectors or matrices (associative and matrix computers), or pipeline performance of calculations. In MIMD systems, separate programs, or blocks and procedures, are processing in parallel (multiprocessors). Systems based on iterative arrays represent a special type. Many of the above systems have achieved a high performance through their parallelism, but very often only for restricted class of problems.

For instance, ILLIAC IV and associative computers, e.g. STARAN, have a very high performance, of the order of 10^2 MIPS, for data that have a suitable structure for SIMD processing, large systems of vectors on which the same operation is carried out simultaneously. Their efficiency to solve problems where the data structure is not so regular drops rapidly, even though they are naturally parallel. These computers are completely ineffective for processing serial problems. Another substantial drawback is the great dependence of the performance of these computers on the method of programming the problem. The programmer has to know the inner structure of the computer to be able to make use of its parallelism and he must himself identify the parallelism in the problem or use a special program to do this. Because of problems in programming, especially when programs written in an existing programming language are to be used, progress in the development of systems with iterative arrays is slow, though these are based on principles which make it possible to take advantage of many levels of parallelism.

In multiprocessor systems, such as C mmp, there are problems with large and complicated interconnection networks which connect the processors and the memory modules and also with the distribution of tasks and synchronization, but in spite of this they are systems which effectively utilize several levels of parallelism.

Many authors [2, 5, 17, 19, 25, 30, 37, 42] have arrived at the conclusion that the central problem in the utilization of parallelism is the basic model for expressing and describing parallelism. Von Neumann's model of computation appears to be unsuitable in this respect, for it is a serial model. Surprisingly, all conventional programming languages and existing computer architectures, either SISD, SIMD or MIMD, are based on this very model of computation. Owing to the serial nature of programming languages, the expression of parallelism in them is troublesome and laborious. The serial nature of von Neumann's model and the problems resulting from it are the main obstacle in utilizing parallelism in the architecture of parallel computer systems processing programs written in conventional high-level languages. Thus, it is necessary first to create a model of a computer system, which would make it possible to express the natural parallelisms of algorithms.

One such model is the data flow model of computation, sometimes referred to as a data-driven system. Closely related is work on the utilization of the principle of single assignment for expressing parallelism.

Work in the field of data flow started approximately 12 years ago. The first work was concerned with questions of parallel models and programming languages, and it can be said that quite a lot has been done in this area. Studies on the principle of data flow [4, 6—8, 15—17, 26, 29, 35, 39] and on the principle of single assignment [9, 10, 12, 23, 32] were later taken up by projects on data flow computer architectures, either as theoretical models [2, 5, 25, 30, 35, 38], projects for practical implementations [11—14, 18, 19, 27, 33] or papers dealing with some additional questions of the organization of data flow computation, performance evaluation, field of application, etc. [1, 3, 20—22, 28, 36]. The growing number of current papers about data flow problems show the increasing interest in the utilization of this principle in the creation of parallel computer systems.

11.2 The data flow model of computation

What are the differences between the data flow model (DF) of computation and the conventional von Neumann's (Control flow, CF) model of computation?

In principle, the difference lies in that what is decisive in the process of computation in the individual models:
— in the CF — it is the sequence of instructions,
— in the DF — it is the availability of data.
In conventional CF computer, the program is stored in memory as a serial sequence of instructions. The program is executed by fetching successive instructions from memory and executing them in the processor. Thus, the course of computation is given by the sequence of instructions in the program — i.e. by the flow of control in the program. It is not possible to execute any instruction until all previous instructions in the program have been executed. If the required operands are available, there may exist in the program instructions that could be executed

already, but these instructions are not executed until their turn comes in the program. This is the main obstacle in the utilization of the natural parallelism of algorithms.

In DF computer, the course of computation is controlled by the flow of data in the program. An instruction can be executed only when all operands are available, i.e. when the instruction is complete. These operands can be fetched as input data or are the product of preceding instructions in the program. Whether an instruction precedes another depends here exclusively on the natural structure of the algorithm being performed and it does not depend on the location of the instructions in memory. Using this method of computation, it is possible to carry out in parallel as many instructions as the given computer can execute simultaneously. After executing the instruction, the result is distributed to all subsequent instructions which make use of this partial result as an operand.

In this way, the DF model of computation exploits in a simple manner the natural parallelism of algorithms. In computer architecture, this makes it possible to create systems which can dynamically adapt their inner configuration to the natural structure of the algorithm being performed.

The principle of the DF model of computation is to be best explained on a concrete example. The data flow program is well represented by a directed graph, which can be regarded as a simplified DF language. The nodes of the graph represent operators — program instructions — and the arc represents uni-directional data paths by which partial results are transferred in the program.

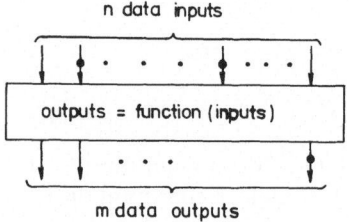

Fig. 1. A symbolic representation of data flow computation.

In general, it is possible to represent the execution of an instruction as a function over n inputs with m outputs, as shown in Fig. 1. A black dot on the data path represents the presence of an appropriate operand or a partial result. An instruction can be executed only when all inputs contain operands. The operator "consumes" its inputs and releases a set of results onto the output paths.

In almost every useable programming language, it is possible to work with a restricted number of instructions. Most data flow languages are limited to two fundamental types of instructions — combinative and separative — with number of inputs and outputs equal to one or two (Fig. 2).

Combinative instructions have two inputs and one output. The output value is a function of the input values. This operator can execute either simple functions, such as addition, OR, AND, etc., or complex functions, such as multiplication, division, or even an entire procedure.

Separative instructions produce two copies of the input data that can be of different types.

Data paths represent the flow of data from one instruction to the next. This is the communication system of the engineering implementation. This communication system can be a simple bus system, but it can also store data in memory using a FIFO (first-in-first-out) system.

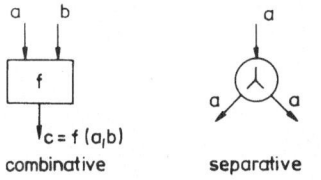

combinative   separative

Fig. 2. The basic types of data flow operators.

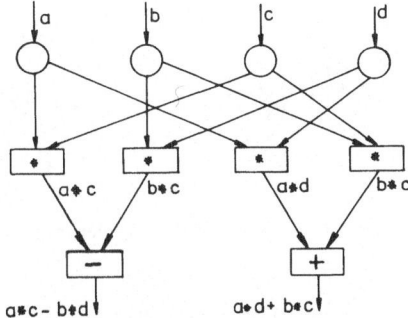

Fig. 3. Simple data flow program to multiply two complex numbers $(a + bi)*(c + di)$.

As an illustration of DF computation, the execution of a simple program that simulates the multiplication of two complex numbers is shown (Fig. 3). Figure 4 illustrates the execution of this complex multiplication program on a DF computer: 4.1 — state before the beginning of computation: all operands are present and the inputs of the four functions are loaded; 4.2 — state after the first cycle: copies of single operands have been produced and distributed to the operators which will use them; 4.3 — state after the second cycle: the partial products ad, bc, ac, bd have been produced and distributed to the next operators; 4.4 — state after the third cycle: the addition of ad to bc and subtraction of bd from ac have been executed; these two outputs form the complex result.

The state of computation is represented by dots on the data paths, representing tokens, which correspond to either input variables or partial results. By means of these tokens, it is possible to represent the dynamics of the computation. But token is a more comprehensive term:

Token — is the value of a variable on the data path which represents the current result of the operation that has been performed by the preceding operator.
A token can contain two types of data:
the data — one or several operands which can be of different types: integer,

real, Boolean, string, but also more complicated data structures, even complete procedures which can be illustrated by a separate data flow graph; control data — the operation code, addresses of results, flags, program code, iteration number, etc. The real contents and format of a token depend on the concrete DF program language and on the architecture of the computer.

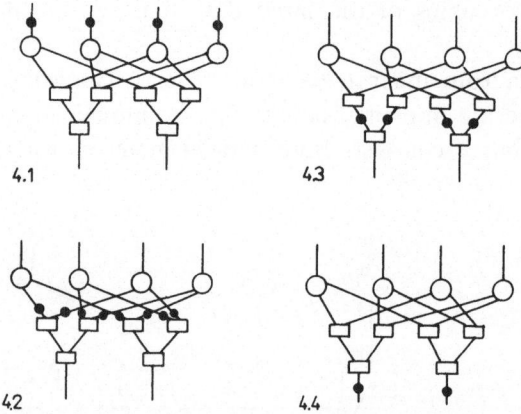

Fig. 4. The execution of the complex multiply program.

A token is a complete independent unit. In principle, it normally contains the data and not addresses in memory. It does not contain any references to other tokens and common units of the computer. Various authors give different definitions of the token, but the differences are not considered important here.

The token is used mainly as a means of representing the dynamics of computation of a DF program written in graphic DF language. It is less frequently used in the description of the architecture and function of the DF computer and is replaced by other terms, as we shall see later.

Thus a token says:

WHAT should be done — a token contains the operation code.

WHERE the result should be delivered — a token contains the address where the result has to be delivered. This mechanism ensures the continuity of the program.

WHEN a computation has to be executed — a method for synchronization. The computation is executed only when a token on the input of the operator is complete.

WITH WHAT the computation has to be executed — a token contains operands on which the given instruction will be executed.

The operator can be in the following states (Fig. 5):

— idle — the given operator has at most one token (combinative) or no token (separative), on the input and no token on the output;

— enabled — all required input tokens are present and it is ready to execute the function;

— active — it executes the function;

— generating — it generates the result, a new token, and sends it to the next operator.

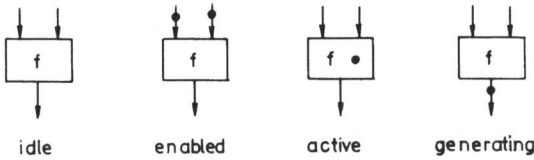

idle   enabled   active   generating

Fig. 5. The possible states of data flow operator.

In the literature, two possible implementations have hitherto been mentioned:

— the operator must not pass from the enabled state to the active state while there is a previous token on its output;

— the operator can pass from the enabled state to the active state irrespective of whether there is one or even several previous tokens on its output. Thus, queues of tokens can be present on data paths.

The question of generating queues on data paths is the key question for DF program languages, the architecture of DF computers and the organization of actions in DF computers. In the first case, when the operator has to wait until its output has been cleared, it is necessary for the processor representing the given operator to inform the preceding processors (operators) that it has executed its current computation, i.e. that it has consumed the token. The first studies in the field of DF [17, 18, 29] are based on this principle. The action of such a computer is based on a feedback interpreter FI [1, 5]. An action where the operator can generate tokens independently of whether the preceding tokens have already been consumed is based on a non-feedback interpreter, NFI [1, 5]. This action assumes the possibility of storing a series of partial results, corresponding to the tokens, during the transition from one operator to another. The memory, as a rule, works on the FIFO principle. The designs in which there are NFI-type actions are described in [1—5, 9, 14, 25, 33, 37]. There also exists an extension of the above concept, in which a series of generated tokens is not stored in the FIFO system, but can be fetched from the queue in an arbitrary order, i.e. single tokens can "jump the queue", which allows a speedup of computation by better utilization of various levels of parallelism. The most elaborate treatment of this problem is to be found in the works of Arvind and Gostelow [1—5], who also have coined the terms: feedback interpreter, non-feedback interpreter and later the terms queued interpreter and unravelling interpreter [5].

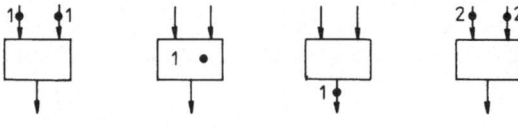

Fig. 6. The execution of computation under feedback interpreter.

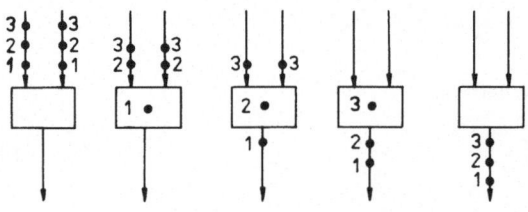

Fig. 7. The execution of computation under non-feedback interpreter with the FIFO queueing of tokens.

The data path can be in the following states:

— loaded — FI: one and only one token is present on it, — NFI: one or more tokens are present on it,

— unloaded — no token is present on it.

For a better illustration of behaviour under FI and NFI, the following three examples are given:

Figure 6 shows the course of computation under FI.

Figure 7 shows the course of computation under NFI together with FIFO queuing of tokens on data paths.

Figure 8 shows the course of computation under NFI together with arbitrary queuing of tokens on data paths.

In the second cycle (Fig. 8) there occurs simultaneous processing of two tokens. This does not mean that in the computer they are processed by the same processor simultaneously, but rather that they are processed by two different processors at the same time. Token 2 can be overtaken by token 3 for various reasons. For instance, the processor can be specialized in processing particular data structures and the data in token 3 can be processed most rapidly, or the volume of data in the tokens can be different. It must be emphasized that token structure can be quite complex.

The data flow model of computation is closely associated with the principle of single assignment (SA), which leads to the design of DF-type architectures [9—14, 23, 28, 32].

The essential concepts in the SA principle are the variable and how it is used in the program. In traditional computer systems one memory location is assigned to each variable.

Different values can be assigned to a variable during the computation, thus various values of the same variable can occur in the memory location at different

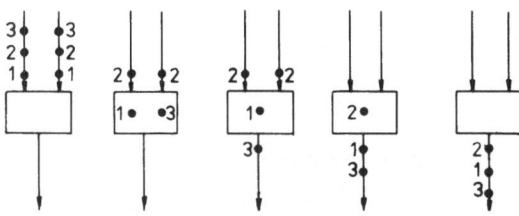

Fig. 8. The execution of computation under non-feedback interpreter with an arbitrary queueing of tokens.

times. Therefore, when a variable is accessed by an instruction, the access time is significant as well as the variable identifier.

In the application of the principle of single assignment the following rule holds true for the variable: a variable may take a single value during computation (and in the iterative computations it holds for one iterative level). For storing a variable in the memory it means that during the use of one variable in the program there exist two periods:

— in the first period one location is reserved for it in the memory, but it has not acquired a value; thus it cannot be read from the memory, but its value can be written,

— in the second period the variable has already taken the value and has been written in the reserved memory location; it can be read many times arbitrarily, but it cannot be changed any more — consequently no entry can be made in this memory location any more.

11.3 Data flow programming

The research into problems of parallel processing of data in the computer and into the representation of parallelism in programming languages has led to the creation of data-flow program languages. Since the purpose of this contribution is to deal with the architecture of DF computers, the DF programming will be given in brief only.

Data-flow languages can have graphical or lexical forms. They can be at the level of high-level programming languages, but also at that of machine languages. Program writing in the DF graphical language is similar to that given in the examples in Figs. 3 and 4. Works on DF languages were the first works in the field of DF.

The most elaborate DF programming languages are those of Dennis [16, 17] and Kosinsky [29]. Others are described in [7, 8, 15, 37]. Some of these languages have also a defined lexical form. This, as a rule, leads to a single assignment language. There are also programming languages based on the principle of single assignment, which have not evolved from graphical DF languages, but have been created as independent programming languages. Most elaborate is the language LAU [9, 10, 12, 23, 32], for which there is practical experience of its application.

DF languages have several noteworthy properties:

— the program writing is clear and in the same way it is possible to write a "high level" as well as a "low level" program;

— DF programs express in a simple manner the natural parallelism of algorithms allow the exploitation of parallelism at different levels;

— it seems to be possible to translate simply from existing high-level programming languages into a DF language [42]. It allows one to use existing programs and to make use of results in DF programming that have been obtained by traditional programming.

The problem of DF languages is dealt with in more detail by Kotov in this book.

One of the most important problems which has to be dealt with and which has great influence on the utilization of parallelism are data structures in DF programming languages. This problem is dealt with in [28, 35] as well as in the publications mentioned above.

11.4 Basic models of data flow systems

Miller and Cocke [30] have designed two models of computer systems which they have called as follows:

— search mode configurable computer (SM),

— interconnection mode configurable computer (IM).

These two models can be considered as basic models of DF computer architecture. The fundamental models are sufficiently general to derive various concrete systems by different implementations of control units, functional units and communication systems. It is also possible to consider these basic models as extreme types and in a particular implementation create a hybrid system by using the principles of SM and IM models at different hierarchical levels of a computer system.

The most characteristic property of both models is the possibility of dynamic reconfigurability of the computer structure to process the task — the DF program — as effectively as possible. The computer adapts dynamically its configuration to the structure of the algorithm. This is done by interconnecting (according to the graph) the processors that correspond to the operators in the DF program of the problem. In the IM type, the interconnection of processors is actually implemented through a large switch — reconfigurability by hardware means. In the SM type, the interconnection of processors is simulated by using a special instruction format — reconfigurability by software means.

Owing to its reconfigurability, the DF computer is potentially able to achieve the same performance as a specialized system, while keeping its general purpose capabilities.

11.4.1 Data flow architecture of search mode type

The search mode type computer (Fig. 9) consists of a memory, a functional unit, and a control unit that has been called "a searcher" by the authors. The functional unit is composed of a certain number of processors, e.g. a network of microprocessors which can be similar, or some processors can be specialized. A searcher is a specialized unit for generating tasks for processors which belong to the functional unit. The memory can have a different structure and it frequently consists of a set of different specialized blocks. Apart from the individual features of different architectures, there are two possible types of memories:

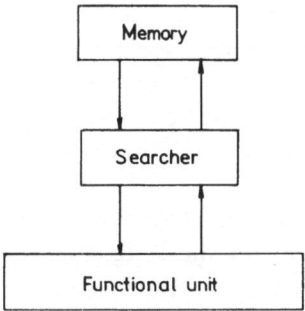

Fig. 9. Search mode configurable computer.

— memory where both data and instructions are stored,
— memory with separate storage of data and instructions.

A free processor asks the searcher for a task. The searcher finds a suitable task in memory or composes it from various components stored in different parts of the memory and sends it to the selected processor in the functional unit for execution. Adders, multipliers, conditional testers, macrooperation (specialized) modules, Boolean processors, I/O processors, universal microprocessors, etc. can serve as processors. The performance of a computer will depend on the type and number of processors, on memory speed, but mainly on the throughput of the searcher which the effective utilization of the processors is largely dependent on. The searcher performs more than a half of the work necessary in traditional computers for the execution of an instruction, by composing tasks that already contain data.

For a more detailed description of the operation, it is necessary to describe a typical instruction format, called executable instruction — EI. An instruction format for executing an operation on two operands is shown in Fig. 10. The name

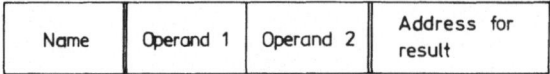

Fig. 10. Format of an executable instruction in an SM computer.

and the address of the result constitute the control part of the instruction and the operands are the data part. The name contains the operation code, the name of the program and other data needed for synchronization, information on the states of computation, flags, etc. Operand fields contain operands (in principle their values, though in some cases, they can also be addresses of the operands in memory), and the address field for the result contains the address of the location where the result is to be delivered to after the execution of the computation. These can be main memory addresses, addresses in scratch-pad memory, address of the next processor, etc. Thus an executable instruction contains all the information needed to execute the instruction and store the result in a selected location. The instruction can be stored in memory in this form, but it can also be generated in this form in the searcher. This mechanism ensures the "logical interconnection" of individual operators in the program and the continuity of the program.

Immediately after the execution of one EI, the processor involved is ready to process another EI — it reports to the searcher and asks for the assignment of a new EI. Thus, the speed of processing an algorithm is dependent on the availability of operands and on the data flow in the algorithm. Consequently, the computation is executed in parallel to such an extent which is allowed by the availability of the data required for the execution of instructions. Thus computation is dependent on the data flow. This mechanism for computer activity ensures the automatic synchronization of computation between all operands of the program. Each EI can be processed at the moment when its input operands are available, but if a processor is not free at this moment, the synchronization of the computation is not lost. Moreover, instructions can be processed in an arbitrary order — the only condition for EI processing is the presence of operands. This property is very promising in designing a parallel computer, since it allows the exploitation of the natural parallelism of tasks as well as good memory utilization, because both the instruction and the data can be arbitrarily distributed in memory.

What is the connection between the terms "token" and "executable instruction"? A token is mainly employed to represent the computation dynamics in the DF program written in the form of a graph; EI is the term used in describing the activity of the DF computer. An example is the best means to elucidate the relationship between the two terms. Figure 11a shows the execution of a function f over operands a and b as it has been represented in the program. In Fig. 11b it is

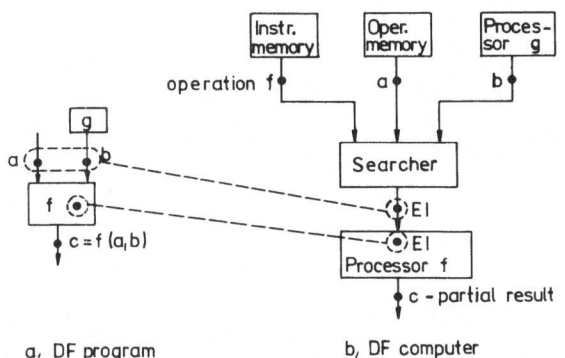

Fig. 11. The connection between tokens and executable instructions (EI).

a, DF program   b, DF computer

shown how an execution of the operation may lead to the generation of the instruction EI and produce the result in the computer. Without loss of generality we assume that operands and instructions are stored in memory separately, that operand b is produced by the processor which corresponds to operator g, and that a stored in is operand memory. It can be seen from Fig. 11 that EI is equivalent to a token when the token is in the operator (Fig. 11a), i.e. when the operator is in active state. EI is also equivalent to the set of tokens a and b when these are on the input of the operator, i.e. when the operator is in enabled state.

11.4.2 Data flow architecture of interconnection mode

As for the SM computer, a computer of IM type can be reconfigured to adapt as much as possible to the algorithm being executed. In the IM computer, reconfiguration is more straightforward — by actual interconnection of processors to form the structure of the algorithm being executed, or part of it. A switch, an interconnection network that executes this function, is the characteristic part of the IM computer (Fig. 12). The switch provides a direct connection between the outputs of one group of processors and the inputs of the next group of processors and it creates a network of processors corresponding to the DF program being executed. As a rule, a set of processors is not sufficient to create a computation structure which can execute the whole program at one time. Thus it is necessary to divide the DF program into blocks of suitable size with respect to the number of processors available at a given time. This is done by a compiler which determines the interconnection of processors, so that the computation structure created corresponds to the graph of the DF program or some part of it. This interconnection is encoded and stored in memory as a set-up instruction for the switch. This set-up instruction is fetched first and sent to a set-up control which does the interconnection of the processors. In this way, the computation structure is ready to

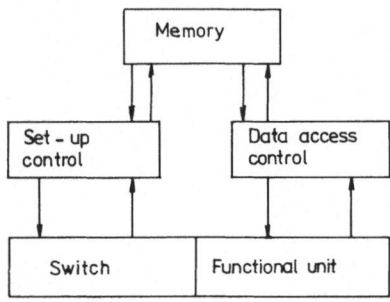

Fig. 12. Interconnection mode configurable computer.

execute the computation of a block of the program, and this is started. The operands and partial results from the computations of preceding blocks are taken from memory via data access control before starting the computation. During the execution of the block, it is not necessary to fetch any instruction and data from the memory, which reduces the load on the data path and the memory. Loops in the block are implemented by direct interconnection of processors. After processing a block, the processors involved and a part of the switch are released and can be used for setting up the structure for another block. In this way, the IM computer appears to be specialized during the processing of one block. It is clear that another block can be set up before the termination of the preceding block, and that individual processors can be released as soon as they have finished their activity in the relevant block, which may occur much sooner than the computation of the whole block is terminated.

11.5 Some architectures of DF computers

11.5.1 Architecture of the data flow computer of Dennis and Misunas

One of the first data flow computers was introduced by Dennis and Misunas [18, 19]. This processor, which they called Elementary DF Processor, has a very simple structure of SM type. It is a specialized processor for some parallel algorithms for signal processing. Programs for the Elementary DF Processor are written in the Elementary DF Language which is relatively simple. It is not possible to implement loops and conditional jumps in it. The next stage was the design of a more universal processor — the Basic DF Processor [19]. This extends the possibilities of its predecessor and is intended for processing programs in a richer language, in the Data Flow Basic Language [17]. This work is only a further step

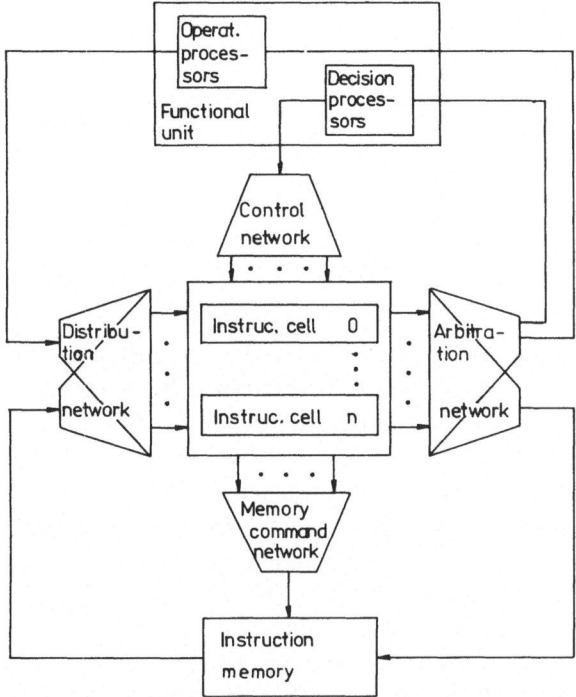

Fig. 13. The basic DF processor of Dennis and Misunas.

towards the final goal, as the authors say. The final goal is to design a universal computer which would process programs in a DF high-level language — having the level of **FORTRAN, ALGOL,** for example.

In the next section we describe the organization of the Basic DF Processor (Fig. 13). This processor is of SM type. Likewise the basic model of the SM computer (Fig. 9), also the Basic DF Processor consists of a functional unit, a searcher, and a memory. The functional unit is divided into two parts — operative and control. Each of them consists of a set of elementary processors, which can be universal or specialized. The searcher is divided into three parts — the arbitration network, the distribution network, and the control network. The memory, which contains a DF program, is organized into a set of instruction cells, each of which belongs to one operator in the program. An instruction cell (Fig. 14) consists of three registers. It contains an instruction whose format is similar to that shown in Fig. 10. When an instruction is complete, i.e. when the instruction code and all additional control data are present in the first register, and there are operands in the second and third registers, it is sent as an executable instruction through the arbitration network to a free operation or decision processor — depending on

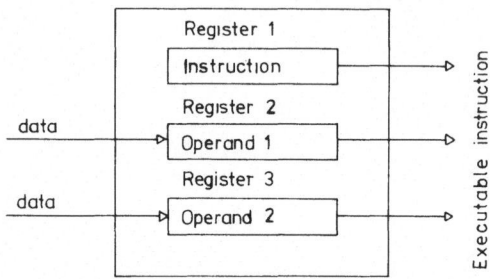

Fig. 14. An instruction cell in the memory of the basic DF processor.

whether this is a computation or decision instruction. After execution of the instruction, the results are sent to the appropriate instruction cells in memory. Their addresses have already been supplied in the EI, they are in the first register where they belong to the control data. The results of the execution of one instruction are operands for one or more subsequent instructions of the program being processed. After the completion of the next instruction, i.e. after the instructions which generate operands for the next instruction have been executed and operands written to the appropriate registers in the instruction cell, another EI is ready for computation. This waits until some operations or decision processors are released. Then, the EI is sent to be processed and the whole process starts again. The number of elements in a functional unit — either operation or decision processors — is considerably smaller than the number of instruction cells in the memory. Many instruction cells can contain complete executable instructions simultaneously and these are transferred into the arbitration network. The task of the arbitration network is to deliver EI's to free processors. If no free processors are available, the decision unit has to place complete EI's in a queue. Since the decision unit has many inputs, the EI flow will be greater at the output than at the input. For this reason, it is convenient to use serial representation of EI's at the input and parallel representation at the output. There is a similar situation in the distribution network, where it is possible to use serial representation of data at the output and parallel representation of data at the input. In this way, the number of transmission paths to memory is minimized but a high throughput is maintained. The original Elementary Processor which was intended for use in signal processing acted in such a way that every instruction cell entered the computation with approximately the same frequency, but with different data, and thus it could manage with a one-level memory — it contained only a set of instruction cells. This does not hold for the Basic Processor. It would be very inefficient to have only one instruction cell reserved for each instruction of the program during the entire time of execution. For this reason, a two-level hierarchy of memory has been designed consisting of two parts, an instruction memory and a set of instruction cells (Fig. 13). The single instructions are moved from the instruction memory for execution. The instructions are stored in the instruction memory when the instruction cells in which they are stored are needed for instructions to be executed earlier.

With this organization, the set of instruction cells creates a cache memory. An associative memory in the set of instruction cells is used for the fast manipulation of data. Further enrichment of the Dennis language, especially the possibility of handling more complex data structures led to further development of the architecture of the DF computer and extension of its application areas. One application is described in [20].

11.5.2 Architecture of the data flow Rumbaugh computer

Rumbaugh has designed a DF multiprocessor which is intended for the execution of programs in the DF language. The Rumbaugh DF language is a modification of the Dennis Basic DF Language (Data Flow Basic Language) [17]. Rumbaugh indicates that the DF multiprocessor is a conceptual model of a new type of computer architecture but does not inted to implement this design in hardware. Activity in the Rumbaugh DF multiprocessor is in accordance with a feedback interpreter. There is no possibility of generating queues of tokens in the computer. The architecture of the DF multiprocessor has a two-level hierarchy.

A token in the Rumbaugh DF language can contain simple data, integer, floating-point, Boolean, etc., but it can also contain DF structures and procedures. The term DF structure is used by the author for a list of elements which can be simple data or simple DF structures. A procedure is defined as any DF program containing no tokens. A token, which contains simple data, is here used instead of the term EI and has a similar format to that shown in Fig. 10. These tokens are processed at a lower level in the hierarchy of the DF multiprocessor. It is the function of the higher level in the hierarchy of the computer to divide a program and complex DF structure, which can be contained in one token, into smaller blocks and assign these to processors at a lower level for processing.

In the Rumbaugh modification of the Dennis DF Language, there are two operators which must be mentioned: **SWITCH** and **UNION** operators. The **SWITCH** operator (Fig. 15) has one set of inputs for data tokens, one control input for the control token and two sets (true, false) of outputs for data tokens. The number of outputs in both sets is equal to the number of inputs. If tokens are present at all inputs, each token is transferred from the input to the corresponding output according to that whether the control token is true or false. In Fig. 15 a situation is shown for a true control token. The **UNION** operator (Fig. 16) has

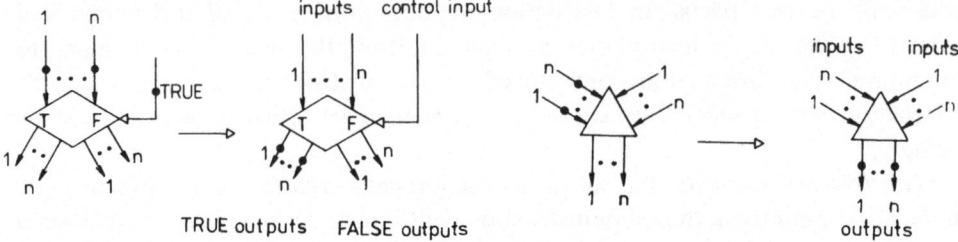

Fig. 15. The SWITCH operator.　　　　　　Fig. 16. The UNION operator.

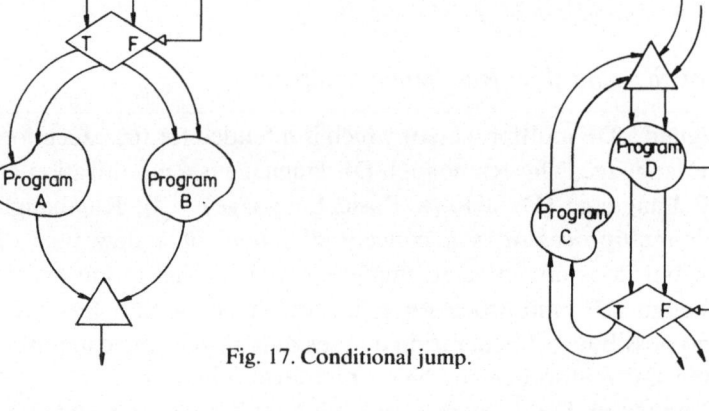

Fig. 17. Conditional jump.　　　　　　　　　　　　　　Fig. 18. Loop.

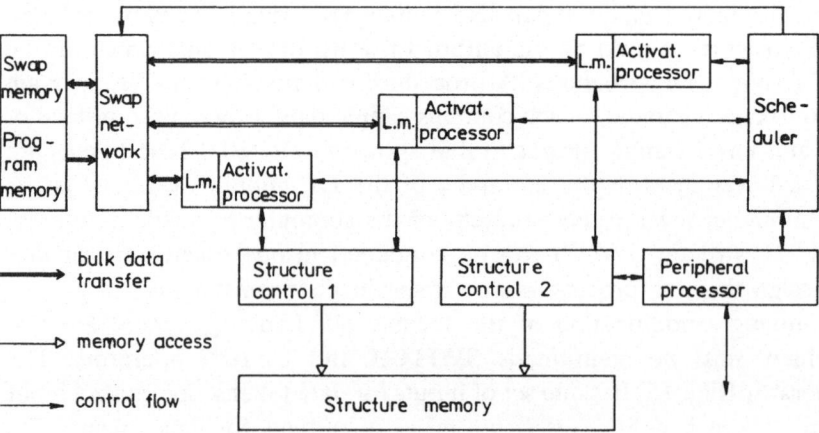

Fig. 19. The Rumbaugh data flow multiprocessor.

a function opposite to that of **SWITCH.** It has two sets of inputs and one set of outputs. Tokens from the inputs are transmitted to the corresponding outputs.

The control operators **SWITCH** and **UNION** allow the use of conditional jumps and loops in DF programs (Figs. 17 and 18). The Rumbaugh DF multiprocessor (Fig. 19) consists of several asynchronous units that make up a two-level hierarchical structure. At the lower level, there are several activation processors with local memory, structure memory and several units for structure control. At the higher level, there are a scheduler, a swap memory, a program memory and a peripheral processor. In each activation processor (Fig. 20), one procedure is stored in local memory and processed in specialized processors which are parts of the activation processor.

The activation processor is a DF processor of SM type. Instructions and data of one procedure are stored in local memory. The local memory has three parts:

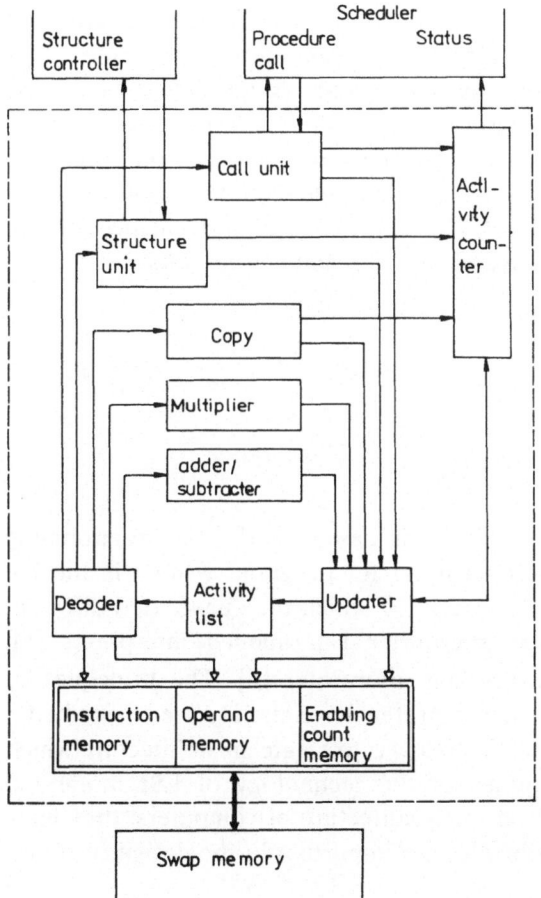

Fig. 20. The activation processor.

instruction memory, data memory and enabling count memory. A DF operator is coded as one instruction. The format of this instruction is similar to that of an executable instruction (Fig. 10) with operand address rather than operands in the operand fields, and in the control part the address of the next instruction as well as the instruction code and the addresses for the result. Operands are stored in the operand memory.

The activity of the searcher is performed by decoder, activity list and updater. The computation is executed in some of the execution pipelines, each of these processors being specialized in one or several DF instructions. Specialized processors can be adders and subtractors, multipliers, Boolean processors, dividers, etc. The processors are mutually independent and can work in parallel, and it is not necessary to synchronize their activity.

Since local memories are of limited size, large data structures are stored in the structure memory. The structure memory is controlled by a structure control. This can manipulate several activation processors.

A procedure that is inactive for some time can be transferred from the activation processor to a swap memory. This is done by the scheduler. A scheduler is an independent unit that generates, controls and completes the activation of the procedure, and assigns it to some processor for processing. Effective activity of the scheduler is of great importance, since the utilization of the activation processors depends on it. The scheduler has to ensure by a suitable distribution of tasks that the activation processors are constantly busy, since the performance of the multiprocessor is determined by the use of the activation processors.

11.5.3 Architecture of the Arvind and Gostelow DF computer

The work of Arvind and Gostelow [1—5] is based on the ID programming language. They have designed a new interpreter for programs written in the DF language [1], an interpreter without feedback for which they have used different names in various articles: feedback interpreter [1], queued interpreter [5], non-feedback interpreter [1], or unravelling interpreter [5]. The principles of feedback interpreters and non-feedback interpreters have already been described.

The aim of the studies by Arvind and Gostelow is to create an architecture which would effectively utilize the possibilities of the technology of LSI integrated circuits. Examining the effect of LSI on the architecture of computers, they have arrived at the conclusion that two principles are important in the design of future computers:

— distributed processing of data by many processors,
— autonomous activity of processors working in parallel.

They regard the data flow model as the model of computation which best satisfies the above principles. The use of the DF principle also follows from the need for asynchronous activity of the processors in the distributed processing environment of future computer architectures.

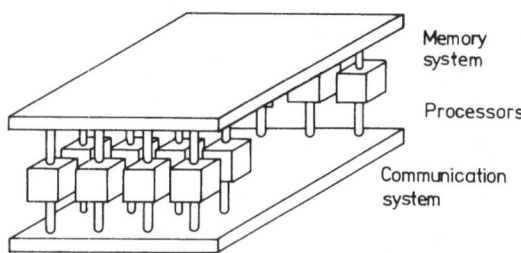

Memory system

Processors

Communication system

Fig. 21. The data flow multiprocessor of Arvind and Gostelow.

Arvind and Gostelow have designed the architecture of a DF computer, in which activity occurs according to a non-feedback interpreter, tokens being arranged arbitrarily, rather than according to the FIFO principle. They have developed this interpreter as a new type of interpreter for processing programs written in the ID programming language which allows a better distribution of computation among processors, a direct consequence of which is a better utilization of different levels of parallelism. The DF computer is a multiprocessor (Fig. 21) consisting of some processors which make up an array, each connected in the same way to the communication system and to the memory system. The processors are dynamically allocated some part of the program during its processing. The allocation process of the processors is based on a mechanism for assigning the name of the activity to the appropriate processor. When a processor completes its activity for the task allocated, it deallocates itself by clearing the assigned activity name. The allocation of processors and their deallocation are not controlled centrally — in the computer there is no central "master" unit which controls allocation and deallocation. In the Rumbaugh computer this was provided by the scheduler.

A characteristic unit of the whole computer is the communication system. The communication system is the medium in which tokens circulate looking for a free processor. As far as the communication system is concerned, the computer has a two-level hierarchical structure. The processors are grouped into columns, each column having one internal bus. These columns constitute the lower level in the computer hierarchy. The internal bus allows communication between processors in one column. Every internal bus is attached to a ring bus through switches B_i and T_i (Fig. 22) which are the terminals of the internal bus. Both the switches in a column, B_i and T_i, are connected via lines R_i and L_i, L_n and R_1 which are part of the ring bus (Fig. 23). This organization of the communication system allows the creation of several independent ring buses allocated to one program or procedure within the whole communication system and the division of the computer into independent, mutually exclusive sections or execution domains (Fig. 24). The possibility of creating execution domains in the communication system is based on the assump-

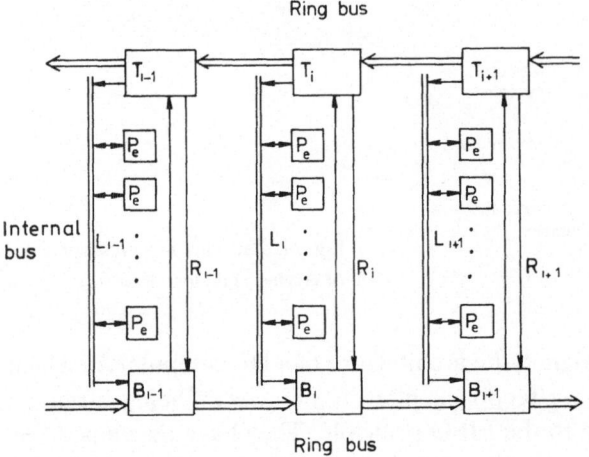

Fig. 22. The communication system in the data flow multiprocessor of Arvind and Gostelow.

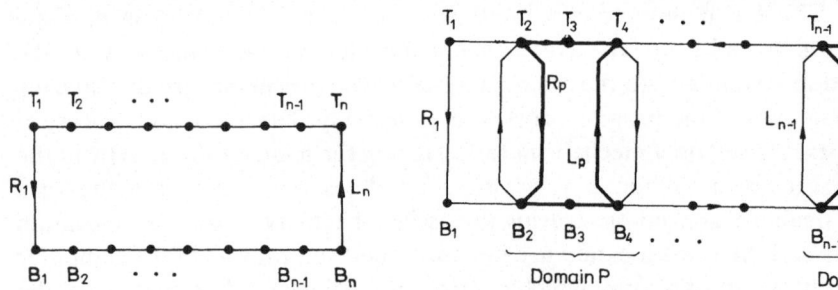

Fig. 23. The ring bus.

Fig. 24. The creation of execution domains.

tion that the DF program has the property of "locality". Arvind and Gostelow suppose that statements (activities) which are "near" in terms of program graph distance should also be near in execution. Specifically, activities within some procedure are normally nearer to each other than to any activity outside this procedure [5].

The communication system is the most elaborate part of the computer. Arvind and Gostelow have also designed possible development of the communication system. The first step is the connection of the terminals of the ring bus, switches T_1, B_1 and T_n, B_n (Fig. 25), so that two ring buses are interconnected at many points. The next step is to create a toroidal structure by putting switches T_i and B_i into one device, so that the two ring buses are merged (Fig. 26).

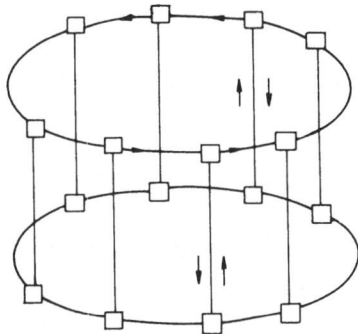

Fig. 25. The communication system with two ring buses.

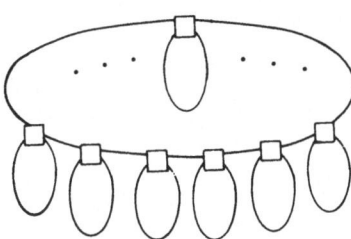

Fig. 26. The toroidal communication system.

In an actual implementation, the buses would be created by shift registers, which provide both functions of the communication system, transmission of tokens and temporary storage. From the aspect of the basic model of DF architectures, the Arvind and Gostelow computer is partially of type IM (the creation of execution domains by means of switches T and B) and partially of type SM. The function of the searcher is distributed among several parts of the computer; it is partly provided by the communication system and partly by the processors themselves. This activity is not controlled centrally. The searcher has two tasks:

— first, to generate an executable instruction — EI,
— then, to deliver the EI to a free processor.

In the Arvind and Gostelow computer, the activity order is reversed. The partial EI's, single tokens, are first delivered to the processor, which afterwards ensures itself the completion of the EI. The process of delivering the EI to a free processor is carried out by assigning an activity name to the processor. This is done by circulating the token in the communication system, so that this token searches for a free processor. When the token finds a free processor, it assigns the activity name which it contains to the processor and this activity name is simultaneously written in the associative memory in the switch T. Then the processor waits for the arrrival of other tokens with the same activity name to complete the EI. The tokens are fetched from the ring bus of the switch T and delivered to the internal bus of the column containing the processor.

The processor itself has four sections (Fig. 27):

— activity name recognition,
— token input and output,

— computation,

— memory system interface.

The functions of the individual sections are clear from their names. The processor is able not only to allocate itself for the execution of an EI by assigning an activity name, but also to reallocate itself after the termination of the computation by erasing the activity name.

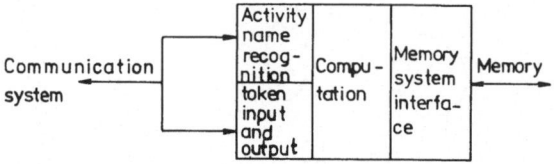

Fig. 27. The sections of the processor.

The structure of the memory system is not yet worked out, but some principles have already been fixed. The main function of the memory system is to reduce the data flow in the communication system. Since the data contained in the tokens can have rather a complex structure and a large size, it is necessary to reduce the size of the token. Thus, tokens only contain pointers — data storage addresses — and not the data itself. This is the main reason why the memory system is distributed and consists of many independent memory units which can be accessed by each processor. Another reason for creating a distributed memory system is the existence of "localities". In a distributed memory system, taking into account the possibility of generating execution domains, it is possible to perform parallel transmissions between several processor pairs, one processor producing data and the other receiving the data, since these are located close to each other. Moreover, with regard to the creation of execution domains, it is probably useful for the processors of the same column to have a faster access to a memory unit in the same columns than the processors outside this column.

The architecture designed by Arvind and Gostelow also seems to be a suitable method for the production of parallel computers of high reliability, since in such a computer there is no central unit and computation can be carried out in any section of the computer. Failure of one, or several processors, need not mean failure of the whole computer, but only a reduction in the performance of the computer. Such a computer system has many levels of gradual degradation.

11.5.4 Architecture of the data flow computer of Gurd
and Treleaven

The design of a universal computer with DF architecture developed at the University of Manchester is based on a profound analysis of the problem of parallelism and on the evaluation of possible CF and DF models from the point of view of the utilization of parallelism [25, 37—39]. The objective of this analysis was to fix the basic requirements a parallel system had to meet if it was to achieve a substantial speedup for various tasks. Gurd and Treleaven arrived at the conclusion that a DF computer model was more suitable for the utilization of parallelism than the conventional von Neumann's (CF) model.

In their design of the DF computer architecture, they started with the idea that "parallelism could and should be exploited at the lowest possible level" [25]. They kept to this principle also in the creation of their own design of a DF computer. In their view, the existence of parallelism at a lower level in the computer supports the existence of parallelism at higher levels. Several types of architecture are given in their publications [25, 27]. Some of these are only auxiliary models for verifying the main properties, or are only stages in the design of the definitive system. There exist other designs and ideas, which, however, have not been published, and therefore are not mentioned here although they are interesting. In the text we mention only one architecture of a data flow computer described in [25].

The architecture of the DF computer designed by Gurd and Treleaven (shown in Fig. 28) is taken from [25]. The authors described this computer as dynamically parallel with separated instructions and operands. In their publications, they introduced the concepts of statically and dynamically parallel systems. These terms relate to the processing method of iterative computations. Systems that cannot

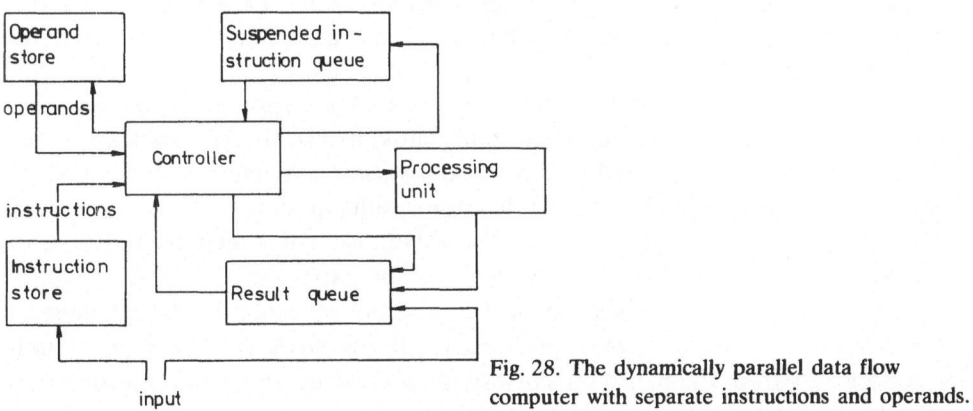

Fig. 28. The dynamically parallel data flow computer with separate instructions and operands.

distinguish various levels of iteration during computation are statically parallel, and systems which can distinguish the individual levels of iteration are dynamically parallel. In this way, dynamically parallel systems allow the start of the $(n + 1)$-th iteration before the termination of the n-th iteration, which results in additional parallelism and speeds up the computation if enough processors are available. In statically parallel systems, it is always necessary to wait for the result of the preceding step. The above dynamically parallel DF computer is of SM type with activity controlled by a non-feedback interpreter. The DF language in which programs are written for this computer is at the level of a machine language. There exist two types of DF operators — combinative and separative (Fig. 2). The combinative operator executes functions, such as addition, subtraction, multiplication, etc. over two operands and produces one result. The separative operator produces two copies of the input operand and is called **FORK. FORK** is a way to allow parallel activity in a DF computer. The computer consists of six units, four of which are memories: instruction store, operand store, result queue and suspended instruction queue, the others are the controller and the processing unit.

The processing unit can be a set of identical microprocessors or a set of specialized processors connected in parallel to a bus coming from the control unit and with outputs to the bus leading to the result queue. The flow of information is one-directional — from the controller to the result queue. In the processing unit, an instruction which has two input operands and produces one result is executed. A free processor asks the controller for the allocation of an EI. After processing the EI, it dispatches the result to suspended instruction queue and then asks again for the assignment of an EI. The controller is a synonym for searcher. Its task is to assemble EI's, the instruction being stored in the instruction memory and operands either in the operand memory or in the result queue. It dispatches the completed EI for processing in a free processor.

The result queue is a memory of FIFO type and contains all partial results produced by processors. The input values of variables and **FORK** results are also written into the result queue. A token is a partial result, i.e. the result of a combinative operator, or a FORK result, i.e. the result of a separative operator. The result queue allows activity by the non-feedback interpreter, since it makes it possible to generate token queues on data paths, to use the terminology of DF programming. The use of RAM memory and associative memory instead of FIFO memory was also examined. Their application results in an increase of speed, but also in an increase in costs. It seems that the use of associative memory will be most promising if prices continue to fall, which is to be expected.

The result queue is also a way to start a program by using the value queue of input variables with the names of subsequent instructions. The control unit formulates EI's from them and the corresponding instruction from the instruction memory.

As seen in Fig. 28, instructions and operands are stored in specialized memory units, the instruction store and operand store. The control unit cooperates with both in generating EI's; it can read from the instruction memory and write to the operand memory and read from it, as well.

The suspended instruction queue is a FIFO-type memory which is used as an auxiliary memory for storing EI's execution of which is postponed for some reason, for example, because in the priority system there are lower priority EI's. It also contains EI's execution of which has become superfluous. For instance, in an iterative computation in which several iterative steps are being processed and the next EI's are being prepared at the instant at which computation is terminated. These no longer need to be computed and for this reason they are placed and then also completed in the suspended instruction queue.

The activity of the computer begins with writing instructions to the instruction store. The calculation is started by storing the value queue of input variables and the names of the next instructions in the result queue. On arrival in the control unit, this tries to assemble EI's from the instructions in the instruction store and from variable values from the result queue. One operand is sufficient for the generation of a FORK instruction, and this instruction is executed by the control unit itself, it does not send it to the processor, but it sends both copies of the operands to the result queue. Thus, no EI is generated for a **FORK** instruction.

Two operands are needed for the generation of an EI. On starting a computation and on the arrival of the first values of variables in the control unit it is not possible to generate EI's, and therefore the value of the variable — the operand — is stored in the operand store where it waits for the arrival of a second operand for the instruction, unless it is a **FORK** instruction, as has been described above. After the arrival of the second operand from the result queue, the control unit formulates an EI, fetching an instruction from the instruction store and the first operand from the operand store. Here it is clearly seen that this is a DF computer — a computer controlled by the data flow from the result queue. The mechanism of storing the first operand in the operand memory is used in the generation of every EI. After the generation of an EI, it is dispatched to a free processor in the processing unit. After the execution of the EI, the partial result is sent to the result queue and is used as an operand for the instruction whose address was given in the EI and is also reproduced in the partial result.

In the computer shown in Fig. 28 there are several buses connecting the individual function blocks. Various data and instruction formats are used for various buses. These formats are closely related to the machine DF language which is used in the given architecture. The graphical DF language and its lexical form at the machine language level have been thorouhgly developed [25, 37]. The individual formats that allow activity by a non-feedback interpreter have also been defined in detail, since each EI has a field for the iteration number and a field called the base address. A more detailed explanation and also some results achieved are given in [25].

11.5.5 Architecture of the LAU data flow computer

LAU is a project for a parallel system based on the principle of single assignment (SA). The basic rule of the SA principle is that during program execution only one value can be assigned to a variable. The computation model that satisfies the SA principle is in fact a DF computation model, since the control of computation is dependent on the flow of data. The original papers were concerned with examining the employment of the SA principle for the representation of parallelism [32] and ultimately to increase the speed of the computer. The result is a high-level programming language, which has given its name to the entire project, LAU (Language Assignation Unique) [9] and a design of the architecture of a computer that is connected with the language LAU [9—14, 23, 33]. The original aim of the creation of the LAU system was to design a system which would execute parallel computations and be a peripheral computer of some general-purpose computer, specialized in fast processing of parallel problems [11]. It has been found during the development of the LAU system — of both the language and the architecture — that it can be regarded as a general-purpose system, since it is possible to program serial as well as parallel algorithms in the LAU language and process them effectively in the computer. For this reason, subsequent work was aimed at the creation of a language and a computer, in particular, with a more universal application than had been intended originally.

The programming language LAU is similar to the programming languages FORTRAN, ALGOL, PASCAL, etc. Experience gained in this respect two years ago has shown that it is as convenient as these languages. But it has the advantage over conventional languages that parallelism can be expressed in it in a simple way and it also allows the natural parallelism of the given problem to be exploited, even though this is not explicitly expressed in the program, i.e. it is a parallelism that has not been declared and identified by the programmer.

The LAU system exploits the following three levels of parallelism [11]:

— parallelism at the level of programs, because parallel execution of several programs — multiprogramming — is possible;

— parallelism within a program; parallel processing of several independent blocks of a program;

— parallelism with a program block; simultaneous parallel processing of several EI's of the same block.

The multiprocessor LAU consists of three principal sections (Fig. 29):

— memory,

— control unit,

— execution unit.

The computer is of type SM, since both control unit and memory take part in the generation of EI's. Both data and instructions — as in a conventional computer — are stored in a common memory. In addition to the main memory, there also are small memories in the control unit which contain bits associated with instructions and data.

The instruction format is illustrated in Fig. 30. Bits C_0, C_1, and C_2 are stored in the control unit in the ICU (instruction control unit) and the rest is stored in the main memory. The fields OP_1 and OP_2 contain the addresses of operands of the instruction whose code is contained in the field OPCODE.

Also the operands themselves can be stored in OP_1 and OP_2 instead of the operand addresses. The field RES contains the address where the result is to be

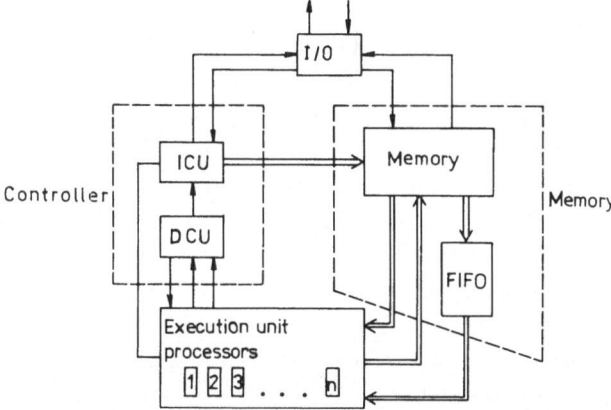

Fig. 29. Multiprocessor LAU.

delivered to after the execution of the instruction. Bits C_1 and C_2 indicate whether the operands have already been computed — i.e. whether they already have a value, and bit C_0 indicates whether it is possible to execute the instructions with regard to the total context of the program and the order of the single blocks of the program. An instruction is ready for execution if $C_0 = C_1 = C_2 = 1$.

OP CODE	OP 1	OP 2	RES

C_0	C_1	C_2

Fig. 30. The instruction format in the LAU computer.

The operand format is shown in Fig. 31. A whole word, except for bit C_d, is stored in the main memory. C_d is stored in the control unit in the DCU (data control unit). The field VALUE is reserved for the operand value. The fields LINK 1 and LINK 2 contain the instruction addresses that the operand will use in this way. The generation of operand copies is guaranteed as well as the flow of computation in the program. One-bit fields L/R determine whether the operand of the instruction will be used as left- or right-hand operand. When the control bit C_d is equal to 1, the operand has already been computed, otherwise not. It is also used to check the SA principle, since before setting C_d equal to 1 a check is made whether $C_d = 0$, i.e. whether a value has not already been assigned to the given operand. The activity of the LAU multiprocessor in processing an arithmetic instruction proceeds in three phases as follows:

— declaration of an instruction as executable in the control unit;

— instruction fetch from the memory and transfer to the execution unit for processing by some processor;

— execution of the instruction by the processor and distribution of the result with appropriate changes of control bits.

Fig. 31. The operand format in the LAU computer.

An instruction is declared executable, when the three control bits C_0, C_1, and C_2 are all equal to 1. It is the task of the ICU to find as soon as possible the combination 111 by continuous scanning of the control bits of the instruction list. On finding such a combination, the ICU sends the address of the instruction to the memory with a command to fetch it. In the memory, the instruction is read at the given address and sent to the FIFO memory, where a queue of executable instructions waiting to be processed is stored. The FIFO memory acts here as a buffer. Immediately after finding a free processor, the first instruction in the queue is sent to this processor for processing.

On receiving an instruction, the processor fetches operands from the memory (if the instruction contained their addresses rather than their values), then it executes the arithmetic operation given by the instruction code (OPCODE), writes the result to the address in memory that had contained an instruction in fields RES and simultaneously reads from this address the next two instruction addresses, LINK 1 and LINK 2, which will use this result as an operand. It writes 1 in field C_d in the CDU for the operand which has been calculated by the instruction and corresponds to the address of the result, and writes in the ICU ones in the fields C_1 and C_2 at the addresses determined by the fields LINK 1 and LINK 2.

Each of the three main units of the LAU computer has a complex inner structure. During the development of the LAU system the architecture has gradually changed. At present, the computer [14] which has been built does not contain all the ideas and concepts that were considered originally [11]. The choice of the final architecture was made on the basis of the results of simulation and contemporary technology, too.

The memory which is common to all processors must be as fast as possible to avoid decrease of the throughput of the whole system. It is possible to obtain a high memory speed by using fast memories and also by a suitable organization within the memory. These problems have already been solved at a high level in traditional computers, and consequently the designers of the LAU system have made use of known principles — they have followed mainly the memory organization of the IBM 360/91.

The memory is divided into eight blocks which communicate with the other units through an input-output multiplexer. In the memory, the principle of address interleaving is used, i.e. sequential addressed are located in different blocks. This organization of memory provides access times comparable to those of the memory with a much shorter cycle time — the virtual memory cycle comes close to the memory cycle divided by the number of the blocks, hence it is almost 8 time shorter in this case.

The buffer of executable instruction waiting for execution is of FIFO type and provides both the function of storing the EI queue and the function of controlling the speed and searching for EI's in the ICU. In this way it is guaranteed that the buffer does not overflow, which would result in a loss of instructions. By generating queues of executable instructions, the activity is controlled by the non-feedback interpreter (NFI). The concept of the execution unit changed most during the development of the LAU system. Originally, the execution unit was intended to consist of a set of various specialized pipelined or pseudopipelined processors that were to cooperate. The specialized processors were to be divided into two blocks according to whether they processed:

— arithmetic and logical instructions, or
— control instructions.

The processors for arithmetic and logical instructions were to be of the following type:

— floating point processor,
— fixed point processor,
— vector processor.

The processors for control instructions were to be specialized in processing single control statements of the LAU language, such as **LOOP, CASE, EXPAND, CALL** and **ACT.** The system could contain several identical processors (either arithmetic or control processors) — if these were needed. The communication with other units was to be provided by the communication processor.

The present concept of the unit, which has also been implemented, is different. The execution unit can contain as many as 32 identical processors, each of them being able to execute any instruction. The processors are microprogrammable, have a width of 16 bits and are based on the AMD 2900 bit slice microprocessor. The execution unit communicates with its environment via six buses, to which all the processors are connected in the same way.

Since the main activity of the control unit is to scan continuously the control bits C_0, C_1, C_2 in the ICU and C_d in the DCU, and to ensure the continuity of programming blocks by means of descriptors in the DCU, the use of associative memories seems to be most convenient here. But at present this is not technologically feasible, and therefore memories of RAM or FIFO type are used, while the activity is speeded up by a suitable organization of writing and reading [14].

An important part of the LAU computer is the communication system. Only a part of it is shown in Fig. 29 — the bus, but not the bus controller. All buses to or from the execution unit are common to all processors. All buses in the system are one-dimensional, so that the throughput of the system can be enhanced as much as possible. The buses are operated by the bus control unit using an algorithm which makes it possible to satisfy a large number of demands within a short time.

At present, the LAU system is in an advanced stage of implementation and it seems that compared to all other DF systems this system is closest to implementation. The programming language LAU has been in use for several years; simulations have been made of various alternative engineering solutions of single blocks and an optimum solution selected on the basis of their results.

Conclusion

In designing computer systems, we have to be able to answer the following three questions:

What is the computer system expected to do? — here, the users' requirements are the starting point;

How should the computer system do it? — thus, it is required to have a convenient theoretical model of the computer system, both the architecture and the programming language;

What is the computer to be made of? — i.e. what technological facilities are required to manufacture all the units of the computer at the required engineering level.

Let us take a more detailed look at the individual questions. From the users' point of view, new requirements arise constantly for the solution of new tasks. Many of them, owing to their size, the amount of computation involved, the precision required, etc., are solved in a laborious way by contemporary computers, or their solution is not possible. Further, users require simplicity in communicating with the computer, which leads to demands for the simplification of the programming process. Other users' requirements are as follows: low price, high reliability, high performance, easy repair, the possibility to adapt the computer to a given class of tasks, etc.

As far as the present technological possibilities are concerned, i.e. the component base, very good results have been achieved over the last years in this field, so that production of large, efficient and at the same time relatively cheap computers is possible now. The second question — how to find a theoretical model of a computer system that would satisfy users' requirements and exploit advances in the technology of LSI production — has still not been satisfactorily answered despite the existence of many computer system designs. At the IFIP Congress in 1977, Professor Chu characterized the situation as follows: "The cost of software would become, if the present trend persists, 90% of the total cost by 1985. In 1968, it was 50%. The technology of semiconductor devices (microprocessors) has reached the point where highly complex hardware can be built reliably and inexpensively. It would be rewarding if the semiconductor technology could be used to solve the problem of software cost. This could be feasible, if the computer architects would re-examine the desk-calculator-like organization and create a new architecture that would help to solve the problem of software".

One such attempt to find a suitable model for computer systems is the data flow model. It seems to be a promising approach to the design of parallel computers and programming languages. The main properties of the data flow model are as follows:

— it has been shown [29, 30, 42], that it will be possible to make use of existing programming work, to utilize existing programs and programming languages, since it is not difficult to write compilers from existing programming languages into the DF language;

— because the inner organization of the computer can be adapted to the structure of the algorithm, it will be possible to achieve the speed of specialized computers for running particular jobs on DF computers and maintain the universality of the whole design concept [3];

— the DF appears to be a very promising design for achieving parallelism, because

> — it allows autonomous and asynchronous activity of the single units of the distributed system [5];
> — the expression of the natural parallelism of algorithms in DF languages and the mechanism of its exploitation in DF computers are simple;
> — DF computers exploit several levels of parallelism in the program [2, 9, 25, 38, 39, 42], and this leads to efficient execution;
> — it allows the use of pipelining as an additional level of parallelism in the processing mode [9];
> — it can be expected that parallel DF computers will also be effective in solving serial problems.

— DF computer architecture allows the exploitation of LSI technology;

— the simple and modular structure of some DF computers allows the construction of a series of computers differing in performance and cost according to the number and type of the processors, the organization of the control unit, the structure and size of the memory, etc. The modular structure should also make it possible that an existing computer can be extended without changing its basic organization;

— the modular structure of DF computers and the regular decentralized organization in some DF computers should lead to a high degree of reliability, based on the many levels in the gradual degradation of the system;

— DF multiprocessors of SM type avoid the use of a large switch which is the limiting factor in some classical multiprocessors.

Most of the above properties are assumptions only, since hitherto there is almost no experience in the use of real DF systems. This is also the reason why it is not possible to specify all the disadvantages of DF systems. These will surely appear when DF computers are in wider use. It can be assumed that higher memory requirements in DF systems will be one of these disadvantages. Additional advantages and disadvantages will result in future from the solution of the currently unsolved problems and from the design of new structures for DF computers.

Some research themes can be mentioned:

— design of DF computers using non-feedback interpreters,
— examination of the nature of complex and comprehensive data structures and their effect on computer architecture,
— exploitation of vector (e.g., bit slice) processing of data in DF computers,
— hierarchical architectures of DF computers,
— questions of reliability and methods of its improvement,
— methods for dividing programs into blocks in an IM-type computer,
— construction of translators for DF languages.

An increased interest in the DF model of computation is shown by the increased number of publications about these problems. There are publications dealing with the formal DF model [26, 41]; in [24] a model is given which is more general and has much in common with the DF model, there are also publications on programming problems; [6—8, 15, 36] deal with DF architecture; [22] and [27] deal exclusively with DF computers; [34] and [40] concentrate on the exploitation of the DF organization in a particular computer. The data flow model of computation is a new concept which makes it possible to create more efficient computer systems — both computers and programming languages. Many authors predict that it will replace the CF (von Neumann) architecture, but this view seems to be too extreme. The development in the architecture of computers will probably be a symbiosis of the two principles, either in using DF and CF principles in one computer, or by producing exclusively CF or exclusively DF computers for different classes of problems.

REFERENCES

[1] ARVIND, GOSTELOW, K. P.: A new interpreter for data flow schemes and its implications for computer architecture. Tech. Report 72, Dep. Inform. and Comp. Sci., Univ. of California, Irvine, 1975.

[2] ARVIND, GOSTELOW, K. P.: A computer capable of exchanging processing elements for time. Tech. Report 77, Dep. Inform. and Comp. Sci., Univ. of California, Irvine, 1976.

[3] ARVIND, GOSTELOW, K. P.: The semantics of asynchrony relationships between two different interpreters of a programming language. Tech. Report 88, Dep. Inform. and Comp. Sci., Univ. of California, Irvine, 1976.

[4] ARVIND, GOSTELOW, K. P.: Programming in a viable data flow language. Tech. Report 89, Dep. Inform. and Comp. Sci., Univ. of California, Irvine, 1976.

[5] ARVIND, GOSTELOW, K. P.: A computer capable of exchanging processors for time. Proc. IFIP Conference 1977. North-Holand Publ. Sci., Amsterdam, pp. 849—853.

[6] ASHCROFT, E. A. and WADGE, W. W.: Lucid: A nonprocedural language with iteration. Comm. ACM, 20, 1977, 7, pp. 519—526.

[7] BÅHRS, A.: Operation patterns. An extensible model of an extensible language. Symp. on Theoretical Programming, Novosibirsk, 1972, pp. 217—246.

[8] BOEKELHEIDE, K.: A high-level, graphical, data-driven language. Proc. of the Workshop: Data Driven Languages and Machines, Toulouse, 1979.

[9] COMTE, D., DURRIEU, G., GELLY, O., PLAS, A. and SYRE, J. C.: Système LAU: Rapport sur le langage évolue. TEAU 9/1, Contract SESORI 74167, Doc. 5/3059, CERT, Toulouse, 1976.

[10] COMTE, D., DURRIEU, G., GELLY, O., PLAS, A. and SYRE, J. C.: Système LAU: Rapport sur le langage machine. TEAU 9/2, Contract SESORI 74167, Doc. 6/3059, CERT, Toulouse, 1976.

[11] COMTE, D., DURRIEU, G., GELLY, O., PLAS, A. and SYRE, J. C.: Système LAU: Architecture multiprocesseur parallele. TEAU 9/3, Contract SESORI 74167, Doc. 7/3059, CERT, Toulouse 1976.

[12] COMTE, D., DURRIEU, G., GELLY, O., PLAS, A. and SYRE, J. C.: Système LAU: Specifications du compilateur et exemple de programmes. TEAU 9/4, Contract SESORI 74167, Doc. 8/3059, CERT, Toulouse, 1976.

[13] COMTE, D., DURRIEU, G., GELLY, O., PLAS, A. and SYRE, J. C.: Système LAU: Résultats de simulation, TEAU 9/6, Contract SESORI 74167, Doc. 10/3059, CERT, Toulouse, 1976.

[14] COMTE, D. and HIFDI, N.: LAU multiprocessor: Microfunctional description and technological choices. Proc. of the Workshop: Data Driven Languages and Machines, Toulouse, 1979, pp. I.1—I.8.

[15] DAVIS, A. L.: DDN'S — a low-level program scheme for fully distributed systems. 1st Eur. Conf. on Parallel and Distributed Processing, Toulouse, 1979.

[16] DENNIS, J. B., FOSSEEN, J. P. and LINDERMAN, J. P.: Data flow schemes. Symp. on Theoretical Programming, Novosibirsk, 1972, pp. 187—216.

[17] DENNIS, J. B.: First version of a data-flow procedure language. Symp. on Programming, Institute of Programmation, University of Paris, 1974. pp. 241—271.

[18] DENNIS, J. B. and MISUNAS, D. P.: A computer architecture for highly parallel signal processing. Proc. Annual Conf. CAM, 1974, pp. 402—409.

[19] DENNIS, J. B. and MISUNAS, D. P.: A preliminary architecture for a basic data-flow processor. Proc. 2nd Annual Symp. on Computer Architecture. IEEE, New York, 1975, pp. 126—132.

[20] DENNIS, J. B. and KEN K. S. WENG.: Application of data flow computation to the weather problem. In: High Speed Computers and Algorithms Organization. Academic Press, Inc. London 1977, pp. 143—157.

[21] DURRIEU, G.: Extension of the LAU System: Global specification of synchronizations in a data driven language. Proc. Int. Conf. on Parallel and Distributed Processing, Toulouse 1979, pp. 149—155.

[22] FRANCESCO, N. DE, PEREGO, G., TOMASI, A., VAGLINI, G. and VANNESCHI, M.: On the feasibility of nondeterministic and interprocess communication constructs in data-flow computing systems. 1st Eur. Conf. on Parallel and Distributed Processing, Toulouse, 1979, pp. 183—196.

[23] GELLY, O. et al.: LAU system software: A high level data driven language for parallel programming. Proc. Int. Conf. on Parallel Processing, 1976, pp. 303—311.

[24] GLUSHKOV, V. M., IGNATYEV, M. B., MYASNIKOV, V. A. and TORGASHEV, V. A.: Recursive machines and computing technology. Proc. IFIP Congress, Stockholm 1974. North-Holland Publ. Co., Stockholm 1974, pp. 65—70.

[25] GURD, J. and TRELEAVEN, P.: A highly parallel computer architecture. Tech. Report, Dep. Comp. Sci., Univ. of Manchester, 1976.

[26] HANKIN, C. L.: Towards a formal data flow model. Proc. of the Workshop: Data Driven Languages and Machines, Toulouse 1979, pp. XIII.1—XIII.12.

[27] HOPKINS, R. P., RAUTENBACH, P. W. and TRELEAVEN, P. C.: A data flow computer with addressable memory. Proc. of the Workshop: Data Driven Languages and Machines, Toulouse, 1979.

[28] KOMP, E. and MUCHNICK, S. S.: Three extensions to LAU and its hardware architecture. 1st Eur. Conf. on Parallel and Distributed Processing, Toulouse, 1979.

[29] KOSINSKI, P. R.: A data flow programming language. Report 4264, IBM. T. J. Watson Research Centre, New York, 1973.

[30] MILLER, R. E. and COCKE, J.: Configurable computers: A new class of general-purpose machines. Int. Symp. on Theoretical Programming, Novosibirsk 1972. In: Lecture Notes in Computer Science, Vol. 5. Springer-Verlag, New York, 1974, pp. 86—298.

[31] MISUNAS, D. P.: Performance analysis of a data flow processor. Proc. Int. Conf. on Parallel Processing, 1976, pp. 100—105.

[32] NICOLAS, J. M. and SYRE, J. C.: Assignation unique et programmation data-driven: une solution aux traitements hautement paralleles. TEAU, Doc. 1/3044, CERT, Toulouse, 1974.

[33] PLAS, A.: LAU system architecture: A parallel data-driven processor based on single assignment. Proc. Int. Conf. on Parallel Processing, Sagamore, 1976.

[34] PRANGISHVILI, I. V., GORINOVICH, L. N., IGNATUSHCHENKO, V. V., KOSTELYANSKII, V. M., LEKHNOVA, G. M., REZANOV, TRAKHTENGERTS, E. A. and SCHERBAKOV, E. V.: Problems involved in the organization of computations in uniform rearrangeable control computer system. Proc. 7th Congress IFAC, Helsinki 1978.

[35] RUMBAUGH, J.: A data flow multiprocessor. IEEE Trans. on Computers, C-26, 1977, pp. 138—146.

[36] SHARP, J. A.: The analysis of data flow programs. Proc. of the Workshop: Data Driven Languages and Machines. Toulouse, 1979, pp. XII.1—XII.13.

[37] TRELEAVEN, P. C.: Exploitation of parallelism in computer systems. Ph.D. Thesis. Dep. Comp. Sci., Univ. of Manchester, 1977.

[38] TRELEAVEN, P. C.: Exploiting problem — parallelism in computing systems. Tech. Report 107, Comp. Lab., Univ. of Newcastle upon Tyne, 1977.

[39] TRELEAVEN, P. C.: Principal components of data flow computers. Tech. Report 108, Comp. Lab., Univ. of Newcastle upon Tyne, 1977.

[40] TRELEAVEN, P. C., FARRELL, E. P., GHANI, N. and JONES, S.: Concurrent computing system design at Newcastle. Proc. of the Workshop: Data Driven Languages and Machines, Toulouse, 1979, pp. VIII.1—VIII.9.

[41] UNGER, E. A.: A concurrent model: Basic concept. Proc. of the Workshop: Data Driven Languages and Machines, Toulouse, 1979.

[42] VANNESCHI, M.: Models and architectures for data-flow computing systems. Note Sci. S-76-17, Univ. degli studi di Pisa, Istituto di scienze dell'informazione, 1976.

Chapter 12

CORRELATION OF ALGORITHMS, SOFTWARE AND HARDWARE OF PARALLEL COMPUTERS

> *"It is easy to design computers, but it is hard to know what kind of computer to design...",*
>
> D. J. Kuck [16]

In the past, the speed of computers was mainly increased by increasing the speed of their logic element. Thus, the memory cycle time has increased by two orders of magnitude. Improvements in technology achieved in the last 20 years have increased the speed of processors by as much as three orders. Today, since the physical barrier of the speed of transfer of an electric signal has been reached, it is possible to achieve additional speed only by improving the computer organization or by using it more effectively. Current technology has made it possible for the processors to be combined into large parallel structures, and by a suitable organization of n processors it is possible to reach an n-fold increase in the rate of computation. Parallelism in computation has brought with it new problems both in the creation of new algorithms and programs, and in the design of computer architectures. Parallel algorithms and programs are closely connected with the architecture of parallel computers, and therefore design and analysis of parallel algorithms and programs cannot be considered independently of their implementation and the architecture of the computer on which they are to be implemented. Several examples are known from the history of parallel data processing, where a valuable concept in the design of algorithms, programs or computers has had a large impact on the efficiency of computation.

Many questions which have not been satisfactorily answered have arisen in connection with the relationship between the organization of algorithms, programs and computers:

— how to design software which would be most efficient for the given computer?

— how to structure the data of a given program for optimal processing on the given computer?

— how to design a language and compiler for the given computer and for the given set of programs?

— how to design algorithms and programs for the given computer, language and compiler?

— how to arrange a set of computer components to built a computer system which would best implement the given class of parallel algorithms or programs?

— how to determine for what categories of computations different parallel computer structures are suited?

These questions are not completely new in the creation of algorithms, programs and computers, new is only the importance which they have for the speed and efficient implementation of computations on parallel computers. Currently, there is no general theory for solving these problems, although partial results have been obtained, mainly be experimenting with existing parallel computers and by the simulation of the solution of such problems using conventional computers. These questions include the cost of the computer organization, a suitable interprocessor communication network, an estimate of the number of processors required for a given computation, the suitability of scheduling methods between processors, the frequency of memory conflicts. Kuck [16] has suggested that it is necessary to create a new complexity theory of parallel computers which would make it possible to describe uniformly the structure of algorithms, programs and computers and the relationships between them.

In this Chapter we give a brief survey of some results achieved about the relationships between algorithms, software and hardware of array processors, pipeline processors, multiprocessors and some specialized parallel computers. A detailed description of the architecture of most of these types of computers is given in the chapter "Parallel Processors and Multicomputer Complexes". Therefore, we will discuss this architecture briefly and only in the context of our requirements.

12.1 Parallel computers

Parallel computers are computer systems consisting of a centrally controlled set of processors which can simultaneously process the data of one program. According to their organization, parallel computers are divided into array processors, pipeline processors and multiprocessors.

Array processors operate on vectors. The instructions of the vector computer are executed in series — like in the classical computer, but they operate in parallel on vectors of data.

Pipeline processors work on the principle of dividing the computations between a number of simultaneously operating functional units activities of which are overlapping.

Multiprocessor computers consist of $n \geqq 2$ processors which operate simultaneously on a common memory, and are interconnected via channels which transmit control commands and data. They are controlled by a single operating system.

A more detailed classification of parallel computers has been made according to the parallelism of their instruction and data streams [11].

SIMD-type computer (single-instruction multiple-data stream) are vector processors with a single instruction stream and a multiple data stream. In [11] they are divided into array processors and pipeline processors. The two systems differ in their structure, but the method of processing programs is similar: each instruction is executed in parallel on many operands.

Each processor of an array processor has a complete arithmetic unit with its own memory, which, however, cannot generate its own instruction stream. The individual processors are interconnected so that common data can be shared. All processors execute a single stream of instructions over different data stored in the local memories of the processors.

In pipeline processors all operands are processed simultaneously by several overlapping instructions. The speedup is achieved by streaming the vectors of operands through an arithmetic unit which is functionally divided into subunits. Each subunit executes a step which is a part of the entire operation: it receives operands, performs its function, transmits the data to the next unit and takes the next elements from the operand stream.

In array processors we try to minimize the number of parallel computational steps, independently of the total number of results. This differs from pipeline processors, where the total number of operations executed should be minimized, since this determines the computation time.

By combining parallelism in the flow of instructions and data we obtain a multiprocessor computer, i.e. an MIMD-type computer (multiple-instruction multiple-data stream). Such a system consists of n independent processors which cooperate with each other during the computation via the common memory. In this computer there are n independent streams of instructions and data. From the point of view of their inner structure, multiprocessors are divided into homogeneous and non-homogeneous [1]. Homogeneous multiprocessors consist of n identical processors. Each of them can independently execute a complete set of instructions, i.e. it can access a common memory, share peripheral units and execute operating system programs.

A non-homogeneous multiprocessor computer consists of non-identical processors, which are often specialized for some categories of tasks, e.g. for implementing the operating system, pattern recognition, arithmetic calculations, Fast Fourier Transformation, sorting, etc.

In SIMD and MIMD computers, parallelism is achieved in a different way. We show this using as example the well-known formula for matrix multiplication [27].

Let A, B, C be square matrices of order n, where $C = A . B$. We assume an SIMD computer with n processors. We write the programs in a language closely related to Algol, in which the notation $(0 \leq k \leq n - 1)$ means the parallel execution of the given operation for all indices of the given interval. The program for the computation of C for an SIMD computer is

```
for i: = 0 step 1 until n − 1 do
begin c[i, k]: = 0, (0 ≦ k ≦ n − 1);
for j: = 0 step 1 until n − 1 do
   c[i, k]: = c[i, k] + a[i, j] × b[j, k], (0 ≦ k ≦ n − 1);
end;
```

In this program, all elements of the i-th row are computed simultaneously. Because each element of the j-th row of **B** is multiplied in parallel by $a[i, j]$, the element $a[i, j]$ must be transmitted to all processors simultaneously, so that they can use it as an operand. Thus an SIMD computer has to allow both a certain level of communication between processors and a fast access to all the relevant data.

For the computation of **C** on an MIMD computer, the algorithm must be made parallel and the subtasks must be assigned to the individual processors. For example, the statements **FORK** and **JOIN** are a suitable method for this [6]. If NV is the label in the program, then the execution of the statement **FORK** NV starts the computation of the independent process at the label NV. Simultaneously, the computation continues in the program at the statement and this immediately after **FORK** NV. On the other hand, the statement **JOIN** unites the independent instruction streams. The statement, **JOIN** n, causes that n independent instruction streams are joined in one stream. The statement following **JOIN** n is not executed until the n-th independent process executes **JOIN**. The program for matrix multiplication in an MIMD environment is

```
for    k: = 0 step 1 until n − 2 do
       FORK NV;
       k: = n − 1;
NV:    for i: = 0 step 1 until n − 1 do
       begin c[i, k]: = 0;
           for j: = 0 step 1 until n − 1 do
               c[i, k]: = c[i, k] + a[i, j] × b[j, k];
       end
JOIN n;
```

The behaviour of the individual processors in the program is similar to the behaviour of processes in SIMD, but there also are essential differences between the two environments. The processors in SIMD are synchronized on instructions, the processes in MIMD need not be synchronized and can also consist of sequences of different instructions.

The execution of a program in MIMD does not depend on the state of the computer. If there is no free processor for a process just generated, this process is queued for execution. When a processor has completed a process, it becomes free and is assigned to another process waiting in the queue.

12.2 Array processors

Different applications require manipulation of large sets of ordered data, such as vectors and matrices. The operations over the elements of these sets are often independent and identical and can consequently be executed in parallel. Their fast computation can be performed in array processors (AP). An AP which is an abstraction of the ILLIAC IV computer is shown in Fig. 1 [27]. The control

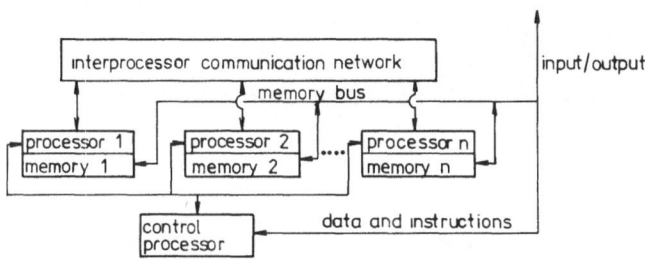

Fig. 1. The generalized perfect shuffle principle.

processor differs from an arithmetic processor because it can also execute conditional instructions which determine the order in which a sequence of instructions is carried out. The instructions are read into the instruction register in the control processor. Every instruction is either a control instruction performed only by the control unit or a vector instruction executed synchronously in all arithmetic processors.

If a processor of the AP wants to communicate with other processors, it has to access them via an interprocessor communication network, which normally connects processors which are physically close together. This network is an important part of the AP, since the effectiveness and speed of a particular parallel computation are dependent on it.

Interprocessor connections should be based on an analysis of the most frequent interactions between branches in the algorithms which are to be executed in the AP. In [21], for instance, the following possible functional relations are distin- guished: one branch on all processors, one branch on some selected processors, all branches on one or several selected processors, each branch cyclically to the next or the preceding branch, and relations which depend on certain conditions being satisfied. But these relations are too specialized, since an interprocessor connection intended for one type of relation is usually quite inconvenient for some other type.

The most flexible interprocessor connection is a total interconnection of proc- essors, in which each processor is directly connected to all other processors. Such a network requires $N(N-1)/2$ bidirectional channels between the processors, and consequently its complexity and cost increases with the square of N. Since the effectiveness of the AP increases with N at most linearly, the complete intercon- nection for a large N is uneconomical and hence unsuitable.

In contrast to algorithms for conventional computers, relatively little is currently known about algorithms for AP's, and therefore many algorithms are at present strongly influenced by the existing interprocessor connections in some AP in use. We describe some possible interprocessor communication networks based on real algorithms [27], paying most attention to the so-called perfect shuffle.

The connection by cyclic shift is the first type of such scheme. If the processors are numbered $0, 1, ..., N-1$, then the i-th processor in this scheme is directly connected with the $(i-1)$-th and the $(i+1)$-th processors, where the value is mod N. For every i and j, the i-th processor is connected with the j-th processor indirectly through $(i-j-1)$ mod N processors, through which the data is successively transferred from the i-th processor to the j-th processor. This scheme results from iterative algorithms of the type

$$x_i = f(x_{i-1}, x_i, x_{i+1})$$

which are typical of one-dimensional partial differential equations. Four-point iteration formulae for two-dimensional equations

$$x_{ij} = g(x_{i+1, j}, x_{i-1, j}, x_{i, j-1}, x_{i, j+1}, x_{ij})$$

and six-point formulae for three-dimensional equations can lead to additional special interprocessor schemes.

Another scheme is a special permutation of some finite number of objects, the so-called perfect shuffle [25]. In it, a set of indices of the vector $x_i = 0, 1, ..., N-1$, $N = 2^m$ is represented in a new set by the permutation

$$P(i) = \begin{cases} 2i & 0 \leq i = N/2 - 1 \\ 2i + 1 - N, & N/2 \leq i \leq N - 1. \end{cases}$$

Another view of this representation is possible via the binary representation of the vector indices. If i is an index with the binary representation

$$i = d_m 2^{m-1} + d_{m-1} 2^{m-2} + ... + d_2 2 + d_1 = (d_m d_{m-1} ... d_2 d_1),$$

then $P(i)$ is the number obtained by the cyclic rotation of these bits by 1 bit to the left: $P(i) = (d_{m-1} d_{m-2} ... d_1 d_m)$, i.e. after performing this transformation m times all processors return to their initial positions.

Switching of registers or processors by the perfect shuffle is of great importance to an effective implementation of several parallel algorithms. We show this with algorithms for sorting, Fast Fourier Transformation and matrix transposition [25].

An algorithm for bitonic sorting is based on the following definition and statement [3].

Definition: A sequence of real numbers $a_0, a_1, ..., a_{N-1}$ is bitonic if:

a) there exists an index i, $0 \leq i \leq N - 1$, such that $a_0, a_1, ..., a_i$ is monotone

increasing and a_i, a_{i+1}, ..., a_{N-1} is a monotone decreasing sequence, or if
b) it can be cyclically shifted in such a way that a) holds.

Statement: Let the sequence a_0, a_1, ..., a_{N-1} be a bitonic sequence. If $b_i =$ min $(a_i, a_{i+N/2})$, $c_i = $ max $(a_i, a_{i+N/2})$, $0 \leq i \leq N/2 - 1$ then the sequences b_0, b_1, ..., $b_{N/2-1}$ and c_0, c_1, ..., $c_{N/2-1}$ are also bitonic, whereby $b_i \leq c_j$ is true for all i and j.

The basic module of a processor implementing bitonic sorting is the "compare-exchange" module

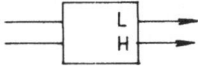

which compares two input quantities and places the smaller one at the L output and the larger one at H. Every module has a masked bit which changes the outputs when it has the value 1.

The structure of a sorting processor for 8 items with perfect shuffle is then

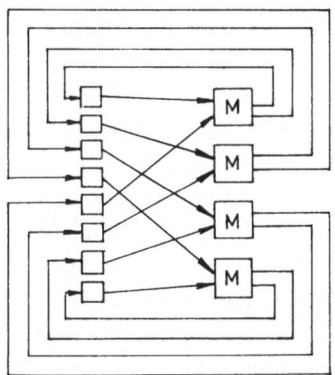

In the memory registers there are elements of the sequence being sorted at the input, and the M modules are "compare-exchange" modules. The computation of masking bits which determine the activity of these modules occurs in every sorting step and involves a perfect shuffle of the state of the mask register. A serial algorithm for bitonic sorting of N items requires time proportional to $N \log^2 N$. On an N-processor computer which is interconnected by a perfect shuffle it is possible to implement $\log^2 N$ steps of this algorithm provided that $N/2$ "compare-exchange" operations can be executed in parallel. Then the speedup of this algorithm is $O(N/\log N)$, which is sufficient for parallel computation.

We note that the best algorithm for interprocessor interconnection of "each-with-four-neighbours" type makes it possible that N elements can be sorted in $O(N)$ steps, i.e. its speedup is only $O(\log N)$.

In the discrete Fourier transformation for the given N patterns of A_k, $k = 0, 1,$ ..., $N-1$, $N = 2^m$, it is necessary to calculate the values of

$$x_j = \sum_{k=0}^{N-1} A_k W^{jk} \qquad (j = 0, 1, ..., N-1),$$

where $W = \exp(2\pi i/N)$. The serial implementation of the FFT algorithm requires $O(N \log N)$ steps. For its parallel implementation, a processor with the same structure as that of the sorting processor is advantageous. Only the module M is in this case a "multiply-add" module, which from its inputs computes in each step simultaneously two weighted totals as outputs. The processor repeats the sequence $\log N$ times: perfect shuffle, multiply, add, shift the result back to the inputs, by obtaining the final result in reversed binary ordering. We can see that for the FFT effective multiprocessor data transfers are as important as a reduced number of arithmetic operations.

The third example of an algorithm that is efficiently implemented by perfect shuffle is matrix transposition. An efficient way to transpose matrices is of great importance to parallel computers, since — as will be seen below — in some algorithms it is necessary to have an equally fast access to the rows and columns of the matrix.

We assume that a matrix **A** of order $N = 2^m$ is stored by rows, i.e. the distance of an element a_{ij} from a_{11} is given by $N(i-1) + (j-1)$. By exchanging i and j in this formula we obtain $\mathbf{A}^T$. It is easy to ensure that after $m = \log N$ perfect shuffles of the binary representation of the index $i-1, j-1$ this is shifted to the representation $j-1, i-1$ which means that an element at a distance of $N(i-1) + (j-1)$ from a_{11} will be at a distance of $N(j-1) + (i-1)$, i.e. a_{ij} has been transferred to the position previously occupied by a_{ji}. Thus we have obtained $\mathbf{A}^T$ from **A** with m perfect shuffles.

Other interprocessor connections similar to the perfect shuffle are, for example, the following illustrations of binary representations of indices [31]:

$$(d_m d_{m-1} \ldots d_2 d_1) \Rightarrow (d_m d_{m-1} \ldots d_2 \bar{d}_1)$$
$$\Rightarrow (d_1 d_m \ldots d_3 d_2)$$
$$\Rightarrow (d_m d_{m-1} \ldots d_{i+1} \bar{d}_i d_{i-1} \ldots d_1) \quad (i = 1, 2, ..., m),$$

where $\bar{x}$ is the negation of x. The first connection implements the exchange of adjacent elements, the second is the so-called inverse perfect shuffle, which is useful in recurrent computations implemented by recursive doubling, the third "cube" connection is similar to the connection in the associative array processor STARAN.

The high effectiveness of AP also requires a suitable data structure and data allocation in memory, since the frequency and amount of cooperation between the individual processors depends on the data distribution between the processors and operators of the algorithm. It is most advantageous when n operands of a vector instruction are situated in n different memory modules; in this case they can be read simultaneously. Least advantageous is when all operands are stored in one memory module and for this reason they have to be read serially. The problems of storing two-dimensional arrays will be discussed later.

When multiplying two matrices of order n, $C = A \cdot B$, i.e. each scalar product is computed by one processor, then the i-th row of A and the j-th column of B must be stored in the memory of the processor which is to calculate the element c_{ij} before the computation can start. In calculating $B \cdot A$ there must be fast access to the rows of B and to the columns of A. Equally fast access to the rows and columns of both matrices seems to be impossible in the given computer architecture.

Suppose we have an array processor that consist of $n + 1$ processors p_i, $i = 0, 1, ..., n$, each of which has an index register r_i via which it is possible to obtain any element from the memory. Let the matrix A, $i, j = 0, 1, ..., n$, be stored in such a way that its i-th column is in the p_i-th processor. If we put i in every r_i, then the elements of the i-th row are obtained in parallel. If we need a j-th column, then n memory cycles are needed to read it, and memory conflicts can occur, if this column is accessed by several processors. This disadvantage does not occur in the so-called skew storing of matrices [15]:

address	p_0	p_1 ...	p_j ...	p_n
	r_0	r_1 ...	r_j ...	r_n
0	a_{00}	a_{01} ...	a_{0j} ...	a_{0n}
1	a_{1n}	a_{10} ...	$a_{i,j-1}$	$a_{1,n-1}$
$\vdots$	$\vdots$	$\vdots$	$\vdots$	$\vdots$
i	$a_{i,n-i+1}$	$a_{i,n-i+2}$	$a_{i,j-1}$	$a_{i,n-i}$
$\vdots$	$\vdots$	$\vdots$	$\vdots$	$\vdots$
n	a_{n1}	a_{n2} ...	$a_{n,j-n}$	a_{n0}

The element a_{ij} is stored in p_k, where $i + j = k \cdot \mod (n + 1)$. Thus, by suitable indexing, it is equally possible to access the rows as well as the columns of A. If we want to obtain the i-th row, we put i in all r_i; if we want to get the j-th column, then we put $(i - j) \mod (n + 1)$ in r_i, $i = 0, 1, ..., n$.

The storage method described requires from every processor to allow a cyclic data shift and to have its own index register. Since these properties are usually included in the computer architecture in any case, skew storing is a relatively cheap way of increasing the effectiveness of an AP.

In [12] it is shown that for some algorithms implemented on an AP with the regular two-dimensional interprocessor network of "each-with-four-neighbours" type, the number of data transfers can be the limiting factor rather than the number of arithmetic operations. It has been shown, for example, that the inversion of a matrix of order N requires $O(\log^2 N)$ arithmetic steps and the multiplication of two matrices of order N requires $O(\log N)$ arithmetic operations. Therefore, the complexity analysis of parallel computations cannot ignore the details of the computer architecture. We discuss these problems further in the chapter on parallel algorithms.

It is obvious from that what has been said above that for a given problem to be effectively implemented on an AP the following assumptions must be satisfied:

a) the calculation can be programmed in the form of vector instructions allowing the parallel computation of identical operations over different data,

b) there must exist connections between the processors which allow a fast data transfer,

c) the operands used in the parallel computation can be read from the memories simultaneously.

If some of these requirements are not satisfied, the calculation will be inefficiently implemented on the AP. Since there are only some types of calculations satisfying these requirements, e.g. linear algebra, the Fast Fourier Transformation, partial differential equations, data sorting, air traffic control, the AP is not a universal computer.

An example of an array processor is ILLIAC IV [2] which was designed mainly for use in nuclear research and weather forecasting. It consists of 64 processors which are arranged as a two-dimensional array. Each of these processors has a memory with a capacity of 2048 words having a length of 64 bits. The processors are controlled by the control unit; each of them has direct access to the input-output units. During the calculation, they synchronously perform the same operation, except that some of them can be blocked by the masking register. Each i-th processor is directly connected to its four neighbours, i.e. with the processors $i + 1$, $i - 1$, $i + 8$, $i - 8$ (mod 64) for data transfer. This interconnection is the same as the five-point scheme of the finite difference method for two-dimensional elliptic equations. The data transfer from the i-th processor to the j-th processor, where the j-th processor is not its direct neighbour, is possible by a sequence of one-step transfers.

For some categories of computations ILLIAC IV is an effective computer; for instance, it inverts a matrix of order 700 in one second at a cost of approximately $ 1.5. But the main problem is the preparation of programs which would make good use of its capabilities. Several programming languages have been designed and implemented for ILLIAC IV. The latest is the language **GLYPNIR** [19] which is based on **ALGOL**-60 with an extension allowing the explicit definition of parallelism in algorithms using 64-word vectors. It was implemented on a BURROUGHS B 6700 computer which contained a program that simulated the ILLIAC IV and was used for program development. Other languages which are being developed are the FORTRAN-based language **CFD,** and the language

IVTRAN which also contains a mechanism for automatic detection of parallelism in the program and allows operations on vectors of any length [19].

A special type of array processor is the so-called associative array processor which contains a combination of matrix processing of data and associative memory. Associative array processors are often used for special purposes, such as data searching and processing in a fast changing data base. That is why they have, instead of passive memory cells small specialized processors capable of executing simultaneously in all memory cells the operation which compares their contents with the word transmitted to them through a channel which connects these processors with the rest of the computer.

An example of an associative array processor is the computer STARAN [24] which is currently the most efficient computer of this kind. It is in serial production and sold by the firm Goodyear Aerospace. Its key feature is an associative array module. It has a multiaccess memory consisting of 256 words of 256 bits each, as well as 256 arithmetic processors and a permutation network. The computer system STARAN can contain up to 32 associative array modules. STARAN differs from other computers in the following features: parallel matrix arithmetic, content addressable storage, bit slice input and output, and the permutation network. Every word of the memory is assigned an arithmetic unit. Each of these 256 arithmetic units processes the data in its memory bit serially. In this way, STARAN can execute in parallel arithmetic operations on hundred thousand operand pairs. For this reason the execution time of arithmetic operations is independent of the number of operand pairs.

STARAN has a so-called associative memory, i.e. a content-addressed memory. Every input word is compared in one memory cycle with all data in the memory matrix; all words that satisfy the given search criterion are identified. Therefore the time for a data search on some key is proportional to the number of bits in the key, not on the amount of data to be searched. An advantage of the associative memory is also, that the data need not be stored in it in some particular order. Input and output operations can be implemented by words or bits for associative operations. In one memory cycle as many as 256 bits of one word can be read or written, or one bit of all words of the memory matrix.

STARAN has also an effective permutation network allowing flexible shifts and data restructuring as well as communication between processors and the memories of the matrix processors. As a result, the speed of the STARAN computer reaches several hundred million operations per second and the speed of the input and output of data up to several billion bits per second. STARAN is suitable for all applications requiring a high computation speed and having a large dynamic data base, or requiring the implementation of identical operations over large data files. Therefore, typical applications of STARAN are as follows: partial differential equations, weather forecasting, matrix calculations, pattern recognition, text processing, seat reservation, protection against ballistic missiles, air traffic control, processing signals from sensors, and data processing. A more detailed description of the STARAN computer architecture is given in the chapter on parallel processors.

12.3 Pipeline processors

Vector transfers between processors and memories can be executed more effectively in a parallel computer, if the vector elements are not addressed individually, since this type of addressing makes the computation considerably longer. But the loss of addressability means that the computation cannot be executed between the elements of a vector, but only between complete vectors. A so-called vector computer of this kind is the pipeline processor (referred to as a PP) whose design is briefly described below.

In adding two vectors of orders n, $\textbf{x}$ and $\textbf{y}$, it is necessary to calculate n sums, $x_i + y_i$, $i = 1, 2, ..., n$. If the addition of two real numbers can be divided into k successive steps of approximately the same duration, such that each step is dependent on the preceding step only, then the sum of two vectors can be computed according to the following scheme, where t is the duration of the longest step:

Time	Steps			
	1	2	...	k
t	$x_1 + y_1$			
$2t$	$x_2 + y_2$	$x_1 + y_1$		
$\vdots$	$\vdots$	$\vdots$		
kt	$x_k + y_k$	$x_{k-1} + y_{k-1}$	...	$x_1 + y_1$
$(k+1)t$	$x_{k+1} + y_{k+1}$	$x_k + y_k$	...	$x_2 + y_2$
$\vdots$	$\vdots$	$\vdots$		$\vdots$
nt	$x_n + y_n$	$x_{n-1} + y_{n-1}$	...	$x_{n-k+1} + y_{n-k+1}$
$(n+1)t$		$x_n + y_n$		
$\vdots$				$\vdots$
$(n+k-1)t$				$x_n + y_n$

One addition is completed after a time kt at the end of each period of time t. Thus the sum $\textbf{x} + \textbf{y}$ will be computed in a time $(n + k - 1)t$, which can be compared to the quantity $n \times$ (addition time of the classical computer) [1].

For example, addition in floating point arithmetic consists of the following steps, where the typical execution time is given in brackets

a) normalization of operands and corresponding alternation of their exponents (100 ns),
b) comparison of exponents (60 ns),
c) shifting of the mantissa of the operand with the smaller exponent (100 ns),
d) direct addition of mantissas (120 ns),
e) normalization of the result (100 ns).

Thus, an addition requires 480 ns. But in the PP, each of these steps is executed in a different hardware section, being shifted to the next section for implementing the next step. Since the longest step, d), requires 120 ns, each step of the computation is assigned the time $t = 120$ ns. Thus, the first result requires 600 ns instead of 480 ns, but every subsequent result is obtained in 120 ns.

On a conventional computer, e.g. CDC STAR-100, the situation is rather more complicated. The execution time R of the operation containing vectors of length n consists of two parts: the start-up time of the vector operation S and the operation times in which all results are computed subsequently. S does not depend on the length of the vectors and ends when the processing of the last step of the first operand pair begins. R is the sum of the time required to start-up the arithmetic unit for a particular vector operation, and of the time which has passed since the start of the last step of the computation of the first pair of operands. The latter depends on the length of the vectors.

Thus, the time R is a linear function of the number of operands and is expressed in 40 ns units, the basic clock time of the STAR-100 computer, as

$$R = S + n/p,$$

where p is the number of results calculated in an arithmetic unit in the basic clock time. The time S is usually much greater than $1/p$. Typical values of S, p, and s (the time of scalar operation) of several instructions of the STAR-100 computer for floating point operations with a word length of 64 bits are as follows:

Operation	S	p	s	$\lceil S/(s - p^{-1}) \rceil$
$+$ $-$	96	2	13	8
$\times$	156	1	17	10
$:$	156	1/2	47	4
$\sqrt{}$	152	1/2	73	3

It follows that:

a) every algorithm should be implemented so that it can have the smallest possible number of vector operations with the longest possible vectors;

b) if short vectors are used, the efficiency of computation decreases owing to the start-up time, e.g. in comparing an operation with vectors of length 1 with vectors of length 100, as much as 97% of the computation time is lost as a result of start-up times [22].

c) for $n > S/(s - p^{-1})$, it is better to use a vector operation than n scalar operations; this is also true if $1/p$ is much smaller than s.

The STAR-100 computer operates with a word length of 64 bits. It has 256 registers and 512 K of main memory. It is intended for scientific and engineering computations [5]. It only operates on vectors, i.e. on sets of words that are stored in n consecutive memory locations $1 \leqslant n \leqslant 65536$. A STAR-100 program must therefore include data manipulation instructions which transform data into vectors. For instance, in contrast to mathematical interpretation, the column of a matrix stored by rows is not a vector. As a result, the addition of two columns ($O(n)$ operations) must be preceded by a special extraction operation ($O(n^2)$ operations) which puts the required elements of the columns into a vector form. Another problem concerns the manipulation of data which are stored in external memory. Since the speed of a pipeline unit is always many times greater than that of transfers from a disk memory or similar peripheral, it may sometimes be advantageous to recalculate the intermediate results rather than store them temporarily on a disk.

Also a small amount of serial computation in the algorithm reduces the total efficiency of the PP. It has been found [33], that if, for example, 10% of a program is executed 10 times slowlier on a vector computer, then the execution time of this program is doubled.

STAR-100 has some instructions, e.g. compress and merge, which have no equivalents in serial computers. Both these instructions employ the so-called control vector. It is the Boolean vector, which can be used to modify some vector operations, e.g. by suppressing the storage or calculation of some vector components.

Let a, b be given vectors and z be the control vector of dimension n. The instruction 'compress' suppresses the elements of the vector a in forming the vector c, depending on the values of the elements of z as follows:

$j := 1$; **for** $i = 1, 2, \ldots, n$
if $z_i = 1$ **then** $\{c_j := a_i \, ; \, j := j + 1 \, ;\}$.

The instruction 'merge' generates a vector c from the vectors a and b, depending on the vector z, as follows:

$j := 1$; $k := 1$; **for** $i = 1, 2, \ldots, n$
if $z_i = 1$ **then** $\{c_i := a_j \, ; \, j := j + 1 \, ;\}$ **else**
$\qquad\qquad \{c_i := b_k \, ; \, k := k + 1 \, ;\}$.

The execution time of the instructions 'compress' and 'merge' are $88 + n$ and $95 + n$.

Both these instructions are used particularly if only some selected data from a long vector is used, e.g. in processing a radar signal or television image only the data which has a certain value is used. Another example is the implementation of the even-odd reduction method for solving a tridiagonal system of linear equations: the separation of vectors into odd and even components is done by the instruction 'compress', and they are joined in a single vector by the instruction 'merge'. STAR-100 has instructions for sparse vector operations. Each vector consists of a continuous set of non-zero components and is assigned a Boolean vector describing its real layout.

Other vector computers which operate completely on the pipeline principle are the Texas Instrument ASC, IBM 2938 and CRAY-1.

We give below an example of the comparison of algorithms for the computation of a tridiagonal system of linear equations, and discuss some problems of their efficient implementation on the pipeline processor STAR-100 [18]. Knowing the duration of the execution of a single instruction of the PP, it is possible to derive explicit formulae for the execution time of a given algorithm, so that different algorithms for solving the same problem can be compared.

Suppose we have the tridiagonal system of linear equations

$$
\begin{bmatrix}
a_1 & b_1 & & & \\
c_2 & a_2 & b_2 & & \mathbf{0} \\
& \ddots & \ddots & \ddots & \\
\mathbf{0} & & & c_n & a_n
\end{bmatrix}
\begin{bmatrix}
x_1 \\ x_2 \\ \vdots \\ x_n
\end{bmatrix}
=
\begin{bmatrix}
d_1 \\ d_2 \\ \vdots \\ d_n
\end{bmatrix}.
$$

The LU decomposition with subsequent forward and backward steps is given by the relations:

$$u_1 = a_1, \qquad g_i = c_i/u_{i-1}, u_i = a_i - g_i b_{i-1} \qquad (i = 2, 3, ..., n), \tag{1}$$

$$y_1 = d_1, \qquad y_i = d_i - g_i y_{i-1} \qquad\qquad (i = 2, 3, ..., n), \tag{2}$$

$$x_n = y_n/u_n, \qquad x_i = (y_i - x_{i+1} b_i)/u_i \quad (i = n-1, n-2, ..., 1). \tag{3}$$

Since all elements of the vector must be known before starting the vector operations, none of these three relations can be implemented on the PP. We compare the serial and parallel implementation of the LU decomposition for calculation (1). In both we write $f_i = 1/u_i$. The first algorithm GE1 does not have vector operations, thus (1) becomes

$$\text{GE1}: f_1 = 1/a_1, \; g_i = c_i f_{i-1}, \; f_i = 1/(a_i - g_i b_{i-1}) \quad (i = 2, 3, ..., n).$$

In the second algorithm there will be two multiplications of the vectors, the first $c_i b_{i-1}$ and the second $c_i f_{i-1}$, $i = 2, 3, ..., n$, i. e.

$$\text{GE2}: \quad t_i = c_i b_{i-1} \qquad\qquad (i = 2, 3, ..., n),$$
$$f_1 = 1/a_1, \quad f_i = 1/(a_i - t_i f_{i-1}) \quad (i = 2, 3, ..., n),$$
$$g_i = c_i f_{i-1}, \qquad\qquad (i = 2, 3, ..., n).$$

Relations (2) and (3) are identical both for GE1 and GE2 with the exception that the division in (3) is replaced by multiplication.

The timing for GE1 and GE2, for the STAR-100 are $273n$ and $312 + 247n$, so that for $n < 13$ the algorithm GE1 is faster, and for $n \geq 13$, GE2 is faster. GE denotes below GE1 for $n < 13$ and GE2 for $n \geq 13$.

We explain the important notion of algorithm consistency using the algorithm for recursive doubling. This algorithm was given by Stone [28] who had noticed that from the recurrent relation

$$q_0 = 1, \; q_1 = a_1, \; q_i = a_i q_{i-1} - c_i b_{i-1} q_{i-2}, \quad i = 2, 3, ..., n \tag{4}$$

it is possible to calculate $u_i = q_i / q_{i-1}$ for relation (1). It follows for relation (4) that

$$\mathbf{Q}_i = \begin{bmatrix} q_i \\ q_{i-1} \end{bmatrix} = \mathbf{G}_i \mathbf{Q}_{i-1},$$

where

$$\mathbf{G}_i = \begin{bmatrix} a_i - c_i b_{i-1} \\ 1 \qquad 0 \end{bmatrix}$$

and hence

$$\mathbf{Q}_i = \prod_{j=i}^{i} \mathbf{G}_j \mathbf{Q}_1.$$

Similarly, it is possible to calculate relations (2) and (3). Thus, recursive doubling provides an effective computation of products of the form

$$p_{ij} = \prod_{m=i}^{i} h_m, \tag{5}$$

where h_m, $m = 1, 2, ..., n$ are given numbers. If $n = 2^k$, then the values p_{ij}, $j = 1, 2, ..., n$ can be summed in $\log n$ steps. If, for example, $n = 8$, then by the following three vector multiplications [18]

$$\begin{Bmatrix} h_1 \\ h_2 \\ h_3 \\ h_4 \\ h_5 \\ h_6 \\ h_7 \\ h_8 \end{Bmatrix} * \begin{Bmatrix} 0 \\ h_1 \\ h_2 \\ h_3 \\ h_4 \\ h_5 \\ h_6 \\ h_7 \end{Bmatrix} = \begin{Bmatrix} p_{11} \\ p_{12} \\ p_{13} \\ p_{34} \\ p_{45} \\ p_{56} \\ p_{67} \\ p_{78} \end{Bmatrix} = \mathbf{P}_1,$$

$$
P_1 * \begin{pmatrix} 0 \\ 0 \\ p_{11} \\ p_{12} \\ p_{23} \\ p_{34} \\ p_{45} \\ p_{56} \end{pmatrix} = \begin{pmatrix} p_{11} \\ p_{12} \\ p_{13} \\ p_{14} \\ p_{25} \\ p_{36} \\ p_{47} \\ p_{58} \end{pmatrix} = P_2, \quad P_2 * \begin{pmatrix} 0 \\ 0 \\ 0 \\ 0 \\ p_{11} \\ p_{12} \\ p_{13} \\ p_{14} \end{pmatrix} = P_3,
$$

we calculate $P_3 = (p_{11}, p_{12}, p_{13}, p_{14}, p_{15}, p_{16}, p_{17}, p_{18})^T$. Hence, for $n = 2^k$ there are altogether k vector multiplications of length $n - 2^i$, $i = 0, 1, \ldots, k - 1$, so that the average duration of each multiplication is

$$
n_a = \frac{1}{k} \sum_{i=0}^{k-1} (n - 2^i) = \frac{n(\log n - 1) + 1}{\log n} \approx n.
$$

Since we have $\log n$ multiplications of this type, the total number of results generated is $n \log n - n + 1$. The serial computation of the LU decomposition with $O(n)$ operations was replaced by an algorithm with a total number of operations $O(n \log n)$, whose parallel implementation requires only $O(\log n)$ vector operations, which therefore produces a speedup. Since the total number of operations is also important, owing to the finite degree of parallelism of the PP, this algorithm will be ineffective above some value of n for the STAR-100. Therefore, we introduce the notation of algorithm consistency [18].

Definition: The vector implementation of an algorithm for solving a problem of size n is consistent if the number of mathematical operations required by this implementation as a function of n is of the same order as in its implementation on a serial computer.

Consistent algorithms are advantageous for STAR-100; but the algorithm for recursive doubling is not consistent. Its duration for STAR-100 is given by

$$
T_1 = (15 n_a + 2432) \log n + 9.5 n - 10 n_a - 230.
$$

By comparing T_1 to the duration of GE, i.e. to T_0, we find that:

a) owing to the term $n \log n$, $\lim_{n \to \infty} T_1/T_0 = \infty$;

b) for short vectors, i.e. for small n, $T_0 < T_1$;

c) for $2^6 < n < 2^{17}$ $T_1 < T_0$, i.e. recursive splitting is more effective for the STAR-100 than LU-decomposition.

If we divide the products in (5) into n/m parts and apply recursive doubling to each part, then the duration of this modification is

$$
T_2 = n \left[\left(\frac{2532}{m} + 15 \right) \log m + \frac{483}{m} - 2.5 \right] - 3m - 10 m_a - 698,
$$

i.e. this algorithm is consistent. If we choose m so that this would minimize T_2, then by comparing T_2 with T_0 we find that $\lim_{n \to \infty} T_2/T_0 \approx 0.68$, where for $n > 2^6$ it is always true that $T_2 < T_0$. A more effective algorithm for the STAR-100 is the algorithm for even-odd cyclic reduction that has been described in more details in another chapter. If a given tridiagonal matrix is stored by diagonals, then the steps of this algorithm can be implemented on the STAR-100 using vectors in time

$$T_3 = 339 \log n + 36n - 601,$$

i.e. the algorithm is consistent, $\lim_{n \to \infty} T_3/T_0 \approx 0.14$ and it is about 7 times faster than GE.

The comparison of parallel algorithms for solving tridiagonal systems of linear equations according to the number of their arithmetic operations, described in [26], has the following results: the cyclic even-odd reduction is the best method for pipeline processors. For array processors it is best only for highly structured systems of equations, e.g. with a symmetric matrix, or constant diagonals. If a system has no special structure and its size is comparable to the number of processors of the array processor, then recursive doubling is the best method.

The cyclic even-odd reduction can also be applied to block tridiagonal systems of equations, but in computers of SIMD type the block matrices must be of the same size, and the need for pivoting causes a reduction of computation efficiency.

12.4 Multiprocessor computers

The problems of multiprocessor computers (MP) are completely different from those of SIMD-type computers. MPS are suitable for a wider range of problems than SIMD; the suitability of an algorithm for SIMD usually means that it is unsuitable for an MP and vice versa. To achieve high efficiency in an MP, the problems of activity synchronization of the processors and of task scheduling between them must be solved. These problems do not occur in SIMD computers, since synchronization is automatic and task scheduling is not needed, for each processor performs the same operations. Consider an MP with n processors, m memory modules and p input-output channels. The main problem of its architecture is to ensure effective communication between these units. One example of processor-memory connection is used to explain the three design possibilities [1]: crossbar switch, multibus and time-shared bus. A similar choice also applies to connections between other units.

Through a crossbar switch each processor has access to each memory, but the memory cannot be accessed by two processors simultaneously. Every connection through the switch transfers complete words and for this reason it must comprise a large number of wires (one per bit). Therefore, a crossbar switch has a high complexity, especially for large n and m. If two or more processors are trying to gain access to the same memory module during a memory cycle, collision occurs. The hardware has to ensure that only one process has access to the given memory;

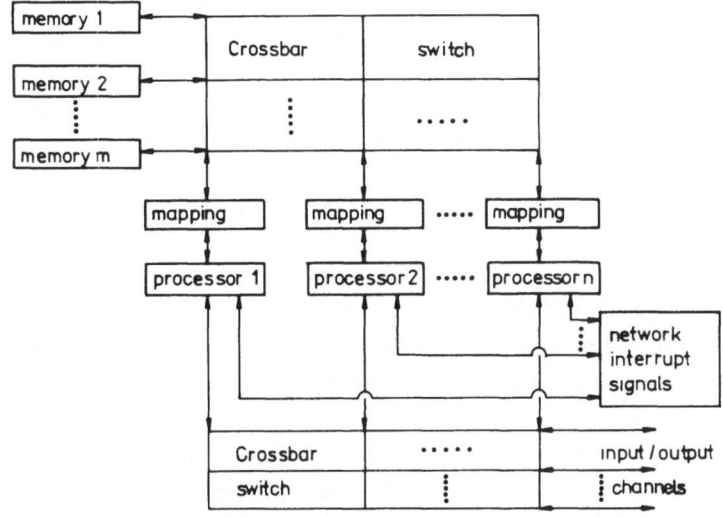

Fig. 2.

the other has to wait in the queue. An example of a crossbar switch **MP** is the C mmp computer, in which $n = m = 16$ [35].

In the case of a multibus system, each processor has access to each memory module via its own bus. Thus the memories have multiple access and each of them contains a device for preventing collisions. In such a system there are fewer interconnecting circuits than in the crossbar switch. It also has more interface modules and is easier to implement. A multibus system was implemented, for example, in the UNIVAC 1108 computer.

In the case of a time-shared bus, all memories are shared by all processors through a single bus. The connection between processors and memories is implemented by standard multiprogramming techniques. From the point of view of modularity, this system is sufficiently flexible, but since there is only one path for all transfers, there will normally be more collisions than in the two preceding systems. A simple example of such a bus is the UNIBUS of the PDP-11 computer.

In Fig. 2 an illustration is given of an **MP** which is an abstraction, based mainly on the C mmp computer [27]. There is multiple connection between n processors, m memories and p input-output channels of the computer. The interconnection processor-memory and processor-I/O channel is implemented by crossbar switches. In a MIMD computer there also is an interrupt network allowing interrupts between processors. There also is address mapping between the processors and memories. Its task is to transform addresses in the processor into real addresses of memory modules. Any change of the program and data locations leads to a change of the mapping function. Memory mapping makes it possible for two or more programs to operate on common or private data. The address which is the result of the mapping is decoded in the switch matrix into the index of the respective memory module and the address in this module. The decoding function is also of great importance to the reliability of the system, since it ensures that if a memory module fails, addresses in the faulty module must not be accessed.

The control of activity of the MP is influenced by the technique of creating, completing and synchronizing parallel branches of the program.

The creation and completion of parallel branches can be solved, for example, by the **FORK, JOIN** technique described above. The synchronization can be implemented, e.g. by operations **WAIT** and **SIGNAL** [7]:

WAIT(*FLAG*); ... **SIGNAL**(*FLAG*);

Before **WAIT** and after **SIGNAL,** statements can be executed by several processors. The part of the program between **WAIT** and **SIGNAL** is the so-called critical section. At most one processor can enter it to execute its process. The variable *FLAG* controls access to the critical section. The operation **WAIT** makes it possible for the process to continue if and only if no other process is in the critical section. When the process has left the critical section, then one and only one of the queuing processes can enter it. The operations **WAIT** and **SIGNAL** can be described as follows:

> **procedure WAIT** (*FLAG*);
>   **begin** $FLAG: = FLAG - 1$;
>   **if** $FLAG < 0$ **then** block this process;
> **end**;
> **procedure SIGNAL** (*FLAG*);
>   **begin** $FLAG: = FLAG + 1$;
>   **if** $FLAG \leqq 0$ **then** start the program
>   blocked by the variable *FLAG*;
> **end**;

At the beginning of the calculation, *FLAG* is assigned value 1. Apart from the implementation of **WAIT** and **SIGNAL,** the absolute value of *FLAG* is equal to the number of processes waiting to enter the critical section. If the process executes **WAIT** and if $FLAG = 0$, then it can continue. If it performs **SIGNAL** and $FLAG \leqq -1$, then at least one other process is waiting to enter the critical section. The variables which are used as arguments in the **WAIT** and **SIGNAL** operations are termed semaphores [7].

The blocked processes are incorporated in the respective queues. Each semaphore has a queue assigned to it, whose elements are the processes which are waiting to enter the appropriate critical section. Every blocking of a process is implemented by the operating system.

In contrast to the collision in memory access which is resolved by hardware, there can also be a collision in the multiprocessor when a processor tries to use the data which is accessed by some other processor. As we have seen, it is possible to solve such a problem by software.

Another problem occurring in the MP is that of scheduling techniques, i.e. determination of the strategy for selecting tasks waiting for scheduling processes, memories and input-output channels. Common resources have to be distributed among the processors so that all system requirements can be satisfied and also the resources exploited efficiently. The main problem occurs if a given scheduling strategy can lead to the situation called deadlock, in which a section of the system gets into a wait state which can be interrupted from outside only. Some results show [34] that the optimal scheduling algorithms are internally very complicated. Therefore, effective heuristic algorithms are of importance in practice. These are simple, sufficiently fast and often give schedules close to the optimal ones. A survey is given in [30]. The disadvantage of heuristic algorithms is that there may occur certain anomalies. Improvement of the system parameters, e.g. increasing the number of processors, or their speed, might lead to a prolongation of schedules obtained by the heuristic method [13].

An example of the multiprocessor computer is the multi-miniprocessor computer C mmp [35], which was constructed at the Carnegie-Mellon University in Pittsburg as an effective computation tool, designed especially for solving problems in artificial intelligence, as well as for research into parallel computation structures and system programming. The C mmp computer system has up to 16 processors, DEC PDP-11 minicomputers, and 16 memory modules, each module having a capacity of 64 K 16-bit words. The connection between processors and memories is implemented by a crossbar switch allowing up to 16 simultaneous memory accesses, provided no accessed words are in the same memory module. Since the 16 bits of the address field of the PDP-11 do not allow access to large data arrays, the C mmp computer contains a mapping device which allows access to the common memory without significant delays. The C mmp attains a speed of 3—5 million instructions per second.

Another multiprocessor computer is the modular multi-microprocessor computer CM* [29]. This system has also been developed at the Carnegie-Mellon University, and it differs substantially from the C mmp in its architecture. The CM* computer was designed with the aim to modularly interconnect processors into a computational system in such way that great computation speeds can be achieved at a small cost. A module of the CM* computer consists of processor-memory pairs. These are connected by a flexible interprocessor mechanism which allows close cooperation between them. By address mapping, all processors have access to the address space of the entire virtual memory. The number of processors, the memory capacity and the channel width are not limited. The first version of CM* consisted of 10 DEC LSI-11 microprocessors. At present a version is being developed which will consist of up to 100 such microprocessors.

In conclusion we discuss algorithms for MP's. Research in this area currently lags behing SIMD algorithms. Kung [17] has achieved interesting results in research on algorithms for MP's. We give a brief description of some of these algorithms.

A parallel algorithm for an MP is a set of processes, which can be executed in parallel and can operate simultaneously in solving a given problem. A process is the execution of a certain procedure in a multiprocessor operating system. A process can be executed by various processors assigned to it by the operating system. Each process has so-called interaction points, at which it can communicate with other processes. The interaction points divide a process into stages.

The duration of a given stage and hence also of the process is usually not constant in the MP. Variations in this duration cannot be foreseen and are due to the following [17]:

a) An MP can be composed of processors of different speed; the speed of a process depends on the type of the processor which it is assigned to;

b) a process can be delayed by conflicts, when several processors wait for access to the common memory;

c) the processor performing the given process can be interrupted by the operating system and the computation can be replaced by other activity, e.g. by a higher-priority process or an input-output operation;

d) in multiprogramming, the speed of computation can be effected by the number and demands of other users of the system;

e) the amount of processing needed for the execution of the given process can be dependent on its input data, e.g. the number of comparisons needed for the sorting of n elements depends on their original ordering; the time of computation of some function is dependent on the value of the independent variables.

From this it follows that the execution time of a stage of any process on the MP is a random variable with a particular distribution function. We make use of this fact in creating algorithms below. Algorithms for MP's are divided into synchronous and asynchronous [17]. In synchronous parallel algorithm (SPA), there are processes some stages of which cannot start their activity until stages of other processes have already terminated their activity. This is achieved, e.g. by the synchronization method already described. Therefore, the durations of the stages of a process are random variables, and synchronization may cause some processes to be blocked at a given time which consequently reduces the total speed of computation. In an asynchronous parallel algorithm (APA), there exists a set of global variables to which all processes have access. If a cycle of the process comes to an end, then this process reads some global variables, and on the basis of these and previously obtained results it modifies some global variables and starts its next cycle. Thus, global variables provide for communication between processes, and the operations on them must be programmed as critical sections. The main advantage of an APA; is that its processes never wait for data, but always compute using the current status of the global variables. Its disadvantage is that processes can be blocked before entering the critical sections. The termination time of the process is the sum of the time of:

1. processing, i.e. of the sum of the times needed to execute all the instructions;

2. blocking, i.e. of the sum of the times in which the process was blocked waiting in the SPA for suitable data and for entering the critical section in the APA.

3. synchronization, i.e. the sum of times needed for the execution of synchronization in the SPA and for the execution of critical sections in the APA.

The time of blocking and synchronization is much longer in the SPA than that in the APA. It appears that there exists a certain equilibrium between these times, i.e. if we reduce one of them, the other increases, and vice versa.

The total duration of every parallel algorithm for an MP is therefore the time which has passed until the termination of the activity of its last process. Let us assume that we always have a sufficient number of processes for the implementation of parallel algorithms. Now, we explain briefly how to design SPA's and APA's for a general iterative algorithm. These problems will also be discussed in the chapter on the design of parallel algorithms.

Suppose we have a convergent iterative algorithm

$$x_{i+1} = \varphi(x_i) \qquad (i = 0, 1, \ldots),$$ (6)

where x_0 is given. A parallel process can be obtained from (6) by parallel implementation of φ, or by using the variation in the time of calculation.

The parallel calculation of φ can be carried out synchronously or asynchronously. Let $\varphi(x)$ be written as $F(g(x), h(x))$. Then

$$x_{i+1} = F(g(x_i), h(x_i)) \quad (i = 0, 1, \ldots).$$ (7)

In an iterative SPA, $g(x_i)$ and $h(x_i)$ are computed in every iteration, x_{i+1} will be computed after the termination of these calculations. It is clear that the execution times of g and h may differ and hence only the time of the function which has been calculated later determines the moment of computation of x_{i+1}.

In an iterative APA, the processes are not synchronized. Let, for example, the computation time of h be much longer than that of g. Then we create an algorithm from two processes, P_1 and P_2, i.e.

P_1: $y_1 := g(y_3)$; $y_3 := F(y_1, y_2)$, **if** S is not **true**;

P_2: $y_2 := h(y_3)$, **if** S is not **true**.

P_1 and P_2 have access to the global variables y_1, y_2. S is the global condition for ending the process. At the beginning of the calculation $y_1 = g(x_0)$, $y_2 = h(x_0)$ and $y_3 = F(y_1, y_2)$. As soon as some process has completed its computation, a new computation starts without delay, making use of the current values of the global variables. If the implementation time of P_1 is smaller than P_2, then

$$x_{i+1} = F(g(x_i), h(x_j)), \ j \leqq i, \tag{8}$$

i.e. this is an iteration different from (7), for which new convergence conditions have to be derived. A compromise between synchronous and asynchronous iterations is the supplementary condition for (8) in the form of $i - j \leqq k$, where k is an integer which ensures that too old values of x_j are not used to compute the function $h(x)$.

Parallelization of (1) by exploiting the time variation of the computation of φ is performed by the so-called simple iterative APA. We generate two identical processes P_k, $k = 1, 2,$:

$$P_k: \ j := i + 1; \quad x_j := \varphi(x_{j-1}); \tag{9}$$
$$\textbf{if } i < j \textbf{ then } i := j;$$
$$\textbf{if } S \textbf{ is true then end.}$$

The variables i and x_i are global; j is the local variable of each processor; i is the index of the variable that was calculated last. Statement (9) is programmed as the critical section. The processes P_1 and P_2 calculate S from input data which are available at their start. This computation can be represented graphically as follows (the length of individual line segments represents the execution time of the process):

P_1: $x_1 \quad x_2 \quad x_4 \ x_5 \ x_6 \quad x_7$

P_2: $x_1 \quad x_2 \ x_3 \quad x_4 \quad x_7$

When P_1 is calculating x_2, P_2 has already calculated x_3, so that P_1 does not calculate the variable x_3 and after x_2 it starts the computation of x_4. Similarly, P_2 does not calculate x_5 or x_6. If each process performs 5 calculations, we have calculated x_7 instead of x_5, i.e. speedup has been achieved. This speedup, however, is not to be obtained by dividing the work between two processes, but by exploiting the variation of the times. The speed of such an APA can be increased further, if the processes which don't perform useful computations are interrupted, and if the cost of the test and the subsequent interruption are not too high.

SPA's are used when the variations in the durations of processes are small and when there is only a small number of processes to be synchronized. APA's are advantageous, when there are great variations in the durations. They are more efficient than SPA's, since they never wait for input values, taking advantage of fast operating processes. They are more reliable, too, because in case of a permanently blocked process, the computation can continue except the blocking occurred in the critical section.

12.5 Specialized parallel computers

In this Section we deal with several special parallel algorithms and specialized parallel computers. First, using an example of matrix multiplication we show how to modify an algorithm to be efficiently implemented on different parallel architectures and then we give a brief description of several computers specialized for narrow application areas. In [10], a distributed array processor (DAP) is described. It is of SIMD type, and consists of 1024 simple processors that have their own memory each and are connected into a two-dimensional array by the "each-with-four-neighbours" system. The processors work on the bit level, so that arithmetic operations are implemented by program. On the system of dimension 32×32, i.e. 1024 processors, which has been in operation since 1976, the following times for 32-bit floating-point operations were obtained: multiplication of two square matrices of order $32 - 16$ ms; inversion of a matrix of order 32 with total pivoting — 29 ms; FFT from 1024 complex numbers — 14 ms. The above times indicate that the DAP is a highly efficient parallel computer.

Algorithms implemented on a DAP should be modified so that it would be possible to exploit all its architecture possibilities. For example, matrix multiplication of $C = A \cdot B$ matrices of order 32 is implemented on a DAP by the following program:

$C := 0 \cdot 0$;
DO 100 $I = 1, 32$
100 $C := C + A(, * I) \times B(* I,)$.

By symbol $A(, * I)(B(* I,))$ a new matrix is assembled whose columns (rows) are equal to the i-th column of A (row B). The corresponding elements of the resulting matrices are multiplied and the results added to C. After 32 steps on C we get $A \cdot B$. Because the mechanism for creating the partial matrices is implemented by hardware it takes only about 10% of the total computation time. It is also interesting that this method does not employ the interprocessor connection of the DAP computer.

The pipeline processor CDC STAR-100 requires algorithms which can be written in the form of vectors. The classical algorithm for multiplying matrices of order n is not suitable for the STAR-100, since a scalar product instruction requires a relatively high execution time on this computer. If $c_j(a_k)$ is an j-th (k-th) column of vector $C(A)$, then a typical vector algorithm is the calculation

$$c_j = \sum_{k=1}^{n} b_{kj} a_k \qquad (j = 1, 2, ..., n).$$

On the STAR-100 computer [20], this algorithm requires

$$(250n^2 - 188n + 94) + \frac{3}{2}n^3 - n^2 + n/2$$

cycles of 40 ns. The algorithm is not suitable for band matrices with a relatively narrow band width or, like every algorithm for pipeline processors, for full matrices of small order. Moreover, in storing matrices by columns it is not easy to obtain A^T on the STAR-100, where successive storing of vector elements is required. Therefore, in [20] a new algorithm — more suitable for vectorization — is described for matrix multiplication requiring matrix storage by diagonals. Storage by diagonals is normal, especially for band matrices. Nevertheless, this algorithm is unusual, because using the diagonals of A and B as vectors, the matrix C can also be calculated by diagonals. Also A^T can be easily obtained from the vectors of the diagonals.

Let d_0 be the main diagonal of C and $d_k(d_{-k})$, $k = 1, 2, ..., n-1$, the first, second, ... $(n-1)$-th diagonals over (under) d_0. The algorithm for the calculation of d_k, $k \geqq 0$ is then informally as follows:

1. Omit the lower k rows of A and the upper k rows of B^T;
2. Multiply element by element the resulting matrices of order $(n-k)/n$ to obtain matrix D_k;
3. The m-th component of d_k is obtained by summing the elements in the m-th row of D_k, $m = 1, 2, ..., n-k$.

The computation of d_k, $k < 0$, is similar — except that in step 1 the upper k rows of A and the lower k columns of B^T are omitted. The time of this algorithm on the STAR-100 is

$$250(3n^2 - 3n + 1) + 3n^3/2.$$

Although the start-up time of this algorithm is about three times longer than that of the preceding algorithm, the algorithms are equivalent for large n. These algorithms are most advantageous for band matrices with small band width. If A and B are band matrices with a band width $2p + 1$, then the band width of C is $4p + 1$ and the computation time of C is only

$$250(2p + 1)^2 + 3n(2p + 1)^2/2.$$

For example, if **A** and **B** are tridiagonal matrices $(p = 1)$ of order 1000, then a diagonal algorithm is more than 48 times faster than the preceding algorithm on the STAR-100.

Now we give a short description of some examples, in which specialized parallel computers have been designed on the basis of a detailed knowledge of the algorithms implemented.

[32] describes a specialized parallel computer for Kálman's filter, in which the calculation is based on basic matrix and vector operations, mainly on the matrix product and matrix inversion. The architecture of this computer makes it possible to implement the product of two square matrices of order n by the following algorithm

1. $k := 0$; **C** := **0**;
2. for $i = 2, 3, ..., n$, shift the i-th row of **A** cyclically left by $i - 1$ places;
3. for $j = 2, 3, ..., n$, shift the j-th column of **B** cyclically upwards by $j - 1$ places;
4. $k := k + 1$; multiply corresponding elements of both matrices and add the resulting matrix to the value of **C** already obtained;
5. shift all columns of **A** cyclically right by one position;
6. shift all rows of **B** cyclically downwards by one position;
7. if $k < n$ go to 4, otherwise end.

In 10×10 matrices, this algorithm is 200—250 times faster than serial matrix multiplication.

Now we shall mention some computers specialized for a particular type of task.

Signal processing is a very important task in various applications. The processing of such a task requires the execution of many independent subtasks of type FFT, linear and non-linear filtering, correlation, convolution, envelope detection, etc., where it is necessary to analyse a large amount of information in real time. Several specialized parallel computers have been designed for signal processing, such as SPS-41, OMEN, CLIP-3, PEPE and AN/UYK-17.

The SPS-41 vector processor [23] consists of 3 programmable processors: the first is intended for controlling data access and sorting, the second — for executing indexed address computations, and the third — for arithmetic operations. Its speed is ≈ 15 million instructions per second, e.g. a 1024-point FFT is executed in 8 ms.

The orthogonal multiprocessor OMEN [32] consists of two processors sharing a joint orthogonal memory. It contains 78 registers connected to 64 processors. This connection can be modified to make it efficient for some special matrix and vector operations.

The parallel matrix processor CLIP-3 [8] has been designed for fast processing of matrices of the illumination intensity of individual elements of a picture obtained by television camera. It consists of a 16×12 matrix, i.e. of 192 processors each having a 16-bit memory, and operating at bit level. The computer CLIP-4 which will contain 96×96, i.e. 9216 processors — each of them having a 32-bit memory, is being built.

The parallel computer PEPE [32] has been designed for processing radar signals in real time for defence against ballistic missiles. It is an associative computer of SIMD type. It has 288 processors comprising a non-structured field in which the individual elements have no topological relationships. The only connection is through the control unit.

The specialized parallel computer AN/UYK-17 [14] for signal processing is described in more detail. Its layout is as follows:

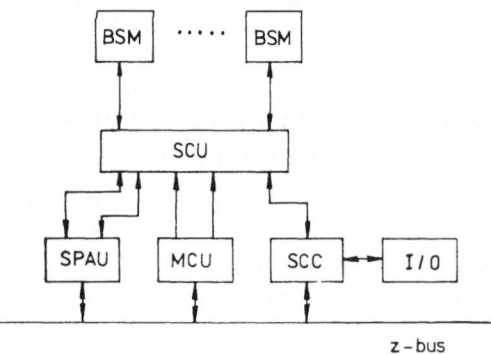

The parallelism of operations of this computer is implemented at both system and instruction levels. At the system level, it is a multiprocessor containing several function units, operating in parallel. The system has a microprogrammable control unit (MCU) which controls the whole system and organizes the data. Main functions of the unit are: data management, scheduling of SPAU work, input-output control, and interrupt handling. A specialized arithmetic processor (SPAU) transforms signals. It executes fast signal processing operations, such as spectrum computation, convolution, correlation and filtering. Other units of the computer collect and store data and control connections between other units. The central memory consists of up to 8 buffer store modules (BSM), which are available to the MCU, SPAU and to input/output data transfer. Each BSM has a capacity of 4096 32-bit words. Transfers between the BSM and peripherals are provided by one or more selector channel control units (SCC).

The store control unit (SCU) computes addresses and resolves conflicts, i.e. it has the function of a switch between the BSM and other units of the system. The intermodular communication is provided by a z-bus which has 16 bidirectional data lines and 14 control lines.

The MCU and the SPAU consist of several modules which can execute parallel operations. Parallelism in the SPAU is exhibited by a recursive filter of order 2 and an FFT. The outputs of a recursive filter of order 2 can be described at any time by the relations

$$w_0 = x - b_1 w_1 - b_2 w_2,$$
$$y = w_0 + a_1 w_1 + a_2 w_2,$$

which require 4 parallel multipliers and 4 adders. The basic unit for FFT computation also requires 4 multipliers and 4 adders so that the two algorithms can be executed by the same hardware.

The activity of the MCU is also carried out in parallel so that a high-computation rate is achieved, e.g. the MCU transposes a matrix of order 40 in less than 1700 150-ns cycles. The AN/UYK-17 system has a modular design and can be extended by additional MCU, SPAU, BSM and SCC units, the intermodular communication being provided by the z-bus and the interrupt device.

Conclusion

In the last section of this chapter we summarize the main problems of parallel computers and give a brief outline of their future prospects.

SIMD computers are not universal computers; they are only suitable for algorithms that can be written as vector operations. The most important problem of SIMD computers is the design of the interprocessor connection which should correspond to the functional relations in the algorithms and the creation of data structures, and their storage in memory so as to allow their effective manipulation. The problem of the synchronization of processors and task scheduling between them no longer exists in SIMD computers. The need to synchronize computation by instructions and the limited possibility for addressing variables are the disadvantages of SIMD computers caused by the lack of a shared store.

MIMD computers are universal computers suitable for solving tasks consisting of several independent subtasks. The algorithms for a particular problem are usually completely different on MIMD and SIMD computers. Their effective execution depends on a suitable synchronization facilities and on effective strategies for assigning resources in the computer. The reduction of delays which are causes of conflicts in memory accesses brought about by both hardware and software represents an important problem of MIMD computers. According to [27], the development of MIMD computers lays behind SIMD computers by several years. In future, SIMD computers will have a high degree of parallelism; for example, according to [4], "it may be that there appear parallel computers of SIMD type with several hundred thousands of processors". For the given SIMD architectures, new special algorithms and data structuring methods will be created and new effective interprocessor connections investigated. There will be further development of languages, translators and program-analyzers which would automatically generate programs for SIMD computers.

Iteratively structured programs are more applicable to SIMD computers; they tend to be less efficient for MIMD computers, owing to the housekeeping connected with synchronization and assignment of resources. Classical numerical algorithms are more convenient for SIMD machines. But it has been shown recently [17] that some numerical computations executed without synchronization in the so-called asynchronous manner can also be effectively executed on MIMD computers. At present, there are MIMD computers which have few processors only. Parallelization of algorithms and programs on them is not complicated. But it is difficult to use MIMD computers which have many processors, since real algorithms seldom contain so many parallel processes, and because till now there have not been developed practical methods for the parallelization of programs for MIMD computers. Besides asynchronous algorithms, there also exist some algorithms based on artificial intelligence which are suitable for MIMD computers. For example, a program for speech recognition that consists of parallel tasks of different structure has been effectively implemented on the C mmp computer. Independent processes in this program are [23]: numerical analysis of acoustic signals, correlation, speech content modelling, generation of hypotheses and selection of the most probable words.

The design of MIMD computers with a large number of processors would only be possible when the problems of creating effective algorithms, synchronization, assignment of resources, automatic parallelization and compilation have been solved at a practical level.

REFERENCES

[1] BAER, J. L.: Survey of some theoretical aspects of multiprocessing. Comp. Surveys, 5, 1973, 1, 31—80

[2] BARNES, G. et al.: The ILLIAC IV computer. IEEE Trans. on Computers, C-17, 1968, 746—757.

[3] BATCHER, K. E.: Sorting networks and their applications. Spring Joint Comp. Conf., 1968, AFIPS Proc., 32. Thompson, Washington, 1968, pp. 307—314.

[4] CHON, S. CH. and KUCK, D. J.: Time and parallel processor bounds for linear recurrence systems. IEEE Trans. on Computers, C-24, 1975, 701—717.

[5] Control Data Corporation, STAR-100 Computer Hardware Reference Manual, 1974.

[6] CONWAY, M. E.: A multiprocessor system design. AFIPS Conf. Proc. 1963, FJCC 24. Spartan Books, Baltimore, 1963, pp. 139—146.

[7] DIJKSTRA, E. W.: Cooperating sequential processes. In: Programming Languages. F Genuys (Editor). Academic Press, New York, 1968, pp. 43—112.

[8] DUFF, M. J. and WATSON, D.: A parallel computer for array processing. Proc. IFIP Congress, North-Holland Publ. Co., Amsterdam, 1975, pp. 94—99.

[9] ENSLOW, P., Jr. (Editor): Multiprocessors and Parallel Processing. Willev—Interscience, New York, 1974.

[10] FLANDERS, P. M. et al.: Efficient high-speed computing with the distributed array processor. In: High-Speed Computers and Algorithms Organization. D. J. Kuck, D. H. Lawrie and A H. Sameh (Editors). Academic Press, New York, 1977, pp. 113—128.

[11] FLYNN, M. J.: Toward more efficient computer organizations. Proc. Spring Joint Comp Conf., AFIPS Press, 1972, pp. 1211—1217.

[12] GENTLEMAN, W. M.: Some complexity results for matrix computations on parallel processors. J. ACM, 25, 1978, 1, 112—115.

[13] GRAHAM, R. L.: Bounds on multiprocessing timing anomalies. SIAM J. Appl. Math., 17, 1969, 2, 416—429.

[14] IHNAT, J. P. et al.: The use of two levels of parallelism to implement an efficient programmable signal processing computer. Sagamore Comp. Conf. on Parallel Processing, Sagamore, 1973, pp. 113—119.

[15] KUCK, D.: ILLIAC IV software and application programming. IEEE Trans. on Computers, C-17, 1968, 8, 758—770.

[16] KUCK, D.: Multioperation machine computational complexity. In: Complexity of Sequential and Parallel Numerical Algorithms. J. F. Traub (Editor). Academic Press, New York, 1973, pp. 17—47.

[17] KUNG, H. T.: Synchronized and asynchronous parallel algorithms for multiprocessors. In: Algorithms and Complexity. J. F. Traub (Editor). Academic Press, New York, 1976, pp. 153—200.

[18] LAMBIOTTO, J. J. and VOIGT, R. G.: The solution of tridiagonal systems of equations on the CDC STAR-100 computer. ACM Trans. on Math. Software, 1, 1975, 4, 308—329.

[19] LAWRIE, D. H. et al.: GLYPNIR — a programming language for ILLIAC IV. Comm. CAC, 18, 1975, 3, 157—164.

[20] MADSEN, N. K. et al.: Matrix multiplication by diagonals on a vector parallel processor. Inform. Proc. Lett., 5, 1976, 2, 41—45.

[21] MIRENKOV, N. N.: Strukturnoe parallelnoe programmirovanie. Programmirovanie, 3, 1975, 3—14.

[22] OWENS, J. L.: The influence of machine organization on algorithms. In: Complexity of Sequential and Parallel Numerical Algorithms. J. F. Traub (Editor). Academic Press, New York, 1973, pp. 111—130.

[23] RAJ REDDY, D.: Some numerical problems in artificial intelligence: Implications for complexity and machine architecture. In: Complexity of Sequential and Parallel Numerical Algorithms. J. F. Traub (Editor). Academic Press, New York, 1973, pp. 131—147.

[24] STARAN: System description. A new class of computer. Goodyear Aerospace Corp., Akron, Ohio, 1974.

[25] STONE, H. S.: Parallel processing with perfect schuffle. IEEE Trans. on Computers, C-20, 1971, 2, 153—161.

[26] STONE, H. S.: Parallel tridiagonal equation solver. ACM Trans. on Math. Software, 1, 1975, 289—307.

[27] STONE, H. S. (Editor): Introduction to Computer Architecture. Sci. Res. Assoc., Inc., Chicago, 1975.

[28] STONE, H. S.: An efficient parallel algorithm for the solution of a tridiagonal system of equations. J. ACM, 20, 1973, 27—30.

[29] SWAN, R. J. et al.: The structure and architecture of CM*: A modular multiprocessor. Tech. Report, Dep. Comp. Sci., Carnegie-Mellon Univ., Pittsburg, 1977.

[30] SHAKHBAZYAN, K. V. and TUSHKINA, T. A.: Obzor metodov sostavleniya raspisanii dlya mnogoprotsessornykh sistem. Zap. nauch. semin. LOMI, AN SSSR, Leningrad, 54, 1975, pp. 229—258.

[31] THOMPSON, C. D.: Generalized connection networks for parallel processor intercommunication. Tech. Report, Dep. Comp. Sci., Carnegie-Mellon Univ., Pittsburg, 1977.

[32] THURBER, K. J.: Large scale computer architecture. In: Parallel and Associative Processors. Hayden Book Co., Rochello Part, N. J., 1976.

[33] TUTLE, P. G.: Implementation of selected eigenvalue algorithms on a vector computer. Tech. Report NPGD-TM-330, Babcock and Wilcox 1975.

[34] VAIRAVAN, K. and DeMILLO, R. A.: On the computational complexity of a generalized scheduling problem. IEEE Trans. on Computers, C-25, 1976, 11, 1067—1073.

[35] WULF, W. A. and BELL, C. G.: C mmp — a multi-miniprocessor. AFIPS Conf. Proc. 1972, FJCC 41. AFIPS Press, Montwale, N. J., pp. 765—777.

Appendix

GENERALIZED PERFECT SHUFFLE

In this appendix the perfect shuffle network interprocessor communication [1] (below PS) is generalized and its applications to matrix transposition, sorting and fast Fourier transformation (below FFT) are described.

1. Generalized perfect shuffle. Assume that $P = \{0, 1, 2, ..., N-1\}$, $N = kn$, where k, n are both integers k, $n \leq 2$.

The following permutation will be called a generalized perfect shuffle of type $k \times n$ (below GPS or $G[k, n]$ or simply G).

$$G(i) = \begin{cases} ki & \text{if } 0 \leq i \leq n-1 \\ ki + 1 - N & \text{if } n \leq i \leq 2n-1 \\ \vdots \\ ki + j(1 - N) & \text{if } jn \leq i \leq (j-1)n - 1 \\ \vdots \\ ki + (k-1)(1 - N) & \text{if } n(k-1) \leq i \leq kn-1 \end{cases}$$

It can be simplified as follows: $G(i) = ki + \lfloor i/n \rfloor (1 - N)$, where $\lfloor i/n \rfloor$ denotes the largest integer less than or equal to i/n. Figure 1 shows the principle of the GPS. There is another representation of a GPS by using matrices based on the work of Fino and Algazi [2].

Definition: Let $N = kn$ and both $a = \{a_0, a_1, ..., a_{N-1}\}$, and $b = \{b_0, b_1, ..., b_{N-1}\}$ be sequences of numbers before and after $G[k, n]$. $G[k, n]$ can be represented by the following matrix product: $\mathbf{P}' \times \mathbf{B} \times \mathbf{P} \times \mathbf{A} = \mathbf{C}$, where $\mathbf{A}$ and $\mathbf{B}$ are both diagonal matrices with sequences a and b in the diagonals. $\mathbf{P} = (p_{ij})$ is the permutation matrix such that $p_{ij} = \delta_{rs}\delta_{uv}$, where $i = rn + u$, $j = vk + s$; $s, r = 0, 1,$

..., $k-1$; u, $v = 0$, 1, ..., $n-1$; δ is Kronecker's δ, $\mathbf{P}^t$ is the transpose of the matrix $\mathbf{P}$. Then the matrix $\mathbf{C}$ is the diagonal matrix with $c_u = b_j a_i$ and $b_j = G[k, n](a_i)$.

The following example shows this representation: let $k = 3$, $n = 2$, then $G[3, 2]$ is represented by the product

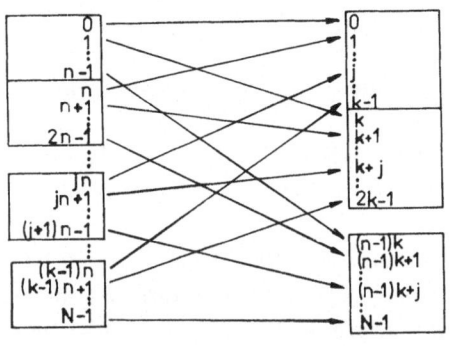

Fig. 1.

$$
\begin{pmatrix}
1\,0\,0 & 0\,0\,0 \\
0\,0\,0 & 1\,0\,0 \\
0\,1\,0 & 0\,0\,0 \\
0\,0\,0 & 0\,1\,0 \\
0\,0\,1 & 0\,0\,0 \\
0\,0\,0 & 0\,0\,1
\end{pmatrix}
\times
\begin{pmatrix}
b_0 & & & & & \\
& b_1 & & & \mathbf{0} & \\
& & b_2 & & & \\
& & & b_3 & & \\
& & & & b_4 & \\
\mathbf{0} & & & & & b_5
\end{pmatrix}
\times
$$

$$
\times
\begin{pmatrix}
1\,0 & 0\,0 & 0\,0 \\
0\,0 & 1\,0 & 0\,0 \\
0\,0 & 0\,0 & 1\,0 \\
0\,1 & 0\,0 & 0\,0 \\
0\,0 & 0\,1 & 0\,0 \\
0\,0 & 0\,0 & 0\,1
\end{pmatrix}
\times
\begin{pmatrix}
a_0 & & & & & \\
& a_1 & & & \mathbf{0} & \\
& & a_2 & & & \\
& & & a_3 & & \\
& & & & a_4 & \\
\mathbf{0} & & & & & a_5
\end{pmatrix}
=
$$

$$
=
\begin{pmatrix}
b_0 a_0 & & & & & \\
& b_3 a_1 & & & \mathbf{0} & \\
& & b_1 a_2 & & & \\
& & & b_4 a_3 & & \\
& & & & b_2 a_4 & \\
\mathbf{0} & & & & & b_5 a_5
\end{pmatrix}
\Rightarrow
\begin{matrix}
a_0 \longrightarrow b_0 \\
a_1 \searrow \nearrow b_1 \\
a_2 \nearrow b_2 \\
a_3 \searrow b_3 \\
a_4 \nearrow b_4 \\
a_5 \longrightarrow b_5
\end{matrix}
$$

The application of GPS to matrix transposition, sorting and FFT is shown below.

2. GPS application to matrix transposition. There are many problems in which it is necessary to have fast access to both rows and columns of a matrix. Parallel computers with GPS handle these problems very efficiently. The following assertion bears this out.

Proposition. Let $A = (a_{ij})$ be a matrix of order $k \times n$. If the matrix A is stored as a vector of data in the Algol fashion (i.e. row by row), its transposition is obtained by one $G[k, n]$.

Proof. Follows directly from the definition of GPS.

The subsequent theorem is a generalization of the previous proposition and of Stone's result.

Theorem. Let A be a matrix of order $N \times k$, where $N = r_1 \ldots r_p$. Then the transpose of the matrix A is obtained after $G[r_1, Nk/r_1]$, $G[r_2, Nk/r_2]$, ..., $G[r_p, Nk/r_p]$.

Proof. It is sufficient to show that if $N = mn$, then $G[n, Nk/n](G[m, Nk/m](i)) = G[N, k](i)$ for $i \in P$. In terms of the first GPS representation we have: $G[N, k](i) = iN - \lfloor i/k \rfloor (Nk - 1)$. We assume (without loss of generality) that: $i = i_1 nk + i_2 k + i_3$, where $0 \leq i_3 < k$.

Then: $G[n, Nk/n](G[m, Nk/m](i)) = (im - i_1(Nk - 1))n - \lfloor (im - i_1(Nk - 1)) /km \rfloor (Nk - 1) = iN - i_1(Nk - 1)n - \lfloor ((i - i_1 Nk)m + i_1)/km \rfloor (Nk - 1) = iN - i_1(Nk - 1)n - i_2(Nk - 1) = iN - \lfloor i/k \rfloor (Nk - 1)$. This completes the proof.

The theorem allows some basic interconnections in various combinations to be used according to the type of matrix.

3. GPS application to sorting. Another interesting property of the GPS is the possibility of its application to the modification of Batcher's algorithm [3] for sorting.

Proposition. Let $a_0, a_1, a_2, \ldots, a_{N-1}$ be a bitonic sequence. By applying the permutation $G[m, N/m]$ we obtain N/m groups of m numbers. For each such group one processor is selected which arranges these numbers in increasing order. The next step is the permutation $G[N/m, m]$. Its result is m bitonic subsequences with the following property (V): no number from an arbitrary subsequence is larger than an arbitrary number from the following subsequences.

Proof. Since the presentation of a formal proof would be too long, only an informal proof is given here. Let $N = mn$. Consider the most general case of a bitonic sequence. This means that it has either the shape

or .

Consider the first case (the proof of the second case is similar). $G[m, n]$ divides the sequence into m sections of n elements (Fig. 2a) which are mutually overlapped (Fig. 2b). The elements in a single column are sorted. It can be seen from the figure how the resultant sequences appear. (For clarity only the first (the lowest) and the m-th (the highest) sequences are drawn in bold lines.) $G[n, m]$ extracts these sequences as can be seen in Fig. 2c, showing that the resultant sequences are bitonic with property (V).

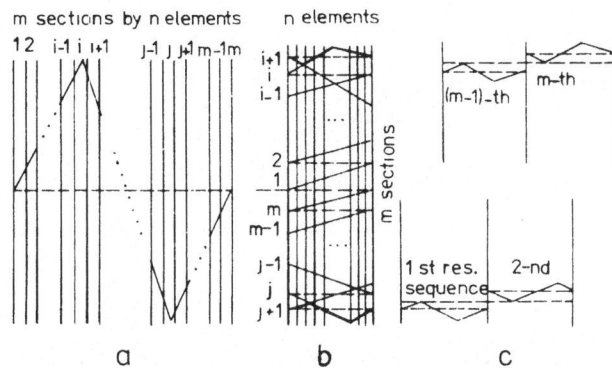

Fig. 2.

Theorem. If $N = r_1 r_2 \ldots r_p$, then the sorted sequence is obtained after blocks: $(G[r_1, N/r_1]$, sorting by r_1 numbers, $G[N/r_1, r_1])$, $(G[r_2, N/r_1 r_2]$, sorting by r_2 numbers, $G[N/r_1 r_2, r_2])$, etc. $(G[r_{p-1}, N/r_1 r_2 \ldots r_{p-1}]$, sorting by r_{p-1} numbers, $G[N/r_1 r_2 \ldots r_{p-1}, r_{p-1}])$, and finally the last r_p-tuples of numbers are sorted.

Proof. Follows from the preceding proposition.

The complexity of our algorithm cannot be compared easily with that of Stone. It can be said, however, that it has a great advantage over it when less than $N/2$ processing elements are available, where N is the number of sequence keys which are to be sorted.

4. **GPS application to FFT.** Consider the discrete Fourier transformation

$$X(n) = \sum_{k=0}^{N-1} x_0(k) w^{nk}, \quad n = 0, 1, \ldots, N-1, \quad \text{where } w = e^{-2\pi i N}.$$

Let $N = r_1 r_2$. Integers n and k are represented by pairs of numbers (n_1, n_0), (k_1, k_0),

$$n = n_1 r_1 + n_0, \quad n_0 = 0, 1, \ldots, r_1 - 1, \quad n_1 = 0, 1, \ldots, r_2 - 1,$$
$$k = k_1 r_2 + k_0, \quad k_0 = 0, 1, \ldots, r_2 - 1, \quad k_1 = 0, 1, \ldots, r_1 - 1.$$

By [4] the FFT can be implemented in three steps as follows:

$$x_1(k_0, n_0) = \sum_{k_1=0}^{r_1-1} x_0(k_1, k_0) w^{n_0 k_1 r_2}, \tag{1}$$

$$x_2(n_0, n_1) = \sum_{k_0=0}^{r_2-1} x_1(k_0, n_0) w^{(n_1 r_1 + n_0) k_0}, \tag{2}$$

$$X(n_1, n_0) = \mathbf{x}_2(n_0, n_1).$$

Proposition. In the computation of $\mathbf{x}_1$, $G[r_1, r_2]$ is used and in the computation of $\mathbf{x}_2$, $G[r_2, r_1]$ is used.

Proof. In (1) we can see that the components of the vector $\mathbf{x}_0$ are divided into r_1 parts (by r_2 components) and the k_0-th components of each part are used in the computation of the k_0-th part of the components of $\mathbf{x}_1$ (if they are divided into r_2 parts — by r_1 components). Then the number n_0 determines which exponents of w are to be used. A similar situation occurs in the computation of $\mathbf{x}_2$. If $N = r_1 r_2 \ldots r_m$, then integers n and k can be represented as follows:

$$n = n_{m-1}(r_1 r_2 \ldots r_{m-1}) + n_{m-2}(r_1 r_2 \ldots r_{m-2}) + \ldots + n_1 r_1 + n_0,$$

$$k = k_{m-1}(r_2 r_3 \ldots r_m) + k_{m-2}(r_3 r_4 \ldots r_m) + \ldots + k_1 r_m + k_0,$$

where $n_{i-1} = 0, 1, 2, \ldots, r_i - 1,\quad 1 \leqslant i \leqslant m,$
$k_i = 0, 1, 2, \ldots, r_{m-i} - 1,\quad 0 \leqslant i \leqslant m - 1.$

Again, by [4], the FFT contains the following $m + 1$ steps:

$$\mathbf{x}_1(k_{m-2}, \ldots, k_0, n_0) = \sum_{k_{m-1}=0}^{r_1-1} \mathbf{x}_0(k_{m-1}, \ldots, k_0) w^{n_0 k_{m-1}(r_2 \cdot r_m)}$$

$$\mathbf{x}_2(k_{m-3}, \ldots, k_0, n_0, n_1) = \sum_{k_{m-2}=0}^{r_2-1} \mathbf{x}_1(k_{m-2}, \ldots, k_0, n_0) w^{(n_1 r_1 + n_0)k_{m-2}(r_3 \cdots r_m)}$$

$$\vdots$$

$$\mathbf{x}_i(k_{m-i-1}, \ldots, k_0, n_0, n_1, \ldots, n_{i-1}) = \sum_{k_{m-i}=0}^{r_i-1} \mathbf{x}_{i-1}(k_{m-i}, \ldots,$$
$$k_0, n_0, n_1, \ldots, n_{i-2}) w^{[n_{i-1}(r_1 r_2 \cdots r_{i-1}) + \ldots + n_0]k_{m-i}(r_{i+1} \cdots r_m)}$$

provided that $(r_{i+1} \ldots r_m) = 1$ for $i > m - 1$, $k_{-1} = 0$. The last step is the so-called "unscrambling":

$$X(n_{m-1}, \ldots, n_0) = \mathbf{x}_m(n_0, \ldots, n_{m-1}).$$

Theorem. In the computation of $\mathbf{x}_i$, $G[r_i, N/r_i]$ is used.
Proof. Follows from the above.
Remark. For the sake of completeness it should be noted that GPS-type networks were known to Clos [5] already in 1953, though they served different ends (switching in telephone networks).

REFERENCES

[1] STONE, H. S.: Parallel processing with the perfect shuffle. IEEE Trans. on Computers. *C-20*, 1971, 2, 153—161.

[2] FINO, B. J. and ALGAZI, V. R.: A unified treatment of discrete fast unitary transforms. SIAM J. Computing, 6, 1977, 4, 700—717.

[3] BATCHER, K. E.: Sorting networks and their applications. Spring Joint Computer Conf. AFIPS Proc., Vol. 32. Thompson, Washington, D. C., 1968, pp. 307—314.

[4] BRIGHAM, E. O.: The Fast Fourier Transform. Prentice Hall, Englewood Cliffs. N. J., 1974.

[5] CLOS, C.: A study of non-blocking switching networks. Bell Syst. Tech. J., 32, 1953, 406—424.